Poverty in Rural America

Westview Special Studies in Contemporary Social Issues

Poverty in Rural America:
A Case Study
Janet M. Fitchen

This case study of poverty in the contemporary United States examines a problem that is widespread but little studied: run-down neighborhoods of intergenerational poverty scattered on the rural fringes of urban areas. Intertwining historical, economic, social, cultural, and psychological material and basing her work on a decade of participant-observation, the author provides a new understanding of the lives and actions of nonfarm rural poor people and identifies the causes of their marginal situation.

Beginning with a typical day in the life of one family, Dr. Fitchen illustrates in specific and personal terms the endemic problems—unsatisfactory employment, low and insecure income, social marginality, inadequate education, neglected health problems, substandard housing, and low self-esteem—that plague rural depressed areas. She describes the ways people perceive their problems and goals, the constraints they face, and the solutions they have developed, looking always for common patterns of thought and action—and an explanation of these patterns—that will be useful to students, practitioners, and policymakers. Among her conclusions are concrete suggestions for breaking the cycle of entrenched rural poverty.

Janet M. Fitchen is assistant professor of anthropology at Ithaca College and does consulting and training work in programs for low-income people.

I have made
a ceaseless effort
not to ridicule,
not to bewail,
nor to scorn human actions,
but to understand them.
                    —Spinoza

Poverty in Rural America:
A Case Study

Janet M. Fitchen

Westview Press / Boulder, Colorado

The paper used in this publication meets the minimum requirements of the American National Standard for Permanence of Paper for Printed Library Materials Z39.48-1984.

Westview Special Studies in Contemporary Social Issues

Published in 1981 in the United States of America by
  Westview Press, Inc.
  5500 Central Avenue
  Boulder, Colorado 80301
  Frederick A. Praeger, Publisher

Library of Congress Cataloging in Publication Data
Fitchen, Janet M.
    Poverty in rural America.
    (Westview special studies in contemporary social issues)
    Bibliography: p. 245
    Includes index.
    1. Rural poor–United States–Case studies. 2. United States–Rural conditions–Case studies. I. Title.
HC110.P6F55 1980   330.973'0926'0880624   80-20069
ISBN 0-89158-868-X
ISBN 0-89158-901-5 (pbk.)

Printed and bound in the United States of America

10   9   8   7   6   5

Dedicated to
the children of Chestnut Valley,
past, present, and future

Contents

Part 4
Conclusion: Causes and Cures

Acknowledgments

This book reflects the influence and encouragement of many people over many years—more people and more influences than I can list here.

I offer particular acknowledgment to the many professors who have shaped and trained my mind as an anthropologist. At Vassar College, John V. Murra and Helen Codere not only introduced me to anthropology but also conveyed to me their love of it. Oscar Lewis and Edward Winter at the University of Illinois contributed further to my anthropological development. Years later at Cornell University, Robert J. Smith and Davydd J. Greenwood helped me to complete my formal training. They also provided the encouragement and critiques that were so important during the research and writing that preceded this book. In the later years of graduate school, I was assisted financially by a National Institute of Health Training Program grant, NIGMS 1256, for which I am grateful.

I also wish to express my appreciation to the many individuals working in poverty settings around the state and the nation who have shared their experiences with me. They work in a wide variety of circumstances as professionals, paraprofessionals, and volunteers. They attempt innovative programs and dedicate their energies to helping alleviate the problems caused by poverty. They have given me valuable insights.

I greatly appreciate the input of a number of friends who have read and commented on the earlier drafts of this book. Their questions and reactions helped me think and rethink my interpretations. In particular, Nina Lambert brought the perspective of clinical psychology and her own expertise to bear on an earlier draft, providing some thought-provoking discussions. Sandra Rosenzweig Gittleman combined her perception as a social worker and as an artist to create the illustrations that enhance this book.

All through the years of my involvement in this endeavor, my husband, Douglas B. Fitchen, has accepted this project as an integral part of my life, recognizing its importance to me and giving me the support I needed. Our children, John, Katie, and Sylvia, have grown up with this project. They have helped me immeasurably with their tacit backing, their willingness to let me follow my own interests, and, on occasion, with their willing labor. Young children's fingerprints still mark the index cards of bibliographies they so carefully alphabetized years ago. I also owe a personal debt to my father, Henderson Mathews, who was ahead of his time in encouraging me to ignore the restrictions of sex-role stereotypes.

Finally, I thank the people who have been directly a part of this study. They have shared their lives and thoughts with me. They have given me many, many cups of coffee, towed my car out of ditches and muddy places, made me feel welcome, given me new perspectives on life, and helped me grow. Most of all, they have provided me the opportunity to carry out the kinds of activities and observations I felt necessary for understanding their lives.

Janet M. Fitchen

Part 1

Introduction

A Day with Mary Crane[1]

About twenty miles north of town, out beyond the suburbs, a narrow side road branches off the highway. It follows along the base of the hill, then winds along the valley and crosses a stream. Flanking the roadside every so often are a worn-down farmhouse, a modest old house trailer, a converted-school-bus home, a half-finished house, and a tar-papered shack. A generation or two ago, there were farms along this road. But now the old fields are completely overgrown, shoulder high in goldenrod and blackberries, with a scattering of young pine trees and small groves of poplars. Only an occasional barn remains standing, sagging and empty. On the slopes behind these abandoned fields, trees and underbrush crowd inside the low stone walls that once enclosed grazing pastures.

Where the road again crosses the stream, a weathered church casts its protective shadow over the cemetery. Further along, the old schoolhouse stands, although it has long since been converted to a home. This was once the lively hamlet of Chestnut Valley, where church socials and school picnics drew a good crowd of families from the surrounding farms. Fifty years ago, there were two stores here, where people stopped in for daily provisions and daily gossip. There was a creamery and a blacksmith, too. But today Chestnut Valley is merely a collection of homes. People who live here now must drive more than fifteen miles to town to work, to shop, to attend school, to join a club, to see a doctor, or to seek help. And today, almost everyone who lives here is poor. The place is what some people call a rural slum, and it has a bad reputation in the surrounding county.

As the road curves on beyond Chestnut Valley, it rises steeply. There is a cluster of four homes huddled with their backs to the wooded hillside, their fronts close to the road. The first is a patched-up two-story house, its kitchen end sagging off to the side. Next is a small tar-paper-covered house; then a small old trailer perched atop cement block pillars. At the end of the cluster stands a larger, but older, trailer with an unpainted plywood entryway attached to the front. In the spaces around the houses, several old automobiles are parked. Partially hidden under the new snow are a car chassis, several

engines, fenders and other parts, and a tripod for hoisting out car engines. An engineless panel truck bulges to overflowing with tan plastic bags of trash, awaiting a spring trip to the dump. Firewood and assorted building and roofing materials protrude from snowy piles. Parked in front of one house are three snowmobiles, the cover missing from one, and an old garden tractor with a homemade snowplow attached to the front. Leaning against each home is a large kerosene drum. An abandoned, doorless refrigerator is stuffed with cartons of old clothing. A long laundry line behind the blue trailer flaps with the frozen pants and overalls of yesterday's washing. Along the road edge are some of the currently licensed cars and trucks, mostly quite old and obviously much used. The mailboxes beside the road are propped up on old oil drums, or hung from leaning wooden posts; none has a name or number on it to identify the people who live there.

The two-story house is the home of Mary and Bill Crane. It is an old house – it was already old and in poor condition when Bill lived there as a young child. Those were hard times; his father was not often home, and eventually he just drifted away. His mother did all she could to keep food on the table and a roof over their heads. Bill remembers eating mostly potatoes, which they grew out back on the hill. Years later, after his mother died, Bill came back to live in the family house, bringing his wife and two small children with him.

Now, in 1971, Bill and Mary have four children and, as Bill says, "They're growing up like weeds in a potato patch." Peter is ten already, and Sandra is right behind him at nine. Ann is almost seven, and Tim, the baby of the family, just turned six last week. During the seven years the Cranes have lived here, the house has been fixed up a lot, with a strengthened foundation and new asbestos shingles on two sides. Just last summer, Bill spent his vacation, with the help of his kid brother, converting the attic space above the kitchen into a bedroom and joining it onto the upstairs of the main part of the house.

Bill, now in his mid-forties, is handy that way. He's always been good at construction work and good at fixing cars, too. But, as his wife, Mary, says, "His only problem is that he can never get one project finished up before he's working on another one." It has been five years since he began the plumbing project.

Mary, just thirty-five, grew up over on the east side of the hill. Her mother still lives there in the old farmhouse. One sister is at home, where she is raising her baby. The other sister lives in a trailer in the back yard. Her stepbrothers both live nearby. Mary's parents were originally tenant farmers, but the landowner sold his property to the state during the Depression. Mary's father managed to buy the house and a little plot of land around it. That took place during the last year he was sober and healthy, thirty years ago. Since then, Mamma has worked the night shift as a hospital janitor to keep the family going. Mamma's "new husband," Shorty, used to work in construction off and on, and now he's on a disability pension.

Mary's family and Bill's have known each other for years. In fact, Mary's grandfather, when he was alive, used to tell stories about when he and Bill's dad worked together digging potatoes and pitching hay over on the Smith farm. And Bill's oldest sister was married to a cousin of Mary's.

But Bill and Mary hardly knew each other as children. Bill was already six-teen and had quit school when Mary entered first grade in the valley schoolhouse. Mary went on to the consolidated high school, where she was a good student and hoped to be the first member of her family to graduate. In her sophomore year, Mary got a part-time job as a store clerk. Then, when a full-time opening came, she quit school, as money was pretty scarce in the family at the time.

A few years later, Mary began going with Bill. She used to ride home from work with him every night. Mary kept her job until she got pregnant and she and Bill got married. It was a difficult delivery for Mary, and the doctor was worried that there might be problems. The baby – they named her Me-linda – was small at birth, and never gained much weight before she died, just short of three months old. That year, Bill worked in a factory in the city, but he hated it, so he quit and went to work for the county on the highway crew. For the last two years, he has been working for the state highway depart-ment.

Their married life has had its ups and downs. Drinking has been a problem, especially for Bill, but sometimes for Mary also. Several times Bill has gone off on a drunk for days at a time. Twice, after bad fights, Mary has packed up the kids and left home. But during the last couple of years, things have gone a bit better for them. Mary guesses that maybe by now, after all these years, she is so used to Bill's tirades that they no longer shake her up so much. Or maybe she is just too tired to do anything about the situation. Anyhow, what *could* she do, she wonders. Besides, their six months apart convinced her that, despite his faults, she really loves Bill – and she needs him. The children need Bill too, she thinks. They seem easier to handle now that the family is back together again.

Still, life is not easy. There has never been enough money to keep up with each day's needs – let alone to pay off the back bills. There are even some bills left from before Bill took his present job, when he was unemployed for most of two years. And it never seems possible to get ahead a bit. So many things have to be put off "until we have enough money" – like fixing up the house. Now that the kitchen attic will soon make bedroom space for the boys, they will have a living room again, and Mary hopes they can convert part of the space into closets, or perhaps build a front entry room for all the boots and snowsuits. It always seems as if there isn't any place in the house to sit down, as if every bit of space is taken up by furniture, clothing, toys, junk—and kids. And after all these years, there is still no running water in the bathroom. Mary wonders if there will ever be time when they will have enough money to be able to fix up the house the way they'd like.

Recently, Mary has been thinking that it would ease the money problems if she went back to work. This year, all the kids are finally in school. But so far, there hasn't even been enough free time for her to go look for a job, let alone actually go to work. It seems to Mary that it is all she can do just to cope with each day's living and family care. There is always something extra coming up that has to be taken care of. The house is almost always a mess; she is usually days behind in the laundry. But, Lord knows, she's sure no one could say she's a lazy person. Once she thought about taking on a night job at the hospital where one of her friends worked or working night shift in a factory, but Bill told her in no uncertain terms that she wasn't going to be taking any night jobs. As for daytime jobs, that would mean arranging for someone to watch the children after school, since Mary feels they are not safe at home alone. They are too much for her mother to handle though, so she'd have to pay someone. And what would she do about all the times a child stayed home from school? So, for this year at least, Mary has decided to give up the idea of getting a job. Maybe next year.

It is already February, only halfway through winter, and it has been a cold winter so far. The kerosene tank is almost empty for the fourth time. Christmas already seems long ago—although the payments on the new TV set will continue for months. There has been a fresh snowfall during the night, and drifts enshroud the cars and the still, dark houses along the road.

*   *   *

Mary Crane gets up quickly when the alarm clock goes off at 5:15. She immediately goes downstairs in her bare feet. She tiptoes past the living room couch where the two boys sleep and goes into the kitchen. She lets the dogs out the back door—it is still pitch black out there—and plugs up the crack with rags. She turns up the regulator on the heater and puts in more kerosene from the can. Going back upstairs, Mary tiptoes past the denim curtain that separates off the girls' room, where they share a bed. She gropes in her dark bedroom for her clothes, trying not to bump into the bed where Bill is still asleep. She dresses in the bathroom, throwing her nightgown onto the pile of clothing that covers the two old TV sets (a secondhand color set that had never worked right and a tiny portable they still hope to fix—Bill had traded some car parts for it). Today's clothes are the same as yesterday's: her husband's old pants and shirt and a navy blue sweater from the rummage sale. She had picked this sweater because it was big and long, covering the protruding bulges where her waistline used to be, before her last pregnancy. Mary leaves the toilet-flushing for later, since she forgot to carry up the bucket of water, and goes back down to the kitchen.

With the ceiling light bulb glaring bright, Mary rubs her eyes. She draws a pot of water from the faucet on the floor next to the pump, lights the stove, and puts the water on to heat. She also lights the oven, propping its door open to help heat the cold, cement-floored kitchen. She clears away the clean dishes and pots from the table, where they had been left to drain the night before, stacking them neatly in the wooden-crate shelves beneath the window. She fixes a cup of instant coffee and sits down with a cigarette, trying to arrange her thoughts after yet another bad night. Still yawning, she puts two eggs and the last scraps of bacon in the pan to fry, and goes upstairs to wake her husband.

Mary is reluctant to wake Bill. He is sleeping so quietly, so peacefully, compared to his violent temper of the night before. When he's sound asleeep like this, his face seems still to have a young-boy look about it, despite the long scar from the motorcycle accident and the grey of his hair. That head must be aching now from all the beer last night. As Mary looks at him, she reminds herself of the decision she had reached before finally dropping off to sleep. This time she would pretend nothing had happened and hope the whole thing would blow over. After all, Bill had been going through a rough time recently, and his temper was so quick these days, he just couldn't seem to control it. But he has been cutting down on the booze. Maybe if she bends over backwards to be loving to him, and to ignore his yelling, things will smooth out again. Besides, for all his faults Bill has been a better husband and father than most of the other men around. At least he doesn't beat her up all the time like Betty's husband does. And he really loves the kids, even if sometimes it doesn't exactly look that way. So Mary taps Bill gently on the shoulder. "C'mon, honey, breakfast's ready."

Bill dresses quietly and comes down. He eats only part of the breakfast Mary serves him, saying, "Save the rest for Tim, he needs it more'n I do." Mary makes some toast in the new toaster Bill gave her for her birthday and, while he eats it, she makes and packs his lunch: two jelly sandwiches and a piece of leftover cake. "It's real cold out today," she says. "If I can get to town, I'll bring you some hot soup at noon. Will you still be working that section of Route 420?" Bill mumbles, "Yeah, I told you we'd be there all week. But your car probably won't start. And there ain't much gas in it. If you do go out, take an extra spare tire along—none of them tires on it are good for much." Bill gets up from the table, puts on his storm suit, pats Mary on the fanny, and sets out.

Mary fixes another cup of coffee, turns on the radio, and sits a few minutes. She massages her stiff neck and runs her fingers through her short brown hair. At 6:45 she wakes the children. Tim skips into the kitchen and eats the eggs and bacon his father left. "Your appetite's really picking up now with them vitamin pills," his mother beams. (Mary has always worried about Tim's being so small. He has hardly grown at all in the last year. Maybe it was just worms, but she sometimes wonders if he, too, has a problem with sugar diabetes.) Peter, always a good eater, fixes himself a big bowl of cold cereal and perches on the stack of tires to gulp it down. Amid yells of "Hey, you got my sock!" and "Mommy, where's my sweater?" all four children finish dressing and put on boots and assorted hand-me-down jackets. As they are about to leave, Mary notices that Ann's nose is still runny. "I think you'd better stay home today, honey. Your cold isn't getting any better." Ann whines that she wants to go to school anyway. At the same time, Tim starts fussing and whining, saying he doesn't feel good, asking if he can stay home. Mary decides that both of the younger ones will stay home today. She calls out her usual last-minute instructions to the departing older children: "You behave yourselves in school today. Don't cause no trouble." The two older children run out of the door as the bus pulls up at 7:15. The sun is almost fully up, but the morning is a cold one.

Already feeling tired, Mary sits down at the three-legged card table to work on a jigsaw puzzle she started the day before. The children turn on the TV and run around the house, then settle down to play with their toy cars. Soon Mary goes into the kitchen to draw water to heat in big galvanized tubs on the kitchen stove. She shoves the breakfast dishes to the far side of the table and pulls the wringer washer out of the corner. (Bill found this washer at the town dump, and it works a lot better than their old one, which now stands in the other corner, with a plywood board on top as a makeshift counter.) Mary goes through the bedrooms and bathroom collecting dirty clothes, throwing them to the foot of the stairs, and then kicking them into the kitchen, where she sorts them by color into four loads. "All that from just two days," she sighs. She puts the first load in, pours in a tub of hot water, sets the machine in action, and goes back to the living room to find a cigarette. She sits down to watch TV – part of a quiz show and her favorite soap opera – then reads through a daily prayer. After this interlude, she wrings out the first batch of clothes, setting them in a pile on the table for rinsing later on, and dumps in a second load.

At ten o'clock, Mary remembers she was supposed to telephone the pediatrician's office to see if the test results have come back. Throwing on an extra sweater, she goes out the front door and walks down the hill. She hurries past the tar-paper house with the barking dog. Bill recently had a fight with Gus. Just two days ago, the sheriff was called to the house on a complaint against Gus. Now, as Mary goes by, she keeps her eyes on the road, just in case Gus's wife is watching her from the front window. Mary would have liked to make the phone call from the Sloan's trailer, but no one would be home there at this time. So she goes on to Newton's. Barb Newton comes to the door in her bathrobe, looking half asleep. "Yeah, sure you can use it, Mary," she responds, "everyone else does." The trailer seems very hot inside, and smells of kerosene and urine. The baby, prancing around in diapers and an undershirt, gives Mary's legs a big hug. Mary places the call quickly. "No," she tells the nurse, "none of the other kids is having diarrhea. But Peter said he had more rectal bleeding yesterday." Assured that the doctor will send in a prescription, Mary hangs up, reminding herself to stop at the drugstore when she goes to town later. She thanks Barb for the use of the phone. Explaining that she must hurry home because of the kids, she departs.

As Mary opens the kitchen door, the children fall suddenly silent. Mary surveys the scene quickly, and shouts, "Tim, get off that ladder this minute before you fall and break your neck. You know what your father said. Stay away from that attic until it's finished. If I catch you up there one more time, you'll really get your ass whipped – and by your father, too." The children skip into the living room and begin jumping on the couch. "And keep off that couch, too," Mary warns, as she starts to put the second batch of washed laundry through the wringer.

Midway through the next batch of laundry, Ann and Tim rush into the kitchen. "I'm hungry, I'm hungry!" "Can we have a doughnut?" Mary's response is almost automatic. "No, you certainly can *not* have a doughnut. Wait 'til lunchtime." "But we want doughnuts *now*," they plead. "Well, you just can't have them now." Tim angrily punches his mother in the thigh. She swats his bottom; he screams louder, "I want a doughnut!" Mary covers her ears. "Oh, all right, go ahead and have your damn doughnut. But that's the only one you get, and you'd both better shut up and be good the rest of the day." The children quickly gobble up their doughnuts and run back to play.

Mary pours herself a cup of lukewarm coffee and lights a cigarette. It's almost time to go to town, so she heats a can of soup and pours it into a thermos. She makes sure the children are bundled up and grabs an old jacket of Bill's. As they leave, Mary pretends to lock the door, even though the lock is broken again—"Just so those thieving neighbors will think it's locked." She rolls a spare tire over from the side of the house and heaves it into the trunk of the car. They all hop in, she hooks the door shut with wire, and coasts the car down the hill until it starts.

Along the main highway, Mary stops to get two dollars' worth of gas and some cigarettes. When she reaches town, she stops at the children's elementary school to complain to the principal. She is angry because they have assigned Sandra to a special education class when, Mary believes, it's really the fault of the teacher that Sandra never learned to read when she should have. But Mary admits that, deep down inside, she is worried about Sandra. Could it be that the spinal meningitis had damaged the child's brain? Will she always be slow, like her cousin Cindy?

Mary drives across town and finds the spot where her husband's highway crew is taking its lunch break. "Hi, honey. Here's some soup." Bill takes the thermos and hands her his paycheck, after endorsing it while leaning on the car. "Did you get that wall paneling yet?" he asks. "Of course not. How could I? What would I use for money?" "Oh yeah. Well, now you can go get it. I'll maybe put the stuff up on the weekend. Then we can get the boys moved into that attic room. Maybe we'll have the living room to ourselves sometimes." Bill continues, "And I want you to get that gasket for the Plymouth and the registration forms from the motor vehicle bureau. I've got to get the Plymouth fixed and registered quick, 'cause I know my truck won't pass inspection—and the sticker ran out last Monday."

Mary heads for the bank, to cash the paycheck (slightly over $110 for the week). She goes to the drugstore and then to the supermarket. She fights off the children's requests for candy and bubblegum balls, and decides she probably can't afford to get the laundry soap this week. She looks up and down the meat counter, settling on five pounds of hamburger (on special this week). She remembers to buy a cake mix and a can of chocolate frosting: next Tuesday will be Ann's birthday. In all, the groceries come to $43.59.

As she pushes the grocery cart to the car, Mary is wrapped in thought. Should she maybe try to get on food stamps again? Two years ago, when her teenage sister Sue was living with them, Mary found that food stamps were a real help. She was able to buy more of the family's favorite foods then, and lots of whole milk. That was the year they bought two whole cases of canned peaches when they were on sale. But the family was declared ineligible for food stamps when Susan moved out again. Now, according to Mary's sister-in-law, there are new income guidelines and maybe the family would be eligible again. But is seems like a lot of trouble to go and get certified all over again.

Mary's thoughts ramble on to other money problems. How hard it is to make ends meet these days! Of course, it would help if they could get on Medicaid: the doctor bills are mounting and Peter is supposed to have more tests soon. And Ann's teeth are so badly rotted that it will take a lot of dentistry to fix them up. And there is still the back bill from the hospital for her own broken arm—the collection agency is after them for that one. But Bill refuses to let her apply for Medicaid. Ever since two summers ago when he got his new job, he has managed to make ends meet—sort of—on his own. He doesn't want to go back to the welfare department again, and he insists that Medicaid is the same as welfare. Mary reasons that it's mainly Bill's pride that makes him this way. He likes to think he can manage things himself. And maybe he could—if there weren't all those unexpected things to pay for all the time. Also, he got in a real argument with their caseworker at social services because she thought she could tell him how to spend his money—what to buy and what not to buy. Mary shudders as she remembers that day. She was really afraid Bill would haul off and hit the caseworker.

"Oh, well," Mary sighs aloud. In another month or two winter will be over, and instead of buying kerosene, maybe then she can squeeze out some money toward those medical bills. As for the water pipes up to the bathroom—well, that will have to wait some more.

Mary makes her next stop at the bakery sales outlet to buy day-old bread and doughnuts. Then, with the children happily eating bananas in the back seat, she drives to the lumber company. There she buys four wall panels—at half price because they are slightly damaged—and ties them onto the roof of the car. Next stop is a car parts dealer, to order the gasket. On the way home, she stops at the courthouse to pick up the forms to register the Plymouth. (She will fill them out for Bill, since he can't read too well.)

Just as they return home, Mary's mother pulls up in the driveway. She is driving the "Fordrolet," a vehicle Shorty put together from his old Chevy that was in a wreck and some Ford body parts that Bill gave him. "Well," Mamma calls out, "I didn't think this old heap was going to make it over the hill today. Clutch is shot to hell. Cripe, it's cold! You got any coffee?" "Sure, Mamma. C'mon in," Mary replies. "Soon's I unload the groceries, I'll make us a pot of coffee."

Susan climbs out of the back seat of Mamma's car. Although she and Mary are half-sisters and widely separated in age, they think of themselves simply as older and younger sisters. Sue bundles blankets around the baby and dashes into the house. Ann and Tim are delighted to see their little cousin.

Both children help unwrap the baby and take turns holding her in their laps and cooing at her. "Look, Aunt Sue! The baby can almost sit up now! Last week she couldn't do that at all."

Mary fixes a pot of coffee and the three women sit at the kitchen table talking. "Did your watch 'As the World Turns'?" asks Sue. "I think he's going to come back to her, I just have that feeling." "Hey, did you hear about Ralphie and them guys getting caught last weekend? And it was all 'cause of that damn dog." "Oh, by the way, don't forget you got to get your license for your dogs. I took care of Prince's license yesterday." "Say, Ellen was over to the house again last night. I just wish she'd make up her mind about that man. Personally, I think she ought to leave him for good." "Oh, have either of you seen Dottie recently? I heard one of her kids has been real sick – the doctors aren't sure what's wrong with him."

Meanwhile, Ann and Tim are playing on the floor with Donna, showing her their toys and trying to make her laugh. Mary watches the baby smile – and sadly remembers the baby she lost so long ago. Susan looks around the kitchen at the piles of laundry waiting to be washed or rinsed or hung up and sighs, "Damn! Looks like I can't use your washer today, huh, Mary? I threw the baby's laundry in the car just in case I could do it over here. Oh well, maybe Shorty will take me to the laundromat tonight." Mamma quickly puts down that idea. "My foot he will! It's Friday night, and he'll be wanting to be out with his buddies." "So," whines Susan, "what does he expect me to do, walk to the laundromat?" Mamma explodes, "Okay, Miss Smarts! Why didn't you think about that before you went and got yourself pregnant?"

Mary gulps down the rest of her coffee and gets up from the table. There's been so much quarreling and ugliness between Sue and Mamma and Shorty for so many years. Back when Sue got kicked out of school, Mary and Bill had taken Sue in because she needed a home away from her parents. Mary hoped she'd be able to help Sue straighten out. At first, Sue had really been helpful with the children, especially when Mary was laid up in the spring. But gradually she started drifting off. Then, when the baby was nearly due, Mamma and Shorty had taken Sue home again. Things were generally better now, but it upsets Mary to hear the old familiar digging, criticizing, and tearing down.

Now Ann and Tim start pulling and tugging on Mary's arm, complaining loudly of hunger. Mary, glad of the excuse to walk away from her mother and sister, goes over to the stove to heat up a can of soup. Mamma and Sue get up to leave. Mamma bundles up the baby, who has just fallen asleep in the corner of the living room. As they go out the door, Mary remembers to ask her mother to watch the children after school tomorrow, as she has an appointment for Ann at the dentist. "I was supposed to take her last week, but something came up and I couldn't make it."

At three-thirty, the school bus arrives. Peter and Sandra and four other children jump off, Pete yelling some taunt back to "Fatback" Newton, who is ambling down the road to his home. The children rush into the house, "Mommy! Mommy! Guess what?" Mary sits down on the couch, the four children crowded around her, to hear about the triumphs and tragedies of the children's school day. She listens and responds with real concern. "Well, don't pay no attention to what those other kids say. You're just as good as they are!" Mary looks carefully at the school papers they have brought home. Peter's spelling and arithmetic papers, though torn and messy, have long columns of "C" marks in red pencil, and at the top the words "very good" or a smiling face. Sandra's papers have more red "Xs" and frowning faces, but Mary consoles, "Never mind, honey. I'm real proud of you anyway. I know you worked hard on this 'rithmetic. Maybe next time you'll get more right. And that's a real pretty picture you made. Will you let me put it up on the wall here?" Ann and Tim, too, press for attention, and proudly tell their older brother and sister about the latest accomplishments of their baby cousin, Donna. Then, one by one, the children drift off into the kitchen to make themselves sandwiches, spread thick with the jam from last summer's wild blackberries.

Mary puts away the rest of the groceries, hiding the special Valentine cupcakes under an overturned pail on the windowsill. Distracted by loud noises from the living room, she rushes in to check. "Cut that out right now! Oh, you kids! Now you've torn my new curtains." (Mary had found the curtains at a rummage sale, and was especially pleased with the color—a perfect match for the begonias and geraniums blooming on the windowsill.) "Get out of here! Get out of this room!" She shoos them out. The boys run out to play in the snow; the girls scramble up the stairs. Mary stays behind to mop up the living room. The warm afternoon sun has melted the snow on the roof, causing a little stream of water to run down the newly painted living room wall and make a puddle on the linoleum. She mumbles something about Bill never getting around to fixing the damn roof, then goes out front to fill up the kerosene can. Coming in, she slams the door shut and sits down on the couch, absentmindedly starting to fold the pile of yesterday's clean laundry. Mary glances at the opposite wall, at the poster of a snowy mountain peak lit up in sunrise. Across the bottom of the poster is printed the "Serenity Prayer." "God grant me the serenity . . . ."

It is now four-thirty and Bill still isn't home. Mary wonders, "Why would he be late today?" Half an hour later, he pulls into the yard. He is greeted enthusiastically by the younger children. "Daddy's home! Daddy's home!" Tim shouts and dances around the living room. Bill knows the question in Mary's mind, and quickly explains. "I just stopped at the diner for coffee. I swear, the only thing I drank was coffee." Mary protests, "But I've had your afternoon coffee ready here for an hour." Bill has no answer, and Mary drops the sub-ject, not wanting to stir things up again. Bill leaves the room to go lie down in their bedrooom. Twice he yells at the children to be quiet.

Mary goes into the kitchen to fix supper. The rinsed clothes are still in the washtub; the clothing that never got washed lies scattered on the floor. She kicks it aside, making one big pile next to the car engine that has occupied a corner for the last six months. She clears off a bit more space on the kitchen table, leaving the jar of peanut butter, a can of evaporated milk, ketchup, and bread in the center of the table. She stacks the unwashed breakfast dishes and coffee cups at one end of the table. Mary cooks a sauce of fresh ham-burger, canned tomatoes, and onions, and pours it over spaghetti. She dumps the puppy, the school books, and her husband's outer clothes off the four chairs and sets plates on the table. One call to the children is enough. They rush in, devour their spaghetti and sauce, eagerly drink their milk, and then divide a can of peaches among themselves. Mary notices that Ann winces from the pain of chewing her food.

Soon after six, the children are back in the living room. Sandra is glued to a Western on TV. Ann is bawling because Tim has taken her wind-up car. Mary yells at Tim to give it back, and swats him on the seat of his pants. She dries Ann's tears on her sweater sleeve, and soon the two children are racing their cars across the room. Peter lies sprawled on the floor, reading a school book in the midst of all the noise. Mary suddenly realizes her own hunger and goes back to the kitchen, where she dishes out a small plate of spaghetti for herself. She sets the remainder on the back of the stove to keep warm for Bill. When the water finally gets hot, she washes the day's dishes and feeds the accumulated scraps to the dogs.

Bill wakes up, and Mary takes him his supper in front of the TV, the children having been sent out of the room. Bill yells out to the kitchen, "Pete, did you get them plugs cleaned on the Plymouth?" Pete answers weakly, "No, Dad, not yet," and slams his book shut. He covers his ears with his hands, hoping to shut out what he knows will follow – the usual tirade. "How come a kid who's so smart in school can't do a goddamn little thing on a car? You'd better get your ass out there tomorrow and get them plugs done or else!" Bill's shouting is cut off by a fit of coughing. When he recovers from the coughing, he remains silent.

Mary rubs Bill's chest with Vicks and pulls a blanket around his shoulders. Bill coughs again, then says, "I shouldn't of gone to work today. This cold in my chest is aching me somethin' awful. And my back is acting up again with this weather." Then he brightens. "Well, I guess we'll be gettin' some over-time this week. On top of last week's overtime, it looks like we'll have enough money to make it through this month." Mary doesn't tell him of her earlier thoughts about applying for food stamps or Medicaid. Besides, counting the overtime pay, they'd probably be over the eligibility limit anyway, at least for this month.

Soon Bill goes back up to bed and falls asleep. Around eight-thirty, the girls hug Mary and go up to bed. Tim is already asleep on the couch, still fully dressed. Peter stays up to watch another show with his mother, who curls up on the other end of the couch and dozes off. At ten, Mary turns off the TV and tucks blankets around Tim and Pete. She carries a pail of water up from the kitchen tap to flush the toilet. Undressing quickly, she climbs into bed beside Bill. She is asleep almost immediately.

Down the road, dogs are barking. A neighbor is leaving for work on the night shift. A snowplow churns its way along the road, past the darkened cluster of houses, headed back down through Chestnut Valley and out to the main road.

2
A Case Study of
Rural Nonfarm Poverty

Poverty persists in isolated enclaves in many regions of rural America. It is a vexing and tenacious problem, but one that has generally been overlooked. When brought to public attention, the problem has usually been misdiagnosed, and the patients have been held responsible for what is really society's illness.

In seeking to understand the problem and its tenacity, we can derive important perspectives from the men, women, and children who actually make up the category labeled "the rural poor." The individuals who grapple every day with rural poverty can, in fact, contribute much insight into this longstanding societal problem. If we were to observe them closely and elicit their perceptions, their hopes, their joys, and their despairs, we would finally see that the problem of rural poverty is not the result of inadequate people or insufficient ambition, as is so often believed. We would find, instead, that the problem of rural poverty is rooted in the sweeping changes that have transformed many parts of rural America over the past century, especially the decline of agriculture and the demise of the small rural community. We would also find that rural poverty exists in a total societal context, including not only economic but also historical, social, cultural, and psychological aspects that are interconnected.

The human problems found in rural poverty-stricken areas are societal problems, societally generated, rather than individual problems caused by individual pathology. The problems of Mary Crane and her family, for example, can only be understood as part of a wider context of time and space and causality. And the remedies must address the underlying societal issues rather than merely providing Band-Aid treatment for symptoms as they affect individuals.

To provide this contextual perspective on the problem of rural poverty, anthropological research has been carried out in a rural depressed community, fictitiously named Chestnut Valley. But this book is not a "community study" in the traditional sociological sense. The community itself is not the subject of

17

analysis, but merely the context, the backdrop. The book is primarily a study of the patterns of action and thought of a number of interacting, proximate, rural poor families, set against the background of their changing community environment.

This book is about the people—individuals like Mary and Bill Crane, their families, neighbors, and friends—who live out their lives in depressed rural enclaves. It describes their world, how they perceive it, cope with it, interact with it. The book is an ethnographic case study, taking one small enclave of rural poverty in upstate New York as a microcosm, as a sample for intensive examination. It is hoped that in-depth analysis of a cluster of interacting families in a particular rural depressed enclave can shed light on similar enclaves elsewhere in northern Appalachia, and on the rural poverty that blights other areas in the United States as well.

The Fieldwork:
Foundations for Understanding Rural Poverty

The idea for this project evolved in 1967, when chance contacts with several rural families forced a realization that poverty was a significant problem in some rural areas, but that it was not well understood. The decision to do research among rural poor people was prompted by a conviction that anthropology can make a contribution to understanding contemporary American society and its problems.

In 1969-70, the setting was selected and basic household data were collected. At that time, the Chestnut Valley area contained thirty-five dwellings—twenty-three located fairly close together in a small residential hamlet and twelve scattered along a few miles of back roads heading out into the surrounding hinterland.

Thirty households were surveyed for basic data in 1969-70. However, since the focus of the study was to be on intergenerational poverty and related problems, ten of these households were excluded from further study because they were socioeconomically somewhat outside the main category of interest. This left twenty low-income households for further research; and it is this sample that forms the 1969-70 baseline for all quantitative data. (Some of the excluded people have been part of this study in various other ways. For example, they have served as important sources of historical background, giving personal accounts of life in the community in an earlier time.)

The total population on which this study is based, however, is much larger than the twenty low-income families living in Chestnut Valley in 1969-70. Over the years, more than twenty additional households were involved in the study. One cause of the expansion of the sample was population increase and mobility. Between 1969 and 1975, there was a net growth of thirteen dwellings, mostly in the countryside. And during those six years, a total of fifty-five families lived in Chestnut Valley at one time or another. As people moved into and out of the area, the cast of characters of the study continually changed. Some of the incoming families were included in the study, and some of those who left were followed up in their new surroundings. Some families came into the area and into the study briefly, then moved out again. The sample was also expanded in another way. The naturalistic, flexible nature of

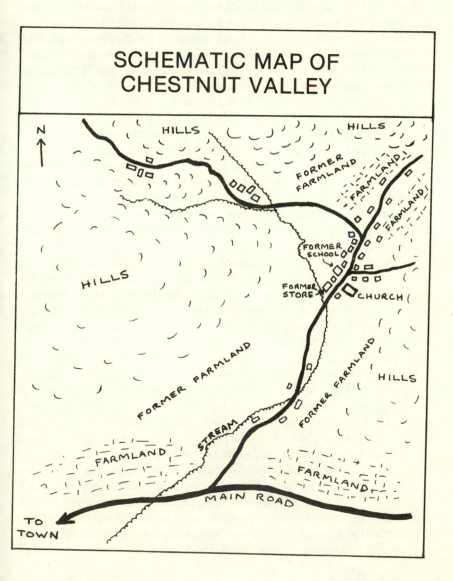

SCHEMATIC MAP OF CHESTNUT VALLEY

anthropological research put me in contact with many other rural poor people living elsewhere, some of them relatives and friends of the people of Chestnut Valley. These secondary contacts provided additional insights into ways that rural people cope with the problems of poverty.

In addition, the sample was intentionally expanded by brief periods of observation, community action work, questionnaires, and informal interviews conducted in other rural neighborhoods. These subsidiary studies were carried out to ensure that the main sample was neither unique nor idiosyncratic, to probe specific issues in a larger sample population, and to add breadth to balance the narrower in-depth observation of the main sample. Data from these one-time-only and short-term contacts added approximately thirty more families to the sample, although these thirty were much less central to the study. In all, the total number of households included in the study was just over seventy; forty were central to the research and, of these, twenty made up the baseline sample. (It is difficult to be precise about the number of households, since there was considerable fluctuation within and among households over the years. For example, a grown daughter and her children might at one time be part of her parents' household, and at another time live separately in a trailer in the yard, making it necessary to count hers as a separate household.)

The portrait presented in this book rests on a decade of observations, interactions, conversations, and co-participations. For about two years, field research was a continuous, everyday activity, though never the total live-in situation characteristic of traditional anthropological fieldwork. Interaction was fairly intensive and included many action projects as well as straight research. During the remainder of the decade, fieldwork was a varying, part-time activity: home visits tapered off to occasional, unplanned occurrences, returned to a more intensive level of daily interaction, then tapered off again, with only intermittent follow-up.

The fieldwork over ten years has yielded reams of notes recording observations, conversations, and impressions of each day's interactions. There are also more systematic forms of data, such as response sheets for topical questionnaires; newspaper clippings recording births, marriages, accidents, court cases, and deaths; tape-recorded recollections; and handwritten bits of life histories. Of course, there are also unrecorded forms of data: images, smells, sounds, and feelings stamped indelibly in the mind.

An important assumption of this research has been that the actors themselves are capable of providing significant insight into their own behavior.[1] There are, of course, some limitations to this position, and we cannot assume that actors are either conscious of, or willing to reveal directly, all their motives and thoughts. However, fantasy, rationalization, exaggeration, evasion, and wishful thinking are all valuable material. Statements affected by liquor and even purposeful lies are also significant and revealing data. The only problem in their use is that the observer must be able to distinguish them from "objective reality." For making this distinction, the long-term and in-depth nature of anthropological research is particularly helpful. The time span of association with informants, and the many different situations of observing and listening, reduced the risk of being naively taken in by conjured-up impressions the informants would like the social scientist to believe. Further-more, as fieldwork progressed, there gradually developed a known context in which to place the verbal data, making it easier to separate fact from fancy, observation from hearsay, truth from gossip. As fieldwork proceeded, the remarks or actions of an individual informant became more understandable, even predictable, and could be interpreted in context, so that they became more reliable and useful as data.

Most of the observations that support this book took place in "naturalistic settings": conversing over a cup of coffee in a kitchen or living room; chatting on a doorstep or in a vegetable garden out back; while waiting in line for food stamps, or accompanying a woman to the welfare office or to a conference at school; while observing children in a school classroom or playing with them at home; while laughing together or wiping away tears. For the most part, these were spontaneous situations occurring in the normal course of daily life, daytimes and evenings, winter and summer, on Christmas Day or on any or-dinary day.

Most home visits were unannounced drop-ins — spur-of-the-moment visits when I happened to be in the area. On all visits, even those that were prear-ranged, an element of unpredictability and surprise was always present. I never knew what to expect as I knocked on a door, nor what we might do or talk about that day. Even when I had a specific topic I intended to explore, it was often postponed because what was happening in the household at that time was much more pressing — and usually more interesting for research. Perhaps a woman had just been beaten up, and wanted to talk things out — or perhaps she preferred not to talk at all, or to talk about the weather. Often, a relative or neighbor had dropped in, and the intended interview session was postponed or interrupted by tacit agreement; on other occasions such a group setting turned into a fruitful session of people expressing their ideas for the future, their discontent with some aspects of the present. Sometimes a hus-band was unexpectedly at home, which either stifled conversation or greatly enhanced the usefulness of the visit. Perhaps a person was drunk or hung over, which could make conversation either impossible or very fruitful for research insights. Perhaps a new grandchild had been born, maybe a relative had just been thrown in jail, perhaps a man had just bought a new television set, or a child had been injured — these events always took center stage.

Happiness often needed sharing; worries and sadness often needed talking out; some situations called for action; some emergencies called for assistance in the form of transportation; and some events and moods had to be ex-perienced alone, while others cried out for a listener. The unpredictability of people's lives became the unpredictability of fieldwork, its essence. The direc-tions research took depended on whatever was going on at the place I hap-pened to be at any given time. Although this necessary flexibility made the fieldwork less systematic, it also enhanced its value, as it afforded me the op-portunity to catch the stream of life in its actual flow. I was compelled to notice the vividness, the urgency, and the sometimes exhausting pace of a life filled with unpredictable happenings and preoccupations. Additionally, unex-pected situations provided insight and data that would hardly have been elicited through a more formal research method, capturing not only what peo-ple say they do, but what they actually do. No preplanned interviews could catch as well the unrehearsed episodes of daily life: the excitement when a young woman returns to her parents with her newborn baby; the tension of waiting to find out what the judge will decide; the diffuse strain that permeates a home when a fight is brewing; the obvious loss of self-esteem when a mother has injured one of her children in a heated test of wills; the reactions and interactions of people as the room where they are sitting sud-denly catches fire; the anxieties over a sick child; the joy and pride of parents who have managed to get new Easter clothes for their children; the relish of men retelling the story of a close call with the police, a near-accident on a motorcycle, an outstanding car once owned. The naturalistic style of anthro-pological fieldwork is particularly suited to enabling the social scientist to "collect" such events as they happen, rather than trying to recapture them through questioning afterward.

The Analysis

Problems

Compiling these diverse observations into written description is a difficult task in itself, but it is only a part of the job, only one step removed from raw data. The important next step is to search for recurrent patterns or themes in the observed data; to extract generalizations from myriad recorded actions and behaviors. For example, family time-lines were constructed to summarize the significant events in the life histories of individual families; these time-lines were then compared for common denominators. Beyond the search for patterns or themes, there is the work of analytical interpretation; seeking out the structural, cultural, and psychological factors underlying the patterns of statements and actions. Through continued contact with many people from the original sample populations, I have been able to test hypotheses against new data, to reject or refine generalizations, and to ask some of the people for feedback on my descriptions and interpretations as they have been developed.

One difficulty throughout the analysis of data has been that it is not easy to generalize. Each family and each individual is in some sense different from all others. Low-income rural residents exhibit the same wide range of behavior that the people of any other socioeconomic stratum do. In any walk of life, some people are quiet and reserved, others are talkative and loud, even vulgar; at any economic level, some women are immaculate housekeepers and other women keep a sloppy house; in any social stratum, there are homes in which children receive open demonstration of affection and homes where little human warmth is exhibited. It is difficult, then, to generalize about the people, or behaviors, or "home life," or values of a socioeconomic stratum. Even more difficult—and potentially more misleading—is the attempt to compare two socioeconomic levels on the basis of such generalizations. Therefore, great caution must be exercised in seeking commonalities and relationships.

In the course of the decade of observation and analysis of rural poor families, some regularities and patterns have emerged, however. These patterns rest on several underlying factors. To begin with, there is a foundation of similarity arising out of ethnic uniformity ("old-stock Yankee"), and out of shared participation in the local version of contemporary American culture (including both the rural, northeastern version and the generalized national version as seen on TV). Superimposed on this base, the constraints of poverty and marginality faced by all of the families of this study appear to operate in fairly regular and predictable ways to yield fairly similar outcomes. Hence, there seem to be common patterns of behavior and action that arise out of the common situation of social and economic marginality.[2] Thus, although individuals and families do vary, and people are indeed very complex, it is possible to draw some generalizations concerning patterns among the rural poor without doing violence to the uniqueness of each individual.

Another difficulty in this particular kind of research with people is that, as informants have occasionally reminded me, there are a lot of things I do not know about the individuals and the neighborhoods under study. This is still true, despite the several years of interaction and observation. At times I have been disturbed that the more I knew, the more I was aware of how much I did not know. However, the complete details of every individual's personal life are not essential to the analysis of general social patterns, and are often quite irrelevant. We can attempt to develop an analysis that is valid and complete enough so that if a previously unknown fact were to come to light, it would fit into the analysis and the predictions already presented. Therefore, there is no need or justification for the social scientists to push, dig, and cajole for every detail of a person's life.

This reluctance to pursue people ruthlessly and relentlessly, to mine them for personal details, is part of a general ethical concern for the needs and rights of the people a social scientist studies. The research and writing of this book have been guided by the ethical principle that the informants on whom it is based should in no way be harmed by either the research process or the publication of the study. Furthermore, people should be made aware that they are, in fact, under study. As soon as my initial activities went beyond casual interaction to become a purposive research inquiry, I told them of my plans. No previous acquaintance took the opportunity I offered to sever the relationship at that time, and only a few appeared to become more guarded in their conversations. From that point on, all potential new informants were told at the outset that I was doing a study to see how low-income people in the rural area get along, the problems they face, the solutions they devise.

In publishing anthropological studies, privacy is usually protected by the use of pseudonyms for communities and for individuals. But this is not always a sufficient safeguard. At times, generalized analysis has to be substituted for colorfully descriptive factual reporting, to insure protection of identities. (For example, in the discussion of causes of marital problems in Chapter 7, no "biography of a marriage" could be included to illustrate the seven sources of stress that are described. Similarly, though fieldnotes chronicled the illnesses and injuries occurring in two families over the course of a year, the data could not be published in that raw and revealing form.) Occasionally, some particular details of a nonsignificant but identifying nature had to be omitted or altered. Thus, in the description of "Mary Crane" and her days's activities, some background facts have been blurred, some details have been altered, and some pieces have been borrowed from observations made in other households. This produces a blend, necessitated by the commitment to protect privacy. However, where details have been altered, the replacements spliced in have come from other observations made in similar situations, and thus they are consistent with, and likely to have occurred in, this case. Mary Crane's day is fact, not fiction, but it has been slightly altered for ethical considerations of informant privacy.

If the risks to the people studied are minimized, the investigator need not wait for a lifetime to pass before sharing the observations with the rest of the world. If research is to have any practical use in formulating more effective policy and programs, as the Chestnut Valley study is intended to have, its results must be communicated. Several informants have actually encouraged me not only to probe their situations, but to help bring a new understanding of it to the rest of the society. It is my sincere hope that their expectations in this regard may in some measure be fulfilled.

Limitations

The analysis presented in this book is based on a very small sample of people in one particular location. Because of this, it did not seem appropriate to pursue the collection of highly quantified data for testing hypotheses. For ex-ample, the reader will find that the role of alcoholic beverages is referred to at several points in this book, but no quantitative material is given. With the small size of the sample, it did not seem worthwhile or significant to attempt to collect precise data on frequency and quantity of alcohol consumption. Fur-thermore, such probing might have jeopardized rapport with people and posed some ethical problems as well.

To the extent that this study generates research questions that it does not sufficiently examine or answer, it should be seen as a plea for further re-search. Systematic research on much larger samples of populations in poverty would allow us to make reliable comparisons among different samples of peo-ple, would enhance our understanding of poverty in general, and would be useful for designing appropriate policy and programs. However, one caveat must be included here: research on "the poor" can be useless and misleading if we do not also have comparable research on "the nonpoor," and on society in general, to provide a context and a basis for generalizations. Too often social scientists—and the public—have made comparisons of "lower-class behavior" and "middle-class behavior" in which the former was researched but the latter merely assumed; in which "real behavior" of the poor is compared to "ideal behavior" of the middle class.[3] The paucity of empirical research concerning other segments of society has led to some unfortunate, misleading, and per-nicious statements about "the poor." So, while hoping that this study might generate future research questions, I do not mean to suggest that research should concentrate only on poverty-stricken populations.

A further limitation of the analysis presented in this book is that it relies on data that did not derive equally from all informants. In anthropological fieldwork, as opposed to random-sample surveys, data are gathered from situations and informants where the investigator has best access. Approx-imately thirty households were only briefly interviewed, and so were known only partially. Of the remaining forty households, some were visited much more often than others. Some homes afforded more up-close observation; some informants spoke more easily, candidly, perceptively. Close personal ties developed with some individuals and families, while relationships with other families remained more formal and distant. The most complete and in-depth data came from a half-dozen families who were intensively involved in the study for long periods of time. As a result, the analysis does not reflect all individuals or households equally, although I have tried to seek balance by using the insights from more closely observed informants as clues to what to probe with other people.

The main effect of this fieldwork bias will be noticed in the predominance of women and children—their words, their actions, and my interpretations of their situations. In fieldwork, I had greatest access to women, not only because of our shared sex roles, but also because of our shared interest in children. Additionally, during many of the hours I spent in homes, women and children outnumbered men. Some men were only briefly around and available for conversation; some husbands would find an excuse to leave the house soon after I arrived. Although I came to know most of the men, and knew some of them well enough to learn a lot about and from them, generally I knew the men in their capacity as husbands, fathers, brothers, or sons of the women I knew. Wherever possible, I tried to correct the feminine cast of the research, for a holistic case study of rural poverty must be done from the point of view of both men and women. Occasionally I bridged the obvious distance between male informant and female investigator by observing and listening in situations where men interacted with other men and boys, and quite often there were husband-and-wife conversations to join. But most one-to-one conversations with men were somewhat formal situations, perhaps because some of the men continued to believe that I was really a spy for the welfare department, or connected in some way with the schools. Despite the effort, the balance of observations, conversations, and activities—as reflected in field notes—was clearly on the side of women and children. Perhaps, however, this emphasis has merits of its own.

Chestnut Valley and Beyond

Even the qualitative, small-sample analysis presented in this book can be generalized beyond the immediate research population. There seem to be striking similarities with rural poverty in other localities, and to some extent also with situations of urban poverty. One can find these similarities in ethnographic studies of other American poverty situations.[4] Similarities have also become apparent through probing the experiences of social science researchers, applied social scientists, human service personnel, and others who have worked among poverty-stricken populations in many areas of the United States.[5]

It is hoped that the observations presented here may help readers to understand a variety of poverty situations elsewhere in America. However, it would require much careful study to assess the degree to which any of the conclusions based on research among white rural poor people in the northeastern United States are applicable to other rural poverty locations, let alone to urban poverty, or to poverty situations with different ethnic or racial variables. The question would be: to what extent do the generalizations derived from this case study in northern Appalachia hold up in the mountains of southern Appalachia, the delta of the Mississippi, the Indian reservations of the Great Plains, the Mexican-American barrios of the Southwest, or the ghettos of the eastern cities? Despite variations in location and details, an in-heritance of economic poverty and social marginality is likely to produce many similar features, no matter where it occurs in our affluent late-twentieth-century society. But until much research is accomplished, caution must be taken in applying conclusions based on one population to other populations with different parameters.

In addition to a substantive understanding of poverty, the book should also have transferability in that it presents a model of inquiry. The holistic ap-proach of anthropology is a multifaceted perspective that views a societal problem from the combined points of view of historical forces, economic situa-tions, social structures, cultural values, and attitudinal factors. Additionally, the anthropological tradition stresses the need to see a situation from the point of view of the people who are in it. Thus, it directs the investigator to seek out and listen to people's own statements of their aspirations and ex-periences. This anthropological mode of inquiry is an antidote to single-factor explanations of poverty and to out-of-context descriptions of poor people's behavior and values.

Why This Book?

This study grew out of the concerns of the 1960s, when the American mainstream and the U.S. government discovered a fact that many Americans had known firsthand all along—that, sprinkled in the midst of affluence, there was also serious poverty.

Over the years since this study began, the public's interest and the govern-ment's commitment to overcoming poverty have gradually tapered off and faded away. Unfortunately, it cannot be said that poverty, too, has become a thing of the past. It hasn't.[6] And because it hasn't, there is still a need for studying and analyzing the problem, and for sharing the perceptions gained in that endeavor. That is the reason for this book.

The people of this study, for the most part, are still poor. But they are much more than that. They are people who love and hate, laugh and cry, work and play. They are grandparents and parents, spouses and in-laws, children and babies, friends, adversaries, lovers, co-workers and neighbors. They are also people whose lives are fraught with problems and who cling to a precarious balance between hope and despair. Their actions in this difficult set of cir-cumstances are generally misunderstood and often judged harshly by the sur-rounding society. And these negative judgments only make the situation worse, for they become causative agents that keep people down, that make them fail, and create the likelihood that their children, too, will fail.

Better understanding, in itself, is therefore necessary and important as a first step to overcoming the problem of poverty in rural America. To furnish a new understanding is the main goal of this book, and it is an expressed desire of the people whose actions and words have contributed so much to the study.

> If people would try to see what it's like from our point of view. . . .

This search for an understanding of poverty in rural America begins in Part 2 with an investigation into the historical forces that brought it about in the first place. In Part 3, separate chapters present ethnographic description and analysis of economic patterns, marriage and the family, patterns of childhood, relationships within the neighborhood, and relationships with the wider community. Part 4 integrates the different threads of the book by delineating the ongoing causes that perpetuate rural poverty, and by suggesting some remedies that could break the generation-to-generation cycle.

Part 2

Historical Background

History: The Trends of Time

Introduction

Over the course of the last hundred years an economic and social blight has slowly penetrated parts of the rural northeastern United States, insidiously attacking the small farming communities of upland plateau and hill regions. The blight began as an economic illness, causing agricultural decline; it later progressed to a social decay, causing the collapse of rural communities. The blight proceeded unrelentingly, with much the same inexorable sweep as was the case in the chestnut blight, which struck the same region and wiped out whole hillsides of stately and useful trees. And just as the succeeding growth was a paltry replacement for the chestnut trees, so the new institutional substitutes emanating from the growing urban centers were never able to compensate for the losses that had occurred in the rural upland areas.

A major long-range effect of this socioeconomic blight has been the tenacious problem of rural nonfarm poverty. Therefore, an understanding of historical forces must necessarily precede an analysis of the contemporary problem of economic poverty and social marginality in the rural areas. And so, we turn now to an examination of the intertwined forces of economic and social history as they were played out in this particular locality.[1]

1800 to 1870

Settlement, Development, Consolidation

Chestnut Valley lies in one of the later regions of New York State to be taken over by white settlers. But once development began, it proceeded quickly, compressing in a short period the same general phases that occurred more slowly in other upland areas of the Northeast.[2] In the first two decades of the nineteenth century, settlers came in rapidly, mostly from eastern areas of New York State and from New England, with some from Maryland and Virginia also. (Among these early settlers were the great-great grandparents of several of the older people now living in Chestnut Valley.) Farmers of greater financial means bought up large tracts of land in the flatter valley areas, while those of more limited means and those who came somewhat later were restricted in their choice of location to hillsides and hilltops. The new residents quickly cleared the forests, developed farms, made roads, built houses and stores, and established schools and churches. In-migration continued until about 1855, when the population reached a peak that was not regained until more than a century afterwards.

Chestnut Valley, like many other hamlets in the region, grew and developed as a small crossroads center, a nucleus of services and people at the center of a surrounding hinterland farming area. In the 1860s, the hamlet was able to satisfy most of the service needs of its residents. The maps of 1867 show that there were twenty-four buildings, about equally divided between residences and business establishments. There was one general merchandise store that also housed the post office; there was also a shoe store, a cabinet shop and harnessmaker's shop, and a doctor's office. Nearby were a tannery and a shoemaker, and there was a mill down along the stream. There were two Protestant churches, each with a parsonage, and one cemetery. (Within a decade, however, one church disappeared from the maps.) In addition to the one-room schoolhouse in the hamlet, two other schools were located in the nearby countryside. The area served by the hamlet was roughly three to four miles in diameter, and included about forty farms.

As in many other upland areas of the Northeast, the period around the Civil War marked the apex of early development and growth of the small agriculture-based community. After that, the number of people and dwellings, the amount of land under cultivation, the number of businesses, and the possibility for prosperity all began to diminish.

1870 to 1920

Gradual Decline of Agriculture

In the closing decades of the nineteenth century, agriculture in Chestnut Valley began its slow decline, just as it did elsewhere in the northeastern upland plateau. The decline was related to national trends: rapid expansion of more productive agriculture in the Midwest; development of modern systems of long distance transportation (first the canals, then the railroads); and the beginning of mass marketing of farm products in an increasingly urbanizing nation.

The severity and extent of agricultural decline in any particular locality was largely determined by local soil and topographical factors. Except for a few valley floors, the predominant soils in the Chestnut Valley area are categorized as marginal or submarginal for agriculture. They are mostly low in nutrients and highly acidic, and contain stones and clay. These soil characteristics, combined with the common slope of 8 to 15 percent, make the land vulnerable to erosion.[3] The rough terrain imposes further limitations on farming: problems of water supply for hilltop farms; lack of running streams large enough for mills; long distances over rough roads to the mills and markets of larger villages.

In the earlier period of subsistence farming on newly cleared land, these limitations of geography, topography, and soil were not particularly restrictive. But in the late nineteenth century, they became significant impediments to further development of local agriculture. It was not so much that the natural resources had changed (although soil fertility had probably been depleted through several decades of use), but that the conditions of agriculture had changed.[4] New technology, agronomic patterns, transportation facilities, and marketing techniques were revolutionizing agriculture in other regions of the United States and in the better suited parts of the Northeast, but they simply could not be utilized here. These poor-soil hill farms were not responsive to the new technology and were difficult to adapt to efficient large-scale production for emerging mass marketing systems. Furthermore, the small-scale family farm, providing the family's sustenance and a limited cash income, was hardly able to generate the cash savings needed for investment in modern agriculture. Those farmers who could afford to do so got out of "back hill farming" in this region, either migrating to modern farms in the Midwest or moving into urban occupations in nearby, growing cities. Those who stayed, and the new farm operators who came in to buy up the hill farms when others left, could only adapt by attempting to find small niches where there was a demand for products that they could successfully raise despite the problems of soil, topography, and limited capital.

The predominant pattern in the first decades of the twentieth century was the small-scale family farm, which supplied products for home consumption, either by people (milk, eggs, beef, lamb, poultry, vegetables, and apples) or by animals (barley, oats, and wheat). Surplus products—cream, milk, veal, grains, and later hay and potatoes—were sold or traded locally. Few, if any, products were produced solely for market. The poor-soil farms were not heavily capitalized, substituting family labor or cheap farmhand labor for cash investment, and bringing a very low cash return to the farmer.

One elderly woman recalled her father's farm as it was about 1910.

> My father had grown up on that farm, and later he bought it from his father. There were 260 acres, but a big part of it was woodland and too steep to farm. My father was a good farmer. He had a hired man to help him, and my brothers, of course. My mother and sister and I didn't do much farm work, as we had work of our own to do.

My father kept around twenty cows and usually three horses and a flock of sheep. He raised a variety of crops, mostly grains to feed the animals, and food for the family. He raised pretty much the same crops his father had. He had grown up knowing which crops did best and on which part of the farm. He didn't have to learn that in books.

The cows were for our own use, and also we took milk to sell to the creamery in the Valley. We raised the bull calves born on the farm to sell as veal calves. What few things we needed to buy, my father often got by trading calves or lambs or potatoes directly. Of course we never had to buy such things as coal for heating, as we cut all our own wood. My father would figure on just two trips a year to the County Seat to buy what he needed, to have our teeth fixed and our eyes fitted. Mostly we provided for ourselves and our needs.

People worked so hard in those days. They didn't expect to get much money. All they wanted was to live comfortably, to provide their family with food and clothes and a place to live. We had a good life, but it was a struggle.

Acquisition of a farm or a farm operation was relatively open during this period.[5] Some men were able to take over or inherit working farms from their families, but purchase was even more common. A young man could save his earnings from working as a farm laborer (either year-round or seasonal), then expand this capital with loans from relatives to enable him to purchase a farm. Renting and share-farming were also common paths toward the goal of eventual farm ownership. These systems allowed a young man to accumulate savings and at the same time to build up a herd and machinery, so that when he eventually purchased his own farm, he would already have the livestock and equipment.

From 1870 to 1920, there was a steady increase in the rate of turnover of ownership of farms, and an increasing mobility of farm families within the area. In a fairly clear pattern, both tenants and owners moved through a succession of slightly better farms, with first-time owners taking over the least desirable locations as the former owners or renters moved up to slightly more productive farms, or left farming entirely. Toward the end of this period, the buyers included families coming back from the Midwest to obtain inexpensive hill farms.

In addition to turnover and mobility, this period also shows an absolute decrease in the number of people engaged in farming. Some farm families moved off the land to nearby towns and cities, and some farm-raised young adults left for urban areas, in both cases giving up agriculture. Thus, the "excess population" was being drained off the land. Most farmland was not actually abandoned, however, since land belonging to absentee owners could be rented or share-farmed by nearby farmers, who frequently used the barns and even the abandoned houses for storage of crops. But some of the most marginal farmland was let go, growing up in brush and scrub trees, evidenced by the fact that whitetail deer began to reappear in the area around 1915, after having been totally absent during the period of most extensive farming.[6]

Despite these trends, farming was still the community's economic base at the end of the period, as it had been at the beginning. But the base was not healthy. On the whole, the farms were generally of low productivity, and few farmers were making a significant cash profit after meeting family consump-tion needs. Older farmers whose sons had moved away to the cities wanted only to get through their last years on the farm. Younger men who remained on the farms could expand their acreage through inexpensive rental of extra land, but they could not expect to prosper. The limited cash profits meant limited cash available for capital investment, and many farmers were locked into such financially uneconomical patterns as the continued practice of pro-ducing their own feed grains. The lack of cash combined with factors of poor soil quality, difficult topography, and difficult farm-to-market transport—and all these factors prevented farmers from wholeheartedly entering into market production.[7] Subsistence farms continued in this area long after much of U.S. agriculture was becoming fully market-oriented.

Changes in the Nature of the Rural Community

Reflecting a period of change in agricultural patterns, the social community, too, was undergoing change and redefinition. Mobility and turnover on the farms affected the social composition of the hamlet nucleus that formed the center of the farming hinterland. The population of the hamlet remained steady and then increased slightly, as some farm families moved inward from their difficult farms, more than counterbalancing those hamlet residents who had left for the larger towns and cities.

During this period (1870–1920), the overall trend in the region was that people of the open-country farms and of the smaller hamlets began to turn outward to more distant communities for more of their service needs. Flourishing villages, towns, and small cities offered a diversity of business ser-vices, government functions, and educational facilities, and these became ever more accessible with modern transportation. The service-dependence on outside communities increased steadily, especially in the early decades of the twentieth century.

Concomitantly, the commercial activities of the hamlets contracted and their volume of trade diminished. By 1920, Chestnut Valley showed a markedly reduced array of services. Two grocery stores remained, two blacksmiths, one wagon shop, a shoe shop, and a creamery where farmers brought their whole milk to be separated, leaving the cream to be made into butter. (Soon afterward, the creamery was closed, replaced by a skimming station, so that farmers had to cart the separated cream to a cheese factory elsewhere.)

Nevertheless, as social communities, the smaller hamlets and their associated open-country hinterlands continued to show considerable strength and cohesion. Throughout the period, the Chestnut Valley community provided social life and social identification for its residents. As late as 1920, a variety of formal institutions united the hamlet with its hinterland in a yearly round of activities. The church had an active ladies aid society, with a membership of about thirty-five, including farm wives as well as residents of the hamlet. The farm bureau and home bureau met regularly in the community. The hamlet school was also the center of a variety of practical and festive events for the public. In 1920, few local people looked to the growing urban centers for their entertainment or social life. This hamlet-and-hinterland social unit was a viable, active community.

1920 to 1950

Severe Agricultural Decline

The dominant theme during the decades after World War I was gradual abandonment of farming as the economic base of the community and as a livelihood and way of life for its families. Many of the poorer farms were unwanted: the older people who had struggled through their last years on these farms died; and their sons and daughters turned to more promising futures elsewhere. Since farms in these marginal agricultural areas were not competitive in market production, they had benefited only minimally from the wartime and postwar agricultural boom conditions.

The price of good local farmland fell to under ten dollars an acre, while some went down to two dollars an acre, putting it within reach of people of quite limited means. From distant cities came industrial workers, some of them first-generation immigrants from eastern and southern Europe, ready to invest their meager savings from years in American mines and factories, hoping to fulfill their dream of becoming independent farmers on their own land. Some purchased their land sight unseen from real-estate catalogues, or viewed under a blanket of snow. "When the snow melted, we found that it was mostly stones and clay." Other new buyers came because they had been squeezed out of competitive midwestern agriculture, attracted by the low prices and the possibility of smaller scale farming. Some families moved to Chestnut Valley after having given up marginal subsistence farming in a similar but even less promising region elsewhere in the Northeast. Typical of this latter pattern is a family with six children who came in the late 1930s from a farm in the western part of the state, "a small farm with ramshackle outbuildings and a bedraggled house with sooty walls and plank floors."

Turnover on farms became particularly rapid in the late 1920s, with both population exodus and in-migration superimposed on the older pattern of mobility of local families from farm to farm within the area.[8] Within six to ten years, a piece of land might be bought, worked, given up as hopeless, and, if possible, sold again. Each new owner struggled until he, too, sank into debt. For those who stayed in agriculture, farming remained, as it had earlier been, a labor-intensive operation in which subsistence production was predominant, capital investment limited, and cheap family labor crucial. It was hardly a profitable venture and many local farmers were poor and in debt.

At the same time, many of those who gave up their low-production farms entered the urban labor market at a disadvantage, often in debt and unable to offer marketable labor skills. They continued to live in their rural farmhouses because it was less costly to do so, but even when they stopped farming, their financial situation did not improve substantially. Thus, by the 1930s, there were impoverished rural nonfarm people as well as impoverished farm people.[9]

In hindsight, it was a period of sharp agricultural decline, but at the time the severity and irrevocability of that decline were disguised or not fully perceived. Land continued to be worked, and people contined to live on farms and to eat from them. But it became progressively harder to break even in farming, and the degree of modernization fell farther and farther behind that of other regions. More farmers met their cash needs by taking on outside work. Highway work, carpentry, or factory work became the sole source of cash for some families. The farm operation was scaled down to production solely for home consumption, and the wives took over much of what remained to be done on the farm: caring for the chickens, a cow or two, a couple of pigs, and a vegetable garden.

A few farmers attempted to adapt to the changing situation by intensifying their farming, specializing in certain cash crops. Often this was a short-term solution, feasible only as long as market prices remained high, competition was weak, and the farmer had good direct access to a retail market. It was during this period that timothy hay, well suited to local soil conditions, became a major cash crop as well as a farm-consumed item. Hay was sold to commercial middlemen who traveled from farm to farm with equipment to bale it to be shipped off, particularly to New York City. (The main consumers were the horses of the city's equestrian police force.) But the farmer received a diminishing share of the market price, and the demand decreased dramatically. Similarly, potatoes became a major cash crop for a time, and were shipped out to the coal mining areas of Pennsylvania. But this market, too, succumbed to competition from other growing areas and to the fall of market prices. Eggs, also, were briefly a market-production item for some farmers.

The Depression years, with prices bottoming out between 1930 and 1934, and remaining low almost until 1940, caused a decrease in the already meager market production in the area, since the proceeds from crop and dairy sales hardly met the cost of production. According to the local newspaper correspondent in 1932, the Chestnut Valley potato crop was going to buyers for twenty-five cents a bushel, down from $2.25 or more in 1920. An elderly farmer remembers when it wasn't even worth hauling the potatoes to town. As a consequence, some families discontinued production for the market. But retrenchment to subsistence farming is, in a sense, a disguised form of agricultural decline, a retreat back to an earlier kind of farming, even less profitable, even less modern.

During the 1920s, some of the least productive land was removed from agricultural use, simply abandoned to the natural succession of weeds, brush, and scrub trees. But there was still a great deal of low-productivity land being farmed. Long before the Depression made it worse, agricultural economists were concerned with the problem of unprofitable agriculture on unproductive land in some regions of New York State. The experts argued that the physical characteristics of the local soil, particularly its poor water-handling capacity, would make this hilly terrain only minimally responsive to such new techniques as the application of agricultural lime and chemical fertilizers. Furthermore, the region still lacked the improved roads and marketing facilities deemed essential to the survival of local agriculture. Hence, the best solution appeared to be to remove the unsuitable land from agricultural use entirely.[10] In the 1930s, the state government carried out an extensive program of buying poor agricultural land (largely submarginal, but including some marginal land) in the central and southwestern part of the state.

Around Chestnut Valley, the state bought a considerable amount of poor quality hilly farmland that was lying unused. Many of these parcels had been sold at least once in the previous decade, or had only recently been acquired by inheritance or foreclosure. Neither absentee owners nor neighboring farmers found it worthwhile to work the old fields, and few young men were willing to take over the marginal operations still extant. In most cases the land was sold eagerly to the state for as little as two dollars an acre. Where houses remained, unoccupied by owner or tenant, they were dismantled by the owner and reconstructed in a nearby hamlet, or added to a farmhouse somewhere else, or even pulled down or burned down by the state. By 1935, much of the submarginal land had been removed from agriculture and had begun its transition to state forest areas, which it remains today.

Individual Histories of Withdrawal from Farming

The gradual and cumulative abandonment of farming is illustrated over and over in the life histories of individual farm families. Elderly residents of Chestnut Valley recall in detail the difficulty of eking out a living from a marginal farm, and the slow process by which they adjusted to changing times. Their nostalgia for the past is definitely tempered by their vivid memories of the all-consuming struggle. As one man put it, "People may talk of the good old times. Well, they weren't. They were the bad old times." The struggle and the gradual withdrawal is revealed in three individual life histories, briefly summarized below.

In the first passage below, an elderly woman who grew up on a farm in Chestnut Valley describes the gradual transition out of farming during her own generation. It is a typical example, starting with a farm that had been settled by her forebears before 1840, and ending with the sale to the state, almost a century later.

After I finished my schooling, I taught three years in the schools of the neighborhood. Then I married and left home. My husband worked as a hired man on a farm ten miles away from my family's farm. He worked there two and a half years, but didn't earn much. Then he worked on a farm nearer where he grew up. But still, he wasn't getting much pay for such hard work. He didn't seem to be getting anywhere. Then he quit and worked a while for the railroad. Finally, he went into carpentry. He started as an apprentice and he worked hard, learned quickly, and advanced well as a carpenter. In 1920 we moved from his family's place to this village.

My older brother lived home until he was thirty years old. He farmed with our father, just like our father had farmed with his father. Then my brother got married and began farming up the road on the next farm. But he just couldn't make it on his own. Father helped him out sometimes with some of the harvesting. Then there were some hailstorms and other things that hurt his crops. So he just gave up farming. He and his wife and their first two children moved to the city [thirty miles away] where he got a job in a factory. [The brother's piece of land was then bought by a neighboring farmer just starting out.]

Then my father died, at the relatively young age of sixty. He just killed himself working on that farm. He had worked so hard on that land, that stone heap! He only just eked out a living. We often said that if he'd picked some other region to settle in, life might have been a little easier for all of us. After he died, my mother wanted to move off the farm. She gave it to my brother. She asked him to take the farm off her hands. He used to come up from the city where he was living to plant some crops on the farm. He'd haul the crops all the way back with him to sell in the city. That was pretty hard. Then he let others use the place for farming. Then, when the state offered to buy the land, my brother sold it to them.

In the passage below, a brief summary of the contours of one man's life illustrates a fairly typical history of farming through the first half of the twentieth century. Mr. Clark, born before the turn of the century, is like many other marginal farmers who struggled most of a lifetime before giving up the farm. Clark recalls his father vividly.

"My dad was a potato farmer, a very good farmer . . . terrific ambition. I remember how he'd almost lather like a horse under the harness; and he wouldn't walk, he'd almost trot."

Clark's father was a tenant farmer, moving through a succession of farms in the township, generally operations small in size and potential. He kept a few cows, once as many as twenty-five, as well as pigs, chickens, sheep, and always several workhorses. Clark's father rented additional land nearby, and concentrated on potatoes (up to twenty acres) and hay. He also raised a variety of grains for the farm animals. At times they had a regular hired man, who was given the use of a tenant house as well as produce and firewood. Normally, extra help would be hired only for the short duration of potato digging.

Clark grew up as his father's main help. He says, "I was practically raised in a potato field." He took the milk to the creamery and the potatoes to town, and did all kinds of field work. His schooling was intermittent, with several moves to different school systems, as his father moved from one farm to another, but he loved to read. He also took part-time jobs occasionally. Later, Clark went to work independently as a hired man on a series of different farms in the area. Then, with his new bride from the farm next to where he had grown up, Clark went into farming on his own.

He rented a series of farms, generally small-scale, diversified operations on relatively poor soil and hilly, remote parts of the community. He could put almost no cash into his operations, except for the small rent. But his labor investment was high. He raised a variety of crops (buckwheat, oats and barley mixture, and hay) for his small herd of livestock (eight cows, three horses), and sold buckwheat for what cash he needed. He felt he could not make a go of it if he bought feed, as some farmers did, particularly as he was not selling milk as a source of cash income.

The Depression years found Clark, his wife, and children living in a house that had been abandoned, getting along with the help of relatives and what little work he could find with other farmers. They moved again to a nearby farm, and then in the mid-1930's, they rented a farm on the same hill where Clark had spent several boyhood years. After a few years of renting, the owner offered to sell him the nearly 200-acre farm for $800, including the house, barn, and grain crib. As Clark says, "Even in those days, that was really a bargain." So he scraped up the money from relatives and became a farm owner. He built up a herd and sold extra calves. He kept about a half-dozen cows, and took milk to the separator in the hamlet, where the cream was sold and the skim milk brought home for calves and pigs. He also raised veal calves to sell.

Clark was typical of those farmers with meager cash resources who could not make the necessary investment to get themselves into the more profitable market of selling whole milk to dairies. "The barn wasn't in any shape to sell milk. It had to pass inspection—and this old rattletrap barn wouldn't. It would have cost a lot of money to fix it up to be allowed to sell milk."

Clark and his wife and children continued a diversified operation, in which they raised virtually all their food and the feed grains for the animals. Although he sometimes planted potatoes on a fairly extensive scale, generally Clark's farming was marginal in size as well as profits. He never invested in mechanized farming, continuing with horses all along. Eventually, though, Clark made enough money from selling small amounts of cream, eggs, and potatoes to pay back his loans.

By the end of World War II, some of the children had left home, moving into nonfarm employment, and Clark's ability to work was severely curtailed by poor health. No longer able to keep the farm going, the Clarks sold the place. With the proceeds, they bought and renovated a rundown house in the hamlet, and Clark's wife took a job in the city.

A few farmers, however, were able to keep above the break-even point. They took advantage of falling land prices to acquire additional land for expanding their operations. Good land could be purchased for about ten dollars an acre in 1920, while poorer land went for between two and five dollars an acre, and marginal farmland could be rented for a dollar an acre. Thus, with a little increased investment derived from profitable farming, from hiring out, or from loans from relatives, some farmers could manage to enlarge and modernize their operations during a period when others were just barely hanging on or giving up. The career path of a farmer who not only hung on to his farm throughout his lifetime, but managed to make it a paying operation, reveals the combination of factors that contributed to success.

Mr. Block was nearly an adult when he came to Chestnut Valley in the early 1900s. His parents had moved here from western New York to take over a farm that had belonged to a cousin. After working for his father and then working a few years as a hired hand, and with the help of loans from family, relatives, and neighbors, plus a bank mortgage, Block was able to buy one hundred acres adjoining his father's farm. He later took on a share-farm operation (half the proceeds to the owner, half to Block, with free use of land and buildings). Subsequently, he purchased this farm, thus owning outright two adjacent farms. He kept a small herd of cows (about eight) for the sale of milk and calves, and grew buckwheat and oats-barley mixture for market. Block's well-kept account books show that he always knew which parts of his operation were profitable, which ones not. And so he shifted from one emphasis to another, specializing now in potatoes, now in eggs. When possible, he expanded his holdings until he was managing quite a large farm, by local standards. However, his enterprise had a greater proportion of crops to dairying than was the case among other similarly prosperous farmers in the area. He purchased modern harvesting machinery as it became available, often paying off the cost and turning a profit by hiring out himself and his tractor and machinery to do harvesting for other non-mechanized farmers. He continued to expand his operation until he reached middle age. Then he began to scale down the operation and took on some part-time carpentry work. As old age approached, and with no children desiring to take over the farm, Block further reduced his crop acreage, eliminated his livestock, and began to live off his savings.

These individual life histories and the aggregate history of the community reveal that the period from 1920 to 1950 was one of severe agricultural decline to the point where farming no longer formed the economic base of the community. Operating farmers comprised a small and decreasing fraction of the community, and they were mostly elderly.

Demise of an Active Social Community

In terms of population size, the total hamlet-and-hinterland community of Chestnut Valley decreased steadily from 1920 to 1950, as more people moved away from farms, and fewer families came in to replace them. However, the population loss was mostly from the open country. The hamlet center actually increased, particularly in the 1930s, as there was a move inward from hinterland to hamlet. Older people who had finally given up the family farm moved to the hamlet to be near relatives and friends. Additionally, some young sons and daughters of farm families took urban jobs but did not want to live either on the isolated farms or in the city, choosing instead the intermediate situation of the rural hamlets. Inexpensive housing was available in the hamlet where, for example, closed-down shops could be converted into homes.

In the early 1920s, the community thrived as a social entity. Community identity and pride were strong. The hamlet-and-hinterland community had a cohesion built out of history, supported by the framework of formal institutions, and reinforced by ties of kinship and marriage, and by informal social relationships. The variety and vitality of Chestnut Valley's activities and organizations during the peak years of the early and middle 1920s is revealed in the weekly "correspondence" sent from Chestnut Valley to the newspapers of nearby county seats. In addition to the many items reporting births, marriages, illnesses, and deaths, the notes about people's visiting and traveling and the vicissitudes of their farming, the weekly news columns also present a picture of a high level of organized activity.

- The church was active, with regular services and a resident minister. A Sunday school was organized, and church socials were well attended. (By 1930, several churches from the township were consolidated into a larger parish organization, sharing an itinerant minister, but there seems to have been no diminution of local church activity until many years later.)
- The ladies aid society of the church was active, meeting monthly in Chestnut Valley homes, with close to forty members.

- A cemetery association supervised the church's cemetery.
- A meeting hall above a store was used for "political meetings and entertainment."
- A Red Cross auxiliary was formed.
- A county library truck delivered books to the school and to the home of a widow who served as community librarian.
- The home bureau (sponsored by Cooperative Extension) held monthly all-day meetings in women's homes, with demonstrations by the extension agents, and occasional tureen suppers. Membership and attendance varied from twenty to fifty women. The home bureau held periodic wiener roasts at the church, to which the community was invited.
- The farm bureau and home bureau combined with the ladies aid society to sponsor activities and education programs in the church. Open to the whole community, the morning programs and evening movies drew a crowd of sixty to eighty.
- There was a men's baseball team that played the teams of other villages of the township.

Perhaps the most important institution in the community was the local school. The elementary school in "the village" (as the hamlet center of the community was proudly called) had twenty or more "scholars" attending, with a succession of young women teachers from the community. There was also one school in the nearby countryside, the second having closed its doors in 1920 because there were "only four legal-age children" in its district.

The school was active in sponsoring public community activities. There were "Christmas exercises," to which the public was invited, and yearly Halloween socials—which were held in the church parlor but sponsored by the school, with proceeds going toward the purchase of books for the school. There were public meetings to decide on questions of district consolidation (at that time, consolidation meant one one-room school combining with another), and public meetings to elect school trustees. These meetings were usually followed by "a social event," with ice cream served. Many families attended, "including children."

Older students had to leave the community if they were to attend high school. They boarded out in rather distant communities, but their progress and their visits home were followed in the local news column, their graduations attended by a host of proud relatives from Chestnut Valley.

There were various public health services available in the community. Occasional free clinics were held at the church, sponsored by the Red Cross or the tuberculosis association of the county. Two doctors from nearby villages and three nurses served at the clinics. A diptheria immunization clinic was held at the school for all children of the community.

Such was the tenor and level of organized activity in the hamlet-and-hinterland community of Chestnut Valley at its high point in the mid-1920s. However, by the late 1920s and all through the 1930's, the character of the community was changing and the rate of change accelerating. As a social community, Chestnut Valley suffered severe and protracted decline. The combined forces of urbanization and modern auto transportation made it increasingly difficult to hold people's allegiance to their home locality, difficult to ensure active participation at the local community level. Some people were attending and joining more active social groups and voluntary associations in the larger villages or in the urban area. But it was not only the pull of the rising urban community that undermined the rural community's social life. Basic transformations resulting from agricultural decline were also having a marked effect. With less farming, there were fewer informal get-togethers of farm families. And as informal interaction decreased, participation in formal organizations declined too. With little money available among hard-pressed farm families, there was little to spend on community social events. In addition, demographic factors took their toll. The high turnover of population and the presence of "outsiders" apparently made it difficult to maintain the sense of community: old-timers felt that the newcomers didn't integrate well. And an aging population structure, resulting from exodus of many young adults, further diminished participation in and decreased the vitality of community organizations. The social community was being eroded.

The World War II era seemed to place a temporary restraint on the pace of social change, and even gave some new purpose and life to old organizations. In 1945, the community retained the school, the church, one general store, and some organized groups. But Chestnut Valley had been able to hold on to only a small portion of its former cohesiveness and social animation, and only a small fraction of its young people. And thus, the community as a social entity had no strength to fight off the sweeping forces of the early 1950s.

1950 to 1970

The Final Collapse

The visual landscape of the rural Chestnut Valley area has changed remarkably. In 1920, according to photographs and local memories, clusters of farm buildings nestled around farmhouses, and big expanses of fields were neatly outlined by hedgerows of trees and interspersed with well-defined woodlots. Only a few areas were receding toward their wild state at that time. Now, in the 1970s, there is a motley mosaic of overgrown fields, brushy pastures, and young forests, with only a very few fields still under cultivation. A few forlorn hay barns stand alone in weedy fields, and along the back roads isolated cellar-holes are surrounded by a green carpet of myrtle, overgrown lilac bushes, and a line of front-yard maple trees.

Only four farms are still in operation, primarily dairy farms, renting additional land elsewhere for hay and corn. (This compares to about forty farms, each quite small in acreage, a century before.) More fields revert to weeds each year, and a diminishing acreage is tilled. Farming now plays a minor role upon the landscape.

Some of the old roads are totally abandoned, and some have no residences along them. By 1960, only eighteen of the original forty-two open-country homesteads that dotted the Chestnut Valley landscape in 1870 still had a usable house standing on the site. But countering this trend, some new dwellings have come in during this most recent period. Beginning in the mid-1950s, a few houses sprouted up along the back roads; by 1970, there were several new clusters of homes, mostly substandard houses and old trailers.

The townships surrounding Chestnut Valley all experienced significant population growth in the 1950s, mainly as a result of encroaching suburbanization. Several townships regained their 1850 population peak by 1960, and have continued growing since then. The Chestnut Valley area has also experienced population growth, but to a lesser degree and from different sources. The people who have come to Chestnut Valley recently are not middle-income suburbanites, but generally low-income rural families with insecure employment histories and low-skill jobs. Often they have come from other declining rural areas, and frequently they have come because of prior ties of kinship and friendship to the people of Chestnut Valley. Like the in-migrating farmers of a generation before, these people have come to this particular spot because the land and housing are relatively inexpensive and the cost of living is low. The major recent growth in Chestnut Valley's population, however, has been due to natural increase of the resident population, as the adult sons and daughters of the poverty-stricken families settle their trailers on their relatives' property and raise their families.

In the hamlet of Chestnut Valley, as well as in the countryside, the visual landscape has changed. The aging houses have suffered wear and tear outpacing upkeep and repair. While only a very few houses have been built in the last half-century, the former schoolhouse, shops, and stores have been converted into residences, or have burned or been torn down.

It is the "social landscape" of the community that has changed most, however—almost beyond recognition. Since 1950, the effective social community has almost vanished. Chestnut Valley, once a viable rural community, has become the victim of urban centripetal forces. It is now totally without formal social, educational, religious, or service institutions, and no longer possesses even a small grocery store. The one-room school was closed in the early 1950s, its pupils bused away to consolidated urban school districts; the church doors are only rarely opened by an itinerant minister; the last grocery store gave in to the competition of suburban shopping centers; and the former local farm and home groups and other social groups have died out or been merged into consolidated township-wide or county-wide organizations.

As the formal institutional structure of the rural community was dismantled, the informal social interaction was also affected. Without the base of ongoing formal institutions, such as the elementary school, even informal interaction became difficult to maintain. Informal social patterns were also undermined by the decline of farming, since the traditional social-agricultural interactions of working and celebrating had fallen into obsolescence. Additionally, informal social patterns crumbled as the population became increasingly burdened with old age or with the daily problems of poverty—or with both.

Today, Chestnut Valley is a vague concept in terms of geographic boundaries. It has no identity as a post office address, a named telephone exchange, a school district, or a local government. And it is no longer considered a socially meaningful entity. As one person said, "There is no longer a community here at all, just people." There is little to unite the scatterings of residents in the hamlet and along the roads of the hinterland. No longer is farming the common interest it once was, providing for daily and seasonal patterns of conversation and communal action. No longer is there an annual round of activities to give meaning and regularity to interaction. No longer are there public places and public activities for the entire community.

Many people spoke of their perception of these changes, their sense of loss.

> These days there's no community feeling. Nobody cares what each other does. It used to be very different. Families would get together. Especially in farming—borrowing machinery and helping each other with the haying. And we had sewing bees and hymn sings and card parties and dances in each others' homes. And neighbors all helped out in emergencies. If you got burned out, all the neighbors would bring you things, help you start over, even let you live with them. And at funerals, we'd all help the family prepare the house and the food. Nowadays, nobody cares. Neighbors don't help each other in emergencies. You have to go to the welfare or the Red Cross or something—and that just isn't the same.

In former times, the people of these rural areas were geographically isolated from the growing, modernizing urban centers. As modern transportation improved, they turned increasingly to the cities and towns for services, goods, jobs, and schooling, although their social needs could all be satisfied within their own local communities. But in the end, this local social community crumbled. Rural people were unable to prevent the eventual disintegration of the social fabric of their small community. The blight that afflicted Chestnut Valley had struck not only at its economic base, but had eaten out its social core as well.

History:
Differential Adaptation to Change

The salient point of this history is that two trends coincided and exacerbated each other: agricultural decline and social collapse. Within this
historical context, we can see specific factors that brought about economic
poverty and social marginality in the rural upland area.

Differential Economic Adaptation

Changes in the economic base of the rural area had different effects on people; some were better able to cope with and adjust to these changes than
others.

Those who faced changing economic conditions from a position of strength
were able to adapt successfully. From interviews, life histories, and family account records, it appears that the factors fostering successful adaptation included absence of debt, availability of some cash resources, access to relatives
who could make loans, possession of a reasonably good farm in the family, access to farm machinery and starter herds from relatives, personal qualities
such as practical knowledge and astuteness in making farm decisions, and, of
course, luck. On the whole, those who came out on top were those who had
the resources and the flexibility to risk innovation, to expand their farming
operations, to specialize and modernize. These farmers were able to survive
price drops and natural disasters—such as crop failure, barn fire, or disease in
the milk herd—that might completely wipe out a marginal, debt-ridden
farmer. For these more secure farmers, the main limitations forcing eventual
withdrawal from farming were ill health, old age, or the lack of sons willing to
take over the farm.

However, many farm people were left behind by the changes of the 1920s,
1930s, and 1940s—left behind and trapped in poverty. Partly this was a matter of insufficient farm management skill. Several people have indicated that
hard work alone was simply not enough.

My brother, even though he was raised on a farm, couldn't run a farm on his own. He was smart enough, but it just wasn't his nature to run a farm. He could do the work all right, but he couldn't plan the farming, couldn't run it on his own.

My son was a hard worker, a good worker. But he couldn't make a go of it. He simply could not do the planning, make the decisions.

People were also left behind because the timing of their transition out of farming was unfavorable. Those who opted out earlier were able to sell their land for a good price and enter the urban economy solidly. Those who clung longer to their rural subsistence-scale operations (because they wanted to or because they had no alternative) found that by the 1930s their farms had become almost worthless, as no one wanted to buy run-down farms. But their skills were almost useless in the urban economy, and there was already a glut of would-be workers looking for scarce jobs. So the marginal operators remained stuck on their farms. They exhausted any cash reserves they had, retrenched to subsistence farming, and went further into debt. Since the demand for agricultural labor had diminished sharply, men were no longer able to supplement farm income or save toward buying a better farm through the traditional pattern of working for other farmers. Unable to get out of debt, unable to get out of farming, and unable to get their money out of their farms, many families were locked into dead-end farming at subsistence levels or below.

Similarly, small-scale entrepreneurs lost money and time trying to readjust their doomed rural businesses to changing conditions of the local community and the national economy. They invested borrowed cash and extra years of family labor to keep a small local shop or store going, only to realize later that the local trade area could no longer support their enterprise. But by that time, it was hard to get a toehold in the business world of the urban center.

For many rural people at this time, the lack of capital, of education, and of experience in nonagricultural jobs made adaptation outside agriculture at least as hard as adaptation within it. Men who did enter the urban job market often remained trapped in low-level jobs due to their lack of appropriate skill and training, and were vulnerable to displacement by mechanization. Some farm laborers and part-time farm operators (both owners and renters) who could not make ends meet on the farm took manual jobs with local highway departments as a part-time supplementary source of income. Gradually road work became a full-time replacement occupation.

The general effect of this period of sweeping economic changes was that a significant proportion of rural people were unable to make a successful transition. People who were already slightly behind at the start fell farther behind. For some local families, poverty became a lifetime condition, rather than a temporary state along the path to success. Residents remember the hardships of the late 1930s.

> There was nothing to eat but potatoes—and only a few of them. Since our mother was sick, we fed the potatoes to her. Us kids got the water they were cooked in—our potato soup.

> I remember seeing my mother crying because Dad was gone and there wasn't any food in the house. I remember seeing Mom doing all the farm work, doing man's work, wearing an old pair of man's shoes. Some years Dad would settle and get a good job, carpentry work or such, and we'd have a few decent meals and clothes.

The differential success of adaptations in the 1920s and 1930s has had long-range implications. Most of the residents of the Chestnut Valley area who adapted successfully during that period have lived out a life of relative security; their children and grandchildren are integrated successfully into the work force of the urban center, full participants in the organized activities and material rewards of modern life. On the other hand, the children and grand-children of the residents who found the earlier transition most difficult are today still attempting to cope with and adapt to a situation that demands more capital, skills, and risk-taking flexibility than they have available. Both then and now, the people with the fewest resources at hand (good farmland in the earlier period; or money, education, or sociopolitical position now) tend to have the fewest and least attractive options for adapting successfully to changing conditions. The limited economic adjustments of one generation have, in turn, placed limitations on the ability of the next generation to gain better access to resources from which new adaptations could be made; and so, poverty begets poverty.

Social Differentiation Without Exclusion

In social aspects also the sweeping changes affected people differently, and tended to produce social differentiation in the local population. But in the earlier period, this did not mean social separation and exclusion.

It is apparent that in the 1920s there was already some differentiation on the basis of prestige or status. From the lists of officers of the formal organizations of Chestnut Valley in that period, it is fairly clear that there were certain prominent families who more or less ran the community. The same names appear over and over in the records as officeholders in local township government, the church, the school, and community groups. But newspaper accounts and elderly people's recollections also reveal that attendance and participation in the organized social life of the community was fairly broadly based, rather than limited to the prominent families.

Similarly, in private visiting patterns, although there were social distinctions, apparently no class of excluded people existed. This conclusion is supported by the recollections of older residents, and also by the weekly newspaper columns, which kept track of who attended a Saturday night social at which farm, who visited whom for Sunday dinner, who was indisposed, and so forth. In these informal aspects, also, there was a circle of top families, interrelated by marriage and associated in frequent visiting.

The factors conferring high standing appear to have been: length of residence in the community, reputation of one's relatives, and prestige of previous generations of the family. But prestige criteria did not significantly restrict participation in the social life of the community. People who were not from "an old family" or "a respected family" might never attain the highest prestige, but they could be, and were, active participants in the social life of the community. Even the economic differences that existed between families did not divide people socially into clearly defined, noninteracting groups.[1] Times were hard, and most people had to struggle. Furthermore, in the self-sufficient family farming that characterized the area for so long, economic differences were not readily apparent in material consumption or style of living.

There were, indeed, a few families who were clearly poorer than most and whose reputation was generally not good. Their economic position is revealed in their patterns of working for many years as low-paid hired men, or in renting a succession of very small, marginal farms, never advancing far up the agricultural ladder. They were also found in such lower-level agriculture-related jobs as blacksmith's assistant. It is clear from recollections of people from both ends of the spectrum that some of these families were often the subject of whispered derision and jokes, or the objects of pity. They were people who, according to the higher-prestige people, "didn't amount to much." Sometimes their intelligence was called into question; often their drinking was cited. But it is also apparent that even these people were very definitely a part of the community, both in thought and in action. Those of lower status participated along with everyone else in the regular activities of work and play, education and worship.

Frequent social interaction among people, no matter what their prestige or wealth, was partly the result of the cooperative nature of traditional agricultural work patterns. Farmers "changed works" at peak harvest periods, with a group of several farm operators helping each other out. Both temporary and regular hired men would accompany their employers and participate fully in both the work and the celebration of its completion. It was a time of conviviality, as well as a time of fever-pitch work. If a hired man did his share of the work at such times, his presence was valued and his reputation as a worker might help to outweigh any other aspects of his standing in the community. In fact, a series of newspaper items shows that the whole community several times intervened with the legal authorities to have a young man let off lightly for a driving-while-intoxicated charge. Behind this action was the fact that the individual had earned a reputation as a good farmhand, and he was needed. It didn't matter that his family was not among the higher-prestige group.

The cohesion among families in the community, regardless of economic and status differences, was also a result of mutual interdependence. Neighborly help in time of crisis, companionship among isolated farm families, and lending of farm and household implements were real necessities. Fortunes and reputations were secondary to neighborliness; being a helping neighbor was a quality that bridged other distinctions. Because family emergencies and disasters small and large were common facts of life, no one could be so secure as to be above participating in this kind of reciprocity, no matter how he might feel privately about a particular neighbor.

The pattern of hired farm labor also contributed to keeping open the social interaction among families of different status, preventing a stratum of poor and rejected people from settling out on the bottom. A young man with no farm to inherit, or an older man who had been unable to do well in farming on his own, could find a secure position working for some other farmer. Often he and his family lived in a tenant house or in a part of the main farmhouse. His worth was judged by his hard work and faithfulness. His limited financial circumstances or the reputation of his parents hardly diminished his and his family's participation in the Saturday socials and harvest celebrations of the neighborhood.

The most significant differences between the poorer families and the rest of the community show up in the education and school experiences of children. Already in the 1930s, in the one-room school, some children were ridiculed. A graduate of the elementary school, looking back some forty years, recalls one family with three pupils in the school.

> It was whispered that their mother had left them, that their father was a drunkard, that the children were left to fend for themselves.

Some of the children from "unfortunate homes" are reported to have been shy and awkward in school, others pugnacious. Some attended only sporadically and were older and bigger than their classmates. Other children were somewhat separated not only by their poverty but also because of the recency of their arrival in Chestnut Valley, where it seemed everyone was related to everyone else, except for the newcomer families. A written recollection of a child's first days at the Chestnut Valley schoolhouse is vivid.

> The kids, strangers, made me feel funny. They stared and giggled, all friends and neighbors and cousins, except me. I was self-conscious in my once-bright polka-dot dress. It was faded now and didn't meet their approval. I slunk down, trying to hide under its sort of grey big collar. I was conscious of a hole in my sock. I felt like crying. No cousins, no friends, no nothing. I wanted to go home.

Beyond grammar school education, the better-off families sent their daughters and most of their sons to high school. The earlier pattern had been to send the "scholar" to board with relatives in a large town where he or she could attend high school. Later, bus transportation made it possible for students to attend high school on a daily basis while living at home, and more children were able at least to begin high school. Many of the children from the more successful rural families completed high school and some undertook further education. Eventually, they became schoolteachers, skilled workers and craftsmen, urban businessmen, or modern farmers—most of them secure socially as well as economically.

On the other hand, the families of limited economic resources and lower reputation rarely sent their daughters to high school; their sons, in some cases, never finish grammar school. The subsequent career profiles of these children tend to be confined to unskilled labor, interrupted work patterns and, in most cases, poverty.

It also appears that marriage patterns and the consequent social ties and residential location began to separate some groups of families from others. By the 1930s and 1940s, the sons and daughters of Chestnut Valley's more pros-perous families were marrying people who had grown up in other, more thriv-ing communities, people whose careers and futures were integrated into the growing, modernizing, urbanizing society. Almost none of them settled down in Chestnut Valley. During the same period, many children of the poorer families were marrying people of marginal backgrounds similar to their own, people from nearby run-down rural areas. Most of them settled in or near Chestnut Valley.

Despite the economic, social, and educational differences among residents, it seems clear that in the period from 1920 until close to 1950, there was no clear-cut clustering of an intergenerational group of derided and despised families living in poverty. True, there was obvious poverty, but "poverty" was neither a social identification nor a derogatory epithet. As one person said,

It wasn't so bad being poor in the old days. A lot of people were poor then, and you weren't an outcast just because you were poor.

Separation of Social Worlds

The subsequent loss of a local community has changed this picture drastically. No longer is there an integrative, cohesive community that can combine the full range of economic differences into a regularized round of activities and an inclusive sense of shared membership. The collapse of the local social community has brought about a cleavage of the population into almost completely separate groups, based on economic and social standing.

Furthermore, the replacement of the local rural community by the distant urban-suburban conglomerate has had markedly different effects on different families. The families who managed to stay above the margin economically, who operated reasonably profitable farms or took on fairly good part-time jobs, also tended to adapt well socially to the new urban-based community. They were integrated into formal organizations and informal networks that spanned a much wider geographic area. As rural depopulation set in—and each hamlet could no longer support its own granges, churches, and ladies' clubs—groups from scattered communities consolidated into single, larger units, often township-wide. The families who were on top economically tended to participate fully in these new, larger units, and thereby established a wide range of social ties. Additionally, they maintained close interaction with brothers and sisters, sons and daughters who had moved out to a wide geographic circle centering on the urban nucleus. These rural people developed networks of relatives, friends, and associates that became increasingly far-reaching. This expanded world became the new focus of their social life, replacing the decaying and insular rural hamlet-and-hinterland community. Even though they continued to live in the rural areas, these families developed wide horizons and a feeling of belonging to a larger, more varied, and more urban community. Their special activities and interests, anchored elsewhere, were more important to them than their home locality, and thus they were able to insulate themselves from the deleterious effects of the decline of the rural community.

For other families in the Chestnut Valley area, however, the range of identification remained significantly more restricted. The very people who were unable to keep on top of the economic changes of the 1920s were the ones most severely affected by the loss of local community. For them, incorporation into the urban community has been much slower and less satisfactory. As new urban institutions took over from rural community organizations, the poorer rural residents were not able to transfer their participation or to forge new social ties. Their relatives, friends, and prospective marriage partners are still mainly concentrated in the depressed rural enclaves, either within the immediate neighborhood or in nearby, similar neighborhoods. The poorer rural people have not been able to enter or to embrace the wider social world: they have not joined, nor do they attend, the educational, fraternal, religious, or voluntary associations of the urban center or its suburban satellite communities. In short, their social connections are restricted and do not integrate them into the new, wider community that has replaced the former rural hamlet-and-hinterland community (see Chapter 10). In this sense the rural poor are now without a community.

Summary: History, Geography, and Rural Poverty

The social and economic history of the Chestnut Valley area reveals that rural poverty has been a fairly long-term phenomenon, and elucidates some of the reasons for its concentration and distribution in a region such as the Southern Tier of New York State.

Historically, the limitations of the natural resource base (that is, the unsuitability of local soil and topography for modern agriculture) have been a contributing factor, producing a succession of unprosperous farmers. In the 1920s, the definite correlation between poor soil and poor people had a close cause-and-effect relationship. Marginal land, by definition, could only support marginal farms, and these brought but meager profit to the families who worked them. Some farmers never made it very far up the agricultural ladder of success before the ladder was taken away by the forces of national and regional economic change. With little formal education and few employable skills, they entered the lower levels of the urban labor market and remained there. They tended to continue to live on family land, sacrificing proximity to jobs for the availability of inexpensive housing on the family homestead and a preference for rural living. Thus, they remained both poor and rural: they became the rural nonfarm poor.

Another important source of the present nonfarm poor population was migration into the area from nearby counties. People occupying marginal positions in their own depressed rural regions came to this area because the urban job situation appeared brighter here. They selected Chestnut Valley as a place to live because of the low cost of land and housing, and because they married into its families.[2]

What all of the chronically poor nonfarm people in the rural area have in common today, then, is that their parents or grandparents made an unsatisfactory transition from agriculture or agriculture-related occupations, in which insufficient resources, unfortunate timing, and large-scale economic trends all worked against their making an advantageous adaptation to nonagricultural pursuits.

The socioeconomic differences that existed at the time this region of the state was being transformed from agriculture have not been erased by time, however, but have become crystallized, firmed, and passed on to successive generations. In the late 1970s, the region was still faced with severe rural poverty, and there is a remarkable correlation between the distribution of chronically poor people and the distribution of poor soil. Why should this be so? The rural poor people of today are not in farming any more, so their limited economic position can no longer be attributed to poor soil quality. By what other mechanisms, then, does the unsuccessful adjustment from agriculture in the 1920s and 1930s continue to affect the families of the 1970s? Why or how have the deficits of earlier adaptations been handed down to subsequent generations? The answers to these questions must be sought at the intersection of the past and the present. The questions will be probed specifically in the concluding section of the book (Chapter 11), where we will seek explanations for the continued persistence of the problems of economic poverty and social marginality that afflict such rural areas.

* * *

These two historical chapters have set the stage, have sketched out the backdrop of history. It is on this stage that the actors of today, the families and individuals who populate this book, play out their lives. It is against this backdrop that their actions, life patterns, thoughts, and words can be understood. The spotlight throughout the remainder of the book will be on the chronically poor people who currently live in and around Chestnut Valley.

Part 3

Ethnographic Description
and Analysis

5

Economics:
Supporting the Family

Introduction

This chapter and the next one examine the ways in which chronically poor rural families manage their various resources toward meeting their needs. The focus is on the means by which a household supports and supplies itself, and on the feelings, ideas, and underlying themes that shape people's economic actions.

A basic assumption of the chapters on economics is that poverty is a much more complex and far-ranging phenomenon than is indicated by the annual income levels specified by the government as "the poverty line."[1] Poverty is not just an income somewhere below a federal guideline; it is an economic situation, an economic niche, and, often, an economic forecast. And poverty has social, psychological, and cultural concomitants as well.

A second assumption is that the economic actions of poverty-stricken people must be examined, not just with reference to dollar incomes, but in terms of people's total economic situation and the larger social, psychological, and cultural context in which economic poverty is embedded. To understand poverty, we must not only record what people earn, but also what they spend; not just their economic actions, but also what they say about their actions; not just what they do in the economic sphere, but also why they do it.

This analysis of economic patterns in their real-life context will challenge some beliefs about poverty commonly held by the wider society. In general, Americans tend to believe that people remain in poverty for the following reasons: (1) they don't work, (2) they spend money foolishly, and (3) they don't aspire to a better life. These popular "explanations" reflect the common stereotypes that poor people are: (1) lazy, (2) spendthrift, and (3) lacking in ambition. And the same stereotypes underlie much of our government's approach to dealing with the problem of poverty. Hence, there are policies requiring "welfare mothers" to take jobs (reflecting belief and stereotype

61

number 1 above); programs teaching "proper" money management to low-income housewives (based on belief and stereotype number 2); and attempts to expand the horizons of the "culturally disadvantaged" (because of belief and stereotype number 3).

Observations and analyses of economic patterns in this one northern Appalachian microcosm of rural poverty challenge the validity of these stereotypes. In fact, the following observed patterns clearly contradict the three parts of the general stereotype.

- Most of the people studied do work—long, hard hours at jobs that give them in return little personal satisfaction and little income.
- Most of the people studied are very clever in stretching what money they have and compensating for the money they lack.
- Most of the people studied do, indeed, have hopes and aspirations for improvement—for their own lives, if possible, but especially for their children's lives.

If the underlying stereotypes are wrong, then the policies and programs based upon them are not likely to be effective in solving the problem of long-term rural poverty.

Making a Living

The Working Poor

The rural families of this study can appropriately be called "working poor," in that most households have at least one gainfully employed member most of the time, but in most cases income generally hovers around the poverty line.

Data from the 1969-70 survey of twenty low-income households indicate that in nineteen of the households, either the husband or the wife was working, and in one case both. In eighteen of the households, men were employed in autumn 1969, though as the 1969-70 winter wore on, the male wage earners in two of these households lost their jobs, due to construction layoffs in one case, injury in another. In the autumn of 1969, there were four households with employed women, although two of these women were laid off in early 1970. In only two of the twenty households were there adult men who had been unemployed for a long period of time. In only one case was there no employed adult.

There is virtually no employment in the Chestnut Valley area, and most workers drive at least fifteen miles to work. The biggest single type of employment for men is with the highway and maintenance crews of the state, county, town, and city. The urban factory assembly lines also provide employment for both men and women. Other employers include the railroad, a metal fabrication plant, a trucking firm, and construction firms. A few men are self-employed in construction or salvage work. The women are most frequently employed by hospitals and other health-care facilities, as well as by motels and educational institutions, all of which regularly need unskilled labor of a janitorial nature, and which accept a high turnover of employees. Both men and women tend to cluster with particular employers, due to the fact that people make their job contacts through their personal contacts: the networks of relatives and neighbors serve as informal employment agencies. Furthermore, certain employers are known to be more apt to hire low-skill and/or short-term workers.

The people are also "working poor" in another, broader sense; although they are poor, work is a basic part of their concept of living, important in their thoughts as well as their actions. For themselves and for their children and their neighbors, they believe in work as the respectable way to support oneself or one's family, and they judge a man harshly who could work but does not.

The belief in the value of work is part of a long tradition. In an earlier time, being a good worker was more important as a criterion of an individual's worth than was his wealth. Men and women built reputations through their work performance in the appropriate spheres of activity in the farm-based community. Hard work as a farmhand was a prime means for a boy from a family of low economic position to gain personal respect and acceptance in the local farming community. Hard work was also essential for climbing the ladder toward economic advancement. Today, in the post-farming era, people still invest years of effort following through on their commitment to the work ethic. Being a good worker, which is interpreted locally as being steady on the job and working hard at it, still is a matter of pride and some recognition.

Despite the high rate of employment and the strong commitment to working, most of the twenty households nevertheless remain poor. Fifteen households out of the twenty had a income on or below the poverty line, which in 1970 was just under $4,000 for a family of four. Income from employment is not only generally low, but also insecure and variable. While a single month's earning might indicate that a family belongs in an income bracket above the poverty line, over the course of a year or several years the income may average substantially below poverty levels. People speak of their earnings in terms of the weekly or biweekly paycheck, rather than in terms of annual income, partly as a reflection of this variability. In 1969-70, men were bringing home $85 and $92 per week for highway crew work; by 1971-72 they were clearing $104 and $111 per week. If these earnings had been steady throughout the year, the annual take-home incomes of these men would have been between $4,400 and $5,800. This would have placed their families above the poverty level only if there were four or fewer members in the households and income remained at that level all year. In most cases, the income adjusted for family size was borderline or below, with respect to the official definition and guidelines. Construction workers at the time were bring-ing in nearly twice as much as factory employees and road crew, but they faced regular winter layoffs and other slack periods of reduced income.

The income figures on which poverty is officially defined are gross income figures, but obviously the household lives on its take-home pay, after deduc-tions for withholding taxes, Social Security, and health insurance. In many cases, the actual amount of the paycheck is further diminished by additional deductions. Some employees may have part of their wages garnisheed for past debts—a kind of after-the-fact installment plan. Some workers purposely have extra money withheld from their paychecks to receive a federal income tax re-fund in April—an unofficial payroll savings plan.

Occasionally, but unpredictably, income is boosted by overtime pay, which may increase take-home pay up to 20 percent. Overtime is viewed as a periodic and necessary financial lift, enabling a family to catch up on back bills or make some long-postponed purchase. In periods of economic recession, however, factories and highway departments cut back on overtime, leaving workers without this cushion and giving them, in a sense, an effective cut in wages.

> We were just scraping by. We were even doing okay. But now, without over-time, it seems like we always come out short.

In some cases, there are also periodic across-the-board pay raises, but these have hardly kept pace with inflation in the cost of living.

> My husband got a raise, but then they upped the insurance and cut out his overtime. So we're right back where we were, except that the price of food and things keeps going up.

Women take jobs as a temporary substitute for or supplement to their hus-bands' irregular, seasonal, or low-paid employment. In households where women are employed, the woman's job is apt to be the main source of income. Of the four employed women in the 1969 sample, one woman's husband was not living at home, two had husbands who were not working, and one woman's husband had a sporadic job history, though he was employed at the time. In seven other households, the wives had an intermittent or fairly regular history of employment, although they were not currently working.

Any overlap period of double income in the family is looked on as a means of catching up on back debts, maybe getting a little ahead, or earning enough to cover some particular target item, such as monthly payments on the purchase of a house or trailer. When the goal is reached, the woman may quit her job to stay home with the children, or perhaps to have another baby.

Men at Work

Working for a living is considered important – both as an economic strategy and as a measure of a man's worth. But often the world of work does not provide sufficient rewards, either financial or social. Commitment to work and dogged persistence in work is not, in itself, enough to raise a family out of poverty. In case after case, a man has worked quite steadily at a grinding, low-paid job – showing up on time, doing what is required, maintaining a fairly good attendance record – and still, ten, fifteen, or twenty years later his family is just hovering above the poverty line.

One reason for this long-term limited earning power is the nature of the regional and local economy. The demand for low-skill employees has not expanded in recent years, and fluctuates with the national economy, sometimes shrinking markedly. Thus, job security is low. The pay scale remains low, compared to the regional cost of living; and advancement opportunities are limited. The faltering growth rate of the national economy in much of this period, particularly noticeable in the decline of the northeastern regional economy, has taken its toll among lower-level employees. They are at risk for unemployment and underemployment, and are caught in the bind of inflation.

The world of work also fails these men in another way: intangible rewards for the jobs they perform may be as low as the cash incomes earned. Factory work, a job on the highway crew, institutional maintenance, and janitorial work do not usually provide either social connections or social status. A man's co-workers are apt to be people he already knows, people in the same socioeconomic position. Although a man who works hard and steadily at a job usually gains some self-respect and recognition from his co-workers and family, his accomplishment is not easily demonstrated or validated in the community. The kinds of employment available are low in prestige – menial tasks that carry a low status and pay too little to allow the worker to purchase a socially approved life style. Thus, hard work brings little social reward and little recognition, as well as too little money.

Some of the jobs men hold do have some definite advantages, however. Highway crew work, for example, though it yields relatively low pay, does offer some job security and the opportunity for overtime work in winter. The nature of the work itself also holds advantages for men who have the physical strength and prefer to work outside. Especially if the job involves operating a truck or other machinery, there is an opportunity for demonstrating personal skill, power, and bravery: men speak proudly of dangerous situations, near-misses, and clever escapes on the job. Additionally, the multiplicity of municipal highway departments (state, county, township, and city) provides an opportunity for a man to be hired at the same kind of job in several different jurisdictions. He can move laterally from one municipal employer to another, since the job skills are transferable. There is also the attraction of having one's friends, relatives, or neighbors as employment contacts and co-workers. But the advantages of these jobs may now be diminishing. Political and economic pressures to control highway maintenance costs lead to reduction or elimination of overtime, and to the institution of more bureaucratic practices in the hiring and administration of highway departments.

Men's attitudes toward their long-range employment future tend to be restricted. A man sees that his co-workers are no better off, and obtain no greater rewards, even if they have been on the job a long time. The possibility of changing jobs offers little encouragement, as he sees that his former co-workers and neighbors have not found things much better in other employment situations. Neither significant promotion nor job-changing for the sake of advancement is common enough among neighbors, friends, and relatives to serve as a model or incentive. And few opportunities exist for learning the skills or proving the capacity to advance. Thus, a man does not see his job as a rung on a career ladder that he can climb upward toward increasingly more satisfying and more remunerative jobs. Rather, he expects only to stay where he is or to step sideways. Furthermore, men perceive job security as more important than advancement. A man who is just making ends meet feels he cannot take the risk of seeking a better job because he might not find one, or the one he gets might turn out not to be what he wanted, or he might not be capable of keeping it.

Better to stick with this lousy job than to be caught with no job at all.

Personal job advancement is also limited by psychological factors. The men of these pockets of poverty are handicapped occupationally by a legacy of diminished self-esteem. They have grown up watching their parents struggle with debt-ridden farms or in grinding, dull jobs that yielded insufficient monetary or personal rewards. They have known their parents' heavy feeling of failure in the world of work. Their own experiences in the competitive world of education and urban employment have further convinced them that failure is the expectation and often the fact. From their observations and experiences of failure, whether firsthand or vicarious, they form limited expectations for their own job futures. They seek, and have found, mainly those jobs that offer the least room for personal initiative and the least expectation of personal development. These low expectations, in turn, become active forces inhibiting advancement in the job world, no matter how strong the commitment to work.

The interaction of limited expectations and limited achievement in the job world is exemplified by the cases in which an employee turns down an offer of a job promotion (from work crew to leader, for example) in which he would be given responsibility over subordinate workers and some limited decision-making authority. The employer regards the promotion as a real chance for a man to get ahead; thus, when the employee turns down the offer, the boss concludes that the man has no desire to better himself. But this pattern is really much more complex. The level of common laborer is considered safe because hard work and good attendance will usually produce adequate results and make failure unlikely, thus providing job security. But in any role involving decision-making and supervision of subordinates, hard work would be only one of several ingredients, and would not by itself guarantee successful performance. Such a job is usually regarded as too much of a risk to the individual.[2] If a man were to advance to a higher position and prove unable to perform adequately, his own personal abilities would clearly be called into question—a risk that a man with low self-esteem is hesitant to accept. Any job with a managerial or supervisory role over other people may seem particularly risky because it requires the very skills about which men may feel least confident. To accept a position of authority over others is thought to invite jealousy, resentment, and certain criticism.

> My husband wouldn't want to be in the middle that way. He'd catch heck from his boss above him and he'd catch heck from the guys below him. No, he'd rather be one of them [the crew of laborers], even if he has to pass up a higher salary.

Thus, many of the men adapt to the security of being steady laborers among their bottom-rung peers rather than advancing to higher positions where they would be faced with decisions to make, and caught between superiors and subordinates. In the lower echelons, a worker avoids further erosion of his personal sense of self-worth by insuring that if something does go wrong, the blame will not fall on him, since he only did what he was told. These considerations also seem to explain, at least in part, the typically lukewarm response expressed both in action and in words to various government-sponsored job training programs that have been proposed or established.

A few of the men have not only failed to advance in their jobs, they have become so discouraged about their lack of success in supporting their families or so burdened by other problems that they eventually lose even their basic commitment to work. Some have worked at a single job for as long as ten to twenty years before surrendering to a growing alcoholism or mental-health problem that eventually causes them to lose their jobs and permanently drop out of the world of work. The life histories of these men usually include a physical disability—perhaps an accident or injury—as the factor that tipped the scale from work to alcoholic unemployment. In the preponderance of cases, however, men exhibit almost dogged determination to work—to get a job or to continue on a job despite its meager rewards, and when they find themselves out of work, most exhibit restlessness, edginess, and self-doubt. Among older men who have worked for most of their lives, this situation causes distress, but among young men who have had little experience in the world of work, prolonged unemployment may have a considerable effect on their future functioning; they may give up trying to get a job more easily than men who have had at least some positive work experiences.

There is a circular feedback operating here. The constraints of being locked into low-status jobs, the lack of advancement, the limited personal involve-ment, development, and pride—all these combine with the low pay to rein-force a man's already low self-esteem. And low self-esteem tends to further restrict a man's potential performance in the employment sphere. Addition-ally, the meager earnings and lack of advancement on the job may restrict a man's satisfaction in his performance as husband and father. This results in further strain on the family, which in turn causes and perpetuates other prob-lems, including the undermining of job performance.

Thus, while most men exhibit a resigned persistence about the necessity of work, the overall impression they give is that they are more tied than com-mited to their particular jobs. For most, the job is merely a job, a respectable though inadequate source of income. It has rarely been possible for men to "work themselves out of poverty" or to earn their way to higher social status.

Working Women

For women, the same general picture of low-level jobs with limited returns holds true. But for women the negative aspects of work are not nearly as strong as they are for men. Fewer women work; they work for fewer years; and they experience less employment-related and personal failure. Women's comments reveal that they have less ego-involvement in their role as income earners than do men. For women, the job is an extra role they assume, in ad-dition to their basic role as mother, wife, and homemaker. Working is not mandatory for their role fulfillment or self-esteem. The money that women earn either supports the family (if there is no income-earning husband) or buys the extras and treats (if hers is the second income). In either case, what is noticed is how *much* she brings home, not how little, as may be the case with a man.

For all of the women who are employed, or have recently been employed, money is the primary reason they give for working. It simply makes life easier if the wife has a regular income, even though relatively low, to supplement the low or insecure income of the husband. Often, too, women state that they prefer working to going on welfare. Besides, if the husband is living at home, welfare support is not usually available, even though his income or his unemployment or disability benefits may be inadequate for family needs.

There are also important secondary reasons why women work or want to work. Employed women, in most cases, have the right to determine how their earnings are spent. Some women find that having their own source of income reduces the friction between husband and wife over how money is spent. If a husband won't allow his wife to spend his earnings on certain items for the house or children or herself, her only recourse is to try to get a job so that she may spend money to satisfy the needs she perceives as important.

Employed women also seem to gain considerable satisfaction from their social interaction with other workers on the job. To a much greater extent than men, women's talk about their jobs tends to center on interactions with co-workers – discussions at coffee breaks, the problems other women on the job are having with their husbands and so forth. And some employed women are simply seeking to get away from the house. Some women clearly keep themselves employed, despite complaints of how hard it is to manage everything and how tired they are, because they do not want to stay home – either in an overcrowded house full of small, noisy children or in a quiet, empty house when the children have all reached school age.

The secondary reasons for working are revealed most clearly when women who have generally been employed are not working, perhaps due to layoffs, the closing down of a factory, injuries, disabilities, quitting, or the birth of another baby. They express dissatisfaction, and exhibit restlessness and sometimes depression, indicating a sense of both social and psychological loss. On the other hand, a woman who has finally obtained a job after being on welfare expresses renewed pride and confidence in herself. The following comments, made by women who were actively looking for work (utilizing both the state employment bureau and informal inquiries among working friends and relatives), indicate some of the reasons and the urgency behind their desire to go to work.

If I could go back to work, we wouldn't be just hanging on like this.

I really have to get out and *do something*. I'm just going nuts here – all alone all day with nothing to do. [All her children are in school or grown and moved away.] I've even taken up crocheting. And I'm so disagreeable – I take things out on the kids when really it's just that *I* get on my nerves all day. Right now I'd do anything, any work, even if it would be against the doctor's orders. [The doctor said that she should not take a job requiring any lifting or even standing on her feet all day, due to a back injury.] As it is, I do all sorts of errands for my married daughter and other people – just to occupy myself. I'm really raring to go! It's been so long since my accident. I'd be so happy! Things seem to go so much smoother when I'm working. I get along better with the kids, and with myself too. And the housework – why I can whip through this trailer in minutes if I have something else to do.

I've got to get me a job. I can tell it's really time now for me to get working. I find myself beginning to give up, and then I know I really better get out and get a job. Something, anything, even volunteer, if it has to be. The thing is, there's so much wanting doing around this house, but never any money to do it, so I can't get at any of the improvements and projects I want to do. So after a while I just give up. Why, this last Saturday, I just stayed in bed all day. When that happens, I know I got to do something quick. I'm so dying to get a job. I'll take anything. If I catch myself in time, keep myself from giving up altogether, get a job so's I can be out doing something and getting some money for all the things we need, then everything will be okay.

The women who have not been employed recently give a variety of reasons for not working. Some say they can't take a job because of problems of transportation and lack of child-care arrangements. However, it seems that these are not always strong deterrents, for most of the women find various ways to solve these problems *if* they really are able to work and *if* a job is available. Rides can be found with neighbors, babysitting with relatives or neighbors. Frequently a women may work night shift, using the family car while her husband is home with the children, or she may work during the day, with her husband on night shift and thus available for after-school care until the mother is home. Furthermore, since the most common pattern is that the woman goes to work when her husband is out of work, transportation and child care may actually not be serious obstacles because the car is available and the husband can be at home.

More significant deterrents to women taking or keeping jobs have to do with attitudes and beliefs about women's roles, and with the relationships between husbands and wives. Some husbands openly disapprove of or actually prohibit their wives from working. Some wives report that their husbands would be jealous of the competition, particularly if the husband is out of work or earning very little. A number of women also report that their husbands believe a woman should be home with her children. One man stated emphatically, "I'm the husband. She's the wife and mother. I didn't marry her so that she could go out and work." His wife said, "No, I'm not thinking about working now. I can hardly keep up with what I've got here at home—four kids, grandma, and a husband that's more trouble than any kid. How could I work too? In a few years, maybe I'll think about working. Right now, there aren't any jobs anyway. So why bother to even think about it?"

Many husbands and wives agree on the division of roles, preferring that the husband work if he can and the wife stay home at least as long as there are young children and maybe until they are teenagers. This feeling seems often to be a reflection of the adults' own sense of having had insufficient mothering when they were children. If at all possible, they want to provide a mother in the home for their children.

Other facets of the husband-wife roles and relationships also discourage women from working. Some women don't work because their husbands express considerable suspicion about allowing their wives to associate with other men. The job would provide an opportunity for women to play around or get involved. Some husbands do not trust their wives to resist such temptation. Additionally, some women do not want to take jobs because they feel that their husbands are too lazy to work unless it is absolutely essential to the family's existence. As the saying goes, "He's the type of husband that, if his wife will work, he won't."

In some cases, or at some times, the woman's low self-esteem also acts as a deterrent to employment, making her doubt that she could get and hold a job. This is particularly true for those women who have been out of the job world for an extended period to raise children. Another deterrent to work is the exhausting demands of keeping house and taking care of the family in a situation of substandard facilities and inadequate equipment. Women who feel overwhelmed or constantly behind in their housework think that it is unrealistic to take on an outside job.

Another deterrent for women is their longstanding health problems: unhealed injuries or illnesses of long ago; exhaustion from continuing overwork and undernourishment; lifelong medical conditions such as diabetes; ignored gynecological problems; and, frequently, "nerves." While these health problems are generally below the acute level, they tend to drag on for long periods, sapping the energy and wearing down the spirit. Women with such conditions find it hard to think in terms of managing a job and the family too.[3]

Despite these deterrents, many women do try to take on a job. A few manage to make a go of it; others give up the attempt, deciding to wait a few years for their situations to change. For a number of women at various points in their lives, the ideal situation as they see it would be part-time employment. But the compromise of a part-time job (or piecework at home) is rarely available in the local employment area, so that a woman must work full-time or not at all. Consequently, women work when the situation at home permits it and when extra income is most needed; and they quit when the strain and inconvenience of working outweigh the monetary or other benefits. Later, they go back to work again; then they quit again. Thus, as individual work histories show, over the long run women have created their own version of part-time employment through their start-stop work patterns. They are likely to continue this intermittent employment pattern in the future, as a way of adjusting the world of work to their own needs and situations.

"Being on Welfare is No Picnic"

Another important source of support is welfare or public assistance. Most of the households studied have had welfare help at some point. At any given time, about one-quarter of the chronically poor families of this study are receiving assistance. In 1970, in the base sample of twenty low-income families, five were on AFDC (Aid to Families with Dependent Children). In 1974, four families were receiving AFDC. Of these four households, the husband was absent in one, in another the husband's self-employed earnings were irregular. In the third, the husband's earned income was too low to cover both household needs and support payments to his children living elsewhere, and the wife was not receiving child-support payments from her former husband. In the fourth household, the husband's alcoholism was too severe for him to obtain or hold a job.

Other households receiving AFDC have included at least one unmarried woman with a baby living as a subunit in her parents' home. In other cases, households have received payments from the welfare department designated for a specific individual in the household, perhaps a foster child or a retarded or disabled relative released from a state facility. But this support is not AFDC and not regarded as welfare.

The pattern observed over the years is that families go on and off AFDC (or in a few cases, home relief) as their situation warrants, using it as a necessary last resort in extended periods of nonemployment or absence of the husband-father. Very few of the entire group of families studied have been on public assistance for long periods of time. (Thus, although two or even three generations of a family might have received welfare support, it is by no means a situation of continuous welfare dependence, which is the usual public stereotype.) In many cases, welfare is merely a supplement to some other income source, rather than the sole support. In no case has welfare brought a family above the poverty level.

Among the low-income rural families, there is clearly a stigma attached to being on welfare. Families who are receiving or have received assistance are sensitive about it and do not talk about it unless there is a particular problem. This stigma seems to be felt more among the older people than the young adults and new parents. However, even on the school bus, children occasionally taunt each other about being on welfare, repeating derogatory comments and allegations they have heard at home. Adults openly discuss the welfare status of their neighbors, frequently exaggerating the amount another family receives and criticizing the way it is being spent.

Living on welfare is definitely considered second-best to earning an income, which is preferred for both financial and social reasons. This becomes apparent, for example, when a man is "temporarily" laid off and has used up all his unemployment benefits, but does not accept "going to the welfare" as a satisfactory answer because he really wants to go back to his job, to earn the family's support and to earn his own self-respect.

A particularly strong objection to being on welfare is its potential control over individual and family actions. People fear—with some justification and some exaggeration—that "the welfare" (meaning the official personnel of the department of social services) will take away their house or land, will force them to sell their cars, will dictate how they must spend their money, and may even take away their children.

Being on welfare is viewed as undesirable particularly because it cuts down the flexibility of individuals to cope with their own situation, because it restricts their options. For example, an unemployed, disabled man might want to spend money buying another wrecked car, so he can fix it up and sell it at a good profit. If his family is on welfare, he is discouraged from generating this extra income, he is not free to make his own spending decisions, to act when the time is right, to maneuver. Likewise, a wife wants to be free to accept a wandering husband back and attempt to keep him, even if it means using some of the meager welfare-budget household funds to satisfy his personal whims. But she does so at the risk of losing her welfare benefits.

In the day-to-day living on the borderline between just barely getting by and not making it, the freedom to act quickly—to make changes in family arrangements, to move to a new location, to spend half the food budget on something else—is an essential adaptation to poverty living. The various restrictions and constant need to keep caseworkers informed of one's doings are thus felt as particularly oppressive. (For example, the requirement that a recipient inform the department of social services before he or she moves to a new location and the paperwork involved are a particular nuisance, and people sometimes get into trouble for not following these regulations.)

These negative feelings about public assistance are superimposed on the traditional rural value of the individual family providing for its own needs. Particularly among older people, reluctance to turn to the government for help is often quite strong. This reluctance, combined with the threat of losing independence and swallowing pride, makes some older people hold out against requesting public assistance, even when their needs are great. The same beliefs inhibit some potentially eligible families from applying for food stamps or medical assistance because they see these programs as part of the welfare system.

Of those who have been on welfare, most do not consider it an adequate or a satisfying means of supporting a family. Recipients may complain that one gets too little money from welfare—and too much supervision.

They are always trying to give you less than they are supposed to.

In return for what they hand out, they meddle in your life, urge you to leave your husband, pressure you to move away.

You have to tell the caseworker every time you do anything.

They try to tell you just how you should spend every penny they give you.

On the other hand, the same people also complain about the large number of "lazy cheaters" who soak up welfare money when they really could work. And some recipients, while they state that they do not like being on welfare, are openly appreciative of its support at a time when no other alternatives seemed possible. On the whole, people want a welfare system that will help struggling families like themselves adequately when needed, and without humiliation. But they see welfare as second-best, an inescapable necessity sometimes, but not the preferred means of long-term family support.

Other Sources of Support

Over the long run, the income level in many households is just barely enough to support a family from one payday to the next. Rarely is income sufficient or secure enough to enable a family to get out of debt or to build up a reserve toward anticipated or unexpected future expenses. But people do have various means of occasionally augmenting household income. At times, earnings may be boosted by putting in overtime, by taking on additional after-hours jobs, or by the wife's working. Household income may also be increased by participation in government programs such as food stamps, Medicaid, and Supplemental Security Income.

There are also important unofficial ways in which people devise substitutes and supplements for employment income and public assistance. They constantly draw on their resources of personal ingenuity and social contacts to obtain small, irregular cash income, goods, and services.

One temporary source of support is other people. Occasionally young men out of school but only sporadically working will continue to draw from their parents' provisions, or will append themselves to the household of a neighbor or girlfriend. A young woman with a baby or small children but no child-support payments from the father may be supported by her parents, either instead of or in addition to collecting public assistance. Although the provision of such support is regarded as part of parental or grandparental responsibility, depending on others is not respected as a long-term means of providing for oneself or one's children.

Junk cars provide a small and intermittent income. Some men invest considerable time, skill, and energy in buying, repairing, and selling or trading used cars and car parts, as well as motorcycles, snowmobiles, home appliances, and other items. This activity does not bring in any steady income, and the amounts for each transaction may be small ($15, $50, $100 or more may be cleared as profit, if labor is not counted), but it provides extra money now and then for general living expenses or for extra expenses such as house maintenance and car insurance. The profit from this enterprise may be collected either in cash or directly in goods needed or desired by the family: a "new" heater or water pump, a TV, or building materials may be obtained through repairing and trading cars or supplying car parts.

There is no evidence that illegal activities have formed any significant basis of financial support, and they are definitely not perceived as an acceptable means of making a living. While illegal activities have been engaged in by some people at some times as a means of obtaining material goods or cash, the game-law violations and the petty larceny, theft, and breaking and entering charges listed against some of the men at various times are mostly the result of youthful pranks or drunken vandalism. They often involve the playing out of hostilities between neighborhood families or specific individuals, but they are not economic activities: they are neither a way of life, nor a way of making a living.

In considering contributions to household resources, it is important to recognize the role played by wives, even when they are not employed. In most cases, it is the woman who spends the time and energy making the trips to town, filling out the forms and going to the various offices to boost family income with food stamps, Medicaid, or public assistance. Women also con-tribute to balancing the household budget by minimizing cash expenses. Women spend considerable time in such activities as going to rummage sales to get cheap clothing; fixing appliances, the house, or the car to avoid repair bills or replacement costs; gathering and preserving wild or garden produce; and doing numerous errands that would require a husband's taking time off from work (such as registering motor vehicles). Women may also earn either cash or goods by doing favors for neighbors, such as giving rides to town and babysitting.

If the family is keeping a disabled or retarded relative or a grandchild, there may be public assistance money coming into the household for that in-dividual, even though the husband may be earning a stable income. It is the wife who does the housework and care required by the extra individual, and so she is, in effect, bringing in a very small income from the government for the work she does in that connection. In all these ways, even women who are not employed are effectively making a substantial contribution to the household's balance of income and expenses. But this contribution is not usually thought of in economic terms by the woman or her husband, and usually goes unrecognized.

Supplying Family Needs

The Cycle of Getting and Spending

The other side of the coin from earning is spending. It is popularly assumed in American society that people remain poor because they are spendthrifts, wasting money foolishly on luxuries rather than sticking to basic necessities, spending without plan, and making no provision for tomorrow. However, a closer look challenges those old stereotypes. What look like unplanned, unconnected expenditures may actually be part of a pattern, a strategy for dealing with the perpetual problems of too little money to cover the household's needs.

Many people are paid weekly on Friday; others are paid biweekly. Welfare checks come once a month in most cases. If the husband is the primary earner, he usually retains control over his paycheck, periodically doling out small amounts of cash to his wife "for groceries." If he earns extra money (from selling fixed-up cars, for example), it is assumed that he is entitled to spend this cash as he wishes. The wife has control over the small amounts of money she acquires, and in most cases she uses such discretionary money to buy clothing and treats for her children. In the case of regularly employed women, the paycheck usually goes toward major recurrent expenses, such as house payments and/or groceries.

The prevalent overall pattern of spending in most households is a payday-to-payday cycle of getting and spending money and being out again by or before the next payday. But in most cases it is not a haphazard cycle. A common pattern of disbursement of income is to pay one or two regular bills each week of the month. The first week's paycheck may go for rent, or for major grocery shopping, or for buying food stamps.[4] The second week, the electricity bill may be paid and perhaps the telephone bill, if there is a phone. The third week the heating fuel bill may be paid, and/or perhaps the second batch of food stamps purchased. The fourth week an installment on a loan or an overdue bill might be paid. In this way, a family just makes it through a month of bills to begin the cycle all over again. Whatever money is left over from bills goes for groceries, for gasoline, and for other household and family needs. One housewife described the tightness of her budgeting system as follows.

> When a month has five Fridays in it, we're really in luck, because there's one paycheck where we don't have to take a big chunk out of it right away to pay a major bill. So we can splurge, like buying a few extra groceries or a new jacket for one of the kids.

Thus, money is spent almost as soon as it comes in, and the night before payday finds a family with little food in the house and little gasoline in the car.

Where the Money Goes

Food generally constitutes a major portion of a family's budget. For families not on food stamps, the weekly cash outlay for food ranged, in 1969-70, from an occasional low of $20 for a family of five when money was very tight, to $80 or more for a family of six. Most noteworthy is the considerable variation among families and within any one family at different times, depending on the amount of cash available.

Most women shop in the large urban supermarkets once a week or bi-weekly, picking up extra items in between at small roadside grocery stores closer to home. In some cases, lack of sufficient storage space and refrigeration necessitates small-quantity buying. Women vary considerably in their shop-ping skills and economical buying habits, but many are real experts. The kinds of food purchased vary considerably from one family to the next. Family tastes, cooking facilities, and the predilections of the homemaker seem to be more important than monthly income in determining the types and varieties of food purchased. However, macaroni products, potatoes, beans, and bread predominate in all households, and when income is lower than usual meat purchases may be eliminated for a week at a time. Families on food stamps generally find that the stamps make a real difference, providing a benefit value ranging from a few dollars to about half of the household food costs. Food stamps also appear to reduce somewhat the fluctuation in the amount of money a family spends on food and the quantity of meat and vegetables purchased.

HOUSING COSTS in these rural areas do not usually constitute a major expense for most families. People have worked out various strategies for keeping down the cash cost of housing to an amount they can generally manage to pay. Many families live "rent-free," perhaps in a house that has been in the family for generations, or in a very modest house that was built or purchased inex-pensively enough to be paid off quickly. One family of seven paid $1,000 in monthly installments to buy their house in the early 1960s, fixing it up over the decade with investments of time and money. Although the house was still substandard, the family was no longer burdened by monthly rent or mort-gage payments. This situation is quite common. Renting a place to live is recognized as causing extra financial strain, and only four out of the twenty families were renting homes in 1972. Rents ranged considerably: one family with three children still at home paid just over $100 a month for a large but run-down house; a family of nine paid $155; two families (ten people) shared a large, dilapidated, isolated farmhouse for $35 a month. A family of four paid $60 monthly on a land-contract for a trailer and a lot that they would own in two years. In a few cases, meeting rent or land-contract payments or property taxes puts too much strain on the family budget. The wife may take a job ex-pressly for the purpose of meeting housing expenses, or the family may move to cheaper quarters.

Increasingly common as a low-cost housing solution is the trailer. Many of the lower-income families, particularly, live in trailers they have purchased, usually secondhand at least. A family may pay less than $1,000 over a year

or two, and can set the trailer rent-free on relatives' land, thus minimizing the monthly cash outlay for housing. This practice gives rise to a familiar sight in the countryside: an old farmhouse with a trailer parked beside it. Trailers are installed either on a relative's land or on a separate lot, rather than in a "mobile home park," for economic as well as social reasons. (In a park, one must pay rent for the lot, must pay for septic and water privileges, and usually must have an impressive-looking mobile home, not a beat-up old trailer.) In 1970, six out of the twenty low-income households in the basic sample were living in trailers, ranging from a very small old-style one in disrepair—really cramped for a family of six— to a large, modern mobile home. The latter was much admired by the neighbors, but it lacked a septic system and a well, and was extremely crowded for its family of ten, despite a wood-frame addition on the front. The percentage of trailers has steadily increased over the decade.

HOME HEATING is apt to be a large, recurrent expense during the long, cold winters (heating season often lasts from mid-October through late April). Fuel is most frequently kerosene, purchased in small amounts and frequent intervals at a combination grocery store–gas station along the main highway. (Some families have switched to regular bulk kerosene delivery to avoid the nuisance of frequent purchasing and the risk of occasionally running out. However, most cannot afford to pay a large bill all at once, and thus cannot take advantage of discount rates on quantity purchases.) Some houses have consistently used wood stoves, and more now are converting to wood due to the high cost of other fuels and the low cost of wood—which is cheap if one obtains a permit and cuts and hauls it himself from nearby state forests.

Whatever the source of heat, some houses are uncomfortably cool and

Whatever the source of heat, some houses are uncomfortably cool and drafty. The most common situation, however, is uneven heating: the main room is so warm that small children run around in diapers and undershirts; the rest of the home so cold that the space is hardly usable in winter. A fan dangling from an extension cord may be hung above a space heater to blow some of the heat into another room. Rags and newspapers are used to cover leaky windows and stuff cracks in doors. The odor of kerosene pervades many houses and trailers. A number of families use the kitchen stove (usually fueled by bottled gas) as an auxiliary room heater.

CLOTHING expenditures are regulated by the amount of money available at any particular time, with a definite seasonal peak before the start of school and cold weather in the fall. Clothes that are bought new come mostly from the discount stores in the shopping centers fifteen or twenty miles away; a family trip to such a store may be a big Friday night event. A large part of the wife's and children's clothing, however, comes from rummage sales around the county. Free, used clothing comes from relatives, friends, and official organizations like the antipoverty programs. Women generally neglect their own clothing needs: the lack of a warm coat and waterproof footwear for the mother is the most frequent hallmark of an overstrained family budget. She considers these items for herself extras she can do without until more money is on hand. But clothes for the children must be provided, not only to keep them warm, but because the mother wants her babies and school children to appear as well dressed as possible.

APPLIANCES AND FURNITURE needed for family living are acquired from many of the same sources as clothing. Most are at least secondhand. An inventory of some houses reveals a surprising number of articles gleaned from the municipal dumps—furniture, appliances, pots and pans. (However, as progress marches on, the old town dump is frequently replaced by a modern, regional "sanitary landfill operation" that greatly limits scavenging because it is far away, patrolled or locked up, and constantly being covered over with earth or other fill.) Some furniture may be donated by acquaintances, traded from relatives and friends, or occasionally bought new or nearly new on time payments. In the past, some families were able to purchase a refrigerator or beds with extra help from public assistance. Almost every family has a television set, perhaps very old and in poor working order, perhaps new. For the house itself, supplies to repair it or to make improvements are obtained by trading, or bought wherever they are cheapest, even if it means traveling a considerable distance, buying unmatched lots, seconds, and material that is not precisely suited to the job.

OTHER HOUSEHOLD AND PERSONAL GOODS are obtained wherever they can be had cheaply. They are often secondhand; if they are new they usually come from discount stores. Toys for children, especially for Christmas, may involve considerable expense, as mechanical and up-to-date television-advertised toys are frequently desired. Parents may begin purchasing children's presents in September, taking out bits of money from the grocery allotment to be sure the children will get the presents they want. But sometimes a child receives toys donated by the Salvation Army or gleaned from the county's dumps.

RECREATION consumes a variable amount of money in different families at different times. Some families go for long periods with almost no money spent on recreation. Many families own snowmobiles for winter recreation, some own a motorcycle, and a few have owned a motorboat for fishing. These items are usually acquired at least secondhand, and prices paid have ranged from $100 for an old snowmobile up to a rumored, but unlikely, figure of $1,000 for a boat. Most such items require money for replacement parts as well.

Some men regularly spend money going out on the town with friends from work, or male relatives, though most drinking takes place at home. Some husbands (and a very few wives and children) regularly go to stock car races. Women rarely spend money on recreation for themselves, unless it is in the company of their husbands. Few families take vacations; at most they take a short trip to visit relatives or to see some major tourist attraction.

MEDICAL EXPENSES are a continuing problem for some families. A few families have outstanding medical bills from years ago; others incur bills that they can only pay off in installments. People purchase over-the-counter and prescription medicines at discount drugstores, and obtain professional services mostly from private doctors and the hospital emergency room. (Relatively few utilize the free well-baby clinics sponsored by county health departments.)

Some financial help comes from insurance plans connected to employment, and from state Medicaid or the federal Medicare program for older people. But families sometimes incur medical costs when they have no insurance, and usually have to pay some portion of costs even when they are covered. There is often confusion about medical insurance or assistance — what it covers, when it expires, how far back it is effective, and whether the family is currently eligible. Medicaid is available to people with incomes below a certain level, even when they are not on welfare, but fluctuating incomes and recertification problems leave many families without coverage. When a family is on welfare, Medicaid is almost automatically available, though it is not retroactive to cover previous medical bills, and does not pay the full bill.

SAVINGS from income are meager, for after meeting various current and past expenses, a family is usually out of money, if not in debt. Occasionally, however, some families are able to come out with a little money left over at the end of some week or month. Small amounts of money may be put away for some particular future goal.

Like I say, there's the future to think about. We'd like to get this house finished so it will be a good place to live in. And we'd like to help the boys towards their future. Our oldest one is starting high school now. He's a good student. Maybe he'll want to go to college. We'd like to help him out the first year if we could.

In some cases, small amounts of cash may be set aside from each paycheck to meet anticipated fixed expenses, such as property taxes or car insurance. Sometimes, however, those little earmarked funds have a way of being spent as petty cash.

When the tax bills come around, somehow there is nothing left in the tax jar.

As we have seen, a few families successfully save by a system of using ex-cessive income tax withholding as a kind of self-imposed, forced savings plan. They regularly plan far ahead which home improvements or other expen-ditures will be made with the spring refund. Very few families have savings accounts in banks, but a few have checking accounts and use these mainly for accumulating and withdrawing small savings, rather than for regular bill-paying. Many families have bills on account with the merchants or loan agencies of the city, usually for such things as tires and car parts, heating fuel, and medical services. Some feel it is important to have such accounts and to keep them paid up to maintain a good credit rating for future borrowing.

Conclusion

Money problems are constant in most of the families and periodic in the others. Conversations frequently turn to the money problem.

> Right now we're kind of stuck for money. We're just making it by. Like, we just keep up with the bills. I just got a new drum of kerosene and paid the phone bill, and our money's about all out. So I couldn't get the one more roll of insulation we need to finish off the bedroom. So, we'll have to wait till next week before we do any more work on that room. *If* there's any money next week.

The stress and worry about getting by is ever-present, but is heightened at certain times. Early winter is often a particularly bad time because of all the expenses of warm jackets and boots for the children, high fuel bills, perhaps a new battery for the car so it will start in cold weather, and the big expense of Christmas presents for the immediate family. All of this comes at a time when some employed men (in construction, especially) face a layoff period or a cut-back in work. As cold weather approaches, women become noticeably more concerned over the insufficient money for meeting family expenses. Marital strains, which seem to be especially prevalent at this time of year reflect the financial squeeze. Occasionally, the strain is sufficiently overwhelming that a man simply can't continue, and will go off on a drunk or in some other way lose his job, throwing the family into even more severe straits, and perhaps forcing them to revert to welfare assistance for a period. But women also feel this seasonal pinch deeply, since the items that must be acquired are within the realm of purchases normally made by women.

> I'm not sure how we're going to get through the next few weeks. We haven't got much food, and the fuel tank is almost empty already, with winter not even begun yet. And I'll have to get things like boots for the kids soon, too.

This chapter on economics has studied where the money comes from and where it goes. In analyzing the income side of the ledger, the observed patterns seem clearly to contradict the notion that people are poor because they don't work and don't want to work. Again and again, the commitment to work has been apparent: work as a way of supporting oneself and one's family; work as a way of gaining the material things one wants in life; work as basic to a man's self-esteem. This conclusion holds true not only for the twenty low-income families in the original sample, but also for the bulk of the fifty other low-income rural families who have been observed and interviewed over the years.

Likewise, the analysis of spending patterns contradicts the public's claim that the rural poor remain poor because they waste whatever money they have by spending it foolishly with no thought for tomorrow. In fact, the low-income people of this study appear quite adept at stretching the available money to make it cover as many of their needs as possible – yesterday's, today's, and tomorrow's.

Economics:
Patterns of Spending

Analysis of Spending Decisions

Money management on the margin of poverty involves constant maneuvering in an attempt to satisfy many competing goals with too little money. Spending behavior in this context is not random, however, but patterned and fairly predictable. The patterns arise out of the needs and goals that people are attempting to satisfy, and from their feelings about those needs and goals.

This chapter explores the social, cultural, and psychological factors that impinge on and shape economic behavior. People, whether poor or affluent, are not economic robots, spending money purely for primary subsistence needs or financial gain. Families in poverty, just like nonpoor members of American society, use their available financial resources for a variety of purposes, including the satisfaction of psychological, social, and status drives. Spending patterns, therefore, cannot be understood simply in terms of dollars and cents, but must be seen in the larger context of people's multifaceted lives.

Almost any expenditure of money involves a decision, and that decision, in turn, rests on values, goals, and perceptions held consciously or unconsciously by the decision makers. In order to uncover these social, psychological, and cultural factors, a most useful approach is to study a number of spending decisions made by different families, and to observe a series of spending decisions made by a single family over a period of time. We can record what was purchased, and what was thereby not purchasable. We can probe the decision makers for explanations of the factors that go into making a decision; we can follow up on people's reactions.

In seeking to identify the underlying values and goals, the most useful decisions to analyze are those that occur when the family has less money than usual because of a loss of income or a large, unanticipated, and unavoidable expense, or the family has more money than usual, either from intentional saving or from a windfall. Analysis of spending decisions made in these circumstances reveals priorities in terms of which needs are taken care of first, which are postponed or given up, and what extras are obtained when possible.[1]

A Specific Spending Decision

Although many families plan their finances ahead and attempt to save toward a desired acquisition or a needed improvement, savings mount slowly and are sometimes sidetracked from the originally intended purpose. Ordinary living expenses nibble away at meager savings; competing goals push in ahead; or the money is suddenly reassigned to some other desired or needed item.

To illustrate the working of these phenomena and to indicate some of the noneconomic factors influencing economic decisions, a typical example drawn from actual cases will be described in detail.

A family had decided that, at last, it would try to get a reliable water supply by having a well drilled. Under the advice of a worker from a county agency, the wife had been setting aside small amounts of money from the household budget toward this goal. Now, in Feburary, she had nearly $100, from months of extra-careful grocery shopping, neglecting her own need for a warm coat and a pair of shoes, and saving what she earned babysitting for a neighbor's child. The husband planned to add to this amount his recent overtime pay of about $100. Later, he would put in any additional overtime pay and the $200 or so he expected from an income tax refund. The financing of the additional $200-to-$300 anticipated cost of the well-drilling was uncertain, although they had talked of taking out a loan. They hoped to have the work done in the spring.

The next time the agency worker returned, she was surprised and dismayed to see, parked on the front porch, a snowmobile. The wife hastened to explain this turn of events, admitting that, in fact, they had spent most of their savings on the snowmobile. She felt guilty and defensive because the family had failed to follow through on what they and the worker had so carefully planned. Their savings were now badly depleted, and the well-drilling would have to be put off again. As the wife said later, "I felt very small, almost like a little child who had been naughty."

After this episode, discussion with the family revealed that the sequence of events was more complex than could be judged directly from the mere presence of a snowmobile on the porch instead of the thumping of a drilling rig in the back yard. In fact, the snowmobile was secondhand, having been offered to the family quite unexpectedly at a bargain price of $300 by a coworker of the husband. The offer came at a time when the family had most of the cash available, with the difference payable in car parts. The opportunity gave them the prospect of obtaining a long-desired item that could provide enjoyment for the whole family and satisfy the children's requests and nagging to be able to participate in a recreational activity highly prized by their schoolmates and neighbors. Both parents felt that, for one of the children in particular, it would be a benefit to be able to participate in snowmobiling and snowmobile-bragging with his friends, as he was currently going through some adjustment problems in school.

At the time, the certainty of possessing a snowmobile was perceived by the couple as a far greater advantage than the somewhat unsure possibility of eventually putting in a well—after many more months of scraping and saving. Furthermore, the prospect of having to take out a loan for the balance of the cost of drilling was of some concern, since the last time they had gone into debt it had been a long, slow process to pay it off.

And so the decision was made. The entire family was excited and pleased. The husband felt particularly proud that he was able to provide this much-desired item for his children. The wife shrugged off the fact that she would have to continue hauling water from the spring out back. "I've been doin' it so long, might as well keep right on."

Financial Management with Limited Finances

To understand such a decision, and many similar decisions made in the face of limited income and definite needs for substantial improvements in living conditions, it is necessary to consider the whole context of factors surrounding and underlying economic decisions.

A family such as this one is perpetually operating on a small income, but is nonetheless faced with making a large number of spending decisions. Decisions have to be made frequently, usually as a series of separate decisions involving rather small amounts of money, each one considered in terms of the financial picture and the family situation at the particular time. Since the money available is limited, and inadequate to cover all demands on it, the family must exercise a temporary limitation of consumption in one area to permit expenditure in some other area. One woman explained it very well.

You have to stop and figure out, and you have three alternatives. You decide you can go without some things and save up until you have enough money to get the thing you're wanting. Or you can keep living the same as usual and go in debt to get the thing. Or you can give up the idea of getting it.

Going way in debt for something is bad. We've done that before, but we don't want to get in that bind again—always shelling out most of the paycheck on a lot of back debts. So, for us, we try to give up some things to save up for something else we really want. But usually we're operating so close that there's not much we *can* give up.

So, sometimes we have to decide that the thing we wanted is out of the question for us now. Like, for example, I sure would like to get the materials so my

husband could add a new room onto this house during his vacation this summer.
I've wanted it for a long time. But now I see that it's not going to be possible
because we can't afford it. So, okay, that's that.[2]

To the extent that a family is able to make ends meet, it does so by constant
financial juggling, not satisfying some needs in order to satisfy others. Certain
living expenditures can be temporarily cut back more easily than others. The
biggest sacrifice is usually made in the realm of housing and household equipment, reflecting in part male dominance in making spending decisions. While
better facilities and furnishings are indeed desired—particularly by the wife,
who spends much more time in the house—they are often assigned a lower
priority or repeatedly postponed. The purchase and installation of a flush
toilet, for example, may be put off again and again. In part this is because a
toilet would hardly bring the enjoyment, pride, and prestige that would come
from possessing a snowmobile. Also, installing the toilet might be useless
without other major improvements, such as an indoor water supply or a septic system, and these cost so much that the occasional bits of money squeezed
out of regular income are only a drop in the bucket. The long period of scrimp-
ing necessary to save up for them may be perceived as unrealistic.

Sacrifices of quality and quantity are also made in other spheres. The food
budget in most households is flexible enough to absorb temporary reductions.
When money is particularly short, a housewife may use her total supply of
reserves and staples, serving meager meals of odds and ends for a few days.
She knows that eventually she will have to spend extra money to replenish
her basic food supplies, but in the meantime, she has released some food-
budget money to take care of some other need. Even in the food budget itself,
there is room for trade-offs to adjust to a reduction in available money. In a
particularly tight week, a housewife will buy mainly cheap and filling foods
(potatoes, bread, macaroni products, beans), omitting the extras she might
like to purchase (meats, fruits, soda pop, and other family favorites). She may
switch to powdered milk or Kool-Aid as a money-saver, may eliminate
desserts entirely. Detergents, cleaning aids, and paper products may be
postponed week after week after week. Coffee and cigarettes, however, are
seldom put off if the family uses them, though the day before payday may be
particularly difficult if a household is down to its last cup of coffee, its last
pack of cigarettes. A housewife may also alter her techniques when money is
particularly tight: one woman reported cooking all meals outdoors on a wood
fire during a six-month period when there was not enough money to pay for
cooking gas. Clothing expenses may be similarly minimized and put off to
allow for other expenditures.

Despite the necessity of frequent, short-range decision making, people also
think in terms of spending money to fulfill long-range desires—usually involv-

ing improvements in housing conditions and provisions for the children's future welfare. But it is difficult to scrimp and save for a vaguely defined future goal when other, more pressing needs are constantly arising.

Practicality and pragmatism force concentration on feasible, short-range solutions. Both men and women pride themselves on their ability to devise inexpensive substitutes. Their overall goal in managing money is to maximize the family's chance of getting through today with a modicum of happiness and a minimum of pain. What cannot be bought today can be substituted for or put on the "hope list." Thus, instead of new chairs for the living room, slipcovers become the substitute goal; but if the money earmarked for slipcovers has to go toward emergency car repairs, the wife throws away the mail advertisement for the $15.98 slipcover-set special, and sews patches on the old couch and chair.

Flexibility

The examination of a number of spending decisions reveals that the crucial factor is flexibility. Flexible spending appears to be essential for coping with poverty, an adaptation to uncontrollable fluctuations in a generally meager income. In the ordering of expenditure priorities and in the amount of money spent for any one priority, an attempt is made to maintain flexibility. The primary strategy is to keep fixed costs to a minimum, particularly fixed cash costs. When a paycheck or AFDC check arrives, fixed costs are usually paid first, since nonpayment would result in trouble with a bill collector or termination of services (heating fuel, rent, electricity, or car insurance may be cut off). The remaining money is allocated among nonfixed costs (food, clothing, recreation, home improvements). People attempt to minimize fixed costs as much as possible so they can maintain the maximum flexibility to decide how to spend their money. Flexibility is basic to the entire process of managing money on an income that is both insufficient and insecure.

Flexiblity in making spending decisions also serves important psychological needs. People seem to enjoy being in a position to decide how to spend their money. They talk about decisions before and afterward, and they show off their acquisitions with pride. The zest for making purchasing decisions and for trading or "wheeling and dealing" among relatives, neighbors, and co-workers is in clear contrast to the observed pattern of shrinking from decision-making roles in the public arena of the employment world. Spending decisions offer the individual the opportunity to prove himself or herself in a situation of relatively little risk to self-esteem and considerable chance of ego-enhancement.

Unfortunately, this same flexibility may also have the negative effect of giving credence to the public's claim that poor people have erratic spending habits and do not plan or budget. Closer observation shows, however, that while spending patterns are flexible, they are not haphazard. Over and over, spending decisions reflect a balancing of a set of needs or desires against the constraints of financial reality. Observed over time, spending decisions reveal consistencies and common themes.

Themes Underlying Spending Decisions

From the analysis of the context and nature of many spending decisions, five basic themes emerge.

Sense of Material Deprivation

One long-run legacy of a childhood of severe poverty may be a certain acquisitive orientation to material items, perhaps a heightened quest for "things." Memories of material deprivation in childhood, of having to do without, of being ridiculed in school for the lack of or shabbiness of certain possessions, are frequently mentioned by adults. These memories apparently foster a situation in which acquiring things becomes important to one's sense of security. These adults may be quicker to buy, perhaps more ready to satisfy a whim, and susceptible to commercial advertising for all sorts of products.

Ironically, this sense of deprivation seems to leave some people unsatisfied even with the things they do acquire. The much-desired item is purchased, perhaps sacrificing needed winter clothing or house repairs, or incurring a husband's or wife's anger. But once owned, the magic fades quickly, the promise of happiness remains unfulfilled—and the quest is on for something else, more, better. Thus, the feeling of material deprivation often remains unassuaged, a nagging appetite never really satiated.[3] (Certainly, this spiral of spending and disillusionment is not peculiar to the families in this sample; it appears at all economic levels in American society, and is part of the basic economic system, played upon by the hucksters of consumerland. But for people who are poor, the money spent to satisfy a craving for possessions makes a more serious inroad in the family budget.)

The material deprivation factor seems to explain a number of the observed actions and attitudes toward the acquisition of things. Some individuals—women especially—are known to be collectors or "squirrels," filling their houses with boxes of free, used clothing, stacks of magazines, dozens of used rugs, and discarded chairs—far more than could ever be utilized by their families. Husbands collect cars, car parts, television sets, appliances, and hardware, partly for the same reason—an insatiable appetite for amassing possessions. Other examples come readily to mind. A housewife may begin in early October to purchase the various parts of a Thanksgiving dinner, to be sure she will have a complete dinner, with all the trimmings, when the time comes. A mother accepts a teenage daughter's clothing splurge, even though it used up some of the welfare money intended for the daughter's baby, because she recognizes that the daughter "has to have something special now and then to feel good about herself." A child, uneasy about the family's food supply, keeps opening the refrigerator door, not to take any food, but just to make sure there is food in it.

The need to assuage deprivation feelings through acquisition may underlie many purchases. The fear of being without, the sense of material deprivation—these may haunt an individual throughout life.

For the Sake of the Children

Like their more affluent counterparts elsewhere in the community, the parents in this study clearly want their children to have more of the good things in life than they had. But there is a difference of degree. Most of the low-income parents experienced a severely impoverished childhood, and thus exhibit a particularly strong urge to provide for their children what they were not able to have. This urge becomes an almost obsessive drive in some cases, and is closely related to a syndrome of low self-esteem and transferrence of goals from self to children, as well as to the sense of material deprivation. Parents may attempt to fulfill this desire in nonmaterial ways, such as in their determination to provide a "good home life with both parents." But if couples are unable to maintain harmony under the stress of overwhelming problems, material gratification may be offered as a substitute and an expiation of parental guilt. (Again, the situation and the reaction to it are not unique phenomena of low-income people—it merely hurts more when "guilt money" is harder to come by.)

The emphasis on providing material items so that the children will not be subjected to the same feelings of deprivation that their parents experienced varies from one family to another, and from time to time. It is particularly strong in relation to Christmas and to the child's experiences in school. It clearly affects some fathers; it frequently and deeply affects many mothers. It lies behind a decision to spend a rather large sum of money to purchase a "luxury item" such as the snowmobile cited in the earlier example, or a brand new television set.

The desperate hope that one's children will find success and happiness—or at least fewer problems—in life underlies many purchases. One woman expressed it succinctly.

Poor people often get over their heads in debt because the salesman can sucker you into buying something for the benefit of your children. The pitch he gives you is, "You don't want to let your children go without. Your children need this. Their school work would improve if they had that. They need this." The poor person falls for this pitch every time because he wants these better things for his children.

As a result of their susceptibility to sales tactics stressing their children's well-being and future success, a few homes have complete sets of encyclopedias (although school personnel often believe that the homes these children grow up in contain no books).

Making a Good Deal

Another consideration underlying many economic decisions is the concept of "making a good deal." With financial resources severely limited and demands on them always in excess of what can be met at any one time, balancing money supply and want-satisfaction requires a constant search for ways to get something for less than normal cost. If a man is offered a good deal on an item that his family has wanted or needed for some time, he may seize the chance, even though it precludes his obtaining some other thing that was actually a higher priority. There is an apparent and expressed reluctance to pass up a good deal—a fear that if you do not take advantage of it when it comes along, you might never again have the opportunity to acquire the desired item.

Just what constitutes a "good deal" depends somewhat on the object or service in question, but low cash price is central. A good deal may be offered by a regular commercial outlet, as in the case of a close-out special on merchandise, or a generous trade-in allowance, or favorable credit terms. If an item is offered by a personal acquaintance who is respected and assumed to be honest about the value of what he sells, the likelihood of the purchase is even greater. Not only is the acquaintance's price apt to be lower than store prices, but the prospective buyer feels a sense of confidence that he will not be cheated. Since not all such private exchanges turn out satisfactorily however, a man weighs his past experiences and his trust in the seller before making the deal. He does not want to be "taken," since this not only wastes his money, but also reflects badly on his judgment. If a man has the money, if the deal looks good, and if other pressing needs can be put off without incurring too much discomfort for the family or displeasure from his wife, he will try to take advantage of the offer. The wife, for her part, will stress the "good deal" aspect as a counter theme to her own disappointment at not having been able to buy whatever item it was that *she* held in priority.

In dealing among friends and acquaintances, there is also the added factor of reciprocity. A man might accept an offered item because he knows that the seller needs cash quickly. By making the purchase, he is insuring that when he is in a similar bind, he can raise cash by selling something to the same man. Thus, a good deal among trading men provides a kind of insurance policy along with the purchased item.

A Matter of Timing

Because of the large number and frequency of separate spending decisions, timing is particularly important. For each decision, the conditions at that particular moment are crucial. People know from years of experience that, for the most part, you can only buy when the money is available. Although installment payments and credit loans are used occasionally, both for essentials and to acquire lower-priority items, the availability of ready cash is a much more important factor in a decision to purchase. It is the timing that often determines whether a purchase is made: if cash is on hand at the same time that an offer of a good deal comes along, a purchase is likely to be made.

Maintaining Optimism and Harmony in the Family

A family's perception of its own well-being is also an important theme underlying spending decisions. While a person may categorically state that happiness can't be bought with money, he or she may nonetheless use money to purchase items that will relieve personal unhappiness or family discouragement, even if the relief is only temporary. (Here again, this is not a pattern unique to low-income people.) As people save toward a high-level goal, as in the case of the well-drilling, the savings may mount up so slowly that the goal begins to seem impossibly out of reach, and discouragement sets in. At such times, with some cash savings on hand, a person is vulnerable to any offer of a good deal on almost any other item. By opting to take up the offer, a man can gain a material item that may bring some immediate pleasure to his family and some recognition to himself as a good provider and a clever dealer. He will rid himself of the burden of discouragement caused by the fact that his higher-order goal seems always out of reach. In any case, for a stress-filled family enduring a long winter in a crowded house, a snowmobile and a working television set make important contributions toward family harmony.

Thus, spending money on desired items that are not absolute essentials is a phenomenon that serves a definite positive function in its contribution to mental health. If the family were to save only toward long-range goals and spend only on "necessities," discouragement could become overwhelming. A wife is often keenly aware of her husband's sense of discouragement and failure as he struggles to satisfy family needs and wants. If he jumps at the chance to buy a used snowmobile or another cheap car, she tries to hide her disappointment, telling herself that if this makes him feel better, her new furniture can wait. Additionally, she may fear that excessive discouragement might lead her husband to drinking. And she emphatically feels that the consequences of drinking to escape discouragement are far worse than the consequences of his spending money on a frivolous but harmless item. So she puts up with, and expects to continue to have to put up with, this pattern of spending. Although such expenditures may cause marital arguments, several women have explicitly commented that it is necessary to be able to spend money occasionally on things that will keep their husbands' and their families' spirits up, to get the family over a potentially dangerous period of discouragement.

* * *

These five themes underlying spending decisions have been discussed in terms of a male decision maker because this is the predominant pattern. However, the same underlying themes, operate in the smaller spending decisions made by women, whether the money they spend is earned by them or by their husbands.

When women do the family grocery shopping, for example, their selections reveal their determination to restrict total food expenditure, their need to adapt to fluctuating amounts of grocery money, and their desire to provide what they consider good food. Women are attracted to weekly specials and other bargains, and tend to stock up whenever extra money is available, for timing, flexibility, and making a good deal are important to them also.

Women are also conscious—more conscious than their husbands—of the fact that spending decisions are a means of satisfying the social and psychological needs of family members. They are aware that their spending decisions can make their children happy or please or placate their husbands. Buying—or not buying—treats for the children, for example, is recognized as an important part of the relationship between parent and child, an expression of love, an expiation of guilt, a reward, a bribe, or a punishment. (Again, this pattern is certainly not peculiar to poor people.)

The importance women attach to this spending role is clearly indicated when they are denied the role. A woman whose husband does the shopping (not uncommon, especially if she doesn't drive) may feel, or even say, that her role as wife and mother is somewhat diminished by the lack of opportunity to make spending decisions. She has one less card to play in the daily game of family interaction.

In households where the woman is the sole economic decision maker, the same underlying themes are apparent—although the goods purchased may be different. For example, few women on their own would purchase a used car if they already had one usable car; and items for the children and the house may take greater precedence than they do with a male decision maker. In most cases, the so-called "female-headed household" is really a subunit of a larger household—temporary in duration and incomplete in structure—and the spending decisions usually involve smaller amounts of money. A single woman living with her parents and supporting her children from AFDC or a paycheck has little discretionary money and almost no chance of accumulating cash, no matter how she scrimps. Women heads of households may differ from male decision makers in that they may attempt to compensate for the fact that their children are growing up without a father. Typical examples of this com-pensatory spending include the regular purchase of candy and expensive toys as treats for children, or routinely falling for cute and stylish (but relatively useless) children's clothing.

The Net Result

General Consequences of Economic Patterns and Underlying Themes

Over time, the patterns of spending described in this chapter have certain predictable consequences. The long-range economic picture for a family following these patterns would be one of consistently consuming all available resources on "just living" or "just getting by," without making any clear prog-ress toward higher goals of improving the standard of living, and without gaining any real relief from the constant anxiety and strain of living at the break-even point. In fact, this is exactly the way the decade since 1969 has turned out for many of the people of this study. A few changes and some tan-gible improvements have indeed been made, such as additions to and modern-ization of houses and trailers. But the struggle to get by has consumed nearly all of the available financial resources, and has left most people still at the break-even point.

It is precisely this lack of observable "improvement" that is so readily con-demned by the larger community. Outsiders ask why the rural families are unable to improve the appearance of their homes, to raise their living stan-dards. Why are they unable to get out of poverty? The answers to such ques-tions are usually shaped by general stereotypes about poverty and the poor.

> Those people either do not know how to live or do not care how they live. They aren't smart enough to manage their money. They are unable to save up for needed improvement. They go on buying sprees, wasting their money on un-necessary and luxury items. They don't care about the future. If they want something new, they get it now—to heck with the future.
>
> No will power. No judgment. If they had to work for the things they get, they might realize the value of a dollar.
>
> They just go on living the way they do without a thought to their future. They'll never amount to anything because they have no aspirations.

Over and over again, the outside community finds its general stereotypes about poor people confirmed in superficial glimpses of the material standards of living in the run-down rural areas. But the larger community is jumping to conclusions, leaping from the visible results of successive economic decisions to imputed moral and mental characteristics, concluding that these people are poor because they are inadequate, both as earners and as spenders of money.

The analysis of the patterned economic behaviors presented in these chapters does not support such allegations. A study of the patterns and underlying themes of people's economic behavior provides new answers to challenge the familiar stereotypes and character defamation. This method can be applied to understand a variety of observed actions that might otherwise be interpreted incorrectly through the condemning lens of stereotypes. The next few pages will examine two common aspects of the rural poverty scene—substandard housing and junk cars—by utilizing the same approach of looking at the total context of factors lying behind particular actions.

Substandard Housing

During the research, special attention was paid to housing, not so much in terms of the condition of the dwellings, but as a way of exploring the needs, problems, desires, and values of the residents. In probing for and recording people's comments about their housing situation and their decisions concerning housing, much was learned about the nature of spending decisions with regard to housing. (For this substudy, the sample population was expanded—lengthy interviews were conducted with a dozen other families not included in the main part of the research and informal discussions with other families living in substandard housing in various rural locations nearby.) The results of the housing study are summarized below.[4]

Those who live in rural pockets of poverty express or exhibit the following main concerns or goals with respect to their housing: (1) to provide shelter for household members, (2) to minimize the cash cost of housing, (3) to be assured of a place to live in the future, and (4) to maintain flexibility to modify living arrangements and adjust housing expenditures to meet fluctuations in family size, household needs, and availability of cash. In these dominant housing goals, we see again the importance people attach to keeping cash costs down and keeping cash expenses flexible to meet changing needs and fluctuating resources. Comfort, convenience, and appearance are of secondary importance—they might be listed as goal number five. Middle-class concerns such as the value of the dwelling and its location for enhancement of social status, or for investment potential, are rarely mentioned.

Given the perpetual shortage of money, it is not easy to meet the four basic housing goals. Over the years, people have developed a variety of strategies to enable them to do so. The most common, time-tested, cost-cutting methods of achieving these housing goals are listed below.

1. Acceptance of housing that is inexpensive because it is substandard or deteriorated or inadequate. (All twenty dwellings of the original sample would have been classified by government census as substandard; eight were significantly below standards.)
2. Acceptance of housing that is inexpensive because it is located in an undesirable, low-priced neighborhood.
3. Willingness to compromise and make trade-offs between ideal preferences and real prospects; to settle for the security of a modest place one can afford rather than the comfort—but insecurity—of a more costly place.
4. Upgrading housing by piecemeal patch-up, repair, and expansion whenever time, materials, money, and optimism are available. (No house is regarded as finished; it is always in a state of being repaired, improved, expanded, or changed.)
5. Attempting to own rather than rent, to gain the security of occupancy and to avoid a fixed monthly outlay for rent. (All four of the renting families in the 1969 sample viewed renting as only temporary, ownership as much preferred.)
6. Use of informal arrangements for financing housing. If one's home is borrowed, purchased, or rented from relatives or friends, payments tend to be smaller, may be paid irregularly whenever cash is available, and can often be paid in goods or services instead of cash.
7. Clustering of houses or mobile homes close together on a single lot, to avoid buying and paying taxes on extra land and to facilitate pooling of facilities. Clustered homes may share a septic system or well, may use a single electrical hookup to save installation charges, and may share appliances such as a telephone or washing machine.
8. Reliance on relatives and other neighbors in active patterns of exchanging services, trading equipment, and providing emergency or overflow living space.

By a combination of these eight strategies, rural people with limited incomes and few prospects for greater prosperity in the near future manage not only to keep a roof over their heads, but also, importantly, to provide themselves with a home in the social and psychological sense. And they do this inexpensively enough so that their limited income can be stretched to meet other family needs.

There are drawbacks to these strategies, however. For one thing, the resultant housing quality leaves its occupants shortchanged in terms of comfort, space, convenience, and sometimes health and safety. Second, the housing is vulnerable to public scrutiny. Critical passers-by and visiting personnel from community agencies and institutions see the piles of building materials in the

yard beside a ramshackle house and remark only on the poor condition of the house and the mess and squalor of the yard. The passer-by is not aware of the perpetual process of repair, upgrading, and modification to adapt to current needs. The passer-by doesn't realize that those building materials, obtained perhaps in trade last fall, are waiting to be joined by some more materials when a little cash is available and will eventually enable the husband to build the new front entryway that his wife has been wanting. The public only condemns, looking at the superficial physical evidence and concluding that the people who live there must be lazy, spendthrift, and unambitious. Once again, the actions that people with low incomes take to enable themselves to get by on what money they have are misinterpreted by the general public: cost-cutting strategies are interpreted as personal slovenliness. Closer analysis reveals that the cost-cutting strategies are essential means of dealing with the economic constraints and social needs characteristic of rural poverty.

The Junk Car Phenomenon

Many of the homes of rural poor people are flanked by junk cars strewn around the yard, a hallmark of a rural depressed area. The outside community often asks why a man would waste time and money on junk cars, why he would clutter up the landscape with old vehicles when his time and money might be spent in more profitable ways.

The first part of the explanation for this phenomenon is that rural poor people must have a way to get to town, but cannot afford to spend much money for cars. Consequently, the cars they drive may only be usable for a short time before they need repairs or give out entirely. Hence, it is helpful to have standby cars, cars that can be fixed, licensed, and put on the road as substitutes, cars that can provide a handy supply of replacement parts. By juggling cars and parts, a man can supply his family's transportation needs at a relatively low cost.

Second, as indicated earlier, the car business is a source of small amounts of cash; profits from $10 to $100 or more can be made if a man is skilled in repair work and has the time to invest in repairing and dealing. The cars in the yard are sometimes thought of and talked of as a bank account. Cars are liquid assets that can be sold or traded quite readily to raise cash or obtain goods.

Third, repairing cars provides a man with a means of using and exhibiting his skills. By avocation he may be an expert mechanic and may derive pride from his ability, although he might not want to be a professional mechanic, perhaps because he is not sufficiently sure of his competence to put himself in a situation requiring its daily validation. (Doing car repairs on his own, he can pick and choose, doing only those he feels confident to handle.) The junk car business allows him to use his skills and his time when he feels like it, not under obligation to a boss, and in a situation that involves more likelihood of success than failure. Car repairing is also a useful skill a father can teach his son, and may form a large part of their conversation and activity together. (Some women, also, are experts, but few engage in car repairing except when stranded along the road, which is a common occurrence.)

Fourth, the trading, buying, repairing, and selling of cars and parts all form an important aspect of the relationships among men in the neighborhood and on the job. It binds men together in a specialty activity, and offers them an opportunity to demonstrate competence to each other. Conversations frequently center on the merits of cars presently owned, formerly owned, or coveted, and on boasts of driving skill and special feats. Many of the men and boys obviously enjoy driving, and spend considerable time fixing up a car to run faster, noisier, more daringly. Reciprocal assistance in working on cars also forms positive ties among neighbors, and dealing in cars and parts is a major content of interaction between neighborhood men. (Interestingly, the fathers of some of these car-trading men were horse traders in their day, maintaining networks of individual acquaintances with whom they carried on an intermittent small-scale trade.)

However, the junk car business does have drawbacks. One problem is that it can consume too much of a man's nonwork time, and his wife or children may resent this as much as they resent the expenditure of money on car parts instead of other family needs. Also, a yard full of auto hulks may be dangerous, particularly for young children at play. Additionally, engines and other car parts, tools, rags, and grease sometimes take up space in the kitchen because there is no garage in which to work on repairs during winter. A wife may periodically nag her husband to haul away the cars he cannot sell, to clear his "junk" out of the kitchen, and he may eventually do so. But gradually, the yard and the kitchen fill up again, not because the man or his family likes it that way, but because this pattern of activity fulfills social and psychological needs and also provides a way to increase income and cut expenses, as well as supplying transportation.

The junk car phenomenon continues, then, because it serves a variety of needs of the residents. But the front-yard auto junkyards are offensive to passers-by and contribute to the public's stereotype of the rural poor. The visual offensiveness of the cars is interpreted by the outside community as a sign of the moral offensiveness of their owners.

Conclusions

Clinging on the Bottom Edge

On both sides of the economic ledger, the rural poor are locked into unsatisfactory positions: their employment income is low, with little prospect of increasing; their family needs consistently eat up the total income, making it unlikely that they can "save their way out of poverty." The poverty problem is entrenched and of long standing—there is an intergenerational history of limited income and self-defeating job experiences and there is a social and psychological legacy of a lifetime of economic deprivation. The resulting money management patterns and job histories lead, in turn, to a perpetuation of the money shortage. Families appear to make little observable economic or material "progress" over the years. And this lack of improvement, in turn, perpetuates the family's low social position and the neighborhood's bad reputation by confirming the stereotypes held by society at large. And so the cycle continues.

However, it is important to understand that these economic patterns exist because in some crucial ways they are positively functional and adaptive. The patterns continue even though the people understand that their economic activities and decisions have not lifted them out of poverty, but have merely enabled them to survive. Survival, in the sense of providing at least minimal food, shelter, and clothing, is obviously both necessary and a goal of the first order. Parents coming out of a period of crisis or multiple problems may be heard to say, with a sigh of relief and a touch of pride, "At least we kept food on the table and a roof over our heads." For families who have spent months or years living in old school buses, in abandoned one-room schoolhouses, in barns, and in tents, the continued provision of food and shelter is not something that can be taken for granted.

Beyond this level of bare existence, the spending patterns are positively adaptive in a second important respect: the maintenance of motivation. While the pattern of taking cash that had been saved toward a higher goal and spending it on a lower-priority item does not help in the long-run improvement of the family's economic and material position, it does have the important positive effect of providing tangible rewards in a system that otherwise seems heavily loaded with punishment. These rewards appear to be important to the preservation of mental health, often keeping a man from giving up entirely. They are also important to the preservation of a family's commitment to the broader economic and cultural system of American society. In a sense, these periodic small rewards are the mechanism by which a man who gains little from the economic system is able to continue to believe in the values of that system. The rewards serve as feedback that allows him to believe that hard, steady work is the way to achieve what he desires in life. They help reassure him that his children will be able to have a better life than he did, that hope is not foolish but both necessary and reasonable.

By these small rewards, rural poor families keep themselves within the mainstream of the American economic system, though clinging on its bottom edge. By the adaptive economic patterns described, most of the families have kept from dropping out in utter despair, severe mental illness, or paralyzing alcoholism. The economic patterns also have enabled most families to continue to subscribe to the socially accepted means for goal achievement. These points are important, for if either despair or deviance places an individual or family too far outside the dominant system, the chances of their ever rising to acceptable status in society are greatly reduced, and the chances for the children to do so are seriously jeopardized also.

By continuing to adhere to the dominant cultural values and norms, poor people remain in a position that allows them to take advantage of any opportunities that might come up as a result of improvements in the general social and economic structure. In a sense, they take a stance that allows them to "just get by" in their present situation, but does not close off any options for moving into a better position, should the system present the opportunity. In a sense, they are ready to take society up on an offer of a "good deal," should one ever come along, and if the risks of accepting it are not too great. In the meantime, each family does the best it can, balancing insufficient resources gained from hard work against never-ending demands, and trying to keep frustration and discouragement within tolerable limits. This economic balance is difficult to achieve and maintain, and society gives those who maintain it little credit for doing so. One woman pleaded for recognition of the effort.

> If people would only recognize that we are trying, that we are struggling with everything we've got. If they would encourage us when we're doing something to better ourselves, instead of faulting us for the way we have to live.

What if

Day in and day out, people in the rural poverty areas operate at or below the break-even point. Only once in a rare while do they get a small windfall to spend – a retroactive disability claim or an accident settlement – and this often goes to pay off back debts, to buy a slightly better car, or for clothes and household appliances long overdue.

Only in fantasy are people relieved of the ever-present constraints that limit their many economic decisions. On occasion an individual will let his imagination roam above the limitations of daily poverty living. Some people wonder aloud what they would do if they "won big" in the lottery or a commercial sweepstakes, or if that "rich uncle" left them a few thousand dollars. In most cases, though, the musings reveal the strains of a lifetime of money management on the brink. A big win would, at last, free them from the constant, crushing weight of debts, bills, and worry.[5] But the envisioned changes in material possessions and living situations are modest indeed. It is not a Cinderella dream, at least for adults, who clearly do not believe in fairy tales and who entertain no delusions of becoming princesses or princes living in palaces. A big, new house in the suburbs is not a part of the dream. If money suddenly became available, they would fix up the present house, or trade it for a slightly better one nearby. The women, particularly, say that they would go on living pretty much as they do, but with fewer discomforts and drudgeries. (One woman wished for an indoor automatic clothes washer with running hot water. She does the laundry now in an old wringer washer on the porch, with water carried from a cistern in the yard and heated on the kitchen stove, then poured into the machine outdoors.)

The limited nature of people's fantasies also reveals a fairly realistic appraisal of their lives. They realize that in their real-life situations, money is not their only problem, merely the most pressing and constant of many intertwined problems. They realize that instant money could not solve everything. But they know that it surely would help. Bogged down by worry, they muse aloud, and their words sum up well the economic picture in these rural pockets of poverty:

If we had all the money in the world, I ask myself, would we really be happy? No, I don't think so.

It's hard this way, with me not working. Every week we use up the money for just certain things. We pay one big bill, then we pay for groceries, then we just have a little left over for other things we need. But this week, I had to tell my family that we wouldn't have nothing but bread and potatoes, milk and stuff like that to eat 'cause we just don't have the money.

If we had *lots* of money? Well, I could get all the clothes the kids could wear on their backs, and I could have nice clothes too. And we could get lots of food. And we'd get a new car—newer than this one anyway. And we'd be out of debt. And we'd fix up the house.

As I say, I don't think having lots of money, being rich, would necessarily make us happy. But if we could just get $150 a week, though, we could sure use it. We could get along much better.

7

Marriage and the Family

Introduction

This chapter analyzes the structures and processes of marriage and family life in rural poverty enclaves. The analysis includes a description of the characteristic features and a delineation of the underlying goals and cultural values pertaining to marriage and family. The chapter seeks to identify the stresses that bear upon the family, the way these stresses affect marriages and families, and the way people absorb or deal with them. The analysis is based on long-term observations of many families, in Chestnut Valley and in other nearby rural depressed neighborhoods. Whenever quantitative profiles are used, however, they are restricted to the original twenty low-income families from the 1969 sample.

Characteristic Features

Three characteristics of family structure and process stand out. They are: the basic nuclear family model, the elasticity of the household, and the high incidence of marital disruption.

Basic Nuclear Family Model

A principal characteristic of the family structure is its conformity to the "standard" American pattern. In conceptual norms and in actuality, the standard nuclear family of a married couple and their young children clearly predominates. In 1969-70, eighteen of the twenty households contained a core married couple. In the remaining two households a single adult temporarily was living separately from a spouse.

In the twenty households, there were slightly more children (fifty) than adults (forty-five). There were children in fifteen households. (Three households had only grown, departed children; one household did not yet have children; and one household contained only an adult male.) In the fifteen households with children, the average number of children in the home was slightly over three, with a range from one to eight. The total number of children born to a family ranged up to ten; in the three-year period from 1970 to 1973, sixteen babies were born in the twenty households.

Elasticity of the Household

Although the predominant pattern is the nuclear family, the second characteristic is elasticity. Individuals, part-families, and entire nuclear families may be taken into a household temporarily. They may break away later, perhaps drift back, and then leave again, creating a shifting household structure. At any time, at least one-quarter of the families are expanded families, with some extra people in addition to the primary nuclear family. But the expansion does not create a permanent family form: families that are expanded at one time may be nuclear at other times, and vice-versa. In 1970, six of the twenty households were expanded. In 1972, there were five expanded households, but these were not all the same households. Only one expanded household remained that way for the two years; the other five had changed from expanded to simple, nuclear composition, while four previously nuclear families had expanded. Over time, then, the family structure is basically a nuclear unit, with temporary expansions to include extra people.

The most frequent form of expansion is the re-inclusion of a grown daughter with her children, if any. Three of the six expanded familes in 1969-70 were of this type, and remained this way for six months to more than two years. In some cases, more than one grown daughter with children were living in the parental home. Occasionally, expansion includes the daughter's husband or boyfriend, but this is usually a short-lived situation. Another common expansion pattern is the inclusion of a sibling, parent, or parents of a principal adult. In a few cases, a grown son and his wife and/or children become part of the parental household for a short time. Occasionally, an unrelated family or individual will be temporarily annexed.

Marital Disruption

A third characteristic of the family is the high incidence of marital disruption. Eighteen of the twenty households contained married couples in 1969-70, but two couples split up soon afterward, and all parties moved out of the neighborhood. One other marriage was in a state of informal separation (in separate domiciles in the neighborhood). In the succeeding five-year period, two more couples broke up. In addition to long-term separations and terminations, five more marriages underwent episodes of serious crisis and temporary separation during the research period.

Evidence of the long-term pattern of marital disruption is also found in those cases where a presently intact nuclear family includes children born of previous marriages. Additionally, the movement of individuals into and out of

Chestnut Valley is very often connected to or triggered by episodes of separation or divorce, or by the formation of a new union after dissolution of a prior one.

In addition to the high incidence of actual breakup, there is a much higher incidence of temporary but repeated and serious family disruption. Violent marital fighting, sudden departure of a spouse, mutual agreement to separate, and accusations or open acknowledgement of extramarital relationships are common in fact, ubiquitous in conversation, and pervasive in thought, fear, and suspicion.

Thus, whether one looks at the development of individual families over a period of time, or at situations in the total sample at one point, severe disruptions in marriage relationships appear to be frequent and characteristic. Although marriage and the nuclear family predominate as the modal type, marital breakup and altered family structure are characteristic also. What are the reasons for this paradox? What do people strive for and why? And why does the reality fall so short of the ideal?

Sentiments and Values Perpetuating Marriages

Family stability or instability is a complex phenomenon, and cannot be understood purely in terms of the statistical frequency of separations and breakups. If we merely count the number of broken and breaking-up families we get an exaggerated impression of instability, because we are using only one of several possible indices of family strength or weakness. Statistical counts of marriage dissolution neglect sentiment and values and tend to leave the erroneous or untested inference that the individuals do not place any emphasis on marital and family stability. In fact, although many of these marriages undergo serious disruption, most couples subsequently reunite, with a strong desire to smooth out the trouble and start over again. All three of the couples that broke up in 1969-70 were eventually reunited.

Many separation attempts – a husband or wife leaving the home, even going into court for initial protective or separation or custody procedures – are aborted because of the strong desire to try one more time to keep the marriage going. As one woman said, "I keep giving him one more chance, hoping that he'll straighten out." Many of the couples in the study had been married for decades, despite periods of intense stress, disruption, infidelity, and brutality that an outside observer might consider significantly damaging to one or both partners and to the children. All but a few of the disrupted marriages were subsequently reconciled. Those few couples who did finally and permanently divorce reached that point only after many attempts to repair their marriages, and the individuals soon established unions with other partners. The *longevity* of some marriages, despite serious and periodic disruptions, may be a more significant social fact here than the rate of breakup or disruption of marriages.[1]

Maintaining a stable, intact family is an ideal strongly held by both husbands and wives. While actual family life may periodically or frequently fall far short of being harmonious, the goal of an intact family is tenaciously held, and tremendous emotional effort is spent attempting to achieve it. There appear to be four chief factors that reinforce the goal of "family."

An Intact Family Is Important for Children

Many of the adults of Chestnut Valley whose lives today are most problem-ridden grew up in disrupted homes. Death of a parent, and periods spent in foster homes and institutions are common in the life histories of one or, in many cases, both parents.[2] As these adults reflect on their present difficulties and their probable causes, they invariably cite their childhood family situations.

> I really didn't have any upbringing. I just existed. And it was always a struggle. Before I was fifteen, I was out in the world alone, getting by however I could, always in trouble, constantly fighting.

> I had no family. I've always resented the fact that they didn't care enough about me to care for me.

> My husband always wanted a relationship with his children that he never had with his father.

> Both my husband and I want so badly for our kids to have the home and childhood that *we* never had.

The lack of a stable family during childhood is viewed as definitely contributory to adult life problems. Now, as parents, men and women fervently hope that their children will have a better life than they had. Providing a two-parent home is considered crucial. Parents believe that as long as a child grows up in his or her own family and, for the most part, receives love and care, periodic upheavals will not seriously harm the child. Parents assume that children are able to see beyond the short-lived fights and squabbles to the overriding fact that their parents love them and that they are doing the best they can to provide a secure home, better than the one in which they were raised.

Fear of Institutional Care for Children

Parents fear the consequences to their children if the family should break up. From their own childhood experiences, from those of friends and relatives, and from experiences with their own children, parents have a deep-seated fear of the possiblity of foster homes or institutional care for children. Divorce or separation might lead, eventually, to having the children put into such a foster-care situation, or even to having them "taken away" for good. Most parents, even those few who may appear to have a rather poor relationship with their children, are chilled by that possibility. Their fear of having the children removed, even temporarily, is partly based on negative feelings about the community and its institutions. Parents are convinced that keeping the family together at all costs is preferable to running the risk of having their children brought up by outside agencies, institutions, or individuals. They say, "no matter what it's like, the kids want to be in their own home."

Dependence of Parents on Their Children

Couples appear to perpetuate a marriage despite its stresses because, consciously or unconsciously, they are dependent upon their children. For many parents, the children are an extension of themselves, a means of self-fulfillment, and an important part of their self-image.

"Without children, there is no family," said one father.

"Where my children are, that is my home," said a mother.

"My children mean the world to me. They *are* my world."

Many women consider the role of mother to be far more important than that of wife, and generally far more satisfying and fulfilling. Some men are emotionally dependent on their children because they receive their main acceptance and admiration from their young children. In times of severe family upheaval, both parents may openly express their personal emotional need for their children. (This need is part of the explanation for the phenomenon of a mother's keeping a child home from school when the child is not ill.) Even estranged parents may recognize that they both have a right and need to continue seeing the children. A divorced woman categorized her relationship with her former husband this way: "We are no longer man and wife. But he is and always will be the father of my children, the grandfather of my grandchildren. So I can never completely cut him out of my life, no matter how much I hold against him for the way he treated me." And so it is hard to make a complete break, and the temptation to try once more postpones a decisive parting.

This dependence of the adults on the children keeps a troubled marriage going because each parent fears that in a separation he or she might be the one to lose the children, either by the simple act of the spouse's removing them, or by the processes of court action. Sometimes a husband attempts to keep a wife in line by instilling in her a fear that he could at any time have her declared an "unfit mother" and have the children taken from her. A similar threat is sometimes used by wives against husbands who do not provide support. Fear of losing the children has many times been mentioned explicitly as a reason for not leaving home. Even women who are brutally beaten believe that if they run away from home to escape domestic violence, they jeopardize their rights to the children. Thus, the ideal of preserving a two-parent home "for the sake of the children" also includes the unspoken need to preserve an intact home for the sake of the *parents*.

Dependence of Husband and Wife on Each Other

Adults also cling to a frequently disrupted and tension-filled marriage because of dependence on each other. This factor was apparent in several cases of long-term but unsatisfactory marriages and in marriages that only broke up after many years of recurrent fighting. Wives, especially, exhibit this dependence, particularly in cases where many years of married life have entailed virtual confinement to the home. In some cases, the wife has had little opportunity to operate as a responsible, independent individual in the wider world. In local phrasing, she has been kept "barefoot and pregnant." The only life she knows is keeping house, bearing and rearing children, soothing everyone's hurts. Even the meals she cooks may be prepared from food that she has not selected, because her husband is the one who drives, the one with the money, the one who gets the groceries. The decisions and interactions involving the big events and the little day-to-day activities may all be made by the husband: whether to buy that trailer or this car, whether to apply for food stamps, whether to take a child to the doctor. For a wife in this position, the contemplation of establishing a separate existence in a world she hardly knows brings tremendous fear and insecurity. This in turn makes her decide that it is better to stay put and take the inevitable blowups than to leave home and try to make it on her own. Her low self-esteem, her limited experience in the outside community, her fear of failure – all these underlie and are combined with emotional dependence on her husband, and give a woman strong reasons to remain with him. Rather than making a drastic change, she attempts to make the best of a bad situation.

In some cases, a wife stays with her husband mostly out of fear of him. On numerous occasions, an unhappy wife consciously decides against leaving home because she fully believes her husband's threats to harm her, the children, or himself if she should leave. Loaded shotguns are powerful deterrents to leaving home in the heat of marital squabbles.

Husbands, also, may keep a poor marriage going because of their dependence on their wives, a dependence more often based on emotional than practical needs. Although men seldom admit their dependence, it shows up when their women do leave them. In these situations, men exhibit a real state of emotional loss, appear helpless in coping with everyday life, and often go on a protracted alcoholic binge. A man whose wife has left him may claim that he can get along without her, and may boast that he can easily obtain sexual gratification with other women. But he may also go to great lengths to track her down and beg her to come home—which, in many cases, she does.

Mixed in with this dependence, there is usually an undeniable and strong bond of affection, and memories of better times together in the past. These, too, act to prolong even a seriously troubled marriage.

Sources of Family Stress

Despite the strong commitment to maintaining a marriage as central to a good home for the children and as emotionally important for the adults, rupture and temporary breakdown are commonplace. The reasons for marital upheaval include both long-term causes and immediate or triggering events.

The triggering event—the last straw—is usually perceived and emphasized by the individuals involved. In most cases, it is a small act by either husband or wife that is reported as having brought on the crisis. The wife may have purchased a relatively extravagant food item, or made an unauthorized purchase for the house. The husband may have refused to fetch the children from the neighbors; or perhaps he has procrastinated in repairing the heater, but is angered by his wife's oblique reference to how cold it is in the house. Sexual promiscuity—actual or imagined, recent or dredged up from years ago—is a frequent fight starter. Either husband or wife may have been seen in some questionable circumstance with someone of the opposite sex, and rumors fly quickly through the neighborhood.

These actions and events, however, are only potential triggering causes: whether or not they actually give rise to a marital fight depends on many factors in the state of the marriage and the individual's emotions. When the marriage has been fairly peaceful for a period, potential triggering events may be overlooked or ignored. However, if one or both individuals are feeling "down" emotionally, or are under the influence of alcohol, small triggering events may be particularly volatile.

Marital fights seem to go through several stages, usually starting with abusive verbal exchanges, goading, and name-calling. Accusations are exchanged concerning factual or fancied marital infidelities of the past or present, and there ensues a general berating and belittling designed to further undermine the fragile ego of the other person. Physical fighting often erupts, and may be brutal, with threats of even greater violence in the future. It is usually the wife who suffers the most physical damage, and furniture and household items are frequently broken. Children, too, may become involved, threatened but seldom physically harmed. They may take sides or merely scream at both parents from the sidelines. Often the row ends in a stormy departure by either husband or wife, and the action and tension subside.

Behind the triggering events that touch off such flare-ups lie long-run, semipermanent stresses on the family and its members. Couples apparently do not recognize or they underestimate these deeper sources of marital stress, dwelling only on the triggering events. But the underlying stresses are festering irritants, as each partner harbors a longstanding and complex list of grievances and accusations. They explain the fact that very minor events so easily erupt into major battles. At most times, a family is under pressure from several stress sources.

Chronic Economic Problems

As discussed in the previous chapters, rural poor families carry a perpetual burden of money shortage, back debts, unsatisfactory or insecure jobs, worry about where tomorrow's meals will come from, and undersatisfaction of felt needs. The financial squeeze is an ever-present source of tension in some households, and the necessity of coping with it, combined with the inevitability of worrying about it, causes an undercurrent of anxiety and tension.

The economic problem may be the triggering cause of any particular dispute, with many marital arguments arising over the expenditure of money: she spent it on a nonessential for the house; he spent it on booze; and so on. Money is also a cause of arguments between parents and children, and these, too, may trigger marital confrontations: a small child may throw a tantrum because his mother refuses to buy a treat to eat; a teenager may sulk for days because the father wouldn't allow her to buy new shoes. In such cases, the parent-child dispute may well end up as a marital fight when one parent takes the child's side in the argument. There are endless small confrontations over money, and criticisms of the way money is spent often enter into marital squabbles, even when they are irrelevant to the argument.

Even when not the cause of a particular dispute, however, the constancy of money problems causes a general tension and anxiety that erode family life. The economic situation is a seething substratum that is constantly present to fuel other problems in the household, to exacerbate interpersonal tensions, and to drain the strength of individuals.

Unresolved Emotional Problems of Adults

Various emotional problems, rooted in childhood, frequently appear as continuing sources of stress in later life. Most of the adults grew up in difficult situations, and many carry into marriage a residue of unresolved emotional conflicts. Because of factors in their early childhood – disrupted homes, deserting parents, abject poverty, foster homes, or homelessness – some adults may find difficulty later in life maintaining close interpersonal relationships. The psychological mechanisms that enabled them, as children, to weather the emotional stress of frequently disrupted family life may actually work against them when, as adults, they attempt to establish and maintain close interpersonal connections. Perhaps in childhood it was necessary for self-protection to limit close emotional ties and to withhold trust. But in adulthood, this insulating shield becomes an isolating wall. This effect was apparent in the case of the man whose childhood consisted of a series of "new mothers," each of whom subsequently left or died: he now reports difficulty in getting along well with his second wife, or any other woman, on a long-term basis.

Some marriages suffer from the fact that they began when the partners had not yet reached sufficient maturity to know what they really wanted or expected in a marriage, knowing only that they needed a refuge from personal and family problems in their parental home. But the emotional needs that give rise to an early escape from the parental home are not necessarily satisfied in the marriage. For example, a woman who married at seventeen, in part because of her need to throw off the controlling hand of her parents, finds that in marriage she is no more autonomous or free than she was in her parental home. The couple has recently been going through a difficult period of struggle for authority, with the wife eventually buckling under to her husband's will—but not without seething resentment that occasionally erupts into hostile rebellion. Likewise, a boy of sixteen has quickly found that establishing a household with his girlfriend and their baby has not magically turned him into a man, and that his problems of getting along with other people have not been solved, but have multiplied.

Built-in Tension Points

Tension may be structured into some families as a result of the family's previous history. For example, if the union is a second marriage for either or both partners, there may be problems connected with the former spouses, or with children of former unions. If the children in the family are from previous marriages or from extramarital relationships, these children may provide a built-in source of conflict between husband and wife. They may argue that "his" children or "her" children are getting inferior treatment, or special consideration, in the family. Accusations of favoritism toward one's own children and accusations of sexual advances toward stepchildren can be a continuing and bitter source of marital disharmony.

In-law problems may also cause strain. Relationships with his or her "people," particularly if they live in the same house or nearby, may provide built-in tension sources.

Presence of Extra Individuals in the Household

Stress in the marital relationship sometimes arises as a result of the characteristic flexibility and expandability of the household. Often the household expands to incorporate an elderly grandparent, disabled adult sibling, or a grown child or grandchildren. This temporary inclusion of others is seen as a fulfillment of one's obligation to help close relatives who have been unable to make their own way in life, an expression of lasting reciprocal bonds of mutual assistance. But it is viewed as neither the preferred nor the normal household situation. People openly state that such an expanded-family situation tends to cause tensions or provide fuel for existing difficulties. It drains family resources of food and money, often causes extra work, and reduces privacy.

The strains of having extra people living in the house show up particularly in the case of the re-inclusion of a grown daughter with her children, the most frequent form of expansion. The daughter may stay in the home because, without a husband, she needs the advantages of free or cheap room and board, she desires grandparental babysitting, and she seeks emotional and social support. In most cases, the daughter is in an anomalous position in the household, as role relationships, lines of authority, and division of labor are ambiguous.[3] Her father may assume a male authority role over both the daughter and her children, especially if the daughter has no man living with her. The young mother may come into conflict with her own mother with respect to the handling of and responsibility for her children. And in some cases, the lines of affect appear to be unclear, even to the children. A child in such a household may as likely go to grandmother as to mother for comfort, and in some cases may even address grandmother as "Mamma." In addition, the young mother may try to assume a disciplinary role toward her younger siblings in the household, as if they, too, were her children.

This lack of clarity in relationships between the basic family members and the annexed individuals is apt to create tensions that reverberate through the household, strains that are exacerbated by the temporary overcrowding of the home. The problem is even greater if only one member of the parental couple is parent to the daughter, while the other member is a more recent stepparent, officially or unofficially. Eventually, the strains may make the daughter move out, perhaps to a trailer or converted bus beside the house, or perhaps to join her husband or another man elsewhere. In some cases, the daughter may soon again need the refuge of a place to live and a family – and once more she will be taken into the home, with the difficulties and strains of the previous stay forgiven and forgotten. Occasionally, the length of stay may be protracted, and more than one daughter may be living at home at the same time. The strain on the central couple is usually apparent, and was described by one woman.

My husband and I need a life together, some privacy. We don't even have a chance to sit by ourselves and talk, or to sit in the living room and watch TV.

And we don't have the time we need to devote to the younger children because my grown girls and their babies are always around. It's so crowded here that my little one still has his bed in with us, and he has no place to play.

But even though parents would like their grown children to move into homes of their own, the parents continue to put up with the strain of an expanded household when necessary because, "she is our daughter, and we can't just turn her out." Marital harmony comes second.

Unsuccessful Role Fulfillment

Because of a host of factors in this multigenerational poverty situation, individual adults may be unable to perform their expected roles to the satisfaction of either themselves or their marriage partners.

The male role pattern appears to present considerable difficulty. The adult male is conceived of as head of household, sole sex partner of the wife, earner of the family's sustenance, provider for the family's secondary wants, and chief authority figure in the household, with the power to make decisions and the authority to carry them out and to use sanctions to secure compliance. In actuality, few men attain even an approximation of this ideal. Many of the male heads of households find that in the jobs they hold they cannot earn enough money to provide what the family needs and wants. And so a man's sense of his own worth may be diminished, in his own eyes and in those of family members. Many of the irritating situations of daily life—the "hungry Thursdays," the chill of the cement kitchen floor, the necessity of sharing shoes and a bed with a brother, the blurry picture on the old TV set—are somehow connected to the vague realization that the man is not successful as a provider for his wife and children. This low self-image is a clear contributor to marital problems.

For the wife, the role expectations are less impossible to achieve. In most cases she can provide her husband with sexual satisfaction and bear children. Mother and housekeeper, as well as mate, are roles she can perform with some degree of success. Whatever the margin of separation between her ideal role and her actual performance, that difference is not totally a reflection on her. For example, her performance as housekeeper may fall below role expectations held by her husband, her neighbors, or by the outside community, as well as by herself. However, the brunt of the blame for this shortcoming may not fall directly on her, but on factors beyond her control, such as inadequate facilities—lack of closets, of hot water, of a washing machine; insufficient money for cleaning supplies; and overcrowding in the house. The blame falls diffusely on her husband, on the job situation, on the fact that there are a lot of people in the household, and on the vague explanation of "that's just the way it is around here." Thus, her performance may not be questioned, her ego not threatened. Outside the home, also, a woman usually escapes the constant exposure to defeat and failure that her husband encounters. If she does take a job, it is an extra role, and she has some leeway to be unsuccessful or to quit without causing damage to her self-evaluation or to her husband's evaluation of her.

The greater attainability of women's role ideals, and the ability to direct blame for unsuccessful role performance away from the self, give rise to a frequently observed pattern in which a wife's ego strength and functioning level appear greater than those of her husband. Although many of the women encounter feelings of failure periodically, and occasionally quite strongly, on the whole the women are less perpetually and consistently assaulted by the sense of failure in fulfilling what they conceive of as their roles.

Although it might seem that this differential success in role fulfillment is a real plus for the women, the imbalance can also be seen as a contributing factor in the tension between husbands and wives. The differential possibility for fulfilling role expectations has been explicitly mentioned by several women, and is apparent in many of the instances of long-term marital strife.

Lack of Roles in the Outside Community

People lack access to secondary social roles in which they could gain a positive evaluation of themselves. This leaves both men and women highly vulnerable to ego damage if their performance in their primary roles (in employment and family) is inadequate. Since there are no other roles open that provide separate gauges of the individual's worth, too much personal evaluation depends on performance of basic husband and wife roles. A man's failure as family provider appears even more crushing than it would be if there were opportunities for him to be successful in other, outside roles. (Even success on a community baseball team or as a member of a volunteer fire department would help. But as we shall see in Chapter 10, the men of the rural depressed neighborhoods do not participate in such organizations.)

It was apparent during the course of observations that individual adults, both men and women, function better in their home and family roles when they are provided with some active nonfamily social role to fill. Success in filling even a temporary outside role apparently builds ego-strength and thus enhances performance in the primary roles. It also takes the mind off family problems. Several women, in the midst of a very demanding and stress-filled home life, have earnestly stated that they would like to be able to give some time to helping out in some worthy cause in the community, like a day-care center or a nursing home. While participation in such outside roles might not put more food on the table, the boost to the self-image produces a sense of well-being that results in smoother relationships in the home. (Some small-scale opportunities for this kind of participation were created during the process of fieldwork in Chestnut Valley, and each time it was clear that the women who participated felt a heightened sense of self-worth during and after the events, for they had given some of their own time, skills, energy, and even money for refreshments to help put on a successful activity for the children of the neighborhood.)

The interaction of primary and secondary roles is by no means a class-bound phenomenon. In the middle class, active community roles may compensate for or support weak marriages. But the people of the rural poverty enclaves do not have access to such substitute or compensatory roles—and one result is stress in marital relationships.

Discharged Aggression

Frequently, marital upheavals result from the fact that the family serves as the place where frustrations generated by experiences in the outside world are released. The many frustrations derived from experiences on the job, in the community, and at school cannot be expressed outwardly and directly, either because the source of frustration is diffuse and undefined, or because there is no avenue or mechanism for redress. Often the individual fears that direct expression of hostility against the perceived source of frustration would entail a large risk which he or she cannot afford to take. The consequences might involve losing a job, even worse treatment for the children at school, being dropped from welfare, being further looked down upon by the rest of the community. Some individuals fear that if they tried to express their disagreement directly to a boss or caseworker, their anger would boil up into furious, uncontrollable rage, making matters much worse. Instead of taking such a risk, frustrations experienced in the outside world are often held in (except when the individual is under the influence of alcohol), and are later vented in hostility toward the family. A marital blowup is much more likely when such pent-up frustrations are present. But many families appear to be accustomed to such venting, as one wife explained.

> Right now my husband is doing the best he can. So we try not to get upset about his angry rages. If someone or something on the job upsets him, he takes it out at home on the family. Even the kids understand this and try to put up with his bad days. After all, its the same for the kids. If a child has a bad experience at school and he suppresses his feelings about it, he'll take them out on the family when he gets home.

This pattern of discharging aggression within the family is clearly not peculiar to the people of this study, or to people in poverty; certainly the bad-day-at-the-office syndrome is well known in the middle class. But the situation in rural poor families is more destructive of smooth family functioning because of several factors: (1) the frequency of frustration-producing experiences is higher; (2) the tolerance level for frustration may be lower, due to insecurity and low self-image; (3) the channels of redress are less accessible; (4) there are likely to be other sources of stress already at work in the family; (5) there may be a greater tendency to express anger in a violent manner rather than verbally; and (6) with the crowded conditions in the home, there may be no space or manner in which one individual can vent his pent-up frustration and anger without immediately impinging on all other members of the family. Thus, discharged aggression is a factor in marital difficulties.

In summary, these seven sources of stress, singly or in combination, press against the emotions and interpersonal relationships of a married couple and of a family. They provide a constant undercurrent of tension that erodes relationships as it erodes individuals. They provide a ready source of friction to touch off a marital row. In the face of these persistent irritants, the remarkable fact is that the marriages last as long as they do.

Processes in Marital and Family Adjustment

Despite these inescapable stresses and strains, people hold tenaciously to the ideal of marriage and an intact family life. Both young adults and older people expect that a marriage will have its stormy periods, but their hope is that their marriage can be better than that of their parents, that their marriage can withstand disruptions, can outlive the fights and separations. An analysis of the dynamics of family adjustment shows how the ideals are pursued, the hopes perpetuated, despite the strains.

Short Cycles of Fighting and Starting Over

It appears that the climactic blowups, caused by relatively trivial triggering events superimposed on deeper strains, serve to relieve a highly charged marital atmosphere. They force unvoiced problems and tensions out into the open, making each partner more aware of the depth of pent-up rage in the other. The blowups also reaffirm the commitment to the abstract ideals of marriage in terms of obligations, rights, and roles. Many of the battles concern accusations of marital infidelity and of failure to fulfill expected roles within the family. The strength of these accusations reveals to each spouse (as it also reveals to the social scientist observer) the esteem in which the marriage and family ideal is held by the individuals. The marital blowup thus serves several positive functions: it acts as a safety valve; it clears the air; and it reaffirms each partner's commitment to marriage and family life. It also sets the stage for "starting all over again," a theme that is quite common in accounts of family history.

One typical example of this pattern, a relatively common occurrence, is that of the wife who has her husband arrested and put in jail for beating her. To the bafflement of others, the wife goes down to the jail the very next morning to take her husband cigarettes and toilet articles. They appear to be on friendly terms. She refuses to press charges, and arranges to obtain his release.

The results of this episode are that the husband has had "the fear of the law put into him," and each partner has realized his or her dependence on the other. The stage is set for starting over again. A harmonious period in the marriage may ensue, perhaps with a pregnancy initiated at this time.

Thus, both the blowups and the re-formations actually serve to keep marriages going, as an ideal and as a practice. The social analyst must look at the many attempts to perpetuate a marriage, as well as at the forces that tear it apart. In this cyclic view of marital blowups and attempts to start over, it becomes clear that despite the high incidence of marital strife, a strong commitment to marriage and family life is indeed present.

The Long-run Cycle of Adjustment

In the developmental history of each family, these short cycles of breakdown and starting over are epicycles on a long-term cycle of adjustment. The long-run adjustment cycle is essentially a response to the varying degrees of stress engendered by poverty circumstances at different periods in the family's development, and there is a clear pattern, despite variations from one family to the next.

Before a marriage partnership begins, either member may be involved in premarital relationships, perhaps with a child born of the relationship. These involvements do not usually entail serious long-term commitment for the future, but may contain many of the secondary attributes of marriage. For example, the young man or woman may very easily slip into the role of unofficial son-in-law or daughter-in-law in the home of the partner's parents. In some cases this entails a very warm relationship between the young man or woman and the unofficial mother-in-law, who in some cases is clearly serving as a substitute mother, providing a relationship that may be almost as important to the young individual as the love and sex relationship with the partner.

In contrast to this tentative arrangement, a marriage relationship, whether or not it is marked by a wedding ceremony, entails a serious commitment and some feeling of intended permanence. A tentative relationship between two individuals may drift into a permanent marriage, including an official legal ceremony. In other cases, each member of the original tentative relationship finds a different partner for marriage. In either case, the new relationship is recognized as the real marriage.

A new couple starts out with high goals, with each expecting a good deal of the other. By the time the young couple has two or three babies and small children to care for, however, considerable marital strife may have developed as a result of several disappointment areas: the inability of each individual to meet his or her own expectations; the inability of each individual to live up to the expectations of the other; and disillusionment over the benefits of marriage itself. And all of these potential sources of stress are heightened and brought into action by the continuing and/or worsening struggle to make ends meet.

The years when the children are young may be dramatic, with many episodes of upheaval – although these are usually followed closely by attempts to start over, in hopes of keeping the family together "for the sake of the children."

By middle age, after twenty or more years of an often stormy marriage, and as the children are leaving home, the picture brightens. The income of the family may be higher, relative to expenses, and the irregular spending patterns of younger days may be more controlled, so that a greater portion of recurrent expenses can be met without strain. The husband and wife seem more willing to accept what they have. By this time, they perceive themselves as having learned "to make do with the things we have and live within the amount of money available." Thus, there are fewer arguments over "foolish spending," and fewer strains over inability to acquire desired goods. They also have learned to accept the faults or drawbacks of each other and "to know that the world isn't a bed of roses, and other people have had rough times also."

Several people have used analogy to describe the lifelong process of marital adjustment. One woman said that making a marriage work is a continuous balancing of both people's wishes, and she compared this to the process of making ends meet through continuous balancing of desires against dollars. The ability to strike this balance is seen as a sign of maturity, not as resignation. "We have accepted our life." Another woman summed up her observations on her own struggle and the balance she had achieved.

> When you're young, you have an idea. For instance, what kind of home you want. You keep striving towards that. But finally you come to the conclusion that you won't get there. Once you accept that, then you can accept your little shack as home. Then you try to make little improvements on it – paint, curtains, paneling. This will satisfy you, at least for the time being. It may not be the ideal home you had visioned, but it's better than what you started with. You have to compare what you have now with what you had in the beginning, not with the best you'd like to have ideally.

But this acceptance, and the peace it brings, usually comes only in mid-life, after years of marital stress, and after the crucial years of raising young children have passed.

The middle-aged period, however, may also give rise to new sources of stress that can create marital friction. Although the children have grown and left the house, they may themselves be going through the stressful phase of early adulthood, encountering problems with marital crises, babies, and financial burdens. During this period, the grown children and their problems may become a preoccupation and a source of worry or dispute between the parental couple. Grown children may periodically return to the parental home, with their own children in tow, coming back to the security of home after having been beaten in their attempt to forge a life of their own in the outside world. As a result of the parents' involvement, conflicts may arise to threaten the newfound harmony of the parental household. Some men complain that their wives give more time, attention—and money—to their grown-up children than they did when the children were little, and more than they ever did to their husbands. A few women have managed to remain aloof from the problems and squabbles of their grown children, but most find their children's dramas as compelling as the soap operas they watch on TV. And because they are their own children and their own grandchildren, they feel obligated to help in any way they can, even if it creates a strain in their marriages.

Eventually, as most of the grown children settle with their familes in independent, if nearby, residences, the older couple may again enjoy a more stable relationship with fewer stresses and less interruption. Couples look forward to this achievement, to being by themselves, less burdened with the problems of children and grandchildren, and free of the extra economic demands. They anticipate this period as a reward for their years of work and worry, and as it arrives, they may find new marital harmony.

However, this later-life situation is not usually idyllc. For one thing, the lifetime of grinding worry, the cumulative effects of undernourishment and limited health care, of many pregnancies in quick succession, of accidents, injuries, heavy smoking and/or heavy drinking combine to make many people age rather rapidly. (Individuals in their mid-fifties are often peceived by outsiders as being nearly seventy.) Poor health in the later years and deteriorative aging problems may provide yet another set of problems and anxieties. Some people are partially incapacitated for many years. Financially, many elderly people are worse off than ever, often subsisting on very meager payments from Social Security (meager because the salary rate and years of employment that determine their benefits were quite low); a pension of some sort, such as a disability payment; or welfare if necessary. They cannot afford to improve their houses, to modernize, or even to repair. For many, however, there is the offsetting fact that nearby and all around them are their children and their grandchildren, who keep them busy smoothing out problems, soothing hurts, caring for babies, giving advice. An elderly individual whose spouse has died may move in with his or her grown children, although others prefer even an inadequate home of their own to dependence and chaos in their children's homes. For a few individuals, loneliness is a painful part of old age, but for most, the support of young family members all around keeps them going.

This, then, is the long-range cycle of marriage and family, much simplified and generalized, but characteristic.

Conclusions

Despite the eroding effects of long-term economic, social, and emotional stress, the family is of tremendous importance in impoverished rural areas. While certain trends in contemporary society have tended to weaken the American family and usurp some of its former functions, the situation appears to be somewhat different among the rural poor. Here, the family remains the major element in the lives of individuals—if only because there are no other social roles and groupings available to them.

Due to the collapse of the local rural community and the failure of the urban community to become a social substitute, the family in these rural depressed areas has been forced to take on extra functions. Because of the social marginality, the rural multigenerationally poor families must provide for their members most of the social and psychological functions that more affluent members of the community satisfy through a variety of secondary relationships and groups. By default, the family is the only group in which poverty-stricken rural people regularly participate on a sustained basis. It is the only social unit with which individuals identify. And, for better or worse, the individual's reputation is inextricably bound to his family's. In addition, the family is a cooperating economic unit, with continuing responsibilities to offer a home, food, and services to its members, even after they have left the nest. In a striking number of cases, the family provides a temporary or semipermanent home to its elderly, its disabled, and its mentally retarded.

The bonds among family members appear to have a high positive valence and considerable permanence, an ability to survive temporary rifts. The family is a fairly self-contained center of affect, activity, and social interaction, largely because there is no other available grouping, either on the neighborhood level or the community level (as will be seen in Chapters 9 and 10). But the family's broad functions also result from traditional cultural values: people believe that the family is and should be a strong, lasting unit. Adults believe that a stable home with both parents present is important for the long-term well-being of their children. And they conceive of family as a continuing entity, with life-long bonds of reciprocity and responsibility to its members. Thus, in sentiment and values, as well as in action, the family is the most significant social grouping.

However, the smooth functioning of the family is continually being threatened and undermined by the many stresses that impinge upon it as a unit and upon its component members as individuals. Family disruption results, despite the desire for family survival. Couples repeatedly try to patch up marriages that are fraught with tension and prone to periodic breakdowns. As the family strives to surmount the stresses and to fulfill within itself the

functions that other people have long since delegated to the secondary and in-stitutional community, it tends to become a separated segment, somewhat detached from other families of the neighborhood (particularly when undergo-ing a rough period), and socially isolated from the people and institutions of the larger community. There is one significant function that the family does not serve. It does not act as a link between its members and the outside world. Parents do not make connections for their children, nor do children forge connections for their parents. The family does not effectively launch its members into the wider community. Instead, the family is a refuge from the wider world.

8
Patterns of Childhood

Introduction

Children are much in evidence in Chestnut Valley, especially in good weather, as small bunches of youngsters play beside the roads that run so close to the clusters of houses. Their old bicycles lean against the houses, their homemade go-carts, their dolls, balls, and torn rubber boots lie scattered on the ground. Inside the homes, the presence and importance of children is abundantly evident in the friendliness and noisy playfulness of children crowded into a small space, and in the frequency with which the topic of children figures in the actions and conversations of adults.

The presence of children is compelling in another way also. In almost every one of the intergenerationally poor families, the children are the promise of the future, the lifetime hope of their parents. And yet, it seems almost impossible to avoid the fact that these children are likely to become the victims of the bitter cycle of economic, social, and psychological problems that has crushed the hopes of one generation after another in these rural depressed areas. To anyone who works closely with the families caught in this cycle, it is hard to avoid the awareness that, despite occasional success stories and the many, many happy moments of warmth and fun, the long-term picture can be tragic. In a decade, we watch a child emerge from an innocent newborn to a sad, defeated youngster, conscious that he just can't seem to do anything right in school; from an eager kindergartner to an eighth-grade truant; from a lovely ambitious young girl to an anxious overtired mother who worries that her own babies seem to be growing up amidst the same kinds of problems and burdens that shaped her own childhood.

This chapter will focus on themes or patterns that characterize the sample of children who were observed from 1969 through 1979. The generalizations are based on unobtrusive observations made mostly in homes, but also in schools and other public places, and on a great deal of interaction and conversation with both children and their parents, particularly mothers, in a variety of settings and during many kinds of activities. For the observation of children, the sample was expanded considerably beyond the original twenty low-income families in the 1969-70 base sample, to include children from several different rural poor neighborhoods. The inclusion of children from well over fifty families provided a greater range of settings for observations and more cases to substantiate the generalizations.

Some important points must be made at the outset. First, the children of the rural pockets of poverty do not form a single, uniform type. The children of any rural poverty neighborhood vary considerably among themselves. Social, psychological, and other factors of the individuals comprising each family, as well as particular situational factors confronting the family as a whole, contribute to the uniqueness of each child's primary environment. No two homes are exactly alike, and no single home environment corresponds exactly to the generalized, synthetic picture presented here. There is neither a typical Chestnut Valley pattern of bringing up children, nor a typical Chestnut Valley child. As in any other neighborhood, as in any other socioeconomic stratum, there are warm, supportive parents and cold, neglectful, or brutal parents; there are parents who are sometimes warm and sometimes cold; there are noisy, chaotic homes and quiet, orderly ones: homes where optimism prevails and homes full of unspoken anxieties. So, also, there are all sorts of children: there are boisterous children and shy ones, tall children and small ones, very clever ones and less bright ones, leaders and followers. There is no one type of child here.

Second, children from these rural neighborhoods are basically very much like any kids in any neighborhood in the United States today: they watch the same TV programs, they memorize the same commercials and wish for the same products; they go to the same kinds of schools, wear the same clothing styles, tell the same jokes; they have the same kinds of fun, get into the same kinds of mischief; and they exhibit the same range of endearing, humorous, thoughtful, and annoying behaviors. In other words, these are not "different" children, not a subculture apart from their contemporary American generation. These children are part of the mainstream of present-day American culture, and they need not and should not be labeled as belonging to a separate category.

Having made these two points, however, it can now be said that the children from these rural depressed neighborhoods do have some *different life experiences* than those encountered by the "typical" middle-class child. They grow up in the midst of problems that are more frequent in occurrence, more severe in degree, and more insoluble in nature than those of the "average" child of the same community and region. And despite the uniqueness of each individual's home environment, most of the children growing up in poverty in rural areas are affected by more or less similar stresses. The common denominators (operating in varying intensities at different times) are: (1) the continuing poverty in which the families are trapped, (2) the constant strain of worry and insecurity that accompanies poverty anywhere in American society, and (3) the deteriorative effect on individuals and on relationships of a continuing accumulation of self-defeating experiences. As a result of these prevailing forces operating on almost all of the families studied, there are certain patterns in the way children grow up in their homes, and certain patterns in the way children respond to and are affected by their home environments and the wider world. These patterns appear to produce somewhat similar long-run consequences in adult life, including restricted life trajectories and limited futures.

This chapter will delineate and analyze ten apparently significant patterns in the home environment and home experiences of children. Although some potential effects of these patterns on children's development will be suggested, psychological interpretations are outside the scope and competence of this ethnographic study. Some facets of the child's interaction in the world beyond the home will also be suggested, although a systematic examination of the role of such important community institutions as the elementary school could not be included in this study.

In addition to observing and analyzing situations and responses, it is important also to seek out people's conceptions, hopes, and aspirations regarding their children. And to the extent that a difference exists between the hopes and the realities, we must ask how people perceive and deal with the disparity. These questions will be addressed toward the end of the chapter.

Characteristics of Home Environments

Babies and Small Children are Cherished

Strong positive attitudes toward having a baby are revealed in connection with the normal occurrences of pregnancy and birth, and women exhibit concern over anyone's difficulty in becoming pregnant or fathering a child. Miscarriages are regarded as a real misfortune, and women tend to count and remember these occurrences in their life histories. Pregnancy is regarded as a state of being, and women often reckon time in terms of their series of pregnancies: "when I was pregnant for Peter." Abortion is strongly opposed as a means of family planning or birth control. Parents do not suggest or urge that their young unmarried daughters abort a pregnancy, nor is a family likely to agree to having such a baby adopted. "That baby will be our flesh and blood. If my daughter can't raise it, I will."

When a baby is expected, the whole family is filled with excitement and anticipation. This seems to be as true for the third or the seventh baby as for the first, as true for the birth of a grandchild as for a daughter or son. The strength of this pattern is indicated by the fact that the excitement is no less when a baby is born to an unmarried teenage daughter.

When it becomes known that a teenage daughter is pregnant (and is not married) the parents may at first be angry, disappointed, or even abusive toward the daughter. But as the baby's birth approaches, the parents not only accept the fact, but may look on it as possibly a good thing. Parents say, "it will help her to grow up," or, "it will give her something to live for, something to care for."(Likewise, in the case of a son whose girlfriend has become pregnant, parents feel, or hope, that becoming a father may make the boy grow up and take responsibility.) In the family of the young parent-to-be, all attention comes to focus on the future event, on the baby itself, not on its origin. As a young mother-to-be departed with her father for the hospital delivery room, her mother called out this last bit of advice. "Now, you just remember, when the pain gets bad, what I've told you before. Just think about what you're bringing into this world! Think about the reward! Then you won't feel the pain."

Upon its arrival home from the hospital, the new baby becomes an individual member of its mother's family, accepted on its own without regard to prior circumstances. It is given all the holding, cooing, and cuddling from its grandparents, parent, and young uncles and aunts that is given to any other baby in the household. As in the case of any new baby, various family members have managed to purchase at least some brand new bedding and layette items, a large supply of diapers (increasingly, disposable diapers), and in some cases a whole wardrobe. Family members may also have assembled used bedding and other appurtenances from relatives and friends. The pattern of preparation and excitement seems no different from that surrounding the arrival of any other baby into a household.

In most homes, any little baby is truly a center of attention for all members of the household. Most fathers, as well as older siblings, appear to derive considerable happiness from interacting with babies and small children, and openly demonstrate pride in a baby's development. Affection toward babies and young children is generally expressed freely and openly, but of course the frequency and intensity vary from household to household, from time to time. With infants, physical caressing, cooing voices, baby talk, friendly teasing, and endearing nicknames are all common.

Babies have a great deal of physical contact with family members. Generally, though not in all cases, babies are held much of the time, whether awake or asleep, by the mother, any other adult, or any capable child. They are handed along from arms to arms, lap to lap. Although one reason for this pattern may be a lack of playpens and baby chairs, even mothers who have some of this equipment seem to prefer holding their babies or asking some family member to do so. Special baby chairs and other furniture are status items, it appears—part of the image a mother, particularly a new mother, has about the things her baby should have. Even the bassinettes and cribs that are handed down through a series of babies may not be used a great deal, as an infant often sleeps in the mother's bed, an older baby often naps on the couch.

For most babies, there are also times when the mother and other family members are too busy or too burdened with anxiety and problems to give the infant more than minimal attention, and it may lie unattended for long periods. And there are mothers who have very little physical contact with their babies, initiating early the practice of propping the bottle rather than holding the baby for a feeding.[1] In such cases, physical contact and warmth depend on the other people in the household. But on the whole, most mothers place a very high priority on "keeping the baby fed and dry and cuddled," and will try to do as much of it themselves as possible.

As a boy child grows "too old for hugs and kisses" (at anywhere from one to three years) affectionate roughhousing becomes a common mode of interaction between fathers and toddlers. At a somewhat later time a mother begins to substitute frequent verbal statements of "I love you," though some mothers continue frequent caressing and lap-holding of both boys and girls well into school age. The verbal and physical demonstrations of affection are spontaneous and genuine. However, with toddlers and preschoolers, as with young school-age children, these expressions of affection may be offered most frequently when the mother is feeling unable to provide any other concrete benefits to the child, when a child is troubled or is in trouble, or when the mother has no control over the source of the child's pain. Perhaps she cannot remove the real problem, but at least she can make the child feel loved in the midst of a difficult situation. (Perhaps, also, the giving of more than usual physical affection reflects the mother's own stresses and needs.)

Love of young children may often be expressed through material objects (as was discussed in Chapter 6, in connection with economic decisions). Many parents would spend their only pennies buying the child some treat, although they may at other times clamp down on the children's begging and nagging for things. Presents on birthdays, Christmas, and other holiday times are viewed as very important, and parents may invest considerable money and ingenuity for months beforehand procuring the things that will make their children feel happy and well-loved at these special times. One mother rationalized her purchase of gifts for the children even though there would be little money for groceries. "I know they're a little old for believing in Santa Claus. But we have to have a little fairyland in their lives because the world is such a terrible place."

Parents also tend to express their love for their children in the form of hopes and aspirations for their future. One young father told how eager he was for his little son, age two, to become old enough so he could read to him about history. The father, himself a high school dropout, had found the subject of history fascinating, and he hoped the boy would too. He kept his old history books from school safely wrapped in a cloth and hidden away until the child was old enough.

Parents tend to be supportive of the childhood aspirations of their youngsters, rarely deflating their boasts of one day becoming a rich person, a famous race car driver, a teacher, a politician—even president of the United States. And many parents encourage and assist their children in the early years of school, urging them on, not letting them give up too easily, express-ing their hope that the child do well in school as the first step toward a more satisfying adult life. This, too, is regarded by parents as an expression of love and caring.

As adults talk about and enact their role as parents, they consciously link their belief in the importance of parental love and attention to their own recollections of having felt unloved by parents when they were young children. They are anxious not to cause the same doubts, pain, and deprived feelings in their children.

> The kids at school used to call me names because my father was drunk and my mother didn't care what I did. So I was always scrapping. I hated school. That's why, when my son was born, even though his father left, I vowed I would do everything I could to bring him up right, give him everything I could afford, and teach him how to behave.

Most parents, even those with large families, are sensitive to each child as a an individual. Their comments and their interactions with the family show that they seek out individual traits in children when they are very young, and appear perceptive to different styles and needs as the youngsters develop.

> All my kids are different. You have to treat them differently. Each one is an in-dividual.

The high valuation that parents place on proper care of children is also in-dicated by the fact that they severely criticize any person who exhibits carelessness and lack of concern about his or her children. In fact, the most caustic criticisms that a family makes about another family often have to do with the abdication of parental roles, and neglect or conscious abuse of the children.

> Why, we treat our animals better than they treat their kids!

The few cases of child neglect or possible child abuse that were observed dur-ing the research period were a subject of real concern to relatives and neighbors, most of whom stood ready to take the affected children into their homes. For although most parents had experienced times of great difficulty over their children, they generally have, as one man put it, "a soft spot in our hearts for kids, for anyone's kids, not just our own." One woman affirmed, "These kids! There are so many problems on account of them. But I wouldn't trade a one of them!"

The Child's Primary Environment
May Include Several Adults

In many families, the infant or young child has a circle of adults who make up his world of interaction: grandparents, aunts and uncles, adult sisters and brothers, and other adults who are periodically and frequently around the house. Many of these are apt to help take care of and amuse him, and so the growing child recognizes a large number of other adults as being connected with his family and with himself.

The child is thus provided with several available parent-substitutes. If his parents at some time are unwilling or unable to care for him or tend to his needs, there are other adults, with whom he is already warmly familiar who can care for him. There are other adults to turn to, other models to follow. The close relationship between children and their older generation relatives has significant effects. Young children tend to approach nonrelated adults, even strangers, quite easily, and to expect response from them. Children who grow up in close association with grandparents, uncles, and aunts carry those relationships with them through adolescence and into adult life. In their turn, these new adults become active aunts, uncles, and grandparents to the next generations of children. The importance of other adults in a child's life shows up also in the fact that kinship terms are common in the speech patterns and stories told by young children. (Not only "Grandma Black," but "my sister's husband," or "my brother-in-law," or "Suzy, my little niece," are common expressions.)

The Home is Apt to be Crowded

Crowding in the home affects many young children, in terms of available space and density of people and activities. There is little space for young children to explore, and they are not encouraged to do so, partly because of the many dangerous or potentially harmful situations, such as a very hot space heater, an unflushable toilet, an open stairway without railings. In many homes, little or no space can be set aside just for children, except perhaps the beds they share. The young child has no place to be by himself, no place to retreat from the commotion of the rest of the household, no place to store his treasures.

In some cases, the crowding results in the child's appearing to be fatigued by overexcitement and overstimulation. Although a routine or schedule for the infant or small child may be attempted, it may be difficult to maintain because of the many distruptions and comings and goings of household members and extra people attached to the household. On the other hand, the child is seldom without people to watch and interact with and learn from, people to tend to his needs. He observes his family's life in close-up and all the time.

The Sibling Bond Is Emphasized

The sibling bond appears early, is encouraged, and usually remains strong throughout childhood and into adult life. The baby, toddler, or preschooler who has older siblings has considerable interaction with them. In many families, older sister and brother often provide a lap for the baby, feed a bottle, rescue a toddler from the brink of danger, remove valued or dangerous objects from a little one's grasp. Older siblings take considerable pride in the accomplishments of the baby, and teach him new tricks to perform, "walking" a six-month-old around the room, teaching a toddler to say words and repeat phrases. Older children eagerly show off the baby's new tricks, both to each other and to visitors, and they appear anxious when a baby is ill. In later childhood, older boys and girls tend, when possible, to include young siblings in their home play activities. By the time the "baby" approaches three or four years, the pride, fascination, interest, and playfulness that his older siblings have directed at him have usually diminished somewhat, perhaps because there is now a new baby. But a legacy of close sibling relationships seems to persist, a feeling of belonging together that outweighs the petty quarrels and day-to-day squabbles of childhood.

The sibling bond is reinforced by parents. They remind a child to "share those cookies with your sister," and "be sure your little brother stays off the road" (using the sibling term more often than the given name of the child). Both fathers and mothers expect older siblings to be concerned about younger ones. Fathers, especially, remind boys to watch out for their sisters, to help them if necessary. Parental praise reinforces the children's acts of sharing and caring, so that such behavior occurs spontaneously away from home as well. A school child will save in his pocket half a party cupcake to share later with a sibling on the school bus, or with a preschool brother or sister at home. Siblings stick up for each other in squabbles at school, and may win parental praise for doing so.

Parents explicitly verbalize their support of a strong sibling bond, and in cases of family upheavals parents attempt to avoid separating siblings. After a difficult period has subsided, a parent expresses pride in the fact that, "at least we were able to keep the kids together." Although childhood squabbling occurs as frequently here as in middle-class homes, the poverty-stricken families seem to have a stronger concept of siblings as a unit, of sibling ties that survive temporary rifts. Perhaps this is due to a realization of the actual instrumental importance of sibling solidarity. There are many occasions when siblings are thrown into mutual dependence—during family crises, for example—so the bond is frequently expressed in action and thereby reinforced.

As the children participate in the outside world, siblings appear to rely on each other to a considerable extent. In school, for example, the interactions between siblings from rural poor families seem to be more frequent and more supportive than interactions between siblings from middle-class families (who sometimes pay no attention to one another). This characteristically higher level of sibling interaction seems to reflect not only continuing parental reinforcement, but particularly the need for protection. Mutual protection of siblings in school apparently arises as a result of the fact that many of the children experience difficulty in initiating and sustaining relationships with other, nonrelated children. This difficulty seems to result in part from children's early perceptions (by age seven or eight in some cases) that they are being avoided or rejected by others. Additionally, the difficulty results from the fact that their parents do not foster, either verbally or in action, social ties with other children, whereas children of more affluent homes receive encouragement and facilitation in developing an active social life and making new social contacts.

The close feelings among siblings appear to last long past childhood. Even in cases where adult siblings do not get along well—and this is by no means rare—there is a feeling of regret that circumstances, in-laws, or alcohol have separated them from each other. And even in these cases, when a crisis arises help will be sought and given among siblings. The basic and longstanding bond of protection and defense continues.

Parent-Child Bonds Persist
Despite Strain and Challenge

Children in the middle years appear to remain emotionally close to their parents. Usually the closer ties appear to be with the mother, for sons as well as daughters. During this period, child-parent relationships may be fluid, changing in intensity not only as a factor of the child's age, but also as a result of the circumstances or emotional ups and downs of the parent or the family as a whole. Such disruptive events as family upheaval, fights, and occasional brutality by a parent rarely cause permanent rupture of the parent-child bond, but they do seem to cause ambivalence of the child toward the parent, unpredictable fluctuation in the intensity of the relationship, and insecurity on the part of the child.

Some children sometimes exhibit exaggerated dependence on parents, clinging physically and emotionally to a parent, more often the mother. Perhaps

this is a semiconscious device designed to force parents to restore normal relationships with the child, or with each other. Some children attempt to remain
physically close to one or both parents as much as possible. One child, for example, frequently stayed home from school "because Mommy needs me," but
it seemed plausible that the child was also staying home because she needed
her mother. In some cases, the pattern of sticking close to a parent arises out
of the child's fear that if he lets his parents out of his sight, they might leave
home, or fight, or go off on a drunk.

Parents, particularly mothers, conceptualize their relationship to a child of
elementary school age in terms of providing love, comfort, guidance, encouragement, and as much of the physical needs as can be afforded. Teaching
the child right and wrong and teaching a child how to take care of his own
needs as much as possible are considered to be a part of the parent-to-child
relationship during this stage. But the preadolescent and early adolescent
ages are considered to be far more complicated, and parents seem less clear
about their role during this stage. Parents feel that teenagers have many more
complex needs, needs that cannot be fulfilled by the simple infant-care techniques of feeding, clothing, and cuddling.

> The older ones—we try to protect them, to soothe their hurts, and to see that
> they get something to eat, that they're dressed clean and decent, and to hope
> they keep going to school, and keep out of trouble.

As they approach their mid-teen years, the children are making a stand for
independence, and parent-child relationships are in a period of redefinition.
Parents express concern about a teenager's behavior, and may become angry
about flagrant defiance, perhaps punishing the child with restrictions on
where and when he can go. But most parents feel that there is little they can
do about their teenagers, either to prevent disapproved behavior or to promote desired behavior. They resign themselves to just hoping.

Although much of the friction between teenagers and their parents appears
to be quite similar to the generalized version in contemporary American life,
children from the rural poverty-stricken areas drift away from home earlier
than their nonpoor peers. Some of them spend considerable time out of the
home—perhaps loafing, eating, and sleeping in a relative's home, or in the
home of a young friend or neighbor. In a number of cases where a young
teenager attaches himself or herself temporarily to another family, one is
struck by the ease and speed with which the teenager develops affectionate
ties with the adults in the host household, and by the ready labeling of the
host adults as "Ma" and "Pa."

The weakening of the tie between parents and their adolescent children is
only a transitional phase, however. The two-way interdependence of parents

(especially mothers) and children (both sons and daughters) continues throughout life, with both obligations and affective content. Grown children are frequently called on for assistance, and are expected to take in a parent in need of a temporary home, and to look out for their parents in old age. (Some do and some don't fulfill these expectations.) Perhaps the strongest expression of the lasting parent-child tie, however, is the continued obligation parents feel toward their children, always standing ready to provide an emergency home-haven. Parents know that they cannot guarantee their grown child a place of respect in society, or a good, well-paid job, or a big inheritance. But the one thing they can offer with some certainty is a temporary home: "You can always come back home." For the young teenager or young adult leaving home, this assurance provides a sense of security.

Discipline Is Primarily Considered Punishment and May Be Inconsistent

Parents conceive of discipline in terms of making a child do what he is told, which is primarily achieved by preventing him from misbehavior and punishing him for disobedience.

There is no typical pattern or general agreement as to what is the best way of preventing or handling misbehavior. Many parents relate their preferred pattern of punishment and control to their own childhood experiences. Some wives think their husbands are too harsh in punishing the children, and a few intercede on behalf of the children. But one woman felt the reverse. "My husband would never punish the kids till it got real bad. He never made them mind because his father was so strict with him when he was small. But I always felt he should have controlled them more."

In some homes, spanking and slapping of small children is rare, and reprimands are verbal and mild, whereas in other homes the situation is characterized by harsh physical punishments with no explanations. In some homes there is a constant tug-of-war between the wills of parent and child. In a few cases, yelled reprimands, verbal insults, slaps, shoves, and being sent to bed constitute a high proportion of the total mother-child interaction for a child of two or three years old.

Punishment patterns also vary from time to time within the same family. At times, the child's misbehavior goes unnoticed and unpunished, while at other times the same act is met with instant, harsh, physical punishment. The main factor that seems to determine the outcome is the situation and tension level in the household at the moment. It is the parent's momentary condition, rather than the degree of "naughtiness" of the child's action, that determines the severity of punishment. In some cases, in fact, it is hard to see the correlation between the child's behavior and the parent's response.

This inconsistency is exemplified by a scene that was typical in many—but not all—homes. A youngster is sitting on his mother's lap as the mother talks and drinks coffee with a visitor. She absent-mindedly strokes the child's hair, caresses his body. Suddenly, she thrusts him down, spanks his bottom, and yells at him, "You get back in that bed, you hear? Hurry up, or I'll swat you for real." He disappears for a while, but soon reappears asking for a drink of water. She satisfies his stated need, takes him up in her lap, caresses him for a while—then remembers again that she wants him in bed. So again she abruptly sends him off, this time with a solid spank and a stronger verbal threat. The pattern is repeated again when he comes out asking to have his sock put on.

From such experiences of inconsistent parental reactions, a child may have difficulty developing a clear idea of the goodness or naughtiness of his own actions, difficulty developing a fixed set of behavioral standards, and difficulty learning responsibility for his own actions. What he may learn instead is to keep a watchful eye on other people, rather than on himself. Certainly the rapid fluctuations and unexpected turns in his parents' actions toward him give an unevenness to his experience of discipline.

Another factor that works against children learning to regulate their own behavior at an early age is the fact that there are usually several older people around to administer restraints and punishments. Most children are kept out of danger and prevented from committing forbidden acts by some older person pulling them away, gently the first time, then subsequently yelling, spanking, and threatening. Younger children are controlled by an external hand and, as they grow older, they may frequently test for reactions to see what they can get away with. A child may also come to operate on the assumption that what he can get away with is all right, and he focuses on the punishment and punishers rather than on the act itself or his own potential for self-control.

The tendency for parents to rely on behavior control that is externally imposed and primarily physical rather than verbal may be functionally important in protecting young children from the many potentially harmful situations in the physical world that surrounds them: makeshift staircases and heating systems, car parts and kerosene in the kitchen. But some children come to depend on external intervention to protect them from harm; and when the child is not closely supervised, accidents happen. Consequently, mothers of school-age children feel that it is unsafe to leave their youngsters unwatched. They assume that the natural tendency of the child, especially a boy, is to get into trouble unless an adult stops him.

These patterns of inconsistent punishment and reliance on prevention by adults may have some negative consequences in the long run. They may underlie some of the behavior-compliance problems some children encounter in school. And the patterns seem to set up or exacerbate the later struggle for authority between parent and adolescent child. As parents sense their loss of control over teenage children, they may lay down stricter rules and intensify the severity of punishments. These tightened restraints, however, are often cited by the teenager as the reason he finally left home.

Still later in life, relationships with an employer or a spouse may be negatively affected by the individual's experiences of inconsistent parental control. For example, a young woman who perceives marriage as an escape from parental authority may find her husband even more restricting and punishing then her parents. For adult men, the lack of childhood experience in exercising one's own judgment and controlling oneself may be part of the reason why they seek out jobs where the decisions are made for them, where they are told each day what to do.

Home Life Requires Adjustment to
Unpredictable Relationships

Long before the child is able to understand conversation, the crises and upheavals of family life are obvious to him. Little attempt is made to shield young children from the turmoil. Several factors appear to underlie this lack of shielding: 1) the crowded living accommodations make it virtually impossible to hide tensions and fights from the children, (2) parents tend to underestimate how much of adult conversation and action a child can comprehend, (3) some parents underestimate the emotional and psychological impact of family crises on children, (4) parents assume that it's all part of family life anyway, and (5) a parent may consciously involve a child in his or her problems as an ally or a witness. In most cases, not only are the crises within the family fully obvious to the children, but also, little attempt is made to seek them out or to soothe their feelings afterward.

Many children learn from experience that crises come and crises go, and that the best thing is to try to forget the crisis once it has passed. But children also learn that they should expect more crises in the future. Although some children give an outward appearance of nonchalance about it, some appear haunted by this expectation. As one seven-year-old said, "Things are going really good now. But I know there's somethin' gonna happen soon. There's trouble on the way." Characteristically, the children whose lives have been fraught with family rupture attempt to stick close to the scene of the action, wanting to be at home if something happens. Some children are apt to stay home from school for this reason, or to suddenly back out of plans to go somewhere, like an overnight trip with a school group. Children may take an active role in trying to shape family affairs and prevent crises. A child may attempt to prevent the parent from leaving home by making a desperate demonstration of dependence—including overt affection, "babyish" behavior, or injury or illness. Since these and other preventive measures don't always work, however, children need to develop strategies for coping with the frequency of family upheaval and other home crises.

They develop a variety of techniques to insulate themselves from the hurt of family crises. Some children learn early not to take the words, threats, and actions of other people seriously. Perhaps they are assisted in this learning by the tendency of parents and grown siblings to tease them.

Some adults, in a playful setting with a toddler, will tease, make threats, ridicule, hit, or grab away a toy. When the child cries, the toy will be returned, the truth told, or a kiss given, to which the child responds enthusiastically. After a moment, a new round of teasing ensues, then reassurance, and so on. Some young children appear quite frustrated and exhausted by this rapid alternation of ridicule and comforting, punches and kisses. Their response is to run off to bed, perhaps sucking a thumb or a bottle, and drop off to sleep. In some cases, these same children exhibited very few overt signs of distress over family fights and crises, as if they had learned not to take people's actions too seriously.

Some children learn to cope with the unpredictability of interpersonal relationships by attempting to remain on the sidelines emotionally. They reduce their emotional attachment to parents, rejecting parental affection even when it is offered. Some children have learned to deny their own needs for interpersonal relationships, to withhold and withdraw from expressions of affection, because close relationships would make them more vulnerable. This pattern of denial of the need for interpersonal relationships seems to parallel directly the way a few children have learned to mute their awareness of physical needs.

One little girl was obviously undernourished, but even when food was offered in school, she refused it saying, "I'm not hungry." In fact, the child's main associations with food had been negative: her parents constantly argued about the amount of money spent on food, and her decayed teeth pained her when she chewed. In response, she had taught herself not to recognize her own hunger. Similarly, she apparently reacted to problems at home by becoming somewhat withdrawn emotionally, rarely expressing affection or even enthusiasm. Interestingly, when this child played with her doll, most of the interaction involved force-feeding the doll, pushing food in its mouth, and bawling it out and spanking it for not eating.

Simultaneously with this emotional detachment process, some children develop new connections with some other person, usually a relative or other neighbor, and spend a good deal of time at that person's house. Young boys may spend most of their out-of-school hours hanging around with teenage boys and young adult men, as they work on cars, hunt or fish, ride around, drink beer, or just "fool around" in the neighborhood. Young girls may try to assume a "grown-up" role early, caring responsibly for younger siblings or nieces and nephews living in the home. They may spend their days in the home of an older sister, sister-in-law, or neighbor, investing their emotions more safely in a substitute family and in television soap operas.

Since interpersonal relationships in a child's family are frequently disrupted, it is functionally adaptive that children learn strategies for predicting, tolerating, or withdrawing from social rupture. But there may also be maladaptive aspects of these strategies. The insulative device of removing or withholding emotional commitment and the self-protective device of forming an expectation that relationships will be ruptured may both have a negative impact in the long run. Both may give rise to an observed adulthood problem of difficulty in developing and maintaining close relationships. The effect of this tendency on marriages was indicated in the previous chapter; the following chapter will trace its effect in producing unstable and volatile secondary relationships in the neighborhood. It is also likely that the necessity of adapting to frequent rupture of primary relationships within the childhood family underlies the observed pattern of rapid changes in intensity of relationships between individuals. A relationship may develop quickly between two people, may become quite intense in terms of frequent interaction and hanging around together, and then may suddenly be blown apart. Because people expect breakdown to occur in relationships, they do not cultivate skills for preventing social rupture, and they make little attempt to reduce or defuse growing interpersonal tension.

In many cases, however, the instability of interpersonal relationships in the home environment seems to have much less long-range psychological effect on the individual than might be expected. One force that seems to be quite effective in offsetting potential emotional damage is the constancy and/or warmth of maternal affection, especially during the earliest childhood years. Some mothers seem both consciously and unconsciously aware of the need to provide a fairly steady base of warmth and affection for their young children.

Children Grow Up in a Dramatic, Action-filled Environment

For many children, life is experienced and perceived as a succession of exciting happenings. Events past, present, and future make up their lives. Their experience of life is that it is dramatic, urgent, and filled with all-consuming events. Even when no crisis or major event is in process, there may rarely be a quiet moment in the day, with people constantly in and out of the house and, in some cases, a great deal of riding around in the car with father or mother.

Another aspect of the action-filled environment is that there may be little time for registering feelings and assessing qualities. Introspective pursuits may be given little opportunity or encouragement, perhaps partly because both parent and child are aware that brooding over troubles may be far more painful than putting them out of mind.

Because children grow up on action and excitement, to be without them may make a child ill at ease. It could be that this action-orientation is part of the reason some children express boredom when things are going calmly, and why some find it impossible, not just dull, to sit through hours of school every day. The action-packed environment may also be a factor in the high level of activeness that is rather loosely labeled as "hyperactivity" by school personnel, pediatricians, and even parents.

In such an action-filled life, the child's perception of time may not be in units, sequences, and routines, but in terms of separate events. In actual experience, there may not be a specific time allocated to a specific activity or, if there is, the patterning or routine may go unnoticed due to the more commanding importance of little emergencies and helter-skelter commotion. Also, parents may not apply such labels as "dinner time" and "bed time," either because there is no specific hour at which these activities take place, or simply because they phrase them in terms of "*you* go to bed now" rather than "*it is* time for bed." Sequences of events may be experienced, and even perceived, but not labeled or related to clocks and calendars. For example, even young children are well aware of the difference between the day before payday and the day after payday.

A child tends to express past time not by reference to calendar years or how old he was or what grade he was in, but by pegging it to impressive events and important people in his life: "the time the baby was in the hospital," "before Mommy had her accident," "after we were burned out," and "when my sister came home with baby Billy." Children also look to a future of events, more than an unfolding process or a sequence of uniform units.

It should be noted, however, that this action-orientation in children's home environments does not reflect a goal on the part of parents, or a sought-after lifestyle. In fact, adults often express a longing for a let-up from the rapid succession of events, for peace and quiet without constant interruptions and things happening. Nonetheless, the life situation is such that action-filled time is both the experience and the expectation; it becomes, also, the framework of perception.

Opportunity to Develop Self-Confidence
May Be Limited.

If there is protracted marital strife in the home, the child may develop guilt feelings, thinking that he is the cause of the trouble, or that he ought to be able to protect his parents from each other. He may feel weak and powerless because he is unable to control the thing that matters most to him—his home security. (When children talk about family fights, very often they include their own actions just prior to the fight, indicating that they see themselves as somehow instrumental in starting the fracas.)

Additionally, the child's self-esteem is inevitably affected by his growing perception of his parents' lack of self-confidence. Some parents give the unmistakable impression that they are wounded creatures who have withdrawn from the world. The children catch these impressions long before they can put them into words, but as teenagers, some talk of their early memories of their mother's total avoidance of public places, their father's defensive attitude about various problems on the job or with "the authorities." Many children sense a connection between their parents' level of self-esteem and their drinking problems. Although some adolescent children have clearly stated that they want to do everything possible to avoid becoming a man or a woman broken down by failure, like their father or mother, in many cases the events, patterns, and examples of failure that constitute their early home environments have serious unconscious effects on the children's own self-images.

The inculcation of low self-esteem in children is certainly not something that parents of the rural poverty areas desire or intend. But it may be an unavoidable legacy of the parents' own sense of failure. A parent with low self-esteem may not be able to teach his child, either by example or by words, how to succeed in the world. All a parent can say to his child may be, "Remember, you're just as good as anybody else." Such a defensive statement, however, may foster rather than prevent the transmission of low self-image.

Most home settings allow in other ways for ego-building and positive development of children's self-images. Some mothers consciously attempt to provide opportunities for a child to demonstrate his skills to others and to himself, to feel good about himself. Mothers say it is important to provide a supportive climate of praise and recognition of individual accomplishment, and to overlook shortcomings. Consequently, many children appear to be quite creative in drawing, building, and problem-solving in their home environment, utilizing initiative and inventiveness to make up for the lack of art supplies, materials, and tools purchased specifically for children's use. But the self-esteem nurtured in good periods at home is not sufficient to carry over into other times and other situations. When a child leaves the supportive environment of home and enters the larger competitive setting of the school, he may request step-by-step directions from the teacher, and may need frequent help, approval, and encouragement to go ahead in a project. Children's lack of self-confidence outside the home environment is, figuratively, written all over their shirts. (In one case, it was even *literally* written on the shirt: a boy's teeshirt slogan demanded, "Love me for what I am!")

The Timetable of Growing Up
Reflects Socioeconomic Factors

In considering the rates at which children grow up, some differences appear between rural poverty home environments and nonpoor home environments elsewhere in the community.[2]

It appears that the period of babyhood and dependence may be prolonged in poor families. Some mothers "baby" a child as long as possible, especially a last-born child or one who remains the youngest in the family for several years. The child may be referred to as "The Baby," and may continue to drink milk from a bottle until he reaches school age. Where this occurs, it appears to be a mother's way of shielding and protecting the child from what she perceives as a very difficult world. It may also be a mother's way of holding onto the mother-of-infant role in which she felt competent.

Children in the five-to-eight-year range sometimes appear to be younger than their nonpoor age-mates. Much of the reason for this is that they have less familiarity with aspects of the community and the world known to the more affluent child, and less familiarity with the kinds of knowledge expected and rewarded by schools. For example, the child of a rural pocket of poverty knows little about the community's museums and public libraries, and has rarely traveled outside his home region—he may never have seen a big city or another state, and may form inaccurate mental pictures to go with the words in his school books. However, he probably knows a great deal more than many of his classmates about how to clean a carburetor, how to apply for food stamps, how to deal with a caseworker, a drunk father, or an accident. (A ten-year-old, though his reading ability may be judged below grade level, may be the one who has to read to his parent the instructions on an application form or a legal notice from the county court.) Unfortunately, the skills and knowledge these children possess are not measured, recognized, or rewarded in school. And so the child of the rural poverty areas may be judged to be "immature," or "backward," compared to his more affluent peers.

The middle years of childhood, in contrast to the earlier years, may be shortened and rushed. Ten-year-olds may periodically be required to serve in child-care roles for younger siblings, even as substitute parents, running the home during a family crisis. By the time they enter their teen years, children from rural depressed neighborhoods often seem to be closer to adulthood in many respects than are their nonpoor age-mates. Although emotionally they may be no more mature than their more affluent counterparts, they have already begun to take on adult rules. Some of the rural children from poverty-stricken homes have already left home by fourteen, perhaps living with a grown married sister or brother. By fifteen or sixteen, when many effectively drop out of school, most of these "children" have had considerable experience of the "real world" as they will find it throughout their adult years: inability to find a job or dissatisfaction with the job they do get; the ins and outs of Medicaid, welfare, food stamps, unemployment insurance; perhaps being in trouble with the law; being sexually active and perhaps becoming a parent; perhaps being married. Thus, by the age of eighteen, the sons and daughters of the rural poverty areas are already launched into their adult world, while their former classmates of a higher socioeconomic level are deciding which college to attend to prepare themselves for the adulthood they will enter four or more years later. Although the parents may regret that their children did not finish high school, they are proud to see them assuming adult roles at an early age.

Parents' Perceptions of Their Children

Most of the children of these poverty-stricken rural homes have, or have had, at least one parent or grandparent who cares, who cares very deeply and tries to translate the caring into action that will help send the child on his way to a satisfactory adult life. But parents often feel that their caring goes unnoticed by the rest of the world.

> Society looks down on us because of where we live and because of our past. But they should give us credit for trying. They should know I'm trying to bring our children up with manners, with honesty. I don't condone them cussing in public. They should know that I try to dress the kids to the best of my ability. I always see that they leave home clean.

Aspirations

Parents want their children to behave and do well in school, and, if possible, to finish high school. They want a son to grow up to hold a steady job, one that is not as low in wages or prestige or security as their own—but not a white-collar job. They want a daughter to have a husband who is good to her, and they want her to be a good mother. Most parents believe that the responsibility for steering children toward such goals is their own, rather than the job of schools or other community institutions. At least some of the time, parents are confident of their ability to help bring about these results.

> If you teach your children right and wrong, if you bring them up knowing how to behave themselves and how to get along with other people, if they learn to take care of themselves and mind their manners, then if they're given a chance, they'll be able to show that they're just as good as anybody else.

Parents hope fervently that their children will fare better than they have. Many of their actions, purchases, and personal sacrifices are shaped by this goal.

> I always said that if I ever had any kids, I would give them what I didn't have when I was a kid. We really gave up ourselves because of the kids. If we only had a little bit of food in the house, they got it and we went without. I've seen the time we've had two crusts of bread in the house and the two boys got it. We went without. We've gone without clothes to give clothes to our kids.

Within this generalized hope for a better future for their children, parental aspirations may be somewhat unclear or inconsistent over time, or may differ between father and mother. In several families, the mother exhibits higher aspirations for the children than does the father, probably as a result of the greater sense of role fulfillment among women compared to their husbands. A mother may cling to her hopes longer, while the father expresses a preference for what he thinks of as more realistic expectations for the child. The child may be caught in the middle.

The mother is usually the parent who is most consciously, explicitly "molding" the children, attempting to give them some guidelines on how to get along in the world, shaping their motivations and expectations. Fathers more often teach specific skills, especially to sons, and when they do attempt to instill values and precepts, it is done with reference to concrete situations, by telling children that they should behave themselves, and stating that certain misdeeds will be punished. In some homes explicit verbal teaching and implicit teaching by example are both frequently evident. However, at other times, the same parents may be preoccupied or bogged down with work and worries, or sick, or hung over. At such times, children's behavior may go uninfluenced by the parents, or perhaps may be unexpectedly punished, often quite severely.

A poignant dilemma faces some parents, who consciously puzzle over what vision of the future, what level of expectation, they should try to inculcate in their children. A mother may dream high, but she knows reality. Just as she manages her own level of expectation, she tries to set a realistic level of expectation for her children, a level that is not frustratingly high but not too low. One mother put her conclusion into words.

> If you tell a child that he can't expect anything more in life than what he's got, when he grows up he will never have anything because he can't expect any more than that. But you can bring up a child to want something better, and to work to get it. You tell him, "If you want something badly enough, you have to go halfway—or more than halfway."

Doubts

Gradually, as the children mature, parents may perceive that circumstances within the family and outside it have given rise to behavior in a child that is working against his or her eventual success. Mothers express concern, even distress, over such behavior symptoms as slow progress in school, disciplinary problems in school, signs of emotional problems, loss of parental control over the child, and minor early encounters with police and juvenile courts. The nagging worry that one's children are headed for a life of problems and poverty comes out poignantly in parents' unanswered questions.

Will what happened to me happen to my kids?

Will my kids, when they get older, live the way I'm living today? Is this a cycle?

We don't want our children to grow up to be like us. We would like our children to have a better position than we had. But will we ever see that happen?

Parents may be unable to discern clearly the causative forces that have acted upon their children to bring about this threat of repeating the parental life history. But they tend to be very alert to the signals of failure in their children. Fathers, especially, may express anger and hostility when a child brings home a "bad" report card, directing the blame outward onto the school and its personnel for not treating the child right, as well as at the child, whom he may berate for "goofing off." Some parents may threaten the child with physical punishment if he doesn't straighten up, may require him to stay in the house after school, or may instill frightening images of what happens to the person who gets into trouble at school—he will end up a drunk like Uncle Harry, or in jail like the neighbor's boy. Other parents quietly accept the reports of poor performance or trouble in school, perhaps because they half expect it, perhaps because they feel that the fault lies partly in their own performance as parents.

Underlying most parents' reactions to children's problems in school, there is usually disappointment and fear, for a negative evaluation of a child means only one thing to the parents: failure. The hopes the parents had transferred from themselves to their children are threatened. The first inescapable evidence that the children, too, may be headed for failure in life strikes at the hearts of parents. Their memories of their own frustrating, underachieving school years are stirred, and their perception of their own failure as adults is heightened.

Acceptance

As time passes, the signals of failure may continue to appear: problems in school, truancy from school, troubles with the law, violent outbursts of temper at home, difficulty in interpersonal relationships. Even those parents who initially showed the highest interest, encouragement, and optimism concerning their children's future may gradually resign themselves to the likelihood that their child isn't going to make it out of the cycle after all.

> This kid is turning out to be just like his father.
>
> I guess that child just wasn't cut out for school.

If parental hopes have been dashed by their older children's inability to succeed, they may pin their hopes on the younger children as substitutes.

> If just one of my children would turn out all right, I'd shout it from the hilltops.

But unless family circumstances have greatly changed or the school environment is very different, one child's chances may be no better than another's, regardless of difference in potential. Some parents exhibit considerable anxiety about the fate of the younger children, and become easily upset over any signs of potential failure.

> Is there any way we can prevent the younger children from growing up with all the problems that their older brothers and sisters have?
>
> All the rest of my children have had problems: look at the difficulties they're in today. That's why I'm watching my little one so carefully. If she's given a hard time in school, I'll pull her right out of there, 'cause I'm not going to have that child ruined too.

An alternative response of parents is to lower their aspirations for the subsequent children, insulating themselves against the pain of more unmet hopes. And since parents perceive that they cannot significantly change the chances for success of a child once he or she has reached the adolescent years, they gradually adjust to accepting "what is." A woman talked with resignation about her sixteen-year-old daughter, whom she had just learned was pregnant.

> At this point, I can no longer take responsiblity for her. I am her mother, and I brought her up the best way I could. I tried to teach her right from wrong, just as I did with all the others. But she never listened. Always had to do it her way. Well, now it's her own life, and she'll find it's not easy. But I can't change that for her now.

Parents learn to be glad for small things, and to stand back and let their children make their own mistakes as they move out into the world, hoping that they'll "straighten out and grow up eventually." Meanwhile, the parents gradually become absorbed in the joys and the problems of having grand-children—new lives and new hopes.

For their part, children also come to limit their own expectations for themselves, to abandon the free, high-level dreams of childhood, to realize that the question of "What are you going to be when you grow up?" can no longer be answered with imagination and limitless aspiration.

Thus, the child and the parent jockey into a mutually shared view of the child's future. A compromise is reached between, on the one hand, the parents' displaced hopes and the child's dreams and, on the other hand, the growing realization that the cumulative experiences of reality are not adding up toward achieving the dreams.

A child of eight was discussing his future with his mother. He proclaimed that he would never live here in this neighborhood when he grew up. "I don't want anybody saying things about me. I'll show them. I can be just as good as they are." But the child's developing lack of confidence that he could actually be and do what he wanted in life began to affect his expressed life expecta-tions. Inability to succeed and perform in an approval-winning manner at school appears to have been an important contributory factor in limiting his dreams.

A year after he made the above statement, the boy's image of his future had shrunk considerably. He and his family were now talking about his future in terms of building a house adjacent to his parents, where he could live when he grew up.

Another boy had always been bright and successful in school, with a flair for learning. While he was small, both his parents encouraged and applauded his pronouncements about a big future. But before the boy reached high school, dreams and realities appeared more incongruent with each other, and the in-congruence could no longer be escaped by fantasy. The father appeared not to understand the studious bent in his son, berating him for his inability and lack of interest in performing "real work" at home, like repairing cars. In his early adolescence, the boy's identification with his father came to outweigh the dream he had shared with his mother—to finish high school, to go on to college and to bigger and better things. He also realized that to climb upward meant to climb outward, away from his family. Even though he felt that he *could* achieve these goals, he became less sure that he *should*. Con-sequently, the boy's school attendance dropped off, his work slipped, he lost interest, and then dropped out of school to become an unskilled teenage laborer.

Although many parents believe that education will help their children at-tain a better life, some of them find that schooling, in fact, seems to contribute no particular benefits. When their children are young, parents are optimistic about education.

> My son [four] is in the Head Start program now, and he's doing beautifully. Right there is where he is beginning to prepare for going to college. [A father with an incomplete elementary school education]

But as children grow older, a more limited vision and a more limited educational goal is accepted.

> About the highest goal any of us here want for our children in education is to have them graduate from high school. But there's a lot of kids that won't get that far. For some, their parents don't really care whether they finish. For others, it will be all the parents can do just to keep the child in school until he's sixteen, just to keep the law off their backs. Only a few parents will see any of their children graduate. [A mother who almost finished high school]

Even those children who have been successful in their early years, and who have had a great deal of help and encouragement from dedicated teachers along the way, may gradually become aware that there are other factors involved in climbing the ladder of success, and that the dreams of childhood may be beyond reach. The realization slowly comes that who you are, who your parents are, and where you live are important determinants of what you will become. This realization may be crippling to the individual.

Conclusions

It seems clear that, in contrast to stereotypes, most parents in these rural poverty neighborhoods do, indeed, care greatly about their children. And they consciously try to bring them up with goals that will lead to a better future for the children. However, parents often find it impossible to translate their beliefs into effective behaviors, to channel their caring into concrete actions that could help bring the dreams to fruition. The outside community sees only the actions, or the lack of actions, and interprets what it sees as being a result of the "fact" that rural poor parents do not care what happens to their children.

Most of the parents, in fact, have an overwhelming concern for the children's security, welfare, and future. But in so many cases, the realities of everyday life in poverty, the stresses of social marginality, and their own sense of failure render parents ineffective or even detrimental in terms of helping their children achieve the dream. Some parents realize and express verbally the negative effect that they have had upon their children's success chances, and harbor guilt feelings about this. Some parents have been hurt so much already that, out of a need for the protection of their already wounded egos, they more or less give up their sense of responsibility and commitment, leaving the child's future to chance, to the child himself, or "to God." At this point, their goal for the child becomes an amorphous one: "that she may be happy in her life, whatever shape it takes," or "that he may eventually straighten out." As the years go by, this limited goal is usually partially achieved, but the higher goal of rising above the poverty and problem-ridden existence of the parents has to be postponed for one more generation.

The patterns of childhood experiences and parental attitudes that have been described in this chapter represent adjustments or compromises between "what we would like, ideally" and "what we know life is like in reality." The patterns of raising children are derived from and adapted to the everyday realities of the home, the neighborhood, and the wider community. But the attitudes and skills the child develops to adjust to his home situation may not be congruous with those that are needed for success in the outside society. Some of the reactive adjustment patterns may be looked down on by the surrounding community; some may be poorly matched to the demands, routines, and expectations of the dominant society. And thus, some behavioral and attitudinal patterns may have negative consequences in rendering children less able to fit into and rise within the dominant community. But, for the most part, these patterns are necessary adjustments to or inescapable consequences of the constant stresses of a life of economic poverty and social marginality.

Neighbors and the Neighborhood

Introduction

The ultimate common denominator among the families of this study is that they all live in neighborhoods of low reputation in the larger urban-suburban community. The small clusters of tightly packed houses, the bedraggled remnants of once-active hamlets, the roadside settlements of trailers – all are characterized by the larger community as undesirable neighborhoods, "bad places to live," offensive to look at, and troublesome to deal with.

One public criticism frequently heard is that the people in the rural poor neighborhoods can't seem to get along with each other. Both fact and fable are cited to "prove" that these rural depressed areas are nothing more than combat zones, arenas of violence, thievery, and disorder. Cooperation among neighbors for any project or goal is deemed almost beyond hope. As a despairing community organizer once remarked, "They won't even *speak* to each other. How can you possibly get them to *work* together?" Most outsiders conclude that rural poor people either do not know or do not care about the way neighbors "ought to behave toward one another."

There does seem to be some grain of truth underlying the stereotype of violence among neighbors, for there is indeed considerable infighting, and it is common to find next-door neighbors not speaking to each other. But the prevalence of antisocial behavior has been exaggerated far beyond reality, and the exaggeration goes unchallenged. Entirely overlooked is evidence of opposite kinds of behavior, of positive social interaction.

The aim of this chapter is to examine the characteristics of social interaction, both positive and negative, in rural depressed neighborhoods. The chapter addresses the question of social disruption within the neighborhood and explores the factors that keep people in the neighborhood despite the squabbles and low reputation. Essentially, this chapter probes a paradoxical statement made by one rural resident.

The people here in this little valley can't get along together . . . but we can't get along without each other either.

151

Social Characteristics of Rural Poverty Neighborhoods

The Neighborhood Is a Social Field
Rather than a Social Unit

The rural neighborhood is actually a rather loose concept. Residents rarely talk in terms of a clearly bounded geographic entity with a roster of people who belong. This is partly because the geographical and social dimensions of neighborhood may not coincide. Some geographical localities, such as the former hamlet settlements, may contain families of a higher socioeconomic level, but these "better off" people are regarded as neighbors only in the geographical sense of proximity. The few residents of higher socioeconomic status essentially live in a different world from their poor coresidents: the experiences and patterns of their lives are entirely different, and they rarely interact.[1] To be a neighbor in the interactive and ideational sense, to become involved with others as a neighbor, is as much a socioeconomic phenomenon as a geographic one. Neighbors are nearby people who share a social stigma.

Rural low-income neighbors do not function as a social unit. Neighborhoods lack the formal structure of institutions and groups. However, a neighborhood is much more than a collection of physically proximate dwellings with a bad reputation. Disheveled and depressed as it may be, the rural neighborhood is a crucial social environment, the social field on which interfamily relationships are played out. No matter how vaguely defined geographically and how lacking in group characteristics, the neighborhood is very important in the thought, conversation, and action of those who live there.

Within this social field, interaction consists of a somewhat fluid and changing collection of separate, dyadic relationships between pairs of households or between individual members of individual households. There is a good deal of visiting back and forth, but each household or individual tends to visit with only one or two other households in any given period. A man and his wife may have quite separate visiting connections within the neighborhood, often with little overlap. Whole families seldom visit each other's homes or interact together at roadsides.

Men's visiting appears to follow lines of job cohorts, drinking friends, and relatives, and is particularly connected with the repairing and trading of cars and car parts, lending of tools, and occasional help in working on a car. Cars are also a main topic of conversation, although deer hunting, fishing, and brushes with the law are also topics of interest. Men who are self-employed or unemployed may be in and out of each other's homes during the day; men employed in urban factories see each other only on weekends and summer evenings outdoors. Occasionally two or three men will spend part of the evening together watching "rassling" on television in someone's home.

Women's visiting mostly occurs during the daytime. The networks of visiting relationships show a predominant and strong pattern of a young married woman visiting her mother or mother-in-law, or vice-versa. Sisters and sisters-in-law, if they live nearby, may also visit frequently or work together at household or gardening tasks, or at putting up food for the winter. Many visits involve dropping off children for babysitting, or going to town together. Although women do not purposely get together for watching television, the TV is apt to be on during visiting, and women exchange exclamations over the heroes and tragedies of soap operas. Women also discuss recent happenings in the family or the neighborhood, gossip about neighbors, and talk of the problems and progress of children, husbands, the garden, and interaction with community agencies.

Visiting between two nonrelated neighborhood women may sometimes become quite frequent, particularly if they both have young children as a common bond and activity, no matter how large an age span separates the women themselves. But the connection between women who are not related is less stable, and is likely to fade or to be ended abruptly by some altercation between the two husbands, or by quarrels between the children of the two families. Sometimes a husband puts a stop to his wife's visiting with a particular neighbor woman because he is suspicious that the friendship will lead his wife into trouble, perhaps into relationships with other men.

Some women, at some times, appear to be social magnets. Their kitchens are filled with a succession of other women who drop in—ostensibly to borrow or return a cup of sugar, some cigarettes, or a tool—but who stay on for coffee and companionship. Small children are often brought together in this manner. At the opposite pole, some women go through long periods of neither visiting nor being visited, interacting only minimally with neighbors. This may occur because the woman has withdrawn from social interaction after some painful episode: for example, she may be recovering from the disgrace of a public alcoholic binge. Or perhaps the woman does little visiting because she is rarely in the neighborhood during the day. She may be employed in the city; she may be spending most of her time with a daughter or mother elsewhere; or she may be one of the women who has access to a car and spends a great deal of time "just roamin' around the countryside."

Children are a source of both positive interaction and estrangement within the neighborhood. For the most part, children get along well, playing together in the roads, yards, and fields. And young children particularly create a basis for mothers to interact and visit. However, older children's squabbles and mischief-making may lead to friction between parents. Conversely, parental squabbles may give rise to verbal taunts and physical fighting among children.

On the whole, the neighborhood relationships are characterized by their fluidity. They are constantly undergoing changes, both in alliances and in intensity. At any given time, each individual has a collection of interactive relationships in the neighborhood. These relationships are always in flux—form-ing, breaking up, shifting, and reestablishing. There are no fixed positions, no permanent groupings. The neighborhood is a social field, defined in terms of proximity, poverty, and stigma. It is characterized by a shifting collection of interactions among individuals and families.

There is Both Permanence and Turnover of Residents

At first glance, a striking characteristic of such rural neighborhoods is the continuity of residents. The same family names have dotted the landscape generation after generation: several names on the plat maps of the 1850s are found on the mailboxes of the 1970s. Longtime residence in the area is com-mon and valued. (In the original Chestnut Valley survey of thirty households, one-third of the families claimed grandparents who had lived in the same part of the township.)

However, this continuity of family names in the rural areas obscures the fact that there is actually considerable residential mobility, mostly within the neighborhood or within a network of several run-down rural neighborhoods in the same region. The Chestnut Valley sample bears out this continuity-mobility paradox. Starting in 1969, changes were recorded for the twenty dwellings occupied by the low-income families in the original sample. From 1969 to 1974, only eight of the twenty dwellings were continuously occupied by the same family, and there were actually twenty instances of families mov-ing. Of those moves, six were moves within the neighborhood, six were moves into the neighborhood, and the remaining eight were moves away from the neighborhood. The moves within the neighborhood were often cases in which part of an expanded family moved to a separate dwelling. The families who moved in from elsewhere were mostly not strangers, for in half the cases they had grown up in the neighborhood, had lived there previously, or had siblings currently living there.

From the point of view of the individual household, the picture is one of a considerable number of residential moves, but within a circumscribed area, a kind of musical chairs among the available cheap houses. Several different pat-terns of geographical mobility occur, primarily related to factors of age and socioeconomic status. The highest frequency of moves occurs among young adult couples, but the range of their moves is the most limited geographically. Many of the grown children of the poorer families spent at least some periods of their early adult years living in the home neighborhoods, perhaps alter-nately living in the husband's and the wife's parental neighborhoods. Their moves tend to be dictated by such considerations as the availability of a more suitable dwelling, the fact of having been "burned out" or "turned out" of a previous home, the momentary state of relationships with relatives, and the fluctuating state of the marital relationship itself. This pattern of mobility in younger adult years tapers off to a somewhat more stable pattern in later years, when more established households remain for longer periods in one location, particularly if they own the home. From the point of view of the neighborhood as a whole, this means that a pattern of mobility of some residents is superimposed on a pattern of residential longevity of others. The additional factor of the circumscribed geographic scope of the moves explains the continuity that overshadows mobility.

Kinship Connections Knit
Neighborhood Families Together

A striking fact about many rural depressed neighborhoods is the dense and overlapping kinship connection or, as it's commonly described, "Nearly everybody here is related to everybody else." For example, out of the twenty low-income households in the 1969 Chestnut Valley sample, fourteen contained adults with a primary kinship tie (father, mother, brother, sister, son, daughter) connecting them to another household in the neighborhood. In eight of these cases, there were two or more ties of primary kinship among households. There are also numerous secondary kinship ties connecting the families of a single neighborhood, including marriage connections, first cousins ("own cousins"), aunts and uncles, and grandparents, as well as many more distant kin connections.

The density of localized kinship ties has been characteristic for generations. In the earlier rural community (for example, Chestnut Valley of the early 1900s through the 1920s) the high degree of interrelatedness among neighboring rural families resulted from geographical and transportational isolation. Today, however, the interrelatedness is due to isolation of a different sort: socioeconomic isolation expressed in selection of marriage partners and in residential location.

The social pool from which marriage partners are drawn is definitely restricted, and bounded by the limits of the parents' residential mobility and their social connections through jobs, kinship, and friends of friends. People from the poorer rural families tend almost exclusively to marry partners from the same socioeconomic level. Although a few households in the sample contain an adult, usually the wife, from a distant county or from out of state, most marriage partners come from the same or a nearby rural poverty neighborhood.

Residential location near parents or siblings has long been a pattern. Men and women who grew up in these rural neighborhoods tended to end up settling in the immediate or adjacent area, originally because of patterns of farm use and ownership, more recently because their limited economic resources have restricted them to neighborhoods of inexpensive housing. Additionally, the emotional and social dependence of young adults on their parents and

siblings tends to make couples settle near their relatives, reinforcing the kinship ties in a neighborhood. The kinship connections also are numerous
because relatively few unconnected people move into such a rural, depressed
neighborhood, partly due to its stigma. For these reasons, a rural, poor
neighborhood is apt to be made up of at least a nucleus of people who are
related to each other, with multiple crisscrossing ties of relationship, both
blood and marriage.[2]

The fact that many relatives live within or near the neighborhood and the
emphasis people place on lifelong sibling ties and parent-child ties produce a
situation in which much of the neighborhood interaction is between people
who are closely related. Visiting, assistance, financial help, and other interactions are all more common among relatives in the neighborhood than they are
between nonrelated people in the same neighborhood.

However, kinship does not necessarily preclude interfamily friction or
hostile relationships in the neighborhood. Squabbles between related families
appear to be as acrimonious and frequent as those between nonrelated
neighborhood families.

> He and his brother just can't get along. They hardly speak to each other.
> They've had some big fights.

But the reciprocal obligations continue despite any chilled relationships.

> Even though he and his brother don't get along, when something comes up in
> the family, like one of their kids getting hurt, or someone getting married or hav-
> ing a baby, then both families will be there. But except for those family occa-
> sions, they do best to keep away from each other.

In some neighborhoods, the population consists primarily of two or three
family lines, and the families may have a history of not getting along well.
One resident explained, "This neighborhood contains mostly two families, the
A's and the B's. By nature, the A's and B's never get along—like the McCoys
and the other ones. They're always running each other down." Even where a
neighborhood consists of two family lines, however, no clan grouping or permanent alliance actually develops among the people of each family line; no
permanent opposition develops between family lines. The absence of a protracted feud appears to be due to three factors: (1) in most cases, there are
crosscutting ties of marriages between the two kinship lines, reducing the
potential for group polarization; (2) individual families move around a lot
within and between neighborhoods, so that the actors in the neighborhood
drama are frequently changed; (3) there is as much potential for strained relationships within a family line as between different family lines.

Tension and Aggression Disrupt
Neighborhood Relationships

Suspicion, hostility, and antisocial acts appear frequently on the neighborhood scene. Most of the disruptive behavior is relatively minor, and frequently related to drunkenness. Scuffles and fights predominate, mischief is common — stealing from each other, and causing minor damage to house, yard, cars, or animals. In cases of severe, continuing, or unwarranted provocation, neighbors may call in the police or sheriff, but most incidents are handled by fights, by retaliation in kind, or by breaking off the relationship.

> The troubles we have with the neighbors are mainly over dogs and children and foolishness. But there have been big things, too. We even had papers drawn up through a lawyer against one neighbor once.

> There was a big fight between him and his neighbor on account of something that was said about his daughter.

> One of these days I'm going to call the law on them. I've warned them to stay off our property and leave our animals alone. The next time we find that something of ours is missing, or if this dog suddenly disappears, I'm calling the law.

More pervasive than the actual antisocial events, however, is the suspicion of wrongdoing. If an animal dies, or a tire goes flat, or "a turkey comes up missing from the freezer," one neighbor will be quick to suspect another, and may plan retaliation before seeking firm proof. Hardly a week goes by without talk of such suspicions.

Even more pervasive is the acrimony with which neighbors talk about each other. Sharp negative criticism and name-calling are common. But the criticism does not follow a linear pecking order: any family is potentially both critic and criticized. Parents may emphatically teach their children that the family next door is not fit to associate with. Meanwhile, the next-door family may be making similar caustic remarks about "them people." A mother warns her child, "Don't you talk that way. You sound just like the next-door neighbors. If you don't watch yourself, you'll end up just like them, too. It may be all right for them, living like pigs there, but in our family it won't do."

Because of these feelings, parents may prohibit their children from playing with certain other children. Although the children usually ignore such restrictions, a child may be ambivalent toward the children he plays with because they are so often cited by his parents as belonging to a family of worthless people. And children may readily hurl verbal insults at each other, based on the derogatory remarks made by their parents. Thus, relationships among neighborhood children can rather easily be punctured by fights and periods of coolness. The hostility often erupts in away-from-home settings — on the school playground, on the school bus, or in the high school.

Adults tend to accept the neighborhood suspicions and squabbles as inevitable. But on occasion, they also express dissatisfaction with the quality of social life in a place where "the neighbors are constantly downing each other." Usually the blame is placed on certain specific people who live in the neighborhood, but sometimes neighbors look at the situation more analytically. One woman reflected, "Parents are always running down the neighbors in front of their own children. It's constant backbiting and name-calling. No wonder the kids of the neighborhood can't get along and are always fighting. Their parents are to blame for it."

A few men indicated that part of the reason for the poor relationships among families was the lack of common neighborhood activities.

> If we only had a recreation center for the kids. A place where they could go and hang around, shoot baskets and stuff. I'd help with it, and I bet some of these other people around here would too. I think something like that would do us all some good. But will we ever see it happen?

Since there are no mechanisms that bring people into regular interaction, they tend most often to express and exhibit some degree of aloofness from neighbors. Even those relationships that become fairly close tend to be fragile: they may either terminate abruptly after an altercation or imagined slight, or they may gradually cool off. There also seems to be a purposeful distancing from neighbors. Several women saw social distance as necessary to coexistence with neighbors.

> If you keep your distance, you can get along with them. The friction arises when you have them around constantly.

> When they start getting too friendly and their kids start hanging around here too much, then something's bound to happen. It's best not to let things get too palsy-walsy.

A common pattern is a situation in which relationships between two families are normally cool, with only occasional interaction.

> I do go over there occasionally, just to let them know I'm still around and not too mad at them.

> My husband won't have anything to do with those people unless he has a car or car parts he wants to sell to them, or if he wants to buy or trade something from them.

Neighbors are Bound Together by Common Problems and Mutual Assistance

Counterbalancing the acrimony, suspicion, and occasional outright hostility, an important characteristic of the neighborhood is a cohesive bond that unites people. Neighbors share a sense of struggle and of rejection by the larger community, and a commitment to helping each other cope with these problems. Several people attempted to express this bond.

> I don't know what the bond is, but it's there. Even though we don't actually get along well, we're the same type of people. We're all having a struggle meeting payments. We're all having a struggle trying to bring up our children better than we were. So we understand each other, and we try to protect each other. Maybe we care about each other and help each other because we know that society couldn't care less about us.

> When you're down and out, you don't have anybody. You're rejected by the community. But you still have the neighbors to visit with. When it comes to down-and-outness, there's a real bond between us. We can depend on each other in that way.

This perception of being the same kind of people with the same kinds of problems and a shared "down-and-outness" is extremely important as a stabilizing factor in the neighborhood, and acts to counterbalance the tendency toward invidious comparison and pejorative criticism.

The bond among neighbors is frequently translated into action, especially when a neighbor is in difficulty. Internal crisis or emergency, or difficulties with the outside world elicit intraneighborhood assistance. There is a clear feeling of protectiveness, of solidarity vis-à-vis the greater forces in life. Even neighbors who may not get along well will rally to help each other. And each action of assisting a neighbor tends, in turn, to reinforce people's awareness of the lasting bonds between them. One woman summed this up very well, using a recent neighborhood occurrence as an example.

> If you got into some sort of a mix-up with the law, everybody will pitch in and put in a few dollars so that a person can get out of jail. As long as you're not in trouble all the time, the neighbors will pitch in and help you get out of trouble if they can. Suppose a neighbor gets in trouble with the law. We may not think that what the person did was right, but we ask, "Why him?" Why can't they nab somebody else who has thousands of dollars? Why pick on this man who is just struggling? For him it is another setback. Now, maybe I don't like the way the guy lives, and my first reaction might be, "I'm glad he got caught; he deserves it." But that's just a surface feeling. We know that each one of us

is having our own struggles, and we don't like to see somebody else take a set-back.

Being a "good neighbor" is something everyone seems to value, and there is a clear consensus on the definition: one who gives assistance when needed, but otherwise does not interfere with another family's business.

> When somebody wants something, or wants to borrow a few dollars to hold him through until payday, he goes to a neighbor.
>
> Whenever anything happens, they'll help.
>
> A good neighbor is one who keeps to his own business. But when you need him he's there and helping.

People's realization that they are all vulnerable to mishap and emergency becomes a crucial factor in regulating neighborhood relationships. No family, no matter how separated or nonsocial, can take the risk of severing all its ties to neighbors, for it is likely to need help at times, and the kind of help that is needed comes mostly from neighbors. Although relationships among families are easily ruptured, most seek to maintain at least a potential for mutual assistance from a few other families. Thus, social rifts are patched up or overlooked; reconciliation or at least an aloof truce can occur after rather heated blowups; and new relationships are nurtured to substitute for old relationships severed. Recognition of mutual interdependence keeps scuffles and fights from totally blowing the neighborhood apart.

However, because there is no institutionalized social structure, there may be little continuity or consistency in the relationships among neighbors. Between one instance of mutual assistance and the next, there is a hiatus in the relationship. Interaction among neighbors tends to be situational, episodic, and disparate. Neither the shared ideal of good-neighborliness nor the perceived bonds between neighbors is strong enough to prevent the divisive occurrences, the social ruptures, that so often characterize the content of neighbor-to-neighbor relationships.

Sources of Strain in Neighborhood Relationships

Chronic Problems and Daily Frustrations Undermine Relationships

A major reason for the instability, volatility, and negative content of neighborhood relationships lies in the difficult circumstances in which most neighborhood families live. Nearly all the residents are burdened by too many problems too much of the time. Crisis is frequent, tension is high, frustration common. Many people are so constantly worn down by money problems and attendant stresses that neither energy nor time remains for tending to the maintenance of harmonious neighborhood relationships.

The frustrations encountered in the outside world are often brought home instead of being channeled directly toward their sources, and are sometimes vented on one's neighbors, in much the same way as they are unleashed on the family. As a locus for discharging aggression, the neighborhood serves a needed function. But in the process of serving this purpose, the neighborhood is undermined by hostility and suspicion. As one man said, "Your neighbors, your wife, your kids—they're like your own personal shock absorbers. When you're going through rough times, they take all the knocks and bumps. But sometimes they get kind of worn out from taking all that."

Status Competition and Regulation
Give Rise to Hostile Acts

The lack of satisfactory social participation in the wider urban-based community leaves the neighborhood as the only accessible social field in which people can hope to gain recognition. Hence, the neighborhood is, by default, the audience to which nearly every resident plays. But there are no lasting positions, no clear-cut rankings, no formal roles. Position in the neighborhood is ephemeral and requires frequent revalidation. Within the neighborhood, there is keen awareness of who has what new status marker: a newer car, a color TV, a deer carcass hanging out front on the first day of deer season, a new porch or entryway added to the trailer.

> That is the way it is here—competition with the neighbors. If one adds onto his house, then pretty soon others do. If one gets a new car, then the other ones have to. Competition, competition, competition. That's all it is here.

This status seeking within the neighborhood often brings dissatisfaction and jealousy, which may be expressed in antisocial acts, such as destroying or defacing a neighbor's new mailbox, scratching his car, uprooting a bush just planted in the yard.

Minor vandalism against neighbors is not just an expression of jealousy, however. It is also one of the chief leveling mechanisms that keeps people from rising above the rest of the neighborhood. Other means of keeping a lid on upward mobility are gossip, gloating, and raising doubts.

> People are always spreading rumors about someone else. Probably they do it because their own back yard isn't too clean, so they don't want someone else's yard to look clean either.

> If a man sees a neighbor driving a newer car than his own, he may secretly be

glad when the neighbor wrecks his car. [And accusations may be made that somebody purposely tried to run him into the ditch in that car.]

If a woman lands a fairly high-status job (above factory or janitorial level), other women may pointedly ask her how she can feel comfortable working with "all those educated people." This casual suggestion may create or increase the woman's feelings of inadequacy to the point where she actually does fail in the job. And when she does so, neighbor women are quick to let her know that it's just what she deserves "for trying to be so much better than the rest of us."

These various efforts keep the neighborhood more or less uniform in its poverty and problem-ridden existence, and thus help maintain solidarity and ensure continued mutual assistance.

Other leveling mechanisms are aimed at keeping a neighbor's status from dropping too low. Residents are keenly aware that the neighborhood's reputation is a handicap to their children's future, and they resent those whose flagrant violations of community standards give the whole neighborhood a bad name. Gossip, criticism, avoidance, and even fights are used to bring into line a person who persistently gets into trouble with the law, one whose alcoholism leads to frequent fighting and vandalism, a parent who makes no apparent effort to keep kids out of trouble.

These various leveling mechanisms all serve positive functions. They preserve the neighborhood as a reference group, a field of potential social relationships, and a source of assistance—which is important to residents because they have no other social field available to them. But the same mechanisms also have negative consequences in that they lead to frequent hostility and continuous suspicion among neighbors.

A related factor undermining neighborhood relationships is that residents know that their neighborhood is scorned by the dominant community. They may even concur somewhat in the evaluation, and feel that by associating with their neighbors, they are themselves tainted. In measuring themselves against their neighbors, they may feel that they are only measuring differing degrees of failure. But the neighborhood is the only available field of social interaction and personal recognition they have. Caught in this bind, ambivalence toward neighbors is almost built-in. This ambivalence probably underlies a lot of the blow-hot–blow-cold nature of neighborhood relationships, and explains much of the paradoxical ways in which neighbors both play to and disavow the neighborhood audience.

Dependence on Neighbors Causes
Ambivalence Toward Them

The many emergency situations that arise in poverty living, combined with the ineffectiveness of assistance from the dominant community, force people into interdependence with their neighbors. The seeking and receiving of emergency assistance tends to strengthen the bonds between neighbors, but it may also have contradictory effects. Asking for help is an admission of weakness or inability to handle one's own problems. Furthermore, it gives the neighbor inside information on personal family matters. A family prefers to solve its own problems and keep private matters to itself. When a woman must use a neighbor's telephone to call the police to report her husband's abusiveness, she is admitting to the neighbors that she can't handle the situation alone, and she is giving them personal information that they may later use against her. Yet she has little choice but to use their phone. The realization of one's full dependence on neighbors in such situations can create ambivalence and resentment. It may also create anxieties that make the individual highly sensitive to any real or fancied rebuff or slight from those upon whom she or he is dependent, thus adding to intraneighborhood strain.

Why People Stay

The rural depressed neighborhood is both a necessary refuge and a comfortable trap. Most of the residents are fully aware of the stigma that their residential location places upon them.

> My wife's relatives won't come visit us because of where we live. This place has a pretty bad reputation, and they want to stay away from it.

> The welfare lady is trying to convince us to move away from here to a better environment.

In addition to being aware of the reputation, many residents, at various times, appear to concur in the judgment. To escape this enveloping stigma, and to escape problems with some of their neighbors, some people wish they could move away. A teenager said, "This is a lousy place to grow up in, and I can't wait to get out of here." Another said, "If people ask you where you're from, you try not to be too exact, 'cause if they know you're from this place, they think right away you must be no good."

But people generally do not move away. And if they do, they move to a neighborhood of similar reputation. Why do people remain in, or gravitate to, rural depressed neighborhoods with bad reputations? This question is frequently posed by the surrounding community, and is often answered in terms of common public stereotypes that cite personal weakness and lack of ambition.

> They just like to stick together. . . . They seem to seek out their own level. . . .
> They have no ambition for anything better.

The question of why people remain in such neighborhoods deserves closer attention. Residents usually answer in terms of the family's specific situation and connections. But long-term observation and probing of people's thoughts and decisions about whether or not to move, as well as study of the moves that people actually make, show that there are several common, recurrent factors holding people where they are.

Rural Preference

A strong preference for living in the country is commonly expressed. People assert that they "could never live in a city," even the small regional cities, which to them are big places.

> I grew up in the country, and I wouldn't live anyplace else.

> It's better for kids. Healthier. They can be outdoors and learn about life. There's less of a chance for a child to get into trouble. In the city, you hear a siren and you worry which of your kids it is. Out here, you know where your kids are, who they're with, and what they're up to.

Although some parents do not feel too confident about their children's activities in the country either, belief in the superiority of a rural upbringing is maintained because people blame children's problems on other factors, not on the rural environment.

Instances of people moving to nearby small and medium-sized cities seem only to confirm the contention that country living is better. Such was the experience of at least five families whose adjustment to city living was observed. In most cases, the urban transplants expressed a real dislike for living in the city and a desire to go back to the country if they could. They complained of noise, security fears, difficulty in supervision of children, lack of yards, trees, and hills, and of the impersonality of city life. These complaints, however, should be seen in the context of the fact that most of these moves to urban areas were induced by negative factors: a split between husband and wife; being burned out of a rural home; or being turned out by a landlord and unable to find another place in the country. The unhappiness over living in the city was therefore partially due to the unhappiness over the triggering events that caused the move; and the longing for the country probably reflected a longing for happier times of the past. Nonetheless, people believe and tell their former rural neighbors that the country is a better place to live than the city. Thus, the preference for rural living is perpetuated. Even young adults who move to an urban area upon setting up an independent household would rather live in the country if they could.

Family and Locality Ties

Kinship ties and ancestral roots in the rural neighborhood are also part of the reason people stay put. Although at times relationships with relatives may produce strains to and beyond the breaking point, the sense of a kinship bond and deep roots persists.

> We've thought about moving away from here, but this is the only place we know. This is where we've lived for so long. And this is where our people are. Anywhere else we'd be strangers. Here, we are at home.

> Several times we've had the trailer hitched up to the car, ready to leave this place, get away from all these problems with my in-laws. But we don't go. We can't. They're his people, the only people he has.

> This is where my grandparents were. We've always lived here. We wouldn't want to leave because we're part of this place.

Desire for Privacy

Another perceived advantage of a rural location is its geographical isolation. The distance from bureaucratic agencies and services, although a problem from the point of view of transportation, is perceived to be an advantage from the perspective of maintaining personal privacy. The location makes families less accessible to "snooping by the authorities." The rural location provides a comfortable separation.

Privacy from one's neighbors is also thought to be an advantage of living in the rural areas. Although in fact houses may be very close together and there is much awareness of the personal family life of neighbors, people can more or less hide in their houses, and can go for long periods without directly interacting with neighbors and family by simply going off into the woods. This opportunity is valued.

Economic Advantages

Economic considerations play the biggest part in determining residential location. Land, housing, and taxes in rural depressed neighborhoods are relatively cheap. The absence of zoning and housing codes in many rural townships is also of major significance—in such unregulated areas people have the freedom they need to keep their housing costs at minimal cash levels. Unfettered by municipal restriction, they can devise all sorts of cost-cutting strategies for keeping cash costs at an affordable level (see Chapter 6). Living in school buses, trailers, or jerry-built houses—and modifying or adding to them whenever and however possible—keeps housing costs quite low.

Other economic advantages of the rural depressed areas include the availability of game and some wild food crops on the hillsides (deer, game birds, rabbit, wild leeks, cowslips, berries, and fruits); free water in natural springs and hand-dug wells; free garbage disposal out back; free firewood nearby; and space in the yard for a vegetable garden, a potato patch, or old cars.

Although transportation costs may be somewhat higher because of the distance from jobs, services, and stores, the total cash cost of living appears to be substantially lower in the rural depressed neighborhoods. For people with very little available cash, unsteady income, and slim prospects for increasing or stabilizing income in the future, these considerations are very important. Anything else is unaffordable. It is not just the low total cost of living in the rural area, but also the economic flexibility that is important. Rural families feel they are able to make adjustments to meet changes in family circumstances.

The isolated rural setting may also be conducive to independence and ingenuity. Here people can attempt to live by the traditional rural ideal of "making-do on one's own" and remaining as independent as possible from government support. Residents also recognize that mutual assistance patterns among relatives and neighbors are an economic advantage that would not be available elsewhere. One woman summed up the economic considerations this way.

> Out here we're different [from people in the city]. We live differently. We learn to make do with what we've got. But we do it on our own. We have the space; we can add on to our house; or we can use our land to plant a vegetable garden to help us get by; or we can keep cars in the yard so my husband can fix them up to sell. It's up to us what we do and how we do it, but we manage to get by.

Social Compatability

Even if money were no limitation, however, other factors restrict people's residential choices to a loose network of run-down rural areas: insecurity about dealing with unknown social situations; the perception of the larger community's stereotypes; and the absence of social connections elsewhere.

The rural poor neighborhood offers a psychological comfortableness in that people know what to expect. In any very different kind of neighborhood, whether in the city, in a suburb, or in a rural village, they fear that they would not know what to expect of other people, nor what others would expect of them. Several women have expressed fear that they would not know the cues for behavior, and they imagine they would feel frightened and insecure.

> Even if I had a chance to live somewhere else, I wouldn't do it. Even if I were given $50,000 to buy a house, I can honestly say that I wouldn't move from here. And I don't think the neighbors would either. I couldn't live in some fancy neighborhood. I wouldn't be comfortable. I'd always have to be behaving in a put-on way. It wouldn't be me. No, I'll stay here.

The preference is to stay where the ground rules are known. For people who are poor, who lack self-confidence, and who occupy a marginal position in the larger community, this seems a reasonable preference.

Avoidance of Risks

Moving to a different place is perceived as risky: the house might turn out to have even greater drawbacks; the new neighbors might be even more quarrelsome; house payments might be unmanageable. One woman analyzed the reasons she and her husband had not pursued a possible chance to move out.

> If we want to improve ourselves, we would have to move away from this neighborhood because it is a bad place to live and a bad address. But if we moved to a better house in a better neighborhood, we would be under too much pressure. We would have a hard time learning how to get along with new neighbors, whereas here we may not get along [with neighbors] but we know what to expect of each other and how to act toward each other. And we would be under the pressure of making house payments, which might be very hard for us. We would not be able to have any luxuries at all, we would lose our serenity. So, even though we do want to better ourselves, we have come to a decision that it would be better for us to stay where we are and try to fix up this house and to do the best we can living here.

This reluctance to risk moving to a "better" location is similar to the men's reticence in seeking or accepting higher-level jobs (discussed in Chapter 5). In both cases, limited expectations and a rational assessment of future probabilities caused people to put up with the inadequacies of the present situation rather than take the risks involved in trying for a better situation.

When the families do move, it is usually to a similar place, and often such moves are made in haste, not planned or desired. Even when people talk about the vague possibility of moving in the future, their ideal seems to be a rural neighborhood, one that is not particularly "high-class" (like the suburbs), but one that is not weighed down by such a bad reputation. They envision, in other words, their own neighborhood or one like it, with somewhat better housing, fewer "undesirable" people, no stigma of being labeled "the worst place in the county."

> If only we didn't have the problem that everybody out there expects all people from this neighborhood to behave badly, to cheat and steal. No wonder some of us get discouraged and quit trying. If we didn't have *that* problem always facing us everywhere we go in the community, then it would be all right living here.

Conclusion

The neighborhood is where people live, where they feel they belong, and the source of their networks of social interaction and mutual assistance. Two salient factors underlie the social dynamics of the rural depressed neighborhood. First, rural poor people are dependent on their neighbors and neighborhood for social interaction and identity. Second, the relationships in the neighborhood are undermined by displaced aggression and ambivalence. Both of these factors result from the inadequate integration into the wider community (which will be explored in the next chapter). The run-down rural neighborhood is the only accessible secondary social environment, but at the same time, its social functioning is impaired. The prevalence of tension and suspicion and the frequent flare-up of hostility keep relationships in a constant state of flux, rupture, and realignment.

From the point of view of the neighborhood itself, the instability of relationships is unsettling, but not devastating. Since the neighborhood is not a social group or unit, but merely a social field from which dyadic relationships are formed, it can withstand rifts. Ruptures and realignments occur, but the neighborhood itself continues to exist as a localized pool of potential relationships.

From the point of view of the individual, however, the effects of these two intertwined factors may be more troublesome. Ambivalence and hostile behavior undoubtedly reduce the effectiveness of neighbor-to-neighbor bonds in fulfilling the psychosocial needs of the individual. Social relationships rupture easily; impermanence is expected. But the anticipation of rupture may, in fact, limit the quality and stability of social interaction that can be achieved. When people defensively restrict the depth of their commitment to relationships with neighbors, they may also be reducing the potential for deriving psychological support from these relationships.

The social marginality of rural poor families—attached to a larger community but unable to participate satisfyingly in it—is a two-edged sword. It restricts people to a very limited social world, and at the same time it undermines and weakens relationships within that limited social world.

10
Relationships with
the "Outside World"

Introduction

People in poor rural neighborhoods sometimes refer to the urban-based community to which they are attached as the "outside world." This chapter will explore the social and psychological dimensions of that designation, and describe the nature of rural residents' interaction with the larger community.

Whether the term "outside world" is actually used in speech or merely indicated in attitude, it is both a statement about the larger community and a statement about one's own identity. The concept is best understood as one part of a duality that exists in many people's thinking. The "outside world" is the "they" of a "we-they" duality; it is all that is not "us."

In this dualistic view, "we" or "us" is defined as "our neighbors, relatives, and friends who are struggling as we are" or, succinctly, "the people at the bottom." "We" is both a personal collection of people and a socioeconomic identification.

The "outside world" of the duality is defined residually as "everybody else" or "the rest of society." It encompasses all that lies outside the personal realm of "us" and "people like us." It refers to the entire urban-based community, its people and its institutions. The "outside world" refers also to people who are perceived as holding low opinions of "people like us." It is made up of "people who look down their noses at us," "people who think they're better than we are."

This polarity between "us" and the "outside world" does not appear to be class-consciousness in the revolutionary sense. In fact, when ideas of class struggle were expounded by young urban radicals in the late 1960s, they fell on deaf ears among rural poor people, who appeared to be totally opposed to notions of revolution and were not interested in uniting with other "poor, oppressed peoples" of the world, or even of the county. Their opposition quite clearly flowed from the fact that what they really wanted was to be accepted by the outside world, not to overthrow it. They wanted a slice of America's pie, they did not want the pie to be destroyed before they got to the table. Almost unanimously, the rural poor did not want to align themselves and their interests with urban poor people or with Black poor people in a "poor people's campaign." They wanted to be identified, treated, and accepted as *people*, not as *poor* people. To carry the banner of poor people was contrary to their long-term hopes. Additionally, urban and Black people, even though they may be poor, are definitely outside the recognized definition of "us." In fact, a fairly pervasive and strong racial prejudice exists against Blacks as a group.[1] Thus, poor people who are different or distant from "us" remained part of the "outside world," and class solidarity never developed.

The phrase "outside world" indicates the extent of the gap that separates people of the rural pockets of poverty from the large urban-based community, the community *to* which they are inextricably bound but *in* which they are marginal participants. It also indicates that the so-called isolation of rural poor people is more than a matter of geographical distance: it is a structural, social, and psychological separation.

Centralization Without Integration

Due to the major social trends of the last fifty years, Chestnut Valley and nearby rural areas have all been centralized into the larger urbanized community. Formal community functions such as education, employment, shopping, health care, government, police, and organized religious activities are now provided by (and only by) the urban-based community. But although the urban community has taken over these functions from the former rural community, it has not been an effective substitute for the people of lower socioeconomic levels in terms of the psychological and social functions of a community. The urban-based community provides neither adequate social participation nor a feeling of belonging and identity for the poorer rural people. They belong to it only in the physical and institutional sense.

Looking at the structure of the relationships from the community to the individual, it is apparent that the various separate institutions of the larger community are in no way unified vis-à-vis each individual rural family. Instead, the many disparate segments and institutions extend separate, parallel connections to each individual rural household. The individual does not experience a *community*, in the sense of a whole system, but a series of separate institutions—a factory, a school, a shopping center, a welfare agency. Identification with the urban-based conglomerate as a unit is thus almost precluded on structural grounds alone.

The connection in the other direction—from the individual to the community—is also fragmented rather than unified. Due to the collapse of the rural communities, there are no local subunits or intermediate-level building blocks to group together clusters of rural people and articulate them to the larger community. No connecting groups link the many separate rural families with the large, distant community. Consequently, each individual rural family relates separately to the central community.

The lack of a sustained social unit at the local level limits poor people's successful participation in the wider community in other ways too. For example, the lack of a local social unit means that there is little opportunity for them to learn and practice in a familiar, close-to-home setting the social roles and behavior required for playing successfully on the broader stage of the larger community.[2]

The lack of structural integration is particularly devastating because it is compounded by substantial attitudinal and psychological barriers, which will be discussed later in this chapter.

Spheres of Participation

For people of rural depressed areas, participation in the outside world is mostly confined to the inescapable spheres of employment, buying, education, formal services, and authorities. A brief run-down of each of these areas shows that participation is restricted, and is often characterized by unsuccessful experiences.

The Economic Sphere

In the economic realm (described in Chapters 5 and 6) people participate at the community's lowest levels, holding its least respected jobs, remaining in its lowest income brackets, and buying its cheapest goods at its least expensive outlets. To the extent they can, people operate outside official economic institutions: they avoid banks, they trade among themselves for goods, and they devise clever substitutes or supplements for cash income.

Education

For most adults in rural depressed areas, formal education was a limited, unhappy, and unsatisfactory experience. Adult memories of school, whether in the old one-room schoolhouses before 1950 or in the consolidated schools since then, are mostly not positive. Some adults stuck with it until graduation from high school; others dropped out in elementary school. The majority made it partway through secondary school—but did not necessarily obtain the skills commensurate with their last completed school year. A few people, particularly women, have resumed an interrupted formal education, taking high school equivalency exams or enrolling in vocational training programs in area adult education programs or community colleges.

Children today all attend distant, centralized, or consolidated schools. Theoretically, their inclusion in modern, high-quality school systems with heterogeneous populations should be advantageous. In fact, many of the potential benefits fail to reach the children of the rural poor families. For many children, the school becomes an environment of failure, a place of defeating experiences, a long series of blows to the sense of self-worth. Because of these psychologically negative aspects, many of the educational advantages and opportunities offered by a large, up-to-date school system are consistently and completely missed by certain children. (This topic will be further elaborated in the final chapters, as it is obviously full of implications for the continued intergenerational problem of rural poverty and marginality.)

Religion

Few families of the rural poverty areas participate regularly in organized church or church-related activities. Some people attend rural and small-town churches occasionally; some send their children to Sunday school and summer Bible school if transportation is provided; but most rarely enter a church. However, they resent the assumption that their lack of church attendance means that they are not religious people. In fact, many individuals hold fairly strong religious beliefs, generally similar to the somewhat fundamentalist emphasis common among the predominantly Protestant churchgoing residents of nearby nonpoor rural areas. But few adults feel comfortable in church. They feel that their reputation, as well as their clothing, sets them apart from other churchgoers.

Sometimes an individual or couple may begin regularly attending church, often as part of a general effort to "live better," to "start over in a new life"—perhaps following a major family crisis. They may express positive feelings about being able to act on their religious convictions, but they shy away from participation in the church's social organizations and clubs, and from any commitment to becoming a member of the church. If they sense pressure to attend regularly and to join, they are apt to stop going altogether.

Politics and Government

In the political sphere, also, beliefs and sentiments may be shared with a wider community, but not reflected in actual participation. A generally conservative political stance is combined with an inclination to see politics and elections as remote from their own problems. Convinced of the political impotence of the individual, especially "the little guy" or the poor person, very few people register or vote. Even though they say that in a democracy everyone has a right to be heard, they think their vote would make no difference. And they are skeptical about the efficacy of banding together in organized political action.

On the whole, interest in political matters and in state and national government is meager and trust is lacking. Typical also is the personalistic approach to politics: a person may "like" some national political figure because he seems to be a "nice guy." A man will "like" a particular state governor because under his administration there was an improvement in salary or overtime benefits for workers on the state highway crew. Several homes still display portraits of John Kennedy, faded and curled at the edges, but conspicuous.

On the local level, attitudes toward politics generally involve more trust, as well as, again, a personalistic approach. People tend to view the personnel of township-level government not as local officials, but as local people. The highway superintendent or town councilman may be someone who lives fairly close by, someone who attended the same school, someone descended from a respected farming family in the township. Even though this officeholder is recognized as being in a higher socioeconomic level, his identity as a local person renders him a personal rather than a political figure.

Administration and Authority

People interact frequently with public authorities and administrators in the county seat. They attend to numerous routine citizen matters, such as the frequent licensing of cars, paying taxes, and so forth; and they encounter regulatory and law enforcement institutions—sheriff, police, and county court.

People rely on "the law," meaning the state troopers or county sheriffs, to come out to the rural areas to break up fights, inspect malicious damage, investigate thefts, arrest neighborhood troublemakers, or to accompany emergency cases to the hospital. On other occasions, however, "the law" comes unasked and unwanted, trying to track down suspected lawbreakers for deeds committed elsewhere in the county. People believe that these law enforcement agents sometimes try to cause trouble, snooping around the neighborhood. Neighbors attempt to protect each other from the law enforcement agencies, refusing to give information or warning each other of highway police checkpoints where unregistered vehicles might be stopped.

Participation in court proceedings is also fairly frequent, and ranges over a wide variety of types and severity of cases. Charges of vandalism, theft, and assault, of harassment and of statutory rape, arise, but they are not frequent, and seem most often to involve offenses against persons with whom the accused has some personal connection. Violations involving automobiles are common: unregistered vehicles, uninspected vehicles, unlicensed operators, speeding violations, and driving while intoxicated. Family court matters also come up frequently: petitions for "an order of protection" against a spouse; child support cases; legal problems involving custody of children; and court hearings regarding "persons in need of supervision" cases, probation violations, and various offenses by juveniles. Most of these encounters are not particularly pleasant, and they reinforce people's desire to remain aloof from the urban community.

Problems in Interaction with Service Agencies

People of rural depressed areas interact with many of the community's human services. Their interactions with service-providing agencies, offices, and institutions form a large part of their relationship with the outside world. Conversely, rural poor people make up a large proportion of the intended beneficiaries or target population and client caseload of many community services. From the viewpoint of the client, the agencies are categorized by the functions they serve. There are providers of money (department of social services for welfare, Medicaid, food stamps); goods (Salvation Army, churches, and other outlets for free food and free used clothing); services (antipoverty agencies, nutrition-education programs, child health clinics); job skills (government programs in various agencies and educational institutions); and counseling (family service agencies, alcoholism programs, mental health clinics).

For a variety of reasons, however, an agency and a rural poor person in need of its service may not come into contact with each other. Rural poor people frequently lack adequate information on available and appropriate services, or the lack of a telephone or a car prevents a person from getting service from an urban-based agency. But there are other, more deep-seated, reasons—having to do with attitudes and perceptions rather than simply information or physical access. Sometimes people simply do not recognize that they have a problem or they deny its existence. Even if the problem is recognized, a person may believe that it is just part of life and cannot really be resolved, so there is no point in going to an agency about it.[3] In other cases, the reluctance to intitiate contact with an agency may be primarily due to fear and a sense of unease about the first encounter. "Will I wear the right clothes, do the right things, say what you're supposed to say?"[4] This fear reflects the basic lack of self-confidence vis-à-vis the "outside world."

Poor people may also resist making connections because they view service agencies as potentially meddlesome, interfering with the individual's ability and right to decide on his own how to handle problems, set priorities, make compromises, and devise substitutes. A related and commonly held perception is that many agencies employ threats—of cutting off financial support, of reporting disapproved behavior to other agencies, or of removing children from their parents. Another deterrent to seeking assistance from community resources is the general preference for standing on one's own—a reluctance to turn to others, especially outsiders, for help. Seeking institutional or agency help is believed to be an admission of personal failure. Going to a mental health clinic "proves" that one is "sick in the head." Shame and guilt about be-ing in such circumstances often prevent people from turning to an outside agency for help.

Despite these deterrents, however, many service connections are made. But even the connections that occur may often be unsatisfactory from the point of view of either the provider or the consumer of such services, or of both. Despite considerable effort and good intentions on both sides, relation-ships may remain negative in tone or minimal in effect. There may be prob-lems in developing a relationship that is deep enough or sustained long enough to achieve a beneficial outcome. Analysis of a variety of individual cases of unsatisfactory or unsatisfying relationships reveals some common underlying factors.

One cause of problems in the agency-client relationship may be the dispar-ity of views concerning the kind of relationship that *should* exist between them. Clients enter the relationships with assumptions, expectations, con-straints, and needs that may differ from those of the service provider. The rural poor client who is reluctant to seek outside help tries to make the situa-tion more acceptable to himself by defining the caseworker-client relationship in a personalistic manner. The client may place emphasis on the relationship between himself and the professional worker as an individual, not as an inter-changeable member of the agency staff. A client who feels comfortable with a particular agency worker may feel that the worker in some sense belongs to him, and may be particularly upset by being switched to another caseworker within the same agency: he may refuse to talk with a substitute, and may ter-minate the relationship with the agency. The client may also feel, perhaps un-consciously, that whenever he needs help the worker should be available to him, rather than being available only during business hours and by appoint-ment. Conversely, when the client feels his need for service is not particularly pressing, he may simply not bother to keep his scheduled appointment.

The personalistic approach to agencies and institutions also works in another way. If a client has had an unpleasant experience with one individual in an agency, he may judge the entire agency negatively, and thus not return to it. On the other hand, if there has been positive experience with one in-dividual in the agency (even the receptionist or secretary), the client may feel more comfortable about interacting with the agency: he has found a way to personalize his relationship with what he would otherwise perceive as an im-personal institution. This personalistic approach to relationships with institu-tions may be a heritage of the small face-to-face rural community. It also reflects people's insecurity about their self-worth, their awareness that the "outside world" as a whole looks down on them, and the real need they have for personal relationships.

Another problem in the interaction between rural poor people and urban service institutions is that of premature termination. After the first several visits, a client may suddenly (and usually without notification) terminate what seemed to be a satisfactory relationship with an agency. This cutoff may reflect different expectations of client and agency. In many cases, the individual seeks assistance only as a last resort. He therefore needs and expects quick relief, assuming that if the practitioner is really any good, the results will come quickly and dramatically. A client may feel that remedies offered by a professional or agency are too long-range to have any effect on the immediate crisis. Or the client may be seeking help for a very specific problem—the straw that broke the camel's back—not the whole tangle of underlying problems. The client may not see the feasibility or necessity of addressing anything deeper than the immediate precipitating event, and may resist the professional propensity to probe beyond the immediate complaint. Sometimes the client finds the professional advice, prescription, or counseling process totally unrealistic and impractical, given the realities of the situation at home. (For example, the mother of three active preschoolers whose doctor instructed her to stay in bed all week, or the distraught woman who was advised by a social worker that she was excessively wrought up and should try not to think about or believe her husband's threats.)

When a rural client perceives that the hoped-for assistance is not forthcoming, he may, in frustration, break off contact. Although neither the client nor the service worker is at fault, each tends to blame the other, when what really happened is that the relationship was hampered from the start by differences in the expectations and perceptions of the two parties.

Another cause of premature termination is that the situation that propelled the client to seek assistance in the first place may change suddenly and drastically. An unexpected alteration in the client's home situation may make continued interaction inappropriate or impossible. A client who was reluctant to seek help in the first place may be particularly quick to terminate the relationship if his or her situation or needs change.

- One woman finally agreed to get help to patch up a difficult marriage. She abruptly stopped seeing the counselor when her husband left home, for she felt her problem was over.
- Another woman several times seeks counseling to plan for a separation from her husband. Plans proceed, and her confidence grows that she can make it on her own. But suddenly the husband either beats and threatens her and she drops the idea of leaving, or he promises to reform and she agrees to give him one more chance. In either case, she sees counseling as no longer relevant, and so she does not go to her next appointment.
- Yet another undergoes all the necessary laboratory tests preparatory to having long-overdue surgery. At the last minute, she cancels the

operation because her husband has gone out on a drunk, her mother-in-law is sick, and there is no one else to care for the children.

Premature termination becomes a self-fulfilling prophecy. Because the relationship is severed before recognizable benefits can occur, the client is confirmed in his belief that social service agencies are of little help. At the same time, agency personnel are confirmed in their belief that some clients do not really want help or do not want to invest any effort in the helping process. Although there have been numerous successful interactions, and a great investment of time, effort, and money in providing effective services, these problems in the interface between rural poor people and the human service network may limit the relationships and perpetuate lukewarm or negative attitudes.

Lack of Participation in Voluntary Groups

The rural poor play little part in the panorama of voluntary organizations of the larger community. The men do not belong to local township fire companies (which draw on a higher socioeconomic level for membership, and function as social clubs). Men who belong to unions tend not to participate in the related social affairs. Although they may associate with co-workers off the job, it is done informally—trading or repairing cars, drinking, or fishing together, not in group activities like bowling leagues or baseball teams. Families who own snowmobiles do not participate in the clubs, organized activities, and expensive outfitting common at higher socioeconomic levels. A few men and women do belong to and attend meetings of Alcoholics Anonymous.

Women rarely belong to or attend groups connected with school or church, or any other formal groups, such as Cooperative Extension's homemaker units. Only a few women have ever been involved in bowling leagues, in networks of Tupperware parties, or other quasi-social events. Although they may maintain active home visiting relationships outside the neighborhood, these predominantly involve relatives or other families in similar poverty areas, and are not organized group activities.

A comparison of formal social interactions of poor and nonpoor families of the same rural region reveals a vast difference in both frequency and type of activities. Even when lower-income people do participate in voluntary groups and activities, they are usually quite different from those of the more prestigious mainstream groups, and participation is apt to be sporadic and short-lived. The difference can be seen in the activities of two rural women, one from a low-income family and the other from a more affluent home.

The more affluent woman served as hostess in her home for three members of a Bible study group, the tiny remnant of the once important ladies aid society of the local church. In contrast, the woman from the low-income family, on the same day, traveled a half-hour by car to attend a Bible study session organized by an agency outreach worker with whom she had become friendly. On another day in the same week, the first woman drove to a neighboring community to attend a large monthly meeting of the local home demonstration unit. The group was made up mainly of elderly and middle-aged women whose husbands or fathers had once been the more prosperous farmers in the township. On the same day, in the evening, the second woman was attending an Alcoholics Anonymous meeting in the urban center.

Children also tend to be minimal participants in voluntary activities. Parents of preschoolers do not generally put their children in organized play groups, formal day-care centers, or private nursery schools. Again, the personalistic emphasis shows: Grandma, a grown sister, or a neighbor is much preferred over an impersonal institution for young children's care. Children of elementary school age tend to be less involved in clubs and activities than their nonpoor classmates. Although lack of money and after-school transportation are often factors, the deeper reasons lie in patterns of social acceptance and self-image. Also, parents do not foster or facilitate their children's participation in clubs, sports, and activities outside school. As children get older, the participation gap widens significantly, so that unless they are encouraged and pushed, poor children in high school participate in few nonmandatory sports or social activities. These are not the boys and girls for whom the opportunity to be on an athletic team provides incentive to stay in school.

Deterrents to Social Participation

Limited social participation in the "outside world" is primarily related to status differences, perceptions of the community, and perceptions of self. Most people of rural depressed areas feel uncomfortable at mixed-status events, and try to avoid them. They may feel, rightly or wrongly, that their presence is not really desired. They feel that they have little to gain from such social participation, for it only confirms their low status in their own eyes and in the eyes of the "outside world".

They [the higher-status people] have no use for us except to be the bottom.

The PTA wants us to come [to meetings] only so they can have someone to gossip about afterwards.

A real deterrent to participating in socially mixed groups in the larger community is the fear of unknown situations where social cues might be misread and responded to inappropriately. This anxiety probably further increases the

potential for making a mistake and incurring embarassment. A related problem is that of inadequate or inappropriate props. With only a limited inventory of clothing, accessories, and other props, the poor person cannot project
a desired image to a status-conscious audience. One woman cited an example
that conveys beautifully the importance of possessing appropriate props and
knowing appropriate behavior, and the insecurity that arises in their absence.

> The PTA dish-to-pass supper really puts pressure on families like us. You have
> to bring silverware. Well, that might be hard for some. And not one of us in this
> neighborhood would know the proper way so far as what to do and what to say.
> How do you act at a buffet? Do you take a little bit of everything so you won't
> hurt anybody's feelings? But if you do that, will they think you're being greedy?
> And what about the food you have to bring to it? I know I'm a fabulous cook for
> my own family, but could it be considered good enough for other people? If I
> brought something, people might know who cooked the dish, from which family,
> and they might not eat it. If my food wasn't eaten, I'd really feel bad. No, the
> dish-to-pass supper scares me, and nobody could persuade me to go. I'd rather be
> home.

Rather than subject themselves to such difficult situations, poor people
simply avoid mixed-status social participation, usually saying they're too
tired, or they don't have transportation or a babysitter. When an individual
does attend a mixed-status activity, he or she is apt to take a brother, a sister-
in-law, or a child for support.

A variety of other factors also inhibits participation in group activities.
There is typically a wait-and-see attitude: until one has some assurance that
an activity or an organized group will be beneficial and successful, people
hesitate to join. As one man told a community organizer, "Show us you can
do something, then maybe we'll get together on it."[5] People perceive no advantage to investing time, social commitment, and emotional resources in an
activity if it has only a marginal chance of some payoff.

Another important factor limiting participation is the unpredictability of
the future. Participation in voluntary activities and organizations requires a
greater predictability of future time, events, and confidence levels than most
rural poor families have. People feel they cannot make commitments for future
dates because of the real possibility that "something might come up" that
would be sufficiently pressing to preclude their attending a scheduled event.
(The "something" that comes up could be anything from having been beaten
black and blue in a fight with a husband or neighbor, to having sick children
with no one to care for them, perhaps a breakdown of the family car, or a sum-
mons to appear in court or at the welfare office.) There is also the fact that a
person cannot predict how he or she will feel, psychologically as well as
physically, on any given day in the future. One cannot be sure that one will

have the necessary confidence when the time comes. And, in fact, anxiety about the upcoming event may reduce confidence to the point where participation, promised a week ago, seems beyond one's capabilities when the date actually arrives.

Furthermore, people are reluctant to create situations in which others have certain expectations of them; they are afraid they won't live up to those expectations. By not committing oneself ahead of time, a person does not incur expectations. When the event actually takes place, the individual may spontaneously decide to attend and participate. Appearing unexpectedly and at the last minute, he is less likely to be a disappointment to others and to himself. (But to community workers, the frustrating fact is that the person often does *not* show up, whether expected or not.)

A particularly significant limitation on the frequency and satisfaction of social participation in the outside world arises from the negative stereotypes that the dominant community holds about rural poor people. Socioeconomic differences and socioeconomic stereotypes can have the same force in a community of fewer than 100,000 people that racial differences and racist stereotypes do in a large urban environment. In the smaller community, individuals are readily identified with the low reputation of their neighborhood, family, and relatives. The individual from a family or locality that is stigmatized as "poor white trash" finds that the community has formed its impression and expectations of him before he has a chance to do anything on his own. The stereotypes not only follow him wherever he goes in the community, they precede him in all his actions within it. A child inherits a reputation, finds it waiting for him when he enters school, his first major contact with the outside world. In a relatively small community, it is difficult to outdistance the stereotype.

One mother felt this stigma keenly.

> My husband's brother's name has been in the paper all the time for this or that crime. Finally, he got put in prison, and that, too, was reported in the paper. Well, my kids are getting teased all the time about their uncle. These kids have really had to pay for it because they have the same last name as their uncle. But *they* didn't do all those crimes. *They* didn't get put in jail. It's not fair for them to have to take all that.

People's perception of their ambiguous, marginal position in the larger community is poignantly revealed in fleeting moments of reflection, and shows amazingly acute sociological awareness.

> The people of the community have their own code and mode. Anybody who does things differently is some kind of animal, not human, according to them.

> Low income people have a fear. It's not because of their income. It's because of

the way the community treats them. They could have a million dollars, but the community would still treat them the same. So they'd have the same fear.

I'm not looking for status. I don't want to be one of them. I'm *not* one of them. I belong here with the people on this road. What I'm looking for is my self-respect and my respect from the community.

We're from the low-income group. Do I expect too much from the high-income people to treat me just like anybody else?

What I want is to be treated equal, to be treated as an individual.

These comments and many others like them were spoken with deep personal feeling, often with bitterness, at times with despair. These perceptions and feelings are at the root of the limited participation in the voluntary groups and activities of the wider community.

Conclusion

The real bind on the people of rural poverty neighborhoods is that they cannot successfully participate in the "outside world" and they feel scorned by it, *but*, at the same time, they do not have the option of withdrawing from and ignoring it. They are inextricably included in the larger community for schooling, work, buying, settling official matters, and seeking help. They are tied to it also by the fact that they share its cultural values, aspirations, and norms. They want to possess the goods that its members consider desirable. They want their children to succeed and gain acceptance according to the rules and patterns of the dominant society. They want to be part of the community in action and in perception.

But since they seldom experience satisfaction in their interactions with the larger community, rural poor people attempt to protect themselves by minimizing participation and avoiding humiliating situations. They see no benefit in increasing their level of interaction. And so, to the extent they can, they maintain their distance.

This aloofness, so clearly expressed in the duality of "us" and the "outside world," is an understandable adjustment to the social and attitudinal barriers that limit successful participation in the broader community. At the same time, there is a longing for something more in the way of a social community, a desire for a community with which one could identify and in which one could operate freely and confidently.

Aloofness from the wider community is not a cultural preference, then, but merely a way of coping with a difficult social situation, a response to a fairly accurate perception of social realities.

Part 4

Conclusion: Causes and Cures

11
Why Poverty and Marginality Continue

Introduction

This chapter will synthesize the economic, social, cultural, and psychological aspects that run through the study. The synthesis revolves around one basic question: Why is the problem of rural poverty so tenacious? Ten causes of the persistence of rural poverty, generation after generation, will be discussed. First, however, some general statements should be made.

1. These ten causes are not separate entities; rather, they are inter-woven, interacting, and tangled together in the flux of real life.
2. The sequence or progression of the causes is, in itself, significant, and the effects of the causes are cumulative. Each derives from the previous ones in the progression; each cause shapes and helps to cause the successive ones.
3. Some of the causative factors listed are not unique, either to the geographic location or to the economic stratum of poverty. What *is* unique is the peculiar concatenation of the interwoven causes, which makes the problem of rural poverty so intractable
4. The ten causes are of two different types. The first five causes listed are *primary causes*. The second five are *derivative causes*, resulting from the primary causes.

Primary Causes

The primary causes of rural poverty are factors embedded in the economic and social structure of American society. They are forces that operate systematically, if not purposefully, to create and perpetuate poverty in some sectors of the population.

1. The Continuing Impact of History

The antecedents of today's rural poverty and marginality are the historical forces of earlier times. But history does not stop; its effects do not cease. Different degrees of success in adapting to sweeping economic changes of an earlier period continue to leave their mark. In the first decades of this century, some individuals were unable to adapt and maneuver from a position of economic strength. They and their children and grandchildren have not yet been able to make up the difference, while the rest of the community has run on ahead.[1] Restricted resources continue to prevent some people from making the adjustments that would enable them or their children to catch up. On the lifelong economic ledger, the balance brought forward for the next generation has often been a debt instead of a nest egg.

In terms of adjustment to social changes, past inadequacies have been carried forward into the present. During the transition from rural hamlet to urban-centered community, some families were slower to forge new ties and new identities in the growing urban-based community. It was a source of concern to rural sociologists studying the regions of New York where farming had declined that some rural families were consistently underrepresented in the granges and churches, the extension units, school groups, social clubs, and community activities.[2] Generally, these were the same families who participated least in new technological and consumer trends such as autos, tractors, and telephones; the people who lived on marginal farms along unpaved roads. Today, descendants of these marginal families still live on parcels carved out of overgrown hill farms, and many still have not become socially integrated.

In the modern complex community, as opposed to the small rural community, there are few social institutions that effectively incorporate poor and nonpoor people in regular interaction. Poverty has thus become a socially isolating condition, and a stigma.

The impact of history, therefore, is that poverty continues to be handed down to succeeding generations, but now with an overlay of social isolation as well. This heritage sits on the shoulders of each generation, slowing them down in their effort to gain a successful entry into the modern social and economic community.

2. The Crippling Economic Situation

Poverty severely affects both day-to-day living and long-run well-being. By any measure, most of the people described in this study are impoverished in terms of the chronic insufficiency of their financial resources to meet their needs.[3] In most families, there is an almost constant shortage of money and buying power. In a condition of perpetual deficit financing, trade-offs are necessary, and certain needs and desires must often go unmet. People plan, save, stretch, substitute, and go without. Adaptive techniques of financial juggling enable them to cope with their poverty, to survive, to derive some pleasure from life, and to raise their children. But the coping strategies that enable people to accomplish this much cannot lift them out of poverty. They remain on the economic margin, hovering around the arbitrary official poverty line, hovering along a vague boundary between just getting by and not making it.

Rarely a day goes by without the consequences of their poverty being painfully obvious to a family: the worried breadwinner is laid off; the housewife wears her tattered rummage-sale coat for another winter; the car insurance bill can't be paid; work on the half-completed front entry stopped when cash and time had to be diverted to car repairs; the hospital is sending threatening notices about the back bill; the kitchen cupboards are nearly empty, and the month's allotment of food stamps is already gone; a child stays home from school for lack of winter boots.

Difficult and painful as these day-in, day-out money problems may be, however, chronic poverty is even more serious in its long-run effects. For example, when cash is limited or unsteady, expenditures for food are low and erratic. Nutritional intake is jeopardized and children may suffer long-range deficiencies in growth, development, and general health. These deficiencies in turn may limit potential lifelong earning power.[4] Similarly, perpetual money problems may also cause deep emotional discouragement, diminished self-confidence, and psychological exhaustion that may, in turn, restrict people's ability to operate at their full potential. One woman spoke of this effect with deep feeling: "When things get so bad that you're discouraged every time you turn around, it seems to take away your ambition. It sometimes seems as if there is no point even trying, because you just can't get anywhere."

Another long-range effect of continued poverty is the inability to win community acceptance. For the most part in modern American society, people are judged on the basis of externally observable factors such as occupation, place of residence, and possession of status-invested consumer goods. The people of the rural pockets of poverty rank low on the first two criteria. And with limited and insecure incomes, they have difficulty acquiring the coveted status symbols, and are therefore unable to project a successful image in the community.[5]

The economic stranglehold of poverty operates like a timed-release capsule. Some of the effects are felt immediately and every day—inadequate resources to satisfy material needs and the constant grinding-down effect of worry and struggle are the essence of daily life. But the economic handicap is also released gradually and continuously over years and generations. Adults may become bogged down and disheartened to the point that their ability to operate in the world of work is substantially diminished. Children who grow up in the emotional and interpersonal tension spawned and exacerbated by economic poverty are more likely later to fall into the stranglehold of an in-secure, insufficient economic status. The economic constraints of poverty are self-perpetuating.

3. Inadequacies of the Social Structure

An important conclusion of both the historical study and the contemporary observations is that in the poverty-stricken rural areas there are neither viable local-level social groupings nor satisfactory structural bridges linking people with the new larger community. This social-structural hiatus is in-timately connected with and constantly reinforcing the poverty of the rural areas. Four negative effects of the inadequate social structure can be cited here.[6]

First, rural people have no local opportunities for prelearning and practicing secondary social roles. Consequently, they may find relating and interacting with the distant, larger community difficult.

Second, social relationships in the primary group setting are weakened or jeopardized. An overload is thrown onto the family, because it attempts to provide social and psychological supports that otherwise would come from participation in a secondary social environment. And, as the stresses from un-successful interaction in the larger community have no appropriate outlet there, they are often discharged within the family and the neighborhood, disrupting primary social relationships.

Third, people have difficulty defining themselves. Lacking a satisfactory identity on the community level, they can only define themselves in terms of their neighborhood and family. But because the neighborhood is denigrated and the family often disrupted, the individual may not be able to derive much strength from either identity.

Finally, attitudinal separation is perpetuated, reinforced by negative stereotypes widely held by the dominant community. In a vicious circle, the attitudinal separation, in turn, makes it harder to build the needed social bridges.[7]

Through these four processes, the inadequacies of the social structure are self-perpetuating. And the structural inadequacies also perpetuate poverty, as they restrict and reduce people's ability to function effectively in the world of work.

4. Barriers to Upward Mobility

A strong desire for upward mobility is evident in much of the observed behavior—particularly in thinking and decision making. People aspire to a bet-ter future, with more security and fewer problems: "to improve our situation," "to make a better life for ourselves and our children."

The crushing fact, however, is that there is very little upward mobility. It is true that some individuals have "made it" out of this poverty situation; and some of today's young adults and children will eventually "make it" after an initially difficult period. But there are few instances of significant upward mobility, and those who do move upward usually have moved out of the area first, thus further reducing the availability of local role models of successful movement out of poverty and marginality. Most adults know they are caught in a rut, making only intermittent and limited headway toward a better social or economic position. Women, in particular, are keenly aware of this, and willing to talk about it.

> Sometimes it seems as if we just aren't getting anywhere. Things happen faster than we can handle them, and we never catch up, let alone get ahead. It's so discouraging. We struggle so hard, but nothing seems to come of it.

Given the economic structure, upward mobility appears nearly impossible for some people. Their limited economic resources are barely adequate to maintain their present low position, and far too meager to propel them upward. Few can gain access to appreciably greater resources than they now command. The lack of economic mobility is attributable to a variety of complex factors. Some are of a broad societal nature: the general structure of employment and wages, and relatively high unemployment rates; the faltering economy of the northeastern region and rising unemployment in nearby urban centers; decreasing local control over industry, leading to plant closings, automation, and an increasing demand for technical or managerial skills.

It is important to note also that certain factors that restrict upward mobility for some groups of Americans living in poverty are not relevant in this particular case. In this example of a rural enclave of poverty in northern Appalachia neither race nor ethnicity, for example, is a pertinent factor. Nor are rural poor people kept at the bottom because they hold different or deviant cultural values: these people share and attempt to live by most mainstream societal values. They believe in the importance of working for a living, and they work hard to obtain widely coveted material items and to achieve other socially approved goals, hoping all the while that they will eventually see their children move up from the bottom into full participation in society and a greater share of its rewards. But believing in these societal values and attempting to live by them is not, in itself, enough to bring about the desired improvement in status.

In the realm of consumption patterns, for example, rural poor people, particularly of the younger generations, are well tuned in to media messages and consumption drives. The currently popular, heavily advertised items (CB radios, snowmobiles, children's toys seen on TV) may be regarded almost as necessities, and their absence leads to feelings of deprivation just as surely as does the absence of food. If a person spends his limited cash to procure these status items, however, he not only suffers hunger pangs from skimping on necessities, he also incurs criticism for careless spending and pleasure-seeking. If, on the other hand, a person spends his money only on necessities, he lacks the socially recognized material items that stake his claim to status. Either way he cannot win status and public approval through consumer goods. For people caught in this bind—people who cannot afford both necessities and status items—one basis of upward mobility, conspicuous consumption, is unavailable.

Nonetheless, people continue to believe in the possibility of upward mobility—someday—at least for their children. The mobility they hope for is really rather modest: a reduction of the painful consequences of their low social and economic position, release from stigma and denigration, and an opportunity for their children to make a decent, less burdened life for themselves.

People believe that education may provide a means for their children to succeed. But public education has not been as effective in lifting intergenerationally poor people out of poverty as it once was in setting penniless immigrants of the late nineteenth century on the road to full participation in the expanding American economy. In educational institutions themselves, there are barriers that reduce the mobility-effectiveness of education.[8] Among these barriers are the negative stereotypes held by the larger community.

5. The Corrosive Stereotypes

Throughout the preceding chapters, we have noted the stereotyped images that American society as a whole has about poverty and poor people. These stereotypes operate on the local level, clearly shaping the way in which the dominant community perceives the people of the depressed rural neighborhoods. Against the background of pervasive stigma in the community, the attempts of struggling individuals, their small successes and achievements, go unrecognized.

> If a kid comes from the town and his name is Jones or Samson or Dominick, then everything's fine. He can behave as he pleases. But if he comes from out here in Chestnut Valley, and especially if his name is X or Y or Z, then they're watching every move he makes. They accuse him of being the cause of every fight in school. They watch him in the store, 'cause they think he's sure to be a thief. They teach their kids to make nasty remarks about his raggedy clothes. They're convinced, before he even does a thing, that he's bad. So he hasn't got a chance.

Some people cry out for individual recognition, rather than group stereotyping.

> Why isn't society willing to allow that we could be a little different from the

others around here? If I'm in a store and the cashier sees my signature on the bill, he says, "Oh, you're one of the Pratts from Chestnut Valley?" I tell him, "Oh, it's only a distant relationship."

Those who are blanketed by these stereotypes despair of ever being able to convince the outside world that they do not deserve the negative judgment. They feel that every action they take is interpreted through the lens of stigma. They know that the stereotypes precede them and their children in their every foray into the outside world. The stereotypes are already there, preventing a man from getting a desired job, influencing a teacher's perception of a child's aptitude.[9]

The most devastating effect of the stereotypes, however, is the degree to which they may be internalized by their referents. Some people who have grown up in the stigmatized neighborhoods, or who carry surnames of stigmatized families, appear to have partially accepted the stereotypes as fact, to have internalized the judgments and turned the condemnation inward. Partial acceptance of the stereotypes compounds the problem of low self-image. Often the damage is done early in life, during the child's first encounters in the larger world, and affects all his subsequent interactions with it. To the extent that the stereotypes are internalized, they also undermine relationships in the family and the neighborhood, and contribute to the high level of ambivalence, suspicion, and hostility.

The stereotypes also can be self-fulfilling prophecies, and people's behavior comes to approximate the very stigma they resent.

If you tell a guy long enough that he's nothing but a drunk, he'll prove to you that he's nothing but a drunk. To survive and have society accept him, he has to be a drunk, because that's what they expect.

There are certain times when my confidence leaves me. In my low times, you can really knock me and tell me I'm no damn good, and I'll go along with the idea. In fact, I'll go out and prove to you that I'm no damn good.

Some individuals consciously try to protect themselves from the corrosive effects of stereotypes.

Society looks at our failures and our mistakes and says, "You'd expect that from them anyway." But those same people, do they ever see the good things we do? Are they willing to admit that we are trying? No. They've already made up their minds that we're lazy or good for nothing. There's no way we can convince them differently. But we have to watch out that we don't let them convince *us*.

Children as well as adults cry out, "I'll show them that I'm just as good as they are." But it is usually a cry of desperation, not affirmation.

Derivative Causes

The derivative causes that perpetuate rural poverty are quite different from the primary causes. I call them derivative, or secondary, because they are results of the five primary causes, results of the destructive effects of poverty on people's lives. Once created, these effects become self-perpetuating, and thus they are also causes of the ongoing cycle of intergenerational poverty. The derivative causes both result from and perpetuate poverty.

6. *Constant Pressure of Too Many Problems at the Same Time*

Many families have a high potential for crisis, which is both a result of and a cause of continuing poverty. The perpetual shortage of money; the inadequacy or unreliability of housing, household appurtenances, cars, and other material goods; continuing health problems at both subclinical and acute levels; the insecurity of jobs; volatile relationships with neighbors; the children's poor performance in school or in the outside world; tensions in the family—all these problems and many more may be present at any one time, forming a pool of potential crises.

Given this potential, the frequency and severity of actual crises is high. Poor families are apt to live in a structure (be it a shack or an old trailer) that is fire-prone. The chance of being burned out is greater and the effects likely to be more disastrous than they would be for more affluent people.[10] Similarly, among women who eat an inadequate diet (as do many of the women studied), the chance of incurring health problems is increased. And, in a chain of causality, a malnourished pregnant woman may deliver before full term, thereby creating a long-range potential for problems in the child. As in so many aspects of life, the actual crises and problems are prevalent simply because the potential for them is high.

With so many potential sources of trouble, there is no way to predict when or where a new and acute problem will arise. There is only the sure knowledge, from the experiences of a lifetime, that crisis is always a likelihood.

> All the little crises that arise. There's not enough money, or you can't pay the bills, or you can't afford enough food. What little happiness that comes, you're ready to grab it and scream it out to the world. But on the other hand, when things do go well, you try not to get too excited about it 'cause you know that before the day is out, something bad will come along.

One result of the confusing and rapidly changing panorama of problems is emotional exhaustion and/or behavioral paralysis. The overwhelmed person is rendered nearly incapable of initiating action: Where to start? What to do?

Faced with several urgent problems, all pressing simultaneously for solution, the family may try to juggle them, just as it juggles financial resources. Temporary patches are applied to one problem in the hope that its resolution can be postponed briefly while attention is focused on more pressing problems. But most families do not have the opportunity or the luxury to cope with problems one by one, for the problems are all jumbled together. They can't pick out a single issue, work on it, get it solved and out of the way, and then go on to the next problem. Few problems are ever settled so completely that they need no further attention. They merely become lesser irritants in the pool of potential crises.

Problems accumulate, rather than being resolved. One reason for this is that individuals who have grown up in problem-ridden families generally lack successful experience in problem-solving, and therefore have little confidence in their ability to solve problems and little faith that other individuals or agencies could help solve them either. This attitude has two long-range effects: problems continue to fester and feelings of helplessness may be increased. The constant pressure of too many problems becomes, in itself, a contributing factor in the continuation of the poverty-marginality cycle.

7. Difficulty of Balancing Aspirations and Achievements

An inescapable fact of everyday reality in the poverty-stricken areas is the disparity between aspirations and achievements. People are constantly faced with this disparity, and they are aware of its power to erode emotional strength. Consequently, they have developed strategies by which they attempt to keep aspirations and achievements in balance.

Poor people consciously and unconsciously regulate their aspirations and their commitment to them. Just as they cannot afford to take financial risks with their limited dollars, so also they cannot afford to take psychological risks with their limited resources of confidence and self-respect. And so they regulate the psychological resources they commit to a specific, distant goal, often telling themselves that it doesn't really matter if they achieve it. They evaluate the potential of a situation, withholding commitment of psychological resources, money, and effort until they can be reasonably sure the goal is achievable. Some people quite consciously attempt to keep their aspirations in line with achievement levels by restricting their aspirations.

> You have to learn not to place your hopes too far above where you actually are . . . because if you fall from high-up hopes, you may never get over it.

> Our eyes are set a little above what we have now, but not as high as what we would like ideally. We aim for something a little better than what we have, but not that much better. Then, if we can't achieve our hopes, it's not a great disappointment. You have to learn to try for a happy medium.

People attempt to reduce anxiety about unachieved goals by stressing the value of the things they already possess, rather than those they lack.

> You learn to come to terms with what you have, learn to accept it. Even though you want to get better, you know you can't. So you work with what you have. And you learn not to be jealous of your neighbor if he gets a new car, and not to make your husband feel bad because he can't get a new car too. Or maybe you are jealous, but you go out and polish up your old car.

> We try to teach our children that it isn't all that important to have brand new clothes all the time and the latest fashions. As long as they look clean and neat, they should not feel badly about their clothes.

People also substitute nonmaterial goals, values, and qualities for unachievable material goals.

> We don't have all the material things, like a complete bathroom or a bedroom for each person. But in this family we have something which all the money in the world couldn't buy: love.

In the eyes of outsiders, goal substitution, goal reduction, and restriction of psychological commitment may be interpreted as "lack of motivation," "apathy," or "improper values." But the strategies seem to be positively functional in that they preserve mental health by maintaining a tolerable balance between aspirations and achievements. The necessity for such maneuvering is pointed up by those cases where individuals have not modified or substituted for high goals, despite repeated proof of their elusiveness. These are the most tragic life histories, individuals who suffer tremendous emotional ups and downs and a great sense of failure. It could thus be argued that aspirations that are too high compared to achievement levels may actually work to perpetuate poverty by causing psychological damage to adults and consequent strain in the home environments of children. By contrast, those individuals who have reduced their goals to a level where some are easily attainable appear often to lead more stable emotional and family lives.

Another common pattern for handling the disparity between aspirations and achievements is to modify behavior in such a way that a sought-after goal becomes irrelevant or out of the question. There are many examples. A child who is frustrated in school by his inability to succeed academically may gravitate to the role of class clown or troublemaker. A teenage girl may become pregnant and drop out of school, or an older woman may bear another child—both may be avoiding setting and striving for other goals. An adolescent boy with some scholastic promise sabotages his eduation by getting kicked out of school. An adult relapses into drinking after a long dry period. In each of these situations the individual has put himself or herself in a position where attainment of a certain goal, or the performance of a certain role, is no longer appropriate or expected, and he or she is thereby released from the frustrations of pursuing it.[11] (Here again, it should be noted that such mechanisms are by no means the unique province of the rural poor. They occur in all segments of our society. They are discussed here because of their frequency in a life situation in which one of the ever-present problems is the difficulty of accepting and managing the gap between goals and achievement.)

When the various mechanisms for fending off the disappointment of unmet goals are not effective, the result is deep, prolonged frustration. This may lead to outbursts of physical violence and destructiveness, in the home, in the neighborhood, or in the outside community. Prolonged frustration may also lead to resignation, to temporarily giving up. People worry that they are "cracking up," and some periodically sign themselves into state mental hospitals when their burdens become intolerable. Some people talk of suicide, and some attempt to blot out their troubles with heavy drinking. They lose hope, and fear they can no longer continue the struggle.

> There's a limit to how much my husband can stand before he gives up altogether. It seems like we just begin to see our way clear towards getting some little thing accomplished, like maybe we have almost enough money set aside to put in a septic tank. Then something big comes along, like our car gives out, or he gets laid off, or one of the kids has some kind of trouble. Then we have to scrap our plans again. He was so disgusted the other night I was afraid he was going to crack up. He just can't take it any more. There's got to be some let-up for him. We have to get some results from all our struggling. There must be some good to come of it all.

Walking this difficult tightrope, making slow and halting progress toward hoped-for rewards at the other end, requires delicate psychological, behavioral, and aspirational balancing, and constant readjustment. People cling to the standard societal goals and norms, however, and strive toward a better future, because they recognize the danger of resignation.

> If we gave up our hopes, we might as well die.

They also cling to their hopes because of their children. Having projected their own unmet aspirations onto their children, their greatest desire is that their children have a better life than they have had. Parents know that if they give up caring and trying, the likelihood of their children's "making it" will be seriously jeopardized. In their children they perceive the best chance for the fulfillment of dreams they once had for themselves. They continue to struggle so that their children may some day achieve those dreams.

Meanwhile, the gap between aspirations and achievements, however it is balanced and managed, continues to be an active cause in perpetuating poverty and marginality because of the damage it does to emotional well-being, family relationships, and general life functioning.

8. The Failure Syndrome

Closely related as an ongoing cause of intergenerational rural poverty is the cycle of failure. Repeated experiences of failure, almost unavoidable for many people, lead to low self-esteem and lack of confidence. This, in turn, leads to limited expectations for oneself that are apt to cause further failures and rein-force the low self-image. The cycle continues, in all spheres of life: on the job, in school, in dealings with community agencies and institutions, in social rela-tionships, and in marriage and family relationships.[12]

Observable behavior and verbalized sentiments reveal the ways people at-tempt to protect what shreds of self-confidence they still possess. They try to regulate their experiences and situations so that the risk of incurring failure is kept as low as possible, partly through assessing situations and hedging on commitments.

> Everything we do is a big stepping stone — if we succeed. But it's hard for us to take disappointments. We've built up such a lot of resentments from all our disappointments. So, we always try to size up a situation and figure out what's in it that could be good for us, and what's in it that could hurt us.

They exercise caution in setting up expectations for themselves, and expecta-tions purposely may be set low. A typical example is the man whose wife has left him. He vows that he will go out and get some other woman to fulfill his sexual needs. But he aims very low, talking of substitute women whom, at other times, he has labeled tramps. With them, he can be sure of success in reaffirming his power over women. These low aspirations, however, reveal both the depth of the wound to his self-esteem, and the urgency of his need for protection from further ego damage. Caution in setting up expectations may also involve setting goals that are short-term rather than long-term.

> We learn to live one day at a time. We try to get through today as best we can, and not worry about tomorrow until it comes.

The efficacy of this short-term strategy would appear to be validated by the fact that it is the foremost tenet of Alcoholics Anonymous. But when people apply the same strategy to coping with poverty, the nonpoor conclude that they are "present-oriented" and "unable to think past today." Consequently, although dealing with one day at a time may preserve the poor person's men-tal health, it may also reinforce stereotypes and add to an internalized negative self-evaluation.

The individual also attempts to reduce the likelihood of failure by manipulating others' expectations of him. He limits his participation in community institutions and organized activity so that participation will not be expected of him. Even in elementary school a child may perform at a level that allows him to stay in the slow reading group, although he might actually be able to do better. Promotion to a higher-level group would increase the risk of failure. Men turn down promotions to more responsible jobs for essentially the same reason.[13]

In many ways, then, people minimize the risks of potential failure. But knowing that not all failure can be avoided, they also build in cushions to soften the impact when it does occur. When people are trying something new, they often keep the old tried-and-true pattern alongside the new, just in case the new doesn't work out. A family will hold on to its former shack, just in case payments on the trailer they're buying cannot be kept up. Parents will assure grown chidren that they can always return home if they can't make it on their own.

The impact of failure is also dealt with, and muted somewhat, by beliefs about the causes of failure. Specific failures are often blamed on forces beyond one's control, thus removing the blame. Some explain events in religious terms: "God has His own purposes" and "His own plan," and "He intends us to profit from our tribulations." (This can explain anything from mental retardation to a teenage girl's pregnancy.) Others cite "bad luck" or a series of "bad breaks." (This might explain a fire, loss of a job, or an accident in a "new" car.) But the lifelong pattern of consistent, repeated disappointments is harder to accept and explain. Long-term failure is usually explained by reference to a deprived childhood, lack of education, other people's interference (all causes external to the self), and by a vague belief that some people are simply more prone to have trouble than others. Hardly ever does anyone say that his or her problems are the fault of the American economic structure; few see themselves as casualties of "the system." Individual operators in the system—the boss, the welfare worker, the judge, or a neighbor—may be blamed, but not the system itself.

People perceive events and difficulties as "happening" to them, rather than as the direct result of the individual's vulnerable situation or his actions. For example, a "burn out" (serious house fire) is not usually connected to the family's living in a highly flammable house heated by an unreliable kerosene stove—it's just another event in an unexplainable series of things that happen.

All the bad things that have happened to us have happened on holidays. When we got burned out it was my birthday. When my first husband died, it was on Christmas. My accident happened on Thanksgiving, and my brother's accident happened on my birthday.

Despite the strategies for testing situations, for managing expectation, for hedging against disappointment, and for externalizing the causes of failure, many people are frequently exposed to personal feelings of failure. Because they must participate in a community in which they do not have the economic resources, social skills, or personal confidence to compete successfully, many individuals live with a fairly high and unremitting sense of failure. Although men seldom mention this feeling, except sometimes when they're drunk, women talk quite freely of their own and their husband's sense of failure.

> My husband is so discouraged. Sometimes he feels as if he's fighting the whole world. And when he gets discouraged this way, he just can't seem to do any-thing right. And that makes him all the more discouraged. He's really down now, and it has me worried.

While it is not true that everyone in Chestnut Valley experiences failure every day and wallows in a pervasive sense of failure, for many people there is a cumulative lifetime experience of failure that generates future failure, because it erodes self-confidence and because it strains family relationships, affecting the children as well. Parents with low self-confidence are unable to instill high levels of confidence in their children. This is the failure syndrome, a vital factor in the perpetuation of rural poverty.

9. Psychosocial Deficits from Early Childhood

The experiences of childhood, first in the homes of a rural poverty-stricken neighborhood and later in the "outside world," have long-range effects on an individual's psychological adjustment and the quality of his social interaction, and thus on the continuing cycle of poverty.[14]

Adults trying to sort out and explain their problems most often refer to their childhoods, to factors of social and emotional deprivation as well as poverty. However, neither the material deprivation nor the social marginality in which they were raised has been eliminated in the intervening years. The same socioeconomic conditions that existed a generation ago and caused the problems now experienced by adults still exist today, and may predispose today's children to suffering the same problems as their parents. This cycle continues *despite* the parents' hopes and their efforts to provide a different and better life for their children.

Any emotional difficulties that parents carry over from their own childhoods will form part of the environment in which they bring up their own children. Unresolved emotional and social problems of one or both parents, *exacerbated by the strain of living in poverty,* may jeopardize the children's home environment and interfere with their psychosocial develop-ment. For example, if family life is often disrupted by fighting and one or both parents periodically leaves, the child may conclude that people are not to be

trusted, and that close attachments are dangerous. To avoid further emotional pain and social loss, a child in this situation may restrict his emotional
involvement with others, acting as if they are not important to him. As the
child matures, he may exhibit difficulty in establishing and maintaining interpersonal relationships, both within his home and in the "outside world."
This effect perpetuates marginality and poverty.

Whatever psychosocial difficulties the child experienced in his earliest
years are often reinforced and worsened by his experiences in the outside
world, primarily in school. Since schools generally reflect the stereotypes and
social separations that exist in the society as a whole, a child from a rural,
depressed neighborhood is usually labeled upon entry into a heterogeneous
school system, and repeatedly made to understand that he, along with his
siblings and his cousins, is on the bottom. His weaknesses are brought out, his
strengths overlooked, and he fails to develop a sense of mastery and control.
For some children, the emotional and social damage incurred in the elementary school years may be an even greater loss than the academic under-
achievement.

In each generation the same poverty and struggle, the same inadequacies of
social participation and support, the same interpersonal unpredictability and
self-doubt—all these form the atmosphere in which crucial childhood experiences take place. The psychological effect on children may be long-lasting,
affecting the environment that they will create when they, in their turn, raise
the next generation of children.

10. The Closing-in of Horizons

The final factor perpetuating rural poverty is a cumulative result of all the
other factors woven together. As an individual experiences years of the
failure, frustration, struggle, and disappointment that are inherent in poverty
and marginality, his horizons close in and he or she becomes locked into a
world of limited hopes and bounded environments.

Some people respond to the narrowed horizons with bitterness, resignation,
and/or alcohol, but most adults eventually accept their situation. Withdrawing into this restricted world, they feel at home in it, despite its physical
discomforts.

I used to have dreams. But gradually I learned to accept what I have and try to
improve it by degrees.

Some people here have been disappointed because they haven't been able to accept the things they couldn't accomplish. Others gradually come to terms with
what they have.

Look at my neighbor. Once she learned to accept the fact that her husband
would always be that way, and that they would always be just getting by, then

she was able to settle down and get some pleasure out of the things she did have.

Horizons become limited also because of fear of the unknown and the anxiety people have about trying new things or subjecting themselves to unfamiliar situations—unnecessary ego risks. Given the inadequate social connections between the fringe and rural areas and the larger community, individuals cannot be assured of success in community participation, and there are no ways to prelearn appropriate roles nor opportunities to forge an identity with outside groups and situations. As a result, individuals who feel marginal to the larger community usually limit their participation in it as much as possible. Their range of identification and interaction remains almost totally restricted to family and neighborhood—while the dominant pattern in American society is moving in the opposite direction.

Likewise, in his choice of role models, the child who once identified with firemen, schoolteachers, nurses, doctors, even presidents, may grow up to identify only with persons in the home environment, because he perceives that it is unrealistic to pattern himself after the models presented to him in the "outside world."

This closing-in of horizons is both a curse and a salvation to young adults. The knowledge that they can always retreat to the safety of home, accepting the limited horizons of the rural, depressed neighborhood, probably has the negative effect of reducing the effort some of them put into making it in the outside world. On the other hand, unless and until the outside world becomes more accessible, the home neighborhood—as both a physical and a socioeconomic niche—is an essential haven for the preservation of the self. Thus, horizons close, and limits may come to feel welcome, rather than constraining.

Conclusion

The causes of poverty in rural America and the factors that perpetuate it are complex. There are no simple villains or scapegoats. There is no single cause. Rural poverty involves a cluster of problems that are the result of a whole set of interacting causes.

The ten causal factors I've discussed, viewed as overlapping and interacting phenomena, provide an explanation for the fact that rural poverty and marginality have persisted with such tenacity generation after generation. The adverse legacy of history (primary cause 1) continues to leave its imprint because it is reinforced by other factors (primary causes 2, 3, 4, and 5). These five primary causes bring about the derivative causes (numbers 6, 7, 8, 9, and 10). And each of the ten causes is also self-perpetuating. Hence, poverty and marginality continue on and on in an intergenerational cycle.

The ten factors analyzed here are *ongoing* causes: they operate now and *will continue* to operate, shaping children's lives and futures—unless significant changes are made.

Changes can be made. Knowledge gained from studying Chestnut Valley could serve as a basis for designing changes and implementing programs that could help unspring the trap in which the people of many marginal rural areas have been caught for so long.

Suggestions for the Future

Introduction

When the burden of poverty and its related problems becomes particularly heavy, Mary Crane sometimes daydreams.

If only there was a magic button we could press to make all the problems go away. Then we could start all over again with no old problems hanging over us. And we'd be able to keep on top of things.

American society as a whole often seems to wish for a "magic button," a swift and sure means of eliminating poverty. Perhaps the War on Poverty was America's magic button, but although we pressed it for nearly a decade, poverty did not disappear. We are beginning to realize that there are no magical solutions.

Poverty will not vanish of its own accord, either in the nation or in one little valley. The problem of poverty in rural areas is *self-perpetuating, not self-curing*. Ignored, it will become ever more intractable, as its causes interact and reinforce each other. Only a conscious and purposeful attempt to eliminate the multiple causes that perpetuate poverty will break the cycle that traps people generation after generation.

This chapter will explore possible approaches for breaking into the cycle of cause and effect. For each of the ten ongoing causes of rural poverty, identified in the previous chapter, some general suggestions are offered, then one particular aspect is singled out for specific remedies and proposals. Here again, it should be stressed that the division of the list of ten causes into two groups — primary causes and derivative causes — is not merely a framework for organizing discussion, but represents a significant dichotomy in reality. The five primary causes of rural poverty lie essentially outside the run-down rural neighborhoods; they are embedded in the larger society, facets of society's structures and processes. Hence, removal of the primary causes of rural poverty will require changes in the society itself. The derivative causes, on the other hand, have arisen in response to the difficult situations created by the primary causes. This fact has two significant implications: (1) attention must be directed first and foremost to the primary causes and (2) if the primary causes are removed, the derivative causes will almost automatically diminish. Thus, addressing the primary causes will pay double benefits.

The suggestions offered in this chapter are not intended as a blueprint for all of rural America, or all poverty, for the data cannot be generalized that broadly. Besides, it is important to realize that the solution to poverty is really many different solutions, each tailored to the particularities of a specific poverty situation, a specific set of needs. The suggestions put forth for this particular case apply only to situations having roughly the same general con-figurations and needs. The suggestions offered in this chapter are also limited in that they do not go beyond or contradict the substantiating data of this study. For example, the chapter does not advocate either major economic revolution or sweeping societal reorganization, for such suggestions would run counter to expressed goals and preferences. Rural poor people want an improved opportunity within the existing system; they want to partake of the American Dream as it is defined in the late twentieth century.

The suggested remedies do involve some changes and new directions on the national, regional, state, and local levels. But all of the suggestions are realistic within the framework of present societal capabilities. Many of them are based on observed situations and programs implemented in various com-munities. If implemented on a more general scale, these suggestions could result in a better future for the people of Chestnut Valley and for people in similar situations elsewhere.

Dealing with the Primary Causes of Rural Poverty

1. Shaping the Impact of History

In searching for historical factors underlying rural poverty, we saw that the people of these upland areas were gradually squeezed out by economic and social changes that swept over rural America during the past century.

Now, in the late twentieth century, significant changes are taking place, and the consequences for marginal rural people look just as serious. National patterns affecting the local situation include: (1) increasing concentration of agriculture only in the most technologically efficient regions, (2) the declining industrial economy of the Northeast, (3) reduction of low-skill entry-level jobs as industry contracts and automates, (4) continuing centralization of community functions, and concentration of programs and services in more densely populated areas, and (5) new land-use patterns related to subur-banization. These new trends are modern parallels of the historical changes that brought about the problem of entrenched rural poverty in the first place. All of these new forces may have serious implications for the future, not only in Chestnut Valley, but elsewhere throughout the region. These forces should be monitored for their potential impact on the people of rural areas. If a possibly negative impact is recognized early enough, it could be averted or controlled so that further socioeconomic displacement could be avoided. At the very least, the negative impact of such trends could be cushioned.

CUSHIONING THE NEGATIVE IMPACT OF SUBURBANIZATION ON HOUSING.[1] As suburbanizing pressures push outward from urban centers, the housing situation for rural low-income residents gets worse. The price of rural land and housing rises markedly; taxes increase dramatically; and the supply of inexpensive rural housing shrinks. People of limited financial resources can no longer obtain old tumbledown farmhouses, abandoned one-room schoolhouses, and vacant house sites, for these are quickly bought up by more affluent exurbanite renovators, investors, and back-to-the-land enthusiasts. Poor people already living in the area cannot compete in this market, and their sons and daughters may be squeezed out because they are left with few options for meeting their own increasing housing needs: they can make over and expand their homes; they can build modest houses on land owned by relatives; or, increasingly, they can turn to the house trailer as the only affordable form of housing.

However, as suburbanization proceeds, not only is there escalation of housing prices, but also elevation of housing standards. As population density increases, housing and sanitary codes are tightened. As new residents settle in, they seek to protect their investment and their image of the rural environment. "Junk ordinances" are enacted and enforced, building permits are required for construction, and zoning laws regulate density and type of housing. Trailers may be restricted to mobile home parks. Municipal pressure is brought against the jerry-built shack, the converted school bus, the cluster of dwellings sharing a single lot and a single septic facility, and against the perpetual process of piecemeal building and modifying of homes.

The net result of these new patterns of rural land use and regulation is that poorer people cannot afford to stay in their home area because their makeshift housing is gradually squeezed out, and they can no longer find or devise the cheap housing they require (described in Chapter 6). Consequently, poorer rural people, especially younger couples, are forced to move farther away from the urban growth center. They move into more peripheral townships or counties, where there is less land pressure and therefore less cost and restriction on housing. They stay there until, once again, the pressures of expanding suburbanization catch up with them, and they are forced to flee to another as-yet-unwanted rural area.

This rural "musical chairs" pattern has serious drawbacks as a solution for coping with these new trends. First, important sustaining ties to family, relatives, heritage, and a place are weakened or broken. Second, impermanence may become a way of life, with a pattern of running away from situations, of searching always for a safe haven elsewhere. Third, and perhaps most important, the connections to a community (its people, its sense of coherence, its schools, churches, and voluntary groups, its doctors and counseling services) become even weaker than they were. Adults move from one community to another without ever plugging in well to the facilities and services they need, without establishing social ties. And the communities to which they move tend to be nonaffluent communities, with insufficient tax base to support a high level of human services. The children of mobile low-income families move in and out of different schools, never getting settled enough to make significant progress. This transience is superimposed on the already difficult problems children from low-income rural families meet in their school experiences, and its detrimental effect has often been remarked upon by school administrators in the area. The market-generated residential mobility could thus have long-term negative effects on a whole generation of rural people.

To deal with the housing pressures now faced by rural poor people, I would suggest a three-pronged approach.

• *Monitor the supply of inexpensive rural housing available for people of limited economic resources, and consider the impact that market forces and proposed municipal regulations might have on this housing supply.* For example, although public sentiment may object to old trailers and shacks as ugly blots on the landscape, ruling out such facilities in rural areas would surely have a detrimental impact on people for whom this housing represents a necessary compromise. Ordinances forcing trailers into mobile home parks significantly raise the housing cost, because most trailer parks charge a fairly high space rental and some do not permit old and modified trailers.

As a general policy, perhaps the concept of protecting rural environments should be more broad-mindedly defined. Is it really a violation of the rural spirit to have a tight roadside cluster of houses and trailers if there is a wooded hillside behind them? Is it necessary for suburban municipalities to set housing-density limits that rule out such de facto "cluster housing?" Can a rural residential area be protected against commercial development without being turned into a highly restrictive and high-priced suburb? Raising such questions will help ensure that new population influx is not inadvertently allowed to squeeze out inexpensive forms of rural housing.

• *Help low-income rural people bring their housing up to a level of greater health, safety, and comfort—a level that more closely approximates community standards.* Since major improvements, such as septic and water systems, cost much more than many rural families can pay, and normal bank loans are far too expensive, government programs for home improvement assistance are clearly needed. But most of these people do not qualify for the low-interest home improvement loans available from the Farmers' Home Administration, as they require far greater economic stability and a higher income than many of the people of Chestnut Valley have. The loan programs have little flexibility in the standards by which they judge loan applicants and their proposed projects: women heads of families have difficulty qualifying; trailers and substandard homes do not usually qualify at all; and land titles must be clear. Obviously, loan programs should be more closely tailored to reflect the specific needs and situations of the people who most need help in improving their homes.[2]

Even if home improvement loans were made more accessible, however, they would not appeal to all rural poor people, since they run counter to traditional strategies for getting by financially, strategies that stress minimization of cash outlay and avoidance of fixed or long-term cash obligations (see Chapter 6). Therefore, in some cases outright grants may be necessary. Several federal programs (Farmers' Home Administration, Housing and Urban Development) are beginning to move in this direction—albeit in very small steps and with difficulty obtaining needed funding levels.[3] Perhaps some assistance might also come from other government sources, such as programs that help small municipalities fund sewer and water improvement programs. Such funds might possibly be used to underwrite the design, development, and installation of septic systems appropriate for clusters of three to six households in rural areas.

• *Help rural people compete in the changing rural housing market by increasing their buying power.* This would imply a more general economic improvement, which will be discussed in the next section of this chapter. Specific to buying power in housing, though, one encouraging development along this line is the extension to rural areas of the federal "Section 8" HUD housing program that subsidizes rent, in which the family pays only one-fourth of its income toward the rent and the government pays the shortfall to make up fair market rent for the landlord. The program may be particularly helpful for young adults, young families, and people with a low but steady source of income, whether from welfare or employment. But the program is not appropriate for those residents who do not have the security of a steady income, those who find it more economical to own than to rent, and those who are currently paying less than the government's benchmark of 25 percent of income for housing. More appropriate housing assistance would concentrate on raising income levels and strengthening income stability so that people could handle their housing needs on their own.

Focusing attention on the need to monitor and improve the *rural* housing situation, however, does not imply that urban housing units are not also needed. Urban housing, affordable and decent, should be available as an option for those rural people who would prefer to move into the cities, as well as for urban people. But it is clear from this study that a move to urban housing, though it may bring improved physical conditions, also has significant drawbacks as a solution for rural people's housing needs. Not only does it weaken important ties to people and places, it also undermines independence and individual initiative. Furthermore, urban housing is apt to be more expensive, both to the individual and to the public, than rural housing. Even when urban housing rents are publicly subsidized on a sliding scale, the occupant may pay far more in cash rent than he would for rural housing. Urban rents, even when subsidized, may be more than a family can afford, thus forcing people to seek public assistance. Thus, the real cost of supporting rural people in urban housing may be far greater than the cost of providing grants for improvement of rural housing.

The general point is that rural people who are poor should have several options for meeting their housing needs, and some of those options should be designed to enable them to remain where they can live inexpensively and maintain important socioemotional supports – and still obtain better housing than they now have.

2. Changing the Economic Situation

It is clear that the people of the rural depressed areas must have more money available to them for meeting their needs and alleviating the constant stress of insufficient and insecure income. However, this study shows that the answer lies neither in "handouts" nor in "incentives to work." Most rural poor people are already basically committed to working for a living, and most of them attempt to live by that commitment. The thrust of change must come in assuring the adequacy of employment: more available jobs, more appropriate jobs, greater employment security, better wages and benefits, and increased opportunity for personal satisfaction on the job.

One useful approach would be to identify crucial points in an individual's life or in the family's development cycle when holding an adequate job would bring most benefits for the individual and the household, and to provide assistance and support at that time to make sure the individual is able to find and keep a job. One such intervention point would be during the late teen/early adult years; another would be at the stage in family development when a woman can realistically consider going (back) to work. At both these turning points, those individuals who have been able to enter the work force successfully have significantly improved their financial, personal, and family stability. Those who have been frustrated by inability to obtain secure jobs appropriate to their needs and abilities at this crucial time tend to become mired in worsening financial and personal problems. These turning points are too important in the lives of individuals and families to leave the individual's employment to chance and the uncontrolled job market. Focused assistance to help people enter the world of work satisfactorily at these important times would have long-range impact.

Coupled with such expanded employment opportunities, however, it seems that a federal guaranteed minimum income, or a negative income tax, would also be needed. This would assure sufficient economic security for all households, including those with no members able to work regularly and those in which the ratio of wage earners to dependents is too low to support its members adequately from employment earnings alone. A combination of employment improvements and some form of guaranteed minimum income is in line with much current thinking on the eradication of poverty in the nation as a whole.[4]

IMPROVING THE ECONOMIC SITUATION FOR WOMEN. This in-depth case study leads to a conviction that the cause of women's economic difficulty is *not* that they are lazy and unwilling to work, or happy to depend on welfare. Some of the women have been fairly steady workers, and others have taken jobs periodically. But their economic status should be strengthened.

Government coercion for women to take jobs (as in the Work Incentive program, WIN) is, however, not an appropriate strategy. The application of economic sanctions—such as cutting off food stamps or AFDC benefits for women who do not register for employment when their youngest child is more than six years old—is not a solution at all, and may be counterproductive.[5] For one thing, this may be unrealistically early for some women to take on the triple role of wage earner, homemaker, and mother. The benefits of a mother's remaining at home, even after all her children have reached school age, may outweigh the relatively low wages she would earn in the kind of job she might get. Second, there may be complicating problems in her home life that make it nearly impossible for a woman to take an outside job, and that may predispose her to lack of success in both the paid job and the home job should she try to do both. For example, she may already be overtaxed by health problems, emotional exhaustion, low self-esteem, marital problems, extra household members, insecurity about the future, problems adequately supervising children when they're not in school, and the demands of doing a lot of housework with inadequate facilities. (Although AFDC and food stamp work regulations include exemptions for medical problems, the diffuse condition of generally poor physical and mental health may be difficult to diagnose and document for exemption.)

Instead of attaching an arbitrary across-the-board work requirement to assistance programs, it would seem much more effective to concentrate on making improvements in the employment situation. This would involve a combination of improving the employment opportunities for women and enhancing their employability. Particularly helpful would be: (1) increased op-portunities to work on a periodic, part-time, and flexible-time basis when a woman's situation warrants and can sustain it; (2) improved education, voca-tional counseling, and job experience for teenage girls and young women out of school; (3) expanded work reentry opportunities for women of middle age, with appropriate counseling, training, and placement assistance; and (4) development or expansion of a system of wage increments for people who per-form well but for various reasons need or prefer to remain on the common laborer level.

Observations of working women in both the young-adult and the mid-life years indicate that women generally benefit in personal as well as financial terms from employment if the jobs are appropriate for them and if other fac-tors in their personal and home life do not interfere. The status or glamour or career-ladder concept of the job may not be the most important factor to a woman from a low-income rural background. Janitorial work in institutions and assembly-line work in factories have been quite acceptable to some women, and are often preferred by middle-age women, for whom the pride of holding a job and earning an income seems to outweigh the career or status aspects of their jobs. Other women desire more people-oriented work, as nurse's aides and hairdressers, for example. The range of jobs available should be as varied as the women and their needs. Individualized assistance in preparing for and finding appropriate work would be far more effective than coercion to take whatever job is available.

Other economic changes for women should be made outside the regular employment sphere, for even women who are not employed participate in the household economy. Women usually take care of the lengthy paperwork and numerous official appointments necessary to supplement the family's income through food stamps, welfare, and so forth. As consumers, women go to rum-mage sales and low-price outlets to save money on living costs. These income-earning or expense-saving activities should be given recognition and credit, for women are using their time and energy to make a direct contribution to the household economy. Restriction of cash outflow is as important a con-tribution to family economics as increasing cash income.

Women should also receive realistic payment for the care-giving services they provide for extra children, physically or mentally disabled relatives, and elderly people whom they keep in their homes. If they were paid for this work, rather than just receiving an allocation of money from public assistance benefits for the home-cared individual, women would also be building up their financial position for the future through Social Security.

It is important to point out that these suggestions for improving women's economic situation should not be carried out in a vacuum. Corresponding improvements in the employment situation for men must also be made, especially since one of the deterrents to women's successful employment is their husband's jealousy over money-earning roles. In fact, any improvement in the income-earning situation of men would almost automatically have the extra benefit of enabling women to participate more successfully in the world of work.

3. Correcting the Inadequacies of Social Structure

This study has indicated two important social contributors to the problem of entrenched rural poverty: the collapse of the rural community and the incomplete integration of rural poor people into the larger urban community.

The question arises whether viable small communities could be re-created in each of these rural depressed localities. The realistic answer would seem to be "no." Societal changes have gone too far to make this a feasible solution. Special interests and activities, rather than locality groupings, now form the basis of social interaction. While it may be that some community institutions may be stirred back to life by energetic local people or newcomers, only in rural areas with a fairly large population and more affluence would significant resurgence of the community be likely to occur. And only with concentrated effort and attention would the poverty-stricken "native" residents be caught up in this essentially exurbanite, educated, affluent movement.

RESISTING FURTHER CENTRALIZATION. Pressures toward further centralization of services, education, and organizations should be resisted at this time. The negative consequences of earlier centralization, as in the school consolidation movement of the post–World War II era, have not yet completely disappeared. Before initiating another round of centralization, more positive steps must be taken to treat the casualties of the last round. State funding schemes should not penalize school districts that resist official plans for merging into larger, conglomerate districts.

Another centralization drive that should not be blindly accepted is the propensity of states and counties to consolidate youth recreation services under county-wide umbrella organizations. This represents one more lost function for the rural township or village (which may be left with little more than snowplowing and dog licensing functions to fulfill—and even these are increasingly being taken out of their hands).

Centralization of recreation, as of education, may throw poorer rural people into a situation in which they feel like outsiders and participate only minimally, if at all. Good local programs, with local input in planning and managing, would attract more people from poorer families. Local programs would serve as a training ground from which youngsters could move out into the wider world of urban-based youth activities, and in which their parents could get a taste of success in planning, organizing, and participating at the local level. There should be more, rather than less, support for small-community programs.

In other municipal functions, such as child care and health, for example, state and federal money has often favored large municipalities and consolidated programs. Federal revenue-sharing funds have to some degree counteracted this tendency, giving townships some decision-making power and program control. The federal government also is beginning to recognize the needs of rural areas, and may be taking steps to help rural areas and small towns get their fair share of federal grants and programs.[6]

BUILDING SOCIAL BRIDGES. New avenues could be built to facilitate successful and satisfying participation by rural low-income people in the social activities and groups of the larger community. This improved social linkage would also contribute to smoother relationships within the neighborhood and family.

One point made clear by this study is that rural poor people do not want to participate as "the poor," as members of "poor people's groups," as "low-income parents," and so forth. Rather, they need and want to participate as *people*—as individuals, as parents, as children—*regardless of income level*. To the fullest extent possible, the community's institutionalized activities should avoid treating low-income participants as members of a separate socioeconomic class—as "the disadvantaged" or as the people from a particular locale—for the stigma of poverty and "bad" neighborhoods is already too strong. Increased public labeling is definitely not beneficial.

A potential, though often overlooked, social bridge to the dominant community is that of volunteer service. Several women have, in fact, expressed a desire to contribute their time to the community, perhaps caring for people who are old, ill, or disabled. But there are no readily available avenues for such participatory contributions. Perhaps if transportation and other incidental costs could be subsidized (on the same basis as the federally sponsored Retired Senior Volunteer Program, which offsets the expenses incurred by senior citizens doing volunteer work), women who are not employed could contribute needed human services to their communities. In so doing, the volunteers would also learn employable skills, make satisfying new connections with the dominant community, and improve their own self-images. A woman whose family life is chaotic and whose children are difficult to handle may make an excellent care-giver outside her own home, and her competent performance may actually improve her functioning at home.

4. Locating and Removing Barriers to Upward Mobility

Several barriers to upward mobility have been identified in this study: (1) lack of economic resources sufficient to provide for both necessities and status goods, (2) absence of social entry points for participating and gaining acceptance in the wider community, (3) pervasive negative stereotypes, (4) the fact that the problems associated with lifelong poverty create such strains that failure and limited achievements come to be accepted as inevitable, and (5) the inability of public education to compensate for socioeconomic handicaps. Since the first four barriers to upward mobility pertain also to the other ongoing causes of rural poverty, suggestions for dealing with them appear under various other headings in this chapter. Here we will concentrate on the educational barrier.

INCREASING THE EFFECTIVENESS OF PUBLIC EDUCATION. As a society, Americans believe in education as the path to economic and social success; and that belief is reinforced by statistics showing direct correlation between income level and amount of education. This view is shared by many poverty-stricken adults of Chestnut Valley, who are well aware of the drawbacks of their own limited educations. For themselves, however, they feel it is too late in life to use education as a tool to surmount their poverty. Thus, they may underutilize available education programs for adults, including basic literacy programs and community colleges. Adult education programs may also be underused because they are not sufficiently flexible in terms of locations, hours, curriculum, bureaucratic requirements, and expectations. Too few programs reach people where they are (geographically, educationally, or financially). For some of the younger adults observed during this study, however, the community colleges have been a very effective bridge into stable and satisfying employment, a significant factor in upward mobility. But not very many have followed this route.

In local belief and practice, it is the education of young children that is stressed as part of the deferred dream of escaping from poverty. And it is here that education falls short. Although the elementary and secondary schools of the region surrounding Chestnut Valley are of high caliber, serving the majority of their students adequately, the children from the rural poor homes consistently do not benefit from their years in school. Many teachers and administrators recognize the problem and are concerned. An administrator in one rural district commented, "We know those kids. They're maybe 10 percent of our school population. We think we know what they need. We try—I honestly think we do our darndest—to be effective with them. But I've got to admit that in many cases—too many—we miss our mark. We do not succeed with these kids." Despite good school systems, despite the touted advantages of a heterogeneous pupil population, despite honest desire to serve low-income rural children better, some children systematically fail to thrive in school. Many children fail to benefit enough from their schooling to succeed in their postschool endeavors.

Several needed changes or redirections of emphasis can be suggested that might increase the effectiveness of education in preparing children from rural poverty backgrounds for successful participation in the wider world.

• *Explode a societal myth.* As a start, the myth that education is *the* key to escaping poverty should be questioned. Since insufficient education is but *one* facet of poverty, better education and more of it would only attack the poverty problem on one front. To say that lack of education causes poverty or that more years spent in school would overcome poverty is to oversimplify the problem of poverty and to misrepresent education. Despite recent educational innovations (such as Head Start), schools have failed, and will continue to fail to lift people out of poverty because it is simply too much to expect schools to be societal panaceas, magic carpets out of poverty.

• *Bury an old argument.* It is time to put aside pointless arguments over who is to blame for the documented fact that children from lower socioeconomic levels are found disproportionately in the lower achievement levels in schools.[7] The frustrated, defensive attitude many educators take comes out in their statements that the children have no worthwhile role models at home, that their homes have no books, and that the "damage" to the children is already done before they come to school, "so it's not our fault that we can't do anything with them." Parents, for their part, say the schools "don't want to be bothered with kids from this neighborhood" and "don't really give our kids a chance." "They don't really educate our kids, don't teach them, just pass them on from grade to grade."

This old argument continues, in words, in attitudes, and in preconceptions; and it influences actions on both sides. As long as the argument is continued, time, commitment, and effort are diverted from the real job at hand—improving schooling for youngsters from lower socioeconomic backgrounds.

• *Build a new relationship.* Schools sometimes reflect the public stereotype that poor people do not care about their children and their children's education. The parents from these rural areas do indeed care. But their caring is not recognized because of several factors: (1) parents may not express their caring in ways that the school understands or expects—such as making sure their children attend school every day and coming in for conferences with teachers; (2) parents may care so very much that they are deeply hurt by any hint of a child's difficulty in school and may consequently withdraw from contact or become hostile toward the school; (3) parents may have unrealistic hopes, expectations, and fears about schools, education, and their children; and (4) parents may be bogged down by too many other problems and crises to pay much attention to the everyday details, notices, and requests that children bring home from school.

Schools could work to build new avenues for parents to express their caring by becoming involved in the enterprise of educating their own youngsters. Perhaps the recent trend emphasizing professionalism in the teaching of young children could be reversed. A parent with limited formal education is particularly vulnerable to the underlying message that parents are inadequate to the task of helping children learn. It would seem possible, instead, for schools to help parents develop skills and confidence so that they could assume a more active role in their children's education. At the very least, such an attempt would improve communication and understanding between parents and schools, would set them up as partners rather than adversaries in the education of children. Especially in the case of young parents whose children are just beginning their school careers, such efforts could have significant effects.

Fundamental to any such efforts, schools should simply adopt the assumption that, unless it is proven otherwise, parents from the rural poverty areas *do* care. Beyond that, schools could try a variety of innovative methods to bridge the school-home gap. Successful methods include: a home-school coordinator or aide to serve as a go-between and facilitator of communication; school-community activities to get children out into the community; and special programs at the school that draw parents in for comfortable, non-threatening, and informal interaction. (Programs and activities at the school are more easily attended by low-income parents if they can bring their children, including babies, and perhaps other relatives as well.)

• *Study the schools.* A school is far more than the sum of its academic programs; it is a gestalt that includes a myriad of social systems, interactional patterns, unplanned activities, and microenvironments. A school could conduct a thorough study of itself as a total institution to see how the children from rural poor families fit into it. The study would encompass not just teaching methods, but every type of academic, para-academic and non-academic situation, every nook and cranny of the school facility, every minute of the school day. It would include a study of the informal social hierarchy and social attitudes that children bring with them, and how these are played out in the school environment.

The study of a school should provide extremely useful insights into what really happens, what doesn't happen, and why both parents and school, as well as children, are often disappointed with the results of schooling. It would point up the particularly supportive and successful microenvironments where children from low-income backgrounds function well and develop confidence. These could be expanded and duplicated elsewhere. The study could identify situations that seem to be most damaging to self-confidence, and raise some questions about points where the school and its children do not mesh well. For example, such a study might shed light on how to handle the problems created by the disparity between a child's home-life pace, which is constantly alive with unpredictable activity, and his school environment, which puts a premium on routine and control.

• *Avoid negative attitudes toward children.* Negative attitudes and assumptions about children from poverty-stricken homes may sometimes slip in despite the best of intentions. These attitudes come out in many little ways: the administrator who believed Sally should not be furnished with free lunch because "it's about time Sally's parents took some responsibility for her"; the frustrated elementary teacher who followed a child out into the hallway after class and shouted above the din, "Richard, *why* do you always have to be like your cousin Joe?"; the teacher who explained to me, "I don't expect to get any place with this child. I had her oldest brother in my class years ago, and I couldn't do a thing with him."

The common thread running through these incidents is that school personnel (probably unwittingly) are judging the child for things over which he has no control, punishing him for the shortcomings (real or imagined) of his parents. The child is blamed for who his parents are, where they live, how they live. He is stigmatized on the basis of what the school thinks his older siblings have done or not done, by the reputations of his cousins.

Schools must become conscious of such judgments to stop them. Otherwise these insidious attitudes toward children can undermine and undo the benefits of even the most conscientious teachers and the most effective teaching methods, for children read these negative messages more clearly and deeply than they read any benign messages.

However, this suggestion does not mean that schools should remove all responsibility and expectations from the children of rural poverty-stricken families. The child should, indeed, be held responsible for his actions, to the extent appropriate to his age and experience, and to the extent that his actions are within his control. The school must set its expectations for the child on the basis of the child, not his relatives; then express approval when the child achieves and let the child know when he has fallen below expectations. Beyond this, schools could actively foster self-accountability through providing cumulative and graduated experiences, coupled with encouraging support. This might accomplish a great deal toward enabling the child to feel that he can deal successfully with the larger world, that he has some mastery and control.

These five suggestions, taken together, are intended to show that schools could be more effective than they are in fostering not only academic skills but also a sense of confidence and competence, which is so crucial to the actualization of children's potentials. Although schools cannot be expected to cure rural poverty, they could do more to prepare children from poverty-stricken backgrounds to deal effectively with the wider world.

5. Combating Corrosive Stereotypes

The people of Chestnut Valley are well aware of the stereotypes and how deeply they corrode. They even have ideas of what it might be like if those stereotypes didn't come between themselves and the community.

The people along this road don't live this way because they want to. They didn't even ask to be born. But if people would treat them like human beings, encourage them when they're doing something good, then maybe they'd try even harder. If they're fixin' up a room, praise them; or if they're out mowing the grass, tell them, "Gee, your lawn looks nice." It would make such a difference to hear that kind of encouragement for our efforts, instead of always criticism for what we don't do.

Can communities, indeed, a whole society, drop their stereotyped thinking? Can they learn to see the good in others rather than judging only in terms of negative preconceptions? The change will not be accomplished by pious sermons in church, by celebration of brotherhood week in school, or by appeals to the collective conscience in newspaper editorials—though such reminders do have their usefulness.

The long-range hope is that the stereotype problem would quite naturally diminish if poverty itself were eliminated through significant changes in the employment picture and general economic situation of rural families. With greater economic stability, there would be less basis for invidious comparison. Superimposed on economic improvement, social bridges between rural areas and the urban-based community would reduce the separateness that fosters stereotypes. New social interaction patterns can be created and developed, and attitudinal changes will follow. However, extra care must be taken, particularly in settings involving heterogeneous mixtures of young children and teenagers, lest situations arise that would either reinforce stereotypes in people's minds or permit discriminatory behavior based on stereotypes. Merely putting children together is not enough; situations must be creatively designed to foster healthy interaction.

FOSTERING BETTER UNDERSTANDING. Careful observation and analysis can supply new perspectives that may eliminate the need to rely on prior judgments. As new bases for understanding people's actions are provided, old errors of misinterpretation and stereotype can be overcome. Three points stand out concerning the use of increased knowledge to combat stereotypes.

• *Look at contexts of behavior.* Looking at economic patterns, for example, it is obvious that poor people have a smaller pie to distribute (less total available money) and they don't know how large tomorrow's pie will be, or next year's pie. Consequently, they may cut their pie differently. For example, the poor people of Chestnut Valley often spend considerably less than one-quarter of their income on housing costs, and do everything possible to avoid the kind of continuing fixed-cash outlay for housing that middle-income people regularly incur. As a result of economizing on housing costs, they sometimes are able to spend a greater percentage of income on leisure and recreation than might be the case for middle-income people, though of course the figure in absolute dollars would still be much lower. The higher percentage allocated to recreation does not mean that the poor are wasting money on leisure, or that they value recreation more than housing; it suggests that, in order to maintain healthy lives and keep some happiness in their homes, the money they are able to save on housing may be assigned to the satisfaction of pleasure needs. Because of their unsatisfying jobs, ever-present worries, inadequate social ties to the community, overcrowded housing, and low self-esteem, rural poor people may have a greater need than others to spend money to bring relief and happiness into their lives.

When a poor family purchases a motorcycle or snowmobile, a fancier-than-necessary car, a color TV, a CB radio set, or a trip to the stock car races, they are emulating the contemporary American pattern of leisure, oriented toward buying heavily advertised fad items. Even poor people feel a need to indulge their desire to be "with it"; and they can sometimes do so because they have reduced expenditures elsewhere. Furthermore, the expenses on leisure-recreation in Chestnut Valley seem to fit well within the general themes of economic decision making, and effectively reinforce people's commitment to earning money. Hence, such expenditures are healthy and sensible patterns—*given the context* in which they are made.

It is the understanding of context that renders spending patterns intelligible, no matter what the economic level of the spender. The spending patterns of poor people in the rural areas are, for the most part, as rational in the poverty context as middle-class spending patterns are in middle-class contexts. But the patterns of one group cannot be judged in terms of the context of another group; one group should not be denigrated because it does not apportion its money according to the designs that other categories of people in other situations find appropriate.

• *Do not confuse quantitative statements about actions with cultural values.* In much of the social science literature, in program design, and in public thinking, there is a tendency to equate statistical norms (frequencies of actions) with cultural norms (learned, shared values). The equation is not merely erroneous, it inhibits understanding and perpetuates stereotypes, as can be seen in the interpretation of marital conflict (Chapter 7). The actual incidence of marital upheaval is indeed high, but the cultural value, the goal for which people strive, was found to be marital persistence, not marital disruption. Marital instability is the result of an assortment of social, economic, and emotional stresses correlated with poverty; it is not the result of insufficient commitment to the ideals of marriage and family life. In the stereotyped view, people's actions are a direct reflection of their preferences, and thus it is assumed that "those people don't value marriage and family living." This confusion between statistical frequency and cultural preference has been fostered by social scientists, particularly by the "culture of poverty" framework, which

has become firmly embedded in the public mind and in the thinking of government planners. It clearly perpetuates false stereotypes and misperceptions.[8]
  • *Design stereotype-free programs.* The understanding of contexts and the
decoupling of statistical norms from cultural norms would help combat not
only the blatant public stereotypes, but also the subtle preconceptions that
creep into programs aimed at "eliminating poverty" by changing poor people,
and teaching them "how to live right." Government programs dealing with
poverty are sometimes built on the assumptions that people are poor because
they don't want to work, they don't know how to save, and they have no
concern for the future. Consequently, the programs often stress dangling incentives in front of people, teaching them skills, and changing their priorities.
But if the underlying assumptions about poverty and poor people are wrong,
the programs not only will be ineffective, but they will be wrong. As earlier
chapters demonstrated, people do not need incentives to work as much as
they need good jobs at which to work. Focusing attention on work incentive
programs will only perpetuate the stereotypes.

Handling the Derivative Causes of Rural Poverty

Thus far, we have discussed suggestions for reducing the five primary self-
perpetuating causes in the cycle of rural poverty and marginality. Before going
on to the other five causes, it should be stressed again that these are
derivatives of the first five. Hence, if causes one through five were reduced,
perhaps along the lines indicated, causes six through ten would almost
automatically be ameliorated. Attempts to overcome rural poverty should
concentrate on the five primary causes. Cures and preventions cannot start
with the derivative causes.

Nevertheless, some attention should be turned toward the derivative
causes. Since these secondary causes have been operating over generations,
they and their negative effects are not likely to disappear instantly when the
underlying primary causes of poverty are attacked. In the common metaphor,
while Band-Aids should not be substituted for treatment of the underlying
cause of an infection, it may be necessary to continue to apply them while the
infection is being treated and the wound is healing.

6. Reducing the Pressure of Too Many Problems

Clearly, the overburden of problems would be lightened if the primary
causes of continuing poverty were removed. Improving and stabilizing the
economic position, primarily through adequate and flexible employment
possibilities and suitable programs for interim income backup, would end the
day-in, day-out worry over "keeping a roof over our heads and food on the

table." This, in turn, would significantly lower the level of stress that insidiously saps energy, reduces effective functioning, exacerbates other problems, and often flares up into anger and violence in the family or
neighborhood. Likewise, improving social connections would reduce the
number and pressure of "too many problems all at once." If avenues could be
created for successful interaction and roles in the secondary community,
primary interpersonal relationships would be less threatened by overloading
and by the pattern of displaced hostility.

However, even significant improvements in the five primary ongoing causes
would not quickly or completely wipe out all the related problems that
burden families; it would only gradually reduce their number, their complexity, and their incessant pressure. The physical, mental, and social wounds
already inflicted by past burdens of problems might continue to fester. People
may need extra social, medical, and counseling services for a long time to
come. Hence, human services for rural poor people must be given adequate
recognition and funding.

DELIVERING HUMAN SERVICES EFFECTIVELY. Attention should be devoted to
improving the quality, nature, and accessibility of human services as they are
rendered to people in the process of emerging from poverty. Two points can
be stressed.

• *Examine the interface between service provider and client.* An understanding of the different expectations held by service providers and by rural poor
people would facilitate a better match between services and needs. It appears
that the most effective and utilized services are those that offer a personal approach, multipurpose workers, and an ability to respond rapidly and flexibly
to urgent needs and sudden changes. Some of the problems in service delivery
include: the need to break away from concentration of services in centralized
city offices, by taking services out to small communities and to homes; the
need to create personal toeholds in the bureaucratic facade; and the need to
minimize personnel turnover in agencies, so that clients who expect and need
personal ties with an individual worker are not, instead, offered only a professional relationship with the agency as a unit.

• *Consider the long-range as well as the immediate benefits of services to clients.*
When social, medical, counseling, and other services are provided, not only
are people's particular problems addressed, but at the same time they also
gain experience in solving problems. Positive attitudes—even the very attitude that problems *can* be solved—are certainly fostered by experiencing
success in solving problems. Skills for dealing with problems are also
developed during the process of successful problem-solving. This secondary
aspect should be given more consideration, for it has long-run implications.
The skills needed to recognize and define one's problems, to locate ap-

propriate community resources, and to utilize them effectively should be taught and reinforced as an integral part of the process of helping people with their specific problems.

7. Altering the Balance Between Aspirations and Achievements

As previous chapters have shown, the poverty that grips generations of people in these marginal rural areas is not due to lack of aspirations. In fact, given the tenacity and complexity of the rural poverty problem, limited aspirations are a realistic response to people's actual and projected situations. Thus, it seems that the popular belief that raising people's aspirations will lift them out of poverty is inapplicable here. More than that, it is also a cruel hoax. High goals, if consistently unattainable, do not lift anyone out of poverty; they may instead destroy the person. And if the damage to that individual's functioning is recurrent or severe, it may limit the chances that his or her children, in their turn, will achieve those higher goals. It is not the aspiration level, but the achievement side of the balance, that must be addressed.

CREATING OPPORTUNITIES FOR ACHIEVEMENT. Opportunities and situations must be created, through reduction in the primary causes of rural poverty, for the achievement of goals.

The economic sphere, primarily jobs, is where opportunities for higher achievement are most needed. But the uncontrolled job market does not usually provide these opportunities. New hiring patterns will have to be encouraged, private-sector involvement solicited, and public-sector jobs created as needed. Again, it may help to target particularly crucial turning points in the lifecycle when the availability of new opportunities for achievement would have the greatest positive effect and would most readily be accepted.

Whenever possible, there should be opportunities for people to try new situations under conditions of limited ego-risk. As poor people hedge against personal failure and are particularly reluctant to take on risks to their self-esteem, new opportunities must be offered with a built-in risk protection. Whether in the realm of better jobs, home improvements, or completed educations, planners should be aware of the risks that potential participants may perceive, and should build in controls or cushions for any unavoidable ego risks. For example, a job training program might guarantee that if a person's new skill has no local market, or the new job proves to be unsatisfactory for the person, or he for it, he will be eligible for another paid training program. When the risks to a person's sense of worth are regulated, he or she is more apt to push on toward higher goals, rather than substituting easier-to-reach goals. The same principle applies to education, whether for young children, teenagers, or adults: risks to the ego should be minimized to make a high-aspiration program acceptable to a person of limited confidence.

8. Overcoming the Failure Syndrome

The self-perpetuating sense of failure cannot be overcome merely by telling people to stop thinking of themselves as failures. But reduction of the primary causes of poverty would almost certainly provide many more experiences of success that, in turn, would help reduce the failure syndrome. For example, if men's earnings on the job were high enough to meet more adequately the needs of their families, they would probably exhibit a considerably greater sense of self-worth, for they would be more adequately performing the provider role that they regard as important.

However, change will be slow. An adult who has lived through decades of failure may continue to be burdened by its psychological effects even after his or her economic situation has been improved, social connections strengthened, and the community's stereotypes muted. Moreover, the failure syndrome of parents may already have been transferred to their children before beneficial changes are made in the family's situation. Hence, we cannot expect a sudden bursting forth of self-confidence: it must be carefully built up and nourished.

PREVENTING INADEQUACY FEELINGS IN CHILDREN. One particular point might be stressed here. According to Erikson's stage theory, the development of a sense of inferiority is most likely to occur between the ages of six and eleven.[9] These are crucial years, when a youngster is changing from a homebound child to an operator in a much wider world. During this time, the experiences both at home and in elementary school can either contribute to or ward off a sense of inferiority. If the parents have low self-esteem, it is unlikely that they can instill confidence, individual initiative, and independence in their children, no matter how much they may wish to do so. Therefore, it is particularly important that the schools and other institutions of the community help. But too often the schools also fail to foster a sense of competence and mastery in these youngsters, thus adding to the sense of inferiority and contributing to the failure syndromes.

Three points seem particularly important if schools are to help break this intergenerational transmission of a sense of failure. First, whatever confidence and security the child does derive from his home surroundings should be recognized and valued, rather than called into question by negative aspersions cast upon his parents, his neighbors, and himself. Second, young children, in schools and in other community institutions, need as much exposure to success as possible. Their microenvironments should be examined and carefully monitored. Situations in which the child is apt to fail should be reshaped or eliminated. Third, children of all ages need to acquire a wide range of skills and tools to build their confidence in dealing with the larger world. Elementary schools have a particular challenge because they work with children at the crucial stage when they are most vulnerable to developing a sense of inferiority, and they are the first potential bridge between family and the rest of the world. By rewarding individual initiative, schools can help children develop moderate risk-taking attitudes and assume independence and learn self-direction.

9. Avoiding Psychosocial Deficits

Here again, the problem will be greatly reduced once the basic continuing causes of poverty and marginality are addressed. But since the healthy development of children cannot wait for such reforms, there must be direct attempts to address this self-perpetuating cause. Erikson's theories of the stages of development sound a warning note here too.

Young children need situations in which to develop basic trust, environments that encourage autonomy, experiences that foster initiative. Because the foundations for these characteristics are laid in the period up to age six, the quality of the child's early home environment is crucial. A holistic approach is needed, to assist the child by strengthening and supporting his home environment, rather than serving the child only in away-from-home settings such as day-care, preschool, and foster care. The supports must be given to the whole household—to all of its members—rather than just focused on the child.

The potential for the home-environment-centered approach is indicated in evaluations of the Head Start program that point out the importance of the out-of-classroom components of the program.[10] A number of program benefits are usually extended to the families of Head Start children. Visits by the social worker and nurse bring to the child's home environment specific services, social contacts, information and assistance that connect the family to other community services. In some communities, mobile programs take educational activities out to the younger siblings of Head Start children; these seem to be effective and well received. Head Start parent groups, regarded as an integral part of the program, not only involve parents in their children's education, but also foster social contacts for the parents. Through Head Start, the child thus becomes a connection between his parents and the wider world, a connection of particular benefit for families who are marginal to their communities. The classroom component of the program is reinforced and enhanced by these supportive services directed to the home environment.

PROVIDING MULTIFACETED SUPPORT FOR FAMILIES WITH YOUNG CHILDREN. A multifaceted attempt to stabilize children's primary environments during the crucial early years at home would break the vicious circle whereby economic, personal, and marital problems so common in the early years of a poverty-stricken household create psychosocial deficits in the children that may, in turn, predispose them to poverty and problems when they become adults. Breaking this cycle is very much a matter of timing, for the family is apt to be under greatest stress just when the children are most vulnerable to incurring long-term psychosocial damage; most likely to develop self-doubt, guilt, and dependence. Conversely, supportive intervention at this time would pay the greatest long-term dividends because it would come at the appropriate period to enhance positive psychosocial development, thereby increasing the individual's chances of breaking out of the poverty cycle.

An example of such a multifaceted support program and its beneficial ramifications could be suggested in terms of the specifics of the family of Mary and Bill Crane and their children.

During the period when Bill and Mary Crane were going through rough times together – he was drinking and she was sick, they were on welfare part of the time, and they separated a few times, with Mary going home to Mamma – there were young children and babies in the home.

Mary's affectionate interaction with their children and her nurturant personality may have helped cushion the effects on the children. There was no problem of child abuse in this case, though several of the common correlates of child abuse were present, perhaps partly because Mary had close relationships with a circle of family and friends.[11] But the level of tension and worry in the household, the periodic fighting between parents, and the occasional splitting up probably caused anxieties in the children and interfered with their healthy development. Some of the children may have developed feelings of guilt, or may have failed to develop autonomy and initiative, since there was no way they could control what meant most to them – their parents and family life. Clearly the risks to the children resulted *not* from any inadequacy in Mary as a mother, but from the fact that many problems pressed in on the family, making her less able to do the kind of mothering of which she was otherwise capable.

Observations in this home and in many others showed that the quality and quantity of mothering given to children was a barometer of how well or badly things were going in the home at any given time. In most cases, minimal nurturing occurred only during periods of tension and upheaval in the home, and thus had very little to do with a woman's adequacy or inadequacy as a mother, very little to do with her valuing of or knowledge about being a nurturant mother. It seems clear that what was needed in those crucial years was neither removal of the children from the home, nor parent education, but a multifaceted support program for the household.

One can imagine a different scenario for the Cranes, based on a coordinated program of intensive services and supports. If Bill had received pay more adequate to the family's needs, or had been given assistance in finding the right kind of job, perhaps he would not have gone through a period of joblessness, changing jobs, and drinking; perhaps he would have felt more adequate as a husband and father, and therefore been somewhat more effective in these relationships. Extra income through a mechanism such as a guaranteed minimum income might have reduced the pressures and worries. And perhaps Mary could have received a small salary as a care-giver for her teenage sister.

Mary might have better satisfied her needs for social contacts and ego enhancement if she could have been involved in supportive interaction with other young mothers. Perhaps this could have taken the format of a playgroup for toddlers. It might even have been possible to organize a cooperative cottage-industry facility, in which the women could have produced some salable item (a craft, perhaps, or piecework for a factory) in a group setting, where their babies and young children could be brought along. Such a set-up might be quite attractive to women who need some income but cannot take on regular full-time work, partly because they do not want to put their young children into a day-care situation they regard as "institutional." Mary might also have eagerly participated in a mobile program bringing educational activities into homes with preschoolers.

Perhaps a home improvement grant would have enabled the Cranes to make their home a more safe, healthy, and convenient physical environment for youngsters. Adequate medical and dental services for all family members might have warded off later health problems, just as food stamps did help the family to eat reasonably well for a period. Various other supports and services might have been offered; though some might have been declined by the Cranes, who would have been actively involved in planning and decisions.

In all, this service package would have been designed by and for the entire household (including Mary's sister when she was living with them) and its entire complex tangle of problems and needs. The support program would not have been continued for more than a few years—just long enough to help the family avert or reduce some of the stresses and problems that can be particularly acute just when young children are most vulnerable. Later, Mary and Bill could well have managed on their own, as they have in fact done.

But in the meantime, the children would not have been negatively affected by the fact that their vulnerable years coincided with the years during which a young couple from a poverty-stricken background is also most vulnerable to economic, social, and emotional insecurity. The long-run beneficiaries are the children, who will become the next generation of adults.

Many aspects of such a multisupport program already exist in many communities: they should be encouraged, sufficiently funded, and coordinated vis-à-vis the individual family. Some coordinated programs for providing multiple supports to the young child's home environment have been tried on a pilot basis and for specific experimental or evaluative purposes.[12] But new ideas must continually be tried out, and successful pilot projects must be put into more widespread practice.[13]

10. Broadening Horizons

People who have grown up in rural poverty enter the adult world when they are in their middle or late teens. Often, however, they find themselves unprepared and unsuccessful at making their own way in the outside world. Consequently, they retreat to the home-haven. The knowledge that this refuge will always be open to them is a necessary security in the face of the high casualty rate they experience. The broadening of horizons can only be accomplished when there is a greater likelihood of satisfactory participation in the community. It may do little good to "expose" youngsters to the wonders of the outer world if the child sees them as belonging only to someone else's world. When restrictions and barriers are removed, horizons will almost automatically expand.

Young people need concrete help in realistically planning for their future and acquiring the variety of skills needed for standing solidly on their own. They need effective education, not just ten or twelve years of attendance in school. Some of the school-plus-employment combinations are particularly effective in this respect, and should be expanded. Basically, the goals of these programs are not so much a matter of stretching horizons as of helping young people reach the horizons they seek, helping them to deal effectively with the demands of adulthood—a stage they enter somewhat earlier than their middle-class agemates.

We can look more closely at the narrow horizons problem by examining one particular example, again from Mary Crane's family. Mary's sister Susan is seventeen, the mother of an infant, living in a somewhat tense situation with her parents, unmarried, and unsure.

Had Susan perceived real, reachable opportunities for herself in the broader community, and had she developed more effective ways of interacting with family and friends, at school and in the larger community, she might not have settled so young in life for narrowed horizons. It is possible that Susan became pregnant and kept her baby not out of ignorance of birth control, abortion, or adoption possibilities, but because she saw no other role in which she could succeed. One thing she could do to prove herself was to have a baby: becoming pregnant and giving birth was a public claim to competence. And Sue's mother, once over her initial anger about the pregnancy, encouraged Sue to keep the baby, hoping that this would make Sue grow up. (Possibly unsaid and unrealized was the fact that Sue's mother saw this new grandchild partly as her own child, as a chance to try again, as a child in whom she could place her hopes, now that her hopes for Susan seemed unlikely to be met.)

When the baby was born, Sue gained a whole bedroom just for herself and the baby—not only a physical gain of space, but an important symbol of her whole new definition and status. And there was a great deal of excitement and attention for both the new baby and for Sue. Her earlier problems were thus temporarily forgotten, sidestepped. But as the novelty of being a mother wore off, Susan's yearnings for friendship, love, and action with other teenagers surfaced again. She became restless at home, felt tied down by the baby, and was bewildered by her conflicting feelings toward the child.

In retrospect, one wonders if the signposts of trouble could have been spotted earlier. Pehaps there might have been other ways for Susan to escape from her unresolved childhood and teenage problems, other ways for her to earn status and recognition, other roles she could have filled, other means of showing competence.

Probably services and agencies and programs for all these needs were available within the community, but as often happens, people like Susan fall through the cracks—or hide in the cracks. By the time Susan was sixteen, becoming pregnant seemed, perhaps unconsciously, the only thing for her to do. At least it would release her from the frustrations of having to try to find a path for herself in the wider community, of having to stand on her own out there.

HELPING YOUNG PEOPLE PREPARE FOR THE WIDER WORLD. It is primarily because adult roles are taken on so soon afterwards that the later stages of childhood are critical in terms of people's horizons. This period is a watershed divide in their lives. And, importantly, late childhood and early adolescence is a period about which many of their parents feel particularly helpless, since the warm hugs, food treats, and verbal reassurances of "I love you" no longer seem appropriate or helpful. In many cases, parents are unable to help children prepare for entry into the larger world because the parents do not feel competent or confident in the interactional skills that facilitate successful participation in the world of schools, jobs, and community living. When the child was younger, the parent sent him off to school with the admonishment, "Now you behave yourself and don't cause trouble." Years later, as the grown child prepares to leave home, the parent's parting words are, "Remember, if things get too bad, you can always come home." Perhaps somewhere in between these two points some effective assistance could come from community programs.

To help young people broaden their horizons, it is essential that early encounters in the larger society be successful. One strategy to increase or insure success might be to provide a special program of specific training in interactive and practical adult-world skills. Small groups of young teenagers or preteens could be brought together in workshops to learn and practice ways of dealing with a boss, customer, social service worker, job counselor, teacher, and so on.

The program could be coupled with an existing youth job training program, and could be operated under the aegis of a community action agency (local antipoverty agency) or a community college. But the practical and interactive skills component would require some autonomy, so that it would not become diluted or diverted by the pressure in employment programs to meet a quota of job placements. Imaginative program design and careful planning stressing hands-on experiential training and keeping the needs, styles, and preferences of the adolescents uppermost would be essential. Assistance in conducting such a program could be sought from a variety of community resources. The instructors could include community employers, agency workers, and youth specialists. Young adults who had grown up in the community might be particularly effective as trainers, sharing the successes and difficulties of their encounters in the adult world. Role-playing sessions would enact job interviews, and dealings with service agencies and licensing bureaus. There could be actual experience in applying for Medicaid, getting a replacement birth certificate, obtaining working papers, a driver's license, or a Social Security card. There could also be sessions devoted to mental health and social skill topics such as how to release anger in a way that won't result in getting kicked out of school, losing a job, losing a girlfriend, or getting in trouble with parents or the law. Other sessions could deal with practical matters such as sex and birth control or nutrition—topics of natural interest and considerable importance for those who may be sexually active and searching for new models to follow, new roles to assume. (Particularly for girls approaching their childbearing years, awareness of the long-range importance of their nutritional health during prechildbearing adolescence could be stressed.)

Such a program would be designed to attract and accept a wide age range, say from twelve to twenty, with as little age separation as possible. The younger participants would be released from school and given school credit for their participation. Rather than wait until they have dropped out of school to participate in such a program, they could use the skills while they are still in school. The program might help them get more out of the remaining time they spend in school, or even encourage them to attend school more regularly or longer.

The extra effort to create and carry out such programs would pay extra dividends. The workshops would directly help young people develop skills their parents hadn't taught them, and thus increase their chances of successful early encounters with the outside world. As a side benefit, their adolescent years might be a little smoother because their newly developed skills could be applied to relationships with peers, girlfriends and boyfriends, and parents. They might be less motivated to leave their homes so early—and less likely to retreat to them so quickly after being knocked down in the first round.

If such programs helped make young adolescents more capable of success-fully dealing with community interactional situations, there would be long-term benefit in enabling them to believe that they *can* get along out there, that their horizons *can* be broader.[14]

Summing Up

The struggle against adversity has long been a central theme in the history of these stony, poor-soil hills—from the first white settlers who cleared the land, through the sons, grandsons, and newcomers who tried to adapt marginal farms to changing agricultural technology and modern marketing. Struggle against adversity is still the dominant theme for residents who seek to provide for their economic and social needs long after most farms have been abandoned and the small rural communities have collapsed. There have always been some individuals who have overcome the odds to win their struggle, but even some of those may have been unduly scarred by the ordeal. Many more have been beaten down by the struggle. Many are handicapped almost from the start, and fall farther and farther behind as they continue.

In the late twentieth century, the forces and circumstances to which rural people must adjust are different from those of earlier times. Today's hurdles cannot successfully be overcome by the traditional virtues of working hard and "making do." Furthermore, the new "community" to which people are in-escapably connected is, for them, merely a rather loose conglomerate of insti-tutions, agencies, and organizations, in which the traditional personal ap-proach does not bring results.

The people have also changed. To a large extent, rural poor people are no longer behind the times; their cultural values and consumption drives are those of the wider society. By and large, the people of these rural enclaves of poverty want to be accepted into the dominant community and society, to become "like anybody else." But they are seldom able to achieve this goal, and are often caught in the difficult position of having undersatisfied needs, unmet goals, and feelings of deprivation compared to the society around them.

Because of this discrepancy, poor people have to make adjustments in their behavior and personal surroundings, devising substitutes for what they lack, relying on each other for help they cannot obtain in the community, project-ing onto their children the hopes they once had for themselves, and insulating themselves against the pain of further rejection and failure by lowering their aspirations, hedging against disappointment, restricting their participation, and reducing their commitment. In all aspects of life, these patterns of behavior represent an attempt to adjust to an unrewarding life situation, and the attempt itself places great stress on personal and social integration.

The behavioral patterns described in this book are mechanisms for adjusting to the difficult situation of continued poverty and marginality. However, these coping strategies are usually interpreted by others as evidence of character defects or faulty socialization, or as proof of deviant values. The struggles of individuals and families usually go unrecognized or misinter-preted. Dogged work brings only the demand that they work harder, or that more of them work. A decision to forgo certain material comforts for the sake of an occasional prestige item brings only condemnation for wasteful spen-ding. And individual initiative to forge one's own compromise solutions draws scorn from the community for living in an unacceptable manner.

The real tragedy of these small enclaves of marginality and poverty is that people are playing a game of life that has been structured in such a way that they are required to play but prevented from winning. Engulfed in an amor-phous urbanized community, they lack social-structural links to give them clear avenues of entry, and social distance is maintained by the force of strong negative stereotypes. Although most people attempt to play the game by the accepted rules, there is little reinforcement and positive reward for doing so. If they attempt to play the game differently, or to stop playing entirely, the penalties are severe. For most people, it is a discouraging and consuming struggle, often taking a psychological toll that makes them even less likely to be successful.

People caught in this bind can only survive by means of the adjustments they have forged, scraping along as best they can, keeping open their options to maneuver and carry on as they see fit in the circumstances. Taken as a whole, these adaptive mechanisms constitute a holding operation, a means of buying time while awaiting the development of a more favorable game situa-tion. Meanwhile, hopes are crushed, energies spent, and potential wasted.

From this perspective, it seems inescapable to conclude that what must be changed here is not the *people* who are poor and marginal, but the *situations* that make them so. If the negative situations that restrict and thwart people were removed and advantageous situations were substituted that enabled people to gain something recognizable from their efforts, society would not have to concern itself with trying to raise people's aspirations and broaden their horizons. If the game situations were restructured to allow some possibility of winning, people would play more eagerly and more successfully; and in playing more successfully, they would become more eager and suc-cessful people. Rural people emerging from poverty will, themselves, raise their aspirations; they will expand their own horizons. The responsibility of society at large is to change and improve the situations, to work to erase the primary causes of rural poverty. The secondary, derived causes, which are no more than adaptations to and results of the primary causes, will not require as much attention.

*   *   *

Entrenched economic poverty and psychosocial marginality need not continue to blight America's rural hinterlands. This anthropological analysis of
one specific case has demonstrated that better understanding of a situation
can provide insight into ways of improving it. The book shows that rural
poverty is a problem with many facets and many causes, that it is a self-
perpetuating cycle; but this final chapter suggests that there are points at
which the cycle could be broken.

Attempts to ameliorate the situation will only be effective, however, if they
fit the specific context in which the problems exist. Solutions must be designed to produce this fit, tailored to meet the specific needs of different ages,
sizes, situations, abilities, interests, and preferences. Just as there is no single,
simple cause of rural poverty, so there can be no single, simple solution.

The development of specially designed, multifaceted approaches to eradi-
cating rural poverty could benefit from additional social research in a variety
of other locations. Research could help identify the particular needs and
clarify the various causal factors operating in specific situations and in the
general category of long-term, nonfarm rural poverty. The focus of such
research on rural poverty (or on poverty anywhere, for that matter) should be
on understanding how poor people perceive and cope with their circumstances, not on demonstrating how poor people differ from some hypothetical middle-class model. It is important to understand poverty situations
well before planning for their amelioration; it is important to understand the
viewpoint of the intended beneficiaries before rushing in headlong with programs. Anthropological research can help fill this need.

This study also indicates that any proposals developed to deal with nonfarm rural poverty must leave several options open to rural people emerging
from generations of poverty, for even in a tiny population there are significant
differences among people. For some rural people, assistance in making a
satisfactory transition into an urban environment may be desirable and/or
necessary. But rural people must not be forced to move to cities as the only
means of achieving economic security, must not be forced into cities as the
only escape from the problems currently blighting rural areas. There must be,
also, the option of improved situations for rural people where they are. Rural
people should not be required to cut off their sustaining roots and ties in the
rural area as the price for gaining a decent position in the wider society.
Similarly, rural people should not be forced by unleashed marketplace determinants into becoming nomadic wanderers, following employment boomlets
around the country or attempting always to find a depressed rural area where
they can set down their trailer home. Our society *can* control and tame the

economic forces that displace people. Our social scientists need not always be studying the casualties of historical processes. The manmade social and economic blight that grips much of the no-longer-agricultural regions of rural America should be subject to more control and cure than was the natural fungus blight that wiped out the chestnut trees of the northeastern hillsides.

Whatever solutions are worked out must build on the strengths that rural people already have. The people of rural poverty are clever at devising ingenious substitutes; they are determined to make do, on their own if possible; they help each other out, care for their disabled members, and maintain lifelong parent-child obligations of providing a home. The people of these rural poverty-stricken areas are extremely perceptive, as the quotations in this book should testify: they could certainly help design programs, solutions, and futures. They are committed to the belief that their children can share in the American Dream; and they urgently want to help their children gain a share of that dream.

Solutions will have to involve changes in society as a whole, and in the many particular communities where poverty-stricken populations remain enclaved on the margins. New opportunities for successful economic participation, new public attitudes, and new social bridges are needed. These can provide the means to make improvement possible. If these better situations become available, the people whose lives have heretofore been dominated by the tenacious blight of rural poverty will eagerly take advantage of them. The people of Chestnut Valley sometimes put a new twist on an old saying: "Where there's a way, there's a will."

Notes

Chapter 1

1. The observations recounted here were made over the course of several days in February 1971, and blended together to construct a realistic total day. In order to protect the anonymity of individuals being studied, family names and place names have been changed. Out of concern for the privacy of informants, identifying personal details have been omitted or altered. (See Chapter 2 for a fuller discussion of the ethical considerations of informant privacy.) The blurring of distinguishing aspects of Mary Crane and her family not only protects privacy, it also produces a family scene that is typical of many others in rural poverty.

The "day in a family" setting is a device Oscar Lewis used in his books (1961, 1966a, and especially 1962) and in his teaching as a vivid means of conveying, illustrating, and summarizing a large number of separate observations made in homes at various times. The device has been effectively used by others (e.g., Howell, 1973).

Chapter 2

1. For an eloquent demonstration of this position, see Lewis (1961, 1966a), the work of Robert Coles (e.g., 1971) and Rubin (1976).

2. I would argue, however, that a "culture of poverty" theory is not applicable as an explanation for similarities in observed behavior in this case – if indeed it is in any case. The culture of poverty theory neither fits nor explains the data. Readers interested in pursuing the debate over the theory are referred to Lewis (1966b) and to critics such as Valentine (1968) and Leacock (1971).

3. A similar position is clearly stated by Stack (1974, pp. 22–23) with respect to "pathology" in Black family structure.

4. For some interesting similarities in observed behavior patterns in urban poverty areas involving different regional, racial, or ethnic variables, see Liebow (1967), Hannerz (1969), Howell (1973), Stack (1974), and Valentine (1978). Some of the studies done in southern Appalachia show many similarities, and some interesting differences. See Weller (1965), Fetterman (1967), Gazaway (1969), Coles (1971), Loof (1971), and Schwarzweller (1971). A multidisciplinary study of a rural depressed area in Nova Scotia shows striking parallels: see Hughes (1960), Leighton (1965), and Stone (1966). Recent studies in Oregon point to pertinent similarities (Newton, 1977).

5. For example, in my own work as a consultant and trainer in poverty-related programs in various states, I have found that paraprofessionals working with low-income families are struck as I am by the many similarities we find in widely separated poverty situations. When I have used "A Day with Mary Crane" as a basis for group discussion, a number of workers have said Mary and her situation sound much like the families they work with in their rural localities.

6. The government's official poverty counts show not only that poverty still exists, but also that it has not steadily declined over the years. A significant decrease did occur through the 1960s, but progress since 1968 has been halting: in 1968, the government counted 25.4 million poor people; by 1973-74, about 23 million were poor; but by 1976, the figure had increased to 25 million. (See Rodgers, 1979, pp. 9, 19-20.)

It is important to note that, contrary to public impression, poverty is a particularly severe problem in rural areas. In fact, the incidence of poverty is higher in rural areas—roughly 25 percent, compared to 15 percent in urban areas and 12.5 percent in the nation as a whole. While approximately 30 percent of the total U.S. population was rural in 1970, approximately 40 percent of the poverty population was rural.

Chapter 3

1. For an overview of agricultural change in New York State, see Hedrick (1933) and Gates (1969). A community study conducted in the Southern Tier region of the state (Vidich and Bensman, 1958) identifies historical trends similar to those operating in Chestnut Valley. Hurd (1879) presents a useful early history, showing population trends.

Useful context for this historical study has come from the many pamphlets published by the Cornell University Agricultural Experiment Station, New York State College of Agriculture, Ithaca, New York. See especially: Warren and Livermore (1911), Vaughan (1929), Melvin (1931), LaMont (1939), Hill (1943), Anderson (1954, 1958).

2. The historical approach to sociological analysis of the sweeping changes in rural society is well illustrated by the Rural Life Studies of the United States Department of Agriculture. The study of Landaff, New Hampshire (MacLeish, 1942) illustrates the less compressed development period in the Northeast.

3. The soils are chiefly Lordstown, Mardin, or Volushia channery silt loam (United States Department of Agriculture, 1965).

4. I am indebted to Professor Stanley Warren of the Cornell University College of Agriculture for a discussion of the handicaps presented by soil and topography in different types and periods of agriculture.

5. Valuable source materials revealing patterns of acquiring farms include old diaries, farm account books, and early newspaper articles. I am grateful to individuals who shared such materials with me.

6. An elderly man vividly recalls his first sight of deer, around 1912. A Chestnut Valley woman, writing a correspondence column for the county seat's newspaper in 1920, felt it newsworthy to report that a pair of deer had recently been seen.

7. See Warren and Livermore (1911).

8. Useful documentation comes from the newspapers of nearby small cities. Each newspaper carried weekly columns from all the rural hamlets in its area. Documenting

farm turnover are many entries such as: "The [Jones] place has been sold to. . . ."; "The [Smith] heirs, all in Massachusetts, have sold the [Smith] farm to. . . ."; "Mr. and Mrs. [Green] have taken possession of the [Waters] place."

9. Conklin and Starbird (1958) note this as a general pattern for the state's low-income rural areas.

10. See Warren and Livermore (1911) and LaMont (1939).

Chapter 4

1. Studies conducted by rural sociologists suggest that there were antecedents for stratification in the late 1920s. In rural areas where agriculture had been seriously declining, there were significant differences in the standard of living and in participation in formal social organizations. (See Melvin, 1931, for example.) In later studies of several rural areas, Anderson (1954, 1958) found that unemployed people ranked lowest in participation in formal social activities and organizations.

2. Conklin and Starbird (1958), in an overview study of low incomes in rural New York State, identified these same two sources of the rural poverty population.

Chapter 5

1. The official definition of poverty is based on a figure that reflects income, household size, and current cost of living. The exact poverty level in a given year is set by the government according to a rather complex procedure, but it is essentially a gross income that would permit a family to obtain a minimally adequate diet if it spent one-third of its income on food.

Further explanation reveals the meagerness and arbitrariness of this definition. The basis for the poverty line is the cost of food. The minimal cost of adequate food for a family of a given size in any given year is figured by the U.S. Department of Agriculture at current market prices (actually using a 1965 index, updated every six months to reflect current Consumer Price Index). This figure represents the current cost of the "economy" or "thrifty" diet plan. Although the Department of Agriculture considers this "economy plan" diet to be nutritionally adequate only for "temporary, emergency use when funds are low," it is this cheaper diet, rather than the USDA's "basic low-cost plan" that is used in calculating the official poverty level.

The annual cost of the economy food plan is figured for each household size. This cost figure is then multiplied by 3, since government studies in 1955 showed that lower income families were spending about one-third of their income on food. The resultant figure represents the annual income a family would need to be able to purchase the economy diet (meeting temporary, emergency levels of nutritional adequacy). Any household with an income below this calculated level is officially poor, and every one above this level is officially not poor.

Various adjustments are made in calculating the poverty level: for farm families (who might not need to spend as much as one-third of their income on food) the poverty level is lower; for Alaska and Hawaii the level is higher; and for households headed by women, adjustments are made upward.

Using this formula, the official poverty level for a nonfarm family of four in 1970 was

$3,968 (this figure was derived from the 1970 cost of the economy diet, $1,323, multiplied by 3). In 1975, due to inflation, the poverty level for the same four-person family was $5,550. Any family of four below this income level was officially poor in that year. As of April 1980, the poverty line for a nonfarm family of four was $7,450.

There is growing awareness, even in government circles, that poverty cannot be adequately defined by absolute dollars per household, particularly when levels are set by such inadequate food-cost guidelines. Federal programs in the late 1970s often included as eligible not only people below the poverty line, but also those with slightly higher incomes, "up to 125 percent of poverty." Many people feel that if income is to be used as the basis of the definition, it should not be in absolute dollars but in dollars relative to the national median income at the time. A new definition of "low income" was included in the Housing and Community Development Amendments Act for 1979, dealing with the Farmers' Home Administration rural housing program: low income is defined as being at or below 80 percent of the median income of the area, as determined by the USDA (Rural Housing Alliance, *The RHA Reporter*, January 1980).

Definitions of poverty—the government's absolute definition and proposed relative definitions—are discussed in Rodgers (1979, pp. 17–38).

2. This pattern of avoiding management/supervisory positions is an interesting parallel to a pattern in the earlier farming period. Some men who had no flair for making farm-management decisions gravitated into the occupational niche of permanent farm laborers, and they remained hired hands for a lifetime, or else went into urban unskilled labor.

3. Roe (1973) conducted a comprehensive multidisciplinary study of the health status of women on welfare in some upstate New York communities. Her team found many longstanding medical and health problems that seriously affected employability and employment history of low-income women.

4. Some explanation of the food stamp program may be useful here. It was phased in nationally in 1969 and 1970, after pilot projects had demonstrated that it would be an improvement over the government's earlier food assistance program, the donated commodities program. For the period of this research, the food stamp program operated basically as follows.

A household certified as eligible is assigned a monthly food stamp allotment amount, determined by household size and composition, and by the cost of the USDA's "economy food plan." In 1974, for example, a family of four was allotted $142 worth of food stamps a month. To obtain the stamps, the recipient paid a purchase price based on the household's income relative to its size. In 1974, the family of four with an adjusted monthly income of $210 paid $59 for their $142 allotment of food stamps, whereas a four-person household with an income of $450 (maximum eligible) paid $118 for the same $142 worth of stamps.

The difference between the purchase price and the allotment amount is called the "bonus." In the first case, the bonus is $83; in the second case it is $24. The bonus is always greater for the household with lower per-capita income. The bonus represents the amount the government is paying into the household's food budget.

The participating family purchases its food stamps at a bank or other designated location once or twice a month, and spends the coupons on food items any time at any participating store. Food stamp purchase requirements, bonuses, and allotments have been revised upward regularly. In 1976, the four-person family with a $210 monthly net income paid $59, but received $166 worth of stamps (a bonus of $107).

In 1979, the food stamp program was changed to eliminate the cash purchase requirement. An eligible family now pays nothing, but collects a packet of coupons equivalent to the bonus level to which the household is entitled (still figured on the basis of household size, composition, and income). The cash that previously went toward purchasing stamps may now be spent directly on food – or on anything else. Those with no available cash can obtain the bonus food stamps, and thus can participate in the program.

Chapter 6

1. For an interesting and relevant study of spending decisions made by rural white poor people in Oregon, see Newton (1977). Her analysis of spending decisions provides concrete evidence that people allocate their meager economic resources rationally.

2. Perhaps it is worth noting here that this quoted passage, like all the others, is verbatim and unchanged. (In this case, the passage was tape-recorded because the informant was so articulate about money management and had so much to say on the subject.) These passages hardly fit the stereotyped notion of inability to defer gratifications or inability to plan for the future. Nor do they bear out the stereotypes that people who are poor cannot express themselves intelligently.

3. See Rubin (1976, pp. 199–200) for a description of this phenomenon among working-class people who grew up in poverty. Rubin also finds that the campers and boats people purchase are seldom used because the owners are too busy taking on extra jobs to pay for the items.

4. For a more complete description, see Fitchen (1977).

5. See Rubin (1976, pp. 161–67) for an interesting description and analysis of how working-class people responded to her query about what they'd do if they suddenly inherited a million dollars. In most cases, the answers were narrow and drab, confined mostly to, "I'd pay off all our debts."

Chapter 7

1. The sample was too small, and the time too short, to indicate whether this natural longevity built upon determination to "try one more time" is characteristic of the current generation of young adults. It would seem that the recent marriages of young people are just as tension-filled and rocky as the earlier married years of the previous generation. Whether today's young couples will stick it out remains to be seen. In any case, they seem no more divorce-prone than the rest of society, and possibly less so. Like their parents, young adults from the rural poverty enclaves believe in the importance of keeping the family intact for the sake of their children.

Parents tend to urge their grown children to marry their live-in mates, and to give a tenuous marriage one more try. However, the young adults are also a part of their own generation: they seem more accustomed to the fact of unwed motherhood, and they are not as concerned about divorce.

2. The high probability that both husband and wife had difficult childhoods is the

result of two factors: (1) the high incidence of family disruption in the preceding generation of rural low-income families, and (2) the pattern of socioeconomic endogamy, in which people from the rural depressed areas are likely to marry people of similar socioeconomic backgrounds.

3. This is in contrast to the more distinct lines and clear understandings between a young mother and her mother in the Black, urban families studied by Stack (1974). There, the very young mother might give over her first baby's care to her mother completely, and in so doing assign over the motherhood role, rights, and responsibilities. Although such an arrangement is not unknown in Chestnut Valley, it is rare, and did not occur during the decade of research.

Chapter 8

1. More of the younger mothers now appear to be breast-feeding their babies than was previously the case, but bottle-feeding seems still to predominate. The observed sample was too small for meaningful quantitative statements.

2. Specific documentation on the timetable of growing up was not obtained, nor was a sufficiently large number of individuals observed going through the successive stages to make definitive statements. Despite these shortcomings, the apparent patterns and timetables seem worth noting.

Chapter 9

1. As stated in Chapter 2, the few Chestnut Valley households who were not long-term poor and were not effectively included as neighbors were not among the families closely studied, for this is not a total-community study, but a study of rural poverty.

2. As the present cohort of people who were young children in 1969 reaches adulthood, it appears (although there are too few cases to be conclusive) that marriage partners are being drawn from a wider geographical area, including not only local neighborhoods but also nearby cities. Partners may come from families who previously did not know each other. Additionally, the selection of residential locations may now include a wider area, including the urban centers, in part because some young couples rent an apartment in the city or a trailer or house in another rural area, using cash assistance from social services if necessary, rather than living in their parents' back yard rent-free.

These new patterns exist alongside the more traditional patterns of mate selection and residence location. If the newer pattern increases, the kin-relatedness of the rural poverty neighborhood would correspondingly decrease. But at present, the kin pattern seems likely to continue because the older patterns are still strong. Furthermore, even those young adults who initially locate outside the home area tend to move back to it later.

Chapter 10

1. Similar racial prejudices were expressed by white, low-income urban residents in Howell's (1973) study in the Washington, D.C. area.

2. It should be noted that the absence of an intermediate-level social mechanism to pull together the multiplicity of parallel ties among individuals or families on one level and institutions or agencies on the other level is not unique to this setting or to its historical causes. Both suburbia and urban metropolis may suffer from the lack of built-in cohesive local-level units joining constituent individuals or families together vis-à-vis the large, amorphous community. But in the case of rural poor people, the situation is more serious because there are also economic, social, and attitudinal barriers to participation.

3. This attitude toward problems as unavoidable things that have to be put up with is apparently very common among poor people. I have found it mentioned or recognized by paraprofessionals working with low-income families in many settings – urban, rural, eastern, midwestern, Black, Puerto Rican, Mexican-American, and American Indian. I would not conclude, however, that this proves the existence of a "sense of hopelessness" or "fatalism" as part of a "culture of poverty." In fact, people seem to believe that problems – in general – are solvable. It's just that they see their own specific problems as unsolvable because they have had no experience to prove otherwise.

4. These hesitancies have been observed in the actions or inactions of many people as they stall and procrastinate after having finally agreed to try to get some help on a problem. When I accompanied individuals on their dreaded first visits to agencies – at their request only – their anxiety was reduced, and I gained insight into how help-seeking looks from the point of view of the seeker.

5. This same wait-and-see attitude was found in southern Appalachia (Weller, 1965).

Chapter 11

1. Conklin and Starbird (1958) saw this as a general pattern in the "abandoned farm areas" of New York State, and as the reason for the continuation of "chronically low incomes of nonfarm open-country residents" (p. 29). They foresaw the problem as likely to continue.

2. See, for example, Anderson (1954, 1958).

3. By both an absolute income standard (such as the government's present definition of poverty) and by a relative income standard (comparing income to the national median) the people of this study would be defined as poor. Even in their best periods, they remain within the income zone defined by the government as "under 125 percent of poverty." Townsend (1970, p. 225) proposed a definition of poverty that is particularly relevant here: "individuals and families whose resources, over time, fall seriously short of the resources commanded by the average individual or family in the community in which they live, whether that community is a local, national or international one, are in poverty."

4. No precise data were obtained on nutritional levels and medical status, but accumulated observations over the years point to a suspicious number of health problems, from mild to severe, that may have been caused, complicated, or prolonged by certain deficiencies in diet, poor sanitation, and other physical situations. Documentation of correlations between poverty and health in a similar population can be found in

Roe's (1973) study of health and nutritional status among poor women in upstate New York. Nutritional problems, dental problems, and various long-term disabilities such as diabetes were found to be common in the low-income sample she examined, and clearly contributed to the spotty employment histories and frequent unemployability that was found among the women. The study included careful medical examinations and lengthy medical histories of more than 450 women.

5. Concerning props for self-presentation, see Goffman (1959). Also of interest here are the striking similarities between economic management techniques found among rural New York's poor people and those reported for rural low-income Oregonians (Newton, 1977).

6. Kai Erikson's (1976) study of the psychosocial effects of the sudden loss of community in the Buffalo Creek Dam disaster provides an interesting analogy. It helps to see what is lacking in places that have more gradually suffered a loss of community, if no substitute is provided. Among other results, he found a "loss of connection," a sense of separation from others and from the self, a difficulty in relating to others, each individual nursing his own hurts, tending his own business.

7. Several studies have shown the effects of inadequate local-level social structure in inhibiting the formation of a definition of the self. Gearing (1970, especially p. 148) illustrates the situation among Fox Indians in Iowa. Powdermaker (1939), in an early study of a southern community, shows that the brunt of frustrations encountered by Blacks in their participation in the wider community falls upon their marriage relationships.

The negative effects of a structural vacuum is analyzed in studies of eastern agricultural migrant workers (Friedland and Nelkin, 1971, and Nelkin, 1970), which reveal a "we-they" polarity. And in a depressed rural neighborhood in Nova Scotia, interdisciplinary studies revealed the negative social and psychological effects of inadequate local-level social structure (Hughes, 1960).

8. Leacock (1971, pp. 9-37) illustrates what she refers to as "structured discrimination" against lower-class pupils in the schools.

9. Excellent examples of the effects of stereotypes may be found in various parts of the Nova Scotia project on "Psychiatric Disorder and Sociocultural Environment" (Hughes et al., 1960, and Leighton, 1965). A related article (Stone et al., 1966) shows that far greater individual success is possible if a man can migrate beyond the reach of the stereotypes, for there he can obtain a good job and have the opportunity to prove himself as an employee.

The stereotypic perception of a marginal and poor neighborhood on the fringes of a larger community is illustrated in Vidich and Bensman (1958). The authors point out that the presence of the "shack people" serves an important social function for the larger community: a baseline, the very bottom standard for invidious comparison. Unfortunately, the authors appear to have swallowed whole the community's stereotypes about "the shack people," for they report that shack people respond only to immediate circumstances and reject or are ignorant of middle-class patterns and life styles (see especially pp. 69-71). Closer observation of the people, rather than reliance on community stereotypes, might have yielded a different explanation.

10. An interesting historical parallel here is that earlier in this century disasters such as barn fires were often the turning point that forced a marginal subsistence farmer to

go under, whereas a more successful farmer–operating on a cash basis, banking his profits, and protected by insurance–could rebuild and continue farming.

11. The same patterns are revealed in Howell (1973, p. 355). Some of his urban
white informants were described as "hard living"–indicative of a life style of intensity,
drama, and liquor that was the opposite of what they claimed to want. This pattern
resulted from their perception of the futility of striving for higher goals, and was "a way
of rebelling against the life circumstances one found himself in."

12. A sociopsychological study that reveals the important role of the failure syndrome in limiting job success is Goodwin (1972). Using quantitative methodology
based on questionnaires, Goodwin reached the same generalization that I have arrived
at by participant-observation. The phenomenon has also been observed by other traditional anthropological researchers: Liebow (1967) and Howell (1973).

13. This minimization of risks does not mean that people are generally cautious in all
things. It is risk of personal failure, risk of ego-damage, that they try to avoid when
possible. Risk of physical danger, on the other hand, is often undertaken, both knowingly and unknowingly, and may serve other psychological needs. Examples of risks
people commonly take, where risk could be reduced if desired, are quite obvious in connection with their use of vehicles. Babies and small children are seldom strapped into
car seats, but sit in laps or stand on the seat. Adults rarely use seat belts. Young boys
court danger doing stunts on bicycles, snowmobiles, and motorbikes. Their older
brothers and their fathers court physical danger and legal penalty in occasional bursts
of high-speed driving, in purposeful skidding on slippery roads, in driving occasionally
without a valid license, registration, or insurance.

14. The concept of psychological deficits derived from circumstances that inhibit or
truncate development at certain critical stages of early life comes from Erikson,
Childhood and Society (1963 edition, pp. 247–69). A relevant view of the etiology,
nature, and results of these deficits in a setting in Nova Scotia much like the one described here is found in Beiser (1965). An especially interesting work is *Appalachia's
Children* (Loof, 1971), which finds almost no emotional deprivation in infancy, but
significant problems of overly dependent personality disorders in children. Loof finds
children have satisfying relationships with their mothers and consequently are well
trained in relatedness, but are not trained well in acquiring controls over their ag-
gressive impulses.

Chapter 12

1. See Fitchen (1977).

2. Even the 1 percent loans available through Section 502 of the Farmers' Home Administration for providing a water supply, sewage disposal, bathrooms, central heating,
and so forth may not be within the grasp of people who simply cannot afford $700 for a
well and water system, no matter how low the interest or how spread-out the
payments. Some people simply cannot commit themselves to meeting payments regularly for up to thirty-three years.

3. By 1978, the province and mandate of the Department of Housing and Urban
Development had clearly been extended to include rural areas and small communities
in housing programs. At least on the level of demonstration projects, both Farmers'

Home Administration and HUD were making progress on low-income housing in rural areas. But significant housing assistance programs have been slow and meager in the rural areas, even by the government's own admission (Task Force on Rural and Non-Metropolitan Areas, 1978). Some loan regulations have been loosened, but increased flexibility on paper does not often translate into action, particularly when funding levels for the loan programs are consistantly far below need levels.

4. Rodgers (1979) evaluates past and current programs for overcoming poverty. He stresses full employment as the most important strategy, but also cites the need for a negative income tax to "provide a guaranteed liveable income to those unable to work" (p. 204). Williamson et al. (1975, p. 211) also conclude their comprehensive review of antipoverty strategies with the view that the negative income tax proposals, if enacted, would have "the greatest potential for a major impact on the extent of poverty and economic inequality in America."

5. For a comprehensive study of the effects on the family of the employment of the mother, see Feldman (1972). This study was based on a variety of research methodologies, including long-term studies as well as quantitative large-scale sampling, to investigate the interaction of work histories and family situations among low-income women in upstate New York communities.

6. At the end of 1979, the Carter administration, noting some of the special, unanswered needs of rural areas, announced its policy for rural America. (See The RHA Reporter, January 1980.) Carter proposed the creation of an Undersecretary of Agriculture for Small Community and Rural Development. This new branch of the USDA could be of great significance for rural Americans. It would identify and assess possible impacts that federal actions and decisions might have on rural areas. It would also provide an official advocate to help rural areas compete more successfully in the scramble for federal funds. This advocacy seems necessary because many federal funding allocation formulas discriminate against rural areas. For example, sparsely populated areas and rural counties that do not have a hospital may be effectively excluded from participation in a federally funded food assistance program, the Women, Infants and Children program (known as WIC). Other examples of funding discrimination against low-density areas are found in education aid formulas, where eligiblity for aid is based on percentages of low-income children in a school district (which may be lower in rural or consolidated districts than in inner-city districts).

New York State has established a specific official bureau to address the needs of rural areas.

7. In 1971, a high-level commission was appointed by the New York State Legislature to look into elementary and secondary education in the state. The commission (generally known as the Fleishmann Committee) came to the conclusion that "the biggest problem in the state is the high correlation between school success or failure and the student's socio-economic and racial origins. . . . [C]hildren from low-income and minority backgrounds fail in school in numbers which far exceed their proportion of the state's total population " (New York State Commission on the Quality, Cost and Financing of Elementary and Secondary Education, 1972, Vol. 1, p. 1.2). The commission report dismisses any possibility of different intellectual abilities correlating with socioeconomic status, stating that it had no "persuasive evidence" that a child's "innate ability correlates with family income, race, sex, parental occupation or ethnicity"

(Vol. 1, p. 1.29). The blame for low performance was laid squarely on the schools. "New York is not providing equality of educational opportunity to its students as long as the pattern of school success and school failure remains closely tied to a child's social origins" (Vol. 1, p. 1.2). The commission went on to say firmly, "the close parallel between school success and the child's socio-economic origin suggests that something is wrong with the way our educational system operates" (Vol. 1, p. 1.29).

8. Stack (1974, p. 71) emphasizes the same point with respect to low-income Blacks in an urban setting in the Midwest. "Statistical patterns do not divulge underlying cultural patterns. This confusion between statistics and cultural patterns underlies most interpretations of Black family life."

9. Erikson (1963 edition, p. 260) says, "The child's danger, at this stage, lies in a sense of inadequacy and inferiority."

10. Lazar et al. (1977, p. 27–31) evaluate a variety of preschool experiences, including Head Start and Home Start. They note the important long-range effects of increased parental involvement, although they admit that the precise effect has not been adequately measured. Unofficial evaluative comments by various personnel connected with local Head Start programs underscore the value of the home-centered components of the program.

11. A follow-up study (Elmer, 1967) of families of urban children who had been hospitalized with injuries resulting from abuse by parents indicates that child abuse by mothers is most likely to occur when the predisposing factors of emotional difficulties of mother, negative attitudes toward child, and lack of adequate social connections for mother are exacerbated in a situation of constant stress such as that fostered by poverty.

12. An effective demonstration project of this sort is reported in *A Second Chance for Families* (Jones, Neuman, and Shyne, 1976). This project, funded by the New York State Department of Social Services, "tested and demonstrated the effectiveness of intensive family services in averting or shortening placement" of children in foster care (p. 124). The evaluation found that a carefully planned program of intensive services tailored to the specific needs of the family was less costly but more beneficial to the child and his family than letting the family fend for itself in the community service network. Both the number of incidents of foster placement and the duration of placement were reduced in families that received the intensive coordinated family services.

13. Funding for such programs might be sought from a variety of sources and categories, including state monies for assisting children (such as, in New York State, the Division for Youth), regional development programs (such as the Appalachian Regional Commission, which includes this section of the state), and federal anti-poverty funds (through the Community Services Administration, formerly the Office of Economic Opportunity).

14. For this type program, private foundations and local employers might provide financial support. Public funds might come from local youth program monies, state youth funds (Division for Youth), and regional and federal grants (Appalachian Regional Commission and Community Services Administration).

Bibliography

Anderson, Walfred A.
  1954   "Social Change in a Central New York Rural Community." Ithaca, N.Y.:
          Cornell University Agricultural Experiment Station. Bulletin 907.
  1958   "Social Participation of Rural Nonfarm Adults." Ithaca, N.Y.: Cornell
          University Agricultural Experiment Station. Bulletin 928.
Beiser, Morton
  1965   "Poverty, Social Disintegration and Personality." *The Journal of Social
          Issues.* Vol. XXI, no. 1, pp. 56–78.
Coles, Robert
  1967   *Children of Crisis.* Boston: Atlantic-Little, Brown.
  1971   *Migrants, Sharecroppers and Mountaineers,* Volume II of *Children of
          Crisis.* Boston: Atlantic-Little, Brown.
Conklin, Howard E. and Irving R. Starbird
  1958   *Low Incomes in Rural New York State.* State of New York Interdepart-
          mental Committee on Low Incomes.
Elmer, Elizabeth
  1967   *Children in Jeopardy: A Study of Abused Minors and Their Families.* Pitts-
          burgh: University of Pittsburgh Press.
Erikson, Erik H.
  1950   *Childhood and Society.* (2nd edition, 1963). New York: W. W. Norton &
          Company.
Erikson, Kai T.
  1976   "Loss of Community at Buffalo Creek." *American Journal of Psychiatry.*
          Vol. 133, no. 3, pp. 302–05.
Feldman, Harold et al.
  1972   *A Study of the Effects on the Family Due to Employment of the Welfare
          Mother.* A Report to the Manpower Administration, U.S. Department of
          Labor.
Fetterman, John
  1967   *Stinking Creek.* New York: E. P. Dutton.
Fitchen, Janet M.
  1977   "Special Housing Problems of the Rural Poor." Washington, D.C.: Rural
          Housing Alliance.
Friedland, William H. and Dorothy Nelkin

1971   Migrant: Agricultural Workers in America's Northeast. New York: Holt,
         Rinehart & Winston.
Gans, Herbert
1962   The Urban Villagers. New York: Macmillan.
1970   "Poverty and Culture: Some Basic Questions about Methods of Studying
         Life-Styles of the Poor." In Townsend, 1970, pp. 146–64.
Gates, Paul W.
1969   "Agricultural Change in New York State." In New York History.
         Cooperstown: New York State Historical Association, pp. 115–41.
Gazaway, Rena
1969   The Longest Mile. Garden City, N.Y.: Doubleday.
Gearing, Frederick O.
1970   The Face of the Fox. Chicago: Aldine.
Goffman, Erving
1959   The Presentation of Self in Everyday Life. Garden City, N.Y.: Doubleday.
Goodwin, Leonard
1972   Do the Poor Want to Work? A Social-Psychological Study of Work Orienta-
         tions. Washington, D.C.: The Brookings Institution.
Hannerz, Ulf
1969   Soulside: Inquiries into Ghetto Culture and Community. New York: Co-
         lumbia University Press.
Hedrick, Ulysses Prentiss
1933   A History of Agriculture in the State of New York (1966 edition). New
         York: Hill and Wang.
Hill, F. F.
1943   Erin: The Economic Characteristics of a Rural Town in Southern New York.
         Ithaca: New York State College of Agriculture, Department of Agricul-
         tural Economics.
Howell, Joseph T.
1973   Hard Living on Clay Street. Garden City, N. Y.: Doubleday, Anchor.
Hughes, Charles C., M. A. Tremblay, R. N. Rapoport, and A. H. Leighton
1960   People of Cove and Woodlot: Communities from the Viewpoint of Social
         Psychiatry. New York: Basic Books.
Hurd, Duane H.
1879   History of Tioga, Chemung, Tompkins and Schuyler Counties, New York.
         Philadelphia: Everets & Ensign.
Jones, Mary Ann, R. Neuman, and A. W. Shyne
1976   A Second Chance for Families: Evaluation of a Program to Reduce Foster
         Care. New York: Child Welfare League of America.
LaMont, T. E.
1939   "State Reforestation in Two New York Counties: The Story of the Land
         and the People." Ithaca, N.Y.: Cornell University Agricultural Experi-
         ment Station. Bulletin 712.
Lazar, Irving et al.
1977   "The Persistence of Preschool Effects: A Long-Term Follow-up of Four-
         teen Infant and Preschool Experiments." Washington, D.C.: Department

of Health, Education, and Welfare.

Leacock, Eleanor Burke
1971   *The Culture of Poverty: A Critique.* New York: Simon & Schuster.

Leighton, Alexander H.
1965   "Poverty and Social Change." *Scientific American.* Vol. 212, no. 5, pp. 21–27.

Lewis, Oscar
1961   *The Children of Sanchez.* New York: Random House.
1962   *Five Families: Mexican Case Studies in the Culture of Poverty.* New York: John Wiley & Sons.
1966a   *La Vida: A Puerto Rican Family in the Culture of Poverty.* New York: Random House.
1966b   "The Culture of Poverty." *Scientific American.* Vol. 215, no. 4, pp. 19–25.

Liebow, Elliot
1967   *Tally's Corner: A Study of Negro Streetcorner Men.* Boston: Little, Brown.

Loof, David H.
1971   *Appalachia's Children: The Challenge of Mental Health.* Lexington: University of Kentucky Press.

MacLeish, Kenneth and Kimball Young
1942   *Landaff, New Hampshire: Culture of a Contemporary Rural Community.* USDA Bureau of Agricultural Economics, Rural Life Studies, no. 3.

Melvin, Bruce L.
1931   "The Sociology of a Village and the Surrounding Territory." Ithaca, N.Y.: Cornell University Agricultural Experiment Station. Bulletin 523.

Nelkin, Dorothy
1970   "A Response to Marginality: The Case of Migrant Farm Workers." Ithaca, N.Y.: New York State School of Industrial and Labor Relations, Cornell University. I. and L. R. Reprint Series, no. 282.

Newton, Jan
1977   "Economic Rationality of the Poor." *Human Organization.* Vol. 36, no. 1, pp. 50–61.

New York State Commission on the Quality, Cost and Financing of Elementary and Secondary Education
1972   *Report of the Commission.* Vol. 1.

Powdermaker, Hortense
1939   *After Freedom: A Cultural Study in the Deep South.* New York: Viking Press.

President's National Advisory Commission on Rural Poverty
1968   *Report of the Commission.*

Rodgers, Harrell R., Jr.
1979   *Poverty Amid Plenty.* Reading, Mass.: Addison-Wesley.

Roe, Daphne A.
1973   *Health and Nutritional Status of Working and Non-Working Mothers in Poverty Groups.* Report to the Manpower Administration, U.S. Department of Labor.

Rubin, Lillian Breslow
    1976   Worlds of Pain. New York: Basic Books.
Rural America, Inc.
            Rural America (a monthly publication). Washington, D.C.
Rural Housing Alliance – Rural America
            The RHA Reporter. Washington, D.C.
Schwarzweller, Harry K., J. S. Brown, and J. J. Mangalam
    1971   Mountain Families in Transition: A Case Study of Appalachian Migration.
            University Park, Pa.: Pennsylvania State University Press.
Stack, Carol B.
    1974   All Our Kin: Strategies for Survival in a Black Community. New York:
            Harper & Row.
Stone, I. Thomas, D. C. Leighton, and A. H. Leighton
    1966   "Poverty and the Individual." In Fishman, Leo, ed., Poverty Amid Af-
            fluence. New Haven: Yale University Press.
Townsend, Peter, ed.
    1970   The Concept of Poverty: Working Papers on Methods of Investigation and
            Life-Styles of the Poor in Different Countries. London: Heinemann.
United States Department of Agriculture
    1965   Soil Survey, New York. Soil Conservation Service.
United States Department of Housing and Urban Development
    1978   "Report of the Task Force on Rural and Non-Metropolitan Areas."
Valentine, Bettylou
    1978   Hustling and Other Hard Work. New York: The Free Press.
Valentine, Charles A.
    1968   Culture and Poverty: Critique and Counter-Proposals. Chicago: University
            of Chicago Press.
Vaughan, Lawrence M.
    1929   "Abandoned Farm Areas in New York." Ithaca, N.Y.: Cornell University
            Agricultural Experiment Station. Bulletin 490.
Vidich, Arthur and Joseph Bensman
    1958   Small Town in Mass Society: Class, Power and Religion in a Rural Com-
            munity. Princeton, N.J.: Princeton University Press.
Warren, G. F. and K. C. Livermore
    1911   "An Agricultural Survey." Ithaca, N.Y.: Cornell University Agricultural
            Experiment Station. Bulletin 295.
Weller, Jack E.
    1965   Yesterday's People: Life in Contemporary Appalachia. Lexington: Univer-
            sity of Kentucky Press.
Williamson, John B. et al.
    1975   Strategies Against Poverty in America. New York: John Wiley & Sons.

Index

Adulthood
early entrance into, 142–143
emotional and role problems, 66–68,
71, 112–113, 115–116
AFDC (Aid to Families with
Dependent Children). See Welfare
Aging, 121
Agriculture, Department of. See U.S.
Department of Agriculture
Agriculture, history of
abandonment of farming, 34–35,
44–45
acquisition of farms, 34, 36–37
decline of agriculture, 32–33, 36–38,
42
Depression years, 37–38
farmers' histories, 38–42
farming patterns of 1900–1920,
33–35
state purchase of land, 38
turnover of farm ownership, 34,
36–37
Aid to Families with Dependent
Children. See Welfare
Alcohol consumption, 25, 67, 81, 83,
93, 194
Alcoholics Anonymous, 177–178, 196
Analysis of data
fieldwork bias, 25–26
generalizability, 26–27
limitations, 24–26
problems in, 22–24
Anthropological study of poverty
holistic approach, 27

naturalistic settings, 21–22
need for more, 25, 231
references to other studies, 233 n1
and n4 (Ch. 2)
See also Fieldwork
Antipoverty programs
assumptions and stereotypes
underlying, 61–62, 219
community action agencies, 228,
243 n13 and n14
Aspirations for children, 91–92, 108
143–145, 195

Beliefs
about causes of failure, 197
religious, 172, 197
Budgeting. See Spending patterns;
Supplying family needs

Cars, repairing, trading, and social
patterns concerning, 99–100
Causes of rural poverty, 185–201
barriers to upward mobility,
188–190
closing-in of horizons, 199–200
derivative (secondary) causes,
192–200, 203–204
disparity between aspirations and
achievements, 193–196
economic causes, 186–188
failure syndrome, 196–198
historical causes, 186
inadequacies of social structure,
188

GENTLEMEN OF SCIENCE:
EARLY CORRESPONDENCE

GENTLEMEN OF SCIENCE

Early Correspondence of the British Association
for the Advancement of Science

edited by

JACK MORRELL and ARNOLD THACKRAY

CAMDEN FOURTH SERIES
VOLUME 30

LONDON
OFFICES OF THE ROYAL HISTORICAL SOCIETY
UNIVERSITY COLLEGE LONDON
GOWER STREET WC1
1984

British Library Cataloguing in Publication Data

Gentlemen of science: early correspondence of the British
    Association for the Advancement of Science.—(Camden
    fourth series; v. 30)
    1. British Association for the Advancement of Science—
    History
    I. Morrell, Jack   II. Thackray, Arnold   III. British
    Association for the Advancement of Science   IV. Series
    506'.041   Q41.B85

ISBN 0-86193-103-3

Printed and bound in Great Britain by
Butler & Tanner Ltd, Frome and London

CONTENTS

ACKNOWLEDGEMENTS

For permission to print material in their care or ownership, we are grateful to the late Viscount Harcourt, and to his daughter, the Honourable Mrs Crispin Gascoigne, whose kind co-operation has made this volume possible; John Murray, Esq.; the Marquis of Northampton; Sir Montague Prichard; British Association for the Advancement of Science; British Library; Botany School, University of Cambridge; Cambridge University Library; Edinburgh University Library; Fitzwilliam Wentworth Estate; Geological Society of London; Institution of Electrical Engineers, London; Magdalen College, Oxford; Northamptonshire Record Office; Royal Society of London; Trinity College, Cambridge; University Museum, Oxford; University College, London (Library); University of St Andrews (Library); and Whitby Literary and Philosophical Society.

It remains only to thank once again those many individuals who have aided our work, and especially Mr Gordon Ray and the Trustees of the John Simon Guggenheim Memorial Foundation whose faith in this project helped us through difficult times. Mr Keith Thomas gave us strong encouragement with this volume, and the practical advice of Dr C.T. Allmand and of Dr I. Roy, his successor as Literary Director of the Royal Historical Society, has been invaluable. Eleanor Hay provided expert secretarial assistance. For identifications we are grateful to William Brock, William Bynum, Harold Jones, Michael Neve and Martin Rudwick. To all of them, and to the Royal Historical Society for generously undertaking to publish this volume, we offer our grateful thanks.

ACKNOWLEDGMENTS

INTRODUCTION

In 1981 we published a study of the origins and early days of the British Association for the Advancement of Science. That study was based on what we believe to be an unexampled record of a nineteenth-century scientific institution, in the form of some five thousand letters written by the scores of individuals whose actions led, directly and indirectly, to the successful establishment of the 'British Ass'. Those letters were retrieved from over seventy institutional and personal archives, scattered in four countries on two continents. Tracking down the letters and transcribing the more 'postworthy' half was a major enterprise. However the central core of letters came from one private library, that of the late Viscount Harcourt. Indeed it was the fortunate discovery of these Harcourt manuscripts in 1971 which led to our whole project, published first in a narrative and analytic form, and now completed with this documentary volume.

Our earlier study (*Gentlemen of Science. Early Years of the British Association for the Advancement of Science*, Clarendon Press, Oxford and New York, 1981; paperback edition, 1982) details the context of the Association's formation, and the course of its 'first cycle' from the foundation meeting in York in 1831 to the triumphant return to that city in 1844. This complementary volume offers a documentary account of the same events, as recorded in the correspondence of the principal actors. These actors, our gentlemen of science, consisted of the twenty-three individuals who held a main office in the British Association in its first six years of existence and who held office again, then or later. A brief sketch of the career of each of these gentlemen of science is given below in the Biographical Appendix.

In this volume we present what we judge to be the 294 letters of greatest significance to the student of early Victorian science and culture. Our principles of selection have been straightforward. We have chosen to focus primarily on the letters written by and to William Vernon Harcourt (1789–1871). Harcourt, the fourth son of the Archbishop of York, was a cultured and influential gentleman. Educated at Christ Church, Oxford, he enjoyed a privileged existence as a Canon Residentiary of York Minster and as incumbent in turn of three local livings. He devoted much time to philanthropic ventures in the York area, and he was the effective founder of the Yorkshire Philosophical Society. A true devotee of science and a practised administrator, he was strategically placed to respond to the passionate but ill-thought-out plan of David Brewster when the latter decided in February 1831 that the time had come to call together a congregation of British men of science in York, 'the most centrical city for the three kingdoms' (letter no. 19).

Harcourt kept the letters he received about the British Association, and drafts of some of his replies. Several of those replies are to be found in the archives of our other actors. It was thus comparatively simple to assemble the 312 letters that survive between Harcourt and one or other of our gentlemen of science. In addition we made transcripts of 168 letters between Harcourt and secondary figures, in our drama. Finally, there were about fifty letters exchanged among our gentlemen of science other than Harcourt, which attracted our attention because of their importance to the subject of our enquiry.

Among the approximately 530 letters that were candidates for publication, many simply repeated themes already explored in other exchanges. Correspondents scattered throughout the British Isles unwittingly repeated the same points, when neither telephone nor rapid travel existed. Again, some of the letters to or from Harcourt were simply not germane to the British Association. It was thus possible to prune the list to 293, which we now publish.

Given our principles of selection and the existence of the Harcourt manuscripts, it is not surprising that though we here publish letters from twenty-three collections, slightly over two thirds are to or from Harcourt, with in-letters three times as numerous as out-letters. In fact, just over half of the letters here presented come from the Harcourt manuscripts themselves. Of those letters about one third (fifty in all) have been previously published in whole or part in volumes xiii and xiv of *The Harcourt Papers*, ed. E.W. Harcourt (privately printed, Oxford, 1880-1905). However that earlier publication is less important than might be supposed. As only fifty copies were produced it is to be found in few public libraries; the letters it prints are on most occasions abbreviated without any indication of the fact, many are erroneously transcribed, and some are misdated.

Considered chronologically, the letters published here accurately reflect the waxing and waning of the interest in the British Association of Harcourt and his colleagues. Sixteen letters come from the years 1824-30. In contrast 1831, the year of the Association's founding, gives rise to seventy-five communications, with no less than eleven from that last frantic, flurried week before the Association first convened. 1832 was somewhat calmer, with but thirty-two letters. From 1833 to 1839 the number varies between thirteen and twenty-five a year. Finally, twenty-five letters span the years from 1840 to 1853.

The letters here presented are often long and always frank. They offer scenes of comedy and bathos. They show the personalities and politics of knowledge, at a time when science was becoming the organized expression of Victorian optimism. With a remarkably modern ring they reveal the fascinations of committee work; the pressures of large meetings; the opportunity to manage the media; the concern with the expense of scientific research; the need to conciliate constituencies; the problems of publication; and the disputes over priorities and personalities which must inevitably accompany any organized attempt at the advancement of science. Above all these letters cast new light on the character of a remarkably talented set of early Victorian thinkers and doers. Harcourt, Whewell, Phillips, Babbage, Brewster, the irrepressible 'Rod' Murchison, and the rest of our gentlemen of science made an enduring mark on the world through their work in and for the British Association. In these letters we see revealed their hopes, their ambitions, and their abilities. The intellectual historian can here ponder the moral ambivalence of a John Herschel, the robust power of a Whewell, and the encroaching vanity of a Babbage.

It has been our privilege to live with the gentlemen of science for the past decade, and to enjoy their energy, their intellect, and their enthusiasms. We shall miss their company even as, through this book, we introduce them to new readers.

JACK MORRELL AND ARNOLD THACKRAY

BRADFORD AND PHILADELPHIA
OCTOBER, 1983

EDITORIAL NOTE

We have chosen to present the letters with modernized orthography and punctuation, and we have extended most abbreviations in the interest of intelligibility. In no case have we interfered with the word order as written. We have provided only a minimum of notes, aimed primarily at identifying individuals mentioned in the letters. We assume that specialists will provide their own gloss on the text, while more casual readers may wish to consult the analysis and the far fuller notes of our companion volume, which offers an exhaustive but we hope not exhausting commentary on the subjects and the actions discussed in these letters. To make this volume complete in itself we have included a full list of manuscript sources, and indexes of names and subjects.

With a few exceptions, we have omitted the formalities of salutation at the start and at the end of the letters. Styles of dates and places of writing have been standardized. The absence of an address for a recipient of a letter means that it does not exist in the original. All editorial insertions in the text are indicated by square brackets; these include dates supplied by us on the basis of internal or other evidence. Excision of irrelevant material in the body of a letter is indicated by points ..., and in a postscript by the editorial [PS omitted].

The *Dictionary of Scientific Biography* and the *Dictionary of National Biography* are referred to as *DSB* and *DNB*. The published Reports of the Annual Meetings of the British Association for the Advancement of Science are referred to as Reports. Thus the *Report of the eighth meeting of the British Association for the Advancement of Science; held at Newcastle in August 1838* (London, 1839) is abbreviated as *1838 Report*. I. Todhunter, *William Whewell: An account of his writings with selections from his literary and scientific correspondence* (London, 1876), who printed some letters now lost, is referred to as Todhunter, *Whewell*.

Most individuals are identified on their first occurrence by a footnote giving full names together with dates of birth and death, brief biographical information, and/or citation of a standard source. Individuals described in the Biographical Appendix are referred to by surname only in the subsequent editorial matter.

MANUSCRIPT SOURCES

Collection	Location
Babbage	British Library, London (Additional Manuscripts)
British Association for the Advancement of Science: Council minutes; Foundation volume	Bodleian Library, Oxford
Brougham	University College, London
Brown, Robert	British Library, London
Compton	Castle Ashby, Northamptonshire
Daubeny	Magdalen College, Oxford
Faraday	Institution of Electrical Engineers, London
Fitzwilliam	Northamptonshire Record Office, Northampton
Forbes, J.D.	University of St Andrews
Harcourt	the late Viscount Harcourt, Oxford
Henslow	Botany School, Cambridge University
Herschel	Royal Society, London
Lubbock	Royal Society, London
Murchison	Geological Society, London
Murchison	British Library, London (Additional Manuscripts)
Murchison	University of Edinburgh (Additional Manuscripts)
Murray	John Murray, Albemarle Street, London
Peel	British Library, London (Additional Manuscripts)
Phillips	Department of Geology, University Museum, Oxford
Royal Society of London: Miscellaneous correspondence	Royal Society, London
Scoresby	Whitby Literary and Philosophical Society
Sedgwick	University Library, Cambridge
Whewell	Trinity College, Cambridge

BIOGRAPHICAL APPENDIX

All have *DNB* entries.

Airy, George Biddell (1801-92), President of BAAS, 1851

The eldest child of a farmer turned excise officer, Airy was a sizar (i.e., subsidized student) at Trinity College, Cambridge, where he was a pupil in mathematics of George Peacock. In 1823 he graduated as Senior Wrangler and first Smith's Prizeman in the mathematics tripos examination. Elected a Fellow of Trinity in 1824, he was Lucasian professor of mathematics at Cambridge, 1826-8, and Plumian professor of astronomy and Director of the University Observatory, 1828-35. Inspired by the German astronomer Friedrich Bessel, he made the Cambridge Observatory a centre for physical as well as observational astronomy. His achievement there led to his appointment as Astronomer Royal, 1835-81. He was knighted in 1872.

Babbage, Charles (1792-1871), Trustee of BAAS, 1832-8

The son of a prosperous banker, Babbage was educated at private schools and at Trinity College and Peterhouse, Cambridge. As a student he was active with Peacock and Herschel in modernizing British mathematics. Graduating in 1814, he soon moved to London, where he spent much of his life and a considerable part of his large fortune on his calculating machines, which Government also subsidized with £17,000. He was a keen worker for the early Royal Astronomical Society. As befitted an unsuccessful Liberal candidate for Parliament, he was a fierce critic of corrupt corporations; he was also the sinecurist Lucasian professor of mathematics at Cambridge, 1828-1839. His soirées did much to give science new importance in London's polite society.

Baily, Francis (1774-1844), Trustee of BAAS, 1839-44, and a General Secretary, 1835-6

The third son of a banker in Berkshire, Baily left school at the age of fourteen to be apprenticed for seven years to a London merchant. After travelling in the United States, in 1799 he became a stockbroker in London. A specialist in annuities and assurance, his commercial success enabled him to retire in 1825 to devote himself to astronomy and the administration of London science. In 1820 he helped to found the Royal Astronomical Society, of which he was the chief sustainer until his death. Though he made no spectacular discoveries, Baily saw the importance of providing useable and accurate resources for astronomers. His work was mainly concerned with precision measurement (density of the earth, length of the seconds pendulum), and with the revision of star catalogues.

Brewster, David (1781-1868), President of BAAS, 1850

The second son of the Headmaster of Jedburgh Grammar School, Brewster was educated in arts and divinity at Edinburgh University. His nervousness prevented him from practising as a clergyman, though in 1804 he was licensed to preach. Until 1838 he earned his living as an editor of scientific journals and of the *Edinburgh Encyclopaedia*, as a reviewer, and as a prolific author of books; his inventions, such as the kaleidoscope (1816), brought him little reward. By 1830 he was the leading British figure in experimental optics, especially polarization; he fought a long rear-guard action against the wave theory of light. As a loyal Whig he was knighted in 1831 and appointed Principal of the United College, St Andrews, in 1838. From 1860 to his death he was the first non-clerical Principal of Edinburgh University, where in 1833 James David Forbes had defeated him in a bitter contest for the professorship of natural philosophy. An evangelical in church politics, Brewster was often zealous, excitable, and unpredictable in the politics of science.

Buckland, the Reverend William (1784-1856), President of BAAS, 1832

The eldest son of a Devon clergyman, Buckland was educated at Blundell's School, Tiverton, Winchester School, and Corpus Christi College, Oxford. In 1809 he was elected a Fellow of Corpus and ordained. In 1813 he was appointed reader in mineralogy at Oxford, and in 1819 reader in geology. In 1825 Lord Liverpool made him a Canon of Christ Church, Oxford, and he resigned his Fellowship to marry Mary Morland, who was an accomplished naturalist. Buckland was a popular and eccentric lecturer in room, field, and cave. He contributed manly Christianity to the Geological Society of London; and, as a liberal Anglican, was the author of a *Bridgewater Treatise* on geology and natural theology. A close friend of Sir Robert Peel and a loyal Conservative, he was appointed Dean of Westminster in 1845.

Dalton, John (1766-1844)

The son of a modest Quaker yeoman, Dalton was educated in a small Cumberland village school, where he also taught during 1778-81. He became assistant and then partner in a far more prosperous Quaker school at Kendal, 1781-93. He then moved to Manchester, where he remained for the rest of his life, teaching mathematics and natural philosophy at the Unitarian New College, 1793-9, and subsequently taking private pupils. Besides the chemical atomic theory for which he is famous, he published on meteorology and colour blindness. As Manchester's leading savant of the post-Napoleonic era, he was President of its Literary and Philosophical Society, 1817-44. He was made an FRS in 1822 and in 1830 received the rare distinction of becoming a foreign associate of the French Académie des Sciences. By the 1830s he was a revered figure as a world-famous yet humble and straightforward Quaker philosopher.

Daubeny, Charles Giles Bridle (*1795-1867*), President of BAAS, *1856*

The son of a clergyman, Daubeny was educated at Winchester School, Magdalen College, Oxford, and Edinburgh University. His wide scientific interests in medicine, geology, chemistry, botany, and agriculture enabled him to supplement his lay Fellowship at Magdalen by medical practice until 1829, and by concurrently assuming three professorships at Oxford (chemistry, from 1822; botany, from 1834; rural economy, from 1840). Though not a great researcher, Daubeny was active and well regarded in Oxford as a temperate reformer and a promoter of physical science.

Forbes, James David (*1809-68*)

A son of Sir William Forbes, the prominent Edinburgh banker, Forbes was educated at home and at Edinburgh University. Though qualified for the law, his comfortable private income enabled him to choose a scientific career. Initially a protégé of Brewster, Forbes successfully opposed him in 1833 in a bitter contest for the professorship of natural philosophy at Edinburgh. His teaching owed much to that of Airy at Cambridge, just as his chief research on the polarization of heat was inspired by the Cambridge advocates of Fresnel's wave theory. A staunch Episcopalian and Tory, Forbes was an effective scientific worker and a determined careerist. In 1845 he was granted a Government pension of £200 *p.a.* and in 1860 succeeded Brewster as Principal of the United College, St Andrews.

Hamilton, William Rowan (*1805-65*)

The son of a solicitor, Hamilton was a child prodigy. In 1823 he entered Trinity College, Dublin, where he achieved such distinction in mathematics and literature that while an undergraduate he was elected Andrews professor of astronomy and, shortly afterwards, Astronomer Royal for Ireland. He was knighted in 1835 and granted a Government pension in 1843. From 1837 to 1846 he was President of the Royal Irish Academy. Undistinguished as an astronomer, his forte lay in mathematical physics and especially in pure mathematics, where his work on quaternions ensured his fame.

Harcourt, the Reverend William Venables Vernon (1789–1871), President of BAAS, 1839, and General Secretary, 1832–7

The fourth son of Edward Vernon Harcourt, Archbishop of York, Harcourt was taught at home by his father before spending five years in the navy. From 1807 to 1811 he studied at Christ Church, Oxford, from which he graduated in classics in 1811. At Oxford he became interested in geology and chemistry through attending the classes of Buckland and John Kidd. In 1814 his ordination launched him on a comfortable clerical career. With powerful family connections and a respected local position, he was the effective founder of the Yorkshire Philosophical Society in 1822. He devoted much time to philanthropic ventures in the York area, which he left in 1861 when he succeeded to the family estates in Oxfordshire.

Henslow, the Reverend John Stevens (1796–1861)

The son of a solicitor, Henslow was educated at schools in Rochester and Camberwell, London, as well as at home by the naturalist William Elford Leach. From 1814 to 1818 he attended St John's College, Cambridge, from which he graduated as Sixteenth Wrangler in the mathematics tripos. A founder and sustainer of the Cambridge Philosophical Society, he was professor of mineralogy at Cambridge, 1822–7, and professor of botany, 1827–61. Married in 1823 and ordained in 1824, he held a succession of livings, the last of which was at Hitcham, Suffolk, where he was active in elementary science teaching. His patronage of the young Charles Darwin was typical of his success in nurturing botany at Cambridge.

Lloyd, the Reverend Humphrey (1800–81), President of BAAS, 1857

The eldest son of the Reverend Bartholomew Lloyd, Provost of Trinity College, Dublin, 1831–7, Humphrey Lloyd was educated at Trinity, becoming a Junior Fellow in 1824. In 1831 he succeeded his father as Erasmus Smith professor of natural and experimental philosophy, and through his work on optics and magnetism was a leader of the Dublin school of mathematical physics. In 1843 he resigned his chair to become a Senior Fellow of Trinity, of which he became Vice-Provost in 1862. Like his father, he was ordained, became President of the Royal Irish Academy (1846–51), presided over a BAAS meeting in Dublin (1857), and ended his career as Provost of Trinity (1867–81).

Milton, Lord: Fitzwilliam, Charles William Wentworth (1786–1857), President of BAAS, 1831

The only son of William Wentworth Fitzwilliam, second Earl Fitzwilliam, Milton was educated at Trinity College, Cambridge. He was Whig MP for Yorkshire from 1806 to 1831, and for Northamptonshire from 1831 to 1833. In 1833, on the death of his father, he became third Earl Fitzwilliam. His huge country house, Wentworth Woodhouse, near Rotherham, was a favourite resort of travelling savants. In addition to his mining, manufacturing, and agricultural interests, Milton was well informed in polite science. He was a natural choice to be President of the Yorkshire Philosophical Society (1831–57), and first President of the Yorkshire Geological Society (1837–57). In London he was three times President of the Statistical Society (1838–40, 1848–9, 1853–5).

Murchison, Roderick Impey (1792–1871), President of BAAS, 1846, and a General Secretary of BAAS, 1836–46

The son of a physician, Murchison was educated at a school in Durham which he left in 1805 to attend the Military College, Great Marlow. Having entered the army in 1807, he served in Ireland, Portugal, and Sicily until in 1814 he retired on half-pay. After his marriage in 1815, he devoted himself to travel and hunting, until in 1824 he began to cultivate a scientific career. He rapidly became a force in the Geological Society of London (President, 1831–3). Not content with his monumental work of the 1830s on the Silurian system in Britain, he extended it eastwards in the 1840s to Russia. In 1846 he was knighted and in 1855 succeeded De la Beche as Director of the British Geological Survey. Through his social position and wealth, his military efficiency, and his personal zest, Murchison attained the beau-ideal of the independent gentleman devoted to science.

Northampton, Marquis of: Compton, Spencer Joshua Alwyne (1790–1851), President of BAAS, 1848

The second son of the first Marquis of Northampton, Lord Compton studied at Trinity College, Cambridge. From 1812 to 1820, he sat as Whig MP for Northampton. Between 1820 and 1830 he spent much time in Italy, succeeding his father as second Marquis in 1828. In 1836 he achieved sudden fame when his popular manners and oratory enabled him to be a resounding success as a last-minute substitute President of the BAAS. He was President of the Royal Society, 1838–48, a writer of poetry, and a keen supporter of organized archaeology. His main scientific interest was polite geology. At his country house, Castle Ashby, he was a hospitable host to wandering savants.

Peacock, the Reverend George (1791–1858), President of BAAS, 1844, and a General Secretary, 1837–9

The fifth son of a curate, Peacock attended Richmond School, Yorkshire, in its heyday. He then entered Trinity College, Cambridge, as a sizar in 1809, graduating as Second Wrangler and second Smith's Prizeman in the mathematics tripos examination in 1813. Having been elected in 1814 to a Fellowship at Trinity, he was successively lecturer in mathematics, joint tutor, and sole tutor there. Ordained in 1822, he was elected to the Lowndean chair of astronomy and geometry in 1836. This post became a sinecure in 1839 when he was appointed Dean of Ely Cathedral. His best work was in theoretical algebra. As a Whig university politician, he was prominent in reforming the mathematics tripos and in founding the Cambridge University Observatory. His powerful positions at Trinity and Ely gave him useful contacts in high places.

Phillips, John (1800–74), President of BAAS, 1865, and Assistant Secretary, 1832–62

Phillips was a scientific Dick Whittington. Made an orphan at the age of eight, he was looked after by his uncle, William Smith, the surveyor. Phillips left school at the age of fifteen, and for nine years he helped in his uncle's work. First making contact with the Yorkshire Philosophical Society in 1824, he was keeper of its museum in 1826–40. Through ardent lecturing and publishing, Phillip's career prospered first locally and then nationally; he was professor of geology at King's College, London, 1834–41, and professor of geology, Trinity College, Dublin, 1844–5. After distinguished palaeontological work for the Geological Survey from 1839, he was successively appointed to five teaching and curating posts at Oxford from 1853, culminating in the professorship of geology (1860–74).

Powell, the Reverend Baden (1796–1860)

The eldest son of a sheriff, Powell entered Oriel College, Oxford, then in its noetic heyday, in 1814. He graduated with first-class honours in mathematics (not classics, as was usual at Oxford). From 1820 to 1827 he was a parish clergyman. Having been elected Savilian professor of geometry in 1827, Powell promoted the cause of physical science at Oxford and engaged in anti-Tractarian controversy from an elevated, latitudinarian standpoint. As Oxford's chief representative in mathematical physics, he worked on optics and radiation; but, unlike Buckland, he was never close friends with his fellow savants in Cambridge.

Robinson, the Reverend Thomas Romney (1792–1882), President of BAAS, 1849

The eldest son of a portrait painter, Robinson showed literary precosity as a child. He entered Trinity College, Dublin, as a pensioner in 1806, graduated in 1810, was a Fellow of Trinity, 1814–21, and a temporary professor of natural philosophy there. In 1821 he assumed a College living, in 1823 he was appointed Director of the Armagh Observatory in northern Ireland, and in 1824 he was made rector of a parish near Armagh. He held these last two posts until his death. Though known primarily as an observer of stars, he was interested in scientific instruments, such as the anemometer. In 1851 he succeeded Lloyd as President of the Royal Irish Academy.

Sedgwick, the Reverend Adam (1785–1873), President of BAAS, 1833

Sedgwick was the third child of a curate and was educated at local schools in Dent and Sedbergh, Yorkshire. In 1804 he entered Trinity College, Cambridge, as a sizar, and graduated as Fifth Wrangler in the mathematics tripos in 1808. Elected a Fellow of Trinity in 1810 and ordained in 1816, he was made professor of geology at Cambridge in 1818. For decades he was the most popular teacher of science at Cambridge, and he greatly developed the museum there. A firm Whig and liberal Anglican, Sedgwick was without any scientific peer as a public orator. In 1834 Brougham presented him with a prebendary stall at Norwich Cathedral, worth almost £600 p.a.

Stanley, the Reverend Edward (1779–1849)

Born into the landed aristocracy, Stanley was educated privately and at St John's College, Cambridge, from which he graduated as Sixteenth Wrangler in 1802. From 1805 to 1837 he was Vicar of Alderley, near Manchester, where he interested himself in education, ornithology, geological lecturing, and church reform. In 1837 his active Whig sympathies induced Melbourne to appoint him Bishop of Norwich. As Bishop, Stanley continued to pursue latitudinarian policies, particularly with respect to non-conformists: he was controversial and extremely unpopular with the Tractarians and with Tory Anglicans. From 1837 until his death he was President of the Linnean Society.

Taylor, John (1779–1863), Treasurer of BAAS, 1832–61

Born into a prosperous Unitarian family of Norwich yarn merchants, Taylor was apprenticed to a land surveyor and civil engineer. In

1798 he became manager of a Devon copper mine owned by Unitarian friends. He was an immediate success, and over the years he obtained significant financial interests in several mining and chemical manufacturing concerns: by 1824, when he launched his Mexican mining adventures, he already controlled about three dozen British companies. Later in life he had extensive mining interests in California and in Spain. His early interest in polite geology, his wealth, and business acumen made him an increasingly important administrative figure on the London scientific scene. Elected FRS in 1825, he was Treasurer of the Geological Society (1816–21 and 1823–43), and Treasurer of University College, London (1842–60).

Whewell, the Reverend William (1794-1866), President of BAAS, 1841

The eldest child of a master carpenter, Whewell attended Lancaster Grammar School and Heversham Grammar School, from which in 1812 he won an exhibition to Trinity College, Cambridge. Graduating in 1816 as Second Wrangler and second Smith's Prizeman, he became a Fellow at Trinity (1817) and later a tutor (1823). Ordained in 1825, he was professor of mineralogy at Cambridge (1828-32), and professor of moral philosophy (1838-58). A reformer with Peacock of the Cambridge mathematics tripos, he published prolificly on mathematics, mechanics, architecture, natural theology, history and philosophy of science, tidology, and moral philosophy. In 1841 his scholarship and attachment to Conservatism induced Peel to secure his appointment as Master of Trinity, a post which he held to his death.

Table of places of meeting and officers: 1831–44

Place	Date	President	Vice-presidents	Local Secretaries
York	Sept 1831	Lord Milton	Harcourt	W. Gray Phillips
Oxford	June 1832	Buckland	Brewster Whewell	Daubeny Powell
Cambridge	June 1833	Sedgwick	Airy Dalton	Henslow Whewell
Edinburgh	Sept 1834	Sir T.M. Brisbane	Brewster Robinson	Forbes J. Robison
Dublin	Aug 1835	B. Lloyd	Earl of Rosse Whewell	Hamilton H. Lloyd
Bristol	Aug 1836	Marquis of Lansdowne	Marquis of Northampton W.D. Conybeare J.C. Prichard	Daubeny Hovenden
Liverpool	Sept 1837	Earl of Burlington	Stanley Dalton Sir P. Egerton Whewell	T.S. Traill W.W. Currie J.N. Walker
Newcastle-upon-Tyne	Aug 1838	Duke of Northumberland	E. Maltby Harcourt P.J. Selby	J. Adamson W. Hutton J.F.W. Johnston
Birmingham	Aug 1839	Harcourt	Northampton Earl of Dartmouth Robinson J. Corrie	G. Barker P. Blakiston J. Hodgson A.F. Osler
Glasgow	Sept 1840	Marquis of Breadalbane	D. MacFarlan Lord Greenock Brewster Brisbane	A. Liddell J.P. Nichol J. Strang
Plymouth	July 1841	Whewell	Earl Mount-Edgecumbe Earl of Morley Lord Eliot Sir C. Lemon Sir T.D. Acland	W.S. Harris C.H. Smith R.W. Fox R. Taylor, jun.
Manchester	June 1842	Lord Francis Egerton	Dalton W. Herbert Sedgwick W.C. Henry Sir B. Heywood	P. Clare W. Fleming J. Heywood
Cork	Aug 1843	Rosse	Earl of Listowel Viscount Adare Hamilton Robinson	J. Stevelly J. Carson W. Keleher W. Clear
York	Sept 1844	Peacock	Milton Viscount Morpeth J.S. Wortley Brewster M. Faraday Harcourt	W. Hatfeild T. Meynell W. Scoresby W. West

THE CORRESPONDENCE

1 *William Daniel Conybeare, Brislington near Bristol, to Harcourt, 17 January 1824*

Werner never answered letters, not even that announcing his election as member of the French Institute. So instead of apologizing for neglect I lay claim to merit for superior punctuality of correspondence. In truth I have had my hands full at our Institution, for which I had a long report to draw up and two introductory papers to get up for the first meetings of our Philosophical Society. For the subject of the former of these essays I took the origin and history of philosophical associations and, as the meeting was thin having been convened only for preliminary business and no paper being then expected, some of my friends thought it would be civil to request me to repeat it at the ensuing [meeting] which was the first regular convention of the Society. This I found myself unable absolutely to decline without affectation while I secretly resolved not to comply, as nothing could have been more ridiculous than an encore on such occasions. Therefore when the time came I had provided a second memoir which I asserted to be a continuation of the first, though in fact it had little connection with it being a general survey of the actual state and prospects of the leading branches of physical enquiry. Getting all this ready, attending numerous committees previous to our annual meeting last week, getting ready lists of all donations of which Miller has brought back a considerable accession from town, etc etc left me little leisure. The first I have had I have employed in answering arrears of letters in which yours comes in turn. Imprimis, I will send the crocodile's head carefully packed but first wish to be allowed to take a cast of it, which I think I deserve for my pains in detaching it from its matrix. I have an opportunity of getting this well and safely done in Bristol ...In many respects I much like your plan of circular lecturers, if *practicable*, though it smacks strongly of being borrowed from the itinerant preachers of the Methodist conference and I set it down as a new proof of your sectarian views. But my if is a formidable one, although the last Edinburgh voice I think proposes an admirable plan of finance which is admitted to be impracticable, but the objection considered is of no moment. The difficulties I foresee are these. How is the collective body of the different institutions to agree in the election? Are they to have our complicity or [act] in council? And when, where and how is it to be convened? Suppose it assembled: will not each district have some promising protégé of its own to support—York advances some Yorkist and Lancaster some Lancasterian—and the hostile votes again blossom? If these difficulties could be got over, and until one sees the plan in a more matured shape it is impossible to judge whether they can or no, such an union would be clearly desirable; for the place of lecturer might by these means be made so eligible as to command much higher talent than could be expected in any other manner. Therefore I am anxious if you prosecute the matter to hear its further progress, and if any plausible plan can be proposed to carry it into execution [I] will endeavour as far as I can to bring Bristol into the league.

I have been endeavouring with some others to get up a Greek committee in Bristol; above my expectation many of the leading literati of the Tory party here were equally active, indeed we have all the literature of the place such as it is with us. But the wealthy of all parties seem very indifferent. I strongly recommended Mr Blagniere when he came here to try York which I think a much more likely field for success in such a cause.

Harcourt MSS

William Daniel Conybeare (1787–1857), *DNB*, expert on fossil reptiles, Anglican clergyman, and a leading promoter of the Bristol Institution and of the Bristol Philosophical and Literary Society; Abraham Gottlob Werner (1749–1817), *DSB*, German geologist; John Samuel Miller (1779–1830), curator at the Bristol Institution.

2 *Sir Humphry Davy, London, to Harcourt, 21 January 1824*

I am much obliged to you and to the [Yorkshire] Philosophical Society for the honour that has been done me, and I wish it may be in my power to promote in any way the objects of their institution. Your election as President will secure both the respectability of the establishment and the correctness and utility of the objects of enquiry.

I will take care that you are proposed as a Fellow of the Royal Society at the next meeting and I am sure all our scientific members will be glad to see your name on our lists.

I remember something of Mr W's letter and I am not sure that he did not write to me on the subject of the British Museum.

I hope to see in two or three years a zoological gallery established and a collection superior to that of the Jardin du Roi: but till our new buildings are completed nothing can be done, though as soon as the plans are determined on, we may make preparations for collecting.

I will bear in mind Mr W's proposition.

Unfortunately Britain now possesses no naturalist who has a reputation that may be called European, and I am afraid we shall long want the genius and arranging spirit of a Cuvier . . .

Harcourt MSS

Sir Humphry Davy (1778-1829), *DNB*, President of the Royal Society of London 1820-27, here acknowledges his election as a member of the Yorkshire Philosophical Society. W was probably Charles Wellbeloved (1769-1858), *DNB*; Georges Cuvier (1769-1832), *DSB*, the French naturalist.

3 *Conybeare, Brislington near Bristol, to Harcourt, 19 April 1824*

I fear you will think me a most remiss correspondent but I have been quite overwhelmed with engagements: first the discovery of a complete plesiosaurus 10 feet long, with all its extremities perfect and a neck exceeding that of the swan and all other δγλιχοδειρα, summoned me to London and there detained me for three weeks. Returned hither I found committee on committee waiting for me, for it was the winding up our first year's proceedings of the Bristol Institution. Here however we have been well repaid by the desired success. I shall shortly send you our report in one or two covers (as its weight may render necessary) but I have not room for particulars at present.

In addition to a new paper on the plesiosaurus aforesaid, I am also drawing up one on fossil crocodiles in which your Whitby head forms a conspicuous feature. I have carefully packed it in a little case adjusted to its shape and sent it to Buckland to take to Chantrey for a cast and to exhibit at the Geological Society [of London] when my paper is read, which will be next meeting, after which it will be immediately forwarded to you. Considering the great labour I have had in laying open the whole of its anatomical details (for when I received it it was completely buried in the shale) I think I have a fair claim for this use of it. Can you procure me a sight of any vertebrae of the crocodile from this locality?

It is not thought practicable at the Bristol Institution to enter into any *regular compact* with any other body as to lectures, but it is thought very desirable that (without such compact) some mutual understanding should be established between the managing committees on this subject: that is, it is believed that if [and] when the Birmingham Council have determined on applying to A or B to lecture there they would communicate their intention and vice versa. Such information might in many *particular* cases lead to arrangements advantageous to both parties, but any more general treaty is not considered advisable.

I enclose an epistle from our Secretary to the geologist Smith signifying his election as an honorary member of our Institution. I do not know where to address him but conclude that you do, and will favour me by forwarding it.

Harcourt MSS

Francis Legatt Chantrey (1781–1842), *DNB*, the sculptor; William Smith (1769–1839), *DNB*, the father of English stratigraphical geology; δγλιχοδειρα means long-necked creatures.

4 *Phillips, Leeds, to Harcourt, Wheldrake near York, 3 January 1826*

About ten days since I replied to Dr Goldie's communication containing proposals from the Council [of the Yorkshire Philosophical Society] for my delivering a course of lectures in February. I felt some difficulty in framing a suitable answer because I supposed the views of my friends had changed respecting the number of lectures which it would be proper to deliver. I receive here £50 for ten lectures. I could not therefore offer a full course at York on the terms fixed by the Council. I proposed 7 lectures on what has been supposed the most interesting part of geological enquiry, the natural history of organized fossil remains. It seems however an imperfection to omit a first or introductory lecture on general principles of geology, and as I have entirely remodelled that lecture I really think it might be an useful exordium. There seems also some lack of conclusion, and if the Council are disposed to stretch their expenditure to £40, I venture to recommend the following scheme of eight lectures.

Lecture 1   as at Leeds omitting some of the mineralogy
     2   on fossil plants etc.
     3   on corallines and radiata
     4   on mollusca and crustacea
     5   on fishes and reptiles
     6   on imbedded *mammalia*. General views
     7   on the animals destroyed by deluge and buried by more recent inundations
     8   a connected view of the whole modern system of geology.

If this meets your approbation and that of the Council, I shall at least not be wanting in endeavour to deliver with effect what may perhaps be my last course on a subject which has awakened in my mind mingled hopes and fears. If another form of explanation be preferred I shall be obliged by the communication. At all events I know that my labours are regarded with favourable eyes.

In compliance with the opinion you expressed on the subject of their fossil fish, Mr George and Mr Atkinson transmitted their drawings to the Geological Society in July, but no notice whatever has been taken on the subject although some applications have been addressed to Mr Webster. My friends, something anxious for the reputation of their fossil, have desired me to mention the circumstance, hoping that if opportunity occurs, you may think it useful to keep in the recollection of the Geological Society the most interesting reliquiae which this country has perhaps ever produced.

Harcourt MSS (Harcourt Papers, *xiii. 204-6*)

George Goldie (1786–1853), a York physician, was a Secretary of the Yorkshire Philosophical Society. Edward Sanderson George (1801–30), a Leeds chemical manufacturer, was a Secretary of the Leeds Philosophical and Literary Society, of which John Atkinson (1787–1828), a Leeds surgeon, was the first Curator and Librarian. Thomas Webster (1773–1844), *DNB*, was Curator of the Geological Society of London.

5 *Harcourt, n.p., to Murchison, n.d.* [*autumn 1826*]

I was much gratified to hear of the success of your researches and of your intention to communicate them to the public. In the truth of your observation as to contemporaneous formations in remote localities possessing a general and not an exact conformity every geologist must now concur; and yet the identity of the fossils from the Red Sea and the Basin of Paris and from the Lake Huron and the mountain limestone of England strongly shows the universal character of the circumstances under which those deposits were formed; and the distance to which well selected characteristic fossils may serve as a good guide is exemplified by the discovery in Yorkshire of the Kelloways rock through the medium of Ostria D. and Ammonitis K. and you will observe that we do not assume this to be the rock of Kelloways merely because we find in it these shells but because we find it in the same stratical position as well as containing the same characteristic fossils. I am impatient to see your list of fossils from Brora and hope since we are as you remark the connecting link for these strata between the south of England and Scotland that we may be able to find you correspondences for the northern deposits as we have already done for the southern.

With respect to the person who should give you an account of the geology of Yorkshire, Mr Smith is unquestionably the man: he has already coloured with exactness the eastern part of the county on the excellent sheet which Carey has lately published and will soon complete the rest; I had a promise from him to have prepared for the press by Christmas the manuscript observations on which his colouring is founded and [I] believe that he has done a good deal towards accomplishing it; you would do a service to a very deserving man if you would make known this intention. Smith has dedicated his life to geological enquiries and has done perhaps more than any individual for the science and is at an advanced age in poverty and dependance. There has been nothing in his conduct or character to diminish the respect due to his exertions in the cause of knowledge and the compassion which his circumstances excite. I have thought that a subscription might be raised for the publication which I have mentioned from the profits of which a small annuity might be purchased for him sufficient to secure his not dying in a poor house, and [I] should be much obliged to you if you would do what you can to forward it. I am sure you would find able and willing friends to this project in Dr Buckland and many other members of the Geological Society.

Mrs Vernon unites with me in begging to be kindly remembered to Mrs Murchison.

Murchison Papers

John Carey (1754-1835), London map engraver and publisher; Matilda Harcourt (1804-76) i.e., Mrs Vernon; Charlotte Murchison (1788-1869). In early summer 1826 on his journey to Brora, Scotland, Murchison had met Harcourt, Phillips, and Smith in Yorkshire.

6 *Sedgwick, Trinity College, Cambridge, to Harcourt, Bishopthorpe near York, 15 March 1827*

Early yesterday morning Mr West called upon me with your letter: and as I was fortunately unengaged with any academic business I was able to accompany him and his brother through the different establishments of the University. We took a hasty view of the buildings, libraries and lecture rooms, during which time I endeavoured to make him comprehend the peculiar nature of our establishments. We afterwards attended a lecture of our new professor of mathematics, on some experimental details connected with mechanical philosophy. I then introduced the two broad-brimmed gentlemen to the Hall and in the evening we heard one of Prof Farish's lectures on machinery. In short your friends saw all that the hasty nature of their visit admitted of and seemed well pleased with their day's work. I am extremely happy to hear that Mr Smith's new map of Yorkshire is in such a state of forwardness. I shall be most happy to subscribe to Mr Smith's work: but it will be impossible for me to recommend it to others till I know something about its magnitude, price, etc. If any bookseller or agent could give me such details I would take care to circulate them ... I have from time to time heard of the proceedings of your Society at York with the greatest interest. I should rejoice if I could make myself an useful member of it.

At the time I published a paper last year on the Yorkshire coast,

I had not heard a syllable of any new observations of Smith on that district. Someone told me that Bird and Young were about to publish a second edition of their work and I hoped that my observations (tho I know them to be imperfect and on that account for more than five years had not thought them worth publishing) might assist them in giving a better classification of our strata.

May I venture to hope that at no remote period you will again be induced to visit Cambridge? I shall rejoice to have an opportunity of showing you any attention in my power and of making you acquainted with our geological collection.

Harcourt MSS (Harcourt Papers, *xiii. 215–6*)

William West (1792–1851), a Leeds Quaker and chemist; Airy was the new professor of mathematics; William Farish (1759–1837), *DNB*, Jacksonian professor of natural and experimental philosophy; George Young (1777–1848), *DNB*, a Presbyterian minister at Whitby and John Bird (1768–1829), Whitby artist and first Curator of the Whitby Museum 1823–9, had published *A geological survey of the Yorkshire coast* (Whitby, 1822).

7 *Lord Milton, Milton near Peterborough, to Harcourt, 16 November 1827*

My name is perfectly at your service, and if I can be of use in furthering the objects of the [Yorkshire] Philosophical Society and any other way it will always give me the greatest pleasure so to do.

I know not whether you have any specimens of the organic remains found in the limestone strata near Milton, but from a cargo which Mr Allen sent to Wentworth a few weeks ago I conceive they must be very rich in those productions, and if they are wanted for the Museum I will give him a hint on the subject.

Harcourt MSS

Lord Milton, a patron and trustee of the Yorkshire Philosophical Society, was responsible by 1827 for a donation of £350 from his family to the building fund for the museum of the Society of which Harcourt was president. Milton's Yorkshire seat was Wentworth Woodhouse near Rotherham.

8 *Phillips, York, to Murchison, Secretary Geological Society, 20 Bedford Street, London, 21 January 1828*

I should sooner have acknowledged my obligations to your kindness in proposing me Fellow Geological Society but that I waited for the opportunity of some friend going to London. Mr Marshall one of our zealous members now setting out on a tour to the Continent has relieved me from this little difficulty and I have now the pleasure to return the signed obligation to good behaviour with £10. 10/- admission fee. I am deeply sensible of the honour which has been conferred upon me and shall endeavour by continual exertions in a favourite science to show myself not a merely nominal member of so useful and honourable a Society. The suggestions of Dr Buckland respecting the n[orth] western valleys of our interesting county I hope to attend to ere long; indeed I am already far advanced in such an investigation. I shall always think myself highly favoured by these hints from head-quarters and beg to request your attention to our Society here, of which there are several members willing to be usefully employed. Allow me in addition to request as a favour that if there be any points *interesting to yourself* on which I can furnish or procure information you will lay on me your agreeable commands. [PS omitted]

Murchison Papers

William Marshall, later styled William Hatfeild (d. 1844), was Curator of mineralogy to the Yorkshire Philosophical Society.

9   *Brewster, Allerly near Melrose, to Babbage, Devonshire Street, Portland Place, London, 3 February 1829*

Permit me to thank you for your very interesting paper which I shall [have] much pleasure inserting in [my] next number of which I shall send you a copy, and [I shall] continue it regularly as often that the journal will be my own property.

I am quite delighted with your plan of a great European Academy. It holds out singular advantages to science, and I wish you would set your shoulders to the scheme. I should like to enlist Mr Brougham in such a cause which I am sure he will enter upon with zeal. If you have no objection I will write to him. Would it not be good to draw out a general view of the plan, which I shall cheerfully publish?

You will probably have heard that the practical astronomy chair in Edinburgh is vacant, and that the professor will have charge of the Observatory. I have reason to believe that it will be offered to me; but notwithstanding this conviction I am desirous to have some certificates of my general scientific qualifications for such an office in case of their being needed. I therefore hope you will oblige me by one, and you would add generally to the favour if you would ask Mr Herschel to confer upon me the same obligation. I wrote him eight weeks ago on other subjects some of which required an answer, and I therefore suppose he must be from home.

The only candidate for the place is a Mr Thomas Henderson, a clerk in the Register House, who I believe is known to Mr Herschel and Dr Young as a clever calculator, and it has been stated to me that Mr Herschel has recommended him, which I cannot believe. If you could give me any other help in this matter it would oblige me much; though I really fear that government will not make the appointment such that I could accept of it without injuring the interests of my family. Do you think Mr Baily, Dr Pearson and Mr South would give me a certificate? I do not know where any of them live.

BL, Add. MSS 37184, ff. 201–202

Brewster edited the *Edinburgh journal of science*; Henry Peter Brougham (1778–1868), *DNB*, shared an interest in optics with Brewster for whom he gained a state pension of £100 per annum in 1829; John Frederick William Herschel (1792–1871), *DNB*, astronomer; Thomas Henderson (1798–1844), *DNB*, was eventually appointed first Scottish Astronomer Royal and Regius professor of practical astronomy at Edinburgh in 1834, the chair remaining unfilled 1828–34; Thomas Young (1773–1829), *DNB*; William Pearson (1767–1847) and James South (1785–1867), both *DNB*, were astronomers.

10   *Brewster, Allerly near Melrose, to Brougham, 14 March 1829*

I have just learned from Sir G. Mackenzie, who had an interview with Lord Melville, that government cannot endow the Observatory of Edinburgh. Lord Melville proposed to abolish the professorship, and to give the salary to the Institution for an assistant observer who could do little more, with such encouragement, than wind up the clocks and keep them in time.

I cannot suppose that Mr Peel can so easily abandon a promise which he has made twice in writing. Sir George indeed says that Lord M was not at all aware of Mr Peel having made any promise, so that I suspect that during Mr Peel's present occupations Lord Melville must be arranging without authority.

Mr Babbage has written to me about the establishment of a great scientific association or society embracing all Europe. The idea has sprung out of the Congress of Philosophers at Berlin (of which I can send you an account if you have not seen one) and has been warmly embraced by many leading continental philosophers. The power of such a body to promote science, and give respectability to the various classes of men who sustain the intellectual character of the age is obvious. Foreign sovereigns would give it every encouragement. There never has been a more ardent patron of science than the King of Prussia is, and I am assured that the infection is spreading through the higher classes in every part of Germany. I wish you would give the subject a thought. Mr Babbage and I would take the oar if you would touch the helm.

Brougham Papers 26608

Sir George Steuart Mackenzie (1780–1848), *DNB*; Robert Saunders Dundas, second Viscount Melville (1771–1851), *DNB*, first Lord of the Admiralty; Robert Peel (1788–1850), *DNB*, Home Secretary, was preoccupied with catholic emancipation in March 1829. The Astronomical Institution of Edinburgh owned an observatory. The Congress of Philosophers was the Gesellschaft Deutscher Naturforscher und Ärtze (founded 1822) which met in Berlin in 1828.

11　*Brewster, Allerly near Melrose, to Babbage, 1 Dorset Street, Manchester Square, London, 12 February 1830*

I have sent you under another cover the sheet of Porisms. I am delighted to find that you are engaged in a work on the Decline of Science in England, the most heart-breaking subject that I know and one on which I would have long ago written if I could have commanded my leisure. It is a disgrace to men of science and to the Royal Society, the natural guardian of English science, that they have not combined in a vigorous attempt to raise public feeling on the subject. Your work will do much, but it would be necessary to obtain the cooperation of political and influential persons in order to produce a practical result. As I do not know exactly the precise bearing of your work, the following ideas may not be of any use to you.

1. One of the causes of the total damper of [men of] science in Scotland is the total want of situations to which they can aspire. Men of science are ambitious of professorships, but owing to the fact that in Scotland the professors are paid by the *fees* of their pupils, their sole object is to fill their classes and to become scientific showmen. It invariably happens that the moment an able man is made a professor there is an end of his scientific career; so that there is not in Scotland at this moment an individual in a university cultivating science.

There are various semi-scientific Boards in Scotland, the Board of Trustees for the Encouragement of the Arts etc, the Lighthouse Board etc; but the commissioners are all unpaid officers and wealthy individuals, who know nothing of the subjects; and the entire management devolves upon the secretary, treasurer, clerks etc not one of whom is ever a person of science. The consequence is that all these boards are more expensively conducted than if they were managed as in France etc by a board of scientific men paid for their labour.

2. A great evil in this country is the want of some order of Civil Merit, which would honour the successful labourers of science. In a poor country this is at least a cheap way of advancing science.

3. The state of the patent laws is another great check to science.

I have read the evidence before the House with astonishment. It seems to have occurred to nobody that a patent should be granted, or rather an invention received, *without any expense whatever*, excepting perhaps the transmission of a model to a national repository. Why should not an invention be property at common law, like a book, which is protected by statute only to enable the author to recover more summarily?

4. I may mention a very striking example of the state of science in Great Britain, connected with myself. After I invented the built up lens, I exerted myself in vain to have it applied to lighthouses, where its vast superiority to mirrors is demonstrable. Several years after I had published my invention Monsieur Fresnel took up the same idea, and proposed it to the Lighthouse Board in France who immediately adopted it after an experimental examination, and arranged a complete system of lighting the coast by these lenses. Even after the superiority of the lens had been thus proved, I have exerted myself in vain to induce the Scotch Board, the Irish Board, and the Trinity House to adopt it; but I have entirely failed; because there is not a scientific man in any of these boards that has the least knowledge of optics. The [accuracy] of the lens is [enormous] and its advantages so palpable that they may be demonstrated to the dullest capacity. I venture to say that if these lighthouse boards were partly or wholly managed by men of science well paid for their labour, there would be an annual saving of many thousand pounds.

I hope you noticed Mr Peel's defence of the Duke of Wellington whom he stated to be a person perfectly convinced that the superiority of England depended on the progress of the sciences and arts.

I was confounded when I saw the Council of the Royal Society announced; and I was so impressed with the belief that something was wrong that in writing on some business to Mr Herschel's brother-in-law I begged he would let me know the reason of Mr Herschel's withdrawing from the Royal Society. I shall weary to see your book, and I should like if you could enable me to give an early account of it in my journal.

BL, Add. MSS 37185, ff. 49–51

Augustin Jean Fresnel (1788–1827), *DSB*; Arthur Wellesley, first Duke of Wellington (1769–1852), *DNB*, then Prime Minister. Babbage's *Reflections on the decline of science in England, and on some of its causes* (London, 1830) was principally an attack on abuses in the Royal Society of London. Brewster was obsessed by the fraudulence of the patent laws, as revealed in the *Report from the select committee on the law relative to patents for inventions*, Parliamentary Papers, 1829, iii. 415–676. For Brewster's built-up lens, invented by him in 1811, see M.M. Gordon, *The home life of Sir David Brewster* (2nd ed., Edinburgh, 1870), 374–86. Herschel's withdrawal from the Royal Society of London began in 1827 when he resigned the secretaryship he had held since 1824.

12 *Brewster, Allerly near Melrose, to Babbage, 1 Dorset Street, Manchester Square, London, 24 February 1830*

I received your drawing for Porisms for which I am much obliged to you. I wish much you could spare ten minutes to my equation, for it will not cost you more, as I am very anxious to have it, for the purpose of using in a paper of mine which is now in the hands of the printer. Would it not be useful to organise an association for the purpose of protecting and promoting the *secular* interests of science? A few influential noblemen and MPs would give great help in forwarding such an object. I again beg to trouble you with an enclosure.

BL, Add. MSS 37185, f. 72

13 *Brewster, Allerly near Melrose, to Babbage, 1 Dorset Street, Manchester Square, London, 16 June 1830*

I ought to have thanked you long ago for your very interesting volume, and for the flattering reference which you make to my labours. I have inserted as an article in [the] next number of the *Edinburgh Journal* a copious extract from the first part of it, and I am now hard at work in writing for the *Quarterly* a review of it, or rather an article on the decline of science purporting to be a review of it; for circumstances partly of a personal nature and partly connected with the *Quarterly* prevent me from entering into the matter of the Royal Society. I suspect Captain Sabine has been ordered to his regiment in consequence of your work. If this is so it would be a great triumph: he surely cannot be a scientific adviser when he is in Ireland.

As I take up the subject under a very general aspect, I feel greatly the want of information on many points, and would therefore thank you for any facts you can give me in reference to the following points.

1. What are the scientific institutions, offices etc which ought to be managed or filled by men of science, such as the Trinity House etc?
2. Are the Academicians of Berlin paid by the government as in France, and what is the amount of their pensions in both countries?
3. What is the income of the Royal Society, independent of the fees, and what is it derived from?
4. Is your machine going on or is it stopped by the withdrawing of the former allowances?
5. Did Sir W Herschel enjoy any pension or allowance from the King, and did the King supply funds for any other telescope but the 40-feet one?

6. Do you know of any instances of liberality to scientific men during the present reign, unconnected with politics?

7. Do you know any thing of the state of science in Russia?

8. Do you recollect of any examples of science being patronised in England since the time of Newton?

If any thing occurs to you that it might be useful to state in such a paper as that which I am writing I hope you will mention it, and I trust you will let me know what impression your book has made upon men in power. It seems to me that this is the moment to do something effectual, and that an association should be organised for reviving science in England. Many of our nobility, though not scientific, would willingly promote such a great object, and an association rightly constituted would have influence enough to direct the existing government to a system of measures which would put England on a level with other nations.

BL, Add. MSS 37185, ff. 229-30

Edward Sabine (1788-1883), *DNB*, army officer and expert on terrestrial magnetism, had been accused by Babbage, *Decline of science*, 77-97, of corruption; Sir William Herschel (1738-1822), *DNB*, the astronomer and father of John Frederick William. For Brewster's polemics, see 'Mr Babbage's observations on the national encouragement of science', *Edinburgh journal of science*, 1830 (July), iii. 58-76, and Brewster, 'Decline of science in England', *Quarterly review*, 1830 (Oct.), xliii. 305-42.

14 *Brewster, Allerly near Melrose, to Forbes, Colinton House near Edinburgh, 10 July 1830*

... My labours indeed are thickening so much upon me, that I must either give up science altogether or retire into absolute seclusion from the world. More than a year ago I promised to Mr Lockhart to write an article for the *Quarterly* on the Decline of Science, but there was no book till Babbage's appeared, which could authorise the insertion of such an article. The article, which is now printing, is about $2\frac{1}{2}$ sheets long, and will I trust be of some use. It is not written under the fear of man, and must give offence in many quarters both high and low.

I begin by establishing the fact, on the evidence of various authors, that science and the arts are on the decline in England. I then show that from the time of Galileo to the present day all the great ornaments of science were honoured and rewarded by their respective sovereign. I show that the living philosophers in all the other kingdoms of Europe are also showered with titles of honour, and I point out how completely the reverse of all this is the case in England. I then show that all public boards which in other countries are filled by men of science, such as the lighthouse boards, Fishery

Board, Board of Trustees, etc are managed by unpaid commissions, and that not even their paid officers are scientific men. I next show that our Royal Societies contain no situations for appointing men of science, and that the few situations which our universities afford, prove the means of extinguishing the scientific character of those who obtain them. I then take up the subject of the patent laws at some length. This wide plan enables me [to] take up many subjects and to bring forward many facts with which the public are little if at all acquainted. I abuse the government and the University of Edinburgh for their conduct respecting the Royal Society of Edinburgh's charter, the transference of their property to the Museum, and the exclusion of the Society from their own collections there. I reprobate the discontinuance of the hourly observations at Leith Fort, and I censure all the three Societies of London, Edinburgh, and Dublin, for having neglected their duty in not stimulating government to acts favourable to science, in not resisting the abolition of the Board of Longitude, and in not recommending to the notice of government such men as Dalton and Ivory.

I am really at a loss to know what should or could be done to place the Royal Society of Edinburgh on a proper footing. Its decay arises more from the general decay of science in the country than from any act of its own; and even if all its mismanagement were remedied, the real evil remains uncured. The first step is for the friends of science to combine in the promotion of national measures for the revival of science. Petitions from scientific institutions and from individuals would produce some effect. Babbage writes me that 'his book is not the only one of the kind which will appear—*one* if not *more* will follow it, perhaps in a few months'. He tells me that reviews of his book are preparing for the *Edinburgh* [*and*] *Westminster Reviews*, and for Férussac's *Bulletin* etc. All this will secure public mention and if men of science and literature would only combine and exert themselves, something might be done especially at the beginning of a new reign ...

Forbes Papers, 1830/41

John Gibson Lockhart (1794-1854), *DNB*, editor of the *Quarterly review*, like his father-in-law, Sir Walter Scott (1771-1832), *DNB*, lived near Brewster; James Ivory (1765-1842), *DNB*, mathematician; André Étienne Férussac (1786-1836) edited the *Bulletin universel des sciences et de l'industrie*, The Royal Societies were those of London and of Edinburgh, the Dublin Society was the Royal Irish Academy. Brewster (Secretary of the Royal Society of Edinburgh, 1820-28) was outraged by its inability to pay the legal costs generated by his own attempts as its Secretary to recover the Society's property from the University museum where it was zealously guarded by Robert Jameson (1774-1854), *DNB*, professor of natural history. Hourly meteorological observations were made at Leith Fort by non-commissioned officers from 1824 until 1828 when the army withdrew its co-operation with the Royal Society of

Edinburgh. The Board of Longitude was abolished in summer 1828. Babbage's book was not reviewed in the *Edinburgh*, the *Westminster*, or in Férrusac's *Bulletin*.

15 *Brewster, Allerly near Melrose, to Whewell, Trinity College, Cambridge, 4 November 1830*

I have just received your letter, and I shall be most happy now and at all times to publish any thing you may send me, even though it be directed, as it will in the present case, against myself.

I wrote the article on the decline of science in the *Quarterly*, and I did hope that there would not be a man of science in England that would not thank me for having espoused *his cause*, and exposed myself to the powers of government from the single motive of advancing the interests of science. I cannot for a moment doubt that you have greatly misapprehended both the object and meaning of the reviewer. You never were more mistaken than in charging the reviewer with entire ignorance of every thing belonging to English universities. The article was carefully revised by a gentleman educated at an English university and I, the author of the article, had obtained the most correct and exact information on the very subjects to which you refer. The mistake is wholly yours in supposing that there was the *remotest reference to Cambridge* etc. The plan proposed refers only to certain professorships which are well known; to *some* chairs, and to *those only* which have £600 and upwards for their value. I *knew perfectly well* that there was no such scientific chair in Cambridge, and I considered the very smallness of the incomes at Cambridge as an argument for dividing professorships that exceeded £600. The chemical chair in Edinburgh is worth £2000 and upwards per annum and when I tell you that that class has never produced a single chemical student of any note I think you will agree with me that the *chair might be divided into three at from £600 to £700 each, one* filled by an *analytical* chemist, *another* by a *popular* lecturer and a third by a *philosophical* chemist.

On the subject of the reviewer's ignorance of the merits of Professors Airy, Sedgwick and Buckland I think you are equally mistaken. The review refers *solely* to the *physical sciences*, and therefore had no reference whatever to the *sciences of observation*. There is no man alive that venerates Cambridge and Oxford more than I do, and few that have a more exalted opinion of the talents of the three eminent individuals above mentioned. I discussed this very subject with Professor Sedgwick when I was correcting the review for press, and I made to him the same observation which I have printed, that I knew of no individual in the eight universities that was engaged *in a train of original research*. He mentioned Professor Airy as occupied with scientific subjects, and he especially mentioned that the advantage might be great of his uniting high mathematical talents with the skill of a practical astronomer. I knew that Professor Airy's time was occupied with popular lectures and with astronomical observations, duties scarcely consistent with a *train of original research*, and when you wrote me that he had been lecturing on the polarisation of light I replied that I hoped he would direct his great powers to that interesting subject. You now write me that he is doing this and you doubtless consider him as engaged in a *train of original research on this subject*. This is in itself a proof that he was not engaged in a train of original research when I wrote the review, as the reviewer uses the cautious phrase of *at present known to be engaged* etc. Now I venture to say that if I had, when I wrote the review, asked Mr Babbage or Mr Herschel if they knew of any person at Cambridge engaged in a train of original research on any subject in physical science, their answer would have been 'there are many men at Cambridge engaged in physical studies and in physical investigations, but none *in a train of original research*'. For example I am always occupied at certain times of leisure with mineralogical enquiries as you are, but I could not say that either you or I are engaged in a train of original mineralogical research. Even your letter is not so expressed as to satisfy me that Professor Airy is so engaged on the subject of polarisation, and I think Professor Sedgwick, had he known this, would not have omitted to mention it to me. Your reference to the *Cambridge Transactions* does not seem to me to justify your view. When Professor Playfair was composing his beautiful papers on the solid of greatest attraction, on barometrical measurements, etc, etc, he certainly was not engaged in a *train of original research*. Had I thought it possible that [the] meaning of this phrase could have been misconstrued, I would have taken great care to explain more fully what I meant. That it has been rightly understood by other professors, personally interested in its meaning, I infer from a kind letter I have this day received from Dr Lardner, who had recognised me as the author of the review. I have also learned that it has given great satisfaction to many influential persons in London who would not have tolerated any thing injurious either to Cambridge or Oxford. I earnestly beg you to read the article carefully, and as I know that the paper you propose to send me will not give me offence I assure you that I shall reply to it in a way that will not offend you and give me an opportunity of doing justice to Cambridge and its distinguished ornaments.

Whewell Papers, a. 201[79]

John Playfair (1748–1819), *DNB*, professor of mathematics and then natural philosophy at Edinburgh; Dionysius Lardner (1793-1859), *DNB*. In his 'Decline of science in England', 327, Brewster had rashly asserted that in Britain's eight universities nobody was 'at present known to be engaged in any train of original research'. Whewell quickly defended Cambridge's teaching and research record in 'Cambridge transactions. Science of the English universities', *British Critic*, 1831, ix. 71-90.

16 *Sir Alexander Crichton, The Grove, Sevenoaks, Kent, to Murchison, 24 November 1830*

Most sincerely do I lament the present state of the Royal Society. I was in hopes, from what our friend Fitton stated to me when he was last down here, that the Duke of Sussex had resolved not to expose himself to a contested election. But if His Royal Highness does stand, I must vote for him not only as one of the oldest friends I have, but from the conviction that *quoad* mere presidency, he will be fully as useful as any of the mere men of science, not excepting the *all* powerful and *omniscient* Warburton. Herschel is unexceptionable in every point of view and not merely unexceptionable but also admirable as far as profound science and the most honourable conduct can make him so; but the presidency of the Royal Society requires a certain state and brilliancy such as Sir J Banks possessed, to do it justice and maintain its éclat; for there is no possibility of satisfying English men of science with eau sacrée or the pure emanations of mind alone. Whether the Irish and Scotch are much more reasonable I leave you and Fitton to decide.

This contest will do infinite injury to the Royal Society; one or other of the candidates ought to be induced to withdraw. If the Duke is resolved to stand (which does surprise me) I think the sincere well-wishers of Herschel ought not to bring him forward but this I say with perfect submission and respect. Oh dear! Oh dear!

Murchison Papers

Sir Alexander Crichton (1763-1856), *DNB*, physician of international repute; William Henry Fitton (1780-1861), Irish-born geologist; Henry Warburton (1784-1858), *DNB*, MP and philosophical radical; Sir Joseph Banks (1743-1820), *DNB*, was President of the Royal Society of London 1778-1820. Augustus Frederick, Duke of Sussex (1773-1843), *DNB*, sixth son of George III, stood for the Presidency of the Royal Society of London against Herschel; on 30 Nov 1830 he was elected by 119 votes to 111, and served until 1838. Such public faction-fighting was uncommon in the annals of the Society.

17 *Harcourt, York, to Milton, 18 January 1831*

You have befriended in a very material degree the Yorkshire Philosophical Society, which has hitherto required the nursing of persons near York as well as the support of more influential names at a distance. I consider it now as capable of going alone and needing a guardian rather than a nurse. It consists now of 250 members, has an income of near £500 a year with a debt only of about £1300. It is fit for the purpose for which it was principally intended, that of a county Museum of natural history and antiquities, and it has collected about it whatever there is of scientific ability or disposition hereabouts, including very good superintendents for the Museum and the Gardens. The superintendent of the Museum has very superior scientific attainments, is modest, sensible and popular, well contented with science and £100 a year. He is well qualified for conducting all the material parts of a philosophical institution. Under these circumstances, both for the sake of the Society and my own, I do not wish to take any longer the prominent part which I have hitherto thought necessary to set such an establishment on foot. It is both my wish, and it is the wish I have no doubt of others, that it should obtain a head and protector of *more consequence in the County of York* than myself. Allow me to say that I think you would do an act of public utility by allowing me now to propose your name to the Society as the properest for that head and protector. It will not demand much of your time, indeed it would require very little; for if an annual Vice-president be appointed he would take the routine duty of the office, and perhaps you would not think it too much trouble to attend the *annual* meeting and at any time at which you might be at York to show your interest in its concerns. I should be very happy to render all the assistance in my power and I am sure that Mr Cholmeley of Brandsby, Mr H. Howard, Mr Wellbeloved and others would do the same. I should not object after the first year to take the office of Vice-president in my turn.

I venture to make this proposition to you as considering a person in your station to be in some degree public property and as believing that you know and feel yourself to be so. But in whatever way you view it I am sure you will excuse the liberty I am taking in making this request; which I do with an *earnest hope* that you may accede to it and that you will allow me at our next Council meeting which takes place on the last day I think of this month to propose you as President of this Society, which is now flourishing in a degree to make the office not unworthy of your acceptance, and which I am sincerely and fully persuaded will flourish hereafter much more under your auspices than under those of any other person in Yorkshire.

[PS] If the immediate acceptance at the present moment should not be agreeable to you, I hope that alone will not induce you to decline it; for a temporary appointment might be made but it would save trouble if you did not object to accede to the proposal now.

Fitzwilliam Papers, drawer Jan–Mar 1831

Francis Cholmeley (1783-1854) of Brandsby Hall near York; Henry Edward John Howard (1795-1868), *DNB*, then succentor at York. John Phillips was superintendent of the Museum. On 1 Feb 1831 Milton was elected President of the Yorkshire Philosophical Society and held office until his death.

18 *Brewster, Allerly near Melrose, to Babbage, 1 Dorset Street, Manchester Square, London, 21 February 1831*

I have just been reading a very interesting account of the different meetings of the German Naturalists drawn up by my friend Mr Johnston, who attended the last anniversary at Hamburg, for the forthcoming number of my journal. The perusal of it, and a suggestion which it contains, has strongly impressed me with the opinion that the cause of science in England would derive great benefit from a meeting of British men of science at York in July or August next. Independent of the considerable scientific interest of such a meeting, [it might produce] some general measures for promoting the cause of science in Great Britain. Will you give the idea a serious consideration, and write about it to Mr Herschel who should be President? The Royal Society of London seems to be gone. So is that of Edinburgh and the Royal Irish Academy has been long ago at an end. This is therefore the time for a general effort, and I hope you will not be backward in giving your aid on such an occasion.

As the transactions of societies are so tardy in their appearance, it seems to me that the organisation of a new scientific journal would be a great object at present. To forward such a measure I would instantly give up mine, and take either an active or a secondary, or no part at all in the management of a new one, as I should be quite satisfied with the position of a contributor. Such a measure however could only be carried into effect by such men as Herschel and yourself taking an active part in it.

BL, Add. MSS 37185, ff. 481-2

James Finlay Weir Johnston (1796-1855), *DNB*, a chemist and protégé of Brewster, suggested in 'Account of the meeting of naturalists at Hamburg', *Edinburgh journal of science*, 1831 (Apr), iv. 189-244 (244) that British meetings of cultivators of science would be beneficial. Johnston's article was dated 23 Feb 1831.

19 *Brewster, Allerly near Melrose, to Phillips, Secretary Yorkshire Philosophical Society, York, 23 February 1831*

I have taken the liberty of writing you on a subject of considerable importance. It is proposed to establish a British Association of men of science similar to that which has existed for eight years in Germany, and which is now patronised by the most powerful sovereigns in that part of Europe. The arrangements for the first meeting are now in progress, and it is contemplated that it shall be held in York as the most centrical city for the three kingdoms. My object in writing you at present is to beg that you would ascertain, if York could furnish the accommodations necessary for so large a meeting, which might perhaps consist of above 100 individuals; if the [Yorkshire] Philosophical Society would enter zealously into the plan, and if the Mayor and influential persons in the town and in the vicinity would be likely to promote its objects.

The principal objects of the Society would be to make the cultivators of science acquainted with each other, to stimulate one another to new exertions, to bring the objects of science more before the public eye, and to take measures for advancing its interests and accelerating its progress. The society would possess no funds, make no collections and hold no property, the expenses of each anniversary meeting being defrayed by the members who are present.

As these few observations will enable you to form a general opinion of the object in view I shall only add that the time of meeting which is likely to be most convenient would be about the 18th or 25th of July.

British Association archives, Foundation volume, 1

20   *Robert Davies, York, to Phillips, Secretary Yorkshire Philosophical Society, York, 9 March 1831*

In compliance with the request of the Council of the Yorkshire Philosophical Society, I have taken an opportunity of acquainting the Lord Mayor and some others of the Magistrates, with the communication contained in Dr Brewster's letter to you, and they desire me to say that they will have great pleasure in doing anything that lies in their power to promote the objects of the society mentioned by Dr Brewster, and they rejoice that York is fixed upon as the place for holdings its meetings.

British Association archives, Foundation volume, 2

Robert Davies (1793-1875), *DNB*, a local historian, Yorkshire Philosophical Society Councillor, and Town Clerk of York.

21   *John Robison, 9 Atholl Crescent, Edinburgh, to Phillips, Secretary Yorkshire Philosophical Society, York, 25 March 1831*

I have received from my friend Dr Brewster your communication to him of the 11 March, and have at the same time been made aware of the announcement made in the April number of his journal of the proposed meeting at York. Since that time I have had conversations with many of my friends (including two who have been present at Continental meetings) on this subject. I find a very general disposition to go into the plan, but considerable doubts as to whether it should have been begun this year in the present excited state of feeling on other subjects. I find also as far as I have yet learned that the months of July and August would be less generally suitable than September (say the first Monday in September) and I should like before any more specific advertisements are made, that you would have the goodness to say what your opinion is on this point.

Having learned from our mutual friend Mr Witham that he would willingly take some trouble in promoting the success of this plan, I have brought him into contact with Professor Pillans and Mr Johnston who have attended different continental meetings (of the German association) and have got them to show him the different lists and programmes, and to explain the local arrangements which are prepared by the authorities of the cities which are in turn fixed on as rendezvous. Mr Johnston is to furnish him with various memoranda on these matters, after which Mr Witham has been good enough to undertake to write to you and others of his friends on the subject; or even, if you should wish it, to proceed to York along with Mr Johnston to give further explanations.

I have written to Dr Brewster to request he may furnish me with the names of any of the eminent persons in the scientific world whose example might induce others to follow them, and whom he may himself prevail on to take an interest in the meeting. When he communicates any such names, and when I have your opinion as to the proper period for the meeting, I shall take steps for making it generally known through the English and French scientific journals, that such a meeting will take place.

British Association archives, Foundation volume, 3

John Robison (1778-1843), *DNB*, an Edinburgh gentleman inventor and Secretary of the Royal Society of Edinburgh 1828-40; James Pillans (1778-1864), *DNB*, was professor of latin at Edinburgh University; Henry Thomas Maire Witham (1779-1844), the Barnard Castle palaeo-botanist. The first public announcement of the proposed meeting, 'Great scientific meeting to be held at York', *Edinburgh journal of science*, 1831 (Apr), iv. 374, revealed July 1831 as the date of meeting and that Robison was interim secretary of it.

22   *Forbes, Greenhill, Edinburgh, to Robison, 7 April 1831*

I have to thank you for your very kind attention to my request, and the most friendly and courteous terms in which my credentials as you rightly designate them are expressed. I shall trust to your communicating to me the result of your application to Dr Hope when it shall be made known to you. The *figure* can no wise interfere, as if there is any, it would merely be the one I drew on the board, and which I can give any day. I am determined not to disgrace the *Transactions* with anything more imperfect than I can help, and if possible will repeat the reduction of the whole of my observations.

Since we last conversed on the York meeting, I have read for the first time Mr Johnston's paper, and I confess it has not greatly warmed my anticipation of it. *Such* a meeting I certainly should not wish to see in England, nor are we likely to seek such a one. But the question is, will it be better? By his own account very little indeed which could be considered the legitimate purpose of the meeting was accomplished. Far too many people to make friends, or if made, to cultivate [well]; and too much eating and drinking and dining to suit our British phlegm.

But as it is to be attempted I would certainly try to make the best of it; I have felt as much as any one can possibly have done the total want of connection with his fellow labourers, which an insulated man may feel; and did I think that such a meeting could produce a permanent good effect in promoting such a community of sentiment in a nation like ours, I should feel very warmly for its success. But at all events, as it is to take place I shall be much disposed to do anything however little I can effect to prevent its falling to the ground. Sir Thomas Brisbane is I think as likely a man as any to [support it] keenly: he has a great deal of influence with Sir James South. Has he been consulted? Is there any hope of the French *savants* taking an interest in it?

By the way, if you approved it, I wish you would suggest to the R. S. Council, that the *Connaissance des Temps* ought to be taken among the foreign periodicals; some past vols are in the library, and besides being an ephemeris, it contains much valuable matter in the 'Additions'.

I am much pleased with article 303 of Herschel's *Treatise*. Were it only as a Scotchman I should be justly proud of it. It is a fine compliment to two of the greatest ornaments of our university.

Forbes Papers, Letter Book I, 348–9

Thomas Charles Hope (1766–1844), *DNB*, professor of chemistry at Edinburgh University and a Vice-president of the Royal Society of Edinburgh, of which Sir Thomas Makdougall Brisbane (1773–1860), *DNB*, was to be President 1832–60. On 4 Apr 1831 Forbes had read a paper to the Society on the variations of barometric pressure near Edinburgh, but failed to have it published in the Society's *Transactions*. Article 303 of J.F.W. Herschel, *Preliminary discourse on the study of natural philosophy* (London, 1830), 273, praised Colin MacLaurin (1698–1746), *DNB*, professor of mathematics at Edinburgh University, and John Robison (1739-1805), *DNB*, professor of natural philosophy at Edinburgh University (and father of this letter's recipient).

23 *Robison, 9 Atholl Crescent, Edinburgh, to Phillips, 29 April 1831*

I find an opinion is daily gaining ground here that it would be advisable to defer the proposed meeting of the cultivators of science to the summer of 1832. The causes of this opinion will readily occur to you, so I need not state any of those which have been urged to me; I shall only add that Dr Brewster who at one time seemed disposed to urge the matter this year at all events, seems now to have become doubtful of the expediency of persevering in the present circumstances of the country.

I should feel much obliged to you if you would have the goodness to ascertain and communicate to me the sentiments of your Society on this matter as if they should still feel desirous that the meeting should be attempted this season, I should endeavour to get some of our friends to attend at all events; if on the contrary the Society should concur in opinion that it would be expedient [to] ly bye for a season, I·should then have notices inserted in different literary journals to intimate the postponement.

British Association archives, Foundation volume, 4

On 22 Apr 1831 a general election was announced with parliamentary reform as the main issue, the first reform bill having been introduced 1 Mar 1831.

24 *Robison, 9 Atholl Crescent, Edinburgh, to Phillips, 1 North Crescent, Alfred Place, London, 26 May 1831*

I heard a few days ago incidentally that you had been for some time in London, and learned at the same time that several friends of science there had spoken of their intention of attending the meeting at York. I am happy to have this confirmed by you, and trust that after all the dubiety which has been felt, a fair attendance may still be looked for. Much will however depend on the efforts of such men as Mr Murchison, and I should have better expectation of the association finding general favour if the promotion of the plan appeared to come from London rather than from Edinburgh.

I have had a good many enquiries of what qualifications were required to become an associate, what were the rules and purposes of the association, and how it was to be conducted. My reply has always been, that all which has yet been proposed has been that an opportunity should be offered to the friends and cultivators of science to rendezvous at York when the formation of an association should be considered and regulations agreed to for its future conduct.

I am not aware that any scheme has yet been prepared, and it is very desirable that some person competent to such a task should take it into consideration, and should bring with him to the meeting an outline to be filled up after discussion with those who may attend. If you know of any gentleman who would undertake this matter, you would contribute much to the success of the plan in engaging him to do it.

In making the announcement by advertisement, it would perhaps be advisable to direct visitors on their first arrival to call at some particular place to inscribe their names and to receive a ticket of admission to the hall of meeting. A list of lodgings might be left at this place for inspection. You will oblige me (if you approve of this) by furnishing me with the name and address of any suitable person for attending to these matters.

On the ticket delivered to the visitors at Hamburg the name, designation and numero of the recipient is written on one side, and on the other is a small plan of the floor and seating of the place of meeting. The benches are all marked with engraved numbers at the extremities, and the particular place appointed for the bearer of the ticket is marked in red ink with his distinguishing numero, so that every one can find his seat without difficulty. Some printed lists were likewise given along with the ticket containing information on local and other matters likely to be interesting or useful to strangers.

I think I mentioned to you before that Mr Johnston, who wrote the account of the Hamburg meeting for Dr Brewster's journal, is in this vicinity and that if you think it would facilitate your arrangements in any degree, I think it more than probable that he would agree to make a run to York to confer with you on what it may be expedient to do in the way of preparing for the meeting.

I shall wait with some anxiety to learn the result of Mr Murchison's efforts among his friends.

[PS] There is an engineer of some eminence in the suite at Holyrood House whom I would ask to accompany me if you think there would be no objection to it. He is a very agreeable and liberal minded man although he has been selected as the instructor of a Bourbon prince. I forgot to say that I do not see any objection to the 3d of October although I should think the last week of September would be more generally convenient in this quarter. A good many junior classes begin on the 3d October.

British Association archives, Foundation volume, 5

Phillips was in London all May 1831 negotiating, fruitlessly, about his possible assumption of a chair of geology at University College. On 25 May 1831 Murchison had issued the first circular about the 1831 meeting, fixing the starting date as 26 Sept; it was apparently written and lithographed by Murchison, addressed London, but unsigned. The junior classes were those of Edinburgh University.

25 *Robison, Edinburgh, to Phillips, Secretary Yorkshire Philosophical Society, York, 8 June 1831*

I have had the pleasure of receiving your letter with the packet of circulars by which I am glad to see I am relieved from any further interference in the affair of the meeting. It might have been as well not to have addressed the circular from London any more than from Edinburgh, as York should be looked on as head quarters until the persons who may assemble shall frame their own regulations.

You have not said whether Mr Murchison or yourself have taken steps towards advertising the meeting in some of the London papers, and in every accessible journal. I fear if this be not done, and if private correspondence be the only means employed to bring the gentlemen together, some idea may get abroad of an intention of confining the association to a particular set. This, however unfounded, may at some future period be urged as a reproach, and it may be well to obviate the possibility of misconception by public announcements. An occasional paragraph in your own provincial paper may be useful to keep up attention, as such paragraphs would find their way into the London and other papers by degrees.

Mr Witham, with whom I believe you are acquainted, promised to take an opportunity of conversing with you on the subject of the subsidiary arrangements for the meetings and of proposing that you should have an interview with Mr Johnston, the writer of the article on the Hamburg meeting in Brewster's journal, who has got a collection of many of the tickets, tables and pamphlets which were distributed to the visitors. There is another gentleman here also who attended that meeting, so that if your own conveniency should admit of your paying us a short visit here, you would have an opportunity of satisfying yourself on many matters of detail which may prove convenient to you afterwards. In the event of your coming here, I hope you will do me the favour of taking up your quarters with me during your stay, and that you will advise me of your approach in time to secure your meeting with Professor Pillans and Mr Johnston.

British Association archives, Foundation volume, 6

26 *Robison, 9 Atholl Crescent, Edinburgh, to Phillips, Secretary Yorkshire
Philosophical Society, York, 26 June 1831*

I had the pleasure of receiving your letter of the 23d yesterday. I
immediately communicated it to Mr Johnston who happened to be
with me when it was delivered. He has promised to write to you
regarding some matters of detail which he thinks may be productive
of convenient arrangements.

I think it is a pity that a general notice has not yet emanated *from
York* as I have some grounds for fearing that an idea may get abroad
that the meeting will be encouraged by a particular party, rather
than by a general feeling among the friends of science; and as parties
have for some time run so high in London, such a notion, although
altogether unfounded in fact, would be very likely to make many
individuals abstain from joining it. If the advertisements etc proceed
directly from York, there will be no fear of any misapprehension on
this score, and every person proposing to attend the meeting will
feel satisfied that he will be likely to have an equal influence with
other visitors in determining on the regulations to be adopted.

I regret to observe that Dr Brewster in his July number has held
out that Mr Johnston and I proposed to draw up some scheme for
the constitution of the association. I have no intention of the sort, as
I think the fewer rules which are made in the early stage of the
business it will be the better, and that such as may be necessary at
the commencement, will come with a better grace if prepared and
suggested by the hosts of the meeting, than if proposed by any other
influence.

Both Mr Witham & Mr Forbes have returned to Edinburgh. I
have seen the latter who appears sanguine as to the number who
will attend. I have not yet met Mr Witham and do not know
whether he may have been successful in obtaining promises. He is
very full of his fossil trees at present . . .

British Association archives, Foundation volume, 7

Brewster, 'Proposed scientific meeting at York', *Edinburgh journal of science*, 1831
(July), v. 180-2, offered draft regulations for the constitution of the proposed association; and he called on Robison, Johnston, and the Yorkshire Philosophical Society to
prepare a code of laws.

27 *Johnston, Portobello, Edinburgh, to Phillips, Secretary Yorkshire Philosophical Society, York, 11 July 1831*

Your last letter to Mr Robison containing the printed extract from
the York paper, which Mr Robison has been kind enough to com-

municate to me, renders it almost unnecessary for me to trouble you with a letter. I felt I believe in common with some others that there was a little unkindness in the London circular, not meant I believe but yet observable in the circumstance that Mr Robison's name was not once mentioned in it, though he had been requested to officiate as interim secretary and had been put forward in Brewster's journal in that character. Mr Robison had felt it as a slight, a thing the more to be regretted as he has acted in the affair in the most liberal and friendly manner.

Partly on this account and partly because the London circular having no name annexed bore no official character I had intended to trouble you with a single suggestion which your last letter shows to be now unnecessary: that a circular if you should think such still necessary and at all events that the advertisements to be inserted in the London and Edinburgh papers should proceed directly from the Philosophical Society of York, bearing from them an invitation (signed by their Secretary) to all persons *interested* in scientific pursuits to repair to York on the 26th of September next then and there to found a society of the cultivators of science in Great Britain and Ireland. Such official documents will set all minds at rest and perhaps still prevent the meeting from being identified with any of the sects or coteries into which the men of science in London as well as Edinburgh are divided.

I am quite of your opinion that the term *zealous* as applied to the patrons of science by Dr Brewster must not and cannot be retained. He did me the honour to send me a proof of the resolutions while they were in the press, but I thought it too late to make any alteration. At the same time some line must be drawn between those who can and those who cannot become members. The efficiency of the society will be destroyed if the terms of admission be too lax. I think therefore the German regulation an exceedingly good one. *All interested* in science are admitted and enrolled and attend all meetings and take part in the discussions; but whenever any matter comes to a vote in the general meeting—that is upon all matters connected with the laws and regulations of the society—only those who have *written* on scientific subjects *vote*. One who has written may be no better philosopher nor more devoted to science than one who has not, but it is necessary to have some line of distinction; and to make the regulation as little exclusive as possible, *one memoir* gives you the necessary title. There is in reality then little irksome in the regulation and it will be chiefly felt during the first day of meeting in your good city. During the entire sittings at Hamburg last September no such vote was taken. You propose popular evening lectures; this I fear will not answer so well as a simple conversazione which I can assure you from experience is by far the most delightful way of spending one's time at these large meetings.

I hope you will be able to make arrangements for lithographing the names of the members as these autographs annexed to the report of the meeting drawn up by the President and Secretary form a very interesting memorial of the assembly.

There are many minor details upon which I might perhaps be able to assist you with useful hints were I in person at York; should you think it desirable I would willingly come to York a few days before the 26th to give you all the assistance in my power.

You of course will be appointed Secretary to the general meeting. Will your Mayor take the office of President?

British Association archives, Foundation volume, 8

On 4 July 1831 the Council of the Yorkshire Philosophical Society appointed a committee, with Harcourt as chairman, to prepare for the meeting. On 5 July this committee agreed to issue from York a circular about the meeting: this York circular, signed by Harcourt and Phillips, dated 12 July 1831, was widely distributed. Brewster had suggested, 'Proposed scientific meeting', 181, that the association should consist of only scientific authors and 'zealous patrons of science'. Lithographed autographs were first produced in connection with the 1833 meeting of the Association.

28   *Whewell, Trinity College, Cambridge, to Forbes, Greenhill, Edinburgh, 14 July 1831*

I am afraid I shall not meet you at York. Even if other circumstances allowed me I should feel no great wish to rally round Dr Brewster's standard after he has thought it necessary to promulgate so bad an opinion of us who happen to be professors in universities. He seems with respect to such people to have the power of imagining the most extraordinary things without a vestige of foundation: and just as he chose to fancy before that we had each a thousand a year (which notion he persists in refering to), he has now chosen to fancy that we are all banded together to oppose his favourite doctrine of the decline of science; though the only professor who has written at all on the subject is Babbage, the leader of the declinists. It requires all one's respect for Dr Brewster's merits to tolerate such bigotry and folly ...

Forbes Papers, 1831/25

29   *Forbes, Greenhill, Edinburgh, to Phillips, Museum, York, 3 August 1831*

I was very glad to see by a circular letter which Mr Robison showed me that the Yorkshire Philosophical Society have taken the meeting ostensibly into their own hands, as it can properly be *fathered* by no other body. I should not have troubled you with a letter merely upon this general subject (of which I doubt not you have already too many) but I feel extremely anxious that the same Society, or yourself individually, would endeavour to do [something] with a very false impression which cannot perhaps in any other way be successfully combated and which if persisted in will infallibly soon bring ruin on the whole project.

I had a letter the other day upon various topics from Professor Whewell of Cambridge and in mentioning Dr Brewster's attack upon professors in their scientific character (which his best friends must allow to be unadvised and most unreasonable) he adds that even if other circumstances permitted he should certainly not think of going to York, *to rally under Dr Brewster's banners*. Now this is truly too absurd. That Dr Brewster originated it there can be no doubt; however Mr Murchison has endeavoured to confine its origin to London and the Geological Society (and I must say he treated his countrymen rather cavalierly on the occasion), but to suppose that on that account the Doctor was to take any ostensible charge, or that even if he did a mere party feeling should keep men who ought to be above such things from joining in a scheme intended for the general promotion of science in Britain, is really vexation.

I believe I mentioned to you that Dr Brewster's nervousness in public is so great that even were he requested, he would be unable to act any conspicuous part at the meeting. And it might nearly be considered the downfall of the association, if the whole constellation of talent at Trinity were thus to be withheld from fostering so infantile a project.

I think you might devise some means for correcting the most erroneous views of the Cantabs: my might in the matter might, as the Trinitarians would say, be equated to zero, but I shall endeavour to do what I can. I rejoice to hear that Babbage will come. He is a host in himself. Is there any hope of Sedgwick? I hear a hope raised that Sir James South may bring the French savans who are to be over at the erection of his instrument.

If you find time to write me a line could you tell me whether Murchison and Lyell are still in London. Believe me My Dear Sir I shall not soon forget the hours we spent together at Oxford: and in hopes of the pleasure of seeing you next month I remain

Forbes Papers, Letter-book I, 396–8

Charles Lyell (1797–1875), *DNB*, the geologist. Forbes hero-worshipped the scientific constellation at Trinity College, Cambridge, which he had first visited in May 1831.

30 *Buckland, Oxford, to Harcourt, Wheldrake near York, 13 August 1831*

I have to acknowledge your two last letters with many apologies for my delay in replying to them. The first arrived as I was on the point of starting for London. The second I found on my return. I should have replied immediately to your first had it been in my power to do so in the affirmative, but I was then and am still doubtful whether it will be in my power to carry into execution the earnest wishes I feel to be present at your September meeting. The kind invitation to Bishopthorpe, which the Archbishop [of York] has done me the honour to send me by your last letter, has added still further to my desire to joining it. I trust I shall be able to do so, but cannot at this moment absolutely promise in the affirmative. The moment I can decide I will let you know.

With respect to sending any paper I must at once state that I have no time to prepare one, but if I come and can be of any use by giving you a lecture upon the caves that have been discovered analagous and subsequent to Kirkdale, I shall be most happy so to do.

I have recently been to examine a cave in Carmarthenshire containing human bones together with the bones of ancient bears but the human are clearly much more recent than the ursine remains. On my return I visited Conybeare who has built himself a most comfortable house on a small living near Cardiff. He was in hopes he should be able to join your meeting.

Harcourt MSS (Harcourt Papers, *xiii. 243-4*)

Edward Vernon Harcourt (1757-1847), *DNB*, Archbishop of York 1807-47, lived at Bishopthorpe Palace near York. The bone-cave at Kirkdale, north Yorkshire, was discovered in 1821 and immediately attracted Buckland's attention. Buckland did not attend the 1831 meeting.

31 *Murchison, Denton near Otley, to Harcourt, Wheldrake near York, 15. August 1831*

I have been on my geological rounds during the last 2 months, in consequence of which I only received *your circular* respecting the York Meeting about a fortnight ago when at Oulton Park. Our host there, Sir Philip Egerton, is certainly to be one of *us*. I use this term, because I presume that Mr Phillips informed you of my *fixed intention* of being present at the York meeting and also of bringing Mrs Murchison with me, who is now here and begs to send her kind remembrances to Mrs Vernon Harcourt and yourself.

It was of course out of my power to act upon your circular quoad the Geological Society, inasmuch as it was dated long after our *prorogation*, but Phillips knows how zealous I have been in forwarding the objects of the York meeting, not only in my own Society but in the Royal and elsewhere. We shall certainly have a very good list. I think you may calculate on Conybeare, Buckland, Greenough, perhaps Babbage, to whom I will write again as his presence would do much; and I will try to secure Fitton.

I am now on my way to see my mother in the County of Durham and would request you to write to me 'Hurworth, Darlington' where (or in the neighbourhood) I shall be [until] the 25 September. I beg you will have the kindness (if Phillips has not done so already) to secure a sitting room and bedroom in a private lodging at York for Mrs M. and myself as I should not like to be so long in an inn. What are your plans? What [is] the programme? Are we all to feed together? It will become a question of 'wie die naturforscher forschen', and as I conceive that persons in very limited circumstances will certainly travel from afar to be present, the prices must be moderate. I was surprised to find that a little druggist of Preston (who has a splendid collection of the limestone fossils by the bye) intended to join us. My *work* has been all along the Welsh and English frontier from Swansea to Flintshire, making repeated transverse sections from the lowest depths of grauwacke up to the coal measures, and I hope I shall be able to make *considerable* corrections in the geological map and to contribute some important zoological data for distinctions in the lower groups. My last few days have been directed to the neglected science of grouse shooting, which I combined with lead mining on the Grassington Moors and with very fair success, killing 11 braces on the 12th. Here our friend Sir Charles has scarcely a bird.

Harcourt MSS

Sir Philip de Malpas Grey Egerton (1806-81), *DNB*, politician and palaeontologist, George Bellas Greenough (1778-1855), *DNB*, London gentleman geologist, and William Gilbertson, a Preston apothecary, all attended the 1831 meeting; Conybeare, Babbage, and Fitton did not. Murchison was President of the Geological Society of London 1831-3. Sir Charles was Sir Charles Ibbetson (1779-1839), who owned Denton Hall and Park.

32 *Harcourt, Wheldrake near York, to Babbage, 27 August 1831*

York having been chosen as the place at which the proposed general meeting of the friends of science is to be held, it seems to be understood to devolve upon our Philosophical Society to propose for the consideration of the meeting a plan to regulate its proceedings. The part which it will fall on my coadjutors and myself to take, in a matter which may possibly prove of no inconsiderable importance to the interests of science, is the apology which I beg leave to offer for troubling you with a statement of my own views upon the subject and requesting your opinion and advice.

The chief objects of the meetings of scientific men which have been held in Germany appear to have been personal acquaintance and a mutual interchange of ideas, objects certainly of great advantage on all accounts yet objects which in my opinion will not continue in this country to draw men of science from their homes, and I think that a society founded on this principle would soon expire.

But perhaps there are higher objects which an annual aggregate meeting of this kind might propose to accomplish, and which would both hold a society together and make it of the highest efficiency in promoting the advancement of science without interfering with the province of any existing institution.

There is no society in Great Britain which has ever attempted, or at least persevered in attempting to give a *systematic direction* to philosophical research. I am not aware that there is any society which has undertaken to look over the map of science and to say: here is a shore of which the soundings should be more accurately taken, there a line of coast along which a voyage of discovery should be made. A society is wanting which will indicate the points that require elucidation, propose problems to be solved, and data to be determined, and either charge such of its members as may be able and willing to undertake the task as an honourable commission, or offer a prize for a particular investigation, or defray the expense of a specific process.

Neither has there hitherto been any society sufficiently independent, deliberative and powerful to possess influence with the government of the country, to claim for science what is due to it and to the interests of society depending upon it, and through the medium of public opinion to lead to a more enlightened and creditable national dealing with men of science and their objects.

If such a society does not exist, if you think it practicable to create it, if you think it might be a powerful instrument in sustaining and advancing philosophy in this country, will you cooperate in giving it that active support which the execution of such a scheme would require?

In that case allow me to say that your attendance at the meeting in September would be of very material consequence. In the mean while I should consider your opinion upon the subject as a great favour, and detailed suggestions on any points in science to which such a society ought to direct the attention of its members would be of the highest value. The time which I have been able to devote to philosophical subjects has been chiefly given to chemical and geological enquiries, and I do not pretend to be able without assistance to present even a competent *illustration* of what might be done by a society professing to point out the lines of direction in which the higher researches of science should move, though to do justice to the plan such illustration ought to be given in proposing it.

My notion of the materials of which such a society should be constructed is that the members of all philosophical societies should be members of this. No limitation would here be useful except that of a respectable character and the being in some manner a contributor to the promotion of science, both which qualifications that condition would secure. The greater the numbers the greater would be the power of the society to accomplish its objects. Committees, consisting of the most eminent men in every science, would prepare the propositions to be laid before the yearly meeting, and the scientific matter of each meeting would be the researches with which the preceding meeting had charged its members or which the prizes had produced. Should a system of prizes be pursued the government might perhaps be induced to furnish the means of giving them, or the members of the society might agree to contribute to them according to their respective tastes and studies. If this system of entrusting particular commissions to particular hands should be adopted, the numerous philosophical societies which have risen up in all parts might be made useful, especially in geology, natural history, and meteorology, by undertaking to render an accurate account of local phenomena; and whilst some experiments were confided to *individuals* the most competent to conduct them, others might be referred to *committees* who might divide among their numbers the labour and responsibility of a complicated research.

It would be of little use to enter further into the details of this plan, till it is known whether the principle is deemed good and feasible by those who are most capable of judging upon it and carrying it to a successful issue. With the view of obtaining the best opinions I have written to the same effect to Mr Herschel and intend to write to a very few other persons, and I shall be greatly obliged to yourself for an early reply. The sentiments of Sir James South or of any other men of science to whom you might think proper to communicate this letter would also be very thankfully received by me.

[PS] Should you come to Escrick before the meeting I should hope to have an opportunity of consulting with you more fully respecting it.

BL, Add. MSS 37186, ff. 136–8

The village of Escrick was four miles from Wheldrake. Versions of this letter were
sent to Herschel, Whewell, and Brewster, 25–27 Aug 1831.

33 *Harcourt, Wheldrake near York, to Murchison, Hurworth, Darlington,
29 August 1831*

I have proposed to Mr Herschel, Dr Brewster and two or three other
persons a scheme for an extended society, to be constituted at our
meeting in September, consisting of the members of all philosophical
societies, and having two objects: the one, to press upon the public
and the government the redress of any grievances under which science may labour and its advancement in a national point of view;
the other, to indicate in every science the researches which are most
required and either to charge certain of their members with them
individually or conjointly, or to offer prizes for their investigation,
to which the government might be induced to contribute. Committees to be appointed at each meeting to prepare the propositions
for the following meeting, and to examine and report upon the
solutions and investigations given in, in consequence of the propositions put forth at the preceding meeting.

If we meet only for the sake of meeting I do not think we shall
ever meet again, but such objects as these might induce our men of
science to congregate once a year and such a systematic direction
given to science might very greatly promote it.

With respect to subordinate arrangements for the present meeting
before we put forth a programme we must know a little more accurately of what materials it will be composed, but my ideas agree
with yours as to subsisting the philosophers cheaply: there must be
an ordinary for each day except that on which, if the numbers are
not too great to prevent it, I imagine they will dine at Bishopthorpe.
On two days at least it should be ruled for all to dine together.
Conversaziones may be held at the Museum every evening; and on
two or more mornings, meetings [held] there at which papers may
be read and debates carried on. Buckland offers a lecture on caves.
This and any other offers of the same kind would be best adapted
to the evening parties, should there happen to be drier matters
enough for the morning. Pray write to me any suggestions which
may occur to you. Can you tell me where Sedgwick is? I will take
care that Mrs Murchison is properly accommodated. It is unlucky
that Mrs W. Harcourt expects her confinement about the middle of
September.

P. S. If Mr Phillips is with you, you will perhaps show him my letter.
I forgot to mention that I have thought it necessary to send notice

to the Duke of Sussex of the meeting and he is invited to Bishopthorpe but we have not his answer yet.

Murchison Papers

Harcourt's wife gave birth to a daughter on 5 Oct 1831, conveniently after the first
meeting of the Association had ended. An ordinary was a public meal provided at a
fixed price.

34   *Harcourt, Wheldrake near York, to Milton, 30 August 1831*

I am desired by the Archbishop to express his hope that during the
philosophical meeting in September you will take up your quarters
at Bishopthorpe. He is to return from an excursion into the West
Riding [of Yorkshire] on the 27th but I shall be ready to receive
you on the 26th if you should come on that day. The business of the
meeting I suppose will commence on the 27th. Neither the present
nor the late President of the Royal Society will be at the meeting
and it is probable I think that you will be called to the chair, an
office however which will not necessarily involve more than a declaration of the value which you attach to scientific pursuits and
your desire to promote them. We shall propose a scheme for the
proceedings of the meeting and I have a plan which I have submitted to the consideration of Mr Herschel, Dr Brewster etc for making
it of a more extensive and permanent utility than merely that of
bringing men of science acquainted with one another. My two objects are these: 1st, to enable them as a body to speak a little louder
in the ear of government than they have yet ventured to do on the
national encouragement due to science; 2nd, to give a more systematic direction to scientific enquiry. If the plan meets with the
support of those whom I have consulted respecting it I will give you
the particulars previous to the meeting, if amidst so many reforms
of another kind you have leisure to attend to them.

We do not know with any certainty what numbers are likely to
attend but I have reason to believe that a good many persons distinguished in science will come and of course more who are not.

Fitzwilliam Papers, drawer Aug–Sept 1831

The President of the Royal Society of London was the Duke of Sussex; his predecessor
was Davies Gilbert (1767–1839), *DNB*.

35   *Babbage, 1 Dorset Street, Manchester Square, London, to Harcourt,*
Wheldrake near York, 31 August 1831

The letter you did me the honour of addressing to me requires no
apology, and being actuated by the same wish for the extension of

knowledge in every direction, I shall freely state to you my opinions on the subject of the meeting at York.

Many months since, Dr Brewster consulted me on the subject and I stated to him at some length my reasons for not being very favourable to the idea.

My friend was not convinced and at his suggestion others have taken it up and the trial is to be made. I have not mentioned those opinions to others, but on the contrary have urged my personal friends to be present and would myself attend if my own affairs admitted. I thought it right to give you this key to my suggestions and will add that I should rejoice at finding the view which I have taken to be unfounded.

I think the constitution which you propose, that this society shall be formed out of all members of other literary or scientific institutions who may be present, much better than that of our German friends who make the author of a certain number of printed pages a member.

The advantages appear to me to arise chiefly from the following circumstances:

1. Persons following the same branches of science become personally known to each other and thus mutual aids are often afforded and their minds derive an additional stimulus from the intercourse; and even in cases where their opinions are at variance the tone of criticisms will lose much of their asperity.

2. It is much easier to arrange any joint observations by conversation than by letter.

3. It is *extremely desirable* that every member should be urged to bring with him such portable instruments as he may employ in experimenting, specimens of the results of any experiment, specimens of anything curious from his own district either in nature or art, specimens of any foreign instruments or objects of the above kind, including of course manufactures. Might it not be possible to have an exhibition of manufactures at each meeting?? I am induced to insist more on this third point from the experience I have had of the great utility (to those who want information) of carrying such portable samples of art or nature as they can convey with them. In several tours of many thousand miles, I have derived great aid from a small collection of things apparently trifling; and in some instances they have been of considerable service in cases of difficulty.

4. The papers to be read at the meetings should not be long and if interesting would be printed by the editors of journals without expense to the society. I rather think plans of experimenting and skeletons for observation in different sciences might be proposed for

discussion; but this could only be considered in conversation not in a letter.

I do not think such a society could ever take the lead you seem to anticipate, for in England especially bodies as well as individuals must take time to acquire character before they exert influence and I doubt if the influence of any body only meeting once a year can be effectual. The late Visitors of the Royal Observatory are an example. I doubt if prizes will be of much advantage. I can scarcely believe we have materials for annual meetings; perhaps biennial may be [well] attended.

Advantage may be taken at such meetings of exchanging the natural history productions of one county for those of distant ones: and wherever there are philosophical societies existing, their secretaries or some of their permanent officers should be put in communication with each other.

The sittings ought to be divided into classes of sciences, in order not to be too numerously attended by persons uninterested.

One difficulty for which I do not see a remedy will arise if, as sometimes happens, persons moderately acquainted with science possessing considerable assurance and fond of hearing themselves speak choose to push themselves prominently forward: professional views often stimulate such persons to become conspicuous and when they are unblessed with any large share of refinement or good breeding they are very troublesome. Perhaps the leading members of the Geological Society of London can give you *the best* advice on such subjects.

Objects for corresponding observations on given fixed days or otherwise; height of barometer every hour during the 24; height of tides during ditto; height of water in great rivers during ditto; also height of rivers every hour during floods or great changes; meteors; temperature of springs; temperature of the sea; members to instruct their neighbours and even the peasantry to look out for aerolites after thunder storms. I have thus given without order the hints which occur to me and shall be truly glad to hear of the success of the proposed meeting.

Harcourt MSS (Harcourt Papers, *xiii. 239–242*)

Skeletons were skeleton instructions.

36 *Whewell, Lancaster, to Harcourt, 1 September 1831*

Without pretending to decide immediately on the probable success of such a project as you suggest of an association among the men of science of this country, I conceive that such a proposal must be looked upon with interest by all lovers of science, and I shall be happy if I can contribute any hints which may be of service to you in developing it. If such a plan could be carried into effect, it would certainly give to the meeting at York a higher utility than that which would be likely to arise from the personal intercourse of those whom such a motive might bring together, though even this may no doubt have very great advantages.

The objects of such an association as you mention would apparently be, to place before its members a view of the present state of science, to select future subjects of examination, and to encourage in some way or other researches on such subjects.

I conceive that such a mode of action might be of very great service to the scientific character of this country. The researches of our men of science have been too much insulated from each other and from what is doing in other countries; and the bearing of what they have done upon the present state of science has not been often clearly placed before the public. This inconvenience might be remedied by the publication of reports, drawn up by well qualified persons, of the recent progress and present condition of the different departments of our knowledge. The annual speeches of the President of the Geological Society, and in some degree those on similar occasions in the Astronomical Society, have been good examples of what such reports may be: and these have been of great use. In most other branches of science we have had no such views presented to the world in this country. In Paris reports of this kind upon science in general are drawn up by the Secretaries of the Institute, and excite much interest. Berzelius every year presents a similar report to the Royal Academy of Sweden.

I offer you the following suggestion as one course of action among others for your consideration. The meeting at York might, in any way that was thought best, select one or two of the most eminent men in Britain in each department of science, and might request them to draw up respectively a report upon their own subject; stating what had recently been done both abroad and here, what is the present state of the science, and what appear to be the points most to be recommended for investigation at present, either in consequence of their importance or their promise of discovery. Such reports might be presented and read at a future meeting either a year hence or at some shorter period. The extent and degree of the interest excited by the prospect of such reports would enable the founders of the association to judge what chance of success the temper of the country gave them; and these reports thus collected would be very valuable guides and materials in all future proceedings. I conceive that any man of science applied to to compile such a report, would feel himself distinguished by the selection, and would feel also the obligation of research and impartiality which such an office would involve. The reports would of course be printed, and the reading and the consideration of them would be a prominent part of the business of the next general meeting. I conceive that, independently of any ulterior steps, the publication of such a view of science would be both very interesting and very instructive.

I will mention a few names which occur in connection with different subjects as examples merely, and nothing more, of the persons who might probably be engaged to give you such sketches of the aspect and prospect of their studies. In *geology* you know how rich in such persons you are. Sedgwick, Conybeare, Buckland, Lyell, etc, etc, would any of them do the work well, and indeed as I have already said it is almost done already. *Astronomy* might be separated into *physical astronomy*, of which the principal cultivators in our own country are, I think, Ivory, Airy and Lubbock; and *observing astronomy*, where you have many good names, Herschel, Airy, Brinkley, etc. In the recent researches about *light* you have Brewster, Herschel, Airy, who have occupied themselves with experiments, and the two latter more especially with the theory. The properties of *heat* are another subject, in which much has been done and much remains to be done. Dalton and Leslie have been our principal discoverers. B. Powell, of Oxford, has been pursuing a portion of the subject; and I believe several of our best chemists have attended to it. Connected with this is the subject of meteorology, which appears to be making considerable progress. Dalton, Luke Howard, and Daniell are the principal persons who have prosecuted it, and the two latter would be able to tell you in what condition they conceive it to be. You probably know much better than I do who are most likely among our *chemists* to take an impartial and enlarged view of the present state of their science: Turner appears to be eminently well informed and candid. I hardly know who at present can be considered as peculiarly well acquainted with *magnetism*: Kater and Barlow may be mentioned. *Electricity* I suppose could be got from some of the chemists as might *electro-magnetics* and *thermo-electrics*. Professor Cumming of Cambridge has pursued these latter subjects with considerable care. In *botany* you have the names of Lindley, Hooker, Wallich, etc, but with this and other branches of *natural history* I will not presume to meddle. You will, I suppose, find no lack of students of them. *Comparative anatomy* is another division of the subject which ought not to be omitted. I should suppose that one of the most difficult of the sciences to speak distinctly and impartially about must be physiology, but it is a very important and apparently a very progressive one. I will only add that Mr Willis, of Cambridge, and Mr Wheatstone, appear to be the persons who principally attend to the subject of *sound*: and that it would be proper, I should think, to make *geography* one branch of your report, which would lead you to Greenough, Beaufort, Basil Hall, and the other London geographers. I have only mentioned these subjects, and these gentlemen, as exemplifications of what you have before you; and I think if you could induce a number of these to join in preparing, by next year, a joint representation of the present condition of British science, and of the views, concerning the points now to be attended to, which its most eminent cultivators entertain, you would do something to give it a fillip.

This refers to a part only of your object: but after such a survey of the place where we are, you would be better able to judge of the mode of advancing. There would be no difficulty in finding subjects to recommend to the notice of scientific men either by means of prizes or in any other way. It would however be desirable to select subjects where we appear to be approaching towards discovery, or where asserted discoveries appear to require confirmation. You know how easy it would be to suggest such in *geology*, if we could send persons provided with knowledge and money to other countries. In *chemistry*, no one in England appears to pursue the subject of *isomorphism*, the most important and promising step, I should conceive, which has been made in the science for many years. The connection between the chemical composition of crystals and their form is another subject where we cannot but hope that something will shortly be known. The condition of the upper regions of the atmosphere as to heat, moisture, and wind, and the physical differences between different kinds of clouds, is another promising subject. Every one probably could mention such in his own department of science.

I can hardly pretend to suggest any thing at present as to the arrangements concerning prizes, funds, etc. As to the materials of the society I would ask, for the sake of consideration, whether it might not be better to make your association consist of all persons who have *written papers* in the memoirs of any learned society. It would be desirable I think in some way to avoid the crowd of *lay* members whose names stand on the lists of the Royal Society.

All committees on memoirs presented or on any subject concerned with science ought to give *public* reports of their views. The neglect of this practice appears to me a serious deficiency in the arrangements of the Royal Society.

I have written very hastily the first ideas which offer themselves, and I must beg you to consider them rather as thrown out for your consideration than as asserted in preference to anything else. I shall be extremely glad to hear that your plan or any modification of it is likely to be carried into effect. I am really sorry that it is out of my power to attend the meeting in person. I am one of the examiners for college fellowships this year and our examinations take place at the same time as your assemblage. I think if you can get such a set of reports as I have described it will be the best beginning for any good plan, and another year will show what can be done.

If I can offer any further suggestions likely to be of service I shall be happy to do so. I shall be at Harrogate probably on Tuesday or Wednesday next, and at Cambridge by the end of the week. At either place your letters will find me.

Todhunter, Whewell, *ii. 126–30*

Jöns Jacob Berzelius (1779-1848), *DSB*, Swedish chemist; John William Lubbock (1803-65), *DNB*, London banker; John Brinkley (1763-1835), *DNB*, Bishop of Cloyne, President of the Royal Irish Academy 1822-35; John Leslie (1766-1832), *DNB*, professor of natural philosophy at Edinburgh University; Luke Howard (1772-1864), *DNB*, London manufacturer and Quaker editor; John Frederic Daniell (1790-1845), *DNB*, professor of chemistry at King's College, London; Edward Turner (1798-1837), *DNB*, professor of chemistry at University College, London; Henry Kater (1777-1835), *DNB*, London retired soldier; Peter Barlow (1776-1862), *DNB*, professor of mathematics at the Royal Military Academy, Woolwich; James Cumming (1777-1861), *DNB*, professor of chemistry at Cambridge University; John Lindley (1799-1865), *DNB*, professor of botany at University College, London; William Jackson Hooker (1785-1865), *DNB*, professor of botany at Glasgow University; Nathaniel Wallich (1786-1854), *DNB*, Superintendent of Calcutta Botanic Gardens; Robert Willis (1800-75), *DNB*, Fellow of Gonville and Caius College, Cambridge; Charles Wheatstone (1802-75), *DNB*, inventor and professor of experimental natural philosophy at King's College, London; Francis Beaufort (1774-1857), *DNB*, Hydrographer to the Navy; Basil Hall (1788-1844), *DNB*, army captain. Whewell's suggestions about reports and reporters were very useful to Harcourt and the Association.

37 *Herschel, Slough, to Harcourt, Wheldrake near York, 5 September 1831*

Returning from a temporary absence I find your letter of the 25th to which I reply with as little further delay as other more imperatively pressing business will permit.

If I felt as strongly impressed as you appear to be with the want in this country and in the actual state of science, of a great, central and presiding power to give an impulse and direction to enquiry, to stimulate, accompany and guide it in its course, to point out unexplored paths, to inspect the map of science and chalk out districts for individual or combined diligence to explore, subdue and fertilise, to distribute to every class of mind its appropriate task and assign its limits, and, as you so strongly and appositely express it, 'to point out the lines of direction in which the higher researches of science should move', as well as to accomplish those other objects of influencing the public opinion, and through its means the government of the country for purposes eminently conducive to the advancement of science, in a more commanding manner and in a way more effectual and less liable to abuse than can be accomplished by existing institutions, or by individual representation, I should scarcely hold any private or personal considerations valid reasons for not immediately obeying the first invitation to lend my humble assistance in furtherance of the object.

It is not my fault, however, if I feel much less sanguine than perhaps I might have done ten years ago, as to the possibility of maintaining and holding together such a body, could it be constituted and brought into action, in a country like this where freedom of action and independence of thought are so highly prized and so energetically asserted on all occasions. Neither ought I to conceal that I entertain great doubt whether in the actual state of science the time is not gone by when bodies of men, however constituted, *can* exercise any powerful directing influence on the progress of knowledge unless in peculiar cases, and when sustained by so uncommon a degree of ardour, self devotion and mutual forbearance in the individuals who compose them, as shall powerfully counteract the fundamental vices of all such institutions. Not but that I am fully of opinion that particular societies, holding in view the humbler objects of affording facilities for the prosecution of particular departments, furnishing funds for the publication of papers relating to their own especial subjects, defraying expenses of experiments or undertakings of which *the whole body* can form an opinion, and affording a fair and open field for the unfettered exertion of genius under the eye of a more intense kind of public (if I may use the phrase) imbued with knowledge enough of the subject to comprehend and appreciate its efforts, may be and have been extensively useful, and will always be so. And I conceive that their utility will always be in the exact proportion to the humility, I should rather say moderation, of their aims and pretensions: to the absence of all attempt to control or direct research, to the degree in which they limit their operations to the affording of facilities, the diffusion of authentic information, and the promotion of a rapid interchange of scientific opinion; to which I may add the establishment of such a character for alacrity and uprightness, as may lead the government of the country to regard them as at once the depositories of the best information on the subjects they profess, and their natural councillors on all such points as can arise to bring them into contact.

You must of course be well aware that the conduct of a great scientific body desirous to preserve or create a high place in public estimation can be no sinecure, and that its claims on those who may take the lead in its management cannot be satisfied but at a sacrifice of time and individual pursuit of no trifling moment to such as feel the value of the one as a means and the importance of the other as an end. I believe there is no one who has mixed in the management of any of the more important existing scientific institutions, who has not felt (severely, if he has been engaged in original research) the enormous drain on time and thought to which a continual interpolation of subjects foreign to the natural course of his enquiries has subjected him. It will be said that such devotion meets its reward and assuredly no one will deny that the public estimation is bestowed with no niggardly hand on those who really deserve it, but that reward which he most desires (it may be) he has not. No contemporary applause can compensate to one who aspires to posthumous fame for the dissipation and exhaustion (for I must not call it waste) of the means which nature has given him to attain it. No sense of *general* utility to the cause of science can supply to one who has an original train of research in hand, the destruction of his opportunities for its prosecution.

From the limited and desultory way in which I have myself cultivated science, it cannot be supposed that I intend to include myself in the number of those who are entitled to claim immunity from any fair share of public duty on the score of more important private pursuits and, had not several of the best years of my life been already more than partially devoted to the business of scientific bodies, I should not think myself justified on the present occasion in alluding at all to my own pursuits. Such as they are however they absorb every moment of that moderate portion of my time which I find it possible to devote to science, and leave me in the present instance only the power of such participation in the prospects of the proposed institution as consists in sincere wishes for its utility and consequent success.

PS   I have no knowledge of Sir J. South's sentiments relative to the intended meeting, nor does my distance from town and sparing visits there allow of my collecting opinions on the subject.

Harcourt MSS (Harcourt Papers, *xiii. 244–8*)

38   *Harcourt, Wheldrake near York, to Michael Faraday, 5 September 1831*

I was extremely sorry to hear that your engagements would prevent your being able to attend the scientific meeting at York at which your presence both in your philosophical and social character, however you may disdain the latter, would have been equally acceptable.

Though you do not come yourself it may perhaps be in your power to send us some scientific novelties, some account for instance of vanadium, the history of which its discoverers seem to be very slow in communicating. You may also have an opportunity of inducing the authors of any new inventions or discoveries which may be afloat to exhibit them on this occasion, and as the Royal Institution is not sitting you are under no temptation to monopolise them. At this time of the year the *lions* may be allowed to perambulate the country.

I hope however that at this meeting we shall do something more than show or see the lions. There are hopes I think of setting an association on foot which may give a fresh and active impulse to scientific research in this country. The plan, respecting which I am in correspondence with Mr Herschel, Dr Brewster, Mr Whewell and others, is to form an association of all members of all the scientific societies in Great Britain to meet annually to receive and discuss reports made to it by committees or individuals selected from among its number on the state of the several sciences and the points in each most immediately inviting investigation, and thereupon to charge such of its members with the proposed researches as may be most competent for the task, either severally or jointly. In particular cases the expense of experiments may be defrayed, or prizes may be offered; and supposing the association to possess not only numbers but character and also some courage and freedom of discussion, it might obtain more influence with the government of the country than science has hitherto enjoyed and command for it some degree of national encouragement.

To give efficiency to such a plan as this it must have the active support of all or the greater part of the most eminent cultivators of science and without some promise of that support it would be in vain to propose it. Will you assist in carrying it into execution? Would you for instance make one of a committee to report on the state of chemistry, the points of theory most requiring investigation and the experimental data to be first established or, supposing such a report made, would you take a part in conducting the researches so designated and resolved upon?

If it strikes you that this plan or any modification of it may help to raise a spirit of enterprise and exertion in science and give a systematic direction to its present loose and disjointed efforts, pray give your mind to it and write me any suggestions which may occur to you as soon as you can, either as to the constitution of the proposed society, or as to the points in science coming under your own observation which it should undertake to have investigated.

Faraday Papers

Michael Faraday (1791-1867), *DNB*, was Director of the laboratory at the Royal Institution, London.

39 *Conybeare, Sully near Cardiff, to Harcourt, Wheldrake near York, 8 September 1831*

I have delayed acknowledging I fear some time your kind letter, having postponed doing so in hopes that I might be able to arrange my engagements etc so as to join your meeting, in which I had promised myself very much pleasure. I regret however to say that my hopes are now finally disappointed, many insuperable obstacles having opposed themselves to my desires in this respect. With regard to one of these I shall I am sure command your sympathy, and that is an indisposition on the part of Mrs C so serious that she must be placed for some time in her mother's house at Clifton in order to command better medical advice than this country place affords.

A friend of mine, Dr Prichard of Bristol, (one of the very ablest men I know) has some thoughts of going over to the meeting and I should be very glad to give him any facilities. You perhaps may communicate some hints as to how he should proceed which would be useful. I forget whether you saw him when at Brislington. He is the author of a work on the *Physical History of Man* which if you have not read I feel sure you will be indebted to me for recommending to your perusal.

Letters will be best addressed to me at Sully as my parochial and family engagements will principally detain me here though I shall often be running across to Clifton.

Harcourt MSS

James Cowles Prichard (1786-1848), *DNB*, Bristol physician and author of *Researches into the physical history of man* (London, 1813).

40 *Harcourt, Wheldrake near York, to Whewell, Trinity College, Cambridge, 12 September 1831*

I feel much obliged by the attention which you have given to my letter and for the suggestions with which you have favoured me, though they make me regret the more that you cannot be present at the meeting. Some of these however are not of a nature to be communicated in their present form to the public and if it is not asking too much I think a letter from you which might be read to the meeting would be some compensation for your absence, a letter I mean expressing the views contained in that which I lately received from you, but divested of the names of persons to whom you thought application might be made, a communication very useful but which I considered in some degree confidential.

I would now beg leave to put two or three questions to you personally.

Should you be asked to give the next meeting of the proposed society a twelve month hence a report upon any branch of physico-mathematical science would you undertake it? And what would be the enquiry which you would prefer? It would of course add much to the value of such reports if they contained in addition to the account of what others had been doing any new researches which the author had been able to make.

If the meeting were to request you to hold an office in the society for a year or for a longer period would you accede to the request? It would be of essential consequence to its success to begin under the auspices of competent advisers and officers of known character.

If this meeting were to propose that the next should be held at Cambridge, do you see any objection? It appears to me that the moving of such meetings from place to place would have a powerful effect in stimulating the science of those places; and if they were to circulate through the two universities, Edinburgh, Dublin, York, and perhaps one or two other towns, this would improve I think the vivacity both of the places at which they were held and of the society itself. I should be anxious to know the sentiments of some of the leading scientific members of your university on this point. Perhaps you would have the goodness to communicate with Professor Airy, Professor Cumming, Mr Willis or any other of your men of science who may be upon the spot, to show them any part of our correspondence, and inform me whether the views on which we are proceeding meet with their concurrence and nay hope for their co-operation, and whether in particular they are disposed to encourage a meeting like the present to assemble at Cambridge in a future year.

I have taken advantage, you see, perhaps to too great an extent, of the permission you [have] given me to trouble you upon this subject. The truth is that the number of persons is very small who have ability or zeal enough to enter with any degree of readiness or spirit into the consideration of plans of this kind, and they who possess those qualities must expect to be proportionably importuned.

Whewell Papers, a. 205[120] (Harcourt Papers, *xiv. 9–11*)

41   *Murchison, Hurworth, Darlington, to Harcourt, Wheldrake near York, 13 September 1831*

I had absolutely procured a frank 10 days ago from 'Michael Sadler' *safely directed* to you, but in one of my geological movements I shot past the post town from whence dated. Having delayed, I must however now expose you to the penalty of postage to congratulate you on the part of Mrs Murchison and myself upon Mrs V. Harcourt's safe accouchement, with every sincere wish that she may be improving rapidly.

I have to thank you sincerely for making me a confidant in your projected scheme for the occupation and objects of our coming meeting.

I think it very likely that Dr Brewster and some of the northern lights may be found good auxiliaries in such an enterprise. But I very much doubt whether you would obtain any real or permanent assistance from the philosophers of the metropolis or the universities, because I fear they might be led to think, that however good the intention of the projectors, and however brilliant the launch of such a scheme, it might eventually and in other hands become an 'imperium in imperio'.

I have always perceived a strong jealousy of any project of this kind when broached; and *even as it is*, I had many battles to fight for the legitimacy and usefulness of our having any meeting at all (out of London).

You will I am sure forgive me for this little hint; and should I prove wrong, and that you can enlist any of the splendid names (Herschel, Whewell, and co) in your enterprise, count upon me as a faithful soldier who will with lungs and hands endeavour to back you gallantly through it.

If such a scheme should have a damp thrown upon it, still rely upon our festive meeting having a *permanent* good effect: we shall rub off a thousand asperities, interchange many scientific opinions and originate numberless undertakings all conducing to the common weal of science. I do not tax you with asking you to write again, but should you have anything to say a letter to 'Egleston' or 'Rokeby' will reach me. I shall be at the former till the 19th, at the latter till I move upon York.

PS I find upon referring to the newspaper that I have been mis-informed as to *the* Mrs Vernon. I hope to find however that I have been correct by my Highland privilege of 'second sight'.

Harcourt MSS (Harcourt Papers, *xiii. 250–1*)

Michael Thomas Sadler (1780–1835), factory reformer, then MP for Aldborough, Yorkshire. Local newspapers had reported that on 6 Sept the Hon Mrs Vernon had given birth to a daughter.

42 *Brewster, Allerly near Melrose, to Babbage, 1 Dorset Street, Manchester Square, London, 16 September 1831*

I was yesterday favoured with your welcome packet. My reply to the pamphlet was in types, but though I cannot avail myself of some of your suggestions, I think you will find that I have anticipated you in all the important ones. I fear it will be impossible to get another review like the former into the *Quarterly*; but I mean to keep up the fire by another article on the foreign pamphlet, containing a refu-tation of the minor points which I had not room to discuss now. Your note respecting Arago and Prony's allowances is very impor-tant; but can it be implicitly relied upon? Arago now has I believe 5000 francs as Secretary.

I am truly distressed at the possibility even of your not being at York. I do not admit the force of your reasons: there will be, at least, TWO good building months after your return; but even if you should be thus put to inconvenience, the great object to be gained by your presence at York deserves every sacrifice. The Revd W Vernon Harcourt, late President of the York Society, and a man of station, of influence, of science, has taken the warmest interest in the establishment of a scientific association for carrying on all the great objects which we all have so much at heart. You will see by the following extract from his letter to me that he is a disciple of your own, and I am sure that we will not carry through this great object without you.

'Neither,' says he, 'has there hitherto been any society indepen-dent, deliberative and powerful enough to possess influence with the government of the country to claim for science what is due to it, and to the interests of society depending upon it, and through the medium of public opinion to lead to a more enlightened and credit-able national dealing with men of science and their objects'.

'If such a society does not exist, if you think it practicable to create it, if you think it might be a powerful instrument in sustaining and advancing philosophy in this country, will you cooperate in giving it *that active support which the execution of such a scheme would require*'.

When I consider that such men as Lord Milton and the author of this extract are about to lend their warmest cooperation to the views of men of science, I feel that it is our duty, *yours* and *mine* especially, to make every sacrifice to be at York; and when I assure you that since the month of May I have not done one thing in my professional pursuits but have devoted all my time to the objects of science, I feel a double claim to urge you to add another to the great sacrifices you have already made. On my knees I implore you to be at York.

BL, Add. MSS 37186, ff. 86–7

The pamphlet was *On the alleged decline of science in England. By a foreigner* (London, 1831) by Gerrit Moll (1785–1838), professor of natural philosophy at Utrecht University. For much of Sept 1831 Brewster was preoccupied with attacking the anti-declinist views of Moll: Brewster, 'Decline of science in England', *Edinburgh journal of science*, 1831 (Oct), v. 334–58. Dominic François Jean Arago (1786–1853), *DSB*, was permanent Secretary of the Paris Academy of Sciences 1830–53; Gaspard François Clair Marie Riche de Prony (1755–1839), *DSB*, was Director of the School of Bridges and Roads, Paris.

43 *Whewell, Trinity College, Cambridge, to Herschel, Slough, 18 September 1831*

... But there is another affair which I should have been glad to consult you about, and if I were not inextricably engaged for this week I would have come over to Slough on the chance of finding you at home and willing to 'trust the ruler with his skies' for half an hour. The managers of the York meeting have applied to me as I believe they have to you for hints about the possibility of managing it so as to make it useful. I do not think there is any chance of exciting the kind and degree of interest about such occasions, which they produce in Germany, but if there be any obvious prospect of stimulating the zeal of men of science and giving a useful direction to their labours, I should be very unwilling to refuse a share in the task of raising the requisite shout: albeit being much more willing to follow my own devices and very doubtful about the chance of doing any great good by this machinery. I shall not be able to go to York; but the advice I gave was to this effect: that the meeting should select eminent persons in each department of science; and beg them to make, by next annual meeting, reports as to the present condition of their respective provinces, and the points where research will apparently be most useful: that the purport of these reports and the

degree of interest which they may excite should be the guide and
basis of future operations of this association if it continue: and that
at any rate such a collection of reports, if it can be procured, be
printed, by which means the wittenagemot will not have met in
vain.

I want much to know whether you see any chance of any good
arising from such a proposition. I put it forth rather as a conjecture
concerning a possibility than as anything else. One of the suggestions
which my correspondent makes is that the meeting may be held at
Cambridge next year if we think it good. One would not repel·
people by any apathy or backwardness when they ask your sympathy in such a case, but at the same time I should be sorry to urge
men of science to come here and make a huge congregation as if we
intended to say we would make it worth their while to do so. If it
really comes to be a question whether we shall encourage the savants
to visit us en masse, it would be very desirable that we should be
able to guess whether the best of them would accept the invitation.
Suppose that it were proposed to hold such a meeting in Cambridge
next year, would you be likely to countenance us by taking an
interest in it, and joining the party? If you do not see any good
likely to come of such a proceeding I shall think there is no great
hope to be entertained of it, and if you keep aloof from the meeting
I shall not expect it to assume the character which would make it
attractive and useful. My enquiries are very hypothetical for I think
it rather unlikely that the proposition to meet at Cambridge next
year will be made on either side. My intention at present is to tell
my correspondent that the visitation of our Observatory is always
held in May; that we shall then be glad to see as many savants as
possible and will do our best to entertain them: and that I will tell
him the precise time as soon as I can. I wish I could have seen
you for it is hardly possible to expound to you how little of sub-
stantiality there is in these speculations but at the same time how
desirous I am of knowing some of your views about this august
proceeding...

                   Herschel Papers, 18. 183 (*Todhunter*, Whewell, *ii. 132-4*)

44 *Conybeare, Sully near Cardiff, to Harcourt, 19 September 1831*

Your very interesting communication redoubles my regret at being
unable to join your proposed meeting, but it increases my hope that
it may lead to some permanent arrangement. For the sake of science
I can warmly express my wishes for this offspring of your efforts
Nunc in annum vivat et [floreat], and may I be able to assist at

many of its future anniversaries. Your proposal for engrafting on this annual reunion of savants a system for effecting such concentration of the talent of the country as might tend more effectually to consolidate and confine its scattered powers, to direct its investigations to the points which an extensive survey thus generalised would indicate as the most important—benefited by all the aid which the union of powerful minds, the enlarged comparison of different views, and a general system of intellectual cooperation could not fail to afford, fills me with visions too extensive almost to allow me to write with sufficient calmness of sobriety. The combined advantages of including at once the most powerful stimulus and the most efficient guidance of scientific research, which might emanate from such a point of central union, seem to me quite beyond calculation. The question must be, do existing circumstances as yet afford a practicable opportunity for actually realizing views like those you have sketched, which if they can be realized would almost give a local habitation and a name to the philosophical academy of Bacon's *New Atlantis*, when 'divers meetings and consults of the united body of depredators, compilers, pioneers etc suggested new experiments of a higher light and more penetrating nature to the *lamps* and thus at length yielded materials to the *interpreters* of nature'.

But to return, is this now practicable? I certainly myself hope and think so, but then the opinion of a poor depredator and compiler insulated in a remote country residence is scarcely competent to pronounce on such a subject. What say the lamps and interpreters Babbage and Herschel? Looking on the general field of scientific folks at present as far as I am acquainted with them, I should apprehend that such a plan is likely to find the most ready and useful allies in the Philosophical Society of Cambridge.

As your meeting is so rapidly approaching I think it best to dispatch these lines at once by return of post so that of course I can do little more than express the interest I feel in your plans. If my ideas under any circumstances are worth anything I can scarcely flatter myself that this is likely to be the case when I can but arrest those which happen to be floating in my mind at the moment and send them off without the slightest reconsideration but yet to exemplify my views of the sort of topics on which such discussion might be expected to throw light. I will venture hastily to mention a few points on which as pioneer I should like to consult the lamps, trusting to your indulgence on the score of said haste if you think them absurd . . .

Harcourt MSS

Much of the first paragraph was quoted by Harcourt in his speech, 27 Sept 1831, in which he inaugurated the Association: *1831 Report*, 9–35 (23). In *New Atlantis* (London, 1627), Francis Bacon (1561–1626), *DNB*, had expounded a utopian, co-operative yet stratified community consisting of merchants, depredators, mystery men, pioneers, compilers, dowry men, lamps, inoculators, and interpreters of nature all based on Salomon's House.

45   *Herschel, Slough, to Whewell, Trinity College, Cambridge, 20 September 1831*

... A certain Mr Vernon Harcourt has written to me about the York meeting. It seemed to me by his letter that the projectors of the thing, having found that a mere meeting for no purpose but to shake hands and eat dinners was not likely to attract much people, had begun to enlarge their views into the establishment of a great permanent central presiding scientific power having for its objects, or part of them, 'to give a systematic direction to philosophical research', 'to look over the map of science and to say here is a shore of which the soundings should be more accurately taken, there a line of coast along which a voyage of discovery should be made', to 'indicate specific points to be elucidated and either to *charge such of its members as may be competent and willing to undertake the task* as one of honour and trust, or offer a prize or offer to defray the expense of a particular process'. And moreover and here seems to me to lie the cream of the thing 'to be sufficiently powerful, independent and deliberative to possess influence over the government of the country to claim for science what is due to it and through the medium of public opinion to lead to a more enlightened and creditable national dealing with men of science and their objects'.

Now there is [in] some of this mere story, some pretension that I question whether we shall ever see realised, and as to the latter part I protest against having anything to do with it. In the first place, I think the only use of people combining into societies is to do what individuals cannot do for themselves or not so well. Now I don't see anything here proposed which will not be done and much better done by individuals in active and *leading* pursuit of particular branches who can and do tell the public (at the same time that they propound their own discoveries) all that they would tell them, of their views of the past and future prospects of those departments and of the promising beats in their preserves, [than] through the medium of a huge society investing itself with a paramount disposing authority; and not only do they execute this duty better because more simply and naturally in their individual capacities but their hints and recommendations do I conceive carry with them in this way a much more persuasive weight than they would coming ex cathedra from a body.

Again no doubt your suggestion about the annual reports of progress is excellent; you have alluded to their utility in your first note to the review of my book, and something of the kind, though less extensive, was clearly in my mind when I wrote that unlucky note which served as a text for Babbage to preach upon and thus (by a strange perversity) has seemed to identify me with all the grovelling and degrading views of the objects and idols of scientific men which have lately made such a hubbub. But in all such reports it is the authority of the writer not the body which gives them weight. Only try the experiment, and taking the subject you *profess*, or any other of which you have and are known to have a full knowledge of and original views respecting, take geology for instance, and write such a report, and announce your intention to continue it and publish it in a book *per se* and depend on it it will be read with eager interest and produce its full effect; or if you saw reason to fear it would not *pay* send it to a reputable journal and let two or three more good men do so, only *keep to the same* year after year, and no man who cares for that branch of science will neglect to possess himself of that journal as it appears.

A thousand bad opinions do not make one good one, a thousand mediocrities don't make up one excellence, nor can a thousand eyes looking through as many spyglasses see as well or as far as one with a first rate telescope. I see nothing in an overwhelming mass of mediocrity which can direct or stimulate or encourage those who would naturally lead the way without them, but much to embarrass and distract, and retard them in their progress. Perfect spontaneous freedom of thought is the essence of scientific progress. If you want a man to climb to the summit of a steeple to overlook the country you choose a stout active fellow who pulls off his coat and to it he goes, hands, legs, and head, but nobody even thinks of dressing him in a gown and wig, or tying a dozen bad climbers or lame men to his coat tail to help him. If you want to win a race you would hardly enter half a dozen horses and harness them altogether.

If any way could be devised more fertile than another in annoyances and disputes and in the long run more self-defeating, it would be the establishment of *scientific preserves* of the kind above mentioned, where particular departments were thus authoritatively, and by what it is meant should be regarded as *the national voice*, dealt out to particular men as matters of trust and honour. Every man who in pursuit of one species of game was led across the fence of another's preserve would be sure to be considered a poacher. The annals of the Geological [Society] exhibit a specimen or two of the kind of jealousy with which any approach to trenching on another man's *own* subject is regarded. No, no, science is a common on which every body has an equal right of occupancy and I trust that every inhabitant would rise up and demolish the first fence that should be erected across a single corner of it. It is often called a *republic* but such a society as is here proposed will make it a *democratic tyranny* with all the vices of the narrowest oligarchy. The very proposal to make it consist of an aggregation of the members of all existing scientific bodies would make it essentially a mob.

However these are objections rather against the crude proposals contained in Mr Harcourt's letter. When the meeting takes place of course it will be seen who takes a leading part and if good men attend, and attend with an intention to take pains and construct it sensibly, and keep it in order, of course in the same proportion will good predominate and evil disappear. I cannot myself possibly attend; and, I confess, I see many more evils to be apprehended than advantages to be expected from any such institution, however I should be very sorry to be thought desirous of throwing cold water on it. But I am certain that if it *is* to come to good, the more modest its outset, and (to a certain extent) the slower its progress, the better; there will be then time for consideration and less to undo. In this point of view your suggestion of making the reports of this year a feeler for the course to be pursued next year is no doubt the best possible. There will be time to talk about it. At present nobody seems to know any thing about it. One great danger in the present excited state of politics is its assumption of a political character, and the avowed object of 'influencing government' will of necessity set this string vibrating in all the speeches etc that will be made.

There is one serious consideration to such as are actively engaged in the pursuit of any particular considerable branch of science that demands much time and thought, who might otherwise be disposed to take a prominent part in such a concern: the great drain on those two articles which it must create, and again the quarrels in which it can hardly fail to involve them ...

Whewell Papers, a. 207[22]

Whewell, 'Herschel's Preliminary Discourse', *Quarterly Review*, 1831 (July), xlv. 374–407 (375–6) had urged the importance of annual reports. Herschel's own note was appended to his 'Sound', *Encyclopaedia metropolitana* (London, 1830), iv. 747–824 (810), which Babbage used in his *Decline of Science*, vii–ix, to claim that Herschel was a declinist.

46 *George Harvey, Plymouth, to Phillips, 20 September 1831*

It was with no ordinary pleasure that I saw the first notice of the intended scientific meeting at York; and I have delayed answering your letter, with the hope that circumstances would permit me to be present at the first of a series of meetings so well calculated to revive the declining energies of science. As however, a course of events which I cannot control necessarily chains me to Devonshire at this time, I must beg of you to present my most sincere regrets to the eminent and illustrious individuals who may attend this most interesting and auspicious meeting.

Of the advantages resulting from what may for distinction here be called *stationary* meetings of scientific men, the world has long had the most abundant proofs; and it is not a little remarkable, now that the subject is brought home to our consideration, that meetings of a *migratory* character have not been long ago established; particularly as Bacon alludes to 'circuits or visits of divers principal cities of the kingdom', as forming a distinguished feature of the *New Atlantis*.

What Bacon foresaw in distant perspective it has been reserved for our day to realize; and as his prophetic spirit pointed out the splendid consequences that would result generally from institutions of this kind, so may we hope that the new visions of glory which are now opening before us may be productive of still greater results than we have yet beheld; and that the bringing together the cultivators of science from the north and from the south, from the east and from the west, may fulfill all the anticipations 'of one of the greatest minds that ever threw glory on our intellectual nature'. At all events let the experiment be fairly and boldly tried. 'Nothing' said Burke, 'tends more to the corruption of science than to suffer it to stagnate. These waters must be troubled before they can exert their virtues'....

I have now only to add my most earnest hopes that the meeting at York may produce all that its most sanguine projectors may desire; that the energies of science may be quickened and revived; that the meeting may be gladdened by every thing calculated to insure lofty notions of zeal for the noble pursuits to which its sittings may be consecrated; and that another and another year may witness the renewal of that harmony and love which, bottomed on the sciences, cannot have a purer and more disinterested source for its origin.

I beg that my name may be inscribed on the list of the intended society of the British Cultivators of Science.

British Association archives, Foundation volume, 64 (paragraphs 1–3);
Phillips Papers, 1831/26 (rest of letter)

George Harvey (d. 1834), Plymouth meteorologist and ship-building expert, taught mathematics at the Royal Military Academy, Woolwich. For Bacon's notion of circuits in his *New Atlantis*, see J.M. Robertson (ed), *The philosophical works of Francis Bacon* (London, 1905) 713-32 (732). For Edmund Burke (1729-97), *DNB*, on the corruption of science, see J.T. Boulton (ed), E. Burke, *A philosophical enquiry into the origin of our ideas of the sublime and beautiful* (London, 1958), 54.

47 *Harcourt, Wheldrake near York, to Milton, Wentworth House near Rotherham, Wednesday [21 September 1831]*

I trust that we shall not be deprived of your attendance at the meeting. It will be of material consequence to us to have you in the chair. The first meeting for business will be on the Tuesday at 12 o'clock and I shall then have to propose the plan of the new society of which the following is an outline. The objects of the Association are: first, to give a stronger impulse and more systematic direction to scientific inquiry; second, to promote the intercourse of those who cultivate science in different parts of Great Britain; third, to obtain a greater degree of national patronage for science and a removal of those disadvantages of a public nature which impede its progress.

The Association to consist of the members of philosophical societies paying a low annual contribution and to meet annually at certain places in rotation.

The General Committee to consist of all members who have communicated any scientific paper to a philosophical society, which paper has been printed either in its transactions or with its concurrence.

The Committee to point out certain subjects to be investigated during the ensuing year and the results brought forward at the next annual meeting, to appoint subcommittees consisting of those members who are most conversant with the several subjects, and entrust to them the selection of the parts of those subjects which most call for inquiry and of individuals to be engaged to give the ensuing meeting a report on the state and progress of that part of science or to undertake original researches into it, and a statement of the particulars in which the aid and contribution of philosophical societies might be solicited.

The rest of the arrangements for the annual meetings to be left to a President and Secretaries, one of whom is to be chosen from among the residents in the place at which the meeting is to be held, with the assistance of any philosophical society which may subsist there.

There will be a public dinner, probably at the concert room, on Tuesday at which all the meeting are supposed to attend. On the

Tuesday therefore we must certainly have you, morning and evening, and as much more of your time as you can spare us. It may probably be most convenient to you and most desirable for [the] meeting if you can give up but two nights, to come to York by 11 on Tuesday morning and to pass that and Wednesday nights at Bishopthorpe.

Sir G. Cayley has reminded us that philosophers are very fond of venison. Can you contribute to the culinary part of science by sending from Wentworth some venison and game?

Fitzwilliam Papers, drawer Aug–Dec 1831

Sir George Cayley (1773-1857), a keen supporter of the Yorkshire Philosophical Society, attended the first meeting of the Association.

48 *Barlow, Royal Military Academy, Woolwich, to Harcourt, 21 September 1831*

I have been favoured with your letter, and should have given an earlier reply, but that I wished to consult the opinions of some of my friends upon its contents. Having done so, I beg to state that I find it is very generally believed that the formation of such a society, however desirable it may be, would be impracticable in this country. Unfortunately many persons who would naturally like to attend are prevented by their occupations; in our institution are four members, Dr Gregory, Mr Christie, Mr Faraday, and myself, who are all prevented [from] joining in such an association by the nature of our duties here; many others I have no doubt are similarly situated. I am much afraid, therefore, in the first place, that it will be difficult to get together a sufficient number of influential scientific men to forward the views suggested in your letter. Persons already subscribing to the Royal, Astronomical, Geological, Geographical, Meteorological, and other societies, would not, I imagine, readily come into the measure of a further subscription to the proposed general association, and I am afraid that little can be expected from the government.

Such at least is my opinion, and of those to whom I have communicated your letter. The object you have in view is certainly highly desirable, but much of it might be attained by the active pursuit of our several societies in their respective departments. In the Astronomical Society, which pursues its object with great energy, almost everything is being done that is possible. The Geological Society might also, I conceive, be the means of urging forward that science as effectually under its present construction as in the general association, the persons by the plan proposed being the same; and the same may be observed of nearly every other society which has a specific science in view, viz, that nothing is wanted but the active pursuit of its particular object; and that no more authority is to be expected by forming the same persons into a new society than they now possess under their present constitution. I should have been very happy to have attended the meeting at York this year, but as I have already stated that is impossible. With every wish, however, that it may be satisfactory to all parties and beneficial to science

Harcourt MSS (Harcourt Papers, *xiii. 248–50*)

Olinthus Gilbert Gregory (1774–1841) and Samuel Hunter Christie (1784–1865), both *DNB*, were professors of mathematics at the Royal Military Academy, Woolwich, where Faraday taught chemistry part-time.

49   *Whewell, Trinity College, Cambridge, to Harcourt, 22 September 1831*

I send you along with this a letter containing some of the suggestions which I mentioned in my letter to you, expressed in a form in which they may be communicated to any of your scientific visitors if you think it useful to do so. I am far from wishing you to notice them except you think they may be serviceable; and I think it very likely that those who are present at the meeting will be much better judges of the advisable steps to take. I shall therefore be very well satisfied if I find you have not thought it necessary to make any use of them. I was much obliged by your considerateness in accepting my former letter as in some degree confidential, which indeed I intended it to be. The suggestions and names were intended to be, possibly, some assistance to you in developing the plan you mentioned; and I would on no account offer my opinions to the meeting on such a subject.

In answer to your enquiries I beg to say, that if I were invited by such a meeting as I conceive yours will be, to prepare a report on the state of the science of which I am professor, I should do so with great readiness and to the best of my ability. With respect to holding any office in your Association I should wish at present to be excused. It is very possible that I may be absent from England the whole of next summer, and it may perhaps be best at first to select your officers from those who are present at the meeting, and are of course the most obvious persons.

If you were to determine to hold the meeting hereafter in succession at different places, I am sure that a large portion of our members would be gratified with your selecting Cambridge. The Philosophical Society, whose members would naturally feel a strong interest in such an arrangement, cannot now be consulted. There might be some doubt about the best time of our receiving scientific visitors, for in the vacation (from June to October) the University is deserted by most of its usual inhabitants, and I should be sorry, for the sakes of many of them, that they should be absent on such an occasion. The following is a suggestion which I beg leave to offer you. The Visitation of our Observatory is always held in May; and on this occasion we have generally had some strangers here, who took an interest in science, and have been happy to see all such. If the party becomes next year more numerous and more distinguished, we shall rejoice the more. I cannot at present tell you the day in May, nor offer any invitation beyond my own; but upon the strength of this you may inform your visitors, if you think it desirable to do so, that we are always glad to see men of science here at the period of our Visitation, and will do what we can to entertain those who may come here next May. Any further arrangements which may be necessary can be made hereafter.

I wish you the best success with your Association, and shall be extremely desirous to hear of its proceedings.

PS I shall be glad if you will have the accompanying letter delivered to J.D. Forbes Esq who is to be one of your visitors from Scotland.

Todhunter, Whewell, *ii. 130–1*

This letter was a private one. Whewell produced a 'Report on the recent progress and present state of minerology', *1832 Report*, 322–65.

50 *Whewell, Trinity College, Cambridge, to Harcourt, Wheldrake near York, 22 September 1831*

As you have done me the honour to ask my opinion on some of the points connected with the intended scientific meeting at York, I shall very willingly mention such suggestions as occur to me on the subject. I should have been very glad to offer them to the meeting in person, but an important college examination in which I am unavoidably occupied leaves me no choice of my movements during the remainder of the month. I am obliged therefore to take this method of expressing my best wishes for the success of the undertaking.

It is very difficult to conjecture how far a society such as you appear to contemplate in your letter might with any chance of being useful take upon itself the functions you describe of combining and directing the researches of philosophical investigators. The men of science who may attend the meeting and who have thus an opportunity of becoming acquainted with each other's views and feelings will be far better able to judge than any absent individual can, of the chance of that sympathy and cooperation in such a cause which its success would require. I will only observe that there can be no want of employment for any zealous labourers in the field of science who are willing to allow themselves to be directed by others. Leaving out of consideration those branches of science in which consummate skill or great talents are requisite to the investigator, there are various departments where, with a moderate preparation, the accumulators and classifiers of facts might be of great use. I need not mention to you natural history and geology as belonging to such a class. I may add that in meteorology, and in the analysis of minerals, we appear peculiarly to require such additions to our stock of materials: in the doctrine of the relations of heat, moisture, and gases many laws remain to be determined or verified by laborious series of experiments: and it might perhaps not be difficult to point out other portions of science similarly circumstanced.

Whether scientific labourers are likely to be stimulated and directed in such researches by a national association, the meeting at York will perhaps judge. If they resolve to make the trial I should conceive that the best mode of beginning would be to obtain a collection of reports from the most competent persons concerning the present state of their respective departments in science. Indeed such a collection of reports is on all accounts much wanted, in order that scientific students may know where to begin their labours, and in order that those who pursue *one* branch may feel themselves in communication with the enquirers in *another*. For want of this knowledge, we perpetually find, in our scientific journals, speculations which show the greatest ignorance of what has been done and written on the subjects to which they refer, and must give a very unfavourable impression of us to well informed foreigners. A collection of reports of such a kind would also afford some means of judging of the degree of interest which prevails in the kingdom with regard to the real state of science, and would thus be a guide and indication as to the future proceedings of the body. I should conceive that if the meeting at York were to select in each department one or two persons among the most eminent, and were to request from them a statement to be presented next year, of the recent advances made in their science, its present condition, and the subjects of research which they conceive to be at present most important and promising, such a request would be respectfully attended to. Such a collection of reports would be of itself highly interesting and valuable, even if no subsequent proceedings were founded upon it. And the proposition of making such a collection would enable the persons directing the association to judge of the degree of national interest which they might hope to excite, and the cooperation, on the part of men of science, which they might look to obtain.

I suggest this without intending to give any opinion of the probable result of the project you mention, which as I have before intimated, I should think it presumptuous to do. But there is one feature in it as you have described it, which I should beg to notice. I should not wish to share in any association which had for one of its objects to influence government in its proceedings with regard to science and its cultivators. I believe that, in England at least, men of science, as a body, will secure their dignity and utility best by abstaining from any systematic connection or relation with the government of the country, and depending on their own exertions. I can easily imagine other persons judging differently, but I should not wish to take part in any proceeding founded on such a judgment.

I have no wish to bring my opinions on the points I have mentioned before a meeting where so many persons will be able to present views of much greater value. If however you think the communication of them likely to be of service I leave them at your disposal. Every one must be glad to pay his homage of admiration and good wishes to the scientific zeal and hopeful spirit of the persons in whom the plan of your meeting has originated. That there is much to be remedied and much to be forwarded in the world of science is abundantly obvious, and your meeting have my best wishes that with them may begin the reform of what is wrong, and the accelerated advance of a new and better era.

Whewell Papers, o.15.47[97] (Harcourt Papers, *xiv. 14–19*)

This was a public letter, part of the third paragraph being quoted by Harcourt in his inaugural speech on 27 Sept 1831.

51   *Prichard, Bristol, to Harcourt, 22 September 1831*

I ought before now to have sent a reply to your kind letter respecting the projected meeting at York but, although very desirous, I have been until today in a state of uncertainty whether it would be in my power to attend it. This I now hope that I shall be able to do, and I have to express my best acknowledgements to the Archbishop and to yourself for the very obliging invitation with which His Grace has honoured me.

Mr Conybeare has forwarded to me the papers to which you alluded in your letter. He expresses, as he has probably done more fully to yourself, his cordial approbation of the plans suggested. I have not quite abandoned the hope that Mr Conybeare may be present at the meeting at which *his* cooperation would be of essential service. For my own part I shall go as a mere spectator, highly interested in the proceedings, but not so vain as to suppose that my presence will be of any use, except to myself.

I have the honour to be
    Sir,
        Your faithful and obedient servant
        J.C. Prichard

Harcourt MSS

52 *Murchison, Rokeby near Barnard Castle, to Harcourt, Wheldrake or Bishopthorpe near York, 23 September 1831*

I beg you will offer to the Archbishop the best thanks of Mrs Murchison and myself for His Grace's kind invitation to Bishopthorpe, which we have much pleasure in accepting.

We go to Lord Tyrconnel's tomorrow to stay over Sunday and leaving Kiplin early on Monday morning hope to reach Bishopthorpe to dinner.

I am travelling with our geological horses, but I shall send them on and post the better half of the road to gain time; and if I reach York before four o'clock I shall call at the Museum hoping to see Mr Phillips, perhaps yourself.

The 3 miles in and out will prevent my dying of 'deipnosophy', a term which I dared not have made use of had I not received a letter from Sedgwick dated Caernarvon in which I am sorry to say he desires me to say to you how very much he regrets that he cannot be one of the 'deipnosophists'.

I have been tracing the Cockfield dyke from the east into the western Durham coalfield and have partially succeeded in connecting it or its embranchments with the Great Whin Sill of Upper Teesdale.

PS Your letter is without date and I am at a loss where to find you. On consulting topographies I perceive I can reach Bishopthorpe without going through York.

Harcourt MSS

Murchison was staying at Rokeby Hall, the home of John Bacon Sawrey Morritt (1772–1843), *DNB*, a fellow Tory; John Delaval Tyrconnel (1790–1853), 4th Earl, lived at Kiplin near Catterick. Sedgwick's fore-cast that the meeting would concern itself with the art of dining was to be amply confirmed.

53 *Harcourt, Wheldrake near York, to Murchison, Rokeby near Barnard Castle, re-addressed Scientific Meeting York, Friday [23 September 1831]*

The Archbishop having been called into the West Riding on business does not return till Tuesday to Bishopthorpe on which day he would have great pleasure in receiving Mrs Murchison and yourself there for whatever time you can favour him with your company. You must however by no means be absent from the meeting on Tuesday morning and will therefore come to York I hope on Monday where we will provide you accommodation for that night.

PS   I perceive that I misdirected my last letter containing an invitation to Bishopthorpe.

Murchison Papers

54 *Murchison, Bishopthorpe Palace near York, to Whewell, Trinity College, Cambridge, 2 October 1831*

Before I entered into the 'British Association' which the meeting at York has given rise to, I was very desirous of *weighing* the men who were eventually *to carry us through*. I was really very mainly induced to join it in consequence of *your* letter to William Vernon [Harcourt]; and I was quite decided in so doing, when I saw the *'calibre'* of the men here assembled, and the promises of support from those who could not attend. I send you a York paper herewith, which will give a tolerable notion of our doings, with the exception of the last day, which was very big with results and at the close of which the meeting was declared dissolved, and that the next meeting would take place at Oxford in June next: Buckland Praeses, *yourself* and Brewster Vice-presidents.

At the close Lord Morpeth made a very eloquent appeal to the assembly, and called on all the inhabitants to thank the men of science for having selected York; and *I* (poor I) in quality of President Geological Society returned thanks in the name of the savans, and proposed a cordial vote of thanks from ourselves to the natives.

I hope you will immediately write to Vernon and give us the full sanction of your valuable name, and allow us to place you on the mineralogical committee in which you have as associates Brewster, the two Allans of Edinburgh, Dr Johnston the discoverer of the new metal vanadium and others. The physical science committee should also include your name. It is now composed of Sir T. Brisbane and Dr Pearson of the Astronomical [Society], Brewster, Scoresby, Forbes and young Potter of Manchester, a very clever fellow.

The chemical committee is also very strong, including Dalton, Henry, Daubeny, Harcourt, Johnston etc.

Of geologists, sat: Conybeare, Greenough and your friend the Praeses with many others. I hope sincerely Sedgwick will join us when he fully knows the nature of the case and I enclose a letter for him.

By a saving clause passed yesterday before the general meeting broke up, and of which you have no account in the newspapers *as yet*, we declare that the objects of the Association are wholly distinct from those of any *established society*; and in truth any one who will go over the list of *very valuable* communications made to this meeting, must see that we shall rob no society of its due.

Scoresby's magnetic observations of the last six months are most curious and novel. Brewster really astonished every one with the brilliancy of his new lights.

Old Dalton 'atomic Dalton' reading his own memoirs and replying with straightforward pertinacity to every objection in the highly instructive conversations which followed each paper, are things never to be forgotton.

The chemical committee at the anxious suggestion of old Dalton have already propounded for their mutual work and solution some very important questions to be answered next year.

Your report on the state of mineralogy will be a great catch for us.

I had no memoir ready myself and did not intend to rob the Geological Society of any thing intended for them, but I found that a poor and hard-working druggist of Preston in Lancashire, who had made some years ago a very important observation (on the existence of shells of existing species of marine shells in the gravel and marls of Lancashire at 300 feet above the sea and at distances of 15 and 20 miles from the sea) was present; I took this opportunity of turning lecturer and having visited those parts this summer I brought out my little druggist with all the éclat he merited.

This is another practical exemplification of the good arising from such a reunion. The Archbishop had all the party on one of the days and it would have gratified the liberality of Cambridge to have seen old Quaker Dalton on his Grace's right hand.

The conversations after the papers have, I again repeat, *been most instructive*; and no one could have done the whole thing better than William Vernon. We had Dr Prichard of Bristol and some good zoologists and were *alone wanting* in botanists.

Pray act cordially with us, and if Adam [Sedgwick], my great master, and yourself will only go along with us, the third meeting will unquestionably be at Cambridge. Rely on it the thing *must* progress: all the good men and true here present are *resolved to make it do so.* Write to me by return of post if only three lines 'P Office Scarborough' and give the enclosed to Sedgwick when he arrives. I shall (with Madame) be at Cambridge before the month is out.

Whewell Papers, a. 209[88]

George William Frederick Howard, Viscount Morpeth and later 7th Earl of Carlisle (1802-64), *DNB*, of Castle Howard near Malton; Robert Allan (1806-63), like his father Thomas Allan (1777-1833), *DNB*, was an Edinburgh banker and mineralogist; William Scoresby (1789-1857), *DNB*, Anglican minister; Richard Potter (1799-1866), *DNB*, Manchester merchant; William Henry (1774-1836), *DNB*, Manchester chemist; the little druggist was William Gilbertson.

55 *Buckland, Oxford, to Murchison, Post Office, Scarborough, re-addressed Lincoln, 4 October 1831*

Many thanks for your long and very interesting account of the last week's proceedings at York at which I regret exceedingly that I could not be present. The whole week seems to have gone off exceedingly well, saving that I think a larger admixture of southern stars with such a galaxy of northern lights would have added to the splendour of the occasion. I presume there will probably be a similar disproportion in favour of the inhabitants of the south at the next year's meeting at Oxford. I had received a letter from Phillips last Friday informing me of my election to the Presidentship for the next occasion, but he did not mention that the society had embodied itself into so substantial a form or had assumed a name and an intention of perpetuating itself which I fear will interfere with some existing societies in a manner that may provoke jealousies and incite opposition. At the same time it will call forth much that would otherwise have remained dormant in possession of its inventors, or at most would have been communicated but to a few. Not the least curious of the communications must have been J Dalton's experiments on the quantity of food taken by a person in health compared with the quantity of secretion and insensible perspiration, the experiments performed on himself. This must have been charmingly edifying to the ladies and would form an admirable sequel to a lecture on coprology. I am glad to see Hutton at work upon the whin-sill and dykes; from his local opportunities I trust he will work out fresh matter. I see you stuck up manfully for old Adam [Sedgwick] who was not present to defend himself and will I trust come home with a rich harvest from north Wales. Your report of your own progress is highly promising and will of course enlighten our Geological [Society] evenings in the next session. Your Preston discoveries are very interesting and I am anxious to know what you will find of tertiary or more recent than tertiary deposits along the east frontier of the chalk of Lincolnshire, especially at the points to which I particularly requested your attention. I quite envy your locomotive powers, tied by the leg as I am here and am likely to be. I have heard nothing of Featherstonhaugh since the first number of his journal, which I trust will do very well for him and be a useful acquisition to geology. De la Beche's *Manual* is an extremely useful addition to our stock in trade and will sell extensively and do much good.

My wife and children are well and all that are old enough unite with me in kindest regards to Mrs Murchison.

Murchison Papers

William Hutton (1798-1860), *DNB*, Newcastle-upon-Tyne insurance agent and geologist; George William Featherstonhaugh (1780-1866), *DSB*, an Englishman living in the U.S.A., had launched his *Monthly American journal of geology and natural science* in July 1831. Henry Thomas De la Beche (1796-1855), *DNB*, *A geological manual* (London, 1831).

56 *Harcourt, n.p., to Whewell, n.d.* [*2-10 October 1831*]

As I understand from Mr Murchison that he has given you an account of our proceedings and of the success which has attended them, I have only to discharge the official duty of informing you that the *Association* have elected you one of the Vice-presidents for the ensuing meeting which is to be held at Oxford in June next. I mentioned to the [General] Committee that it was not improbable you might be absent from England next summer, but this did not alter their determination to request you to accept the office. Dr Buckland was elected President and Dr Brewster the other Vice-president. Dr Daubeny and Mr Powell are the Secretaries for Oxford; the London committee consist of Mr Greenough, Mr Murchison, Mr Yates and I hope Mr Babbage; the Edinburgh committee of Mr Robison, Mr Forbes and Mr Johnston; the Dublin, of Dr Lloyd and I believe Mr Hamilton and Sir C. Giesecke; a Calcutta committee is also likely to be formed of some very zealous promoters of science there.

The object of the committees is to put down the names of persons desirous of becoming members of the Association and to forward its views in their respective districts, and if you should find that there are persons at Cambridge willing to act upon such a committee it may be desirable to establish one there. I have every reason to believe that Professor Sedgwick is favourably disposed to our proceedings and I hope that the Oxford meeting will be attended by more of the members of your University than have been able to be present at that which has taken place here. A copy of the rules which have been adopted shall be sent to you as soon as possible with lists of the scientific sub-committees, in which as well as in the office of Vice-president we are desirous that your name should appear. The rules are founded on the principles which I have before stated to you, care has been taken as far as possible to avoid giving offence to other societies. Several subjects of scientific enquiry of much importance in chemistry, geology, meteorology and natural philosophy have been proposed to be prosecuted and several persons have undertaken to pursue them who may be expected to execute them well; thus Dalton has insisted on more accurate and multiplied experiments to establish the primary data of chemistry and will take a part in them; Dr Daubeny is to examine the question from whence the metallic principle developed in plants is derived. Mr Scoresby has undertaken important magnetical observations, Mr Forbes barometrical, etc. Dr Brewster is to give some account of the progress of optics, Mr Johnston of chemistry abroad as well as at home, and we are in hopes of obtaining from you an account of the state and progress of mineralogical science which I am directed to request at your hands. The same kind of view of physical astronomy an application is to be made to Professor Airy to undertake. In geology the effects of electrical action are to be taken into consideration. You will receive a *Report* of these and the rest of our proceedings as soon as it can be prepared. But in the meanwhile we hope you will allow us to insert your name as Vice-president.

Whewell Papers, a. 205[123]

James Yates (1789-1871), *DNB*, London Unitarian minister, and Bartholomew Lloyd (1772-1837), *DNB*, Provost of Trinity College, Dublin, had attended the 1831 meeting; Sir Charles Lewis Giesecke (1761-1833), professor of mineralogy at the Royal Dublin Society, did not serve on the Dublin committee. A Calcutta committee was nominated but was ineffective.

57 *Buckland, Christ Church, Oxford to Harcourt, Wheldrake near York, 9 October 1831*

I hope you received a week ago through my letter to Mr Phillips the notice I sent him of my adhesion to your plan, which he then announced to me, of holding the next meeting of the British Association for the Advancement of Science in Oxford in the month of June next, and my acknowledgement of the honour that has been conferred upon me by my nomination to the office of President on the occasion. I feel that I owe much of this to your personal kindness and am more than before filled with regret that it was not in my power to be present at your recent meeting at York, which I am glad to find admitted on all hands to have gone off so well. The honourable conjunction also in which I am placed with respect to the Vice-presidents and [Local] Secretaries is highly gratifying. My only fear is that the jealousy of many existing societies may be excited by what will perhaps be a more than imaginary interference with papers that would otherwise have been sent to them; and although the British Association professes that it will studiously avoid all such interference, I see not how in practice this profession can be strictly adhered to. I believe that it will absorb certain papers that would have gone to other societies, but at the same time I admit that by pointing out and fixing subjects of enquiry it will cause much to be done that would otherwise have remained untouched for want of a stimulus; and if the general good of science be thus advanced, though somewhat to the detriment of existing societies, this comparatively trifling injury will be infinitely overbalanced by the promotion of general good.

You do not mention what is to be the specific duty of the proposed local committees. I presume it will be chiefly to collect recruits and papers. The subjects you mention as already undertaken are all highly interesting in their respective departments. I shall be happy to receive a copy of the rules as soon as they are prepared. Could you send me a few duplicate copies for distribution among persons whom it may interest, such as Lord Grenville, Lord Stowell, etc? If my name will be of any service in the sub-committees you are welcome to use it. I think the two subjects submitted for geological enquiry extremely apposite to the present state of that science.

Harcourt MSS (Harcourt Papers, *xiii. 254-5*)

William Wyndham Grenville (1759-1834), *DNB*, Chancellor of Oxford University; William Scott, Baron Stowell (1745-1836), *DNB*, M P for Oxford University 1801-21.

58 *Whewell, Trinity College, Cambridge, to Murchison, Post Office, Scarborough, re-addressed Lincoln, 10 October 1831*

I have been away from Cambridge and am only just returned to find your account of the York meeting for which I am exceedingly obliged to you. I had heard before that the business went off 'excellent well' but I had not heard that they had elected me Vice-president, and am in no small degree surprised at the selection as well as much gratified which, looking at the character of the meeting, it is impossible not to be. I cannot yet get over the feeling that I shall be out of my place, having done nothing for science except study and expound the discoveries of others, and being thus put in a position better suited to a person known by original labours like my worthy Praeses and brother Vice. I may add that my brother Vice-president, excellent fellow as he is in many ways, is labouring along with other people, to make science such a business of brawling, that a man may well be disposed to avoid any ostensible connexion with it: especially if he has got abundance of other employments. However as you working sçavans have thought it right to put me in such a situation, I will do the best I can not to disgrace your choice. I will write to Mr Harcourt as soon as possible to accept the appointment and to offer my best services which will be very cordially given. But I will wait till tomorrow that I may be able perhaps to send one or two names for a Cambridge committee, though being just arrived I do not know if any body is here. My task of giving a report of the state of mineralogy will I expect be a very pleasant employment.

I can see abundance of good things that such a society may do: one matter which requires multiplied and extensive fagging is meteorology, which I hope Dalton will set them to work upon. I was in the north during the summer and made the acquaintance of the old Quaker philosopher. I had a great admiration for him before and my admiration for him was much increased by knowing him. He is indeed a most excellent person and I can easily imagine how much of the right character he would give to the meeting. I used to fancy, in looking at him, that Newton must have been as much like him in person and manner as it appears that he certainly was in the face.

Perhaps you are not yet aware that honours have of late being [sic] falling thicker than usual on some of our men of science, and with somewhat of better judgment than in the case of the knight of the 'objectif'. Herschel, Babbage, Ivory, and Nicolas (of the Antiquarian controversy) are to have, or have already, the Guelphic order. Moreover Konig is Sir Charles Konig in some way or other in consequence of walking in the Coronation procession: so when you come to London you will have to call a lot of your friends by new names.

I rejoice to hear there is a chance of seeing you in Cambridge and am especially delighted to hear that Madame is coming. I shall be here from this time till December so do not give us the slip. If you let [me know] when you are coming it will be the better. Sedgwick [is still] hammering in Wales. Darwin, who accompanied him at first, is just on the point of setting out as naturalist with Captain Fitzroy who is to complete the survey of the south end of America.

I expect he will bring you home the tip of Cape Horn for the Geological [Society].

Murchison Papers

Whewell's brother Vice-president was Brewster; Sir James South was the knight of the objectif; Nicholas Harris Nicolas (1799-1848), *DNB*, a London barrister, had attacked the Society of Antiquaries with Brewsterian zeal; Charles Dietrich Eberhard Konig (1774-1851), *DNB*, was keeper of mineralogy at the British Museum. In Oct 1831 the Guelphic order was conferred on Brewster, Herschel, Ivory, Leslie, and Charles Bell (1774-1842), *DNB*, the anatomist, who were soon also knighted. Charles Robert Darwin (1809-82), *DNB*; Robert Fitzroy (1805-65), *DNB*.

59 *Whewell, Trinity College, Cambridge, to Harcourt, 11 October 1831*

I am much obliged to you by your information respecting the proceedings of the meeting at York. I am much gratified by their election of me to the office of one of the Vice-presidents of the Association, and the more so when I consider the characters of the other officers appointed. I shall be extremely happy to forward the objects of the Association as far as lies in my power, and am only sorry that they have not selected for the office to which I am appointed a person more distinguished for his contributions to science.

I shall have great pleasure in preparing for the Association a statement of what appear to me to be the present state and prospects of mineralogy. I presume this is to be produced at the next meeting which I think I understand is to be in June next at Oxford.

I shall probably in a short time be able to send you the names of other persons who will endeavour to forward the objects of the Society. I am but just arrived in Cambridge and have as yet had no means of making any enquiries.

Whewell Papers, o.15.47[98]

60 *Murchison, Lincoln, to Buckland, Christ Church, Oxford, 12 October 1831*

Yours of the 4th must have made a tardier journey than I anticipated, but I found it here today on my arrival. I cannot recollect whether or not I sent you a *York Courant* with an account of our *finish*, so I forward to you a [*York*] *Herald* with the *dramatic* conclusion, in which *I* endeavoured to perform my part with all the feeling that *was in me*, though far short of the sensational *efflorescence* of my Lord Morpeth. I must put you right as to your *mis*conception of the *objects* of the annual Association of science.

I especially propounded in committee a declaratory clause which by the consent of the general meeting *was adopted*; and in our last committee meeting of Monday it was resolved should form *the preamble* to our bill and in some such form 'And whereas the objects of the meeting are declared to be in no wise an infringement on the duties or avocations of *any established* society but namely these'. This will relieve you from all anxiety on that score. Again I must correct you as to old John Dalton's *secretions*: all [such] like effusions were read to the *men* of science only and in the *morning*; the ladies were never treated with a peep into the cloaca which *you alone* know how to render sweet in the senses of females, and therefore I hold you bound at the Oxford *gala* to enable them inwardly to digest all such matters. But joking apart I seriously assure you that the thing did go off well, remarkably well, and the more shame that few or none of you *southerns* were present. 'Nimium me crede colori', for I can confidently state that you will be inundated with men from beyond the border next meeting. In the first place we are certain of Brewster, Johnston, Robison, Forbes etc all of whom have not only promised papers but have in answer to the respective calls made upon them by their several subcommittees (as you will see by the printed programme when forwarded to you) agreed to write specifically in answer to queries proposed. By this you may infer we are not mere 'men in buckram'. On Monday we did much work in committee on all these points, particularly in chemistry and mathematics—as President Geological Society I propounded but little, and that little of a very general and speculative kind, which I knew would never see the murky light of Somerset House, being too proud to admit that so active a body as our own could require papers on any matters *purely geological*, but only on such correlative questions as those (alas many they are) in which we require the aid of great *feelosophers*.

We left the Archbishop's on Tuesday for Scarborough and in taking leave of that amiable and agreeable prelate, he shook me by the hand and said 'Perhaps when we meet again I shall be plain Mr Vernon'. I could only exclaim 'God forbid my Lord, I cannot endure to hear of such possibilities'. What a comment all this is on the cursed reform bill; however I had the thanks of all the party at Bishopthorpe for having kept them out of such tattle for many days. I went to Hackness and passed a day with old Smith in his own tabular hills and another at Scarborough. Smith is steward to Sir J Johnstone and has a most [little] [box] in a beauteous valley but he is discontented because he says he cannot work on in geology. I have bethought myself of a scheme to set him up and do *us* good: viz to apply to the government to give him a small salary as 'Geological colourer of the ordnance map'; Smith to colour the same at

the discretion, and under the general direction of, the *Council* of the
Geological Society. I have mentioned it by little to Phillips and he
warmly approves of it as the only course which can do his uncle and
ourselves real service, inasmuch as colouring maps is his *forte* and his
ambition. Of this however nothing till we meet when we can all
consult ...

Murchison Papers

The speeches of 1 Oct 1831 by Lord Morpeth and Murchison were reported in *York
Herald*, 8 Oct 1831. From 1828 the Geological Society of London had met at Somerset
House. Sir John Vanden Bempde Johnstone (1799–1869), of Hackness Hall near
Scarborough, protector of the ageing William Smith. The scheme to employ Smith
as geological colourer came to nothing.

61 *Babbage, 1 Dorset Street, Manchester Square, London, to Harcourt,
Wheldrake near York, 12 October 1831*

I was quite gratified to find the scientific meeting at York answered
so much better than I had anticipated and I hope from such a
commencement we may anticipate results advantageous to science.
It was out of my power to attend and fortunately I had not left
town as I had during that week some business at the Treasury
relative to the calculating engine, which would have been impeded
by my absence. I shall of course be most happy to be considered a
member although I was last year necessarily absent, but I do not
wish my name to be put on any committee merely because my
avocations are so numerous that it would be quite impossible to
attend to it. I congratulate the Association on so auspicious a beginning and hope that I shall have the pleasure of becoming personally
acquainted next year with many of its most zealous supporters.

Harcourt MSS

62 *Whewell, Trinity College, Cambridge, to Harcourt, 14 October 1831*

I do not know whether the mention made in your letter to me of
the intention of the Association formed at York, to apply to Professor
Airy for a report on physical astronomy, was intended to be considered as official. I have mentioned it to him, and I have reason to
believe that on a direct application he would undertake such a task.
I need not, I conceive, mention how valuable he would probably
make the result of his labour.

I imagine that the thing requested of him should be an account
of what has recently been done in facilitating or extending the investigations connected with physical astronomy, and any suggestions

which he can offer as to the points which it is now most desirable for mathematicians to bestow their labour upon. I think any request of this description would fall in with the views of the Association, and I presume it might be advisable that you or some person officially authorised should make an application to him to this effect.

I may add that Professor Henslow, our professor of botany, will be happy to forward in any way the views of the Association. Professor Sedgwick will be here in a few days.

Whewell Papers, 0.15.47[99]

63 *Harcourt, Wheldrake near York, to Whewell, Trinity College, Cambridge, 17 October 1831*

I have written to Mr Airy and am rejoiced to hear that there is a probability of his acceding to the request of the [General] Committee. We are printing with the regulations of the Association lists of the sub-committees for promoting the several branches of science and of the local committees for assisting the general objects of the Association, and think it highly desirable that Mr Airy's name should appear with Sir Thomas Brisbane's, Dr Brewster's, Mr Forbes's, Dr Pearson's, Mr Scoresby's, your own, and I believe those of Sir J. South and Mr Hamilton on the sub-committee for mathematical and physical science. I shall be obliged to you to obtain his permission for this and the permission of Mr Henslow to add his name to the sub-committee of zoology and botany, on which are those only of Dr Prichard and Dr Daubeny. If you wish a corresponding secretary for Cambridge to be added to those for London, Edinburgh, Dublin, Oxford and York, have the goodness to mention who will undertake the office. The Secretary of the Royal Society of Edinburgh is our Secretary there, Dr Daubeny and Mr Powell at Oxford.

We wish also for permission to add the name of Professor Sedgwick to our sub-committee for geology. When you can furnish me with answers to these requests we can go on with the printing and I will send you copies immediately.

One of the resolutions of the Committee was that you should be requested to use your utmost efforts in the name of the Committee to procure from some competent individual a report upon the European progress of *mathematical* science during the year 1831. Would Mr Hamilton of Dublin be likely to undertake it, or have you any one at Cambridge?

The Committee have resolved that geologists should be requested to examine strictly into the extent and the truth of that part of the theory of Mr É. de Beaumont and its application to Great Britain and Ireland in which it is stated that the lines of disturbance of different strata are not parallel to each other and that those of the same age are parallel. Would Professor Sedgwick undertake to promote enquiries on this point in conjunction with Conybeare, Buckland, and any other of the members of the sub-committee and to make a report?

It was resolved also to invite botanists to compose local floras to be presented at the next meeting, and enter into such other researches as may be useful towards determining between certain plants and the soil and strata on which they grow. Would Professor Henslow take a part in promoting this enquiry?

Mr Phillips has undertaken with such assistance as he may procure a systematic catalogue of all the organised fossils of Great Britain and Ireland hitherto described with such new species as he may have an opportunity of accurately examining, with notices of their localities and geological relations. There are several important questions propounded in chemistry, especially respecting the true specific gravities of gaseous elements, and I should be glad to know whether we are likely to have the assistance of Professor Cumming and whether in that case we may add his name to the chemical sub-committee.

It is of importance to publish good lists of names and it is of still greater importance to engage good men to go to work.

Whewell Papers, a.205[122]

Jean Baptiste Armand Louis Léonce Élie de Beaumont (1798-1874), *DSB*. Robison was Secretary of the Royal Society of Edinburgh.

64 *Brewster, Allerly near Melrose, to Harcourt, Wheldrake near York, 19 October 1831*

I am very glad to find from your letter that you have been so successfully occupied with the interests of our Association, for I had some fear that you would suffer from the labours and anxieties to which you were peculiarly exposed during our memorable week at York. Do not suppose that you can take too much upon yourself. The Association owes much of its success to your individual exertions, and much to the patronage it received from the Archbishop and all the members of your family. For myself I can truly say that the week I spent at Bishopthorpe was one of the happiest in my life, and that I have felt the great kindness I received under its roof as an ample reward for all the sacrifices I have made to science. I hope this example will not be lost upon those whose local position and whose elevated rank enable them to countenance the annual meetings of the Association ...

I think I heard you say that you would be in London early in winter. I find that I shall be obliged to be there about the end of November, or early in January, and if we meet there we might do some good to the Association, and prepare for the prosecution of our respective labours. Mr G.P.R. James of the Royal Society of Literature agrees to become a member of the British Association. He will pay his subscription to Mr Robison in Edinburgh. Mr Harvey and Mr Forbes both write me in great anxiety for an account of the proceedings at York.

Harcourt MSS

George Payne Rainsford James (1799-1860), *DNB*, a historical novelist, was a neighbour of Brewster.

65 *Phillips, Halifax, care of E.N. Alexander, Esq., to Harcourt, Wheldrake near York, 20 October 1831*

I have just received a letter from Forbes begging for no delay in the issue of the Circular and *Report*, and for a transmission to the *Philosophical Magazine* of an authorized report of the proceedings, including of course or rather joined to your address, for insertion in the November number. I do believe this to be very important, especially as Forbes has purposely delayed to receive names for the Association until there should be some regular statement before the public.

Murchison engaged to get the report introduced into the *Philosophical Magazine*. Permit me to say your own sending it would answer as well, and be more certain. I believe this must be considered to depend wholly on you, and if you judge that a short statement would be better than a long one for the *Magazine*, every body would be willing to acquiesce in it, but some account does appear needful. Mr Forbes' letter abounds with most grateful allusions to yourself.

I am much interested in the geology of this vicinity and with the general spirit among the members of the infant society here. My audience exceeds 100. I have been twice underground and have made one or two experiments on temperature rather interesting but not very conclusive.

Harcourt MSS

Edward Nelson Alexander (d. 1859), a Halifax attorney, was Secretary of the Halifax Literary and Philosophical Society (founded 1830).

66 *Airy, Observatory, Cambridge, to Harcourt, Wheldrake near York, 21 October 1831*

I have received your letter conveying the request of the [General] Committee of the British Association that I would prepare a report of the state etc of astronomy, and that I would become a member of the sub-committee for promoting mathematical and physical science.

I shall be most happy to draw up such a report as I am able, and to offer suggestions on those points which have struck me as most in want of improvement. At the same time I should be glad (at least if the subject of astronomy is divided and different parts of it intrusted to different persons) to understand more precisely the limit of my province. In one sentence you have mentioned physical and practical astronomy: in another physical only. Am I to discuss both? Or to touch but lightly on the practical astronomy? And is the physical astronomy to include every thing thaepend on the theory of gravitation? If there is to be no other report than mine, perhaps it would be best to leave these points wholly to me; in that case it would be taking unnecessary trouble to answer this letter.

With respect to the wish of the Committee that I should become a member of the mathematical sub-committee, I beg to represent that I could be of very little use in that capacity. I am sometimes almost oppressed with engagements, and though I can undertake specific business for which time enough is allowed, I could not always attend to the business of a committee. I must therefore most respectfully decline this invitation, at the same time that I beg you to convey to the committee my wish to give every assistance in my power. I shall have great pleasure in attending to any particular point on which they think that I can employ myself with advantage to their proposed objects.

Harcourt MSS (Harcourt Papers, *xiii. 259–61*)

67 *Harcourt, Wheldrake near York, to Forbes, Edinburgh, 25 October 1831*

Though Mr Phillips' lectures at Sheffield have deprived me of his assistance I have not left the business of the Association to stand still. The delay in printing has arisen out of the wish to include the names of the members of the sub-committees and the circumstance that some distant persons were put upon them whose permission it was necessary to obtain. I have answers now either negative or affirmative from all except Sir J. South, and only want information from you whether Dr Brewster is Sir David, K G O and whether Mr Johnston is not F R S E and whether he claims any other capital letters. I have sent to the *Annals of Philosophy* a summary of our objects and rules and list of office bearers and local committees and a statement of the reports on different sciences which have been undertaken, among which you will be gratified to find Mr Airy's on astronomy.

Pray consider well the recommendations of the mathematical and physical [sub]-committee, namely, that a series of observations on the magnetic intensity of the earth be made in different parts of England under the auspices of the Association; that a series of electro-magnetic observations similar to those made in Cornwall be carried on under the auspices of the Association; that measures be taken to obtain a series of hourly meteorological observations in some central part of England and in some part of the south of England; that the committee in India be requested to obtain a series near the equator; that endeavours be made to procure a satisfactory exposition of the theory of the moist bulb hygrometer; that Mr Stevenson be requested to report upon the waste and extension of the land on the east coast of Britain, on the question of permanence of the level of the sea and land and that individuals be requested to correspond with him on the subject; that authentic observations on the decreasing temperature with increasing height in the atmosphere be collected from all quarters. It rests with you chiefly to set these things in train to be executed, to point out the measures which we should take, and to draw up a short theoretical and practical statement with respect to each of them to be inserted and circulated in our *Report*. It may be advisable to print directions and queries on the subjects proposed for enquiry in a separate form for more general circulation. Let us take care not to issue a brutum fulmen or promise more than we can undertake in any degree to perform.

Forbes papers, 1831/39

Robert Stevenson (1772–1850), *DNB*, lighthouse engineer. Johnston was piqued that he was not a Fellow of the Royal Society of Edinburgh. The summary of the Association's objects appeared in the *Philosophical Magazine*, 1831 (Nov), x. 387–98. By then *Annals of Philosophy* had been subsumed by the *Philosophical Magazine*.

68 *Forbes, Greenhill, Edinburgh, to Harcourt, Wheldrake near York, 2 November 1831*

I regret extremely that the accident of being addressed simply to Edinburgh, prevented me from receiving your very kind and welcome letter till today: and I lose not a moment in answering it as far as I am able. I shall be much vexed if any unintentional delay should retard the appearance of the *Report* about which you have taken so much trouble.

As to Dr Brewster, he is not yet Sir David, not having been in London to be knighted, and I do not think it likely that he assumes any letters distinctive of the Guelphic order: indeed I am not sure what they are. Neither Mr Johnston nor Mr Robert Allan are members of the Royal Society of Edinburgh. Mr Johnston is MA but I believe nothing else.

I am a good deal perplexed about the physical queries but most anxious to do everything in my power as a member of the committee, which you may think right, and also to goad the memories of other members, which is no sinecure. But in what form an application to *individuals* is to be made I am a little at a loss. It is, as you observe, a subject for consideration, and as the members of the committee are separated there is some difficulty in accomplishing it: should the queries be forwarded in the name of the Association, and in the form of a resolution, that A be requested to do so and so? Or should the committee correspond through some of their members? This doubt occurs I think only with regard to Scoresby on magnetic intensity, Stevenson on the German Ocean, and Lubbock on the tides (who by the way I think you do not mention). Now, Scoresby having been at the meeting, no ceremony need I think be used with him except to write and ask whether the person he thought of would positively undertake to do the experiments to purpose, without some assurance of which I do not think the Royal Society [of Edinburgh] would be justified in sending the instrument to England. As to the second, I could answer, I think, for having the application made to Mr Stevenson in a proper way, if we had a distinct proposition from the central Committee in the form of a resolution of the Association or otherwise. With regard to Mr Lubbock making a report upon the tides, if you can forward an application to him from the central Committee through any good channel and will let me know in time, I shall write to him on the subject and give him some information I had from Scoresby which might perhaps the more dispose him to the task.

Respecting the Indian committee and establishment of the meteorological register there I shall write to Dr Brewster and speak to Mr Robison about it. I think an hourly register in the south of England might easily be managed and I think nothing could be better than that the central Committee should correspond with Mr Harvey about it who is both a very zealous man and apparently anxious to promote the objects of the Association.

I shall be most happy to draw up short notices as you propose of the nature and objects of the queries, and will perhaps get Dr Brewster to assist me. You must be aware that being the only member of the natural philosophy committee in Edinburgh I labour under considerable difficulties in the way of cooperation, but I shall spare no pains to forward any object you may consider desirable and only beg you to develop your hints so that I may not appear to take undue responsibility upon myself. You will perhaps favour me with a more particular notice of what you think these abstracts of queries ought to be and whether you wish them immediately forwarded for the principal *Report* or whether you will confine them to a subsidiary paper. I write all this in the perfect conviction that the mechanism of the whole affair must turn upon one individual and the noble exertions you have already made in the institution and conservation of the Association, leave us to wish for no better hands to whom its principles and structure should be intrusted.

I am delighted to hear of Airy's acceptance. It at once secures all the aid of Cambridge talents, and after that the Association *must* stand and be heard of far and wide. I hope Babbage has written favourably: I have only had a short letter from him since my return home. Besides the larger *Report*, I hope you will furnish us with a statement in a single page of the objects and nature of the institution for the purpose of giving to proposing members: whenever I receive that I hope to make large levies. When you send these (which should be addressed to John Robison, Esq. Royal Society apartments) will you request Mr William Gray to forward some printed £5 receipts.

I shall take the liberty of enclosing this to the Archbishop which I hope will not be inconvenient. In anything in which I can be of use to you be assured of my most ready assistance and believe me to remain with the truest esteem and regard

Forbes Papers, 1831/42

William Gray, jun (1806-80), a Secretary of the Yorkshire Philosophical Society 1827-37 and with Phillips a Secretary to the 1831 meeting of the Association. His father, Jonathan Gray (1779-1837), was Treasurer of the Yorkshire Philosophical Society and first Treasurer of the Association 1831-2. The instrument of the Royal Society of Edinburgh was a standard Hansteen needle.

69 *Murchison, 3 Bryanston Place, London, to Harcourt, Wheldrake near York, 3 November 1831*

The first letter which I write after our *first* meeting at Somerset House is this to yourself, and if I have not written to you 'chemin faisant', it was merely because I had no wish to add to your load of letters, without being able to communicate something satisfactory to you respecting the British Association for Science etc. During the course of my journey from York (via Lincolnshire, Norfolk and Cambridge) to town, I have, you may rest assured, exerted myself to the utmost in propagating our York doctrines, and I am happy to say with as much success in the provinces as I *now* flatter myself they will be received with in the metropolis.

At Cambridge where I spent 4 days with Whewell and Sedgwick comfortably lodged in the great quadrangle of Trinity during all the movement of the county election, I flatter myself I was of considerable use in explaining much of the real objects of the Association and in defending controverted points on which 'doctors differed'. Whewell, for example, was of opinion that we should have no publication; others thought we should have no subscription; all of which points they now understand are no longer capable of being discussed as the *constitution* of September 1831 has been solemnly ratified, and will I hope flourish many a year without the necessity of a *reform*. Whewell will send you a list of Cambridge adherents, in which of course you will see my friend Adam Sedgwick's name, of which please to make prominent use. If Sedgwick has not written to you, take this as his letter for he frequently omits these duties, and understand from me that he is heartily *with us*.

I picked up a very good recruit in the Rev'd Edward Stanley of Alderley, Cheshire, whose subscription of £5 I have received; therefore insert him in your list as paid, and application to be made to me. I only reached home 24 hours before the Geological [Society] meeting, and have no doubt from the tone and disposition with which the accounts of our doings were received that when the London committee begins to work effectively (as soon as our little secretary Yates arrives) that I shall have the pleasure of sending you a most powerful and numerous catalogue of men, good and true. In your own department I have already hooked the first chemist of the metropolis, Dr Prout, who has authorized me to add his name; this you will be happy to do without delay. Buckland and Whewell have by correspondence agreed to call the meeting for the 3rd week of June next.

At our [Geological Society] Club dinner yesterday I held forth con spirito on the glories of York, and if I may say to your face that which I gave out behind your back, the Vice-president was lauded (as in candour, justice and gratitude I was bound to do) for the origin, plan and success of *the whole undertaking*.

Babbage sat on my right hand yesterday at dinner; he is with us, but at the same time denies that either Herschel, himself, or anyone engaged in original researches which occupy all their time and thoughts, can be expected to join in *committees* or give memoirs. Sir J. South expressed the same sentiment, although both their names are to appear in our lists.

As I wrote to congratulate you on the accession to your family by anticipation allow me now to do so after the event has happily taken place, and to add Mrs Murchison's congratulations and remembrances to Mrs William Harcourt.

I particularly request that you will express to the Archbishop and Lady Anne Vernon how deeply and sincerely both my wife and myself were affected by the kind reception we met with at Bishopthorpe and that we shall for ever recur to that visit as one of most perfect enjoyment and delight. We also beg not to be forgotten by Miss Georgiana Harcourt, although I had no chance of making that profound impression on her mind which was effected by the great northern star of our meeting, who is so fully alive to the polarizing beams of a female eye.

Harcourt MSS (Harcourt Papers, *xiii. 261-4*)

William Prout (1785-1850), *DNB*, London physician and chemist; Lady Anne Vernon (1760-1832) wife of the Archbishop of York; Georgiana Harcourt (1807-86), was Harcourt's youngest sister. Brewster, an experimental optician, was the great northern star.

70 *Whewell, Trinity College, Cambridge, to Harcourt, Wheldrake near York, 4 November 1831*

I have delayed answering your last letter on various accounts, one of which is that I have now mislaid it and cannot lay my hand upon it. I will however speak to such points as I recollect. With respect to the report on the recent progress of mathematics I do not know any one so likely to do it well or to give it authority by his name as Hamilton. We have several young mathematicians of promise here but none to compare with him if he will undertake it. In proposing it, however, care must be taken to distinguish the department intended so that it shall not include Airy's province of physical astronomy. Perhaps if he be informed that Airy has undertaken such a portion of the subject it will be the best way of avoiding confusion. Observe Airy's department is not astronomy, as I observe it stated in some of the reports, but *physical* astronomy, that is the mathematical mechanics of the science. A report on astronomy would be a good thing but I hardly know who could be asked to give it. If Dr Brinkley, the *present* President of the Astronomical Society, would undertake it, it would be an admirable arrangement every way; but at any rate avoid the late President or we shall have to repent it. Perhaps as there is an Astronomical Society such a report is less wanted.

Professor Henslow will be glad to join any committee where he can be useful, so if you will let him or me know what he can do we will see about it. I believe I may say the same of Professor Cumming who intends to form one of the party next year. So does Mr Willis, our experimenter on vowels, an admirable mechanist. We shall, I have no doubt, send many more, for the members of the University are only just coming together, and all I have spoken with seem well inclined. I have not attempted any array of committee or secretaries, as I do not think there is any necessity for it here.

Dr Buckland wrote to me to make enquiries about the most suitable time for the meeting, and to meet the convenience of Oxford and Cambridge it appears that the third week in June will answer best. Mr Murchison, who has been here for a few days, informs me that this time will also do well for the geologists, so you will consider whether there is any objection to it.

I am afraid I may have answered your enquiries very imperfectly, but I shall be happy to give you further information on any points which I have omitted.

Whewell Papers, o.15.47[100]

Whewell had a consistently low opinion of Sir James South, the 'late President' of the Astronomical Society.

71 *Brewster, Allerly near Melrose, to Harcourt, Wheldrake near York, 5 November 1831*

I write you at present in consequence of having received letters from Mr Johnston and Mr Forbes expressing great anxiety to receive any account of the proceedings of the meeting at York, or any printed regulations of the Association which you may have drawn up. Mr Forbes was desirous of this information previous to his beginning to recruit for members, and Mr Johnston wished it in order to give accuracy to an account of the meeting and of the Association which he is now preparing. He writes me that he has received from Dr Daubeny a box of specimens from Earl Fitzwilliam's iron works, with valuable hints on the subjects to be investigated, so that this part of the machinery has already begun to move.

I had a letter a few days ago from Whewell on the subject of the Association. He says that Airy has engaged to draw up a report on the present state and prospects of physical astronomy, and he expects that several 'Cambridgemen' will interest themselves in the projects of the Association. He is anxious to hear whether his own report on mineralogy is to be written in conjunction with Mr Thomas Allan and me. I shall write to him that though we are not associated with him in this duty, we shall transmit to him any information we can collect, and that I shall procure for him from Berzelius the latest intelligence respecting Swedish mineralogy.

I shall be very glad to learn from you how the Association is advancing, and how many members have been added to it.

I am very anxious that the Association should be able to establish at some military station in a central part of England a series of hourly meteorological observations. Perhaps you could learn where such stations are.

PS Be so good as insert as a member of the Association Lieut Colonel Ferguson of Huntley Burn who is entitled to admission as a member of the Highland Society.

Harcourt MSS

Lieutenant Colonel James Ferguson and his brother, Sir Adam Ferguson (1771–1855), *DNB*, both lived at Huntley Burn, Melrose, and were near neighbours of Brewster.

72 *Harcourt, Wheldrake near York, to Forbes, Greenhill, Edinburgh, 9 November 1831*

I had forgotten in directing to you that good names are so much more common in Scotland than they are with us. I have written to Mr Hamilton at Mr Whewell's desire to ask him to undertake the mathematical report, and to Mr Lubbock to ask him for a report on the actual state of our information as to the height and periods of the tides on our coast and on the data remaining to be obtained in order that the Association may exert itself to procure them. It would be well for you to write to him also with the particulars to which you refer and with which I promised that you would furnish him. By tonight's coach I believe will be sent our short printed statement which will enable you to send us a list of members for the fuller *Report*. I have sent the geological subjects of enquiry to Sedgwick to redress and to put into a tangible practical shape and I should be glad if you would do the same with those which I sent you, in readiness for the *Report* which we are preparing for the press. If you have any wish to consult with us here upon any points in them I shall be most happy to receive you at my house for any time that you can spare. Dr Brewster, Mr Whewell, Mr Scoresby and yourself are I believe the most competent advisers of those who are on the sub-committee as to the manner in which the questions shall be put, so as to answer the end of putting them. But I am persuaded you can do it as well without the trouble of much correspondence. I will write to Mr Scoresby to make the enquiry respecting his undertaking the observations on the magnetic intensity.

[PS] I have the most favorable accounts of the reception of our plans at Cambridge and in London from Mr Murchison.

Forbes Papers, 1831/44

73 *Harcourt, Wheldrake near York, to Sedgwick, Trinity College, Cambridge, 9 November 1831*

In consequence of a letter which I lately received from Mr Murchison I have considered myself at liberty, without waiting for a direct communication, to add your name to the list of members of the Association and of its geological sub-committee. You will receive immediately a printed statement of the objects and rules of the Association with the names of the members of the sub-committees etc. This will be followed by a fuller *Report* of the proceedings of the late meeting and the enquiries recommended by it, some of which require a little redressing. It required so much time to arrange other matters that these enquiries were not in all instances enough digested and reduced to a practical shape. The sending forth any thing like a 'brutum fulmen' is by all means to be avoided and I would therefore beg your particular attention to the enquiries proposed by the geological sub-committee before they are issued ...

Sedgwick Papers, Add. MS 7652/1A/41A

74 *Harcourt, Wheldrake near York, to Scoresby, Liverpool, 11 November 1831*

You will remember that one of the resolutions of our committee was 'that a series of observations on the magnetic intensity of the earth be made in different parts of England under the auspices of the Association; that for this purpose Mr Robison be requested to procure from the Royal Society of Edinburgh a loan of the instrument in their possession, and to put it into the hands of Mr Scoresby who undertakes to make the observations as extensively as possible'. Mr Forbes and Mr Robison wish to know whether you intend to make the observations yourself or whether the person to whom you propose to commit them will undertake to make the experiments effectively, without some assurance of which the Royal Society would probably not feel justified in sending the instrument to England. In publishing the *Report* which we are now preparing for the press it will be desirable to add to the scientific notices such explanations and instructions as may practically conduce to carrying the objects of them into effect without which many of them will prove a mere 'brutum fulmen'. I would beg you therefore to give your particular attention to this resolution and to consider in what manner either by requesting particular persons whom you may be able to name to cooperate in making particular experiments or by a more general invitation and explanation of the object, with which you can furnish us for the *Report*, we may be enabled to put [it] into a tangible shape and give it real effect.

I should be glad also of any suggestions from you respecting another resolution which followed this, namely, 'that a series of electro-magnetic observations similar to those made by Mr Fox in Cornwall be carried on under the auspices of the Association'.

The Association has been joined by all the principal men of science at Cambridge, and in London we have associated Babbage, South and Prout; and as soon as the statement of our objects, and of which I have begged Mr Phillips to forward you copies, is circulated we shall probably be joined by many more. We wish to print in our *Report* a list of members and shall therefore be obliged to you to send us a list of any recruits whom you may pick up.

Scoresby Papers

Robert Were Fox (1789-1877), *DNB*.

75 *Brewster, n.p., to Harcourt, n.d. [18 November 1831]*

I went to Edinburgh on Thursday last and remained till Tuesday, for the express purpose of making arrangements with Mr Robison, Mr Forbes and Mr Johnston respecting the Association. Mr Forbes had unfortunately gone to Argyllshire and has not yet returned, so that we could do no effectual business without him. Mr Robison received the copies of the rules of the Association when I was with him, and we were much satisfied with the manner in which they are drawn up.

On the receipt of your letter which followed me to Edinburgh I would have written instantly to Lord Brougham about the hourly observations at York; but until I learn from you the amount of the interruption which takes place in the occupation of the barracks, it would be needless to apply; for unless the register could be carried on during that interruption it would be entirely useless ...

I fear that I see in the horizon of our Association a small black cloud which if not dissipated may yet overshadow us. I was not prepared for the refusal of Babbage, South and Henry to enter our committees, and I hope it is not owing to the cause I am about to notice.

In Lord Milton's address, and I think also in yours, the *direct* encouragement of science by government was reprobated; and I think you also mentioned that science was not declining in England. Although these opinions were hostile to mine and I believe to those of *nine tenths* of the active men of science in England, yet I heard them with no other feeling than that of regret that any controversial topic should have been agitated. I had indeed entirely forgotten them till a London magazine was put into my hands last week in Edinburgh in which I was taunted by name for having listened without replying to your observations on the non-decline of science. On the same evening I received the first sheet of Mr Johnston's account of the York meeting in which, without any communication with me, he had felt it his duty to animadvert upon Lord Milton's opinions. The present ministry are determined to give a direct encouragement to science, and the Duke of Wellington assured Lord Ashley that if he ever again came into power he would conduct himself differently to science and scientific men. I have at this moment before me an original letter, from Lord Melville to a friend of his own, in which he states that it was always a grievance with him that the government did not do enough for men of science. Here then we have the concurrence of all political parties in the necessity of a direct encouragement, and it will appear a strange anomaly that the President of the British Association should tell all the science of England that her cultivators should not be directly encouraged by the government. The inconvenience and risk of introducing such discussions are very obvious; and I feel such a deep interest in the success of our Association, that I shall never again refer to the subject; and I hope that from the present moment it will pass into utter oblivion.

Since writing the above I have received your letter of the 17th. The exact state of the case with regard to the origin of the York meeting is this. Without the slightest communication with any person whatever I conceived the idea of the meeting, and wrote to Mr Phillips the letter in which I requested the sentiments of your Society and of the public bodies at York. I then announced to Mr Robison, Mr Johnston and Mr Forbes what I had done, and they all cooperated with me in the heartiest manner in our future proceedings. Mr Murchison deserves the highest praise for his liberal and active services. He advocated our cause against the illiberal opposition of Captain Hall and others and deserves our warmest acknowledgements. But all that we have done would have gone for nothing without your zealous and unremitting exertions, without the kind patronage of the Archbishop, and without the active cooperation of the officebearers and members of the Yorkshire Philosophical Society.

I should like much to receive from you as soon as possible a list of the members of the Association. Mr Forbes, from whom I have just heard, says that he is about to send you a list of members. Sir John Sinclair desires me to forward to you his name.

The cabalistic letters K C G will sufficiently describe the adjunct to which you refer, but their omission in mention is to me a matter of indifference.

I earnestly trust that this horrid pestilence will not invade your interesting county. The uncertainty of its character, and its slow progress at Sunderland have in this quarter removed much of the alarm which its first appearance excited. Many intelligent physicians in Edinburgh conceive that it has already done its work in that city in the modified though severe cholera which prevailed there in summer, and we had in this parish an unusual number of cholera patients in May and June.

We must use the means and trust the result to providence.

If you have not seen Mr Douglas of Cavers's pamphlet entitled *Prospects of Britain* I would recommend it to you as containing an anticipation of our new Association, which he seems to have long contemplated. He is a Cambridge man and the representative of the great house of Douglas.

Harcourt MSS

Anthony Ashley Cooper, 7th Earl Shaftesbury, styled Lord Ashley (1801-85), *DNB*; Captain Hall was Basil Hall; Sir John Sinclair (1754-1835), *DNB*, statistician and agriculturalist. James Douglas of Cavers, near Hawick, lived about ten miles from Brewster's home; Douglas's *The prospects of Britain* (2nd ed., Edinburgh, 1831), 58, 60, proposed the formation of a voluntary national society to promote science. Harcourt was keen to inaugurate hourly meteorological observations at the York barracks; for Milton's speech of 27 Sept 1831, see *Yorkshire Gazette*, 1 Oct 1831; for Harcourt's views about the non-decline of science in his speech of 27 Sept 1831, see *1831 Report*, 11; the London magazine article was 'The decline of science denied', *Mechanics' magazine*, 1831-2 (22 Oct 1831), xvi. 63; for Johnston's strictures on Lord Milton's views, see Johnston, 'Account of the scientific meeting at York', *Edinburgh journal of science*, 1832 (Jan), vi. 1-32 (9).

76 *Brewster, Allerly near Melrose, to Phillips, 19 November 1831*

Private

I send you notices of my four papers which I think convey a correct idea of their contents. You can alter them as you choose.

I may mention to you *confidentially* that in writing yesterday to Mr Harcourt I stated to him the risk to which the Association is exposed by the introduction into his address of the controversial points respecting the non-decline of science, and by the circumstance of both him and Lord Milton having reprobated the *direct encouragement of science* by the government. These things I had entirely forgotten, though I felt their inconvenience at the time; but when I was in Edinburgh last week, there was put into my hands a London magazine taunting me by name for having heard Mr Harcourt's observations without replying to them, and on the same evening I received a proof (that of Mr Johnston's account of the York meeting) in which without any communication with any person whatever he has felt it his duty to reply to Lord Milton's observations. These I believe will be found to be the reasons why Babbage and South will not join our committees; and if something is not done to prevent it, our Association will find its grave in Oxford. Herschel, Babbage, South, Leslie, Henry, Harvey, Johnston, Brown, are unanimously of opinion that the mathematical and physical sciences (not the natural history sciences) are rapidly declining, and can only be saved by the direct encouragement of the government; and if the President and Vice-president of the British Association avow opposite opinions, on topics on which they are unable to judge, and publish these under the sanction of the Association, all the above individuals and the crowds which think with them will withdraw from the Association. I never will withdraw on any such grounds; but if the office bearers of one year attack opinions supported by *nine tenths* of the Association, the office bearers of another year will be compelled to defend their opinions, and the house thus divided against itself will not long stand.

When Mr Harcourt wrote to me about the Association he said 'Neither has there hitherto been any society, independent, deliberative and powerful enough to possess influence enough *with the government of the country to claim for science what is due to it, and to the interests of society depending upon it, and through* the medium of public opinion to *lead to a more enlightened* and creditable *national dealing with men of science and their objects*'. This passage convinced me that Mr Harcourt and I held the same opinions, and that it was to be a specific object of the institution to obtain *national encouragement* to science and consequently to scientific men.

Mr Harcourt seems therefore to have completely changed his views, and I have no doubt that this has taken place from the good motive of securing the co-operation of Whewell who is crazy about the decline of science, and hostile to government doing any thing for it. But if *one* Whewell is gained *twenty* are lost to the Association, and one of its leading and grandest objects sacrificed for ever. If you see this matter in the light that I do, you may yet stay the impending evil. If you do not agree with me, let the matter instantly be forgotten . . .

I trust Mr Forbes will induce you to visit Edinburgh this winter or spring. If you do I hope you and Miss Phillips, to whom I beg my best respects, will pay Mrs B and me a visit either on your way to Edinburgh or from it or both. The chevy chase runs through Melrose on the mount road to Edinburgh.

PS   Be so good as give my best compts to Mr Taylor & Mr Gray.

British Association archives, Foundation volume, 76

Robert Brown (1773–1858), *DNB*, botanist; Ann Phillips (1803–62), sister of John, was his housekeeper from 1829 until her death; William Taylor (1790–1870) a York Anglican minister and inventor. With characteristic zeal Brewster gave four papers at the 1831 meeting of the Association.

77   *Harcourt, Wheldrake near York, to Milton, Wentworth House near Rotherham, Monday [21 November 1831]*

I send you the newspaper report of your speech at the scientific meeting, to revise compress or enlarge, for the publication of the proceedings which we are preparing for the press. In what you said the most material point is the view of the assistance which a government can give to science, a subject much debated now, some scientific men forming too high an estimate of it and some too low; and the fact being, that in this country from our love of war very little has ever been done by our government for the arts of peace. Though I believe the report enclosed is a pretty correct account of what you said but, as it is now liable to be circulated through Europe, you will probably like to correct it a little more.

[PS]   I shall be obliged to you to return me the newspaper report and to send me the corrected one as soon as you can.

Fitzwilliam Papers, drawer Aug–Dec 1831

78   *Harcourt, n.p., to Whewell, n.d. [late November 1831]*

You will see by the enclosed letter, which I will thank you to return to me under cover to the Archbishop, that my application to Mr Hamilton to give us a report on the progress of mathematical science has not been successful, but perhaps the objection might be surmounted by a direct request from Cambridge. I mentioned in my letter to him that the progress of *pure* mathematics was the subject of the proposed report. If you think it in vain to repeat the application you may perhaps be able to think of some other person to whom it may be entrusted; but of course it had better not be done at all, than done indifferently. We should be glad to name the person who is to undertake it in the *Report* of which we are preparing the materials.

The chemical committee are invited to endeavour 'to ascertain the relative weight of the several elements hydrogen, oxygen and azote, or which is the same thing the specific gravity of the three gases, in such a way as would ensure the reasonable assent of all competent judges; also, the proportions of azote, oxygen, etc in the atmosphere, and the proportions of azote and oxygen in nitrous gas and nitrous oxide; and the specific gravities of the compound gases in general; and to communicate the results to the next meeting at Oxford'. Dr Prout writes to me on this subject that for the last 4 or 5 years almost the whole of his leisure has been devoted to the atmosphere, particularly its weight and composition. The results he hopes will prove very interesting and important. They will comprise observations on the relative expansion of the air and mercurial thermometer shewing that the present views on these points are quite erroneous; on the tension of vapour, on the weight, etc., of the atmosphere at all seasons, on the specific gravity of hydrogen, oxygen, azote and carbonic acid, etc., etc. And he hopes to send to Oxford a sketch of some of the particulars at least, though the whole investigations may not be completed. In the mean time he also hopes that some one else will take up the same points and adds that it would be well that this should be done independently and the results compared, which is likewise strongly the wish of Mr Dalton who proposed the questions. Dr Prout observes that in this case it will be necessary that we should use the same weights and measures and those which he employs are the national standards as adjusted for him by Captain Kater. He is afraid of not getting many if any London chemists to join us on this, all being fully occupied with other things. It is of no use to ask any but very accurate experimenters to undertake such researches; whom have you at Cambridge? There is Professor Cumming whom you might perhaps induce to take a part in settling these highly important data of chemical theory.

I am in hopes of obtaining from Mr Powell a report upon radiant heat which I have no doubt will be valuable. I am very anxious that much really good work should be done at the Oxford meeting which will stamp the character of the society.

[PS] I conjecture Mr Hamilton's backwardness to be real, but I believe misplaced, modesty; but I am not personally acquainted with him.

We shall be glad of a list of the Cambridge members of the Association.

Whewell Papers, a.205[118]

Azote was nitrogen.

79 *Johnston, Broughton Crescent, Portobello, Edinburgh, to Harcourt, York, 27 November 1931*

I have just received your letter of yesterday and I sit down immediately to answer it now in order to do away as early as possible the impression which has been conveyed to you, I know not how, regarding my commentary on Lord Milton's speech. What I have said will, I trust, when you see it, give dissatisfaction neither to you nor to Lord Milton. My account of the meeting is in the press. It occupies only two sheets and is printed thus early as it is to form the first article in Brewster's *Journal* and consequently will not be published till the 1st of January. By that time yours, I suppose, will be in circulation. Had I been aware that a corrected copy of Lord Milton's speech was to appear in your *Report*, I might have deferred the remarks I have made to some other opportunity. It is possible, however, that when it does appear it may be taken up by some one else. The only point to which I have adverted is to his Lordship's opinion as to the best mode of encouraging science. As an individual I have argued in favor of *direct* encouragement but in no form or language that can either offend his Lordship or provoke controversy. On the contrary, it has been a matter of regret among us northern men that you should have introduced the decline of science in your address; for as you may have seen a writer in the *Mechanics' Magazine*, Mr Rotch most likely, has argued that since Dr Brewster did not rise and oppose you therefore he must have agreed with you. This I insert mainly to show you that I personally think he's excessively sorry, deeply interested as I am in the society to do anything or say anything that might keep any man from lending it his best support. My account is a journal of the proceedings with a few remarks interspersed in which, though far beneath what they deserve, I endeavour to convey to the people of York our sense of their zeal and hospitable attention. I hope there is not a word in it that will give offence to any individual. It would be a bad return to make for the high gratification I myself experienced. I would send you an early copy did I know how to address you under cover, so as to save you the postage which it is not worth.

I have been aware for some years of Prout's investigations and I hope it may prove as he says and that some definite results may be obtained. I fear very much we have none here in the north who would join us. Dr Thomson, as you say, is too theoretical and besides he refuses to join our society. I had a letter from him a few days ago in which he says that he believes all societies are in reality injurious to the progress of science and that he has no desire to become a member. I am afraid he has been neglected. I doubt if he ever received any circular to attend the meeting.

As for myself I am really unqualified for the task. With some instructions from Dr Prout I might by practice obtain some approximate results but I doubt much if I could produce any by next meeting. I do not, however, say no to the proposal if I saw I could do any good . . .

Harcourt MSS

Benjamin Rotch (1794–1854), a London barrister, attended the 1831 meeting of the Association and was elected to the sub-committee on the mechanical arts; Thomas Thomson (1773–1852), *DNB*, professor of chemistry at Glasgow University.

80 *Milton, Wentworth House near Rotherham, to Harcourt, 28 November 1831*

Of all audiences I find that a philosophical society is the most difficult to address, for I have carried your letters and my own speech about in my pocket for several days in the hope of some propitious moment arriving at which I might reduce the latter into a shape more worthy of a destiny, which I never anticipated for any offspring of mine, that of being introduced to the notice of foreign critics. The propitious moment however has never presented itself and I am constrained to return it with some few verbal alterations which will make it run somewhat smoother. Upon the disputed point, I should not like to omit from the printed report an opinion which I expressed when speaking, especially as it is one which I hold most deliberately and stated intentionally; the omission would look as if I had changed my opinion, or was afraid of avowing it. I hope the latter part will not get us into a fresh correspondence with Mr Salmond but I cannot say less of you or more of any one else.

I think you will easily fit the corrections to their proper sites.

Harcourt MSS

In his speech Milton had lauded Harcourt as the founder of the Yorkshire Philosophical Society, an ascription disputed privately and publicly by William Salmond (1769–1838), a York gentleman geologist: see, e.g., *Yorkshire Gazette*, 12 Nov 1831 and the privately printed exchange of letters in Oct 1831 between Milton and Salmond (3 pp., no title, copy in York Minster Library).

81 *Forbes, Greenhill, Edinburgh, to Harcourt, Wheldrake near York, 1 December 1831*

I fear you have thought me dilatory in communicating to you for the *Report*. The fact is that I was anxious to have a *tolerably* respectable list of names to send you, and perhaps you are well enough aware of the difficulty of stimulating people when the excitement of the moment is past to wonder that it has required some sacrifice of time and energy to obtain even those now sent, a great many of whom I am sorry to say have put down their names merely as a favour to myself. Be this as it may I shall have nearly £100 when the money is all collected.

The outlines for the *Report* will I hope be of the description you wish. It was very difficult to keep within the narrow limits and yet enter at all upon the subject. I submitted them to Dr Brewster who approved of them all. Would it be worthwhile to try and collect any in astronomy or the higher sciences? Sir James South's query about the satellites ought to be inserted if it had any companions. I hope the printers will be able to read my scrawl. I shall be happy to correct the proofs if you think it worthwhile.

I had a letter from Lubbock yesterday, not very satisfactory; but he seems to overlook the object of the Association in thinking we want to get what he gives to the *Philosophical Transactions* or *Philosophical Magazine* and yet he begs me to try to get him data from Scotland which is exactly what his report should express the want of and beg the Association to endeavour to procure.

I am sorry to hear from Dr Brewster that Hamilton has declined to report. I think the Cambridge men should be again applied to: probably Challis or some of the younger men would feel a pleasure in being asked.

Murchison is an invaluable man and will not desert us; always incite him to keep attention in London towards the Association. He is on the new Council of the Royal Society.

Do not be discouraged in your laudable exertions by any checks which the most disinterested efforts often receive even from the mere inconsiderateness of friends. Let me know if in any way I can be useful to you and believe me (in haste) with great esteem and regard

PS   Since the York meeting I have become a F.G.S. and am a member of the Royal Geographical Society.

Forbes Papers, 1831/50

James Challis (1803-82), *DNB*, a Cambridgeshire Anglican clergyman. In 1831 the annual subscription to the Association was £1 and life membership was £5. The outlines were recommendations and notes about questions in physical science drawn up by Forbes for *1831 Report*, 48-52.

82   *Harcourt, n.p., to Milton, n.d. [late November–early December 1831]*

A few words more on the direct encouragement of science as regards *persons*. Undoubtedly I should be very sorry to see any system of encouragement adopted by which men of science in England should become servile pensioners of the ministry but I am no less sorry to see them under the present system, when exerting the rarest intellectual faculties in the necessary scientific service of the state, chained down in a needy dependance on a too penurious government.

If, said one whose opinions on all subjects deserve the highest attention and on none so much as on the advancement of science, if the fathers of the sciences are ill fed 'et patrum invalidi referant jejunia nati'. Yet to this day philosophy has been kept upon a kind of parish allowance, and in the abstract sciences has been proportionably unprolific. One English statesman did indeed give so much direct encouragement to science as to make Newton Master of the Mint; but it was not till he had been compelled to beg hard at great men's doors; it was not till the discomfort of his circumstances had contributed to unsettle his mind, and it was a *kind* of encouragement which turned the first of philosophers into a common man of business. Lately our best practical astronomer was made a bishop, an appointment which deserves to be applauded if the astronomical bishop can take due care of his diocese without giving up the stars. In our universities direct encouragement is given to a few professors, and these professorships are supposed to be comfortable things; but they are certainly not made comfortable by the sufficiency of their endowments which are less now than the bequests left in the unexecuted will of Bacon for founding professorships 200 years ago. If our professors have a competence it is earned by cramming the elements of algebra etc. into undergraduates' heads not by attending on the service of science. Even thus much direct encouragement, however, is thought too much by some and we have men 'whom fortune has placed in a senate but whom nature intended for a pawnbroker's shop'; we have senators in this year 1832 [sic] who can muster a party and make a patriotic effort to effect a saving in the salaries of professors.

The best kind of porcelain is too refined a manufacture to be maintained in a country without direct encouragement; and how can it be expected that mathematics should maintain its professors without assistance from the state? As things stand at present the deeper and drier a man's studies are, the drier and more sparing must be his diet. For bread many of our first men of science are driven to mercenary practices which add indignity to poverty, which have no leisure, and indeed no soul for great achievements.

I cannot see any reason why with proper precautions men of science should not be helped to study for the public good, as well as statesmen to act for it; nor do I see why they should not be as independent on fixed salaries, as statesmen in places, revocable at will.

At the present moment there is a man of science and more than one friend of science at the head of affairs. Our starving philosophers are some of them indulging no unjustifiable hope that the fortunes of philosophy may be mended by their influence. You cannot wonder that they should be unwilling to have it proclaimed ex cathedrâ from the midst of themselves that there is something illegitimate in the direct encouragement of science though they are ready enough to own that there is something in it very *un-English*.

At this moment a strong effort is making to obtain for the grey-headed, disinterested, and almost pauper philosopher, Mr Smith that encouragement and reward which his public services deserve. In the present system it is a matter of interest to obtain it; on a better it would be an irresistible claim.

After considering what I have now said you would perhaps have no objection to substitute, for the expressions you have used, the following: 'one of the most effectual methods of advancing science is to remove the obstacles which oppose its progress' or 'but perhaps the most effectual method of advancing science is' etc. Speeches are seldom fit to be published exactly as they are delivered: publication involves a new and more deliberate exercise of judgment and the publication[s] of societies particularly require revision.

I think your speech must end in our *Report* with the words 'It will redound to the honour of this Society to have been the first to set the example'. I am the principal editor of the *Report* and am averse to publishing at length the compliments you paid me. It will be enough to say 'Lord Milton concluded by pronouncing an eulogium on his predecessor in the office of President of the Society'.

[PS]   Mr Johnston writes to me that he has not received the iron ores. Will you take the trouble of enquiring how they were sent and addressed?

Fitzwilliam Papers, BK

Harcourt was in fact quoting not Bacon but Virgil, *Georgics*, III, 128, slightly inaccurately (weak offspring show up the weaknesses of their fathers). Newton's patron was Charles Montagu, 1st Earl of Halifax (1661–1715), *DNB*; John Brinkley was the astronomer bishop; Brougham, then Lord Chancellor, the statesman. Johnston's work on iron and its ores, suggested at the 1831 meeting of the Association, required specimens from the Fitzwilliam iron-works.

83   *Harcourt, n.p., to Murchison, n.d. [very early December 1831]*

I find myself writing about the concerns of our infant Association, last in order, to its best friend, secure, whether I write or not, of his zeal and prudence. What pugnacious people your contrymen are on the other side of the Tweed. I discovered the other day that our friend Mr Johnston, who is going to print I suppose in Brewster's *Journal* an account of our late meeting, meant to animadvert upon Lord Milton's remarks about the direct encouragement of science. I have begged him to let it alone and to wait for an *authentic* report of our President's speech, not trusting too much to his own recollection. This is the only cloud I have yet observed in our horizon. The question is one which affects the pocket on the one side, and on the other the spirit of independence. Our northern friends are not indifferent to the former consideration, and our comfortable English professors are warm with the latter, and our own business is to keep such powerful elements of strife at rest. Forbes and Brewster are at work upon the questions of the physical committee to put them into a practical shape and fit them for publication. On the geological I have consulted Sedgwick and Conybeare. They both agree that the question of electric charges should be limited to veins: it will thus reduce itself to a continuation of Mr Fox's experiments. Do you know him or can you send me his address? I have also asked Sedgwick and Conybeare to unite in drawing up a report on E. de Beaumont's lines of disturbance as regards England and I believe they will undertake it; they have both materials of their own for different parts of England and Wales, and Phillips will furnish them with valuable additions to their stock; but they will want cooperation from other quarters; I mentioned Mr Hutton and some others to Sedgwick and he promised to parcel out the work to different hands, but I mistrust him in this, knowing from your testimony and his own confession his aversion to writing letters. If you would assist I should have more confidence, that the allotments of labour would be actually made, and made immediately. There is Mr Mantell in Sussex, and there are others who will occur to you, bearing in mind however that it requires a geologist of more than the common retail-dealing kind to enter into such an enquiry. You ought to be a handsome contributor yourself.

We want names of members to print in our *Report*. I hope you will add to our chemists Dr Turner and Faraday, and induce the former who has time to work. We are very much in want of a sound chemist or two in addition to Dalton and Prout, from the latter of whom I have great expectations.

I shall see Mrs Murchison and yourself I trust in the spring. My wife desires her kind remembrances. We are very busy at York about keeping out the cholera.

Murchison Papers

Gideon Mantell (1790–1852), *DNB*, Lewes surgeon and geologist.

84 *Brewster, Allerly near Melrose, to Harcourt, Wheldrake near York, 5 December 1831*

Your letter to Lord Milton is admirable, and perfectly unanswerable.

Nine professors of the English universities receive a direct pension of £100 per annum each from government; and it would be a strange infatuation to maintain that scientific men *who are not professors* should not (if they need it, and merit it) obtain the same direct encouragement. Those *nine* professors are not the tools of government. Nay a pension given for life in place of making its holder a *tool* makes him independent of government. A pension during pleasure has certainly a *tendency* to produce servility though practically speaking it has the very opposite effect on well regulated minds.

I earnestly hope you will be able to begin the hourly observations with the thermometer at York on January 1st 1832. The thermometer should be large, placed in a free northern aspect, and free from artifical heat in winter and from the sun in summer. Our observations at Leith Fort were made by the Serjeants of the Guard, and we gave them annually as a *present*, not as a *fee*, £10 or £12. I enclose one of our schedules.

I have already written to Mr Harvey to have a similar one established at Plymouth. I expect to meet at Minto tomorrow with Captain Elliot, Secretary to the Admiralty, who will no doubt write immediately to Plymouth to obtain some facility from the local powers. If the Association shall succeed in getting even *one* year's thermometrical observations at these two points, it will do more for the science than has been done for a century.

I sent the rules of the Association to Lord Brougham. I heard from him today, but he said nothing about the Association ...

I would willingly write to Professor Hamilton about a mathematical report, but it is my conscientious belief that there is not one man in England who can venture to do it. There is no man solely devoted to mathematics, and sufficiently acquainted with what has been done abroad. Hamilton [is] intensely occupied with inquiry into his 'systems of rays', but with his occupations in the Observatory, he can not have time to study foreign mathematics. Airy is I think similarly circumstanced.

In Scotland we have not one mathematician, and scarcely an individual pursuing science ardently excepting the pilgrims to York. I am in great haste.

Harcourt MSS

George Elliot (1784-1863), M P for Roxburghshire 1832-53. The Plymouth meteorological scheme was implemented, that at York apparently not.

85 *Murchison, Up Park, Petersfield, to Harcourt, Wheldrake near York, 5 December 1831*

I was favoured with yours of—before I left town, where I was attending to my duties both as President Geological Society and as one of the *new* Council of the Royal Society.

I know your disposition too well not to infer that you will be glad to see a *gathering* of many of the working men of science around the old parent body. For my own part I was one of the extreme dissidents, and had quite made up my mind to the uncomfortable doctrine that the old lady Royal Society was doomed to die from atrophy; but when I found the attitude which the Duke of Sussex with great good sense and moderation had assumed, I began to change my notions. On enquiry I learnt (and from unbiassed authorities) that he did his duty carefully and zealously at the Greenwich visitations and on every possible occasion. I found Pettigrew dismissed, and so sincere a desire evinced to enlist all the savans on H R H's side, that the 'cordons bleus' of his former Council were all scratched out and a list prepared with representatives of each branch of science in due proportions. On this I gave in my adhesion and dined with the Duke at Kensington the eve of St Andrew's Day where he gave us a [sumptuous] entertainment being the first in his new apartments. Sedgwick, Buckland, Lyell, Greenough, Whewell and the great majority of my Society approve *entirely* of my conduct,· but there are dissidents. These I hope with time and good humour may come round in the end. In the mean time the old Society is getting many good papers from Airy (the *irregularities* of *Venus*), from Ritchie on electro-galvanism, and much [is] expected from Faraday as he has about completed a grand new discovery establishing the identity between magnetism and electricity.

But enough of the Royal which will I doubt not work on very well, and we of the Geological are *progressing* marvellously; and now to our York joint stock company, of which you are the father. I had always considerable misgivings as to the conduct of that Scotch chemist, i.e. in respect to *bien séance* of the man, but I never could have imagined that he should [have] decrepitated in the manner you describe and still less that our excellent and disinterested President should fall within his explosive range.

However we must rejoice that things were got together as well as they were, considering the combustible materials we had to deal with. You really have no conception of the irritability of some of my countrymen. I find among other phenomena of this sort that old Fleming (or as Sedgwick now calls him, *Phlegm*-ing) *is furious* with my predecessor and for what? Not because he, Sedgwick, said anything *against* him, but because in his last speech and confession of faith wherein he abjures that old heresy of diluvialism (to which I am sorry you still cling by the bye) he the professor should not have given the merited honour to old Malagrowther as the *first antagonist* of Buckland!!

With regard to recruits for our Association I do not think we shall *enrol many* till towards our reunion at Oxford; and as I never inhabit London regularly till New Year's Day I do not before that time expect to work systematically as a recruiting sergeant. There are objectors, as I have often told you, and many men in the Royal Society (such as Lubbock and others) think there are already *too many* societies, and of this party H R H the President is very likely to form one.

Notwithstanding all this we shall flourish, Lyell and 2 or 3 other good names may already be put down, Leonard Horner, for instance, who has written me an excellent letter from Bonn, enclosing a long translation of Hoffman's account of the new volcanic island, in which he not only fully approves of every part of our programme with which I had acquainted him, but promises to bring over [?] for our next, and I must say that if we could secure such men as Mitscherlich, Goldfuss, Leonhard etc, our meeting would have a much higher character. *I* shall attend to *this point particularly.*

The reports from various geologists on the applicability of de Beaumont's theory to the lines of elevation in England is a very legitimate subject. It is one on which I shall of course *be previously* compelled to fire off all my ammunition on the occasion of my anniversary oration. I have already in my hands 2/3 of Lyell's new volume and I may tell you that he flatters himself he will completely destroy the whole of the system i.e. the only part of it which as a system *is new*, viz the *synchronous* elevation of parallel chains. It is not by parallel rulers and examination of great maps à la Humboldt that this question *can be settled.* And I so far agree with Lyell that if the things called 'single epochs' should prove great indefinite and *indefinable periods of time*, embracing vast *zoological* discrepancies and differences between their extremes, that then we must reject the most bewitching part of the scheme. I have too much to say on this to give even an outline but I tend to the belief that my friend Élie has been *vastly* overrated. Necker de Saussure in the Alps, Conybeare in Wales, and *Germans* without end are showing him up as erring in his parallelisms, but Lyell will do the thing 'en philosophe', and endeavour to reduce the matter to incongruous nothings by *strict zoological data.* As Sedgwick has let fly so valiantly (I think somewhat prematurely) in the Frenchman's favour he will of course ride his horse on. We should always be careful of adding incense to the French puff.

I am delighted you are coming to town. Can you not manage to be at the anniversary of the Geological? Or do you intend to defer to the end of May and so join the great debacle upon Oxford?

I am labouring hard to get the volume out and am only retarded by Fitton's green sand, the illustrations of which by the bye will be quite beautiful (coast views, sections etc); and I flatter myself that the maps, views, sections and fossils of the eastern Alps will render this part 'unique'; all our portion of it is done. I have plenty of new matter from my late tour to make some memoirs: at all events I could give one long one on the younger edges of the grauwacke along the Welsh frontier coupling it with the ridges of igneous rock which burst through it, most of which are very ill known, but I have no time to set about the task. When in town I have so many committees to attend, Royal, Geographical, Naval and Military, Athenaeum, etc, besides the management of the Geological, that my spare minutes are few.

Brewster is to be Sir David as soon as he comes to town.

You are certain to make next meeting a good one and I commend all yoIndeed all sorts of 'rapports' on the Élie de Beaumont system *must elicit truth.* If the thing be nothing more than a bold assumption, the sooner it is annihilated the better, otherwise we shall have 20 or 30 years not in truth hunting but in bolstering up the hypothesis on one side and knocking it down on the other.

Mrs Murchison unites with me in best remembrance to Mrs V. Harcourt.

Harcourt MSS (Harcourt Papers, *xiii. 268-73*)

Thomas Joseph Pettigrew (1791-1865), *DNB*, the leader of a court clique; William Ritchie (1790-1837), *DNB*; John Fleming (1785-1857), Scottish Presbyterian minister and naturalist; Leonard Horner (1785-1864), *DNB*, geologist, educationalist and factory inspector; Friedrich Hoffman (1797-1836), German geologist; Eilhard Mitscherlich (1794-1863), *DSB*, professor of chemistry at Berlin University; Georg August Goldfuss (1782-1848), professor of mineralogy at Bonn University; Karl Cäsar von Leonhard (1779-1862), *DSB*, professor of mineralogy at Heidelberg University; Friedrich Wilhelm Heinrich Alexander von Humboldt (1769-1859), *DSB*, the famous environmental scientist; Louis Albert Necker de Saussure (1786-1861), Genevan geologist. The Greenwich Visitors inspected the Royal Observatory; the Scottish chemist was Johnston; Sedgwick, Murchison's predecessor as President of the Geological Society of London, had rejected diluvialism in his presidential address of February 1831; Malachi Malagrowther was an 1826 creation of Sir Walter Scott; Lyell's new volume was his *Principles of Geology* (London, 1832, Jan), ii. Fitton's green sand paper 'Observations on some of the strata between the chalk and the Oxford oolite in the south-east of England' was eventually published in *Transactions of the Geological Society of London*, 1836, iv. 103-378; for Sedgwick and Murchison, 'A sketch of the structure of the Eastern Alps ...', see *Transactions Geological Society*, 1835, iii. 301-420.

86 *Milton, Milton near Peterborough, to Harcourt, 5 December 1831*

I can have no objection to the alteration you propose as it does not at all compromise my opinion upon the main point, upon which I am still doubtful, notwithstanding the powerful arguments you adduce in favour of greater protection and favour to scientific men. Our difference of opinion may perhaps have its origin in a very remote region of our thoughts, the explanation of which would take up too much time. To the finale of my speech I can have no objection except that it might imply that I had been unmindful of your claims and I should not like (even through your own instrumentality) to be exposed to such a charge. My short time here is so much occupied that I wish you to excuse this very hasty scrawl.

Harcourt MSS

87 *Harcourt, Bishopthorpe near York, to Whewell, Thursday [8 or 15 December 1831]*

I am delighted to hear that Mr Peacock will give a view of the progress of the calculus in his report. Will the proper description of what he undertakes be 'a report on the state of mathematics including a statement of the progress of the differential and integral calculus'?

We are printing our *Report* which I hope will be ready about the end of the month and which are to be distributed to the subscribers. We will send to Cambridge a surplus for members who may be subsequently added. Mr Turner would be a valuable addition to our list, and on the strength of what you say I will write to him to enquire whether he will help to satisfy Mr Dalton's doubts on the primary data of chemistry. I wish we could get Professor Cumming to give us some account of those parts of electricity which he has studied. I hear that Faraday has made important discoveries on the connection of magnetism with electricity, but do not know their exact nature. May we expect from Professor Henslow any aid in respect to Dr Daubeny's enquiry and the invitation to botanists to state the habitats of plants as to geological position, soil, etc.? At our next meeting I hope you will set the chemists seriously to work upon isomorphism, which is one of those questions that requires to be settled, and needs good workmen well directed. Mr Johnston, a member of our chemical committee and a hard working analyst at Edinburgh, writes to me that he has found carbonate of lime occurring in some minerals in which it had not been before observed and presenting a[n] additional illustration of the truth of the isomorphic doctrine and he is pursuing the subject further.

I should recommend your receiving the subscriptions or compositions and when they amount to a considerable sum sending a draft for the amount to our Treasurer, Mr Jonathan Gray, York.

Whewell Papers, a. 205[119]

The *1831 Report* was published February 1832.

88   *Whewell, Trinity College, Cambridge, to Harcourt, Wheldrake near York, 19 December 1831*

I understand what Peacock intends to give us to be a report on the recent progress of analysis, including the differential *and integral* calculus. Some of the most important parts of what he will have to say refer I believe to the latter portion of the subject so it may be as well to mention that in particular. Henslow is quite ready to do all that he can. He says that Relhan's *Flora Cantabrigiensis* is so complete that there is little to be added for this part of the country, but that he will give, as a further contribution to such knowledge, a notice of the distribution of our plants according to the soils and strata which they affect. He mentions, too, one or two other subjects to which he wishes to invite the attention of botanists, and which a meeting like that contemplated will be a good opportunity of considering, as, 1 A list of the plants found in England concerning which it is doubtful whether they are introduced by man, the poppy for instance. Their history may be best traced by being pursued by persons in various parts of the Kingdom. 2 A list of plants concerning which it is doubtful whether they are varieties or species. This question also can best be settled by the comparison of information from various quarters. Any contributions to such lists will be desirable. He cannot he says take upon himself a report on botany for this year, but he proposes to write to Lindley to enquire if he can undertake anything of the kind. What I have requested him to suggest is 'an account of the principal questions recently settled or at present agitated in the philosophy of botany, either here or abroad'. It is very important that we should have such information in all the leading sciences. Lindley is I believe the best person to supply such a statement, and if you can any way enforce the application to him it may be useful. Brown is incomparably the first of our botanists, but perhaps less likely to give himself to the exposition of other people's labours. If we could get anything from him it would be well worth having. He was at the meeting at Heidelberg two years ago.

Professor Cumming will give us some account of the present state of thermoelectrics and the related subjects, either from his own observations or from those of others.

Dr Turner has an intention of making the meeting at Oxford an occasion to come to an agreement of the English chemists on various important questions of nomenclature, etc, on which there is now much doubt and confusion, and a necessity for some change. Probably however he would not wish this to be announced, and it might not be desirable, as claiming beforehand an authority to settle such points might generate resistance.

When I sent you the name of Mr Rothman FAS I meant F R Ast S, which I believe the former letters do not indicate. He is also a Fellow of Trinity College.

I will see about collecting subscriptions shortly.

I wish you could make any thing of Sedgwick. He is cordially well disposed to us; but declares that he cannot be at the meeting being under the necessity of taking the field in Wales in May. So we shall have neither his company nor any contribution from him.

I should be very glad indeed to get the chemists to work at isomorphism. One important point is to measure very exactly the crystalline angles of the substances analysed. If Mr Johnston has been making mineral analyses, this would be a valuable addition to them.

Whewell Papers, O.15.47[101]

Richard Relhan (1754-1823), *DNB*, wrote *Flora Cantabrigiensis* (Cambridge, 1785-93); Richard Wellesley Rothman (1800-56), Fellow of Trinity College, Cambridge. In 1829 Robert Brown attended the congress of German savants at Heidelberg. Sedgwick found it possible to attend the 1832 meeting of the Association.

89 *Johnston, Portobello, Edinburgh, to Harcourt, Bishopthorpe near York, 22 December 1831*

I have to acknowledge the receipt of your two letters of the 1st and 8th of this month and to thank you for the many judicious corrections you have been kind enough to propose in my account of the meeting. I have to regret that the whole impression was thrown off before you had received the copy I sent you, and I do so the more that your suggestions are all decided improvements. I am happy to find that the concluding paragraph seems to give general satisfaction, the commencement I do not like so well myself, and your alteration would certainly improve the style. I have not spoken rashly, however, in regard to those who 'had set their faces against it'; yet I agree that it would have been better omitted since it is susceptible of a wrong application. I do not understand by those who have opposed the meeting, persons who have merely not taken any active share in the arrangements, but those who have actually done what they need not have done to discountenance it; and for my applications I have not crossed the Tweed.

I hope you have not taken amiss my allusion in a former letter to your remarks on the *decline*. The manner in which you introduced them was unobjectionable and I am not sure on second thoughts that it was not judicious to introduce them, as showing that the meeting was not the work of a party, but that men of different sentiments were eager to promote it. For myself I do not think *all* science on the decline, but as to the physical sciences perhaps you have arrived at the true medium: they are stationary. I believe all are of opinion, even Dr Brewster himself, that the offensive articles to which you refer as the work of *our* party had better never have been written. He is a man of an ardent mind and when his pen is in his hand his thoughts carry him away. I had a hurried note from him the other day in which he informs me he had just stumbled upon a remarkable discovery which perfectly *astounded him*. I am waiting anxiously to hear from him what it is.

I am sorry I have done you injustice in my critique on the manner in which the regulations were propounded. Your observations have convinced me that you adopted the most proper course and I would now willingly omit the passage. For myself I never dreamt of any opposition.

I had a letter last night from Mr Hartop, informing me that he had sent off to Mr Phillips a box of specimens of iron for me; you were kind enough to offer me others from *Low Moor*. I shall be very glad indeed to receive them ...

Dr Daubeny informs me he has sent an article to Jameson's journal which will consequently appear in a few days in which he hopes to have given a satisfactory reply to the objections against the volcanic theory, those I suppose which were broached at the [York] meeting. I am glad to learn from him that the meeting is likely to find a good reception at Oxford.

I had requested Dr Greville of Edinburgh to undertake a report of the state of cryptogamic botany, but he informs he has 3 years work before him; but he has no objections to be placed on the botanical committee. Perhaps you will be kind enough to insert his name.

Harcourt MSS

Henry Hartop (1786–1865) was manager of the Fitzwilliam furnaces at Elsecar near Rotherham; Robert Kaye Greville (1794–1866), *DNB*, the Edinburgh botanist. Low Moor Ironworks were near Bradford.

90 *Harcourt, Bishopthorpe near York, to Murchison, Thursday [8, 15, or 22 December 1831]*

It is not a bad thing for the Association to have a friend or two in the Council of the Royal Society, and I am very glad to hear that you are settling your disputes; for it is better to be governed by any one than to be in a state of anarchy and I believe the Duke is likely to make us a better President than could reasonably be expected from a prince of the blood. I am afraid however that your return to what you irreverently call the old Lady has damped your ardor for the service of a young Mistress, for though I had less expectation from London than any other part of the King's dominions I did expect a few names from thence for our *Report* and I do not discover from your last letter whether you even authorise me to add *those you name* such as *Mr Horner* etc to the list we are preparing. The best thing you have done for us in London is the obtaining us aid from Dr Prout. I hear from Mr Whewell that Dr Turner also will join us; and we have succeeded in obtaining an excellent reporter in the highest departments of mathematics in Mr Peacock. Depend upon it though you must not mention this in the Council we shall do more for science next June at Oxford than the old Lady (for whom however I have a high veneration) has done, as far I mean as the old Lady herself and her advisers are concerned, for fifty years past. What are these discoveries of Faraday? I am rejoiced to hear of them; if they are of the consequence which you ascribe to them it will set the stagnant water of philosophy in motion. I knew you are too full of work of your own and of Lyell's logic to send us any names but you may get Mr Yates to do so and quickly for our book is in the press.

Murchison Papers

In 1831 Faraday discovered electromagnetic induction. The book was the *1831 Report.*

91 *Murchison, Nursted House, Petersfield, to Harcourt, 29 December 1831*

When you know that from the 1st of November to this day I have not been *above a week* in London, you will not hit me so hard for neglecting the objects of our Association. I circulated your printed statements, eulogized the concern publicly and privately, and got a few good names. Many persons not unfriendly to our cause defer the subscription till the ensuing term day at Oxford, and still more think 10 times before they add even £1 per annum to their numerous scientific calls.

Receiving your letter in the country I immediately wrote up to Greenough requesting him and Mr Yates to forward their list of recruits. In truth however you do not want noses; and the next sittings will add such a catalogue of *good* names to those of the founders of the Association that we never can retrograde. I go to town on Monday with Mrs Murchison to remain permanently till June, and we are now mainly doing what I presume every one else is occupied with, eating Christmas fare with our relations.

This morning's post brought me a letter from Sir J. Johnstone dated Bishopthorpe on the affair of W. Smith. He says that you agree with him in opinion that we (geologists) will never derive much benefit from Smith's exertions as 'Colourer of the Ordnance Maps under the direction of the Council Geological Society', for that Smith *is really not skillful* in the manual labour of that department, except with the assistance of Phillips; and Sir John further inclines to think from his knowledge of S's character that he will not like to *work under the direction of others*. Now as Sir John may still be at Bishopthorpe, I wish you to commune with him.

The question simply is this: 'are we more likely to obtain an allowance from the government for duties to be performed by Smith, or as a mere sinecure pension?'

As *I had strong grounds* for presuming that in these times of public economy, no mere pension would be granted, I thought of the creation of the appointment above named, as one which would enable the government to satisfy the Humists, would gratify old Smith in giving him active employment in the field, and would really do us much service, by connecting us more intimately with the advance of physical geography. But before I ever thought of propounding my scheme to the Council of the Geological Society, I wrote to and *consulted with Phillips*; and having received from him a most satisfactory *approval* of the plan, with the suggestion *on his own part* that his uncle should be regulated in his principles of colouring and working by the Council of the Geological Society, I did then think that I was fully authorized to broach the matter to the Council; and although it met with their entire approval the further consideration was adjourned till I might have an opportunity of feeling the pulse of the ministry on the subject. It was through Lord Morpeth that I intended to do so, and my delight and surprise were equal when on my last visit to town I found that he had anticipated all my wishes by a direct appeal to Lord Lansdowne which he called upon me to second. This was done forthwith and all my views as expressed to you were given to Lord Lansdowne.

I adhere to my opinion, and I am borne out in it by Phillips, that Smith's *forte* is mapping a country geologically; having stated this gravely, and after mature reflection, and after consultation on the very point with Phillips, I cannot recede. The government has the case fully before them and may decide as they please. If Sir John is at Bishopthorpe and that you consult with him and Phillips on the subject you may perhaps feel disposed to indite something to me which I may receive before our next Council day the 4th January. If the appointment be made, rely on it there must be some regulating principle, and the terms of restraint may be drawn so leniently as not to wound the 'amour propre' of the old man. I am glad Sir John quite agrees with me respecting the MSS being placed in the hands of Phillips, and I am further rejoiced to hear that you are sanguine in your estimate of the quantities of good matter (at this time of day) which these reams may contain.

Mrs Murchison begs to unite with me in every good wish and compliments of this season to Mrs Harcourt and yourself.

[PS] To put you into full possession of all I have done I have induced my wife to copy my letter to Lord Lansdowne.

Harcourt MSS

Henry Petty Fitzmaurice, 3rd Marquis of Lansdowne (1780–1863), *DNB*, then Lord president of the council; the Humists were disciples of Joseph Hume (1777–1855), *DNB*, an advocate of financial retrenchment. The scheme to employ Smith failed, but in early 1832 he was awarded a state pension of £100 per year.

92 *Forbes, Greenhill, Edinburgh, to Harcourt, Wheldrake near York, 13 January 1832*

You have probably heard before this of Dr Brewster's accident which prevented his communicating with his York friends, which he requested me to explain to you. I am happy to learn that he has nearly recovered from the injury which it occasioned, and without any permanent damage to his eyesight which was much to have been feared, as the explosion of the nitric acid tube took place right in front of his eyes when he was examining some phenomena which it presented during heating.

I am very glad to learn through Mr Phillips and Mr Robison that the business of the Association goes on prosperously and that the *Report* is nearly ready for circulation, which is very desirable. If it be not too late I should like to see the proof sheets of the queries I prepared. I want to add something about Dalton in the hygrometric one.

I am rejoiced to see that the Association has already given an impulse to meteorology. Mr Phillips writes me of the energy with which he means to set about it in Yorkshire. Mr Whewell has written me at great length on the subject of the meteorological report in which he seems to take great interest.

I had some time since a most unsatisfactory note from Mr Lubbock who seems to look with a jealous eye as Vice-president Royal Society upon the Association. He fears that he will have nothing to communicate to the Association besides what he *has* published or *may hereafter* publish in the *Philosophical Transactions* and *Philosophical Magazine*. He showed that he understood very little of the nature and objects of the Association for he applied to me for data about the tides in Scotland, the very object which his statement to the Association ought to have mentioned as a desideratum and endeavoured through them to procure. I wrote a few lines on the subject to Murchison and begged him to try and put Mr Lubbock aright on this point, as he is in the Council of the Royal Society. I am just going to write to Mr Scoresby about forwarding to Mr Lubbock the observations on the tides he mentioned to me. The Royal Society [of Edinburgh] has agreed to give the instrument for magnetical intensity for the purposes desired by the Association and Mr Robison has a private hand next week by whom it may be forwarded to Liverpool. I am glad that a man like Dr Traill has agreed to take up these various experiments, more especially as he formerly spoke against the York meeting when I met him in spring. I hope he will be active and travel diligently over the country.

Can you tell me if any plan has been thought of for having associated foreign members? Professor Necker of Geneva who is here at present is a peculiarly fit person and takes great interest in the body. He is one of the *redacteurs* of the *Bibliotheque Universelle* and I shall beg him to make the existence and objects of the Association as much known as possible on the continent and furnish him with some of the circulars.

I really think no time should be lost in bringing out the *Report* with a view of making it extremely perfect. The period of the Oxford meeting seems already approaching. I think the annual subscriptions should be made payable for the intervals of the meetings. Thus the present one for September 1831–June 1832. Pray instruct me on this. Since I sent Mr Phillips a list of names I have got two more:

Revd John Sinclair A M Oxon, F R S E; and John Abercrombie M D, F R S E, First Physician to the King for Scotland.

Forbes Papers, 1832/9

Thomas Stewart Traill (1781-1862), *DNB*, then a Liverpool physician; John Sinclair (1797-1875), *DNB*, Edinburgh Anglican clergyman; John Abercrombie (1780-1844), *DNB*. The Association established foreign corresponding members in 1834.

93 *Harcourt, Bishopthorpe near York, to Milton, 21 January 1832*

The annual meeting of the Yorkshire Philosophical Society is on Tuesday the 7th of February. As this is the principal meeting of the year, at which the Council make their report and the elections take place, should parliamentary business or any other cause render it impossible for you to attend, it may be proper to write a letter to the Council which may be read to the meeting lest the Society should think itself neglected. Circumstances having hitherto prevented you from being present at any of our meetings, it may be thought that the Presidency is merely nominal which it will not be I hope in the ensuing year, the public business not being likely to be so absorbing as during the last. The Vice-presidents who will probably be elected this time to supply your place when you are absent are Henry Howard, Francis Cholmeley, Charles Wellbeloved, and James Atkinson. I ought to remind you that our annual dinner is also on the 7th of February, in case you should think proper to perform the same service to the Society as you did to the Association in supplying it with venison or game.

I will *send* you the *Report* of the latter as soon as we have printed it, that of the former I am also drawing up.

Fitzwilliam Papers, B. 15

James Atkinson (1759-1839), *DNB*, York surgeon.

94 *Brewster, Allerly near Melrose, to Harcourt, Wheldrake near York, 22 January 1832*

As I am only beginning to have the use of my hand I am obliged to write you very briefly. I have had a most providential escape for which I have reason to be deeply thankful ...

I cannot resist sending you an extract from a letter of Sir John Herschel's, dated January 1st 1832, respecting our Association.

'On reperusing one of your former letters I perceive a mention of a wish on your part that I should become a member of the new scientific Association. It escaped me in my first perusal owing to the difficulty of the handwriting. I have not yet been able fully to make up my mind on the subject. On the one hand I should be sorry to appear indisposed to further by any means in my power any under-taking which held out a prospect of real and extensive utility to science. On the other I have my hands already too full to volunteer the *slightest additional labour* or sacrifice of time. My present impres-sion therefore is rather to observe in silence, but with deep interest, the course it takes at its second meeting, and hold myself meanwhile unfettered by any pledge'.

Harcourt MSS

95   *Buckland, Christ Church, Oxford, to Harcourt, 25 January 1832*

I am very glad you have written to me respecting the time of the proposed meeting here in June as you have not rightly understood the matter in supposing that it is to begin on the 23rd.

On consulting the Cambridge men it was found that the week most convenient to them will be the 3rd week of June beginning on Monday the 18th; the 2nd week being Whitsunweek will be occu-pied with examinations at Cambridge and the 4th week with ex-aminations here.

The first week in July will be our Commemoration week and therefore not convenient. Under these circumstances therefore it seems highly desirable that in the *Report* you are printing notice should be given that the meeting at Oxford will begin on Monday the 18th of June.

Harcourt MSS

The 1832 meeting at Oxford did indeed begin on 18 June. Commemoration at Oxford was the annual celebration in memory of the founders and benefactors of the University.

96   *Harcourt, Bishopthorpe near York, to Forbes, Greenhill, Edinburgh, 27 January 1832*

In my opinion our *Report* will be read with increased interest in proportion as the Oxford meeting is nearer at hand and with more desire to know what *will* be done there than what *has* been done at York. Having however received Mr Harvey's reply this morning I am now possessed of all the information which I require. I had found in a correspondence with the Board of Ordnance that they were smarting from what they called 'a very unpleasant correspond-ence' with the (late) Secretary of the Royal Society of Edinburgh about the observations at Leith Fort, the history of which you probably know though I do not. I wrote therefore to Mr Harvey to advise him by no means to apply to the Board or to any of the London authorities for military aid in making the meteorological observations but to try his influence with the local commander, and I had the pleasure of hearing from him today that he has been successful with Sir John Cameron. You will find when our *Report* comes out that I have a good deal changed the arrangement of your meteorological remarks for the purpose chiefly of putting into the mouth of the committee the recommendations of what is to be done and into that of 'some of its members' the comments thereon; with the propriety of which I have no doubt you will be satisfied and shall not lose time by sending you the proofs. They will now do very well for the *Report* and may be useful to persons of some skill in the subject, but for *general circulation* I desiderate the addition of some plain and popular directions; for the lower class of observations in this science are very easy and there are a great many individuals who *can* make them and *do* make them, though to little purpose in general, and you should give these people such instructions as will assist them without giving them the trouble of going to abstruse books which they will not read and cannot get; such instructions as Faraday has given to *the lowest capacities* in his minute and practical account of chemical manipulations. If you can furnish me with any thing which you think would be useful in this way in a short space of time I would print it with the recommendations for more extensive circulation.

I have received some suggestions respecting botany from Dr Greville which point to a scheme that has long occupied my thoughts in respect to all the departments of *natural history*: a survey of the whole kingdom by collecting from counties accurate local surveys of their respective districts. It was with a view to this that I first planned the Philosophical Society of *this county* and I hope we shall in time do our part of the work in meteorology as well as other sciences which call for local observations over an extensive field.

Will the third week in June suit your northern lights for the Oxford meeting? Have the goodness to answer this question as far as Edinburgh is concerned. I am afraid your city is in imminent danger of a visit from this, to the lowers [sic] orders of people, very formidable malady. I assure you notwithstanding numerous occupations in respect to this as well as many other subjects I do not lose a day or an hour in forwarding the *Report* as far as I am myself concerned.

[PS]   Mr Harvey says 'Major General Sir John Cameron is disposed in every thing to attend to the wishes of the British Association and I expect in a short time to receive a communication from him authorising me to fix a thermometer in some approved locality when the observations will be begun'.

Ought you not in your meteorological instructions to appoint some plan of comparing thermometers with a standard? Will you suggest that deputies from societies and other observers should bring their thermometers to Oxford for comparison? Answer me this promptly.

Murchison's question respecting chemical and galvanic agencies which had produced *certain* widely extended changes in the strata was too vague. What could the chemical committee make of it, unless he told them something more accurate about those changes geologically?

Forbes Papers, 1832/16

Sir John Cameron (1773-1844), *DNB*, was Commander-in-Chief of the Western District. Brewster was the late Secretary of the Royal Society of Edinburgh; M. Faraday, *Chemical manipulation* (London, 1827). The formidable malady was cholera.

97 *Brewster, Allerly near Melrose, to Harcourt, 1 February 1832*

I wish much to have your opinion of *two objects* which I think can be accomplished by the British Association and which would tend much to promote British science.

1. The first is to have a *monthly* journal of science called the *British Journal of Science* published in London in place of the *four* journals which are now in existence. All that the Association could do would be to patronise it. All the *four* scientific journals are I believe carried on without any remuneration to the editors who have therefore no motive for exertion. In order to save themselves from loss the editors are obliged to insert popular papers, totally unsuited to such works; and in consequence of the editors being acquainted with only one branch of science, their numbers abound with the most contemptible articles which disgrace British science in foreign countries. In order to make a good scientific journal, all the best papers from the *four* different journals would be required.

Though I receive no remuneration whatever from my *Journal*, I do not intend to discontinue it; but I would willingly do so in order to carry into effect the plan I mention; and I should have no objection if required to take a department in the general journal. All the *four* editors might do the same, and we should then have one good journal made out of the whole. If you view this in the light I do, I would write to Mr R. Taylor, the editor of the *Annals of Philosophy*, and ascertain his sentiments, and if they are favourable application might be made to the other editors. All this might be done independent of the Association but, with their approbation and aid, it would be done more efficaciously.

2. The *second* object is a more [arduous] one and has been suggested to me by some discussions in [the] Royal Society of Edinburgh relative to the giving up the publication of their *Transactions* which cost them £200 annually without any return. I propose that there should be only *two* sets of *Philosophical Transactions*, viz: one for mathematics, physics and chemistry; and another for natural history including zoology, geology, mineralogy and botany.

The Royal Society of Edinburgh, for example, would send their papers to the Royal Society London, and the consequence of this would be that good papers only would be published; and that the different societies would save their funds for scientific purposes in place of wasting them in publishing an annual volume of which 2/3rds is of questionable value.

As the British Association contains members belonging to all the different existing societies they would have no difficulty in getting such a plan executed if it should appear practicable on further consideration.

I need not point out to you the advantages which the readers and purchasers of journals and transactions would derive from such arrangements. I beg you will excuse this scrawl.

Harcourt MSS

Richard Taylor (1781–1858), *DNB*, naturalist and London's leading scientific printer. Brewster's second scheme did not materialise, but his first did in part with the publication in July 1832 of the first number of *The London and Edinburgh magazine and journal of science*, edited by Brewster, Richard Taylor, and Richard Phillips (1778–1851), *DNB*, the chemist.

98 *Forbes, Greenhill, Edinburgh, to Harcourt, Wheldrake near York, 1 February 1832*

I enter into the feeling of the want you express, though I can hardly hope that the enclosed very hurried note will answer your object, yet perhaps you will take the trouble to revise it. For fear of detaining you I have been obliged to expedite it *currente calamo*.

I am *extremely delighted* to hear of your success with Mr Harvey: you were quite right to attempt nothing through the Ordnance. The termination of the Leith observations was rather an unfortunate business. I am quite ready that you should correct my queries in any way you choose.

When I was asked by the [General] Committee at York how June

1832 would suit Edinburgh, I stated that the *summer* classes of the University (which were only a few) would indeed be meeting, but that from the way in which the professors had held back at the first meeting I did not consider it an object to consult their convenience. Jameson, who is the principal one perhaps, I can answer for it would not come. I have not been able to persuade him to become a member. Otherwise I should think it would suit Edinburgh well, if indeed it were worthy of consideration which I am afraid its scientific character hardly entitles it to. The cholera will probably be better met here than any place it has yet visited. The Board of Health and Medical Police is on an excellent footing and all that art can do will be done.

The comparison of thermometers is a very important object and should certainly be taken into consideration by the next meeting, but I believe the difficulties are too great for an immediate remedy to be devised. Even supposing all the instruments collected at Oxford no one would have time to undertake the laborious task of comparison, the labour of which I know something of, having been hard at work upon the standards of the Royal Society here.

Forbes Papers, 1832/19

Forbes enclosed some meteorological notes for the *1831 Report*.

99 *William Henry, Manchester, to Babbage, 1 Dorset Street, Manchester Square, London, 19 February 1832*

There is an enquiry in the letter, with which you were lately kind enough to favour me, that ought to have been answered at an earlier period. Mr Dalton has never received from government any pension or honour of any sort. The honours, indeed, which it is in the power of government to bestow, would be totally unsuitable to his habits and station, and I should think painful to him rather than agreeable. But confessions, which I have drawn from him in conversation, have led me to believe that he would rejoice to be relieved, in part at least, from the burthen of teaching the elements of science, and in being able to devote his time to the revisal of his scientific labours, and to the extension of enquiries which he has left incomplete.

Of Mr Dalton's eminent claims, no one who is acquainted with the history of science in this country can entertain a moment's doubt. If he has not furnished any important improvements to the practical arts, he has established general principles, from which practical rules of great value must necessarily flow. He has exalted, too, the scientific renown of his country among the nations of

Europe, and in future times will be one of those whose names will shed lustre on the present age.

If, as I earnestly hope, any thing can yet be done to retrieve the character of the nation from the reproach of unmerited neglect of Mr Dalton, there is no time to lose. Though his temperate habits exempt him from general bad health, yet I have lately noticed, with regret, the effect of casual illnesses, and his slow recoveries from them. I am not aware of his precise age, but believe it to be about 64 or 65.

Any other particular which you may wish to learn respecting Mr Dalton, I can readily obtain through indirect channels; for I have not given him a hint of our former or present correspondence on the subject.

I made one unsuccessful attempt to obtain the information which you request respecting births; and I will try other sources till I either succeed, or find that success is unattainable.

PS   Will you do me the favour to thank Sir J Herschel for the letter enclosed in your last. If he knew its cordial effect, I am sure he would rejoice in having written it. The approbation of such persons as Sir John Herschel and yourself is the best of all rewards, and the most powerful of all incitements. Having been stopped from further experiments by the difficulty of finding subjects, I am endeavouring to gather out of the immense mass of errors, absurdities, and false-hoods, facts enough to form the groundworks of some general laws respecting contagion.

BL, Add. MSS 37186, ff. 260–1

In 1833 Dalton was given a government pension of £150 per annum, a mark of favour first announced at the 1833 meeting of the Association.

100   *Harcourt, Wheldrake near York, to Brougham, 23 February 1832*

Private

If it is true that under all the pressure of public duties you still sometimes find time to attend to the 'studia umbratilia philosophiae' you will perhaps feel some interest in the *Report* which I have sent you of an attempt by a new Association to stir up the slumbering spirit of British science.

I wish there may be grounds for the hope which I know some persons entertain that this subject is likely to receive from our states-men the consideration which is due to it in a national point of view, but which it has never yet obtained at their hands. I doubt indeed whether we have ever had till now, with the exception of two names, those of Bacon and Montagu, a minister holding a high rank in the councils of the state who has given any attention to science, or has appeared to consider its influence on the character and resources of the country. Of late years an opinion broached by a popular and in some respects profound political writer, and implicitly adopted by many less profound readers, has led to the reception of a theory that the sciences require no *bounty* and should be left like other commodities to rise and fall according to the natural demand. With these philosophers coincide the practical economists, to whom the saving some pounds of the public money seems the highest political wisdom, and who carry into the legislative assembly of a great nation the principles and spirit of a pawnbroker's shop.

Whilst the vulgar mind is thus abundantly reflected in the senate, there is no one, or next to none, who represents there the views of scientific men, or pleads the cause of science; and the consequence is that the national treatment of its objects and cultivators is far, very far indeed, from being liberal or enlightened. It has no recognised claim upon the public, and if occasionally by knocking hard at a minister's door it obtains an alms, he gives as if by stealth and under dread of correction, and takes care, in case of detection, to be able to palliate the job by having shown at least a very frugal mind.

Thus, for instance, a man in humble life without other instruction than that which he has given himself, a common practical surveyor, seizes instinctively on the true principles of philosophical investigation and applies them to create a new science respecting the structure of the earth. He forms the bold conception of a geological map of England and executes it with unremitting ardour and industry. He pursues his researches into minute detail and publishes similar maps of several counties. His public-spirited labours improve, or tend to improve the value of every estate in the country. In the mean while he has sacrificed to these objects a lucrative profession, and his means of subsistence fail before his gigantic plan is completed. The man himself sinks into indigence and a precarious dependence upon the humane consideration of an individual; the works by which science has been enlarged and other men enriched produce him an income of perhaps £20 a year. Under these circumstances the geologists of England take up the cause of their master; strong interest is made in his favour; sanguine hopes of success are indulged; the government are induced to recommend a pension, and this extraordinary man receives from the wealthiest nation in the world—what? an annuity of £100 a year, a pittance insufficient to render the short remaining space of life independent, even to one who would be content to live upon a crust, so that he might be enabled to roam again freely over the country to perfect those investigations which he has always loved better than money.

Could any means be contrived by which the government and the legislature might be better advised than they have been on scientific subjects there might possibly be less parsimony and at the same time fewer jobs; there might be an enlarged system of protection and encouragement to science, and a better management of its existing establishments; every thing in public affairs on which it could throw light might be more wisely conducted; it might not happen to us again to sign away half the tin trade of the habitable world by a stroke of the pen; and we might manage to take more timely precautions when threatened with a pestilential disease.

Such consequences we might hope to see if it should ever be determined by our rulers to establish a public office and to make a minister for scientific affairs and public instruction, being himself a scientific man of the highest character, holding an official seat in the House of Commons and a responsible station in the executive government.

In the mean while with many apologies for so long and free a letter I remain

Brougham Papers, 16001

Harcourt was referring to the opposition to bounties of David Ricardo (1772–1823), *DNB*, as shown, e.g., in P. Sraffa (ed), *The works and correspondence of David Ricardo. Volume 1. On the principles of political economy and taxation* (1817) (Cambridge, 1951), 301–26. The practical economists were the supporters of Joseph Hume. Harcourt's illustration concerned William Smith and his patron, Sir John Johnstone. In 1825 the tariff on tin was reduced from £109-5-0d to £50 a ton. The disease was cholera. Harcourt's scheme of a minister for science and education was not implemented.

101   *Harcourt, Wheldrake near York, to Forbes, Greenhill, Edinburgh, 23 February 1832*

It would be much I think for the benefit of our objects if you would undertake a review of the *Report* of the British Association, which you have either received or will receive in a day or two, in the *Edinburgh Journal of Science*. I shall make the same request to Mr Whewell as regards one of our quarterly English journals, and I have written to Mr Taylor to beg him to insert the preface and the recommendations of the committees in the next number of the *Annals of Philosophy*. I have not published the more popular meteorological remarks which you sent me, thinking that the publication of observations and queries of this kind had better be delayed till the Oxford meeting which will give time for having them well digested and then put forth with full authority.

We have sent a number of copies besides those of subscribers to be distributed as from the [General] Committee to such persons as it may be thought fit. Pray tell Mr Robison that some copies should be transmitted to Calcutta to the persons named for the committee and accompanied by a letter or letters to the proper persons. It would save time and trouble if he would communicate with these gentlemen himself on the part of and by the desire of the General Committee; but if more ceremony than this is really required, he will have the goodness to send me the form of address and which I know nothing about and should be writing to the wrong person or with a wrong direction and send my letter to the West Indies perhaps instead of the East. It would be much better however for Dr Brewster and himself to undertake the correspondence.

I hope at the meeting in June you will come practically prepared, as I have recommended in the preface to the *Report*, with a well arranged plan to set societies, individuals, and all the world at work upon meteorology. I have ventured in the report of our own Society and also I think in dressing up the botanical recommendation to allude to the examination of the temperature of rain, which I conceive to be a legitimate subject of enquiry not attended to and of some consequence at least to botany. It does not seem by any means clear that it would not be found to differ, as well as in snow and hail, from that of the lower part of the atmosphere.

I am afraid neither Edinburgh nor London can be considered safe from cholera in a terrible form if the disease does not exhaust itself before the spring advances. When do you move south?

Forbes Papers, 1832/29

Forbes reviewed the *1831 Report* in *Edinburgh journal of science*, 1832, vi. 360-75. The 'report of our own Society' was *Annual Report of the Council of the Yorkshire Philosophical Society for 1831* (York, 1832), 3-4.

102 *Harcourt, Wheldrake near York, to Whewell, Trinity College, Cambridge, 23 February 1832*

You will receive nearly at the same time with this letter the first *Report* of the British Association which I hope may prove a good advertisement for the Oxford meeting. I think it would tend greatly to promote and perhaps in some degree to regulate that meeting if you would yourself undertake a review of this *Report* for the *Quarterly Review* which I think is published in April, or for the *Quarterly Journal of Science*. I have written to Mr Forbes to make the same request to him as regards the *Edinburgh Journal of Science*, believing him to be not only a clever but also a judicious man.

I have alluded slightly in the preface to one point which I think of the highest importance to the future character and utility of the

Association, namely that persons who wish to make it serviceable to any science should come to the meeting with distinct, practical, well digested propositions, founded upon just views of what is the proper and peculiar business of such an Association. This might be fully made out in a review and suggestions put forth of the objects to be looked to in this light in various sciences; and if you could do thus much before the meeting in any of our periodical journals you would I am sure perform a most valuable service.

Whewell Papers, a. 205[124]

Whewell did not review the *1831 Report.*

103   *Brewster, 1 Dorset Street, Manchester Square, London, to Harcourt, 4 March 1832*

Although I can scarcely command a single idea in the whirl of occupation in which I am involved, yet I must write you a few lines on the subject of our Association. Both Mr Forbes and I have studied the *Report* and are delighted with it. It will open the eyes of many prejudiced persons here who look upon the Association as a work of supererogation, and it will alarm those who view it with jealousy and fear.

I have endeavoured to explain its objects and advantages to the former; but it is impossible to disarm the hostility of the latter, as it is founded on the good though mistaken motive of a regard to existing institutions.

I understand that the Duke of Sussex regards it as injurious to the Royal Society, but I could not say upon good authority that this is the case. In a conversation I had with His Royal Highness on Thursday he made no allusion to the subject. I have had, however, discussions with the Vice-president, Mr Lubbock, the ablest member of the Council and can state to you his views. In answer to all my arguments that we are the auxiliaries of other societies, that we are doing what they never proposed to do, and cannot do so well as we, he asserted that through the Duke of Sussex's influence they *could* do more for scientific interests than we could, and that they *could* also establish hourly meteorological observations and take measures of the variation etc of the magnetic intensity. I replied by stating what you and Lord Morpeth *had* done for Mr Smith, and what the Association had done and was doing for science. Mr Lubbock then put the subject on another footing. He said that nobody could form an idea of the difficulty of obtaining proper persons to do the business of the Royal Society, that the indifference of the members was great, and that the occupation of the time of the leading members of the Royal Society with the business of the Association would prevent them from working for the Royal Society. This, I believe, is the real source of hostility to the British Association; and though it is not a fair one to urge, yet it is not an improper one to feel.

Colonel Colby and Bellenden Ker, Esq, have agreed to become members, and though I have not succeeded in getting the name of Mr Robert Brown, yet he has almost yielded and so has Dr Fitton. Dr Prout is, I am told, preparing an account of some researches for the Oxford meeting. I shall be here till the 14th or 15th, and shall be glad to receive any suggestions from you which may enable me to be of use to the Association.

Harcourt MSS (Harcourt Papers, *xiii. 284–6*)

Thomas Frederick Colby (1784–1852), *DNB*, Director of the Ordnance Survey; Charles Henry Bellenden Ker (1785–1871), *DNB*, London barrister. In spring 1832 Brewster went to London where he stayed with Babbage.

104 *Harcourt, Wheldrake near York, to Daubeny, Oxford, 8 March 1832*

You will perceive by the preface to the *Report* of the Association that I have not been inactive in promoting the success of the Oxford meeting and have obtained it the promise of many valuable contributions. The *Report* will prove I hope an efficacious advertisement, and of the thousand copies which we have printed I should think from five to seven hundred will be distributed before long. What more is necessary to collect the meeting, and to manage it after it is collected, will chiefly rest on the shoulders of the Oxford office bearers. You will have to issue as many circulars, or more, with an earnest request for answers, in order to enable you to form an estimate of the numbers with which you will have to deal. My expectation is that those numbers will be very considerable and that you will require a much larger General Committee room than sufficed at York. The subcommittees must meet, as far as it can be arranged, in separate apartments, or if necessary at different hours. I hope however that the sectionary plan of the German meetings will not be followed except for the purpose of transacting the particular business of these committees. Even such tough matter as a report on the integral and differential calculus should in my opinion be read in the public meeting, though two thirds of the auditors may not understand it; and this is an extreme case. It will scarcely be possible to get through the business of the meeting, without reassembling, as we did here, after dinner; but for this *'chasse café'* something lighter of digestion than the integral calculus should be selected. I trust the constitution of 1831 will be adhered to as much as possible, for if you begin legislating again, you will get no scientific work done. The only chance of managing the meeting is as far as you can to keep every man to his science.

I consider the future fortunes of the Association to depend chiefly on the success of the Oxford meeting and however agreeable it may be it will not really have succeeded unless it produces fruits of substantial and extensive utility. Every means should be employed to get work done, and produced, on the subjects proposed in the *recommendations* which have been put forth in the *Report*. You see in the preface how far I have been able to proceed in this; but much more should be done before the meeting. I hope you will apply to all the really good chemists of your acquaintance to contribute to the elucidation of the chemical questions which are before us, especially Dalton's; I am sorry to find that the Cambridge laboratory is not in a state to enable Professor Cumming to assist in this; but Oxford will I dare say be prepared with suitable implements and with her own experiments. In like manner pray do what you can with your botanical friends, communicating to them the recommendation which originated with yourself and which after consulting Professor Henslow and Dr Greville I ventured to enlarge. There are also other of the recommendations the objects of which you may be able to advance by similar applications. I intend writing to Dr Buckland on the subject of those which relate to geology as well as on other points. Dr Brewster and Mr Forbes are in London, the former at 1 Dorset Street, Manchester Square.

Daubeny Papers, 400

At the 1832 meeting of the Association there were four sections for the conduct of scientific business; there were none in 1831 at York.

105 *Murchison, 3 Bryanston Place, London, to Harcourt, 12 March 1832*

Thanks for your letter and parcels. We dined at the Archbishop's on Saturday, when to my horror I heard it whispered that our Royal President was not favourably disposed to the *British Association*. 'Inter pocula' I only begged to express my disbelief of the surmise, resolving to make out the truth or untruth of the tale by a speedy journey to Kensington. Yesterday morning your beautiful copy of the *Report* fortunately arrived, so that I instantly set out on my voyage of discovery and requested an audience.

I am now happy to tell that HRH received the donation very graciously, and further expressed himself very good-humouredly respecting the *cause*. Seeing, however, that he was as ignorant of the *real nature* of our new Association as any well-fed prince might be supposed to be, I requested him to read over the objects proposed, which putting on his spectacles and laying down his cigar he did, *reciting them aloud*. I then took the liberty, perceiving that he had taken the bait, of expounding some of the practical good results, such as old Smith's reward and many other things, and urging the [Lord] Chancellor's good will, and making H R H intimately believe that the *shove* we are trying to give to science, would really reanimate the Old Lady herself. He cordially assented to *all the doctrine*, and authorized me to inscribe his name in the list of members, saying he would do all he could to forward our views, and promising faithfully to read every word of your discourse, in consequence of my eulogium of it.

I had previously been authorized by Mr Children the Junior Secretary to add his name and I have today written to Roget, the other Secretary to enlist him if possible. Sir David [Brewster] is, as you may believe, delighted with the result of my mission and he has himself done good service in obtaining the names of Fitton and others.

Could you not if the press is not broken up strike off an additional list of members? At all events such lists in a report form may be prepared when you come to town.

Copies of the *Report* should *by all means* go to the savants at Paris, Berlin, Bonn, etc, and as Phillips mentions another envoi to Mr Yates this point should be attended TO SPECIALLY.

Babbage is interesting himself in the concern and I shall not forget your [letter ends here]

Harcourt MSS (Harcourt Papers, *xiii. 289-91*)

H R H the Duke of Sussex was President of the Royal Society of London, of which the two Secretaries were John George Children (1777-1852), *DNB*, and Peter Mark Roget (1779-1869), *DNB*.

106 *Daubeny, Oxford, to Harcourt, Wheldrake near York, 15 April 1832*

I feel much obliged by the hints contained in your letter, and hope that we shall have the further benefit of your assistance in making the preliminary arrangements for the ensuing meeting, and that for that purpose we shall see you here at least as soon as the week previous to that in which it takes place. I have indeed on my own authority suggested to a few of the more active members the propriety of meeting before the time; on Monday all will be confusion, and I rather think that it will be found difficult to get through the business in a week without much management even though we adopt the expedient of dividing occasionally into sections, which you deprecate, and which I agree with you should be avoided as much as possible ...

Harcourt MSS

107 *Babbage, Wimbledon Park, London, to Daubeny, 28 April 1832*

I am anxious to suggest to you a few hints for our meeting in June feeling as I do very confident that such annual assemblies may be productive of great advantage to science and that, if we each contribute to the general stock, you [sic] resident committee will be best able to arrange the materials. Amongst the advantages of such assemblies are that scientific men mix more in general society, and that the more intelligent amongst the upper classes and amongst the wealthy manufacturers associating with them get a little imbued with love for science. Thus we shall ultimately get public opinion to bear upon science and consequently the quacks and charlatans will more readily get detected and discountenanced. Mr Boulton is I think a resident in Oxfordshire; if so he should be invited and any other great manufacturers should also be applied to.

I think also that *ladies* ought to be admitted at some kind of assembly: remember the dark eyes and fair faces you saw at York and pray remember that we absent philosophers sigh over the eloquent descriptions we have heard of their enchanting smiles. It is of more importance than perhaps you may imagine to enlist the ladies in our cause and the male residents throughout the county will attend in greater number if their wives and daughters partake some share of the pleasure. If you will only get up an evening conversazione for them at Oxford I will try and start a ball for them at Cambridge.

Next, pray let us arrange our next meeting for Manchester instead of Cambridge. I have talked with many Cantabs and with Lord Milton about it and we agree that it can be done very prettily, that it is too academical to select in successive years Oxford and Cambridge, that it is a fit respect to Dalton, a proper compliment to the manufacturing interest (which depend upon it is destined to become the great support of science).

As to work for the meeting I think my letter to Brewster with a few notes might be read (see Brewster's last journal) and that we might organize a committee to collect and print the constants of nature and art and present it at the meeting at Manchester as a *result* of such associations. Could not a grand septennial or decennial meeting be held in London at which foreigners might attend?

Amongst things of minor importance pray remember to give publicity to the fact that the Royal Society intend *if* they can get 200 subscribers at *cost price* before July next to print the abstracts of the papers read at their meetings since 1800 and also a classed catalogue. Do not let them fail for want of support. The Duke of Sussex will be a millstone not on his own account, but because it is in the nature of one class of persons to pay undue deference to rank, and it interrupts freedom. I do however sincerely hope that no indiscreet fool or flatterer will bring him prominently forward in the shape of President Patron or any other form for our British Association, for if any such attempt is made it is impossible it can be carried with unanimity and any discussion on such a point cannot fail to place the Royal Duke, the University of Oxford, the British Association, and perhaps a few individuals in a most unfortunate position. It is as well by considering this amongst the most judicious to confer upon the means of preventing it.

I shall take up my residence at Merton with Mr Head my old travelling companion. If you are not acquainted with him pray let this letter be an introduction for him and as you are a professor it will not be contrary to etiquette that you should introduce yourself to him.

I do not think I have had any opportunity of expressing how much I felt delighted by your volume on the atomic theory. The historical part is highly interesting and the collected view you have taken of our present knowledge on the subject is a valuable present to English science. It will I hope bring more before us one of the most important branches not merely of chemical but of other physical sciences.

Excuse these undigested hints. If I can do anything for you in London (whither I return in a few days) relating to our meeting I will try my best.

Daubeny Papers, 400

Matthew Robinson Boulton (1770-1842) of the firm of Boulton and Watt; Edmund Walker Head (1805-68), *DNB*, Fellow of Merton College, Oxford. Women were admitted to the general meetings and lectures at the 1832 meeting of the Association, but not to the scientific sections. Babbage's scheme for scientific constants came to nothing: see his 'On the advantage of a collection of numbers, to be entitled the constants of nature and of art', *Edinburgh journal of science*, 1832, vi. 334-40. The Duke of Sussex became a member of the Association in 1832 but was never its President. Daubeny's volume was *An introduction to the atomic theory* (Oxford, 1831).

108   *Brewster, Allerly near Melrose, to Harcourt, Wheldrake near York, 28 April 1832*

I ought long ago to have apologised to you for having passed your door on my return from London without paying you the visit which I had offered and from which I had anticipated so much pleasure. I left London, however, with such a severe and alarming cold that I was utterly unfit for society, and had no alternative but to get home as fast as possible.

I was the more unwilling to make such a sacrifice as I had brought with me all the apparatus for showing you my latest experiments on the absorption of light, which might perhaps have been of some use in directing your chemical enquiries to some points that might otherwise escape your notice.

I am now busy in drawing up my report on optics, and in writing some papers for the Association. Although I felt that there would be a sufficient number of reports without mine, and that I might employ my time more usefully for the Association, yet I was convinced when reconsidering the matter that I could not well avoid fulfilling the task which I had undertaken.

You will no doubt have heard that the Duke of Sussex is to be Buckland's guest during the meeting; and that Airy and Whewell and Sedgwick are to be attended with a tail of about 50 or 60 followers. All the talent of the metropolis has threatened its presence, and the south of England is to push forward a debacle of naturalists which will no doubt be met by another from the manufacturing districts. I am really beginning to be alarmed at the magnitude of the machinery which we have put in motion, for I cannot see how we are to construct, and where we are to place, the fly-wheel by which its movements must be regulated. If we could count upon receiving for the future the same powerful aid which has sustained it during its first year, my fears would be somewhat abated, but this we cannot expect; and I do not see how the scientific power of the Association is to be directed, and how even its ordinary business is to be managed, unless by a regular Board or Council composed of the leading cultivators of each branch of science and literature, having a permanent existence, and having its secretaries at least paid by government. According to our present constitution there is no executive entitled to act, and no body entitled to deliberate, till the general meeting of the Association; so that if an occasion should occur on which it was necessary either to appeal to the government or to take any other very important step, the opportunity would either be lost, or an authority would be exerted which the main body might not be disposed to recognise. I wish you would give this matter your most serious consideration, as it appears to me that the success and permanence of the Association will depend on the manner in which we shall meet the difficulty which I have stated.

You will perhaps better appreciate the correctness of my views from the following case. I have long thought that one of the greatest scientific desiderata in England is a *physical observatory*, erected and endowed by the government. No better arguments for this are necessary than those on p. 26 of your Address and pp. 213, 214 of Sir J. Herschel's *Discourse*. To these arguments I can add others more specific. I have now made almost all the experiments on the defective lines of the spectrum, whether solar or artificial, and its other properties, which an individual can do in a private house and with private instruments. If I had the use of apartments sufficiently long and sufficiently lofty, such as those of a public building only can be, and had large instruments, I know that the most important discoveries would be instantly made respecting the constitution and properties of light of all kinds; and therefore I feel that optics is now in that state that, like astronomy, it can be studied only by national assistance. What a grand subject, for example, is that of the defective rays in the light of the stars, from which we might gather almost the kinds of combustion which supply their light. The refraction of ordinary heat, too, and the determination by means of the defective lines of all the data for the construction of achromatic telescopes, are subjects of national interest which the government should investigate. Besides these enquiries, all the phenomena of magnetism, meteorology and electricity would be observed in accordance with the plan adopted in the physical observatories which, through Humboldt's influence, have been established in various parts of Russia, and in the Island of Cuba. Now though the British Association might be supposed the best channel through which the government could be urged to erect such an observatory, yet I am so satisfied of its want of an executive power, and am so sure that such a scheme would be opposed by great numbers and would be supported by only a few enlightened individuals, that I intend to submit the plan directly to the Lord Chancellor. If the Association had an executive Board, then the physical section of that Board would alone be entitled to consider the scheme and upon their report the General Board could, through its President, convey its wishes to the government. But in our present state this would not be very practicable, and I do not see how any great measures could either be matured or executed. I have no doubt that some such fears as I have stated have occurred to yourself, and have perhaps suggested plans more practicable than those which I have mentioned. The Oxford meeting seems to me the proper occasion, if there is an occasion wanted, for giving form and stability to the huge unwieldy monster, the philosophical Frankenstein, which we have called into existence. I fear much that the cholera is going to assail your beautiful county, but I daresay you are well prepared for it. The continued increase in Edinburgh keeps us in considerable anxiety.

Harcourt MSS (Harcourt Papers, *xiii. 291-5*)

For Brewster's report on the recent progress of optics, see *1832 Report*, 308-22. In June 1832 a Council was established to deal with the Association's business between meetings. The views of Harcourt and Herschel on physical observatories are in Harcourt's inaugural speech, *1831 Report*, 26, and in Herschel, *Preliminary discourse on the study of natural philosophy* (London, 1830), 213-4. Brewster's scheme for a government physical observatory found no sympathy with government or with the Association.

109 *Harcourt, n.p., to Brewster, 4 May 1832*

With respect to a physical observatory, I do not know what Humboldt's plans have been, except so far as regards his copper houses for magnetical experiments; but it is easy to conceive a national establishment for observations and experiments of a certain order which would be in the highest degree desirable, and to which the only impediment which forbids us to hope that it can soon be realized, is the state of the national finances. Should these improve, as I trust they will, and should the government assign a few thousands a year to the support of such an establishment, I do not think that much objection would be raised even by a reformed parliament, or by the country, jealous, and often ignorantly jealous, as it now is, of the public expenditure. At such a moment I conceive that our Association might exert itself to promote this object with the greatest effect. Let a committee of the best men be appointed to draw up a report on the manner in which science is affected by the laws and taxes, and on the manner in which it might be promoted by public encouragement—a sound and eloquent politico-scientific report; let this report be adopted by the following meeting of the Association, and embodied in a petition to the legislature, with the signatures of all our eminent men of science and with the support of all its patrons. This would have weight, much greater weight than anything that an individual in office or out of office can say or do, much greater weight also than the application of any scientific council.

Quoted by Brewster, 'The British Association for the Advancement of Science',
North British Review, *1850, xiv. 235-87 (276-7)*

The opportune moment for a politico-scientific report on laws and taxes was postponed by the Association's managers until 1858: W. Fairbairn, 'The patent laws. Report of the committee of the British Association', *1858 Report*, 164-7, William Fairbairn (1789-1874), *DNB*, Manchester structural engineer.

110   *William Henry, Manchester, to Whewell, 6 May 1832*

I beg to apologise for not having replied sooner to your letter, conveyed by Mr Kennedy, on the plea of indisposition which has thrown me into arrears with various duties.

It is impossible to feel otherwise than highly gratified by the manner in which you estimate the claims of this town to stand next in succession to Oxford, as the place of meeting for the scientific Association. To myself, there is every inducement to hold out the greatest encouragement to the plan, for though frequently laid aside, so as to be disqualified from joining in any public business, I might still enjoy in my own house the society of yourself and other lovers and cultivators of science, leaving any thing more to the chance of my actual condition at the time.

As it appeared to me perfectly consistent with the object of your letter to communicate its purpose to Mr Dalton, I ventured to do this a few days ago. Our chief doubt is as to the means of accommodation for the meeting. The building belonging to our Society, having been erected when comparatively few members constituted it, is on too limited a scale even for our ordinary occasions. The hall is inconveniently crowded by 50 or 60 persons, and a lecture room over it is not adapted to contain many more persons. The house of the Natural History Society, which it rents for the purpose, is filled in every part by its collections; and at this moment that Society is contemplating a building for the purpose. The only room at the Royal Institution which (if no lectures be then going on) could be had for the purposes of the Association, is the Theatre, which is fitted up to accommodate about 700 persons. When the Institution is more nearly completed by the appropriation of funds as they come in, we should probably be able to offer in that building more complete conveniences for a large assemblage. But at present we have not in the town any thing in the way of a suite of rooms, adapted for the various committees and public meetings of such a body.

It is extremely probable that our Society will send a deputation to the meeting at Oxford, which will afford an opportunity of obtaining from its members any further information which you may think desirable.

Mr Dalton desires me to say that the Cambridge Society's *Transactions* were safely received; as the secretaries ought to have acknowledged. The volumes of our Society's *Memoirs*, to which you allude, were given into the care of Mr Willis of Caius College, and the volume just published was sent by coach, directed to the Philosophical Society, Cambridge.

Whewell Papers, a. 206[62]

John Kennedy (1769-1855), *DNB*, Manchester cotton-spinner. Henry's Society was the Manchester Literary and Philosophical Society. The Association did not visit Manchester until 1842.

111 *Daubeny, [Oxford], to Babbage, 1 Dorset Street, Manchester Square, London, 29 May 1832*

Will you allow me to consult you in confidence on a point which as [a Local] Secretary of the British Association I am interested in settling, but which it is a matter of some delicacy to enquire about except amongst friends.

The University [of Oxford] are talking about the propriety of conferring honorary degrees on a few of the leading savants not already belonging to an English university, and amongst the rest the name of Ivory has been mentioned. We are of course not unacquainted with his irritability of temper and eccentric habits; but these, if not pushed to an extreme which render him a *marplot* in any society in which he may be thrown, ought not to operate either against him as a member of the Association, or as a candidate for a degree conferred expressly with reference to scientific attainments.

It has been hinted to us however that 'he has *of late become* very eccentric', and my informant further writes that the remarks he has heard are of such a character that he has thought it as well to put me on my guard respecting him.

Now it has occurred to me that you would possibly be able to tell me more in detail how the matter stands, so as to prevent those who suggested the giving a degree to Ivory from getting into a scrape with the University, or the latter from adopting a recommendation of which they may afterwards repent. No hint of the kind has as yet been given to the person alluded to, neither has he intimated his intention of being here, so that in case of any doubt arising as to the propriety of the step proposed, the academical body might fairly say, that they merely made a selection from the number of them who had intimated some intention of coming.

We have adopted the suggestion about popular lectures, and the admission of ladies, and I hope we shall have a dinner on the Tuesday for the members in general.

PS   The intentions of the University respecting degrees being uncertain should not be as yet mentioned.

BL, Add. MSS 37186, ff. 440-1

In the event honorary doctorates were conferred on four non-Anglican members of the Association (Brewster, Brown, Dalton, and Faraday).

112 *Brewster, Jetsall's Hotel, Adelphi, London, to Harcourt, 9 June 1832*

I enclose a letter on the subject of the patent law which I received in 1827 from the Lord Chancellor (then Mr Brougham) from which you will see that any movement on the part of the Association will in all probability be well received by the government. As a bill is about to be brought forward relative to the Lord Chancellor's salary, and as the abolition of all patent fees would affect the measure, this appears to be a very fit time for doing something on the subject; and the more so as the improvement of the patent laws is referred to as one of the objects of the Association.

I may also mention to you that Mr Lennard, M P for Herefordshire, who formerly brought up the bill for amending the law of patents (which bill was stopped by the dissolution) is willing to bring it forward again, and Mr Bellenden Ker, a great friend of the Chancellor's, was anxious that I should meet him and Mr Lennard for the purpose of making arrangements on the subject. Mr Ker is a member of the Association and will likely be at Oxford.

I will thank you to preserve for me the Bishop of Cloyne's letter. I have heard that the object of leaving the age for ordination at 32, was to prevent persons in business, or engaged in other professions, from entering the Church. If this is the case it would not be applicable to me who never was engaged in any secular profession.

Harcourt MSS

Thomas Barrett Lennard (1788–1856) was M P for Maldon, not Herefordshire; he was chairman of the select committee on patents which reported in 1827. Brewster, an evangelical Presbyterian, was toying with the idea of being ordained in the Church of England through the influence of Brougham, of John Brinkley (Bishop of Cloyne), and of the Archbishop of York.

113 *Harcourt, Wheldrake near York, to Phillips, Royal Institution, Manchester, 2 July 1832*

It was proposed at Oxford that I should be perpetual Secretary to the British Association and that you should be Assistant Secretary with a salary; the latter of these propositions decided me to accede to this arrangement, on condition of a permanent Council being formed from which we might receive instructions, and of a change in the title of my office from *perpetual* to *general*, with an understanding that the arrangement should be considered as an experimental one. I stated to the [General] Committee that the offer of a salary to you was the inducement which weighed with me to accept so arduous and so undefined an office; and upon being afterwards asked by the Council what I thought the salary should be, I told

them that if you did all that the Association had a right to expect
from a person holding such a situation, which implied the giving up
much profitable time to its affairs, you ought not to receive less than
£100 a year. This was the universal opinion and it was settled that
this sum should be offered you. R. Phillips the chemist was a candidate for the office and there would doubtless have been many
more; but there was no question of any person but yourself. It is at
my request that the appointment stands on the footing of an experiment and if it is found to answer it will undoubtedly be continued. We shall have as much and indeed more to do than we had
last year. The publication will be a full size octavo volume and is to
be put in hand immediately, the arrangements having been nearly
completed with Murray for printing it; but in the first place all the
materials are to be revised by us and by such persons as we call in
to our aid and this ought [to be] done forthwith. I should therefore
wish for an interview with you as soon as possible, and if your
lectures have commenced should be glad if you could condense them
so as to leave as short an interval as possible before I see you.
Between this time and October there will be a good deal of correspondence requisite: you will have many letters to receive and many
to write, and should postpone some of your occupations, on accepting this office.

Phillips Papers

John Murray (1778–1843), *DNB*, published the *1832 Report* and its successors.

114 *Phillips, 44 George Street, Manchester to Harcourt, Wheldrake near
York, 8 July 1832*

I was very glad to receive from you a more explicit account of the
nature and motives of the appointments of the General and Assistant
Secretary of the Association, and upon the whole I really think the
meeting could not have done better. Not having the smallest notion
of their actual decision, till *Mr Salmond* told me of it, I was quite
prepared to welcome Whewell and Forbes as our permanent officers,
but this would I do believe have cost much jealousy and rivalry,
from which the present appointments may perhaps be free. Moreover I do not well see how they could choose any other persons to
overlook the building than the architect and his clerk of the works,
who began at the beginning.

I think it will be a heavy and increasing labour, both on account
of the probable growth of the business, and the difficulty of maintaining the right tone and temper of the Association. I should think

the last in particular will require a very watchful eye. Our ship is fairly afloat, *now for good steerage*.

The kindness of your expressions towards me is very gratifying and I am charmed to find you are not an Honorary but a *General* Secretary, though I confess I see no other objection to the change of this word to *permanent* (as Cuvier's was), except the danger of jealousy which could not so well enter the Institute as our Association. I have very nearly completed my essay for the *Encyclopaedia*, so far at least as to set Daubeny to work, and can lay it aside. I am also willing to postpone the further survey of the north west of Yorkshire so that all my time till October is at your command. The lectures here are unfortunately fixed by the Governors (as I had no notion of what has happened) for Monday and Thursday this July 2, 9, 16, 5, 12, 19.

I will try to alter the arrangement so as to extinguish the lectures of the middle week and to spend that period in York, but if that be impracticable I can leave Manchester by mail on some Thursday or Monday (the former is preferable as giving Friday, Saturday and part [of] Sunday) and meet you as you may appoint. This letter will probably reach you on Wednesday morning; if you reply by a letter on Wednesday evening in the post before 6 or 7 it will I expect reach me on Thursday morning and I can be ready to quit Manchester Thursday evening or the following Monday evening as you may desire.

There is a general notion here that smoke is *anticholeric*. The number of cases is not considerable, 24 or 40, abundant precautions are taken, and the people it is hoped will behave better than they did at York. But one case of riotous stopping of the cholera cart (taking a woman to the Hospital) has occurred.

Harcourt MSS

Phillips was lecturing at the Royal Institution, Manchester. The essay on 'Geology', co-authored with Daubeny, was published in *Encyclopaedia metropolitana*, 1835, vi. 529-808.

115   *Buckland, Christ Church, Oxford, to Harcourt, 10 July 1832*

You will have received a copy of the treaty I at length made with Murray who has affixed his name to the contract. I left it with Mr J. Taylor who with Babbage and Murchison was to sign a counterfeit and send it to J. Murray. It is every thing I would wish and he does not require any suretyship against loss by the transaction. In fact there can be no loss as the Association will, in case of any residuary stock coming to the market, be disposed to buy it up for the use of future members. Murray is now ready to begin printing the moment you send him instructions to begin with the *Report* of last year. I presume the *Report* itself will stand precisely as it is. Of the preface you are better able to judge than I am whether it should retain its form and place as part of the last year's *Report*. If so, it should be preceeded by another preface introductory and explanatory. At all events Murray is ready to begin instanter and I have supplied him with a copy of the last year's *Report* and your fiat will be the signal for him to commence with page 1.

I have written this day to Conybeare desiring him to send his report on geology to you as soon as possible. It is I imagine all but quite finished, as in a letter to me a week ago he spoke of printing it immediately on his own account in case it should not be wanted for the *Report* of the British Association.

I have explained to him that if he wants to add a section it must be at his own expense as we print only unadorned treatises and pay only for letter press. And I have exhorted him to send his section immediately to Gardner to be engraved at his own expense. I dare say you will get Conybeare's paper in a fortnight. I have also told Conybeare that Prichard's paper can not be printed among the reports. I requested him to prepare a short abstract of it, to be published among our announcements of results.

At Murray's request I drew up a short table of contents of the forthcoming volume including the *Report* of last year and Conybeare's report on geology. He wanted it for immediate insertion among his advertisements. It was hastily done and probably imperfect and it will be probably better for you to send him an improved edition of it.

I have desired Conybeare also to send you an abstract of his remarks on Élie de Beaumont's theory immediately. Of Mr Johnston and his report I know nothing. I will write to J. Taylor and desire him to send you the book you ask for containing the names in ruled columns. The account in the *Annals of Philosophy* of the Oxford meeting was by Harvey at the request of Sir D. Brewster. I was just in time to overhaul it and eject certain 'efforts hanging upon willows' etc so as to leave at least no harm in it.

I trust you will undertake to make a good analysis of the *Reports* for the *Quarterly* or *Edinburgh* by the time the volume is ready for publication and that you will make arrangements with Brewster to get a good review inserted in the *Edinburgh*. You say rightly that then will be the proper time to answer the petty attacks that are made by *The Times* and others on the society as 'useless and childish'. The censure passed on jokes is a matter of taste and requires no answer. Conybeare's allusion to Dalton is incapable of justification and must be passed in silence. In the *Medical Gazette* of June 30, page 426, is a complaint evidently written by some disappointed son of Aesculapius who could not get a hearing for his paper on magnesia and rhubarb and calling out for larger provision next year for medical reports. The name of Mr Broughton is mentioned as a dissatisfied author of a paper. Who is Mr Broughton?

I have consulted Brodie and Green and have written to Sir H. Halford to obtain from him, as I have obtained from Brodie and Green, a decided opinion. Should the practise of medicine be excluded from the objects of the society? If not the Association will become a receptacle of papers that ought to go at once to the medical journals. Had we not better next year meet the objections stated in the *Medical Gazette* of June 30 (which you had better order your bookseller to get for you price eight pence) by dividing our sub-committee no IV into two parts, no IV to contain botany and zoology, and no V physiology and anatomy; and omit altogether the word medicine, including as much as we want of it, viz the philosophy of medicine, under physiology? or, to prevent cavil and complaint on the part of the profession, would you make no V to contain physiology, anatomy and the philosophy of medicine? I think this would be better as it would by implication exclude the practise of medicine.

I spoke in the former part of my letter vaguely about a review of our proceedings in the *Quarterly* and the *Edinburgh*, but to be more precise I have asked Whewell to write a review of them for the *Quarterly* and I hope you will write also a similar review and through Brewster get it into the *Edinburgh* if you are not by your personal communication in contact with the editors of that important tribunal. I need not suggest to you that in these journals is the proper place and time for reply to our assailants by appeal to facts.
[P S omitted]

Harcourt MSS

Gardner was probably James Gardner, a London mapseller to the Ordnance Survey; Samuel Daniel Broughton (1787-1837), *DNB*, a London surgeon, gave a paper to the 1832 meeting on the progress of physiological research: *1832 Report*, 589-92. Benjamin Collins Brodie (1783-1862), and Joseph Henry Green (1791-1863), both *DNB*, were London surgeons; Sir Henry Halford (1766-1844), *DNB*, President of the Royal College of Physicians, London, 1820-44. Harvey's review 'British Association for the Advancement of Science', was published in *Philosophical Magazine*, 1832 (July), i. 77-82. No review appeared in the *Quarterly*, and none in the *Edinburgh* until Brewster, 'British Scientific Association', 1835, lx. 363-94. *The Times* denunciations appeared in an editorial on 28 June 1832. For Conybeare's facetious remarks about Quakers and Dalton, *Fraser's magazine*, 1832, v. 750-3. *The London Medical Gazette*, 1832, x. 426-7, complained about the meagre provision for medicine at the 1832 meeting at which physiology and anatomy were joined with zoology and botany to make a scientific section; at the 1833 meeting anatomy and medicine constituted a separate section.

116 *Buckland, Oxford, to Harcourt, Wheldrake near York, 1 August 1832*

I am glad you approve my bargain with Murray. He has taken over our terms, all but the number of separate copies to be allowed to each author. Of that limitation Conybeare complains. Will you refer to the contract of which I have no copy and tell me precisely what it is? I think Murray engages to give to the Association gratis 20 copies of the volume and there is no mention of copies of single papers to the individual authors. If so, it is still open to each author who wishes for copies (like Conybeare) to treat with Murray for any given number subject to approbation of Council. I am very glad to have reason to infer from your letter (for I know it by no other means) that Murray will employ Taylor as the printer of our *Report*. It is wise in him to do so.

Your method of proceeding with the papers is not only the best but the only practicable method during the next 2 months, wherein it will be impossible to collect a committee in London, and if possible they conjointly could not look over papers. I think I had better send on to you Conybeare's paper when I get it as it will take but little time and on the whole I should prefer so doing. I will tell him not to speculate on the moon.

Dr Turner will be a capital person to correct the press if in London, as I trust he will be. Fitton is somewhat dilatory (witness his Green Sand paper that has been in hand 7 years) but I dare say would be ready to assist, though I fear not to accelerate. You say nothing to my proposal about your undertaking a review for the *Edinburgh* in which if you chose to divide the labour no doubt Brewster would assist you, and I assume his having access to the pages of this *Review* either for himself or his friends.

Whewell says he can not possibly find time to review for the *Quarterly* but says he will ask Sedgwick, whose style in his 2 Geological Society speeches would do admirably, now that we have no Dr Ure to be served up and sliced. I have written to ask him, but perchance my letter may miss him at Aberystwith. Will you also write to ask and urge him to it as a duty arising from his office of President elect and direct your letter to Cambridge 'to be forwarded'? Though he would not write till his return and be thus in time for the Christmas *Quarterly*, still if he declines we should be looking out and engaging somebody else. One or other of our 3 letters I trust will reach him.

You speak of a paper on physiology but do not say who it is that has been applied to. At Conybeare's suggestion I desired the Dean of Bristol to sound Dr Riley (for whose high competency both the Dean and Conybeare are answerable) whether if applied to for a report on comparative anatomy he would undertake it for us. If I obtain from the Dean information affirmative, it will be for the Council then to make application to him officially. The application of chemistry to the arts is another subject of vast importance. Would not Dr Turner do it admirably? If he declined, is R. Phillips of Birmingham, who must know that part of it well which is practiced in Birmingham, also competent to a general view of the subject, or would he be willing?

Another subject, the application of science to navigation (if we could get a joint stock paper by Scoresby, Harvey, and Harris all now in Devon) would be well done, but such an amalgam is impossible. Scoresby alone, I presume, would do it best of the three. Can you think of any better? Yates went through Oxford a week ago on his way to Malvern to stay a month there and then go to the Lakes or elsewhere. I did not ask him if any notice was sent to members of Council that they were elected, but most of them met at J. Taylor's on the Tuesday you were present in London. I will ask about Green and Greenough whom, as being on the London committee of last year, we ought to have on our London Council. You had better write yourself and ask Prichard to send you his paper and tell you what his own wishes are respecting it. I am very slightly acquainted with him, not more than you are.

I have Whewell's permission to see his report on mineralogy in its way from York to London, as I was unable to listen to 5 sentences when it was read but I heard that we have something to unlearn about Haüy's theories and am anxious to see what it is. Will you therefore have the goodness to send me the paper when you have done with it and I will forward it to Murray . . .

Harcourt MSS

The Dean of Bristol was Henry Beeke (1751–1837), *DNB*; Henry Riley (1797–1848), a Bristol physician, never produced a report for the Association; René Just Haüy (1743–1822), *DSB*, French mineralogist. In the first of his two addresses as President of the Geological Society of London 1829–31, Sedgwick had attacked Andrew Ure (1778–1857), *DNB*, *A new system of geology* (London, 1829). No report on navigation was produced by the Devon trio, not least because William Snow Harris (1791–1867), *DNB*, the Plymouth inventor, was Harvey's bête noire.

117   *Airy, Edinburgh, to Harcourt, Wheldrake near York, 5 September 1832*

I have been wandering for several weeks in the Highlands in such a manner that it was impossible for me to receive any letters on the road. Yours of July 23 was just too late to find me at Inverness, and I only received it the day before yesterday at Glasgow. I lose no time in answering it though I have in these two days been in almost too great hurry to have considered it properly.

With respect to my report there is a distinction to be attended to which doubtless has not escaped you. As to the *matter* it is written advisedly, and any material alteration in this would destroy its character as my report: it would no longer contain what I feel and what I wish to express. As to the *manner*, it is written in haste and probably admits of much improvement.

I will make my remarks on yours seriatim, in the way of explanation principally. If I have misunderstood your object, I beg that you will set me right. And I entreat you to believe that if I should not in consequence make any alteration, it will not be from inattention to your suggestions (which shall be carefully considered) but from differences of opinion and the necessity under which I am placed of judging for myself.

I understand that you do not object to the paragraph pp. 74, 75, beginning with 'There are other points' and ending with 'views may be incorrect' except on the ground of inconsistency with three sentences in p. 77. My meaning would perhaps be more clearly expressed if in p. 75 I had said 'there ever can be so strong a connection' or something like this expressing degree: and if in page 77 I had said 'the growing intermixture' (though it has grown very little yet). As to the 'observation of planets and regular comparison of observations with tables' it is at present confined to myself: and that part of 'physical astronomy' in which 'much has been done in England within the last five years' has engaged the attention *only* of persons *unconnected with observations*. (One paper by myself, which seems to form an exception to this, was principally written before I dreamed of having any connection with observations.) In these two sentences therefore there is nothing inconsistent with the preceeding paragraph.

With respect to the account of English observers generally, I think that you have not interpreted my statements correctly. Perhaps I may with propriety state to you in the first instance (for practical knowledge) that the work of a mere observer is the most completely 'horse-in-a-mill' work that can be conceived. The beau ideal of an observer of the highest class is (as a friend has well expressed it) 'a compound of a watchmaker and a banker's clerk'. Most of the observers that I know (and certainly those who attract most attention) are far below this standard. You will see therefore that the *mere observer* is a person very very far below the *mere chemical experimentalist* (the character with which you have associated him). Having premised this, I will beg you to remark that I have given to English observers the highest praise which as mere observers they could receive. I have said that their instruments are excellent, their observations accurate and numerous, their plans well arranged, their purpose steady, and I would say more if I could. If then I have said that I consider English observers as below foreign observers, it is not because they are deficient in their character of mere observers (in which on the contrary they are pre-eminent) but because that character is essentially low. And the worst of its lowness is that it affects every arrangement of the powers of an observatory. For instance, I could partly forgive our ignorance of the theory of the small planets and comets if we had produced any observations of them: but from our being *mere* observers we have not known that there were such things to be observed, and consequently we have not even 'merely observed' them. The principle of division of labour will not apply because the physical astronomer has no control over the observing astronomer. I think you will find that I have not been too severe upon our mere observers.

As to the distinction between persons on whom the public has a claim (I understand you to mean official observers) and those on whom it has not, I do not generally allow it. To put a case, if a private person buys a telescope and makes some observations, however rude, and keeps them to himself or publishes them bare, certainly no one has a right to meddle with him. But if such a person publishes strictures upon the conduct and efficiency of observatories: if he writes letters in the newspapers, and publishes and industriously circulates pamphlets of the same tone: if he presents himself to the government as the representative of English astronomy, I conceive that he is 'perfectly fair game'. That this is the character of all English observers I do not say: but it certainly is of some: and I do not think there will be any misapplication of remarks upon these.

I do not feel much inclined to discuss the propriety of particular expressions and shall only recall to your consideration that whatever opinions are contained in them are the result of more extensive acquaintance with what has lately been done (partly from personal knowledge and partly from research expressly made for this report) than I believe any other Englishman possesses *at this moment*, not as extensive as some *might* possess if they would take as much trouble.

To conclude, I am desirous of presenting what appears to me to be the truth in a clear shape and in a form which will give the *least possible* offence: to give no offence is not possible. I shall be glad to revise this part of the report (as well as some others) because as I have said it was hastily written: and I shall be very glad if I find that I can alter any part so as better to suit your opinions providing my meaning can remain untouched.

I really do not recollect at present the subject of heads V I I and I X.

If at a week from this time you will direct Murray to send me the M S addressed 'Observatory, Cambridge' it will I think be sure to find me at home. I will carefully consider all your remarks. If any part is now printed or printing, I would be obliged by your putting 'Mr Ivory' for 'Sir James Ivory' where it occurs.

Harcourt MSS

The pages under discussion were published as Airy, 'Report on the progress of astronomy during the present century', *1832 Report*, 125-189 (184-6). Sir James South saw himself as the representative of English astronomy.

118 *Buckland, n.p., to Harcourt, Wheldrake near York, 5 October 1832*

In reply to yours of the 30th Sept, I beg to say I think what you have said of the degrees will do quite well. I will write to Phillimore, and ask him whether he would like to have any part of his speeches printed, but I am almost sure he will not, and I think he [always] has refused to accede to my applications of the kind. Therefore I shall not place the matter before him in a very urging form. His speeches were very neat as they always are but can not be very recondite on the subject of chemistry or botany as he had (I was told) never heard of Dalton or R. Brown till the day before he was called on to present them for the degrees. Tell it not in Gath. I am very much obliged by what you have had the kindness to do in compounding a speech for the Theatre by contributions from that in the Hall and am very glad you have introduced what I said about Lord Grenville. Your instructions to Taylor will I take for granted be attended to and the proofs sent to me here.

It does not occur to me at present to wish to make any additions to the account of my field lecture which having been 4 hours long and de omnibus rebus would be an endless task. I will thank you if you think it desirable to add the apposite note to the words 'Artesian wells'. I will transcribe it on the next page. If Phillimore (as I expect he will) should wish nothing more than you have said to appear about his speeches, I will not write to you further on that subject. I fear it will be long before the *Report* appears if the proofs go to Germany for correction. What is become of Johnston's report? I sent off Conybeare's a month ago to Taylor and the section 3 weeks ago to Gardner.

[P S omitted]

Harcourt MSS

Joseph Phillimore (1775-1855), *DNB*, was Public Orator at Oxford University. For Harcourt's compounding of two speeches by Buckland, see *1832 Report*, 96-8.

119 *Whewell, Trinity College, Cambridge, to Harcourt, 16 October 1832*

I have been absent from Cambridge and moving about from one place to another of late which has prevented my answering your last letters sooner. I hope no inconvenience has arisen from the delay which should not have occurred if I could have helped it. On looking at the recommendations of some of our committees, as you have sent me them, I cannot but apprehend that they are in several instances too general and wide to be likely to produce much good. For instance 'the improvement of the thermo-barometer' and 'the improvement of the achromatic telescope' are no doubt very desirable objects, but I hardly see how they are more likely to be answered by our saying so. I am afraid that this applies in a great measure to most of the recommendations when no particular person or persons are indicated as likely to give some answer to the questions proposed.

The reports which you state as promised will make I think a very good collection and I do not see any strong necessity for going beyond what you mention as already undertaken. With regard to Clark's on physiology I have a word to say. He appears oppressed by the extent of the subject and young Henry, as Airy tells me, is very willing to undertake a part of it. If therefore we could make a division we might obtain a better report from the two together than from either separately. Clark says he is ready to agree to any form of subdivision of physiology, and to let Henry choose his part; dividing either according to functions, as respiration, nutrition, etc, or according to the development of the individual as foetus, life, death. I do not know whether it will be easy to manage this matter, or whether you think you have authority to apply to Henry. If you do it would be well if Henry would suggest some partition of the subject, for I do not think Clark will do so, though he certainly wishes to get rid of part of the task. I do not know whether you have asked Baily for a report on pendulums: perhaps a review of what has been done on that subject might come better from some other person than from Baily who has been so much an actor in this line of research. You mention that we have no report on comparative anatomy. Buckland has got some man at Bristol, Riley I think is the name, who is held by all the knowing people that he has talked with, to be well qualified to give us a report on that subject, and who is well disposed to work for us. If you ask Buckland about this he will be able to give you any further information if it be wanted.

With regard to Miller's notation, he says that he conceives the symbol $\ddot{A} + A$ rather than $\mathring{A} + \ddot{A}$ will be best on the account you mentioned, so it will be well to put it in that form.

I omitted to mention that the report on the resistance of water to steam boats which you mark as questionable appears to me to be of doubtful value except we could be sure of wording it so as to fall in with the precise views of some very [clear] and well informed man who might answer our queries. I do not think enquiries on practical subjects couched in general terms will be found of much use.

Some time ago Mr Phillips enquired concerning a paper of Mr Lacy on the spectrum. Coddington says that the paper may be stated to have been 'on the analysis of the solar spectrum, illustrated by diagrams', but that it was not a paper of which it is necessary or desirable to preserve a fuller memorial.

I hope I have noticed the most important points in the memoranda which you sent me, so far as I have any thing to say about them. We cannot say any thing about the arrangements here next June until our new Vice-chancellor is appointed, which is November 4.

Whewell Papers, O.15. 47[107]

William Clark (1788-1869), *D.NB*, professor of anatomy at Cambridge University, wrote a 'Report on animal physiology', *1834 Report*, 95-142; William Charles Henry (1804-92), a Manchester physician, produced 'Report on the physiology of the nervous system', *1833 Report*, 59-91. William Hallowes Miller (1801-80), *D.NB*, professor of mineralogy at Cambridge University; Henry Coddington (d. 1845), *D.NB*, Fellow and tutor in mathematics at Trinity College, Cambridge. The paper given by Charles Lacy, vicar of Tring, was not mentioned in the *1832 Report*.

120 *Buckland, Christ Church, Oxford, to Harcourt, Wheldrake near York, 24 October 1832*

By the inclosed you will see that our hopes of a review of the proceedings of the British Association from the pen of Sedgwick are at an end. My letter written nearly 3 months ago has only reached him on his return to Cambridge and it seems impossible before Christmas that he should have leisure to attend to such an article as we want for the *Quarterly*. Whewell is equally occupied and I know not where to look unless our Cambridge associates will get up a joint stock review for the spring number of the *Quarterly* and appoint Whewell or Sedgwick to the office of redacteur. I should be sorry to leave ourselves to the mercy of any chance critic who may be disposed to mockery and slaughter, but I see no other means of preventing it than by a Cambridge combination review.

I believe we confided to you the task of announcing the merits of our proceedings in the *Edinburgh* trusting to the influence of Sir D.

Brewster for admission of the same to its potential pages. As the whole subject will have passed through your hands, the matter will be to you of all persons in the world the most familiar. Relying therefore on you and Sir D. Brewster to take care of the *Edinburgh* I am very anxious about the *Quarterly* and know not where to look beyond Cambridge. Conybeare would do a good deal of it very well, but I fear his want of tact and discretion. If he would contribute a portion to a joint stock review and Whewell or Sedgwick consent to reduce the whole, it may be a means of relieving us from our difficulty and hazard of being at the mercy of any unfriendly persons who may be inclined to laugh at us.

In your last you were kind enough to tell me that you would desire Taylor to forward to me for correction the pages which would contain what was said by myself. Having yet heard nothing from him I concluded he is not yet advanced so far with his printing of the proceedings. I called at Gardner's 10 days ago and found that he has engraved Conybeare's section and sent it to him for corrections so that there will be no delay in the geological report.

Harcourt MSS

121   *Buckland, Christ Church, Oxford, to Harcourt, Wheldrake near York, 5 November 1832*

By last night's post I returned to Taylor the corrected sheet of the termination of the meeting in the Music Room on the Saturday night. I have to thank you for the good amalgam you have made of my 2 speeches in the Theatre and New College Hall; Daubeny I expect will lament his fallen stars. I have struck out the name of Cuvier which stood in Lord Northampton's speech associated with that of Buffon under the imputation of superficial knowledge, and have left Buffon alone.

My chief object in writing now is to remind you that many persons here were not pleased at having their names incorrectly printed in the last year's proceedings. You know how touchy little folks are upon this point, and therefore let me beg you to send the list of names of the present members to one of our Oxford Secretaries. I mean to desire Taylor to send the proof of the list of names for correction to Dr Daubeny with a request that he should correct them which belong to Oxford and add their proper designations.

With respect to the review for the *Quarterly*, I have already sent a letter both to Whewell and Sedgwick and as you know they have both declined; but as the idea of a joint stock has been started, I think a letter from you to each of them offering your own contribution also would be effectual.

I have lately heard that Forbes is to remain abroad for 2 years. If this be so you can hardly look to him to provide for the *Edinburgh*, and from Johnston's specimen of taste in the matter of the German meeting we should hardly look to him. Brewster would I doubt not contribute his department towards the joint stock.

I have been much edified and gratified by Phillips' paper in the *Annals of Philosophy* on the fresh water characters of the great coal field.

Harcourt MSS

For the speech of the Marquis of Northampton, see *1832 Report*, 108–9. For Johnston on the German meeting, see 'Account of the meeting of naturalists at Hamburgh', *Edinburgh journal of science*, 1831, iv. 189–244.

122 *Baily, 37 Tavistock Place, London, to Harcourt, 6 November 1832*

I have been favoured with your letter of the 27th ultimo, stating that at the late meeting of the British Association it was resolved by the mathematical and physical section to request me to draw up a report 'On the recent theoretical and practical history of the pendulum'; and desiring to know whether it will be in my power to comply with that request.

To this letter I should have made a more early reply; but, having been absent from London during a portion of the interval that has elapsed, I had not an opportunity of writing to you so fully on the subject as I wished.

I assure you I have every desire and disposition to promote, as far as my humble means extend, the laudable objects of the Association; and would most willingly embark on drawing up the history to which you allude, if I thought I could do it in such a manner as would reflect credit on the Association, and be satisfactory to myself. But, I fear the [General] Committee have made too favourable an estimate of the subject, and of the proposed writer. The recent theoretical and practical history of the pendulum lies in a small compass, and has been very ably drawn up by Professor Airy, so that, in fact, I should have very little more to do than to repeat what he has already written; unless, indeed, I were to enlarge on my own recent experiments, which are probably the most numerous that have yet been made. But, I hope I may be spared this species of self-commentary, as it would not come well from such a quarter.

It appears therefore, to me, that under all the circumstances of the case, I cannot persuade myself that anything which I could draw up on the subject, would be either new or interesting: and although I regret my inability to meet the wishes of the Committee, yet I trust they will attribute it to the true motives here assigned, and not to any desire to obstruct any of their proceedings.

With my best wishes for the success of the Association,

Harcourt MSS

For Airy and Baily on pendulums, see respectively: 'Figure of the earth', *Encyclopaedia metropolitana* (London, 1830), v. 165-240; 'Report on the pendulum experiments made by the late Captain Henry Foster', *Memoirs of the Royal Astronomical Society*, 1834, vii. 1-378.

123   *Murchison, 3 Bryanston Place, London, to Harcourt, Wheldrake near York, 23 November 1832*

Your letter was, I can assure you, perused with unaffected sorrow by Mrs Murchison and myself, on whom the kind attentions of the revered parent you have lost have made an indelible impression. We sincerely condole with the Archbishop and all your family on the irreparable loss you have sustained.

On the receipt of your letter I summoned a Council at which Greenough, Turner, Yates and myself being present, it was resolved that authors of reports should have a certain number of them, say 25. Of *foreign* distribution we can say nothing, for *how* limit the author in the 'modus operandi'? We feel convinced that in this point we must conform to the usage of every other society, and in consequence we have directed Buckland, who made the *improvident* bargain with Murray, to rearrange it either by *love* or *money* so as to accomplish our ends.

Since this missive was forwarded to Buckland, I have seen publisher John, and I find he stickles for his rights. He says it is a *principle* with him in his trade, never to allow of separate copies and that authors' copies are never granted, *except by societies* which publish on *their own* account. He admits the reasonableness of my demand and says he will at once *give up his agreement* and allow us to publish as we please; on pressing him to allow the 20 copies of the volume he has already conceded to authors, to be split up into as many fasciculi as there are authors' reports, he says he *will consider* of it. Buckland must settle it.

Harcourt MSS

124   *Brewster, Allerly near Melrose, to Babbage, 1 Dorset Street, Manchester Square, London, 3 February 1833*

I ought to have written you long before this; but I have scarcely recovered from my astonishment at the result of the Edinburgh election. That Forbes, who with all his merits is literally ignorant of

9/10ths of the branches of science which constitute natural philosophy, knowing nothing of mechanics, hydrostatics, and hydraulics, little of optics and as little of astronomy, should have been preferred to such men as Dr Ritchie and Mr Galloway, is the most scandalous job that the history of science records.

Mr Forbes's family is extensive, respectable, wealthy, and highly influential, forming the nucleus of the Tory party in Edinburgh. They and their connections own the principal banking house there, and their pecuniary influence was enormous. The electors to the chair were principally shopkeepers who either had cash-accounts in the above bank, or who received pecuniary accommodations or who were employed by the Forbes, or who were promised employment by them. So powerful was the personal influence used by them with my supporters in the [Town] Council, that *every* Tory customer was sent to canvass them; and as the Tories form the bulk of the wealthy community in Edinburgh, such an appeal was not easily put aside.

In addition to this enormous personal and family influence, politics were brought into play. The Town Council is essentially a Tory corporation, and as they are about to be reformed by the Burgh Reform Bill, they hate the government and their supporters. One of the Council was the brother of the beaten Tory candidate for Clackmannanshire; another the brother of the beaten Tory candidate for Leith; and another four were of the committee of the beaten candidate for Edinburgh, a partner in Sir W Forbes's bank. All these and others united as one man to support the Tory candidate for the chair, and as I had taken an active part as one of Captain Elliot's committee in Roxburghshire against Lord J Scott, the Duke of Buccleuch's brother, the whole influence of this family and its dependents was brought into action.

Notwithstanding all this influence the Town Council durst not have carried their job through, if their wishes had not been backed by the testimonials of *Cambridge* and *Oxford professors*, and other English philosophers, who certified what was notoriously, and what was not within their knowledge. This mass of testimony was invariably appealed to, and not unreasonably, by illiterate men, to prove that they could not be doing wrong electing Forbes.

Many of these, if not most of them, were procured dishonourably. Sir James South may have shown you Forbes's letters to him. In these applications it was stated that he stood at my request, or with my approbation, and that I had no chance of success and did not mean to present testimonials, all of which were substantially false. Sir John Forbes and Mr C Forbes assured me and others that their brother would not on any account oppose me; and on this understanding I recommended that Forbes should stand in order to bring himself into notice. All the other candidates offered to withdraw in my favour. He *alone* refused. I can scarcely trust myself to speak as I feel of his conduct.

In resigning I was guided by the best advice in Edinburgh; but though I was really not a candidate on the day of election yet I was put in nomination and beaten. I had *13* friends in the Council and Forbes *20*; but on the ground of my not being a candidate one of my friends voted for Forbes, and *three* declined voting, as it would have injured them in their business without doing me any service.

Had Herschel accepted of the Provost's invitation to come forward he also would have been vanquished. The Provost has been my warmest and most ardent friend, and has made great sacrifices in his generous support of me ...

BL, Add. MSS 37187, ff. 408–11

On 30 January 1833 the Town Council of Edinburgh elected Forbes to the chair of natural philosophy at Edinburgh University, his chief rival being Brewster, his chief Scottish patron. Thomas Galloway (1796–1851), *DNB*, professor of mathematics at Sandhurst College; Lord John Douglas Montagu-Douglas Scott (1809–60), brother of Walter Francis Scott, fifth Duke of Buccleuch (1806–84), *DNB*, was the unsuccessful Tory candidate for Roxburghshire in 1832; Sir William Forbes (1773–1828), father of James David Forbes; Sir John Stuart Forbes (d. 1866) and Charles Forbes (d. 1859) were elder brothers of James David. The Lord Provost of Edinburgh was John Learmonth (1789–1858).

125   *Whewell, Trinity College, Cambridge, to Harcourt, Wheldrake near York, 20 February 1833*

I have not been able sooner to answer your enquiry when the next meeting of the Association must take place. We held a Council of the society the other day in London, on the Geological [Society] Anniversary, and it appeared that the only time which was convenient was the week beginning the 24th of June. We shall therefore begin to issue letters of notice and invitation for that date very soon. If you see any very strong objection to that time mention it; but if not send any suggestions which occur to you as to what ought to be stated in our letter. I had hoped to be able to send the *Report* along with our letters to some of the foreigners, but I am afraid from what I hear of the still unprinted portion that this will not be possible. I cannot state much more respecting the ensuing meeting than the date of it; but I will send you our letter as soon as it is agreed on.

We shall I have no doubt be allowed the use of any of the University rooms which we may want and shall have a grace passed for that purpose; but we have not yet determined when we are to meet nor indeed any of the details of the business. We will do something in this way soon, the time being now fixed.

I will try to get Airy to give a lecture, for I do not think we shall get any paper from him. Miller and Turner I hope will make something of their task. I am surprised to find that Clark and Henry have not come to any agreement on the partition of their subject as I supposed I had put them in correspondence for that purpose months ago. Clark seemed to me to wish to get rid of part of the subject, and I thought they might have managed to divide it. I hope Dr Henry will prepare a report on a portion of physiology and let Dr Clark know what portion he has taken. This will secure us against losing both which I should be very sorry for; and I should think it would suit Clark so far as I could collect from what he said when we last talked on the subject. He has been absent from Cambridge, and is only just returned so that I have not yet had an opportunity of speaking to him about your enquiry and I will not delay my letter on this account. I do not know that any thing can be done about the pendulum report. Baily says that he considers Airy by his article in the *Encyclopaedia Metropolitana* has done so much of it that little remains to be done. We will make further arrangements as soon as we can and let you know them.

Whewell Papers, O.15.47[111]

A grace was a formal resolution of the University Senate. At the 1832 Association meeting W.H. Miller and Edward Turner had been asked to do research on mineralogy and atomic weights respectively.

126 *Conybeare, Sully near Cardiff, to Harcourt, Wheldrake near York, 23 March 1833*

A late visit to Bristol has convinced me that that place would under present circumstances afford such peculiar facilities for the meeting of the British Association in '34 that I have written to Buckland on the subject, and you will see from his answer which I enclose that he enters warmly into the same views. But as you have less local acquaintance with the neighbourhood I must perhaps explain them to you more at large.

In the first place we have there an influential man just cut out for our *local President*, Mr Harford of Blaise Castle. He is a man who having inherited one of our large Bristol fortunes travelled a good deal in Italy, enriched his house with one of our best collections of pictures and on his return, feeling that he had less classical advantages than he wished, resided at Cambridge for a couple of years and there became a very respectable scholar, as he has shown by a very pretty translation of the Agamemnon of Aeschylus which he has published. Although literature and the fine arts are his great taste, he has always actively endeavoured to promote the cause of science and was the great supporter together with our friend Beeke of our [Bristol] Institution. Now from his situation and local rank he can do what he likes with our Corporation, being very popular with them, as they are all Conservatives and he, though very moderate, is of the same party. His residence at Cambridge has made him very intimate with all the best men there with whom he has zealously kept up his connection and he knows many of our Oxonians; all his habits would make him an excellent mezzo-termine between our academical Presidents and those of our large towns. I find that he would be very favourable to our visit, and quite delighted to fill his home with some of his old Cambridge friends, etc. Through him also I have sounded all the leading men of his own party and found them greatly gratified with such a prospect. For my own Whig friends I can answer, but old Bright the head of them is too aged to be very active. In the last election my old Whig party and the Conservatives coalesced against radical unions, etc, which I firmly hold we ought to do generally.

Now as to a local committee, Daubeny who has always been so active for us would be especially so in this his own city. He indeed first suggested Bristol and Harford to me. Prichard would be very useful and if the thing should be settled I know no place where so efficient a one could be organised. Though as not locally resident I should not wish to take any nominal office myself, you might count on my most active cooperation. I consider Bristol to have very peculiar advantages. There we should equally command Bath, where John Duncan would zealously work for us so we should have two strings to our bow. The Cathedral of Wells would send us Goodenough, and from Gloucester I think its Bishop would be glad to renew his acquaintance with his old Trinity friends. Our Institution would afford admirable accommodations to our meetings and sections and as I have ascertained the cordiality of all our leading people I am sure that nothing of the most hospitable reception would be neglected. You have already been in the north and midland districts. The west of England seems naturally your next move. Pray think this over and answer me speedily. I shall write also to Sedgwick and Murchison and if you all think favourably of the project I will according to Buckland's suggestion obtain a regular invitation from our Philosophical Institution which shall be signed by all the leading names of Bristol.

Harcourt MSS

John Scandrett Harford (1785–1866), *DNB*, translated *The Agamemnon of Aeschylus* (London, 1831); Richard Bright (1756–1840); John Shute Duncan (1769–1844), *DNB*, was the leading spirit of the Bath Royal Literary and Scientific Institution; Edmund Goodenough (1785–1845), *DNB*, Dean of Wells Cathedral; James Henry Monk (1784–1856), *DNB*, Bishop of Gloucester.

127   *Forbes, Edinburgh, to Murchison, Athenaeum, London, 30 March 1833*

I have just received your most kind letter and am indeed gratified in every way at the manner in which you have kindly taken up my cause at the Athenaeum. I shall be most curious to hear of your final success, as I should hope to have an opportunity of making use of my privilege this summer.

I cannot delay an hour in writing to you about the Association, having taken the deepest interest in its coming here next year, and being horrified at your proposal to put us off for *three years*. I entreat you *as a personal favour* to keep the matter open: and in the meantime I can prove to demonstration that your reasons are null and void. First. You say that Dublin has secured a prior claim to Edinburgh. This I positively deny. It was specifically understood both at York and Oxford that Edinburgh from having to a great extent originated the meeting at York should have the first visit: this you will see I have distinctly expressed in the enclosed letter to Sir T Brisbane which I send *for your private perusal* and can easily be substantiated. Hamilton got no promise of anything and I am ready to swear that the representatives of Edinburgh entered a *caveat* against Dublin being first visited. It was a private offer on both sides: neither the Royal Irish Academy nor the Royal Society [of] Edinburgh interfered at all. Everyone present must be aware of the decided feeling expressed towards the prior claim of Scotland.

Second. Then as to Bristol, the idea is a new one. Liverpool was spoken of, but as far as I recollect not the other, nor do I think it a good position. But putting this out of the question what I object to is your considering Edinburgh as a *university town*, and therefore that it ought not to follow Cambridge. This is quite a mistake. The University gives no character to Edinburgh and I fear will give little to the meeting. You must be perfectly aware that it is *not* an academical place, and that the University has nothing to offer: it has *no status, no funds, no power*. In short you must never think of the University when you come here, nor compare it in the remotest degree with Oxford or Cambridge. I assure you, you are proceeding on a fallacy and I beseech you not to let your friendship for Conybeare prevent the exercise of justice and of patriotism. My dear friend you are a Scotchman and though a deserter, should not quite forget what is due to your country. Only look back to York and remember what Scotland did for the Association: was there any talk of Dublin, or Bristol then?

Now I must again press you to remember that you are not to consider Edinburgh a university town. You must know as well as I do that it gives no character to it whatever, and that we poor wretched professors can do nothing as a body. To *prove* it to you, in turning in my mind in what quarters to look for support I never thought of applying to the *Senatus Academicus* though I have applied to the Royal Society, the Highland Society (who have come nobly forward), the Presidents of the College[s] of Surgeons and Physicians (whose offers of their utmost services are now before me), the Duke of Buccleuch, Marquis of Lothian and other noblemen, and a host of individuals. All your reasons go exactly the way to prove the reverse of what you wish: that Edinburgh must come, to *separate* the university meetings at Cambridge and Dublin; and as for Bristol I cannot tolerate the idea of such a slur upon Scotland.

My dear Murchison do not commit yourself. I dare say you think I am mad. But the more you think of my reasons and the feelings that prompt them the more I am sure you will see their force. Only tell your friends not to expect in Edinburgh such hospitality as England has nobly lavished and such as *university towns* can furnish.

Forbes Papers, Letter book II, 10–12

John William Robert Kerr, 7th Marquis of Lothian (1794–1841). Forbes wrote to Brisbane as President of the Royal Society of Edinburgh. Until 1858 Edinburgh University was run by the Edinburgh Town Council.

128   *Murchison, Athenaeum, London, to Forbes, 2 April 1833*

I have the pleasure of informing you that you have this day been elected a member of the Athenaeum on our '*distinguished*' list.

Your double letter frightened me a little at first. Your enthusiasm, (which no one values more than myself) has made you run away with the erroneous impression, that I had been *gained over* by Conybeare and was a complete Bristolian. In truth I really never had thought much of the matter and never should have known that either Edinburgh or Bristol were spoken of except from your hints and from a communication which Conybeare *made to Sedgwick*. I also heard Buckland and others express themselves favourably respecting Bristol, but not by any means as *comparing* it with 'Auld Reekie'. I have taken no steps and am in no degree compromised, but how the deuce my dear friend is one to divine that all these steps were *taken* and secured by *you*!!! On thinking the matter over I have thought it best to write direct to Sedgwick and acquaint him with all you have been doing. How far the weight of Scottish appeal will carry the day I will not now decide, because you are so vehement in your desire that I am afraid of adding stimulus, but be assured that *no one* is more intimately acquainted than number 1 with the efficacy of the Scottish band, and if you extract from the savans of this metropolis *the Scottish desertee* as you term me, you will not find that there was in *the first year* one single metropolitan of any weight save Greenough. Do not fret yourself, but converse rationally with Whewell, Sedgwick and others thereon and the award I have no doubt will be equitably adjudicated.

I am going to Cheltenham tomorrow and only staid in town to bring you into this Club.

Pray do not place me 'en mauvaise odeur' with my countrymen, but *do they really* wish for us next year?

Forbes Papers, 1833/23

129 *Buckland, Christ Church, Oxford, to Harcourt, Wheldrake near York, 9 April 1833*

Conybeare has sent to me your letter respecting the meeting of the British Association in 1834 requesting me to communicate with you on the subject. I am strongly of opinion that of all towns in England Bristol is the best: Liverpool has lost in Dr Traill its one scientific man, and although they sent last year a civil offer of their rooms, it was only in reply to an invitation of ourselves which we rather unceremoniously forced upon them. I have not the least idea that we committed ourselves to go there in any specified year, and imagine that the good merchants there would readily absolve us. Bristol on the other hand under the Presidentship of Mr Harford, a Cambridge man who would go and learn his work in June next, would set us a going upon so good a travelling system that we could hardly fail afterwards.

Another reason why I caught readily at Conybeare's proposal of Bristol was that it seemed to get rid of the unpleasantness of a meeting at Edinburgh so soon after the contest between Brewster and Forbes which cannot but have left some unpleasant feelings and may cause want of cooperation among the leaders of our Association at Edinburgh. How this matter stands between them I know not; but Murchison, who passed through here just after I had received Conybeare's letter, told me that he has heard from Forbes who is furious at the idea of the society not coming to Edinburgh next after Cambridge and tells him that the University will not invite but that the Royal Society of Edinburgh are preparing to receive or rather to invite us. Now I know not who are the members of that Society, excepting those who came to York and Oxford, who are likely to bestir themselves and certainly unless the Royal Society has better accommodations than it had in 1824 they could not hold for the number of visitors we had at Oxford.

Of the accommodations of the Bristol Institution I have no doubt. There are at least 4 large rooms besides the Theatre which holds 300; for any larger number that may want to dine or meet together there is a room which may be hired that will hold 800. In short the accommodations of Bristol are as perfect as may be wished, and Clifton [offers] plenty of pleasant summer [lodging] places, and convenient proximity to London, Wales and Ireland. Until I hear more of the proposals and capabilities of Edinburgh I must suspend my judgment, but between ourselves I am rather afraid of the obtrusive zeal of Forbes situated as he now is with respect to Brewster. You can probably tell me more of what they are doing or contemplating at Edinburgh. I will only answer for Bristol as being after York the most desirable of our provincial towns. My allusion to Conybeare's Deanery rests on the fact of his appointment by the Bishop of Llandaff to some small office of a Rural Dean, which having no pay he expects may be permitted to survive reform.

I hope that many days will not elapse before the last year's *Report* comes forth. It will I think do more good to the next meeting by coming forth now, than if it had appeared in the autumn of last year...

Harcourt MSS

The Bishop of Llandaff was Edward Copleston (1776-1849), *DNB*; Clifton a delectable suburb of Bristol.

130 *Yates, 49 Upper Bedford Place, London, to Harcourt, Wheldrake near York, 27 April 1833*

In reply to your letter received this morning I have much pleasure in informing you that the printing of the *Report* is now completed. Dr Turner and I met this morning at Mr Murray's to learn from him the price at which he will sell us the volume. He promised to send me the information next Monday. I also saw Mr Babbage this morning and showed him the *proofs* of a circular, which I had prepared agreeably to your request. This proof only waits for Mr Murray's answer, and will then be returned to Mr R. Taylor, the printer.

I propose to send sufficient quantities of this circular to the various local treasurers, with a list of the names to be allotted to each, requesting them to direct and forward the letters. In this way we may save postage to the members without violating the Post Office regulations. Also copies of the volume will be sent to the several depots; and the quantities for each appear to be as under:

Oxford 50, Cambridge 50-100, Dublin 50, Edinburgh 40-50, York 50, Bristol 5-10, Liverpool 5-10, Manchester 25, Birmingham 5-10, Newcastle 5, Plymouth 5.

At a meeting of the greater part of the Council held about the end of February a list of *foreign* societies and individuals was fixed upon, to which copies of the *Report* were to be sent. Of this, I believe, Dr Daubeny has the charge. But I am not aware that any thing was fixed about the supply of editors in this country. But I will immediately forward your letter to Dr Turner, directing his attention to that point. It appears to me that any thing of that kind may be left to the *publishing committee* without the authority of a Council. The publishing committee consists of yourself, Dr Buckland, and Dr Turner; at all events we should be glad of your *recommendation* of the editors to be sent to.

A few days ago I wrote to Mr Phillips about the arrears, and inserted a rough copy of the circular which I proposed to get printed.

I may observe that in several instances I have written to Mr Phillips, as a mere matter of detail, but, if I ought rather to communicate with you as his principal, I should have the greatest pleasure in doing so. In one instance when I supposed the matter could be expedited by sending direct to him, it was rather delayed as he happened to be in Manchester at the time.

PS I have directed Mr Taylor to print about 20 separate copies of the list of members. Would it not be desirable to have some of them interleaved in a quarto or folio sizing, to be sent to the local treasurers or secretaries in order to receive additions or corrections?

Harcourt MSS

131 *Mary Buckland, n.p., to Whewell, Trinity College, Cambridge, 12 May 1833*

How ungrateful you must have thought me for not answering your kind letter! Nothing but domestic anxieties that entirely shut out all schemes of pleasure from my thoughts would have prevented my writing to you long ago. My father's health has been in so precarious a state that I was in constant expectation that his disorder would terminate fatally. Thank God! He is so much better that we have every reason to hope he will recover.

Then, Frank fell sick of the measles, and I was kept in hot water for some time expecting the rest of the children would sicken, but they did not. Then I fell sick myself but you shall have no more bulletins of health, so now to business. I certainly had misgivings that I should be *de trop* at Cambridge but when gentlemen write so persuasively as Mr Whewell and Mr Sedgwick, my heart must have been much harder than it is to resist the wishes of such kind friends. Dr and Mrs Thackeray politely requested us to be their guests, but we think we shall be much more independent in a lodging. I say *we*, for my husband and self are a sort of Darby and Joan couple, and *I*, at least, should not relish his being in College while I was left to my own devices in a lodging. Probably Mrs Murchison would like to be with us; this I will learn from her forthwith, and I have tried to persuade our friends the Chantreys to go to Cambridge, and when I have heard from these persons severally, I shall trouble you again on the subject of lodgings. For ourselves it matters little how or where my spouse and I get accommodated, so that we are not very far from Trinity: till I know whether Mrs Murchison and Mrs Chantrey would like to be with us, or near us, it would be giving you useless trouble to seek a lodging for our party.

You ask how the Bridgewater treatise goes on; I wish I could say that it had gone off with éclat as yours has done. The geology is finished but the mineralogy had advanced but little. As the geology was utterly unintelligible without plates, there has been endless trouble about them. By way of encouragement to my husband's labours, we have had the Bampton Lecturer holding forth in St Mary's against all modern science, (of which it need scarcely be said he is profoundly ignorant) but more particularly enlarging on the heresies and infidelities of geologists, denouncing all who assert that the world was not made in 6 days as obstinate unbelievers, etc etc. We have had two sermons about the Flood concerning which he has a theory, but his hearers cannot justly make out what it is, and we are to have next Sunday a sermon on the universal conflagration by which the earth is to make its exit from among the planets. Alas! My poor husband. Could he be carried back a century, fire and faggot would have been his fate, and I daresay our Bampton Lecturer would have thought it his duty to assist at such an 'Auto da Fé'. Perhaps I too might have come in for a broil as an agent in the propagation of heresies, *merely* a mechanical one however, for if I venture to utter a suggestion or to make an observation I only get the answer that the lady in the French song did under similar circumstances:

Qui vent ouir, qui vent savoir
Comment les savans aiment;
Ils aiment si *brutalement,* ce sont de si *brutales* gens,
Qu'on les entend toujours disant Taisez-vous.

And this *brutale* prohibition I am condemned to endure because my husband's writing master allowed him to form shapeless characters in lieu of legitimate letters!!!

    William desires his kind regards to you and all friends.

Whewell Papers, a. 66[31]

Mary Buckland (d. 1857), was the highly accomplished wife of William Buckland; Francis Trevelyan Buckland (1826–80), *DNB*, their eldest son; George Thackeray (1777–1850), *DNB*, Tory Provost of King's College, Cambridge. Buckland's Bridge-water treatise was his *Geology and mineralogy considered with reference to natural theology* (London, 1836); Whewell's his *Astronomy and general physics considered with reference to natural theology* (London, 1833). The Bampton Lectures for 1833, delivered at St Mary's church, Oxford, by Frederick Nolan (1784–1864), *DNB*, were published as *The analogy of revelation and science* (Oxford, 1833). Buckland's scrawl was notoriously illegible.

132   *Whewell, Trinity College, Cambridge, to Harcourt, 12 June 1833*

I am quite of your opinion that we ought to get the committees of our sections together, and to try to provide subjects of consideration for the sections when they meet, and very likely subjects for prizes; this latter is a point which I have not considered. This is the more desirable as the contributions which hitherto have been announced for our Cambridge meeting are not very numerous, nor, with the exception of the reports, likely to be of very great importance. It will not however be easy to collect many persons at present, for all our Cantabs are absent; even most of those who will be at the meeting. I think however that I can set a few men to work who will do something in this way, enough to set us agoing.

    I hope you intend to come some days before the Association meets, the sooner the better. If you will let us know we will have rooms in College ready for you whenever you choose, from the present time, and shall be all the more glad to see something of you before the bustle begins.

    At any rate I think we must, as J. Phillips suggested in a letter to me, have a meeting of the Council of the British Association here on Saturday the 22nd. I shall be much obliged to you if you will inform Mr Yates our Secretary that this is the opinion of the President and myself, and request him to summon the Council for 11 o'clock on Saturday the 22nd to meet at the President's rooms. We shall then be able to make all the arrangements that we have not previously made; and I dare say shall have business enough. I hope you will be there.

If Mr Phillips is still in town pray tell him that I shall attend to the suggestions which he has given: any that we doubt about, we can discuss when he comes. Inform him also that I shall find rooms for him in College when he arrives.

Mrs Buckland (who comes on the 22nd) sends me word that Arago is coming: this will be very good. You may have heard that our musical people here have tacked a musical *coda* to our philosophical movement, which is more likely to increase our numbers than our philosophy: but will keep us I hope in admirable humour.

In the hope of seeing you here soon

[PS] Mr Stevenson informs me that his report is not prepared: can you ascertain whether Mr Rennie's is ready and whether he will bring it and read it himself?

Whewell Papers, o.15.47[114]

George Rennie (1791–1866), *DNB*, produced his 'Report on the progress and present state of our knowledge of hydraulics as a branch of engineering. Part I', *1833 Report*, 153-84. Grants of money for research, not prizes, were first awarded at the 1833 meeting of the Association.

133 *Yates, Trinity Hall, Cambridge, to Murray, Albemarle Street, London, 22 June 1833*

A meeting of the Council of the British Association for the Advancement of Science has been held this morning, at which it has been determined to procure from London a reporter and a police officer, and I write to beg your assistance in obtaining them. A most excellent reporter from the House of Commons was engaged last summer at Oxford, and we should be glad, if possible, to have him again. But we must leave it to you to do for us the best you can. We wish the reporter to be engaged from Tuesday morning till Friday evening, and you will have the kindness to make terms with him and to inform us what they are.

Also we wish you to send a police officer to frighten away thieves, and do every thing pertaining to his profession.

The Council trust you will excuse this trouble.

[On the outside of this letter Yates wrote: 'To be delivered immediately, and half-a-crown to be given to the bearer, if punctual'. In another hand: '1 guinea per diem and travelling expenses']

Murray Archives

134 *Harcourt, Trinity College, Cambridge, to Matilda Harcourt, Cliff,*
Scarborough, Tuesday [25 June 1833]

I know not whether I shall have time to say more than that we have
had a very satisfactory opening of a great and splendid meeting.
Sedgwick on Dalton's pension was very good and Whewell gave an
able and eloquent analysis of our volume of report[s]. We had last
night an open discussion in the Senate House where Dr Robinson,
the astronomical professor of Armagh, like a true Irishman took the
field with undaunted and eloquent volubility, when we were in want
of one courageous enough to open the debates in the Senate House
on the subject of the aurora borealis and the falling stars; he
was followed by Scoresby, Professors Airy and Christie, Sir John
Herschel, Dalton, and Whewell.

Tonight the geologists in their turn are to have a field day and I
suppose we shall turn out a provincial dissenter from the orthodox
doctrines of the science, Dr Boase, and hunt him down, for the
amusement of the ladies. I very much wished, dearest, that you
could have been here last night for it would have interested you to
have heard the Herschels and Airys speaking on some of the most
mysterious phenomena of the heavens. I have made many new acquaintances worth making. Nevertheless, in the midst of all this
excitement, when I lie down on my lone couch I think of you, love,
and wish that you were partaking with me of these high intellectual
enjoyments.

Harcourt MSS (Harcourt Papers, *xiii. 317–8*)

Henry Samuel Boase (1799-1883), *DNB*, a Penzance physician, was attacked for
holding the unorthodox view that veins in rocks were formed at the same time as the
rocks themselves. In 1833 Dalton was granted a state pension of £150.

135 *Johnston, Durham, to Harcourt, York, 4 July 1833*

The bustle and press of business at Cambridge prevented me from
informing you of my intention to apply for a chair or readership of
chemistry about to be established in Durham and of requesting you
to favour me with a testimonial. The situation is not likely to be one
of much emolument but it would serve to identify me with the
science, and probably give me facilities for the prosecution of my
labours which I do not at present possess. Since my arrival here I
have learned that a chapter is to be held on the 20th of this month
at which some appointments will probably be made as there is some
desire of commencing partially in October next. I wish therefore to
have my application made and testimonials sent in before that time.
I am not aware how far my being a member of the Church of

Scotland may be an objection in the eyes of some of the chapter; by Dr Gilly I am informed that his opinion is that it will be no objection at all. At all events I come forward as a candidate only upon the understanding that this circumstance shall not operate to my disadvantage.

After collecting and printing my testimonials I intend to revisit Durham about the 10th of this month with the view of waiting personally upon such members of the chapter as may then be in town; and though I cannot urge you to do anything further in my behalf than to furnish me with a testimonial, your acquaintance with the members of the chapter might enable you to give me letters of introduction which would be of considerable service to me on my return to Durham.

I did not at the time see the force of your objection to the proposal of monthly reports. The remarks of the Marquis of Northampton in regard to identifying Professor Whewell's address with the Association, completely satisfied me that you had taken the proper view of the subject.

I return to Portobello tomorrow where I shall be happy to hear from you at your earliest leisure.

Harcourt MSS

William Stephen Gilly (1789–1855), *DNB*, was a prebendary of Durham Cathedral. Johnston was appointed reader in chemistry at Durham University later in 1833. The General Committee of the Association had decided that Whewell's *Address delivered in the Senate House at Cambridge, June 25, 1833* (Cambridge, 1833) was merely his report of his own speech.

136 *Whewell, Trinity College, Cambridge, to Harcourt, Wheldrake near York, 27 July 1833*

I send you our preface in its present condition. If you have any suggestions to make *respecting* it, I think you had better address them to Henslow as I leave Cambridge in a few days. I believe Henslow expects to have the book ready for publication in a very short time. I saw him in London when I met Buckland, and discussed with him your plan of foreign corresponding members. We agreed that the plan was excellent, but we thought that with so few members of Council as we would assemble it might not be advisable to bring it forward at present, especially as it may be equally well carried into execution if resolved upon in the autumn. The application to government was made on Wednesday last by appointment with Lord Althorp. Herschel, Airy, Baily were the deputies, and it seemed to be thought that no others were necessary. They were very favourably received. The sum to which they limited their present application was £500. The previous delay was necessary in order that they might ascertain the amount of the work to be done which Airy examined with care. I have received an answer to my application to Liverpool about the tides and when I have consulted Lubbock we shall probably set our calculator to work soon. I hope you retain as agreeable a recollection of the Association as we all do here. Sedgwick, who was a little out of order, is much improved by a visit to Leamington which he has just finished. I believe he and I move together shortly. Perhaps my travels may lead me to York in which case I shall try to find you. In the mean time letters will be forwarded to me from Cambridge.

Harcourt MSS

This letter was written on the margins of the proofs of *Lithographed signatures of the members of the British Association for the Advancement of Science, who met at Cambridge, June 1833. With a report of the proceedings at the public meetings during the week; and an alphabetical list of the members* (Cambridge, 1833). Harcourt's scheme for foreign corresponding members was implemented in 1834. The successful application to John Charles Spencer, Lord Althorp (1782–1845), *DNB*, Chancellor of the Exchequer, was for £500 to pay for the reduction of planetary observations made at the Royal Observatory.

137   *Harcourt, Wheldrake near York, to Henslow, Cambridge, 29 July 1833*

I return the proof sheet of the preface according to Whewell's desire to you. I think the statements in the first page and a half would be clearer and more correct if you should think proper to adopt the alterations which I have suggested. I should be glad to have the half sheet containing Whewell's letter returned when you have done with it.

I am in some anxiety about your publication of the *unrevised* speeches. I hope you have in fact revised them all with care. Where you cannot give the speakers an opportunity of revising themselves, it is necessary at least to be *extremely cautious*, both for the sake of the feelings of the individuals and the credit of the Association, [so] that you print nothing in any one's name which is either absurd or in bad taste. A newspaper editor of speeches either leaves out the nonsense of a speech or contrives to turn into sense, and you must exercise a still more vigorous excision and a choice transmutation. I dare say you have done this, but the allusion in the preface to *the responsibility of the reporter* leaves a doubt with me whether you are taking your own share of responsibility which is not a small one in giving publicity to these extemporaneous speeches. I know by experience the difficulty and delicacy of the task you have undertaken and feel that I should myself be annoyed (though my sensibility on such matters is a good deal blunted) at reading a foolish speech of my own in print whether faithfully reported or not. When I have had to do what you are doing my method has been to pick out the most valuable parts of a speech and not to scruple to dress up the phraseology of them a little better than the reporter and I have generally found the speaker well satisfied with this treatment.

Henslow Papers

The letter refers to *Lithographed Signatures*.

138   *Baily, 37 Tavistock Place, London, to Harcourt, 31 July 1833*

As you would probably wish to know the issue of the interview which the committee, appointed by the British Association, had with Lord Althorp relative to the grant of a sum of money for the purpose of reducing the planetary observations made at the Royal Observatory at Greenwich, I beg to state that Sir John Herschel, Professor Airy, and myself (Mr Gilbert being in Cornwall) waited on his Lordship; who expressed his willingness to second the object of our wishes, and said that he would speak to Lord Grey on the subject. I have since learnt that, on the very same morning, he did go to Lord Grey, who *immediately* acceded to our request; and a warrant will be made out for the sum proposed.

As none of us could give a reasonable estimate of the total expense of these calculations, we thought it best to ask at once for the sum of £500; with an understanding that if it should exceed that amount, and we could show that *that* had been well laid out, we should be at liberty to apply again for a similar sum. And the matter thus rests with this understanding.

I cannot but congratulate the British Association on this occasion; as I am very sure that it will, as much as anything they have done, tend to raise it in the estimation of scientific men, and to show its utility and public spirit. And I am still more sure that the result of the enquiry and investigation will, in the hands of the learned professor who has undertaken the task of revising the planetary theory, add to the scientific honour of the country.

I hope at the next meeting of the Association to be able to report considerable progress in this business;

Harcourt MSS

Charles Grey, 2nd Earl Grey (1764-1845), *DNB*, was Prime Minister; the learned professor was Airy.

139   *Herschel, n.p., to Sedgwick, Trinity College, Cambridge, 3 August 1833*

I this morning received an official notification from Lord Althorp that £500, for which the British Association applied to government for the purpose of reducing the planetary observations from 1750 to 1830, under the superintendance of Professor Airy, is granted and a note from Lieut Drummond states that that sum is payable at the Treasury to the order of Professor Airy or Mr Baily according as it is wanted.

I ought not to omit mentioning to you that so far from the slightest hesitation occuring or the least difficulty being made, Lord Althorp (on the committee waiting on him to explain what was wanted and why) conferred with Lord Grey the same morning on the subject who *immediately* assented to the proposal. I consider this highly creditable both to the government and to the Association in which feeling I am sure you will agree.

I should also add that in the course of our communication with Lord Althorp it was stated by us that the above sum *might not* suffice, that the operation *might* be expected to cost a thousand, but that we limited our application in the first instance to £500, intending to economise that grant in the strictest manner, and only to make further application in the event of being able to show that the first had been efficiently and advantageously expended. From the manner in which this was received (though no positive pledge of course was given us) I should presume that no difficulty would probably be made in the event of a further grant being necessary to complete the operation, or carry it on to the construction of new and improved planetary tables.

I hope you have not suffered by your exertions in the cause of the meeting. What a week!

Herschel Papers, 15.422

Thomas Drummond (1797-1849), *DNB*, was Althorp's private secretary.

140   *Henslow, Cambridge, to Harcourt, 8 August 1833*

I will write to Mr Yates and consult with him about the meeting of the Council. Whewell is away and does not return for a few weeks. My own opinion is most decidedly against employing Mr Murray any more. My chief object in writing to you at present is to confer about the report we are preparing. I do not consider its present shape as that in which it ought to appear, as we have not carefully revised it so as to correct grammatical errors and misprints; but I confess that I see nothing to find fault with in the general character of it. The reporter's account was most defective and it has cost us no small pains to reduce it to its present shape. You will observe that I am not the only person who have worked at it: Sedgwick,

Whewell, Lodge, Peacock, Brown, have corrected parts, and the three former especially have looked over the whole. Peacock has a copy now. I have sent others to Mr Taylor, Mr Yates, Dr Daubeny, Mr Phillips, [and] Lodge and before it goes to the press I am anxious for the opinion of all. I really think that you take too high a view of what is required in such a publication. No one expects any thing of dignity in such a statement: all that is called for is a simple memorial of *what* took place, and as nearly as possible, of *how* it took place. To alter the speeches into prepared orations would take away the whole charm which they possess as exhibiting the unpremeditated sentiments of the speakers. I and several others considered the account we are preparing would be highly gratifying to those who have seen no accurate report of the proceedings, and nothing but the very erroneous statements which have appeared in the papers and elsewhere. Still, so far as I am concerned, I have no care for the publication and will correct and alter to suit the taste of others as may be thought best. With three friends to assist me last night, we directed above 800 of the circulars, and I have given the rest to a clerk to finish for us. You will, I trust, excuse me if I have delivered my own view freely, but having lived long enough to know that it is impossible that we should all think alike upon any subject whatever, I always consider it best to state plainly my own opinions and then abide by what the majority wish, without any care for the consequences. I verily believe that we shall gratify very nearly the whole of the Association by appending this report to the signatures, and that they will be the better pleased to find the speeches given as nearly as possible in the language in which they were delivered. I don't think we can suppress it after the Syndics have so liberally offered to print it for us. It cannot be considered an act (or a very deliberate one) of the Association, but of a few only; for it forms no part of our regular proceedings. I therefore do think that you view the matter with too severe a judgment; but in saying so pray don't suppose that I am in the least annoyed, and that I am unwilling to stop the publication, and burn the letters if it should seem most advisable to do so. I am willing to suggest and to act for the members of the Association to the best of my power, but have no desire to support any fancies of my own that may be unpleasant to *them*. *Quere.* If we find a Council cannot conveniently be called, might not a circular be sent to the members requesting their opinion as to Murray's publication. I see that I am the only member of Council in Cambridge, but I am quite ignorant of the London members and I think a circular would be a ready and efficient mode. Will you, if you consent, prepare one, and I will get it lithographed if you choose a printer.

Quere. Would you recommend my sending the report of any of the speeches to their authors?

PS   I see you mention *rough Mss* as sent you by Whewell, but as you have not got the *proof sheets*, you may perhaps find that we have already done something towards altering them into a fitter shape for publication.

Harcourt Papers

John Lodge (1793-1850) was Fellow of Magdalene College and University Librarian; John Brown (1776-1850), Fellow of Trinity College, Cambridge, and Vice-master 1830-42. The report under discussion was that included in *Lithographed Signatures* which was printed by Cambridge University Press. Murray had published the *1832 Report*.

141   *Harcourt, Bishopthorpe near York, to Yates, 13 August 1833*

The subject most immediately requiring the attention of the Council is the question respecting the manner of printing our transactions. I am disposed to think that we may *dispense with a publisher*, that with so many members and so cheap a publication we run no risk in doing so, and that it will be a great advantage to have the power of fixing our own price (which ought in my opinion to be lower than it has been) and of accommodating our reporters more liberally. I think however that we should do well to adhere to our former printer (Mr Taylor), whose practice in the correction of scientific matter and as I suppose superiority also in command of type over our provincial printers are material considerations. Of the expense of printing a volume of five or six hundred pages such as our last *Report* Mr Taylor can supply an accurate estimate and I do not conceive that much need be allowed for advertising.

As to the notices for the collection of the arrears I should recommend your advising with Mr Taylor respecting the form of them. A form of notice being agreed upon I suppose you will send lithographic copies to the local treasurers to send out.

In a letter to Mr Whewell about six weeks ago I stated at length a plan for appointing foreign correspondents which I requested him to submit to the Council. He communicated it to Dr Buckland who agreed with him in approving it and if he is in London I have no doubt he will lay it before the meeting; but in case he should not I will now restate the particulars.

The plan is. 1. that the Council in the name of the Association should nominate the following foreigners corresponding members of the Association:

1st, M Oersted, Copenhagen;
2d, M Rudberg, Stockholm;
3d, M Kupffer, St Petersburg;
4th, M Mitscherlich, Berlin;
5th M Gmelin, Tubingen;
6th, M Amici, Modena;
7th, M De La Rive, Geneva;
8th, M Quetelet, Brussels;
9th, M Babinet, Paris;
10th, Mr Featherstonhaugh, America.

2d. that through these members our invitations should be transmitted to foreign savants.

3d. that they should be severally requested to furnish our annual meetings with a brief written statement of any important discoveries in science which may have been made in their respective countries *during the year preceding the meeting to which the communication is made.*

4th. that certain expenses which may probably attend the getting these statements drawn up and transmitted shall be defrayed by the Association and that *ten* pounds shall be placed annually at the disposal of each corresponding member for this purpose.

If the Council shall think well of this proposition I would undertake to correspond with the persons nominated. The list which I send Sir D. Brewster and myself drew up together. If any of the parties should decline the service they might be requested to name any person whom they had reason to think would be willing to undertake it.

I have taken measures with Mr Phillips to collect the reports and abstracts as soon as we can for the [*Report*] and I have no doubt we shall obtain them earlier than we were able to do last year and get them printed sooner. We propose to print the united recommendations of the committees etc immediately or as soon at least as they can be properly corrected.

I have received letters from Mr Baily and through our President from Sir J. Herschel announcing the success of the application to government for the reduction of the astronomical tables and will beg you to communicate Mr Baily's letter to the Council and to return it to me.

British Association archives, Minutes of General Committee, 1832

Hans Christian Oersted (1777-1851), *DSB*, Danish physicist; Fredrick Rudberg (1800-39), professor of physics at Uppsala University; Adolphe Theodor von Kupffer (1799-1865), physicist, of the Academy of Sciences, St Petersburg; Christian Gottlob Gmelin (1792-1860), professor of chemistry at Tübingen University; Giovan Battista Amici (1786-1868), *DSB*, Italian microscopist and astronomer; August Arthur De La Rive (1801-73), professor of physics at Geneva Academy; Lambert Adolphe Jacques

Quetelet (1796-1874), *DSB*, Belgian statistician and astronomer; Jacques Babinet (1794-1872), *DSB*, professor of physics at the Collège Louis-le-Grand, Paris. Murray published the *1833 Report*.

142 *Harcourt, Bishopthorpe near York, to Herschel, 23 August 1833*

I had very sincere pleasure in communicating to a late meeting of the Council of the Association the announcement from Mr Baily and yourself of the success which has attended your application to the Treasury. It is valuable not only on account of the importance of the object itself but as shewing the influence of our annual meetings in calling forth the exertions of men of science and in giving those exertions their due weight with men in power.

My chief object in troubling you with this letter is to request a statement from you of the nature of your communications to the Cambridge meeting. One of these is mentioned in the minutes of the Committee as 'an account by Sir J. Herschel of his instrument called the actinometer and of the principle on which it is adapted to the measure of the intensity of the solar rays'—the other as 'a paper on the absorption of light by coloured media in reference to the theory of undulation'. Any abstract or summary of this account and paper would be a valuable addition to the 'abstracts of communications' which we are proceeding to publish, if you are not too much occupied by your preparations for your voyage to be able to send it me.

Herschel Papers, 9.226

In autumn 1833 Herschel went to the Cape of Good Hope to do astronomical research. From 1832 the standard format of a *Report* was commissioned reports on the state of various sciences, followed by abstracts of papers given at the last meeting.

143 *Harcourt, n.p., to William Charles Henry, n.d. [early autumn 1833]*

It was my practice in editing the former volume of the transactions of the British Association to look carefully over the reports before they went into the printer's hands and communicate freely to the authors the observations which occurred to me, leaving it to them to make what use they pleased of the criticisms which I offered and I had the pleasure of receiving for the most part their ready concurrence in the revisions proposed. I am too imperfectly acquainted with physiology to trouble you with many remarks upon your report. I have however had sincere gratification in reading so clear a statement of the progress of one portion of these enquiries; and the more so because in the physiological writers into whose works I have dipped I have been usually struck with the prevalence of indistinct ideas and inconclusive reasonings, a defect common undoubtedly to

almost every science in its infancy. I fear from the expressions in Dr
Clark's letter that it is doubtful whether we are to expect the execution of his portion of the undertaking and in that case I hope you
will proceed to complete the task which you have begun by giving
us in a second part the history of muscular irritability and going on
to the other subjects adverted to in your introductory pages.

Mr Rennie and Mr Challis have in like manner given the first
parts of enquiries of which they will add the sequel at the next
meeting. I was in hopes that Dr Clark's contribution might have
given some general description/remarks on the true spirit of physiological enquiry, and of its importance together with some cautions
respecting the manner of exercising the right of making cruel experiments. It is impossible to read the work of some of the French
school and to observe their wanton multiplication of useless experiments involving much suffering to the unfortunate objects of them
without disgust. I trust that if Dr Clark fails to treat of these points,
you will not leave them entirely untouched.

There is only one part of your report on which I have any criticism to offer and that is near the conclusion. I think the terms, in
which Sir C. Bell's doctrine of an exclusive system of respiratory
nerves is spoken of, somewhat too peremptory to be properly employed in a report of this nature. The expressions to which I see an
objection are these: 'this doctrine has not received the concurrence
of *the more intelligent* physiologists of this country or the continent';
'Dr Alison has *completely demonstrated the unsoundness* of this part of Sir
C. B.'s arrangement as well in the individual nerves thus classed
together as in the general principle on which the entire system rests.
*It is somewhat remarkable that in the last digest of his opinions published 4
years after the appearance of Dr Alison's paper Sir C. B. should have attempted
no refutation of his arguments*'. These remarks, considered as addressed
to a living and distinguished philosopher, appear to me too strongly
controversial for the equable spirit of one of our reports. You would
I conceive find no difficulty in giving Dr Alison's arguments their
due weight without shewing any want of deference to the opinion
deliberately persisted in by Sir C. Bell.

In the last line of your last page but one the grammatical construction is imperfect and the meaning in consequence obscured.
The following paragraph (the last on the last page) strikes me as
unnecessary; and the same respect for Sir C. Bell's opinion, even
though it should prove to be erroneous, which leads me to *wish* the
former expressions modified would make me strongly doubt also the
propriety of placing this statement under the head of 'facts have
been fully ascertained'.

Harcourt MSS

Sir Charles Bell (1774–1842), *DNB*, discoverer of the distinct functions of the nerves; William Pulteney Alison (1790–1859), *DNB*, professor of theory of medicine at Edinburgh University. Henry's published 'Report on the physiology of the nervous system', *1833 Report*, 59–91 (88–90) was suitably revised. Henry did not produce a second report.

144 *William Charles Henry, Manchester, to Harcourt, Residence, York, 23 October 1833*

I beg to express my sense of obligation to you for the attention you have done me the favour to bestow on my physiological report and for the trouble you have taken of conveying to me so fully your valuable remarks and suggestions. Of these, I need scarcely assure you, I shall avail myself with much pleasure, and with entire deference to your judgment, when the proof sheets are submitted to my revisal.

I entertain, as I have indeed expressed in various parts of my report, the most profound respect for the high genius of Sir Charles Bell, and consider his discoveries as beyond doubt the most important accessions to physiological science of the present and past centuries, and I admire and value them the more warmly, that they have been made at the smallest possible expenditure of animal life and suffering. It would therefore have given me the greatest concern, to have discovered that I had employed any terms, that might be interpreted into want of deference for that distinguished physiologist, and I feel particularly grateful to you, for having enabled me by more temperate and qualified expressions, to avoid such misconstruction. As regards the question of a separate respiratory system, I believe I have not overstepped a truthful and impartial criticism, in the decided preference I have assigned to the arguments of Professors Alison and Mayo. But I perfectly feel that the expression of this conviction is in no way inconsistent with the due and most respectful consideration of the opposite opinions of Sir Charles Bell; and I earnestly hope that the manner in which I shall endeavour to combine these objects will be sanctioned by your approval.

Harcourt MSS

Herbert Mayo (1796–1852), *DNB*, professor of anatomy at King's College, London.

145 *Buckland, Christ Church, Oxford, to Harcourt, Wheldrake near York, 20 November 1833*

If you have not yet seen a gross attack upon the British Association on page 7 of the preface of Mr Nolan's absurd and mischievous

Bampton Lectures, preached last year at St Mary's Oxford, it is in my humble opinion highly expedient for the interests of the said Association and of the University that you should do so, and should take up the subject in a manner which no man can do so well as yourself to set the question at issue before the public on its right footing in the form of a review of some half dozen enthusiastic scio- lists that have inundated the world with anti-philosophical volumes which nobody has taken the trouble to contradict; but as the character of Oxford and the British Association are committed by Mr Nolan's work you will I am sure do a most important service by taking up your pen and reviewing the whole question in the *Edinburgh Review*.

Murchison was here 10 days ago and was outrageous at a work of a similar class by Captain Fairholme entitled 'Geology of Scrip- ture' written in utter ignorance of the very elements of the subject which he endeavours to reconcile with the letter of scripture even to its minutest details. Of this work he wrote to Sedgwick begging him to castigate the author in the *Quarterly* together with Granville Penn, Sharon Turner and the rest of that school; and now that Mr Nolan has added his Bampton Lectures to the list it still more behoves the President of the British Association to defend it against the imputa- tions of his preface as well [as] to defend geology and all other sciences from the misrepresentations that pervade the whole volume.

A very good review of Mr Fairholme has just appeared in no XV of the *Presbyterian Review*, Newcastle, November 1833. But this in no way supersedes the necessity of a general and masterly statement of the bearings of the whole question, which I trust you and Sedgwick will forthwith prepare for the *Edinburgh* and *Quarterly*. I am person- ally interested in [the] doing of this because I wish the way to be prepared for the due reception by unscientific persons of the facts which will in my Bridgewater Essay be set forth in a manner which will not admit of the usual subterfuge of all this school in a denial of their existence; and they have for the most part so committed the truth of sacred scripture upon the nonexistence of these facts that their establishment involves the believers of Penn, Nolan and Co in a necessity of disbelieving the sacred records.

The time is now arrived when this school must be put down, singly they are unworthy of the notice of any scientific man. But it is not unworthy of any one to take up the question in its general bearings, and an extract or 2 from each author will slay them in detail with their own weapons.

I must of course say a little in the introduction to my Bridgewater, but must be very brief. I earnestly hope you will take the matter in hand forthwith.

Harcourt MSS (Harcourt Papers, *xiii. 321–3*)

Granville Penn (1761–1844), *DNB*, author of *A comparative estimate of the mineral and Mosaic geologies* (London, 1822); Sharon Turner (1768–1847), *DNB*, had just produced the fourth edition of his *The sacred history of the world as displayed in the creation and subsequent events to the deluge* (London, 1833). George Fairholme, *A general view of the geology of scripture* (London, 1833) was slated in *The Presbyterian review and religious journal*, 1833–4, iv. 345–80, which was published in Edinburgh and not Newcastle. Nolan gave the Bampton lectures in 1833, not 1832. Neither Harcourt nor Sedgwick fulfilled Buckland's request.

146 *Robison, 9 Atholl Crescent, Edinburgh, to Murchison, Vice-president Geological Society, London, 20 January 1834*

... I wrote yesterday to Mr Yates the Secretary of the Central Committee to suggest that no time should be lost in sending down detailed instructions to the local office bearers of the British Scientific Association on all points which the Committee may deem it their duty to consider as in their province. It may seem early enough to begin preparations now, but so few useful persons will remain in Edinburgh after the winter sessions are over, that if the essential arrangements be not made at present, there will be confusion and mismanagement in the end. I have urged the expediency of fixing the meeting in *the first week* of September, as I am assured we can get the Parliament House, the Courts of Justice and the great libraries at that period, without fear of interruption, while we could not rely on them later. There are other reasons, but that one seems sufficient to determine the point. The great extension which the Association has taken and is likely to maintain will now make the correspondence very laborious if it be considered expedient to conduct it in the manner which has been thought necessary while the Association was forming, and while attendance at the meetings was made a matter of solicitation. It is to be feared, that if a constant repetition of the same efforts which have hitherto been made, be expected to be continued, many persons who might otherwise be willing to give their services, will be shy of undertaking a task in which they may fail, or be obliged to neglect their own affairs to accomplish; for the sake therefore of the permanency of the system, it is desirable that its machinery should gradually be reduced to the greatest degree of simplicity compatible with entire efficiency. With this view it may be considered whether public advertisement in properly selected quarters, may not in most cases be substituted for circular letters.

There was a good deal of joking in various journals last year, on the proportion which the time which was spent in lauding the Association and in interchange of compliments, bore to the time employed in business. I should apprehend there will be little danger of such observations being called forth by the proceedings of the approaching meeting as you are aware that our President is more accustomed to military brevity than to academic prolixity. There will likewise be less opportunity for personal compliments, as I do not anticipate the possibility of there being more than one entertainment given; and, as at the dinners, at the ordinaries nothing of the kind will be expected. With regard to the latter the idea which prevails here is, that in order to render them as attractive as possible, no private dinner parties should be allowed to withdraw the stars, or to create invidious distinctions, but that all those who wish to entertain their friends or strangers during this week should do it by giving breakfasts, on any scale they like. I hope that this plan may not be misapprehended, but be attributed solely to the desire to make the general effect as good as possible. You are so well acquainted with the peculiar circumstances which must more or less affect the arrangements here, that you are perhaps better qualified to give a general sketch of a good plan than persons on the spot who may insensibly be swayed by local prejudices. I should therefore consider any observations which you may be disposed to communicate to me as being exceedingly valuable, and if you will indulge me by such a communication, I shall, if you desire it, consider it confidential. I do not know whether you be acquainted with Lord Greenock, but if you be, you will not be surprised to learn that he is likely to be a most valuable and zealous co-adjutor in all our measures. I should make an apology to you for this long rambling letter written in the midst of many interruptions, but I trust to your zeal in the common cause to overlook any defects in my efforts to advance it. [P S omitted]

Murchison Papers, Edinburgh University Library, Gen 523/4

Charles Murray Cathcart, Lord Greenock (1783-1859), *DNB*. The 1834 President was Brisbane, a soldier and astronomer.

147   *Daubeny, Oxford, to Harcourt, York, 3 February 1834*

I send for your perusal through your brother the concluding portion of my strictures on Nolan. If you have an opportunity to send them and the previous parts to Phillips of York he will be glad to peruse them. You have probably heard of the death of poor Dr Williams. His appointment as Librarian I understand is the object of much canvass; the other, namely his botanical professorship, I have great hopes of obtaining, my only opponent a physician in London, having withdrawn. I shall prize it greatly, less for the emoluments than for the facilities it will afford me in the experiments I am carrying on. Allow me to suggest with respect to the time of the Edinburgh meeting that it ought to be *early* in September, the German meeting held this year at Stuttgart being fixed for the 19th or 20th of September, and it would be a pity for the two to clash. I have thoughts of being at both.

Harcourt MSS

George Williams (1762-1834), *DNB*, was professor of botany and Radcliffe Librarian at Oxford University; Daubeny succeeded him as professor of botany. Daubeny's strictures on Nolan were published anonymously as 'Apology for British science', *Literary gazette*, 1833, 769-71, 789-92.

148 *Forbes, Edinburgh, to Harcourt, Wheldrake near York, readdressed to Archbishop of York, Grosvenor Square, London, 16 March 1834*

Having learned from Mr Robison that he has some hopes of your paying us a visit here, I cannot help writing two lines to endeavour if possible to make your determination complete. Not merely do I speak from the abstract pleasure I should have in seeing you (which I fully believe I need not insist upon) but because you could by your advice save a multitude of dubitations as to the *leading* arrangements for September which have very much fallen upon myself, as having taken part in the previous meetings. We contemplate very material changes in the arrangement of business chiefly with a view to make the thing more colloquial and easy and less of *hard work*. You above all other persons I should wish to consult, for you know the cordial admiration I have of the manner in which you have directed previous affairs, looking upon you as I do, as the father and founder of the Association, and the mainspring of all our past meetings. Do therefore, my dear Sir, be persuaded to favour us with a visit of a day or so and let us benefit by your advice and direction. Even the choice of apartments (of which we have no want) is a difficult one and perhaps better to be decided on by a stranger than a native.

For the affairs of the Association or anything else except professorial business I have had little time to spare; but am now approaching the close of an anxious and laborious session; though by the kindness of a good providence, less anxious and laborious than I had expected. And I have reaped the best reward of my exertions in finding that they have given satisfaction and that I have found pupils zealous and anxious to second my endeavours towards a higher standard of education than has hitherto been attempted. Pardon this digression about myself, and pray accede to our wishes.

Forbes Papers, 1834/7

149   *Harcourt, Wheldrake near York, to Forbes, Edinburgh, 25 April 1834*

Not being aware that Mr Robison was on the point of quitting Edinburgh I wrote to him yesterday to propose coming to him on Wednesday next. This morning I have a letter from him in which he says that he shall set off for the continent in a few days, and that you are also going, but that it is probable you will both return by the beginning of June. Unless therefore these plans should be in any way interrupted I shall defer my visit till that time. Meanwhile if you will pay us a visit here instead, on your road south, we shall be most happy to see you. I shall endeavour to persuade you not to tie us down in September to *unremitting* ordinary dinners, and not to alter the practice of meeting *daily in general session*. I wish also to suggest, in the reprint of the *auroral instructions to observers* in our *Report*, that it should be recommended to make *direct* experiments on the *electricity* of the atmosphere as connected with this phenomenon. I am not aware that such experiments have as yet been made or proposed, but the present state of our knowledge as to the connection of electrical with magnetical phenomena and the fact of the deflection of the needle during the aurora appear to me to call for observations of this kind; let me know what you think of this and whether you could not establish at Edinburgh an apparatus for observing atmospherical electricity, and apply it on these occurrences to detecting electrical currents to which the magnetical deflections may be attributed; and whether you would not add some direction to this effect to the auroral instructions.

[PS]   The mail from Edinburgh gets into York in the morning after our letters leave it, we are therefore liable not to receive letters from thence till the following morning. Pray tell Mr Robison, if he has not yet left you, that if I do not hear from him to the contrary I shall consider my engagement to him as standing for the early part of June, and repeat to him how glad we shall be to see him here and to have the honour of a visit from Mrs Robison if she accompanies him south.

Forbes Papers, 1834/9

150   *Airy, Observatory, Cambridge, to Harcourt, Wheldrake near York, 28 April 1834*

Nothing was mentioned to me by Mr Phillips about making observations on the electric state of the atmosphere, and it did not then occur to me (foolishly enough) that such a thing would be desirable, though now that you have mentioned it I quite assent to the importance of such observations in conjunction with aurora observations and perhaps many others, as far as I know anything on the subject.

Now my acquaintance with this subject is a very general one, as I never made any experiment on the electricity of the air. Would you have the kindness (at your leisure) to let me know what is the kind of apparatus required and how troublesome the observation would be? I can then give a tolerably definite answer as to the possibility of observing here: meantime I will answer generally that if the observation were troublesome I could not undertake it in any way; if easy, I could perhaps myself undertake for *occasional* observation (though my time is very much occupied), or I could undertake that an assistant should make *regular* observations *if a fee were paid him:* my assistants are so ill paid that I could not undertake it without. I wish that at Edinburgh instead of making an observatory for meridional instruments they had made a meteorological observatory: for I am sure that it would have been more useful.

Harcourt MSS

151   *Forbes, Edinburgh, to Harcourt, Wheldrake near York, 29 April 1834*

Many thanks for your kind letter. I regret excessively that your visit has been so long postponed that Mr Robison's departure prevents your being with us tomorrow as you intended. I consider it of great consequence that *you* and *he* and *I* should have a meeting as soon as may be. If you were to be in London within a fortnight or so (which I hope is not quite beyond possibility) we should be all there as well as Phillips and Murchison whom we would wish to consult. My time has been so much taken up that I have been able to think of the matter but by snatches. In *general* my principle is to deviate as little as possible from past practice, in which I am sorry to say Mr Robison and I do not wholly agree, as he not having been at the last meetings is full of views of his own, which I do not feel myself quite entitled to oppose definitely without being supported by you and others who I am sure will agree with me. It is therefore of the utmost consequence in order that things may go on smoothly that we should come to some understanding with your assistance. The only innovation I am anxious for is the diminution of the general public meetings, which I hold to be dull and useless, but I beg distinctly to explain to you that I have steadily set my face against an edict which Mr Robison wanted to promulgate against private dinners; in fact I prevented this from being done.

I do not think there is *any* one capable of giving such good advice as you on the subject generally, and you will always find me anxious to promote what you think best. Do, my dear Sir, try to meet us in London. I leave this on Saturday and *do not intend being back till July*. I had made all my arrangements for going by steam which prevent me *for the present* from accepting your kind invitation to Wheldrake. I am sure however that unless Mr Robison had accompanied me we should not have made much progress towards a final understanding of the mode of proceeding.

About the aurora; common electrical observations are so exceedingly vague and unsatisfactory that I should not attach much importance to them. In fact we must view the needle *simply as an indicator of electricity*, and as *by far the best*. It has occurred to me however that some sort of electromagnetic apparatus might be employed to measure the effect. However I had much rather have good magnetic observations than (so called) electric ones. The imperfection of magnetic instruments and their enormous price are however discouraging, but I hope some day to see them carried on here.

Pray write to me as soon as you can to the *Athenaeum Club, London;*

Forbes Papers, Letter book II, 162–4

152   *Robinson, Armagh Observatory, to Harcourt, York, 28 July 1834*

As the founder of the British Association, you will I hope excuse the liberty which I take in writing to you and requesting you to consider the propriety of having Dublin as the place of meeting for next year.

Notwithstanding what was said last year of the necessity of conciliating the manufacturing class to our objects, and of the danger of connecting ourselves with universities, I submit that on the simple ground of superior accommodation Dublin should be preferred to any of the English towns which are likely to come forward. Trinity College, Dublin, authorizes us to offer its resources which afford facilities for the sectional meetings surpassing (I think) even those of Cambridge. It has four fine lecture rooms of which that of the professor of natural philosophy is richly furnished with apparatus, especially optical; and the chemical is attached to a good laboratory, while the University Library is at hand in case of any reference to books. *Across the street*, in the house of the Royal Irish Academy (which joins Trinity College, Dublin, in our invitation) are two large rooms, one already arranged as a lecture room; the other a library, which can be adapted to the same purpose, and at ¼ mile distant is the magnificent theatre of the Royal Dublin Society. The lecture room of the Geological Society also is offered. For the general meetings, the Examination Hall of Trinity College, though not equal to the Senate House at Cambridge, will accommodate about 700 persons, but if it be too small, there is a public room in Sackville Street which we will procure.

I need, I suppose, scarcely add that there is not the slightest cause for apprehension on the part of any member of the British Association from the disturbed state of Ireland. *That* threatens *us* only; *you* will be perfectly safe and treated with kindness even in its wildest parts, and in the metropolis there is as little chance of any annoyance as in London itself. But on the other hand, if there be a spot in the British dominions where an impulse to the cultivation of science is peculiarly wanted, it is here, and I know of no ground where the presence of our Association would produce a more abundant harvest. At present our scientific bodies are in a state of asphyxia; you I hope will be their *Humane Society*.

Harcourt MSS

153 *Hamilton, Observatory, Dublin, to Harcourt, Wheldrake near York, 30 July 1834*

You may remember that at a Cambridge breakfast you conversed with me on the subject of the Association visiting Dublin, and seemed even inclined to support the proposal if such had been made that they should do so in the present year.

I therefore trust that you will not be displeased to hear (what has perhaps already reached you) that all the scientific bodies of Dublin have resolved to request the Association to visit this city in 1835 and hope that you will support this request in the General Committee at Edinburgh.

Harcourt MSS

154 *Forbes, Greenhill, Edinburgh, to Harcourt, York, 8 August 1834*

I hope that you are now beginning to think of turning your steps northwards. I write to beg you to make this house your own during your stay, the longer the more agreeable. Though a little out of town I think we shall prevent it from being at all inconvenient and the College is very accessible. I had a letter from Whewell yesterday who is on his way north and who I hope will be also with me, Dr

Chalmers being most unfortunately too unwell to join the meeting. Whewell says he had written to Oersted and Quetelet at your desire. Dr Lloyd of Dublin has already arrived. I do not write more because I hope you will very soon join me.

Forbes Papers, Letter book II, 173

Thomas Chalmers (1780-1847), *DNB*, Presbyterian minister. Dr Lloyd was Humphrey Lloyd. Greenhill House was on the south side of Bruntsfield Links, Edinburgh.

155   *Harcourt, n.p., to De La Rive, n.d. [August 1834]*

I entertain a hope that the approaching meeting of the British Association for the Advancement of Science at Edinburgh the beginning of next month will afford me an opportunity of renewing the acquaintance which I had the pleasure of making with you here some years ago.

At that meeting it will be proposed to add to our body, as foreign *associates*, a certain number of men of science residing in different parts of Europe; and it is hoped that the being thus attached to us may prove an inducement to them to attend our annual meetings or when such personal attendance may not be convenient to furnish to those meetings some account of any new investigations or remarkable discoveries which may have been made in their own country. I should be much obliged by your informing me whether in case of this plan being executed you would have any objection to your name being placed among the associates. Geneva is one of those places which has always been distinguished for the pursuits of science and there is no person more capable of giving an account of the progress which it is making there than yourself. I am happy to hear that we are likely to receive from M Arago some account of what is going on in France.

Harcourt MSS

Arago and De La Rive attended the meeting at which they were elected corresponding foreign members.

156   *Robison, n.p., to Phillips, Museum, York, 22 August 1834*

My only reason for not sooner replying to your letter of the 11th was my desire to be able to communicate particulars of your billet while among us. You some time ago stipulated for a romantic view, so I wished as far as possible to fit you well; I think I have now done so, as I have got an invitation for you from Mr Cowan an eminent paper maker who occupies Moray House in the Canongate and takes great pleasure in keeping up every thing as nearly as possible in the state it was in when Mary and her brother rendered this house and its romantically situated gardens the scenes of many important transactions. You will not be without interesting associations of a more modern nature here, as the scenes of Hutton and Playfair's labours are spread out before the windows of the house, and the path of the Lelly of St Leonards and the track of the Laird of Dumbie dykes form the foreground of the picture. Mr Cowan has left me a note of invitation (addressed to you) for yourself and Miss Phillips, and he has offered 2 more bedrooms, so that you may be able to make up an agreeable coachful for going home together after the evening meetings. I shall not let billets be given for these rooms in order that you may arrange your own partie carrée.

On your arrival here I should recommend your going first to Mackenzie's Hotel in Castle Street which though not a house of the first fashion, is a most comfortable & reasonable one. I shall then have an opportunity of introducing you to Mr Cowan before you go to his house.

I am very anxious to impress an agreeable character on the ordinaries by discouraging the forming of private dinner parties, which would have the effect of robbing the assembly of the most eminent ornaments, and making the ordinaries appear the refuge of the neglected. I preach to my friends that they ought to exhibit their hospitality by giving Scotch breakfasts to all on whom they can lay their hands; and in pursuance of this doctrine, I mean to attend the ordinary daily, and to accept and offer no dinners; but I shall expect that such of my friends as approve of my views, will give me marks of their approbation by congregating round the breakfast table daily at 9 o'clock. I shall count on you and Miss Phillips whether you like my plan or not, because I know you have a certain weak side towards good coffee, by means of which I hope to seduce you to my party. Will you have the goodness to promulgate this to my kind friends at York, and to say that I shall be proud to have their support on these occasions?

I am happy to say that notwithstanding all the gloomy reports, my friend Monsieur Arago is not going to fail me. He and Mr Pentland were to leave Paris together yesterday for London; they will spend some time on the road, and will be here from the 3rd to the 6th of September and remain to the end of the week of the meeting.

[PS] The Craigleith Quarry is I am told likely to prove a great bore. The person who is working it, is preparing a shot of 60 feet deep, which will require some barrels of gunpowder to fill it; and, as Mr Cubitt calculates, will throw down 20,000 tons of rock in one huge heap of ruins. This will beat the Cambridge fireworks hollow, and there will be no Provost Thackeray to segregate the spectators who I trust may not meet the fate of St Stephen.

I am inundated with offers of absurd communications. One man proposes (if the Association will pay him for it) to prove that the moon has no gravity, and that its shape is that of a large round boat, floating on a vortex of vapour!

Phillips Papers, 1834/16

Mary Queen of Scots (1542-87), *DNB*; her half-brother was Lord James Stewart, Earl of Moray (1531-70), *DNB*. James Hutton (1726-97), *DNB*, the geologist, was interested in the crags of Holyrood Park, which are visible from Canongate, the lower portion of the Royal Mile. The path and the track feature in Scott's novel, *The heart of Midlothian*. William Cubitt (1785-1861), *DNB*, civil engineer; Joseph Barclay Pentland (1797-1873), *DNB*, traveller and explorer. At the 1833 meeting of the Association at Cambridge, George Thackeray, Provost of King's College, refused to allow the gates to be fully opened so that members of the Association might witness a fireworks display in the College grounds.

157   *Robison, Royal Society, Edinburgh, to Phillips, Museum, York, 5 October 1834*

I have received your parcel and am glad to learn that you are gradually getting rid of the effects of the Association fever. The excitement and over-exertion incident to the present mode of proceeding in the meetings of our overgrown body, are evils which loudly call for remedy. It is now obvious that laws and arrangements which were very suitable to such meetings as were originally contemplated, are no longer appropriate in the present circumstances of the Association, and that something must be devised to relieve the pressure arising from the simultaneous rush for tickets on the first day of meeting, and also to diminish the rapidity and to give some interruption to the unceasing flow of the stream of business during the period of the meeting.

It appears to me that, as the greatest pressure for admission will always arise from the residents at the place of meeting, great relief may be obtained from it by transferring the power of admission from the General Committee to the Local Council and office bearers of the Association. Two advantages would result from this: the admission of resident members might be begun and completed, before the arrival of the real effective supporters of the institution; and time would be given for due discrimination in the admissions. At present a list of candidates is formed in a hurried manner, so that it is impossible to ascertain even the personal identity of the applicants; the list is then presented to the General Committee who know nothing of the merits of the candidates, and are besides too busy to be able to attend to such matters. At all events time is lost, and when the list is passed, the tickets have to be prepared and issued to persons who are impatient at losing their right of entry for a moment.

The scrambling for ladies tickets is likewise a serious cause of difficulty and confusion. It is plain from what occurred here, that many persons applied for admission with no other view than to obtain a cheap week's amusement for the females of the family. It is impossible to issue ladies tickets to every member, and it is impracticable to draw any line of selection which will not cause dissatisfaction to those who are left out. I should therefore be inclined to suggest that no ladies tickets should be given excepting to permanent members who have compounded for their fees. Many persons will then compound who would otherwise have been mere intruders for a season, and no one will be able to boast that they and their female friends have eaten more in refreshments than the price of their ticket would have purchased. The Local Council might be allowed the privilege of issuing ladies tickets to members who may subscribe a certain amount to a local fund for refreshments. With such checks as these the influx of ladies would not occasion either embarrassment or discontent, and the company would be more select, than I regret to say it was here.

The exertion of both body and mind which is required to sustain the state of permanent activity during 12 hours per diem throughout a whole week, is too great even for those who float on the surface, and to all the office bearers and others who take part in the duties is overwhelming; and judging from the effect on myself, I would say paralysing. The great accession of business which has arisen from the extension of the numbers and influence of the Association, seems to demand a corresponding extension of time to transact it in. It would therefore appear nearly indispensable that a greater number of days should be devoted to the sectional meetings. The same necessity does not however exist in respect to the evening meetings, which may even be reduced to three with advantage, as this would allow of some repose to those who wished for it, and would admit of the strangers enjoying something more of *private evening society* than has hitherto been possible. I think this sort of relaxation would be very generally relished, and it would tend to promote a more intimate union between the strangers and the resident members than has yet obtained in the hurried public intercourse of the 5 or 6 days' meetings.

If my suggestions appear to you worthy of attention, I hope you will found a new scheme of regulations for the consideration of the central Council, and that you will endeavour to have a plan adopted in sufficient time to admit of the Dublin office bearers becoming fully acquainted with it before they require to give their notices or begin their preparations.

I have had a long letter from Mr W.C. Taylor, the sub-editor of *The Athenaeum*, on the subject of reporting the proceedings of the meetings. He seems to take a very fair view of the case and to be aware of the impossibility of the secretaries doing anything to assist him *during the time of the meeting*. I have recommended him to confer with you in London on the measures to be taken previously to the next opening, in order to give all practicable facilities to the preparation of a fair account of the proceedings.

I have thrown [this] together in a very desultory way, but I fear that if I defer [sending] it off as it is, I may not again find a quiet hour while the matter is fresh in my mind. I trust therefore to you to extract the grain from the chaff and to sow it where it may fecundate.

I am glad to learn that my much esteemed friend Mr Taylor is better again. I can hardly say that I regret his absence from this, for it would have been very tantalising to have had him here a second time and to have been unable to profit by his presence. I feel as if I had been defrauded of my expected pleasure in seeing many friends who were actually here, but with whom I never exchanged words. Present if you please my kind regards to Miss Phillips.

[PS]   Is there any chance of your being able to give a short course of lectures here during the winter? You can hardly doubt now of the success which would attend your doing so.

Phillips Papers, 1834/21

William Cooke Taylor (1800–49), *DNB*, ensured that *The Athenaeum journal of literature, science, and the fine arts* gave copious accounts of the Association's meetings. Robison's friend was William Taylor of York. Robison's plan for ladies' tickets was implemented in 1835, but not his proposal for lengthening the meetings.

158   *Harcourt, Bishopthorpe near York, to Lubbock, 13 November 1834*

I have been much occupied lately or I should sooner have written an explanation of the grant of the British Association for the tides. The grant was for the *discussion* of observations and it was made by a special resolution payable by the Treasurer to *you* or *your* order. These were resolutions of the General Committee and leave I think nothing for the Council to determine on those points. Respecting the publication of the results the Council which meets next week will decide; but I have no doubt they will allow them to be offered to the Royal Society, expecting however from you for their own transactions a general account of what you have done.

Your name was placed upon a committee, as Mr Phillips has informed you, of which the object is to induce the government to establish a magnetical and meteorological observatory. I have a hope that this may be accomplished and made independent of the astronomical Observatory. Let me beg you, if you have not already had a meeting, to see Mr Baily, who is also of the committee, on the subject.

Lubbock Papers, H57

The Association's committee established in 1834 to lobby government for a magnetic observatory, separate from the Royal Observatory, Greenwich, was unsuccessful.

159 *Leonard Jenyns, Swaffham Bulbeck, Newmarket, to Harcourt, Bishopthorpe near York, 20 December 1834*

I beg to acknowledge your letter and to thank you for the kind manner in which you have noticed my report. I shall not regret the labour which it has cost me, if it gives satisfaction to the members of the Association, but I have been deeply impressed with the arduous nature of the task which had been put upon me, and it is not without great distrust of my own powers that I now offer to the public the result of my endeavours to complete it. I am glad to think that you approve of the general tone in which it is drawn up; as it has been a great object with me throughout to avoid that severe and prejudiced criticism, which as well as yourself I have noticed with much pain in many recent works of our countrymen on zoology, mixed up as it has often been with angry feeling and uncharitable censure.

My principal object however in troubling you with this letter is to reply to some remarks which you have made on one or two parts of it, and which it would be great disrespect on my part if I were not to notice. And 1st, as to Linnaeus I am sorry you should think (for others perhaps will think the same) that I have any wish to depreciate his merits as a zoologist, or to undervalue what he did in his day towards the advancement of the science. So far from it, I consider that we are under great obligations to him; and to see this it is only necessary to compare his works with the crude and ill digested compilations of the older authors (Ray and Willughby cepted). His *System Natura* was on the *whole* a great step and far beyond any attempt which had been before made to arrange animals systematically and in conformity with some general principles.

His arrangement of the *invertebrata* was certainly far from natural, but that of the *vertebrata* has decidedly been the groundwork, whereon those have built who have appeared since; that it was not more perfect was not the fault of himself, but must be attributed to the *comparatively* little progress which had up to that time been made in the knowledge of animals, and of their true structure. If you ask, why I have not stated as much as this in my report, I have only to answer that it refers to a period of time anterior to that at which I take up the subject, and in consequence I hardly felt called on to say much of Linnaeus, or to point out his real merits with any particularity. The little allusion which *is* made to his system, was simply an introductory step to the speaking of those reforms which were effected by Cuvier and others towards the end of the last century. If I appear afterward to have treated it harshly, in reference to those who for so long afterwards adopted it as their sole guide, it was not from any blindness to its just value and utility when it appeared, but from a sense of its utter insufficiency to meet the wants of the science at the present day, and from a wish to show the error of those naturalists who would let things remain just where Linnaeus left them, without a single effort to carry on that improvement which no man was more alive to than Linnaeus himself, as will be seen from an examination of his *twelve* successive editions of the *Systema Natura.*

With respect to your 2nd remark, as to the natural system being the true object of zoology, I think if this appears to you as too restricted a view of the subject, it may arise (but I beg to state it with great deference) from your not having a sufficiently enlarged idea of what is meant by *the* natural system (of which there *can* be but *one*) as contradistinguished from all artificial systems. The latter, being founded on some arbitrarily assumed principles without any reference to the *value* of organs or the true subordination of characters, may serve very conveniently as a kind of dictionary in which you may learn the name of any animal, but without getting any thing further in its history. The *natural system* is the plan of the creation itself in which, supposing we had attained to it, we should see every animal placed according to its *true affinities*; these affinities being deduced, *not* from a comparative view of any one isolated organ which we may choose to take up as a principle of arrangement, but from that of its structure as a *whole*, and its manner of life as dependent upon its structure. Consequently, knowing the place occupied by any animal in such a system would be in fact the key to its whole history. It is clear that this system (it seems to me nearly the same thing whether you call it *the natural system* or the *system of nature*) is more the *beau idéal* of the science, to which all our efforts tend, than what we have attained or are ever likely to attain *in toto*; but enough has been discovered of it to render it extremely probable that it is established upon (i.e. the order of affinities follows) some general laws, with respect to one of which we have already more than a glimpse; I speak of *circular groups*. It is also clear that the advancement of our knowledge respecting this system, depends upon our thorough acquaintance with the entire organization of animals, as well as their habits, economy etc, so that it involves every other consideration, which cannot be said of any artificial system, and which, last, it would be miserably mistaking the true end of the science to put up as the leading object of zoology. I do not know whether you may be able to refer to Cuvier's *Règne Animal*, or I would direct you to his introduction (p. 8 etc) to that work, in which you will find *his* views on the subject, I think, much in accordance with what I have stated. He concludes with saying 'la méthode naturelle (supposing we had attained to it) *serait toute la science*, et chaque pas qu' on lui fait faire *approche la science de son but*'.

Sincerely hoping that I have not *bored* you with these details, into which I have been rather unconsciously drawn

Harcourt MSS

Leonard Jenyns (1800–93), *DNB*, vicar of Swaffham Bulbeck, wrote 'Report on the recent progress and present state of zoology', *1834 Report*, 143–251, of which 248–51 compared continental European and British zoology. Carl Linnaeus (1707–78), *DSB*, the famous Swedish botanist and taxonomist; John Ray (1627–1705) and Francis Willughby (1635–72), both *DNB*. Until the 1860s advocates of the natural system of taxonomy classified living things on the basis of organs or organ systems deemed to be of fundamental physiological importance, whereas artificial systems reflected the arbitrariness of human concerns and convenience. The obscure theory of circular groups, i.e. that all natural groups of animals return into themselves forming circles, was promulgated chiefly by William Sharp MacLeay (1792–1865), *DNB*. For Cuvier's views on the natural method see his *Le Règne animal distribué d'après son organisation* ... (Paris, 1817), i. 12.

160 *Harcourt, Bishopthorpe near York, to Forbes, Edinburgh, 15 January 1835*

I hear from Phillips that you make a point of our publishing *all* that you said of me in your preliminary discourse at our late meeting. I claim no right as an editor to modify your expressions but as a friend I beg the omission at least of one passage which is, you will see, superfluous and which may be misunderstood as I misunderstood myself at first reading. The passage I mean is 'the much more signal merit of bringing that idea to bear'. The comparison is in fact between the merit of originating the idea and the carrying it into execution, but my first impression was that a comparison was intended between the merit of Sir D. Brewster's idea and mine, and it might happen that he or others on a hasty perusal might fall into the same mistake and take some offence at the expression which with your leave therefore I will omit.

One of the grants of money at Edinburgh was that of £100 to a committee for magnetism and meteorology. Will you undertake to be secretary to that committee and draw up a plan of operations and recommend methods of expenditure? If you go to London in the spring you might call the committee together to discuss your project, or communicate with them by letter.

I have corresponded with Mr Baily about the application to government respecting national magnetic observations and ventured to recommend the asking for a distinct magnetical observatory near London and a salaried observer independent of the Greenwich establishment. The committee met but agreed to wait till some government was established. The new Premier will appreciate better the claims of science than his predecessors, if he can but stand, and I should be sanguine as to the success of this request. Your Aberdeen Provost etc have denied their scale till it is safe to send it by water!! I have written to them to urge a speedier loan of it; but have not as yet received any answer.

PS   Have you or has Brewster any interest at Aberdeen? I think you might officially second my request to the magistrates and convince them that their scale would travel well enough by land, by coach for instance if a person were charged with the care of it. It will be too late if not sent immediately as I have told them on Baily's authority.

Forbes Papers, 1835/2

In his *Address to the British Association for the Advancement of Science ... at Edinburgh, 8th Sept 1834* (Edinburgh, 1834), 6, Forbes had praised Harcourt, not Brewster, for being the establisher of the Association. As editor of the *1834 Report*, Harcourt felt uneasy about reproducing Forbes' address in full. The new Prime Minister was Peel. Baily's 'Report on the comparative measurement of the Aberdeen standard and scale', *1835 Report*, 91–2, was an early example of the Association's continuing preoccupation with standards and units.

161   *Forbes, Edinburgh, to Harcourt, Bishopthorpe near York, 18 January 1835*

It would be quite impossible to refuse acceding to your wish were it much more unreasonable. You will admit that correctly speaking, the true sense of the passage was distinctly expressed, but it is best to avoid even the *appearance* of evil, and such a comparison as you allude to, it would have been equally invidious and unbecoming in me to make. I therefore request you to *omit* the words 'much more signal'. Any corrections or alterations or omissions in *any other passage* of the thing I beg you to make without consulting me. *If you prefer it* in p. 6 say simply 'suggested by Sir D. Brewster'.

I hope Phillips told you that I also wrote to say that I had no wish about the address except the benefit of the Association; and I wish to repeat most distinctly, and *without any reservation*, that I shall not feel in the least degree mortified by its omission on any account, and I think if you have any doubt of the value of *continuing* the practice ad infinitum you had better take advantage of a willing scapegoat. I beg you to think seriously of this. If you feel decidedly for the *continued* practice I can send a corrected copy to Taylor to whom I am sending at any rate.

It would be impossible for me to take much trouble at present about the meteorological committee; but when I go to London (about May) I should be very happy to be of use. I have in fact been already over-worked with a paper on the polarisation of heat I am just bringing out which seems to me important. My professional duties will fully occupy me for some time.

I saw your sister's marriage mentioned in the newspaper; I wish her all happiness.

Did Phillips see the magnificent aurora of the 22nd December?

Harcourt MSS

In the *1834 Report*, p. xiv, Harcourt expunged from Forbes' address the embarrassing phrases and names, simply noting that Forbes had described the share which some of the Association's founders had taken in planning and conducting it. Forbes' research 'On the refraction and polarisation of heat', *Transactions of the Royal Society of Edinburgh*, 1836, xiii. 131–68, gained for him the Rumford medal of the Royal Society of London and the Keith Prize of the Royal Society of Edinburgh. No sister of Harcourt had just married at this time.

162   *Forbes, Edinburgh, to Harcourt, Bishopthorpe near York, 3 February 1835.*

As I fear you cannot remain in ignorance of the article on the Association in the *Edinburgh Review*, it will at least, I am persuaded, give you the same satisfaction as it affords me to show you that my views respecting the share of the utility and precise extent of your exertions in the foundation of the Association were once those of Sir D. Brewster himself. In an article on the Association in his *Journal*, written by me at his desire and published by his sanction, I used as explicitly as possible the terms I did the other day: 'Mr Vernon Harcourt the real originator of the *permanent* (printed in *italics*) Association', Brewster's *Journal*, 1832, vol. vi, p. 364. In fact it was a matter so notorious between us that neither then nor since did I dream of offending him by stating it. My authority perhaps you are not fully aware of, viz. your admirable letters to Sir D. himself before the York meeting and in regard to which we united in wondering at and applauding. It was just because Sir D., yourself and I are perhaps the only three individuals who know the whole history that I have always stated the fact broadly, which I shall never repent of, nor retract. Thus you see that the Edinburgh reviewer is at least put completely in the wrong.

[PS omitted]

Harcourt MSS (Harcourt Papers, *xiii. 342-3*)

Brewster, 'The British Scientific Association', *Edinburgh review*, 1835, lx. 363-93 (371-4, 390-1) asserted that he, not Harcourt, was the founder of the Association. For Forbes' view, 'First Report of the British Association for the Advancement of Science', *Edinburgh journal of science*, 1832, vi. 360-75 (364).

163 *Humphrey Lloyd, Trinity College, Dublin, to Harcourt, 8 February 1835*

The day after I received your letter I sent a portion of my report to Mr Phillips and believing that he would communicate the circumstance to you, I thought it unnecessary to send a formal reply to your letter. I send this day a large portion of this long delayed paper, and will forward the remainder in the course of a fortnight at farthest. Had I been aware at the outset of its probable length, or of the labour and time which it would require I should certainly have attempted only to prepare *one part* for the present volume but such an arrangement became impossible from the accident of my *commencing with the second*. Its length has arisen unavoidably from the line which I selected (which was to compare the *explaining powers* of the two theories of light) and which of course compelled me to enter into detail. The line might perhaps have been better chosen, but this I hope will be *useful* and I think it will be found tolerably complete.

We have made considerable advances in our arrangements here with reference to the approaching meeting. Having organized a local Council (which is now composed of the local officers, the provisional secretaries of sections, and a few other members who attended the last meeting) we have entered into correspondence with the different public institutions in Dublin which have shown an interest in the matter, have fixed upon our places of meeting, taken steps to make the objects of the Association more generally known here, and to admit the Irish members at once, and receive and forward recommendations of persons not privileged, and lastly set on foot other arrangements more purely local such as a subscription fund, etc.

We have chosen as the place of the *general meetings* our large public room (we call it the Rotunda), a circular room 80 feet in diameter and which will contain 1500 persons. Immediately adjoining is another fine room, which will accommodate about half that number. We intend to fix our *ordinary* there, and I believe that 300 may dine there. With respect to the *section rooms* we are not so well provided as Edinburgh, for you are aware that our University is modelled on the plan of the English universities and is therefore not so complete in its professorial establishment as the Scotch colleges. We shall therefore be compelled to *scatter* a little and place 3 of the sections in the [Trinity] *College*, 2 in the *Royal Dublin Society*, and one in the *Royal Irish Academy*. These places are however not more widely distant than the section rooms at Cambridge; and we shall endeavour to obviate as much as possible the inconvenience, by placarding at an early hour each morning the bill of fare of each section in the place of *general rendezvous*, which will be the Hall or Theatre of the University. We shall also have a sketch of the *sectional district* on the back of the tickets to furnish the requisite geographical knowledge.

When the proper time for making such a communication shall arrive, we mean to propose through you to the central Council that we should be allowed what schoolboys term a *half holiday* on *Wednesday* (the evening of *Saturday* I believe the Association does not claim) and on *these two evenings* it is proposed that the members should assemble merely for the purposes of acquaintanceship. There are public gardens, adjoining the public rooms, which may be made available on these evenings.

I may add that the public bodies in this city have taken up the matter in a very cordial spirit, and that we have every reason to hope for the success of the Dublin meeting.

Harcourt MSS

Lloyd's 'Report on the progress and present state of physical optics', *1834 Report*, 295–415, helped to consolidate the position of the wave theory of light at the expense of the particle theory.

164 *Harcourt, Bishopthorpe near York, to Forbes, Edinburgh, 13 February 1835*

Who could believe that a man of any mind or character would of a sudden sit down to depreciate or condemn all the proceedings in which he has concurred and cooperated in his capacities of Vice-president, reporter etc for the last three years; nevertheless the breaking out again of the old Cambridge grudge and the malice against yourself I fear indicate but too plainly the mint from which the unworthy review proceeds. I am very sorry for it both on account of the author, for whom I entertained sincere feelings of respect and friendship and on account of the mischief which I fear he may do to the Association. I have never claimed the paternity of it; but on the principle of Solomon's judgement he who does would after this scarcely have his claim allowed.

The less notice anyone takes of this review I am persuaded the better for the interests of the Association as far as regards the personal part of it, though it may be our duty to vindicate the principles we have adopted and the practice we have followed in the management of its affairs. The personal question must not be brought forward at all events in our transactions; and therefore we must omit the paragraphs in your address that relate to it, not omitting however the statement of the improvement which we conceive we have made on the German system. I propose to insert a note respecting the omitted part to the following effect: 'Professor Forbes here introduced a statement of the share which some of the founders of the Association had respectively taken in designing and executing the plan on which it has been conducted'. Under the present circumstances it is plainly improper for me and might be injurious to the Association to edit the controverted statement or to admit anything which might give rise to further personal dispute.

Forbes Papers, 1835/3

165   *Forbes, Edinburgh, to Harcourt, Bishopthorpe near York, 22 February 1835.*

As I have already told you I have no concern whatever about my *address* except as concerns the Association. I *now* think however that for the sake of the Association it should be printed, containing as I think it does, a fair and candid statement which the *Edinburgh* has been quite unable to answer. With regard to THE passage, my only doubt is whether it would not be stooping too far to take it out; on the whole perhaps I would rather have it left, but you have my full consent to do what you please, or rather what you think best for the common cause: provided that it is not *smuggled* out, but some such note put to the passage as you proposed. On the whole, however, looking purely to the character of the Association, I believe it might fully better be left as it stands. The review I fully believe can do no harm. I have heard nothing but absolute disapprobation of it.

I suppose my poor friend the author, for whom I feel most sincerely vexed (infinitely more so than either for the Association or myself), will hardly appear at Dublin; and from a letter which reached me the same day with yours, from Cambridge, you may readily believe that he had better not appear *there*.

I hope the *Report* will soon be out. I trust you will not wait for trifling communications or abstracts, the *onus* of omission of which must lie with the authors not the society.

My present intention is to go to London by York in the end of April: so that I shall have a chance of seeing you in one or other place. I have some doubt whether I shall be at Dublin, as I meditate an excursion with Arago to the south of France.

[PS]   May I write to you under the Archbishop's cover?

Harcourt MSS

Neither Forbes nor Brewster attended the 1835 meeting.

166   *Hamilton, n.p., to Whewell, Cambridge, 6 April 1835*

I have just been saying to Mr Peacock that I trust you and many others from Cambridge will attend the Dublin meeting; as to you, we can't do without you.

Did you read the article in the *Edinburgh [Review]*? By Brewster? Hard knocks at all of us discussers and debaters. Sly hope that there will be no new influx of eloquence in Dublin!

But seriously, much thought ought to be given, and I have given scarce any, as to the proper future functions of so vast a body which seems to be in some danger of being crushed under its own weight, like Herschel's Man in the Sun. Should there be no falling off in Dublin, as I have yet no fear that there will, can we hope that in Bristol or Liverpool the present plan will continue to work well? And even if there be no falling asunder, nor outbreak of the 'fierce democracy' (I only mean if the huge mass of members shall continue contented with their comparative obscurity, while a few persons necessarily occupy the chief attention and control of the meeting) yet ought we not, as lovers of wisdom and of our country, to consider carefully to what end or under what guiding idea so great a power may be best wielded; keeping of course our fundamental laws inviolate, and remembering gratefully that even if the Association were to be dissolved tomorrow, it would still have already accomplished great ends by its brilliant and delightful meetings at Cambridge and other places. I speak to stir up your mind, not as having formed any definite conception much less any plan in my own. Indeed, I have not been so busy as I ought in my post as [Local] Secretary, but in my various conferences with Professor Lloyd upon the subject of arrangements, I have found him always so clear and practical that I had nothing to do but assent to what he had already conceived. Our local Council meets every three weeks, and we think we are getting on well.

[PS omitted]

Whewell Papers, a. 205[107]

167   *Murchison, 3 Bryanston Place, London, to Peel, 6 April 1835*

As a Trustee of the British Association for the Advancement of Science, I am desired by the Council of that body to request you will honor a deputation with an interview on the subject of the Ordnance Survey.

Feeling how seriously the progress of various branches of science has been checked by the want of this Survey in the central and northern parts of England and in Scotland, I moved a resolution at the general meeting of the British Association in September last, which was warmly approved of by all the noblemen and gentlemen then present, and it was unanimously resolved that an application should be made to His Majesty's government to endeavour to procure an additional grant of money for this neglected department of the public service. I am aware, Sir, that it is unnecessary to point out to a person of your acquirements the numberless instances in which the want of such a survey must be severely felt, particularly in all the commercial and manufacturing districts, whether they contain mines or are destined to be traversed by rail-roads and canals: but I would humbly venture to call your attention to this point, that although all the leading trigonometrical data were fixed many years ago, and complete materials prepared for the publication of maps of large tracts in the south of Scotland, the Survey at *its present* rate of progress will not reach the banks of the Forth in the life time of the present generation.

I may add that many men of influence and of all political parties cordially unite in supporting this application, and I cannot but entertain the hope that if an enlightened minister who has already proved himself so kind and judicious a patron of science, should express sentiments favourable to this project, that a British parliament would gladly accord a sum to restore the Survey to *its original* position, and thus place its prosecution upon the same standard of advancement which it has attained in other European countries.

BL, Add. MSS 40419, ff. 150–1

This letter was overtaken by Peel's resignation as Prime Minister on 8 April 1835. By

1840 the Association had successfully lobbied government to accelerate the Ordnance Survey of England and to resume that of Scotland.

168   *Humphrey Lloyd, Trinity College, Dublin, to Harcourt, 30 May 1835*

I am directed by the Dublin Council of the British Association to communicate to you its views with reference to the conduct of the approaching meeting, and to request that you will submit them to the central Council for its consideration.

It is recommended by the Local Council that the general meetings of the Association should take place on *four* evenings of the week only, namely, Monday, Tuesday, Thursday and Friday, and that the evenings of *Wednesday* and *Saturday* be dedicated to the purposes of recreation and to the promotion of social intercourse and friendship among the members.

With respect to the management of the evening meetings, it is suggested that the authors of the reports to be brought forward on the present occasion be requested to prepare *popular summaries* of them to be read at the evening meetings. And that *discussions* be then provoked in some of the debated topics which may be signalised by the authors. Members competent to take part in such discussions may be easily put in possession of the nature of these debated questions, through the intervention of the provisional secretaries of sections appointed at Edinburgh.

As to the formal business of announcing the proceedings of the sections, it is thought that it should be limited almost to a mere enumeration of the titles of the papers read, but that a fuller account of such papers be printed from night to night, for morning distribution among the members.

I may add that our public rooms and gardens are well adapted to the purposes suggested for the evenings of Wednesday and Saturday, and that one of these rooms may be devoted to the same purposes on *every evening* of the week by those who prefer recreation to labour and scientific excitement. It is scarcely necessary to say however that, whatever be the plan adopted by the central Council with relation to the evening meetings, we shall cordially unite all our efforts here to make it effective.

Harcourt MSS

By the 1835 meeting a compromise was reached: it allowed most evenings to have a scientific character, while permitting more mixing and recreation.

169   *Humphrey Lloyd, Trinity College, Dublin, to Harcourt, Bishopthorpe near York, 31 May 1835*

Enclosed I send you a letter containing the suggestions of the Local Council here, as to the management of the evening meetings, to be submitted to the central Council as soon as can be conveniently done. The first part of the proposed arrangements (namely to have *holiday* evenings on Wednesday and Saturday, so as to allow the members opportunities of becoming acquainted) was thought of long since; and I mentioned it in a letter to Mr Phillips some time ago, stating at the same time that I would send it to you for the formal consideration of the central Council whenever you thought it expedient.

Within these few days however I received a letter from Mr Phillips containing a collection of the views of several of the influential London members, the principal of which was that there should be *but two general meetings*, both before dinner, and that the *evenings* should be *entirely* given up to recreation and amusement. I immediately called a meeting of our Local Council to enquire whether in consequence of this information they would modify their intended recommendation. They were almost unanimously agreed that an innovation to the extent suggested in Mr Phillips' letter would be dangerous: that the *popular* part of the body would have just cause for complaint if it were thus completely dissociated from all participation in the interest of its proceedings; that the change proposed might have the effect of placing the meeting in a less dignified position in the eyes of the public; and finally that it would probably separate from the Association a considerable and most respectable portion of the *Dublin public*. It must be admitted however that the Association would suffer more from an ill-managed *scientific display* than from the abandonment of all attempts to give a scientific character to the evenings, and it is with the view of meeting the objections against the conduct of the last meeting, that [we] propose to substitute *discussions* for *lectures*. Such discussions would naturally spring out of the many related topics brought before the Association in the reports, and you may remember that a most successful [venture] of the kind arose in Cambridge from the views put forward in Mr Taylor's report on mineral veins. I do not think that the reporters would hesitate to take upon themselves the small additional trouble of preparing a popular account of some of the leading points in their report, and of mentioning beforehand briefly what these topics were, in order that members competent to take a part might be not altogether unprepared. I need not add (what I have said in the enclosed letter) that we will cordially unite to work out any plan which may be adopted by the central Council, but you will perceive that there is no time to be lost in obtaining the final decision of the Council on the subject. I am sure that you will give these things your best consideration and that any modifications you may suggest will be conducive to the interests of the Association.

Harcourt MSS

At the 1833 meeting John Taylor's evening lecture on mineral veins provoked a lively discussion.

170 *Bartholomew Lloyd, Provost's House [Trinity College, Dublin], to Harcourt, 1 June 1835*

Hearing that I might be anticipated by some other Hibernian if I were longer to defer my application, I venture so long before the meeting of the Association in Dublin to request you would do me the favour to stop at my house on that occasion. You will naturally wish to know whom you may expect to meet, and on that subject I can only say that I have written to make the same request of Baron Humboldt but have not as yet received his answer; that whilst in Edinburgh I visited Dr Chalmers who will join us, if permitted by his physicians, and has promised me the pleasure of his company subject to that condition; and that from Mr Whewell I have obtained a direct promise. I hope to be able to provide for the other gentlemen of the universities in the chambers of our fellows, so that if you know of any who are likely to attend, you would greatly oblige by favouring me with their names, together with any other information you may judge to be useful for my direction.

Harcourt MSS

171 *Harcourt, Grosvenor Square, London, to Humboldt, 28 June 1835*

I have been directed by the Council of the British Association for the Advancement of Science to inform you that you have been elected a corresponding member of the Association. This body bears some resemblance to that which of late years has held annual meetings at Berlin, Vienna, Hamburg, etc. It assembles yearly at different towns, having met successively at York, Oxford, Cambridge and Edinburgh, and being now summoned to meet on the tenth day of August next and during the following week at Dublin.

The object of the Association is not only to bring the men of science of our own country together and to concentrate their efforts for the accomplishment of those objects which require combination, but also to cultivate a closer acquaintance with foreign philosophers, and to obtain earlier and more accurate knowledge of the progress of science among our neighbours.

With this view especially it is that it desires to associate to ourselves individuals of scientific eminence in different countries, whom it hopes to induce either to be present at its meetings, and to take a part, as Mess Arago, Quetelet and Moll have done, in the discussions of our sections or when that is impracticable, to be favoured by them, or through their means, with communications relative to any thing particularly deserving of scientific notice which may have occurred from year to year in their respective countries.

Should it be in your power to attend the approaching meeting of the Association at Dublin, no endeavour I am sure will be wanting there to render your visit agreeable and convenient to you.

[PS] If you will inform me by what conveyance I can transmit to you the three volumes of *Reports* which the Association has published, I shall be happy to send them to you.

Harcourt MSS

Humboldt did not attend the 1835 meeting or send a paper.

172 *Humphrey Lloyd, Trinity College, Dublin, to Harcourt, Nuneham Park, Oxford, 30 June 1835*

I received your letter of the 26th instant and am happy that our suggestion as to the evening meetings has met with the approbation of the Council. The evening of Monday (I presume) will be entirely occupied by the new President's taking the chair, and the report of one of the [Local] Secretaries.

Professor Hamilton has undertaken the latter, but as the new volume of the reports will not be in his hands much before the week of the meeting, he will be compelled to confine himself to the general character and prospects of the Association and to the objections which have been urged against it. Dr Lardner has promised to give us a lecture on his favourite subject, locomotion and steam power, on one of the evenings and as he will bring over a large collection of working models and diagrams I feel satisfied of the success of the lecture. The third evening I suppose may be best occupied by a discussion, and as the geologists are the most expert in this line, I think we should leave this in their hands. If you see nothing to object to in this, I will consult Phillips about it immediately. I am sure there will be no difficulty in finding a theme.

As to the vacant evenings, we have space enough under shelter, and gardens adjoining, which we propose to light up if the weather should be favourable. Our reception committee will be prepared to do their duty in introducing foreigners and strangers, and on the whole I have hopes that we may be able to avoid the opposite errors of being either too frivolous or too dull.

We have made our arrangements respecting the ladies so as (I hope) to avoid dissatisfaction. Any who favour us so far as to come across the water will of course be accommodated, and we have limited the number of tickets for those of this side of the channel by a rule of which none can complain.

The meeting promises to be a *very* large one, and the difficulty of making satisfactory arrangements will of course be proportionally great. The University will be able to lodge 30 or 40 within its walls, and has promised to give us a dinner to about 300 (the largest number that our Hall will entertain). I have some hopes that the [Royal] Dublin Society will do something of the same kind, but I very much fear that we have not succeeded in awakening the Dublin people generally to a sense of the importance of the meeting, or of the honour conferred on them.

May I ask you to have the enclosed put in the way of being forwarded to Berzelius? We are here so much separated from all means of communication with the Continent that we are obliged to rest much on the kind assistance of others more central and better known.

Harcourt MSS

173 *Humphrey Lloyd, Trinity College, Dublin, to Harcourt, Nuneham Park, Oxford, 2 July 1835*

I am compelled to trouble you again on the subject of the evening meetings. I have received this morning a letter from Mr Yates, containing the resolutions adopted by the central Council with reference to our proposal. The first two of these are as follow: '1. That the first general meeting of the Association take place on the evening of Monday, August 10th. 2. That there be three other general meetings, viz. on the evenings of Tuesday, Thursday and Friday'.

Can there be any mistake in this? In your letter of the 27th ultimo you mention that the Council agreed to leave the *alternate* evenings open, and you add that *Monday, Wednesday*, and *Friday* evenings will be those of business.

I wish to know how this matter stands, as we are about printing a circular (for distribution here) containing as much detailed information as we can respecting the arrangements.

I have written today to Phillips to say that we hope that he will be with us *at least* a fortnight before the 10th.

Harcourt MSS

174 *Phillips, care of Professor Lloyd, Trinity College, Dublin, to Ann Phillips, Penley Grove Street, York, Saturday [1 August 1835]*

Though I do not fear your growing anxious to hear from me, yet having ten minutes to give to you, en voici. My stay at Mr Lloyds has been and will be very agreeable, and as he is a most excellent man of business my labours are not very heavy. Yet, as they are of a kind to make my presence in Dublin necessary all the preliminary days, I have only had one trip to geologize in the vicinity. The generosity of the Irish members is extreme: nearly £1000 has been raised to make the cost of their visit as light as possible to the strangers, who will have only 5/- to pay at the ordinary (wine included). Many will be lodged like me in Trinity College, some in private houses, but most in lodgings which are troublesome to obtain. There will we hope be a good but not perhaps a *very* large meeting. Beaucoup des Ecossais ne viennent pas. Il y a peu d'étrangers. Some, the stars of England come not (as Buckland, Airy, Peacock). But enough will come. The admissions are regulated according to a plan of mine which seems to leave little room for confusion or delay. The General Committee has red, the foreigners have blue, the Irishmen yellow and others white tickets. On the platform (that source of jealousy) we shall admit only officers and councillors. Ladies will be admitted by ticket. Tickets for ladies given only to strangers and to Irish members who subscribe to the local fund. There will be promenades, a military band, open gardens and gay refreshments. Three or four public dinners and breakfasts, a trip on the railway etc.

I dined on Sunday with the Provost (Dr Lloyd), on Wednesday a party at home, today with Mr Robert Hutton, on Sunday with the Provost, on Wednesday at Captain Portlock. I have seen Dr Greene, breakfasted with Hutton twice, Revd G. Smith once. *I am well*. My uncle is invited to College rooms. Let him bring what you have to send.

There is a Reception Committee Local Council. On Monday (3 Aug) we begin to admit new members (already 400 or 500!) and issue tickets. Dublin is a gay merry place full of fashion and not a little beauty. The houses are mostly brick: the public buildings fine. Air good. Climate mild.

[PS] I went to Howth north of Dublin on Thursday. It was a lovely day. The Bay is very fine.

Phillips Papers, A19

Robert Hutton (1785-1870), a retired merchant, became MP for Dublin 1837-41; Joseph Ellison Portlock (1794-1864), *DNB*, of the Irish ordnance survey; George

Sidney Smith (1807–75) was a Fellow of Trinity College, Dublin. Phillips' uncle was William Smith.

175   *Buckland, Oxford, to Harcourt, 2 August 1835*

I have this morning another letter from Mr Samuel Turner of Liverpool stating that Hamilton has written to him proposing to alter the day of the sailing of the *William Penn* from the 9th to the 7th August. I inclose this and a copy of my reply.

Oxon, 2 August 1835

Copy

Dear Sir,

Immediately on receiving your last, announcing Sir J. Tobin's liberal offer of a passage to the members of the British Association on Sunday the 9th, I transmitted it to the Secretary of the Association, Mr W. Vernon Harcourt, and suggested to him the expediency of immediately giving publicity to it in all the circulars he might be sending as Secretary, and also in the *Philosophical Magazine* and *Literary Gazette*.

I accordingly find the invitation twice repeated in the *London and Edinburgh Philosophical Magazine*, 1 August, and have no doubt of its being at this moment circulated over England in various notices and publications which it is now too late to alter or countermand. I have no doubt therefore that great numbers of the Association will come to Liverpool on Saturday in reliance on the public invitation thus made. I am also certain that had this invitation been given for Friday, very few individuals would have been found to accept it, as it would involve the sacrifice of half the present week, in addition to that which must be passed in Dublin.

It is however of no importance to consider whether Friday or Sunday would be most convenient to the members of the Association. The invitation has been given for Sunday and there is no time to retract it.

I can easily imagine that our kind and hospitable friends in Ireland are anxious to receive the members of the Association in the week preceeding the meeting, but I know too well the value of time to the classes of persons who attend, to think it would have been possible by any notice to get a large number to go over on Friday. Professor Powell and Dr Daubeny, the 2 Oxford [Local] Secretaries, are entirely of opinion with me, and will write this day to Professor Robinson and Dr Hamilton to this effect. Mr Powell will go to Dublin Friday by the ordinary packet, and Dr Daubeny has made his arrangements to go by the *William Penn* on the 9th.

I have written today stating all this to Mr Harcourt, but it seems to myself, Daubeny, and Powell too late to make any change if it were desirable.

As it will be impossible for me to go to Dublin I can only offer my best thanks for your [Liverpool] Institute's invitation to myself.

Yours,

Etc etc.

I have not yet heard of the arrival of Agassiz in London. I trust he will come in time and bring the fruits of his labours with him and that you will be able to get for him another grant of £100 in consideration thereof. Also pray remember the begging box for Mary Anning's annuity.

Harcourt MSS

Samuel Turner (d. 1847) was the Liverpool agent of the Bank of England and the Association's treasurer in Liverpool. Sir John Tobin (1762-1851), a Liverpool merchant, had offered a free passage to Association members from Liverpool to Kingstown on his best steam vessel, *Sir William Penn*, on 9 August. In the event, the ship sailed on 7 and 9 August. At the 1835 meeting Agassiz was awarded a second grant of £105, not £100, to aid his research on British fossil fish. Buckland succeeded in obtaining an annuity for Mary Anning (1799-1847), *DNB*, the discoverer of various saurian fossils. Jean Louis Rodolphe Agassiz (1807-73), *DSB*.

176 *William Henry, Pendlebury, Manchester, to Harcourt, York, Sunday evening [2 August 1835]*

I received this afternoon a letter from Mr [Samuel] Turner dated Liverpool August 1st informing me that 'at the particular desire of the Dublin Committee, as conveyed by Professor Hamilton, the day of sailing of the *William Penn has been* changed from the 9th to Friday the 7th instant to start precisely at six in the morning', and that 'the directors of the Kingstown Rail Road have just arranged for the conveyance also of the members to Dublin as soon as the vessel reaches Kingstown harbour'.

I trust, therefore, that under these circumstances you will be able to accomplish the intention, at which you hint, of leaving York on Tuesday. To meet this contingency, I will be at the Mail Coach Office at the Royal Hotel on the afternoon of that day to accompany you hither, or, if you should travel in any other manner, and should not then have arrived, you will do me the favour to follow me to Pendlebury (four miles from Manchester, the Bolton road). We dine on that day at 5 for the accommodation of the Revd Mr [William] Turner of Newcastle-on-Tyne who will visit us en famille and has some distance to go over in returning with his friend for the evening. Wednesday we can devote to Manchester, and on Thursday an hour and 20 minutes will take you as early as you like to Liverpool. As I must write to Mr Turner of that plan, I will mention the probability of you being in time for Friday's vessel, for I doubt the practicability of her making two voyages in time.

My servant waits to convey this letter to town and I can only add my expressions of regret, and those of Mrs Henry, that Mrs Harcourt is prevented and that by indisposition from accompanying you.

[PS] I this morning drew up the form of an invitation to the British Association to meet here the next or any early time.

Harcourt MSS

The Kingstown–Dublin railway was the first Irish line to be built. William Turner (1761–1859), *DNB*, Newcastle-upon-Tyne Unitarian minister.

177 *Conybeare, Sully near Cardiff, to Harcourt, Wheldrake near York, 24 August 1835*

I answer your note instanter, though only to state my own private opinions, but I will forward your letter to a *confidential* friend of mine at Bristol, Mr Clark, who is to be one of our [Local] Secretaries, who has judicious *tact* enough to feel the ground there and I will let you know the feeling of folk there as soon as I hear.

My own original idea when I proposed Bristol as a place of meeting was formed more in the infancy of the Association and when at the Oxford meeting it seemed very doubtful whither it would repair after Cambridge. The idea then *generally* entertained as to presidents in the commercial towns seemed to be that, when there was no nobleman so connected with the place as to make us *certain* we could rely upon his willingness to officiate, we ought to take the Mayor or some other leading man who would make the Corporation civil to us etc. Under this impression I thought my friend Scandrett Harford of Blaise Castle exactly the sort of person. I can describe him to you in two words by telling you that he is exactly the Roscoe of Bristol, with a very complete library, a good collection of pictures, etc etc, with every accommodation of house, etc, which a splendid income can procure, and the great promoter of the scientific institutions etc of Bristol though himself rather literary than scientific. Feeling a desire to improve his classical attainments he resided two or three years at Cambridge and is intimately acquainted with and highly esteemed by Whewell and all the best men there. I therefore thought him exactly the beau ideal of a mean proportional between your *academic* presidents and your future *commercial* ones, according to the anticipations of '32. I found Buckland, Whewell and every one else I mentioned the thing to at the time entirely agree with me and they all knew the individual well and his *facilities* for the office. However it seems that this year the proposition of his name was not smiled on by your Committee, and I of course have no wish to press the point. Passing him over therefore I should think it more desirable *myself* to select if we can some person of decidedly *superior station*, such as were suggested by proposing the names of Lord Lansdowne and Lord Granville Somerset. I however of course have no means of knowing as yet, whether either would accept the office, nor do I quite understand whether Lord Lansdowne's not being yet a member of our Association would be a fatal objection in point of form. I should think were he otherwise willing this could readily be got over by his sending his name in now, but the whole matter seems really to depend on the question whether the appointment would be *agreeable to his feelings*. I believe you are acquainted with him. Could not you ascertain this point? I think I can fully answer that no sort of *political* objection would be felt. All the friends of the meeting are perfectly aware that all politics must sleep in the shade for the season. As to the other nobleman mentioned, Lord Granville Somerset, he would of course be acceptable to the Corporation etc, but I don't know whether there is any reason to suppose he would take it. But I hope to let you know better how the land lies within a week, and only write at once that you may consider over the subject in your own mind previously as to what you will recommend.

As to Davies Gilbert I have on the first flush of the matter some little doubt. He is not at all more distingué than Harford, and without his best facilities for doing the thing well, I think it would be somewhat a slight passing over Harford for him; and I doubt whether he would like going to the expense of hiring a house for a fortnight in Clifton, which it would seem the President if he has no residence of his own in the neighbourhood might be expected to do.

I am happy to hear that all the influential people in Bristol seem to engage in the cause heart and hand and will, I believe, spare no trouble or expense to make the meeting go off thoroughly well. Bristol also at present contains within its bounds very able assistants indeed for the mathematical, physical, chemical, zoological, anatomical and botanical departments. I may perhaps be over partial to my own western metropolis, but I very sincerely believe that at the present moment taking all those different branches into account, and its peculiar facilities for geology, its excellent Museum, rising Zoological Garden, etc, it is hardly rivalled by any other provincial town in its capacities for receiving the Association worthily, and I am sure the meeting will further all my own views in creating a spirit of still more active support of our Philosophical Institution, etc. So I shall be delighted to cooperate. I shall be anxious to learn from your experience whether it is desirable to exert oneself on the spot to direct attention to the questions proposed by the sections, get at new materials, etc. I have filled my sheet so that I must resort to first page to subscribe myself.

PS   After all very likely the Bristolians may be quite content with Davies Gilbert. I will let you know presently.

Harcourt MSS

George Thomas Clark (1809-98), *DNB*; Charles Henry Granville Somerset (1792-1848), *DNB*, was a staunch Tory; William Roscoe (1753-1831), *DNB*.

178   *Buckland, London, to Harcourt, 27 August 1835*

Your plan I think obviates all difficulties. Call it West of England and you include Gilbert, under whom both Conybeare and Prichard will readily act, and Bristol will not be jealous if it were possible to add Harford as a 3rd Vice-president. It might be better as far as regards Bristol feeling, but this is not I think within our rules. I will see how they manage the evening meeting at Bonn and report to you.

Your notion that the evening performances of the British Association are the worst part of their proceedings is very true and at the same time flattering to those who have been called upon to take part in them.

Never mind me but do not say as much to Dr Lardner.

Agassiz is intensely grateful for the support he has received and says it will ensure the completion of his work.

I have just left my eldest boy at an excellent school near Oundle and embark for Ostend Saturday, hoping to return the 1st week in October. Address me should you have occasion at Bonn from 17 to 24 September.

Harcourt MSS

In 1835 the Gesellschaft Deutscher Naturforscher und Ärtze met at Bonn.

179   *John Yelloly, Woodton Hall, Bungay, Norfolk, to Harcourt, 2 September 1835*

I am happy in having had a little conversation with you, relative to the British institution, during our voyage from Ireland. I do not at all wonder at the wish expressed by you at the General Committee of being liberated from the large mass of onerous duties, which have hitherto attached to the Secretaryship; but at the same time, I feel very strongly how important it is for the interest and well-doing of the British institution that you should continue to hold some official situation in it, and thus maintain the right of taking an influential and monitory part in the management of its affairs. Secretary general, joint Secretary, Secretary extraordinary, or joint Treasurer, would all be designations which would connect you permanently with the society, and allow you to do just as much or as little as you pleased in its concerns; but I would be inclined to prefer the last, because it would not interfere with your holding the offices of Vice-president and President.

The society, I am convinced, cannot lose you as an officer without risk; for it is hardly possible that Mr Baily, or any of the members of the society, should be able to exercise the same salutary influence, and perform the same duties which you have so successfully done. A young man, receiving a salary and acting to a certain extent under your influence and inspection, seems, as far as I can judge, the most promising description of person for carrying on, conjointly with Professor Phillips, the active duties of the Association.

I hope you will excuse my troubling you with these remarks; but as you consented to hold office *merely* for the present year, I am anxious to press upon you the importance of your determination as to the future, on the permanent interests of the society.

During my stay in Edinburgh last year, I arranged with my old friend Dr Thomson, the professor of pathology, the basis of 2 or 3 communications on general pathology, in accordance with your views on the subject. I had hopes of finishing the first in about 3 months, which would have been in time for its being submitted to the Council, previously to the printing of the last volume. I was unfortunately, however, deprived of the use of the necessary books till after Christmas, from the Library of the Royal Medical and Chirurgical Society being shut up till their new house was ready for its reception and I then thought it too late. This will account for my apparent neglect; but my general interest in the British institution you may infer from a communication which appeared under the signature of X.Y.Z. in Brewster's *Journal* of last month, and which I should hope does not differ materially, though it may perhaps in some respects, from your views on the subject.

Harcourt MSS

John Yelloly (1774-1842), *DNB*, Norfolk physician, 'Suggestions respecting the ensuing meeting of the British Association for the Advancement of Science', *London and Edinburgh philosophical magazine and journal of science*, 1835, vii. 118-23; John Thomson (1765-1846), *DNB*, professor of pathology at Edinburgh University.

180   *Robison, Edinburgh, to Phillips, Museum, York, 23 September 1835*

I have duly received both your late packets and have done the
needful with their contents. The letter for Professor Johnston I put in
the post for Portobello although I have not heard of his being there
& rather conjecture that he is either abroad or at Durham. Professor
Graham's I shall convey to Glasgow myself in a day or two.

I wrote you a hurried note a short time ago by a Russian General
Officer, the Count de Ste Aldegarde, whom I hope you have seen
as he is my beau ideal of a finished gentleman and a highly accomplished man.

I am sorry to say that the general feeling does not, as far as I
learn, accord with your account of the success of the Dublin meeting.
Every one I hear speak of it asks 'if this struggle for pre-eminence in
feasting the Association is to continue, what will be the consequences?' and it is said that either the philosophers will be put hors
de combat by indigestion, or more probably that few towns
will be found willing to receive such pampered guests. It may be
well for the scientific fame of the Association if Bristol prove a Barataria for them, and a rigid physician preside at their banquets to
inculcate moderation. Seriously speaking there appears to be a certain taint of ridicule beginning to be attached to the proceedings in
the eye of the public not only in this country, but on the continent,
and the letters I get from Paris contain many sly jokes about the
speeches and the gourmandise so *vauntingly* displayed at Dublin.

Dr Robinson's attack on Sir David Brewster has likewise had a
bad effect and like the machine infernale of Louis Philippe turned
many frondeurs into supporters. Certain persons who have not
spared Brewster either in their conversation or in their writing now
defend him and exclaim against the astronomer. I am sorry for Mr
Harcourt who must have suffered much when his name was so
recklessly brought forward in the negative praises bestowed on him
by the other.

I shall be happy to learn at your leisure what prospect you have
for the meeting at Bristol, and whether you are likely to have such
influence with the local directors there as to enable you to put
matters on a more wholesome footing and to get the feeding department reduced to its proper subordinate level: this, and a cutting
out of all occasions for oratorical display, are I suspect essential to
the future health & *respectability* of the body.

The Saturday morning discussion of the General Committee
appears to have offered the same difficulties as were experienced on
former occasions. The fixing the next place and time of meeting will
always be likely to lead to a long debate when the debaters are so

numerous and so ill prepared for fair argument. Might not this part of the business be taken out of the hands of the General Committee by the Central Committee [ie Council] advertising *previous to the meeting* that invitations and propositions for receiving subsequent meetings of the Association should be addressed to the Central Committee some time before the actual meeting, and that on the first day of it a special committee should be named to take all these communications into consideration and to report to the General Committee on the Saturday morning? By this means the ground of discussion would be much narrowed, and a determination previously come to by those most able to judge rightly, could be supported by a little concert.

I assure you that it requires all the attractions of steam power to make me determine on using the high seas instead of the highway on my route to London; I always hesitate between the desire of seeing my kind friends in York and the expediency of getting forward or backward in the shortest possible time. The next excursion I promise myself will be to St Petersburg, and as Hull is the best port of embarkation for Hamburg, I shall have I trust next May an opportunity of renewing my acquaintance with the walls of your Museum, where we spent such interesting hours in 1831. En attendant have the kindness to remember me to Miss Phillips & to Mr Taylor.
[P S omitted]

British Association archives, Miscellaneous Phillips bundle

Thomas Graham (1805-69), *DNB*, was professor of chemistry at Anderson's University, Glasgow. At the 1835 meeting of the Association Robinson had publicly denounced Brewster for wielding 'the concealed dagger of a lurking assassin': *Athenaeum*, 1835, 642. In the early 1810s Barataria, a stretch of coast south of New Orleans, was the haunt of pirates and smugglers. By 'machine infernale' Robison was referring to the republican bombing in Paris during the early part of the reign of Louis Philippe (1773-1850).

181   *Harcourt, York, to Forbes, Athenaeum, London, 1 October 1835*

I hope you will take a bed here on your road to Scotland, when we can talk over Dublin and the Pyrenees. Of Dublin I will only say now that it appeared to me a perfectly successful meeting at all points. There was no foundation at all for the comments you may have seen as if a sacrifice had been made of science to gastronomy (vide Lockhart, I presume, in a note on the British Association in the last *Quarterly*). The sections never worked better as far as I saw of them and heard from others.

Bristol will be a severe trial and the meeting may probably not be so numerous as those which have preceded, but I dare say it will answer well enough notwithstanding. We have not yet chosen a President. I am fearful of venturing on politicians for the chair such as Lord Lansdowne who has been named or Lord Granville Somerset of whom Conybeare speaks. I suggested D. Gilbert as a west country man but the Bristolians do not think him enough connected with their city: I should have liked to have proposed Conybeare but do not think he would get decently through the dinners and Prichard is too quiet. Have you any recommendation to offer?

Your sisters were here and seemed much delighted with our music. [PS] What Robinson said about 'the skulking assassin' he had better have let alone.

Forbes Papers, 1835/39

Lockhart's footnote, *Quarterly Review*, 1835, liv. 466, attacked the 'gastropatetic turtle-philia' of the Association. Forbes spent the summer of 1835 on the continent.

182   *Harcourt, Residence, York, to Lubbock, 29 Eaton Place, London, 6 October 1835*

I send you a transcript of the resolution passed at Dublin to place sums of money at your disposal for the discussion of tides etc. A copy of the same I understand was transmitted to you before which appears not to have reached you.

'Why do you not come to these meetings?' is a question you will say I have no right to ask, nor would I, if your presence at them were of less consequence. What I have said on this subject in the last number of the *Philosophical Magazine* is true: that the utility and ultimately the existence of the Association as a scientific institution depends on the attendance of persons like yourself at its meetings. [Then follows in Phillips' hand]

British Association for the Advancement of Science

At a meeting of the Committee of Recommendations

Dublin 13 August 1835

Resolved that the old grant for the discussion of observations on the tides be considered as ended, and that the new grant for the payment of work already done, and the further prosecution of the subject both with regard to the Brest and the Liverpool observations be £250 (payable to Mr Lubbock). Also resolved that £10 be placed at Mr Lubbock's disposal for making transcripts of such portions of that discussion as he may think proper.

John Phillips
Assistant General Secretary

Memorandum

Mr J. Taylor will pay any portion of the sums above granted to Mr Lubbock's orders. A copy of the grants made at Dublin has been forwarded to him.

Lubbock Papers, H58

For Harcourt's remarks on the importance to the Association of master-spirits, 'Official report of the proceedings of the British Association for the Advancement of Science, at the Dublin meeting, August 1835', *London and Edinburgh philosophical magazine and journal of science*, 1835, vii. 289–315 (291).

183   *Prichard, Bristol, to Harcourt, York, 3 November 1835*

I write according to your request [to] express to you my humble opinion upon the points to which your letter relates.

Whenever the subject has recurred to my mind I have felt persuaded that the Marquis of Lansdowne is the most eligible person for the office of President of the British Association at the ensuing meeting and I still entertain the same conviction. In Bristol particularly, where a peer of his rank would be held proportionally in higher estimation than elsewhere, it would give great éclat to the meeting of the Association to have such a person appearing at its head.

It cannot be questioned that Davies Gilbert has high merits and is altogether a most unexceptionable person, but I think his claims are of that kind which requires a little consideration before they will be remembered. He was for a short time President of the Royal Society, but was it not under particular circumstances and as a sort of interrex?

I fully agree with your opinion that it would be highly injurious to the Association were any man set at its head who is chiefly known as a politician. On that as well as on other considerations Lord Granville Somerset appears to be out of the question. Indeed I wonder that he was ever mentioned. But do the same objections hold against the Marquis of Lansdowne? I should think certainly not. They might have been argued with greater force against the first President to whom, however, as far as I know, no exception was ever made. The Marquis has long been known as a patron of letters and of learned men. He is himself a man of letters and of highly cultivated mind. He has long been a very eminent and meritorious member of the Bath and Bristol Agricultural Society, which was until of late the only thing approaching to the character of a scientific association in this part of England. In that Society he has been accustomed to preside over the meetings of the gentlemen inhabiting this and the neighbouring districts. I believe that Lord Landsdowne has been of late rather quiescent in politics. If it is worthwhile to advert to the feelings of the Bristol people and the natives of this vicinity in general towards Lord Lansdowne, it may be observed that he has lately acquired their good will in a point on which they feel even more acutely than with regard to politics: I mean their own interest. I understand that he has pleased the people of this country very much by taking their side in the discussion and contest about the Western Railway. Besides being high in the peerage Lord Lansdowne is an excellent orator, which is a most desirable qualification in a president, and these two recommendations would ensure a degree of éclat to his appearance at the head of the Association, which would fall to the lot of no other individual yet mentioned as a candidate for that distinction.

I happened lately to see a lady who is well acquainted with Lord and Lady Lansdowne, and I asked her if she thought the Marquis would like the office of President of the Association. She said that she was confident that he would be greatly delighted with it. Of course I only said that I had heard a rumour of some probability of his appointment.

I have expressed my opinion freely upon subjects over which I have perhaps scarcely a right to have an opinion. For this your request excuses me.

Harcourt MSS

184 *Murchison, 3 Bryanston Place, London, to Whewell, Trinity College, Cambridge, 21 November 1835*

Just as he was leaving town yesterday, W V Harcourt received a letter from one of the Secretaries of the British Association at Bristol (Mr Clark) stating that Dr Jerrard his Co-secretary had resigned, and calling upon the Council in London to appoint a successor. The local Council at Bristol recommend the Revd V F Hovenden, M A, formerly fellow of your good college and now resident in Bristol as a person well qualified to supply the place, and Harcourt desired me to enquire of you, Sedgwick and others, whether you conceive that Mr Hovenden will answer our purpose.

In case of your answer in the affirmative, I shall call a Council and confirm the appointment. Our President is Lord Lansdowne; Vice-presidents [are] Harford of *Blaze* Castle, Conybeare, Prichard.

You will be glad to learn that we have got Lubbock back into the Council of the Royal Society. At our last meeting I felt so strongly the untowardness of his secession, and seeing nothing in his letter to us which prevented our electing him into *our Council*, albeit he had resigned the office of *Treasurer*, that I made a motion for the purpose which was unanimously carried it being felt that his continuing to act with us would materially contribute to our well being. I also wrote to him a strong private letter and the result is that he accepts our offer, saying at the same time that 'he does not consider that by so doing he at all compromises the opinion he entertains of *the manner in which* the President has *treated* the Society'.

Peace therefore is preserved for the *present*, but ere' another election day arrives, we must be prepared with *an effective* President or a revolution will take place. Ponder well on this.

Harcourt added my name to *your* Antarctic Committee which now consists of Brisbane, Franklin, Whewell, Drummond, Greenough, Gilbert, Sedgwick, Airy, Christie, Barlow, James Ross, Dr Robinson, Peacock, Murchison. I only consider myself as whipper-in; but as a Vice-president of the *Geographical* [Society] and being certain of meeting *Barrow* our President tomorrow and knowing that *he* will eventually be the person to lead the government into the project or make them repudiate it, I wish you to *cram* me by return of post, with instructions for my guidance in the initiation of this adventure. When the project is matured and that *you have drawn* out your memorial, for such it must be, then let us go as a deputation say on about St Andrews Day to the Chancellor of the Exchequer on which occasion Peacock and yourself will have great weight with Spring-Rice.

[PS]   I shall be in town till the 4 or 5 Dec then out of town for a month.

Whewell Papers, a. 209[98]

Joseph Henry Jerrard (1801–53), Principal of Bristol College; Valentine Fowler Hovenden (1807–90), gentleman of Sion Hill, Clifton, Bristol; Sir John Franklin (1786–1847) and James Clark Ross (1800–62), both *DNB*, were Arctic explorers; Sir John Barrow (1764–1848), *DNB*, was Secretary of the Admiralty; Thomas Spring-Rice (1790–1866), *DNB*, was Chancellor of the Exchequer 1835–9 and a loyal son of Trinity College, Cambridge, where Peacock and Whewell were tutors. The Association had set up in summer 1835 a committee to induce government to send an expedition to the Antarctic to pursue magnetic research; by spring 1836 this committee was defunct.

185   *Whewell, Trinity College, Cambridge, to Murchison, 3 Bryanston Place, London, 22 November 1835*

I doubt whether Hovenden would be a very useful [Local] Secretary. He is a man of elegant attainments and amiable character but I should not expect him to be so active and business-like as our Local Secretary ought to be. At the same time if he were to take up the office with zeal he has talent and character enough to do it well, and if he has been sounded and is willing I should think it no bad choice. My own judgment would be that we should have a man who knows the more intelligent indigenes of Bristol and its neighbourhood well, for I have no doubt that there are enough of them to support us efficiently if they are properly applied to. It would seem to me that the people who are most active in the Bristol and Bath societies are the best persons for us, for they must know who take an interest in science. For my own part I have no doubt that without very bad luck we shall go on very prosperously at Bristol, for it was clear that we had at Dublin more vitality than ever; but nothing would be so troublesome as a panic among our local officers. I think Lord Lansdowne as President is a good appointment and also the Vice-presidents. A Mr Stutchbury with whom I have corresponded about the *Bristol tides* seems to me an intelligent and zealous person.

I am glad you have got Lubbock in to the Council, one of the many good things you have done in the way of peace-making. But still I am vexed with his resignation of which his retaining office makes the absurdity still stronger. We must as you say see about a new administration of the Royal Society if anything is to be done with it.

As to the south pole, when I was last in London I had an interview with Lord Minto and he told me that he did not think the government would be likely to accede to such a recommendation, and that he did not think they would even send out a *north* west expedition again. This latter point you can ascertain from James Ross or Barrow for I suppose Ross will be the navigator if anything of that kind is done. If it is I think good reasons may be shown for a *simultaneous* expedition to the south. I send you a draft of a representation on the subject which I drew up and which you can return to me next Saturday when I shall be in town. We might add that sending out such expeditions is anything but prodigality, for the officers and men when they come back are improved to the amount of the sum expended so that all the discoveries are clear gain. But without knowing the disposition of Barrow, Beaufort, and the Admiralty in general to such a scheme I should not advise risking the *prestige* of the British Association by drawing down a refusal.

As we have no frankers here you must be content to have my budget in a double letter. I hope you dine with HRH on Saturday. I was sorry I could not join your party on Thursday.

Murchison Papers

Samuel Stutchbury (1798-1859), was a Bristol geologist; Gilbert Elliot, 2nd Earl of Minto (1782-1859), *DNB*, was 1st Lord of the Admiralty 1835-41.

186 *Phillips, n.p., to Harcourt, Bishopthorpe near York, 3 February 1836*

Sedgwick's great labours in the geology of Yorkshire make me very anxious to sub-join his name to yours in the dedication of my volume. He has worked the oolites, magnesian limestone and western border, from 1822 (when I met him in Teesdale) to this day and has just published a valuable paper on the Pennine fault.

To the Revd W Vernon Harcourt F R S, F G S etc who, as (First?) President of the Yorkshire Philosophical Society, proposed for its principal object the elucidation of the geology of Yorkshire, and laboured earnestly in the prosecution of it;

and
The Revd Adam Sedgwick F G S, F G S

Woodwardian Professor in the University of Cambridge whose splendid geological career began with researches in this his native county,

This volume
is most respectfully dedicated by their friend and fellow labourer
The author.

As I do not doubt of your accordance in the propriety of showing this mark of respect to Sedgwick, who, in point of fact, has done quite as much in the geology of Yorkshire as myself and began in the same year (1822), I have sent him a copy of the sketch on the other side, and now I shall be glad of your permission to place your name first in the page, with some such expressions as these set down, not as a mere compliment, but as a matter of undoubted right and bare justice, or less than justice. (See Objects of the [Yorkshire Philosophical] Society p. 6.)

The notion of a dedication is in my mind of this sort: it ought to embody some historical truth, bearing on the subject matter of the book, and peculiarly characteristic of the individuals named. This in substance I hope is secured in the sort of sentiment which is expressed in the sketch which I send: and this, happily, is my last or nearly last page, and in a few days the last plates will be received and my head will cease to ache. *It is my last volume* (except a supplement to volume 1) *on topographical geology.* I have neither health, spirit, nor hope of leisure to try any other ground. Happy shall I be if for some few times more I may wander through the western dales, and climb some of the beautiful mountains, which have been to me a land of philosophical romance, sources of health, and antidotes to care, but I dare not think of undertaking a minute survey of the coal tract. This must be left to practical men versed in the works and acquainted with localities. I think I shall make a geological map of the county and then my task is done.

Harcourt MSS

J. Phillips, *Illustrations of the geology of Yorkshire: part 2. The mountain limestone district* (London, 1836) was dedicated to Harcourt and Sedgwick. The principal aim of the Yorkshire Philosophical Society was to elucidate the geology of Yorkshire.

187 *William Fairbairn, Manchester, to Harcourt, 2 April 1836*

In accordance with instructions received from the British Association, I have been collecting specimens of cast iron from the cold and hot blast. Being now fully prepared for the experiments, I am induced at the request of Mr Hodgkinson to state that we have procured upwards of fifteen different samples from the Welsh, Scotch, Yorkshire, Staffordshire, and Shropshire manufacture. A seeming reluctance has been evinced in some quarters to give information, but notwithstanding this desire to withhold such facts as were deemed essential to accurate investigation, we have nevertheless obtained sufficient data on which to found pretty accurate results.

Mr Hodgkinson and myself will be glad to have your opinion and advice and it will afford us great pleasure to receive information on a subject so intimately connected with the arts and manufactures.

Harcourt MSS

Fairbairn and Eaton Hodgkinson (1789–1861), *DNB*, retired Manchester pawn-broker, were given a grant at the 1835 meeting of the Association to compare irons produced by the hot and cold air blast furnaces.

188 *Baily, London, to Harcourt, 2 May 1836*

I should have answered your letter of the 16th ultimo before this time, but have been waiting Mr Airy's return from Cambridge, to which place he is gone to deliver some lectures. I now find that he will stay longer than I expected; and as I propose to go to Scotland at the end of this week, to view the annular eclipse of the sun on the 15th instant, I shall not be able to see him till my return.

I have written, some time since, to the Bureau des Longitudes respecting the reduction of the stars in the *Histoire Céleste;* but at present have not received any reply.

The determination of the constant of nutation is in progress.

The determination of the difference of meridians hangs on hand; and nothing I believe has been done on it. The parties interested in the question have not stirred to effect it.

I understand that something has been done as to the application to government respecting a magnetic voyage to the southern pole, but with what effect I am not aware. There was a meeting of the Council of the British Association some short time back, but I was not summoned to it, and did not know of its existence till after it was over.

I observed that several of the recommendations are ordered, but no person is appointed to carry them into effect; in consequence of which they remain a dead letter. This should be remedied in future.

I have written to the Secretary of the Leeds Philosophical Society informing him that there are no copies of my *Account of Flamsteed* undisposed of, the whole edition having been distributed, and no chance of any new edition.

Harcourt MSS

At the 1835 meeting of the Association it had been agreed: to urge the French government to pay for the reduction of the observations of stars published in the *Histoire céleste française* of Joseph Jerôme Lefrançaise de Lalande (1732–1807), *DSB*, this lobby being unsuccessful; to calculate the constant of lunar notation; and to determine the differences of meridians between six British observatories. The Secretary of the Leeds Society was William West who wanted Baily's *An account of the Revd John Flamsteed, the first astronomer royal* (London, 1835).

189   *Whewell, Trinity College, Cambridge, to Harcourt, 27 May 1836*

There are some points which I should like to urge at the next meeting of the British Association at Bristol, and I should be glad to know your opinion about them beforehand. There is a man there, by name Bunt, who has been working very hard at the tides with a view to constructing tide tables; and has become so much fascinated with the subject, that he has given more time to it than will be repaid him by any return he is likely to get. His results appear to me to be valuable as an addition to our knowledge of the subject, and I should wish to propose to purchase his calculations from him, or in some other way to make him some recompense. He is likely to go on with the subject, and to do more than he has yet done. If I were authorized to employ a certain sum upon him, it would be exactly what Lubbock has done in the case of Dessiou.

Another matter connected with the tides is the execution of our ancient scheme of fixing the relation of land and water, at least at one or two points. The observations of tides at Liverpool and Bristol have been so multiplied and so well analysed that the position of the measuring scales, with regard to the sea level at those places, may be considered as very exactly determined. I would therefore propose that these scales should be well connected with the natural features of the country in some clear and permanent manner, so as to afford a point of comparison in future times. I think this is the only way of executing the scheme, formerly recommended, of ascertaining the permanence of the level of land and water.

Nothing has been done respecting the antarctic magnetic expedition. At one period Captain Beaufort, the Hydrographer, sent me a message that there was a ship which we might possibly have if we asked for it. But I found that there was no chance of this, and that, if sent at all, it would go to the north, as it has done. I found also that nobody, except Murchison, came to the meeting of the committee held on this subject, so that I thought it better to wait than to urge the point weakly and ineffectually. Next year, with Sabine's report in circulation, we shall have, I hope, a better chance.

I have not yet heard of the time of meeting at Bristol, though it is now late for it to remain uncertain. I hear too that Phillips is ill, which I regret very much.

There is an election to take place soon, in which the Archbishop of York is an elector (one of four), and in which we Cambridge men are somewhat concerned; I mean the Mastership of Downing College. Of the candidates, Starkie, though in other respects an excellent man, would, I think, be objectionable as a non-resident lawyer; Dawes has taken a living, which would also take him away. Worsley is, as appears to me, a candidate every way unexceptionable; and being a person of very conciliating character, very great accomplishments, and very desirous of making the College more effective for the purposes of good education than it has yet been, he would, I think, be a great gain to us. There are few persons of whose religious principles and right intentions I think so highly, and he is a very general favourite both for his literary and conversational endowments. You will not think me superfluous in saying so much, for, of course, it must be the wish of the electors to choose the person most likely to manage the College well; and you can communicate what I have said to the Archbishop, or not, as you think best.

I shall be in London soon, where I may perhaps meet you.

Todhunter, Whewell, *ii. 237-8*

Thomas Gamlen Bunt, a Bristol surveyor, was paid from 1836 by the Association to work on tides under Whewell's supervision; Joseph Dessiou, of the Hydrographer's Office, had done similar work for Lubbock. Sabine's 'Report on the variations of the magnetic intensity observed at different points of the earth's surface', *1837 Report*, 1-85, was crucial in the successful lobby of government in 1838-9 for an antarctic magnetic expedition. Thomas Worsley (1797-1885) was elected to the Mastership of Downing College; Thomas Starkie (1782-1849) and Richard Dawes (1793-1867), both *D.NB*.

190   *Harcourt, Bishopthorpe near York, to Murchison, Bryanston Place, London, 13 June 1836*

The circuits having been arranged and the time of the Bristol Assizes fixed for the 12th [August], as Mr Yates writes me word, we now know that we may abide by our intention of holding the meeting on the 22nd, a time which I trust will insure the attendance of our President and the sooner it is announced the better. I shall not be able to attend the Council meeting, which Yates proposes to call on the 18th, but I have written to him what occurs to me on the points which he has to bring before it. We shall meet I hope at Bristol, whither I shall go in good time and Phillips will be there a fortnight or three weeks before to assist in the arrangements. Forbes will come from Scotland but not Brewster, who however I am glad to hear is prevented only by the distance. The female part of my family is at Scarborough where I reckon upon joining them in about a fortnight and staying for a week or two; beyond that I shall probably not move from home till I go to Bristol.

Murchison Papers

191   *Yates, 49 Upper Bedford Place, London, to Harcourt, Bishopthorpe near York, 20 June 1836*

The annexed extract from the minutes will inform you of what was done by the Council of the British Association on Saturday.

No resolution was adopted relative to the further preparation of the 4th volume, as the conduct of it had been entrusted to you; but I mentioned the suggestions, contained in your letters to Mr Richard Taylor and myself, and it was the opinion of all that it will be advisable to add the list of members and to bind in the volume the *proceedings*, which were published in a separate pamphlet, and of which there is quite a sufficiency on hand. The volume will not even then be so large as some of its predecessors. The press is at present stopped for want of proofs, which were sent to Professor Lloyd at Dublin, and have not been returned.

I have written to several places in Belgium, Holland and Germany to give notice of the time and place of the meeting and to invite scientific foreigners. I shall write also to Paris and to Caen for the same purpose.

I am preparing to send to Bristol the names of those who will attend the meeting, especially the more distinguished members, both to assist the Local Committee in allotting apartments or providing accommodation in private houses, and that our noble President may be properly supported. I understand he will be quite prepared to be with us at the appointed time.

At our Council on Saturday we had some conversation on a subject on which I should be desirous of conversing with you when you come to town, viz the revision of the list of the Council, and the appointment of the President and Vice-presidents for Liverpool, supposing that to be the place of meeting. My own impression, regarding at once rank and station, character, scientific attainments, and decided and constant interest in the welfare of the Association, to which I must add popular manners and talent as a speaker, is that the Marquis of Northampton is the fittest man. But it was answered that he has no connection with Lancashire. Mr Whewell was therefore named. I then mentioned Sir Robert Peel, who was born and for some time brought up in Lancashire, who is still very much connected with the county, and who has been a member from the beginning of our Association. I was pleased to find that this suggestion seemed to meet with approval of the other gentlemen who were present. I hope Mr Whewell, to whom we are already so much indebted, would not object to take office again as Vice-president under Sir Robert, and one or two Liverpool men, chosen on account of their official situation as well as character and attainments, might be joined with him.

Harcourt MSS

192   *Humphrey Lloyd, Trinity College, Dublin, to Harcourt, 26 June 1836*

I received your letter yesterday, but too late to return an answer by the same day's post. I have already had a letter from Mr Taylor, and another from Mr Yates on the same subject, and returned the proofs on the day in which the first reached me.

It is scarcely fair in Mr Taylor to lay upon my shoulders the whole amount of the blame due to delay. I received the last proofs (or revise) on the 13th of this month, and returned them on the 20th, being obliged to keep them *one week* in order to communicate with Captain Sabine who is joint contributor with me in the paper. The original proofs remained in Mr Taylor's office *nearly a month*.

The Provost, Sir William Hamilton, Mr McCullagh, and many other of the Dublin members of the Association hope to be in Bristol before the 22nd [August]. Mr McCullagh will have a very beautiful discovery in the wave theory of light to lay before the physical section, and I am happy to add that the difficulty unravelled is one of those put forward by the Association among the desiderata of this branch of science.

Harcourt MSS

James McCullagh (1809-47), *DNB*, Fellow of Trinity College, Dublin, announced at
the 1836 meeting his theory about the laws of double refraction in crystals of quartz:
Athenaeum, 1836, 623. The joint paper was Lloyd, Sabine, and J.C. Ross, 'Observations on the direction and intensity of the terrestrial magnetic force in Ireland', *1835
Report*, 117-62.

193   *Yates, 49 Upper Bedford Place, London, to Harcourt, 19 July 1836*

Having heard that Professor Moll was in town, I called at his lodgings, 71 Great Queen St, Lincoln's Inn Fields, but did not find him
at home. I think it might be important to the success of one of our
evening meetings if you could induce him to give a short lecture,
describing, for instance, the process of making a new channel for the
Rhine, or exhibiting on a large scale some of his own magnetical
experiments. Drawings or apparatus could easily be provided before
the meeting.

I inclose a note from Mr Ward, a surgeon in Wellclose Square
near the Tower. His method of growing plants under glass excluded
entirely from the outer air is described in the *Transactions* of the
Society for encouraging Arts, Manufactures and Commerce, and is
a very valuable, as well as curious, discovery. If you were near that
part of London, I wish you would call to see it. I think that with a
view to our meeting in Liverpool in 1837, it would be a very good
plan to appropriate a sum, say £25, to growing plants in this way
under the direction of the Committee of the Liverpool Botanic Garden in conjunction with Mr Ward, Sir William Hooker, Dr Daubeny, and Professor Henslow, so as to have the plants ready to be
seen at the Liverpool meeting. They would be a novel, attractive
and beautiful object of attention, and at the same time be an aid to
botanical science on account of the facilities which this method affords for bringing plants from abroad. Some weeks ago Mr Aikin
had some glass cases of plants in John St, Adelphi, showing the same
process.

[PS]   I go to Bristol on Thursday.

Harcourt MSS

Nathaniel Bagshaw Ward (1791-1868), *DNB*, discovered that tightly glazed cases
preserved plants, a discovery which gained him an Association grant of £35 in 1836
and much publicity at the 1837 meeting of the Association; Arthur Aikin (1773-
1854), *DNB*.

194 *Robison, Royal Society, Edinburgh, to Phillips, Philosophical Institution, Park Street, Bristol, 28 July 1836*

I duly received yours and have delayed replying to it only because
I have been uncertain whether it would be in my power to attend
the meeting at Bristol. I have now reason to hope that I may be
able to do so, and that I shall arrange matters so as to accompany
Sir D. Brewster and any other friends who may propose to join us.
In this case we shall probably arrive in Bristol about the 18th or 19th.

On receiving your letter I had some communication with Sir D.
B., Mr Johnston &c on the subject of the arrangements which would
be most likely to contribute to the success of the meeting, and found
that they agreed in opinion that by attempting to do too much, and
within too short a period, the result of previous meetings has been
less satisfactory and agreeable than it might have been under a
different arrangement. I have found also a very general idea prevailing that more opportunity should be given for the assembled
members to find one another out, and that the meeting on the whole
should be regarded more in the light of a rendezvous for making
acquaintance with one another than in that of an opportunity of
making communications which, in the majority of cases, may be
better made through the press. In accordance with this impression,
I venture to suggest that two at least of the evening meetings should
be unoccupied by formal business, and that if a proper locality be
procurable for the purpose, a sort of levée or promenade should be
substituted, at which an opportunity would be afforded of regularly
presenting strangers to the President and staff of the Association,
and of allowing the members to find one another out which has
hitherto always been a matter of difficulty and uncertainty. The
private dinners which have been so hurried and inconvenient hitherto, might be less objectionable if restricted to days on which the
levées are fixed and a general understanding come to, that the ordinaries should be well supported on the other days as they are more
essential parts of the general arrangement than any hospitality
which can be shown to favoured individuals and which will always
be more or less a cause of dissatisfaction to those not included in
them.

I should also venture to suggest that the whole week should be
given up to the public business of the meeting and that the meeting
of the General Committee with the concluding arrangements should
be deferred until the Monday of the following week, by which means
time would be given for preparing the business, and much desultory
discussion and loss of time would be avoided.

Professor Forbes has just returned to Edinburgh from an excursion in the north and on my mentioning to him what I had proposed to Sir D. B, and proposed to mention to yourself, he says he entirely coincides in these views and considers the leaving some evenings free as an essential arrangement for the future success of the Association. He leaves this in a few days for London on his way to join you in due time.

While I remained in Paris I was occasionally asked when the Association would hold a meeting in London or its vicinity. The very cheap rates of travelling between Paris and London seem to have awakened a desire on the part of our Parisian friends to profit by them.

[PS] Holding the proposed levées need not prevent any persons disposed to give lectures from doing so, if separate rooms can be alotted for the purpose and audiences be found willing to attend on them.

Phillips Papers, 1836/34

The Association has met in London only once in 1931.

195 *Phillips, Philosophical Institution, Bristol, to Harcourt, 3 August 1836*

I have not yet fully comprehended all that has been done here, but there are some things worth communicating with respect to the *preliminary* arrangements adopted. In the allocation of the sections considerable difficulty has been experienced, but there is sufficient accommodation for all. I made only one change in these dispositions, viz to give the General Committee as the elite of our corps scientifique, the singularly beautiful apartment of the Chapter House next [to] the Cathedral. The other rooms are in general large enough or *too large*. The geological room is in the Institution. It will hold 350 *if crammed* and so we imagine it may be necessary to enforce almost absolutely the law as to exclusion of ladies from the sections.

The Theatre will seat 1600 or 1800 persons.

Admission of members. This is accomplished to the extent of 400 + and applications still come in and *may increase*. The rule has been to have names mentioned in the Local Council (a very large body) and *there* to require the nomination and seconding of two *well known* members *of Council*. Thus persons who wish to compound, to pay to the local fund, and individuals of known merit have *all* been elected and not one yet refused. But now comes the tug of war, viz to decide on the claims of persons who wish to rush in en masse at the end.

Scientific business. Very little yet done in the way of preparation. There are provisional secretaries of considerable merit, and many communications are announced. It has been proposed to have 3 evenings for public lectures, addresses, etc. (including the first opening meeting on Monday evening), and to give on every one of the five first evenings all the usual stuffing of ices, jellies, etc in the Theatre. I wish it may be possible to arrange one *promenade* in the Zoological Gardens but I fear it may not be done.

Ordinaries. Very good arrangement and low prices for 500 persons to dine in one room.

No public dinner nor (as yet) public breakfast is talked of. I have discouraged it by all means.

Lodgings. There is a committee (Daubeny and others) to see to this. I suppose you have some invitation already, if not you will be well cared for. 300 (I guess) will be located in private families, and there is something done as to lodgings for hire and hotel prices.

Arrivals. Sir D. Brewster, Robison, Lubbock, Lloyd, Dalton, C. Henry, Hamilton, Mitscherlich, Parigot, Schumacher, etc are to come. I have a letter at last from Brewster and think all his displeasure is ended. Conybeare not come yet, and seldom here. He *must not be excited.*

Whewell is to give some exposé or other with apparatus but I know not its meaning.

I will write again soon.

PS   I will write today to Gyde and Harris. It will be best not to print the names of committees for they are most crudely selected or rather collected.

I have requested Mr Gyde not to print the names of the committees. They are really *too bad* a *collection.* This whole matter must be reformed!!

Harcourt MSS

Julien Jacques Louis Parigot, (b. 1806), then teaching mineralogy and geology at Brussels University; Heinrich Christian Schumacher (1780–1850), *DSB*, the Danish astronomer; Charles Gyde (d. 1865) was the manager of Richard Taylor's firm which printed the *Reports.* At the 1836 meeting Whewell displayed an improved version of his self-registering anemometer. The committees which embarrassed Phillips were the many research committees which did nothing.

196   *Phillips, [Bristol], to Harcourt, 5 August 1836*

I found the [Local] Committee had issued tickets to ladies to a great extent, and for every evening of the week excepting Saturday, under the notion that every evening was to be occupied by the usual formal or lecturing display. In this condition I reflected on the best means of extricating ourselves from the very painful dilemma of totally reversing the arrangement or of changing it to a better one. I decided to recommend (after many letters urging the same sort of thing) that only 3 of the 5 evenings should be spent in the Theatre, and the remainder in the Zoological Gardens and great nursery ground of Mr Miller. Thus the ladies will not be balked of their tickets and the great object or avoiding the dangerous and laborious trial of patience in the Theatre for so many evenings attained.

I have also succeeded in causing an agent to be sent around to ascertain really what accommodation can be had as to lodgings. It is a shameful thing that many gentlemen who have been *invited* to private families here have not *noticed* the kindness and it is not easy to say whether the inviters may not think it right to take other guests. Are you located yet? If not, does Mrs H come? There is great and real desire among the wealthier classes of any liberality of sentiment to make every exertion in the cause of public and private encouragement of the Association, and as far as I see the scientific pretensions of the place are very considerable.

Three reports are already announced and several replies to recommendations, besides other communications.

It is resolved to admit reporters to the evening meetings: several good *thoughts* have been formed as to the dispatch of section business and to the making known the order of the following day's proceedings, but I doubt rather our power of *working through* these plans. However I shall soon see, as I find great kindness and desire to second my wishes. The Theatre is likely to be a very capital room for speaking *sotto voce* which will suit the mass of our orators. There is a proposal to supply the place of J.S. Harford *absentee and en voyage* by Sir R Vivyan (or Vivian), Conybeare and Prichard being either too *excitable* or too tame. What do you think of it? If you dislike, pray write instanter. I do not much like it myself but deem it a *nonessential*.

I have seen all the rooms and they will *do*, some very well. The statisticians do not like my giving the beautiful Chapter House to the General Committee, but I have shown them the clear truth that the room in which the General Committee should be received (on the Saturday) should not be an auction room! I will however *try* to get them a better room but may *not succeed*.

Harcourt MSS

Sir Richard Rawlinson Vyvyan (1800–79), *DNB*, MP for Bristol, did not act as a Vice-president. Philip John Miller, a seedsman and nurseryman, owned a garden at Durdham Down, Bristol.

197   *Phillips, [Bristol], to Harcourt, 8 August 1836*

I have found the means of finally adjusting every thing as to sectional and other rooms and can promise certainly a successful issue on all matters of mere form. Today the [Local] Council adopted right views as to the working of the 'Location Committee' and appointed a secretary of it. They also finally decided on affirming the plan of admission and division of the labour of the reception room which I had drawn up, so that on all these points I have ease of mind.

As to the evening meetings, we have great embarrassment and must not yet decide what is to be done on some evenings. I mean whether to grow hot in the Theatre, or cool in the gardens of the Horticultural and Zoological Society, or in the groves and picture rooms of Mr Miles, who is dying to invite Lord Lansdowne and some of the grandees to his splendid mansion. But it is doubtful whether he will do good or harm by this. I have great hopes that the ordinaries will be well supported. 5/- a head (plus charge for wine) is the price and it is sure to be agreeable. We have fitted up the theatre thus* so as to let every one of *2400 persons!* see and be seen.

The admission of members is to the extent of 450 and nearly all these will have ladies tickets. Say in all 500 and 400 so Bristol will give 900 attendants in the evening. In addition say 600 or 700 strangers with 300 ladies = 900 × 2 = 1800 total and there are 2400 seats of which *1600 are excellent.*

It is imagined that the geologists and botanists may take excursions, on a certain day if they choose, the chemists see the Bath and Hotwell waters, the astronomers may find it worth while to enquire as to Mr West's telescopes which are of extraordinary make and value.

Three reports only announced; many researches will be brought in and other communications in tolerable abundance. But *I dread the evening meetings* and it is difficult to tell what to do on this point. I propose Monday, Wednesday and Friday in the Theatre and Tuesday and Thursday elsewhere. The foundation of the new iron bridge at Clifton is to be laid by Lord Lansdowne on the 27th [August] in the evening. Will you write to me as to the evening meetings any general views for I *have no data* to give you, not knowing of *even one evening performer.*

PS The [Bristol] Institution is in very creditable condition. Goldie has little practice, but excellent health. He is a failure and a sad one I fear. Von Raumer, Moll, Mitscherlich come. I shall go down the collieries here to get temperatures, and have hopes of collecting many other notices of like matters.

Harcourt MSS

Philip John Miles (1774-1845), Bristol merchant, banker and Conservative MP, of

Leigh Court, Somerset, owned an extensive picture gallery; William West (1801–61), a local artist, rented the old windmill on Clifton Down, Bristol, and styled its tower an observatory; Frederick Ludwig Georg von Raumer (1781–1873), historian. At * Phillips inserted a sketch.

198   *Lansdowne, London, to Harcourt, 19 August 1836*

It is with the greatest pain that after having made every arrangement for leaving town on Saturday afternoon, and for being at Bristol on Monday I find myself obliged to abandon that intention in consequence of the alarming illness of my eldest son.

May I beg of you to express to the committee of the British Institution my regret at not being able to meet them on an occasion to which I had looked forward with so much interest.

Harcourt MSS

Lansdowne's eldest son, the Earl of Kerry (1811–36), died on 21 Aug. The Marquis of Northampton acted as emergency President.

199   *William Charles Henry, Manchester, to Harcourt, York, 29 September 1936*

You will probably have learned, through other channels, the irreparable loss, under the most painful circumstances, I have lately sustained. I cannot but regard the constant intellectual excitement of the Bristol meeting, operating upon a too sensitive frame which for some months previously had been rarely visited by refreshing sleep, as the cause of that sudden delirious paroxysm, which overloaded my poor father's clear intelligence and high moral principle and during a moment of fevered agony subdued his habitual and vigilant self-control.

I venture now to request that you will have the kindness to express to the Council of the British Association my most grateful sense of the honour they were pleased to confer upon me, in appointing me one of the [Local] Secretaries for the Liverpool meeting, an honour which I am now under the painful necessity of most respectfully declining. You will readily understand my feelings of total incompetency to take any action or conspicuous share in proceedings now so bitterly associated with the sad fate of one, whose affection towards me has been ever most ardent and tender.

Harcourt MSS

On 2 Sept 1836 William Henry committed suicide in the private chapel of his home.

200   *Forbes, Edinburgh, to John Taylor, 8 December 1836*

I understand from Mr Robison that he has countersigned Mr Russell's demand on the funds of the Association, for experiments on waves, etc. Mr Robison having communicated to me on a former occasion Mr Russell's statement of his progress, I find that a considerable proportion of the expenses incurred are purely *personal* expenses, as of travelling, lodging etc. You may perhaps recollect that at Bristol I declined having anything to do with Mr Russell's intromissions; but believing the case to be as now stated and that payments have been made or may be made from the funds of the society on such demands, I cannot suffer any private feelings which would altogether induce me to stand muted in the matter from protesting *in toto* against such misapplications of the funds of the Association which it is quite obvious must open a door to a system of unrestrained jobbing.

I cannot conceive that anything beyond the expenses in instruments and mechanical aid employed can fairly form an item in accounts which are not accounts of engineers, but which should be merely supplementary to the principal's own zealous exertions in a scientific cause.

You will oblige me much by saying whether such demands have on any former occasion been made upon you as Treasurer and whether Mr Russell's accounts have been presented in that distinct and precise shape which the greatness of the pecuniary concerns of the Association makes it necessary should be insisted on.

Harcourt MSS

At the 1836 meeting of the Association, John Scott Russell (1808-82), *DNB*, the naval architect, and Robison were awarded their first of several grants for research on the characteristics of waves and on the contours of ships.

201   *Harcourt, n.p., to Murchison, n.d. [late 1836]*

I am glad you postponed sending your letter till you had communicated with me for it is very desirable that on subjects of this degree of importance we should consult and act together.

The resolution of the General Committee, 15th August 1835, was this: 'that it be recommended to the Council to *consider* and *report upon* the most effectual means of obtaining an international protection for scientific and literary property in published works', a recommendation materially different from that stated in your letter 'that the Council be requested to take such measures as should from time to time appear to them to be desirable to promote such views'. What the Council were intended to do was to *make a report to the General*

Committee and the General Committee were afterwards *to take such measures as they thought fit.*

If the Council then are of opinion that there are circumstances which make it expedient for them to express their sentiments *immediately* without waiting for the authority of the general body it will be necessary to adopt a form of communication somewhat different from that of your letter. I would propose the following.

Sir [Guizot]　　The Council of the British Association for the Advancement of Science, having been informed that a commission has been appointed under the authority of the French government to deliberate on the best means of securing literary property, and being apprised of the interest which you take in every question of public policy which may affect the progress of knowledge, has directed us to submit to your consideration and to that of the commission the view which the Association entertains of the importance of some international arrangement for the protection of scientific and literary property in published works.

The propriety of thus extending the principle of securing to intellectual labour its just remuneration, and the expedience of encouraging authors by this means to adapt their works to the wants of other countries as well as of their own, will immediately occur to yourself, Sir, and to the enlightened members of the commission as among the chief reasons which have led the British Association to this conclusion, nor are they indifferent to the reflections that such a reciprocity whilst it advances the cause of literature and science will also tend to form an additional tie in the friendship of nations.

To place these views in a practical form the Council wish to invite the attention of the commission to the following general proposition. It is desirable that authors of different countries shall enjoy the exclusive privilege of publishing their works or translations of them in every other country, 2 for a limited period of time and 3 under the same conditions as if they were natives of that country, notifying their intention at some public office of record.

We have only further to add, Sir, that in the opinion of the Council that there are no countries between which the establishment of such a mutual understanding would be of greater reciprocal advantage than between France and England.

We have the honour to be, Sir,
　　With sentiments of the highest consideration

Harcourt MSS

On 9 Jan 1837 Harcourt and Murchison wrote to François Pierre Guillaume Guizot (1787–1874) about the desirability of international copyright: British Association Council minutes, 9 Jan 1837. Guizot did not reply.

202 *Phillips, York, to Harcourt, 16 March 1837*

Though I have only partially heard concerning you, the short statements made by Mr [William] Taylor have given me much anxiety on your account and if indeed, as he I think said, there be any thing doubted concerning the action of the heart the less trouble you take on any subject whatever the better. Do not therefore think of answering this letter, which is chiefly meant to tell you that I am going tomorrow for the third and last time to Lancashire, and among other things I intend now to visit Liverpool to see what is doing in respect of apartments and preliminary arrangements.

Mr Challis will probably ere this, have sent his paper to R. Taylor; if not yet, *Daubeny* and *Richardson* will find him full employment for a month. Should your stay in town be prolonged, and you may wish to consult me I will come to town a little earlier than I proposed (end of April). (My hands are so cold I can hardly write.) ...

I have found so many demands on my time last year, and this year expect so many more that in justice to the Yorkshire Philosophical Society I have informed the Council of my inability to devote in future *any fixed portion of time* to the duties which I have now performed for 12 years. It is open to the Council to adopt their own view and decision on the matter, but my conscience tells me that in thus restoring to the Council the appointment confided to me I am merely doing the commonest justice to them and myself, for it is not the amount of labour but the extent of time which I can no longer appropriate without utter neglect of my own health and studies. Inevitable engagements take me from home 5 months this year, and though by the favour of the Society this might not be construed into neglect of duties, it rendered my resignation unavoidable. Don't let this annoy you: there is plenty of time before 1838 to adopt a final determination but I assure you it is from no slight knowledge of my own mind, health and prospects in science that I have taken so decided a step *without any impulse from without*. For the last two years I have felt overworked, or rather overburthened with various occupation and *responsibility* and now that I have a prospect of some relief, the natural tone of my mind is beginning to return and I can plan the execution of some further publications.

Simpson is elected to the Hospital. Goldie thinks of settling in Lendal. The Swimming Bath is reviving on a more moderate plan of expense. The [Yorkshire] Blind School exhibition was greatly applauded and more subscribers have been added. Hoping that you may not long languish in doubtful health, with compliments to Mrs Harcourt.

Harcourt MSS

John Richardson (1787-1865), *DNB*, explorer and naturalist, wrote a long 'Report on North American zoology', *1836 Report*, 121-224; Thomas Simpson (1788/9-1863), was a York physician; in 1840 Phillips resigned from the Keepership of the Yorkshire Museum.

203   *Phillips, Royal Institution, Liverpool, to Harcourt, 6 April 1837*

I think you will be glad to hear that in all that regards the accommodation of the members of the Association, Liverpool promises well. The sectional meetings can be fixed in and near the Royal Institution, a capital part of the town, quiet, and near the lodging streets, and not too far from the Town Hall where the evening promenades and all the arrangements for reception, admission, etc can be completely arranged. For evening meetings, such as we have had before, the Amphitheatre offers great space (3000 seats); the Rotunda will do well for models and exhibition of inventions; the dinner can be given to 400 in Lucas's Rooms near the Amphitheatre and also near the Town Hall. Five sections may be at and within a stone's throw of the Royal Institution but every section room can be reached from any other in less than ten minutes: the two rather removed being medical (in a medical institution) and statistics in a handsome apartment. None of the rooms holds less than 150, the geological room 450; in *all 1800*. With regard to fêtes, etc if advisable, the Botanical Gardens may furnish 100 yards of tent in connection with a grand conservatory 1 mile from [the] Royal Institution.

Manchester taking one evening, Friday, as well as morning, the *evening meetings* may be 3, Monday, Wednesday, Saturday. Promenade and rafraîchissements, Tuesday, Thursday. Steam boat and railway trips may be had but I doubt the propriety of them.

Then as to the interest felt in Liverpool. It is not yet excited and much care and delicacy must be used in fanning the embers. Jealousies as to political and other disunion have induced me to recommend the first step to be thus. That the local officers should NOT constitute the Local Council, but with care and judgment select names of leaders of institutions and public or influential bodies, who are likely to work, and to get these declared as Local Council by the London Council, e.g. Mayor, Recorder, Rectors (2) etc. Thus a great evil may be avoided, for as one of the officers is not very popular (Turner) and is a somewhat talkative person, many of the good old Conservatives are likely to be shocked by the fact of his nominating or appearing to nominate the Council. He is a most worthy man, but less prudent than Currie (Whig) and Walker (Tory). Traill should be written to from hence (I have advised Walker to do so). Finally the aspect of trade in Liverpool is too alarming to allow of any *second step yet:* no one can think of any thing but the American packet and return of the lost bullion. They have fêted me, and what is of more importance have easily followed my reasoning and given no trouble.

Lord Burlington is totally unknown here, and political feeling very strong and not easily repressed. I am going away tomorrow to Lancaster and hope to see you in York, but if not then in London. Harris offers to fill an evening, and I think we may find a way of rendering the dull reports (or else fulsome reports) unnecessary as part of evening performance. I trust you are much recovered or quite well.

Harcourt MSS

William Wallace Currie (1784–1840) was 1st Mayor of the reformed corporation; Joseph Need Walker (1790–1865) was President of the Royal Institution, Liverpool; Turner was Samuel Turner; William Cavendish, 2nd Earl of Burlington (1808–91), *DNB*, was President at the Liverpool meeting, at which Traill gave the key-note address. The day in Manchester was planned as a tribute to that town's scientific importance.

204 *Murchison, 3 Bryanston Place, London, to Babbage, 13 April 1837*

Your memorial is so perfect, that no one can improve it. I am ready to be your squire whenever you fix to have an encounter with the little Knight of the Red Tape.

BL, Add. MSS 37190, f. 101

On behalf of the Association Babbage and Murchison, armed with Babbage's memorial, met Spring-Rice (Chancellor of the Exchequer) and Charles Edward Poulett Thomson (1799–1841), *DNB*, President of the Board of Trade, about the remission of duty on scientific instruments. The lobby was successful.

205 *Phillips, King's College, London, to Harcourt, St Clare, Ryde, Isle of Wight, 27 May 1837*

At the Council today, Yates being ill, I acted as secretary to the meeting. We got through a great mass of business, but for want of a list to be furnished by the Liverpool secretaries of men proper to join the Local Council this thing is postponed to June 9th, when the last meeting will be held. I shall go home on Thursday morning (if possible) with a dipping needle of some value to do my mountain work for the credit of old York.

Memorandum of things done at Council. 14 persons present!
{Earl of Burlington, Marquis of Northampton.

Report and progress as to duty on instruments: favourable.

Report and progress as to copyright: nothing new.

Report and progress as to Brest tides: nothing new.

Local Council to be named 9 June.

Circular adopted. I have made some improvements to help the issue of tickets at Liverpool greatly, added notice of model room etc.

Sub-committee of 5, Babbage, W.V. Harcourt, Powell, Murchison, Phillips, to meet on 9th of June at 1 p.m. to consider and report to the Council meeting *at* Liverpool as to the propriety of proposing a change in the qualification of members to be on the General Committee (object [is] to admit certain office-bearers of institutions and exclude mere writers of papers in magazines).

The Manchester day to be given up (I have found by letters that it would not do at all).

Secretaries of sections to print in the morning daily a list of papers which *have been read* and a similar list of those *to be read on the day*. (This is intended as a substitute for reading the report of the chairman of each section, which the whole meeting appeared to think intolerable because of the mode of doing it and the necessity of changing the plan of evening meetings as follows.)

Evening meetings for business *only two*, an opening and a concluding meeting. Not more than *two* evenings of the remaining four to be devoted to *general* lectures, exhibitions, etc and no such lecture to be given except previously authorized by the Council (chair to be taken and no discussion allowed). At least two evenings for conversation, promenade, etc.

Ladies admissible to *all* the evening meetings and bring others, provided that no mere speechifying (except on the last day) shall take place.

Mr S. Harris's experimental lecture on defence of ships from lightning accepted.

Some facilities for the newspaper editors allowed (inspection of papers etc).

Mr Whewell to be asked to accept office of Vice-president as the Bishop of Norwich cannot come and Dalton is ill.

Murchison to support applications now making as to Ordnance Surveyors starting to work in Scotland.

Nothing else of moment.

I was asked what you thought of the evening meetings. I replied Mr Harcourt desires them to be changed, so that on the one hand the dignity of the society shall not suffer by the production of ill arranged or unsuitable discourses or exhibitions, and on the other the public who expect gratification at the evening meetings, and wish to enjoy the opportunity of friendly conversation shall have their opportunity. To distinguish between evenings of business and lecture evenings on which ladies may properly and with pleasure attend and be instructed as well as amused. For these objects the evening meetings must be rearranged, and the labour which they bring upon the officers and others lightened. I stated that you valued the reading of the reports, and the lectures as a means of *uniting* the now divided body. On this head many suggestions were made and very fully and actively discussed, but the result was the adoption of Mr Babbage's motion, which was a revised outline of a plan of mine, to print daily a correct *list* of what *had been done*, and what was *to be done* in each section. This is the duty of each [sectional] secretary and will be easy for him and save me a world of anxiety and alarm. Upon the whole I am of opinion this plan and the change of the evening works will greatly benefit and simplify our arrangements and leave us more time for *thought*, and more hours for the recommendations.

Harcourt MSS

Phillips contributed to the work on the magnetic inclination and intensity in Britain done by Sabine, Lloyd, Fox, and Ross: 'A memoir on the magnetic isoclinal and isodynamic lines in the British Isles ...', *1838 Report*, 49–196. The Association had approached the Bureau des Longitudes about the publication of the tides measurements made at Brest 1806–30; the French were uncooperative. The Bishop of Norwich was Edward Stanley. From 1834 recommendations about research and grants were made to the General Committee by the Committee of Recommendations.

206 *Murchison, 3 Bryanston Place, London, to Harcourt, St Clare, Ryde, Isle of Wight, 26 June 1837*

Knowing that it is almost certain we of the British Association must take to *Newcastle next year*, and being very desirous in my capacity of General Secretary not to be without good cards to play, and fancying that I understand the method of succeeding in that region (from pretty good local acquaintance) I have made a 'démarche provisoire'.

In casting about in my own mind who ought to be our Praeses it occurred to me that the Duke of Northumberland was the proper man, whether you look to his station, his love of science or his popularity. I was also moved to this demonstration because I felt that it was highly desirable to break the spell of having any appearance of *one-sidedness*. I had, however, no notion, or rather very little hope, that the Duke *would* like such an office in case we went to Newcastle, and I therefore perceived that my friend Lord Prudhoe could be the President, as representing the Duke.

On opening the case to Lord Prudhoe he at once declined for

himself but offered to be an ambassador to his brother, and through him I lea[rned] that the Duke will be very happy to take the duty, if the office be proposed. I presume, nay I am sure, that I know your mind well enough to be confident that you will approve of this tentative, and that in the event of our deciding to go to Newcastle I should propose the Duke of Northumberland as President.

The Duke's position in the north is a tower of strength.

I have also had a conversation with the Bishop of Durham who will be delighted to do all in his power and to give us the best of Auckland Park ...

Harcourt MSS

Sir Hugh Percy, 3rd Duke of Northumberland (1785-1847), *DNB*, a Tory; Algernon Percy, 1st Lord Prudhoe (1792-1865), *DNB*; the Bishop of Durham was Edward Maltby (1770-1859), *DNB*.

207   *Phillips, Philosophical Institution, Birmingham, to Harcourt, St Clare, Ryde, Isle of Wight, 6 July 1837*

Unfortunately I can not well leave Birmingham till the 15th instant (unless it were from the 11th to the 13th inclusive) and as I wish to have some conversation with you as to the Liverpoolians *before I go there*, I am desirous of learning what chance there is of my meeting you in London. Would it be better for me to return *home* on the 15th and join you in London at a later day, or shall you prefer to see me on the 16th, Sunday, or 17th, Monday, or 18th, for I must not be long in town else my magnetic survey will be of small extent? I do not mean that this is of much importance, except for my health which needs many appeals to the air of the mountains, and never appeals in vain. I have just been discussing with Mr *Follett Osler* the principles and practice of his new anemometer which has worked very well and hope he will be induced to give the proofs of its good work at Liverpool. It would help greatly to correct our now somewhat rude notions of atmospheric phenomena did we really know the laws or limits of variability of the wind at *one point*, but there ought always to be *three* points exactly determined for the purpose of calculation. This subject of instruments is a very serious one, for our future progress in meteorology requires exact, numerous, and corresponding observations on a uniform plan and at a great expense. Mr Whewell's instrument I think will be of inestimable value in deciphering the meaning of the indications of the thermometer, wet bulb, electrical instruments, etc, and Mr Snow Harris highly approves it.

There is an attempt making by the Philosophical Institution here to obtain for themselves and other such bodies an exemption from local and national taxes; they hope to engage the Association in favour of their supplication. It may require an Act of Parliament: the pressure of these taxes is very injurious on many useful establishments (Bristol, Newcastle, Hull, Liverpool, Birmingham, Worcester) etc.

Though I hardly expect you *will* get to Liverpool, I trust you will get so well that you *might* go there with safety and comfort. It will be *less* exciting than previous meetings I feel confident.
[PS omitted]

Harcourt MSS

Abraham Follett Osler (1808-1903), *DNB*; in 1837-8 the British Association's General Committee and Council declined to lobby government about the remission of taxes and rates on buildings used for scientific purposes. The Philosophical Institution, Birmingham, paid 11% of its income in tax.

208 *Harcourt, St Clare, Ryde, Isle of Wight, to Phillips, Philosophical Institution, Birmingham, 9 July 1937*

The week before last being in town for two or three days I abstracted the chemical papers in my possession and sent the abstracts to the printer, having as regards Mr Crosse only left out what was palpably irrelevant, and taken care to let every alleged fact rest entirely on his own credit. The compunction however which I feel at being in any degree accessary to the publication of experiments in which I have no faith, and the general impression which I entertain that these abstracts of miscellaneous communications run up more on the debtor than creditor side of our account with the public, lead me to recommend strongly that this should be the last publication of them by the Association. Its own proper transactions are now become sufficient to fill an annual volume, and care should be taken to keep up a supply of good work from hands on which dependence may be placed.

You must not depend on me for any further work respecting this volume. I shall not object to revising any sheet which you may wish to pass through my hands; but without the original documents I fear my revision will be of little value. You must make sure of having it out before the meeting.

I think you have failed to receive two letters which I directed to you in London, in one of which I transmitted to you a proposal to *lecture* here; though that I suppose is out of the question, possibly if you come up to London you might contrive to pay us a visit; we can give you a bed and should be very happy to see you. The communication is very ready and the trip might not be disagreeable. If you cannot accomplish this I fear we may not meet till late in the autumn.

I hope you have taken care of my little crystals from the baked slate. Send them me if you can.

Phillips Papers, 1837/33

Harcourt was uneasy about appearing to give the Association's sanction in its *1836 Report* to the research of Andrew Crosse (1784-1855), *DNB*, who had created a sensation at the 1836 meeting when he described his views about the ability of electricity to produce crystals from solutions. Harcourt wished the *Reports* to contain only reports and research commissioned by the Association.

209 *Murchison, Beach Hotel, Littlehampton, to Harcourt, St Clare, Ryde, Isle of Wight, 11 July 1837*

You did not favour me with a yes or no to my last of date a month back.

I do not wish to charge you with duties, but the point on which I consulted you, and which it is essential for us as *ministers* to be agreed upon, is the President elect for 1838.

I told you that in my opinion it was impossible to pass by the Duke of Northumberland. He is in fact Patron and chief of their Natural History Society [of Northumberland, Durham and Newcastle-upon-Tyne] and has always *favoured science;* besides he is beyond all reach of cavil. And as there is no leading man of science there, no Dalton or Faraday to put at the head of it, we should take care to fix upon the man whom no one can gainsay.

Again we should not have the semblance of one-sidedness in politics and seeing that our two last chiefs have been Whigs, it is very desirable that an honourable but not bigotted Tory (like the Percy) should now be our Praeses. I got Lord Prudhoe to broach it to the Duke, very little thinking his Grace would take the bait, but *he did* and having expressed himself *most ready* to do his best if the office were proffered, I do not see how *I* can draw back.?

What do you think of beginning from the Liverpool date to make our affair *biennial*? It is infinitely too hard a drag on those who would wish to be always present. Besides, by permitting your best cards to be present at foreign reunions in the intervening years, you would command a most brilliant biennial and the communications would be of stouter materials with much fresh stimulus. What say you? I am *quite anxious* to make it from *this September* biennial. Hoping to hear good accounts of your little invalid and with best remembrances from my wife and self to Mrs W.V.H.

[PS] We have been here ten days for my wife's sea-bathing. I shall be here a week longer, then in town for 3 or 4 days. After that a fortnight at Up Park and Nursted near Petersfield. I am too busy with my book to go far from London. In August I shall go in to Staffordshire to give a last touch to certain Silurians and then drop down to Liverpool via Oulton Park, Sir Phil. Egerton's.

Harcourt MSS (Harcourt Papers, *xiii. 357*)

The idea of biennial meetings was floated by Murchison 1837–41 but not taken up by the Association. Harcourt had taken his family to the Isle of Wight, where he hoped the health of his eldest daughter Louisa would improve. She died in Jan 1839 aged twelve years. Murchison was finishing *The Silurian system* (London, 1839).

210 *Sir Francis Alexander Mackenzie, Conon near Dingwall, to Murchison, 3 Bryanston Place, London, 20 July 1837*

[Over the address Murchison scrawled:
Augt 8th answered. Stating that there was no objection to the introduction of agriculture as a branch of science but *impossible* to form a new section, already too many to be accommodated or managed; recommend it to be amalgamated with the statistical (statis & agricultural section)]

I was asked by a great many people last year at our Bristol meeting to take some steps towards having agriculture brought forward more *prominently* in one of our sections and I have had a good deal of correspondence since then on the subject, but like all other things no one excepting Sir David Brewster really gives me any assistance and I am left to eke out my way as I best can. Now I hear that you are against us and won't have any thing to do with mother earth till she has proved herself a patriarch and seen at least one deluge; therefore I cannot better apply than to you to know what are the [General] Committee's objections to what seems so universally desired. Let me I pray into the secret of your dislike to a subject which was so interesting to Davy and which would interest hundreds of our country squires amongst whom I have always understood it to be one of our great objects to encourage a thirst for science instead of the more common thirst for claret etc. I have before me now a letter from Sir C. Gordon, Secretary of the Highland Society, 'conveying to me their concurrence in the great importance of every attention being given to agriculture as a science'; and unless you are afraid that the section will be better attended than your geological one which is a fear unworthy of geology (in its great depth) I know not the reason of a seeming unwillingness to allow the lairds squires and yeomen of Britain enrol their names as members of the Association and call the aid of scientific research towards obtaining that greatest of all blessings to an Englishman, plenty of good cheer. I won't trouble you with more on the subject as I suppose that we shall have a very strong memorial signed at Liverpool this year, but as you are au fait in the secrets of your divan pray let me know if we shall expect much opposition from you and upon what grounds. I have been in this country for a month and our weather has been delicious; the country never looked better. Pray offer my kind regards to Mrs Murchison.

BL, Add. MSS 46127, ff. 146–7

Sir Francis Alexander Mackenzie (1798–1843) and Sir Charles Gordon of Drimnin, near Oban, were Scottish improving landowners. In 1843 agriculture was admitted to the Association via section B (chemistry and its applications to agriculture and the arts).

211 *Phillips, Royal Institution, Liverpool, to Harcourt, St Clare, Ryde, Isle of Wight, 10 August 1837*

I arrived here on the 8th evening and have already obtained an aperçu of the état des affaires. All the notions of political feeling seem to be falsified by the event or rather the thing is completely neutralized by the measures adopted in consequence of forethought. The Council here and (Sub) Committees are hard at work and it will need some care to prevent them from over-running the ground. I think I may be able to prevent any mischief on this head, but already as to ladies tickets the course was become oblique and needed rectification. I think also the plan proposed in modification of my own to concentrate the *sections* round the Town Hall, in the midst of the bustle, not good on many accounts, so that I hope it will be re-exchanged for the old one.

There is a good spirit among the public bodies, and I expect a fair subscription for expenses. We shall try to reduce these to a minimum.

The Council meeting has passed very satisfactorily.

14 August

We have rearranged our section meetings nearly as I had first proposed. Members are elected daily.

Some subscriptions are received. There appears no doubt of the meeting being well attended. Buckland is abroad and will not come home in time. I hear *nothing at all* of Traill.

Tomorrow morning I shall supply R. Taylor with the last Mss he is to expect from me and I think it will be as much as he can do to produce the volume [*1836 Report*] in time for Monday 11 Sept. I go tomorrow for 3 or 4 days to the Isle of Man to magnetize and make myself well for I am hardly so at present. My kind host Mr Walker goes from home tomorrow also, but since we have adjusted many of the preliminary measures there appears no reason why Mr Wallace Currie and myself can not get through the rest of the business and let Mr Walker have his *grousing* in Glen Dochert, Perthshire. He will return in 10 days or so, and Traill, *it is said*, comes on the 18th.

Lord Derby has written to offer all the help he can give, but this is not thought likely to amount to more than an inspection of his Aviary as the Old Lord gives no money even to charity without grave consideration.

Colonel Sykes is to present a report on the statistics of Deccan.

Last year an Italian MD of eminence, *Manni* of Rome, called on me at York after the Bristol Meeting, and passed part of the day. He promised to send to Liverpool a copy of a large bust of Maecenas recently found and then in his possession. I thought it a pleasant speech and was vastly astonished yesterday to be informed of its arrival, a marble bust by Thorwaldsen, homage to the British Association. He wishes it to be put in a fuller situation where the world may see it and not be called upon to pay shillings. It is not quite easy to find this in Liverpool!

I trust you are all enjoying prospects of improved health, and that my young friend received her botanical work via Longman's whence I ordered it to be sent to Grosvenor Square.

[PS] I dined at a mighty Mayor's feast here the other day with Parke, the Sheriffs and 45 others. This is the country of turtle par excellence, never knew such a place for dinners!

Harcourt MSS

Edward Smith Stanley, 13th Earl of Derby (1775-1851), *DNB*, opened his menagerie at Knowsley to the Association; William Henry Sykes (1790-1872), *DNB*, formerly of the East India Company; Pietro Manni, a Roman physician and antiquary, had attended the 1836 meeting; Bertel Thorwaldsen (1770-1844), the Danish sculptor, lived in Rome 1820-38; Parke was probably James Parke (1782-1868), *DNB*, the judge, who attended the 1831 meeting of the Association.

212 *Murchison, Leamington, to Harcourt, St Clare, Ryde, Isle of Wight, 20 August 1837*

Having failed in seeing my scientific friend, to meet whom I halted here today, I think I cannot better employ an hour at my hotel than in writing to you, awaiting a frank which I shall procure tomorrow from my host Lord Dartmouth.

I was so very busy my two days in town that I should scarcely have had time to hunt out Babbage, but I stumbled on him at midnight in Regent Street returning from an explosion of Vesuvius in the Surrey Zoological Gardens so we walked home together. I found him in desperate bad humour, not with *us*, but with things in general and Whigs in particular. The machine and its prodigious expenses are breaking the poor fellow's heart: he declared it was impossible he should go to Liverpool; that he could not *afford* it, explaining that he lost £200 for example by going to Dublin, which I found to mean that owing to his absence things went wrong, calculations erred, and workman's time was thrown away. I tried to reason him into better humour by allowing him to expend the whole of his ire *upon* the Whigs, and I should not be surprised that he comes to Liverpool after all.

He *approved highly* of Peel as a future President and I have no doubt would be charmed to be his Vice Lieutenant, in that the Duke of Wellington and Peel are demi Gods in his eyes compared with the scrubby timid Whigs.

The *real* history of his sulkiness quoad Liverpool, i.e. the most cogent reason with him, Lord Burlington! Babbage has a strong feeling that Lord B. *deserted* all his best and warmest Cambridge supporters and utterly forgot *their* sacrifices *for* him; he therefore declares he will not go a yard to swell the train of such a poor devil (Babbage was chairman of his committee).

I will write to Brewster from Sandwell.

Tomorrow I am to meet old Corrie the Great in Birmingham to judge of capacity and capability; you shall hear the result. Phillips had gone to the Isle of Man for a few days by a letter from Joseph Walker who was at Liverpool *till the 16th*. He is now grousing but is to be at his post again on the 2nd at latest, William Currie acting ad interim for both.

Sandwell, Wednesday. After gay cliffing and geologizing I reached Birmingham and found old Corrie waiting. I inspected all the sites proposed to accommodate us. They appear ample. The New Schools, an exquisite building by Barry, furnishes 2 very large and 2 moderate sized halls, enough for 4 sections within the same building provided they can make out committee rooms. The Philosophical Institution having a good laboratory and a theatre will do for the chemical, the Medical School and theatre for the medical, and the rooms at their Court House for the statistical. This leaves the great Town Hall free for our general assemblies with an excellent large room under the organ for the General Committee. As to scientific secretaries I could not learn much though I think old Corrie could manage this; the inventor of the anemometer might be one, but this I say not advisedly and only having seen the machine not the man. I find from Corrie that although he is of the *low* party at Birmingham he is *most anxious* to have Peel as President and has already discussed the matter warmly with his friends of that clique some of whom were very violent against the nomination, but he has or is bringing them round. I charged him to obviate all this before he came to Liverpool, for that if Birmingham was selected Peel must be the man. As this has all come from *themselves*, and Babbage is also amicable, there can be no doubt of *what ought* to be done. Write to me at Liverpool so that I may have the letter when I arrive on the 5th or 6th.

Harcourt MSS

William Legge, 4th Earl of Dartmouth (1784–1853) owned Sandwell Park, near Birmingham; John Corrie (1769–1839), Unitarian minister, was President of the Philosophical Institution, Birmingham; Charles Barry (1795–1860), *DNB*, the architect. Burlington was M P for Cambridge University 1829–31; the inventor of the anemometer was William Follett Osler.

213 *Phillips, Royal Institution, Liverpool, to Harcourt, 25 August 1837*

Though I grieve to trouble your retreat with any thing tending to disquietude, it seems hardly possible to delay longer asking your views on two material things connected with the Association on which you have made a large venture of your own reputation, as well as lavished most precious time and deep reflection. In this Association we may behold the type one and indivisible of all human efforts to augment and establish knowledge. We propose
1. Certain objects
2. Appoint certain means for their fulfilment.
So long as you have held, virtually at least, the guidance of our ponderous machine, I, at least, have supposed myself to know what objects we aspired to: *combination* of adequate means in the acquisition of *data* wanted for the amplification of theory; *selection* of specially gifted persons to make the required generalisations and amplifications. You leave us (I am afraid) without a successor of adequate influence, and disinterested conception of your plan, to keep our vessel on the right course. Say you put it in the hands of a *select body* (Committee of Recommendations), they require larger powers and longer durations and cannot long escape opposition and censure. Give it to the *Council*, a more unfortunate delegation (according to my observation) can hardly be. There *station*, rank et id genus omne, will stifle your simple flower of philosophy, or turn it into a double and fruitless gewgaw. What *single man* do you know who will give his life to the growth of knowledge in other men;

neither blinded by special views of the value of science, nor personally interested in the theoretical questions which must arise, and the verification of which may turn the whole strength of the Association into a fruitless path of research?

I see only one clear course: (1) let the committees of science be bound together and *kept together* for their year of duty; (2) let each committee present a report at every meeting of the steps taken in its own field of research; (3) let them also respectively prepare for printing their own report of the proceedings had in their section at each meeting; (4) out of these let their demands for special reports and researches arise, a very hasty business as now done; (5) let all this be submitted to the Committee of Recommendations *after the meeting*.

Then as to the publication. Will it not be best to divide our volume into 3 things? 1. Recommendations etc with annual supplements and explanations (give it away to members). 2. The reports etc published as before. 3. The notices: let these be given to the journals etc or if collected for members let them consist *exactly* of the reports of the committees of science.

Powell talks of a paid secretary of notices. I cannot conceive of what use such a being could be: but a change of our present plan is really demanded, by the dignity of our object, which suffers greatly in my eyes by the scraps of commonplace which compose the bulk of those notices. I expect to be roughly handled for throwing away whole sheets of the merest schoolboy theses on this occasion. Thus you see I have written loosely chiefly to give you a sketch of what fears are in my mind, in hopes that you will find it good to tell me, for my guidance, how you think of the delegation of your powers *if you resign them;* and what are your views as to the *volume* on which there seems somewhat of ferment. If you do *resign* the Secretariate, Whewell, Babbage, Peacock, seems to me the best man, and you ought to be named as a Vice-president for the next meeting.

PS   I had nearly forgotten to say that, as I told you, the localities here are capital, but the waves of science are very slow and shallow. There is no excitement, little money yet raised, and only 100 or 200 members elected. They say it will grow with a great ratio. Be it so!

Harcourt MSS (Harcourt Papers, *xiii. 365–8*)

In Sept 1837 Murchison replaced Harcourt as senior General Secretary, a succession which worried Phillips. The notices were of communications made at a meeting.

214   *Burlington, Holker Hall near Kendal, to Harcourt, 3 September 1837*

I am extremely obliged to you for the instructions you have given me as to my duties at the approaching meeting of the Association.

Your letter should have been here two days ago, but it has only arrived this morning.

I have attended only one meeting, that held at Cambridge, but I hear from everybody that hitherto so much has depended on your exertions that I am very apprehensive your absence on this occasion will be a very serious obstacle to the success of the meeting.

Nothing occurs to me at present which you have not mentioned in your letter, but if I should want your advice on any point, I will not hesitate to avail myself of your permission to trouble you with more letters. You have rather alarmed me by telling me how much you expect me to do on Monday evening. I trust your anticipations of Dr Traill's inefficiency will not be verified, for I fear my speech will be but a poor substitute. I am very anxious to receive the last volume of the Society's transactions [ie *1836 Report*] and am much obliged to you for ordering it for me.

Blanche goes with me to Liverpool, and will I hope feel strong enough for the evening parties.

Harcourt MSS

Blanche Georgina, Burlington's frail wife, died in 1840.

215 *Harcourt, St Clare, Ryde, Isle of Wight, to Phillips, 4 September 1837*

1. The selection of scientific surveyors to map the terra cognita of our knowledge and to cast a prophetic glance over the terra incognita; 2. the selection and combination of enquirers, and the supply of means, for the purpose of obtaining the data wanted for the improvement of theory: these are the objects which the Association has sought to fulfil and in which it has already had as much success as could perhaps be expected in so new and difficult an undertaking. As for '*the selection of generalisers and improvers of theory*' that I suspect is above our mark, but we may undoubtedly be of the greatest assistance to them and may sometimes even excite their inspirations.

The various machinery which we have set a going for the attainment of these ends has been at work for six years and we have had sufficient experience of it to know the practical value of every wheel. Now with respect to committees our general experience is that all cooperation expires with the meeting, except that kind of cooperation which consists in individuals taking each his own road towards one concerted point; we find indeed occasionally that two or three persons may be associated together with advantage for some definite object which they have at heart; but we have not found it practicable nor do I believe it is practicable to execute the plan of keeping on foot in the intervals of the meetings permanent committees of sciences to correspond and consult together for their advancement. I would not therefore counsel a repetition of this attempt. Yet I am fully alive to the importance of a better matured system of recommendations and I would suggest with that view that it should be an instruction to the sectional committees to appoint some person or persons to report to the next meeting what data are wanting to determine important points of theory in procuring which the resources of the Association might be available: such reports would furnish the best materials for the deliberations of the committees.

With respect to the publication of our transactions I have before given you my opinion that it would be better on all accounts to confine it in future to the reports and recommendations of the Association and the researches instituted at its instance. As to the miscellaneous matter which comes before the sections, if the General Committee were to choose some respectable journal and to instruct the secretaries of the sections to request the authors of any valuable communications to furnish an abstract to the editor, all difficulty and responsibility on that subject would be happily at an end. The recommendations should I think continue attached to the transactions and earlier copies of them might be sent to the members of committees etc and given to other members on application.

On the last point, my retirement from my office of Secretary, I will say first that it is the post of all others which had I been without a profession I should most have desired to fill, and secondly that had I felt equal to it together with other duties I would not have given it up. As it is I shall send by Murchison a formal and final resignation. Most heartily do I wish that Whewell could be induced to accept this office for a couple of years: it would be nothing but play to him and of incalculable service to the Association. I am sure there is no advice I can give of so much consequence as that every effort should be made to accomplish that object.

[PS]   Pray look after the reception of our associate De La Rive.

Phillips Papers, 1837/45

216   *Murchison, Liverpool, to Harcourt, Bishopthorpe near York, 18 September 1837*

The Liverpool coach has not been upset and the meeting has gone off remarkably well, notwithstanding *wind and weather*. I arrived on Thursday and cast about to find how the land laid and foresaw very soon that in all essentials connected with this meeting there would be perfect success and so it has turned out. The conversazione, Snow Harris's lecture, and above all a splendid dinner or dejeuner to 2500 persons in the Botanical Gardens have all proved good and satisfactory. There has been more intermixture and intercourse and less of wrangling and sparring than at any former meeting. I am now speaking of the mass. There appeared, however, early in the week two or three great nebulae in the horizon which it required all my energy and skill to disperse. 1st. A colossal head of *Maecenas* had been sent by an Italian Doctor *Manni* to the British Association as a recompense for their kindness to him at Bristol, and this head was *to pass through us* to Liverpool par les mains as the French say of one Dr Bryce; and it was currently reported that all our affairs on Monday were to begin with an exposition of this head in our great amphitheatres, where it was to be served up with a sauce of Dr Bryce's preparation. I smashed the dish, for I saw that it would be a delightful 'morceau' for John Bull and all our friends gastropatetic, particularly as Lord Nugent was present etc. I deferred it to the Saturday night, together with Old Tobin, that we might have all the trumpets together after the real science of the week had been completed.

Another and a *thicker* nebula arose. Friday evening had been left blank in the progamme. The Mechanics' Institute seized on it, issued a flaming prospectus and handbills 6 feet long, announcing that the British Association, Earl of Burlington and Marquis of Northampton were to attend!!! I at once resolved to run (though in an amicable manner) an opposition coach. I instantly bespoke the great amphitheatre, and recollecting your old opinion that the meeting should never separate without some evening assembly at which the proceedings of the sections were brought before the public, I resolved at once to ask each president of a section not to give a detailed and prosy abstract of all that had been done, but to present in a condensed view (each taking about 20 minutes) *the spirit of his section*. The plan *took*. Faraday promised and the presidents or persons they appointed went through their parts. I need not tell you that a few hours after I took the step my placards were all over the town with the names of my 7 dramatis personae. It has been the best thing of the week. Lord Burlington went to the Mechanics' Institute for 20 minutes, told them he was there in his private capacity and not as President British Association, gave them good advice and was much applauded. I cannot mention him without assuring you that we never have had a better chief.

I should say he was *the* best. In public, though [not] gifted with the power of fluent oratory, his manner is impressive and his thoughts clear and his promptitude and decision *very remarkable* in so young a man. I cannot speak too highly of his conduct in the General Committee at which we had long and in some respects stormy debates. I much regret that Lord Burlington was not here on Saturday to attend the General Committee, of which Lord Northampton was the chairman, for if he had some awkward points might have been parried. At that meeting we resolved to modify that law concerning qualification for General Committee on which you and I had so much talk, and which *we foresaw* would give so much trouble. The *statisticians* fanned the flame and your 'intellectual Atlas', Whewell, poured in such a deluge of aether that I feared a terrible combustion. They gave me credit for getting through without loss of temper. In fact Whewell told them totidem verbis that the statistical section ought never to have been admitted and went much too far. *We* all know how this originated, but having the section once established it was our bounden duty to keep its members in good humour. They took fire at not being one of the bodies named whose publishing members are admissible to the General Committee, and the result of a long debate was their admission and that of the Geological Society of Dublin, etc. In the meantime this discussion had let loose the angry feelings of deputies and provincials and a storm was brewing. To expedite business we resolved to have two other meetings [of the] General Committee, one on Thursday at 3 at which the place of meeting and officers for next year were to be appointed, the second to be devoted (viz Saturday) to the calm and exclusive consideration of the reports and recommendations and money grants. No sooner had Saturday passed over than a rumbling whisper passed my ear that *the people of Newcastle* (unknown to any member of the Council or to any of the present Vice-presidents or General Secretaries) had actually sent a *deputation* to *Lord Durham* to ask him to be our next chief and *that* he had assented!!!

Ascertaining this melancholy and unforeseen fact on Monday morning, as soon as the sections met, and learning from little Johnston of Durham that he, Harry Witham and Mr Hutton had been the doers, I consulted with Lord Northampton, Lord Burlington and others and immediately wrote to Lord Durham stating the whole case. In order to prevent any misconception I told him that there had been so very universally expressed an opinion that the next President if selected from the nobility should not be Whig and that the leading members of the Association had recognised this opinion to show clearly to all that science was of no party. I added that in an entire ignorance of any step being taken by the men of Newcastle (neither the General Secretaries nor any members of the Council having heard of it) a motion had been made to the Duke of Northumberland who had signified his willingness to act if elected. I then begged permission to write in His Lordship's name as Vice-president, with a due amount of puff etc. This last proposition was made because the men of the north said Lord Durham would act in that capacity. No answer arrived till Friday morning. In the meantime on Thursday we were obliged according to notice to go into the case of the next place of meeting and we had a very full committee. Receiving applications from Newcastle, Birmingham, Manchester, Sheffield, and Cheltenham, a long palaver ensued. Old Corrie of Birmingham made us a most touching and eloquent harangue which surprised every one, but he did it in a quiet and gentlemanlike manner which was certain not to provoke angry feelings. I cannot here go into the details, but the case was decided hollow in favour of the coal-hole long before the meeting; and after eloquent and neat speeches from Hamilton and others Newcastle was unanimously carried with a full understanding that Birmingham would be our next place of meeting. Sir W. Hamilton then proposed the Duke of Northumberland, and was seconded by Brewster, Peacock, Sedgwick, Whewell and Baily all of whom brought out in succession such a series of proofs of why he ought and must be our chief in the north (several of the *deeds* previously unknown to me: several *thousand pounds* for scientific objects) that all responsibility was taken from me and His Grace was with warm acclamation proclaimed President.

And here I must tell you by way of interlude that Lubbock broached as a principle (not objecting to the Duke) that we ought always, if possible, to take a scientific chief. I cheered the sentiment [warmly] and stated that it was our wish to act on it from time to time whenever a favourable opportunity occurred. But I called on Professor Johnston to state whether in his opinion there was any such person in the north of England; on which he and all the men of Newcastle declared there was no such person and that they were all *now* agreed that the Duke of Northumberland was the man. *I* then proposed the Earl of Durham, stating that should ill health or any other cause prevent the Duke's attendance Lord Durham would from his great talents and power of conducting public meetings make us a most efficient President and this passed. Our other officers were: Vice-presidents, the Revd W. Vernon Harcourt, Prideaux Selby, Esq; [Local] Secretaries, Hutton, Johnston and Adamson. I will [not] tell you all that I endeavoured to say of you when I proposed your name as V P or how enthusiastically the proposal was received. I then announced your resignation as General Secretary and proposed as your substitute the *Revd Professor Peacock*, which was much approved of.

In pursuance of your wishes I tried hard to get Whewell but in vain, and my next cast was Peacock who has taken it for the year though the latter part is between ourselves. I have so thorough a reliance on Peacock's good judgment and *temper*, and his *manners* are so infinitely preferable to those of Whewell that in *managing men* which is our great difficulty, I cannot tell you how gratified I am with my new coadjutor.

All went off charmingly when on Friday morning a fierce gale set in from the north-east in the form of a letter from Lord Durham, desiring me indignantly to withdraw his name from any list of officers and talking of 'rational' beings, etc.

Lords Burlington and Northampton were both shocked at this impatient and angry reply, while the men of Newcastle were all in dismay. I saw at once that the only course was to substitute the name of the Bishop of Durham for that of the Earl by merely announcing on the morning of Saturday, that his Lordship declined. This was highly approved and all ended very well.

The result, however, has given me much trouble for my business is not to quarrel with or expose Lord Durham, which I might have done by reading to the Committee and shortly publishing his intemperate absurd and perverted letter to me, but to keep all men in peace. I have though (and Burlington approves) written what I hope you will consider a dignified but yet a polite letter such as will save the Newcastle men from his ire and preserve the balance if possible, with a long private letter to Witham and company who are going to pacify him. I have done this simply to save the Association from discord.

Entre nous the whole of this is owing to Phillips having given the men of hot rolls and butter reason to think that they were to do *the whole thing* and, before it was even certain that we were to go there, that they were to depute to and therefore to elect a President. Such a precedent should never be established. They should have corresponded with you or me before they *thought* of such a thing.

I have toiled my fingers off and stretched my heart-strings to set all to rights. 'T was well you were not here, for the agitation would have been too much.

I shall be at Cheltenham in a week where you may write if you please. Afterwards for 2 days in London and after that at Nursted. [PS] The sections here have been excellent, and Sedgwick as president of the geological surpassed himself. He smitted the hearts of all the ladies of whom we had 300 daily in our gallery at the Mechanics' Institute.

Harcourt MSS (Harcourt Papers, *xiii. 359–65*)

Charles Bryce was a Liverpool surgeon; George Nugent Grenville, Baron Nugent (1788–1850), *DNB*, the radical Whig; John George Lambton, 1st Earl of Durham (1792–1840), *DNB*, a leading Whig politician; Prideaux John Selby (1788–1867), *DNB*, the Northumberland ornithologist; John Adamson (1787–1855), *DNB*,

Newcastle-upon-Tyne attorney and antiquary. *John Bull*, a Sunday newspaper, was a fierce critic of the Association. The new Mechanics' Institution, Liverpool, was opened on Friday, 15 Sept 1837. At the 1833 meeting of the Association, the statistical section was established clandestinely and its existence reluctantly accepted by the General Committee as a fait accompli.

217 *Murchison, Cheltenham, to Charles Wentworth Dilke, the Editor, Athenaeum Office, 2 Catherine Street, Strand, London, 27 September 1837*

Private

I had no time when at Liverpool to look into the public journals, and as long as I saw that the proceedings of the British Association were successful I was satisfied. In reading over the published accounts I naturally turned to your journal as one which has *been always very happy* in giving an excellent sketch of these meetings. I am quite aware of the many difficulties your reporter has to contend with and I will not therefore go into details concerning the sectional meetings. In running my eye over the account of the proceedings of the geological section I perceive that my name is omitted on several occasions and also all notice of several points of some geological importance on which I spoke at some length. Again in the account of Wednesday's proceedings it is stated that Professor Sedgwick *suggested* the subscription for Brennan the miner. Whatever merit this subscription had, it was *my suggestion* and as such announced from the chair. In fact it would not have come so well from my friend Professor Sedgwick as from one of his auditory who were so moved by his pathetic description. But to pass from these personal affairs (which though trifling you will perhaps correct) to a topic of general interest connected with the future success of the Association in which as General Secretary and Trustee I am warmly associated, I must allude to your account of the meetings of the General Committee on Thursday & Saturday. Of the first I would only say that in stating the opinions of Mr Lubbock and two or three other gentlemen concerning the superior fitness of *scientific* men to fill the office of President, it would have been kind and courteous towards the Council and the officers of the Association to have said that Mr Murchison the General Secretary endeavoured to explain how under existing circumstances the selection of such a scientific chief was *impracticable*, in which statement he was borne out by the men of science of the north of England. The Council have never abandoned the principle of taking a man of science for their chief when *an opportunity* occurs, but how was this to be done at Liverpool? How at

Newcastle? I will not here enter into the discussion of this point, but as much was said to place this matter in an *amicable train* and as no notice is taken of anything which I did or said, I may complain of the *impression* which is left upon the public mind. I now pass to the account of Saturday's meeting [of the] General Committee (p 706). On that occasion (though not mentioned) I was the person who received the letter from the Earl of Durham and as such I stated (not the Earl of Burlington) that the Earl of Durham had declined the office of Vice-president, and I proposed the Bishop of Durham in his Lordship's place. You then state truly 'that no explanation of this circumstance was given or demanded in the meeting' but the statement which follows though 'brief' is not 'fair', and this I am sure you will acknowledge when I place the *facts* before you.

The general or London Council did *not* write (as you state) 'to the *local authorities* to make the necessary arrangements in order that they might be laid before the General Committee'. A moment's reflection will convince you that the general or London Council, which is the governing body between the weeks of annual meeting, *could* not communicate with a body *not in existence* and whose *creation* would depend upon the vote of a future meeting of the General Committee. The simple truth is that some scientific gentlemen of the neighbourhood of Newcastle, conceiving that they were authorized (though they never had been so instructed by either of the General Secretaries or any member of the London Council), did tender the office of future President to the Earl of Durham. Though a mistake, this act proceeded from a zealous desire to perform duties which these gentlemen conceived to be within their province and I am far from wishing to impute the slightest blame to them.

In the mean time however the proper authorities (agreeable to former practice) had felt their way as to a future President *in case* the *General Committee* should decide upon visiting Newcastle, and the Duke of Northumberland having been applied to had consented to act if elected.

You will therefore perceive, that if the gentlemen of Newcastle had not taken upon themselves the duties of the *Officers* of the Association, no dilemma or difficulty would have arisen.

As the case then stood, it appeared desirable to say as little about it as possible, but simply to propose the Duke of Northumberland as President, because the proper initiatory steps had been taken concerning his Grace's appointment.

At the same time, as it was suggested by some of the gentlemen from Newcastle and Durham that the Earl of Durham would be gratified in having the office of Vice-president offered to him, a letter was written to that effect, explaining the official steps which had been previously taken. His Lordship declined the post and it was then our duty to supply his place.

After the warm and well merited encomiums which were passed upon the Duke of Northumberland by the most eminent men of science from all parts, for his Grace's *munificent* and *repeated* donations to promote scientific objects I need say no more of the propriety of the appointment (Sir W. Hamilton, Sir D. Brewster, Professor Sedgwick, Professor Peacock and others spoke with great effect on the subject).

I have written this letter for your information in order that a kind feeling should be kept up between the various parties of which our large body is composed and between whom there is in reality no difference of opinion on any point of importance connected with the *operation* of the Association when the facts are properly explained.

That the Liverpool meeting went off remarkably well is generally acknowledged and that its success was in great measure due to an increased facility of social intercourse is not to be doubted. It is to this point, which has been materially modified in relation to former meetings, that I have most directed my attention as well as to afford ready access to every one who was really desirous of acquiring information. I venture to hope that your observer at Liverpool will on reviewing the general result not give occasion to any one to think that the official duties I had to perform, which were undertaken at a considerable loss of time accompanied by the retardation of a large work now in press, were inadequately performed.

[PS] I shall be in town at the end of the week.

Murchison Papers, Edinburgh University Library, Gen 523/2

Charles Wentworth Dilke (1789–1864), *DNB*, edited *The Athenaeum*. In Murchison's eyes the offending pages were *Athenaeum*, 1837, 697, 706. Daniel Brennan was an intrepid miner who saved the lives of four colleagues when the sea broke into a submarine part of a colliery at Workington.

218 *Murchison, Nursted House, Petersfield, to Dilke, 7 October 1837*

Your packet of Tuesday only reached me yesterday. I hope you will not for a moment think that I am actuated by *any personal feeling* in the points alluded to. I have always said and still think that your journal contains much the best account of the general proceedings of the Association, and any small errata on points of science are not of great moment for these will be corrected in our volumes. But it is I repeat of *great importance* to our *future* welfare, that the public should not be led to think that there is *bad management in the Council, that Lords are preferred to men of science*, and *that confusion is arising from jarring interests.* I ask you to look at your two short accounts of the proceedings of the General Committee on Thursday and Saturday; and if you are of opinion that they might produce such impressions, if unexplained, I would ask you in fairness to place the matter in a clear light by simply stating the facts. Besides the correction of the press I therefore herewith subjoin a little statement, of which you can make any use you please, not as *my document*, but as information you have gained from the most authentic sources. My sole object is to preserve the peace. Had this not been the case I might by a direct letter to the editors of the daily papers have published correspondence which would set all this matter at rest, but I have no intention of so doing.

The Presidents past and elect as well as every person of influence in the Association appreciated the motive.

Murchison Papers, Edinburgh University Library, Gen 523/2

219　*Sabine, Tortington, Sussex, to Phillips, 4 July 1838*

I hope you have received through Mr Gyde, who kindly undertook to send them to you, *eight* copies of my report on the magnetic intensity, one for yourself, one for the Bishop of Durham, one for Mr Vernon Harcourt, and one for Professor Johnston (the Local Secretary). May I ask your friendly aid in forwarding the three last named copies to their respective destinations, the copy for the Bishop of Durham to be accompanied by the note which I enclose? There will remain *four* copies at your disposal; and should you desire more they shall be sent to you as soon as your letter reaches me. I have already supplied copies to nearly all the leading members of the Association who were in London last week. It is desirable, that the means of forming an independent judgment, on the subject of a south polar magnetic expedition, should be furnished to all those members who may be expected to take a prominent part in the conduct and proceedings of the Association at Newcastle: for I am assured that on the one hand it will not fail to be brought under discussion there, and on the other I am assured by a competent authority to judge, (Captain Beaufort), that if the discussion terminates in the adoption of a suitable recommendation to government, it will certainly be done. The force that the recommendation will carry will depend, (or *should* depend) on the number of concurring supporters, of those whose judgments are of value on such a point, *after a due consideration.* I have endeavoured in my report to bring together as much of the materials on which a judgment should be formed as could be condensed within the space, and it is now my object to put the report into the hands of all those whose concurrence is desirable. I am rejoiced to say that Sir J Herschel, whose opinion must carry great weight, is a warm advocate, for the measure, and for its recommendation by the Association. Do not therefore scruple asking for copies if you can make them useful as there are nearly 50 left. Captain Beaufort and Ross are occupied in preparing themselves with all the *nautical* considerations which may require to be taken into the account in a plan of operations. I am going over to Ireland to see Mr Lloyd and Dr Robinson before the meeting, to talk well over such a comprehensive scheme as would embrace weekly simultaneous observations in stations appropriate to each of the principal magnetic centres, in addition to determine the lines of dip, force, and variation in the southern hemisphere. Should you be so kind as to favour me with any suggestions, bearing upon any part of the subject, either as to the plan itself, or on points which may be likely to influence its *successful* discussion at the meeting, I am sure you will not spare the trouble. I will only add that nothing which I can do shall be wanting; but that some one of more weight and influence than I possess must be looked to to bring it forward ...

You were very kind at the Liverpool meeting in securing me a most convenient lodging: can I ask you to do me this great favour a second time? Mrs Sabine will be with me; a couple of rooms, with facility of breakfast and tea would be all we should desire. But if the sitting room were large, we could accommodate the more in holding consultations etc. Pray let me know when you propose to leave York for Newcastle, that I may have the power of finding you either at one or the other a few days before the meeting in case I see occasion to do so. Excuse this very long letter and believe me with our united very kind regards to your sister,

Phillips Papers, Box 9

Sabine's wife, Elizabeth Juliana (1807-79), was an accomplished translator of German and French scientific works. Sabine had 250 pre-prints made of his 'Report on the variation of the magnetic intensity observed at different points of the earth's surface', *1837 Report*, 1-85. It confirmed the importance of a British voyage to the south pole area to study magnetism, a project for which the Association successfully lobbied government, 1838-9.

220 *Phillips, Royal Institution, Manchester, to Harcourt, St Clare, Ryde, Isle of Wight, 7 July 1838 (till 27 July)*

Though I have not written to you for months you will not believe that I have had no occasion to write, but in fact, knowing your occupation to be extreme and that you had causes of anxiety, I chose to incur the reproach of neglect rather than give you trouble. Perhaps I should not now trouble your flowery retreat, but that I feel very anxious on two or three points connected with the Association, and you alone can resolve my perplexity. 1. Shall you take your post of honour at Newcastle? 2. If so, will you take your post of work in the Committee of Recommendations? 3. Have Mr Murchison or Peacock written to you concerning the corresponding members list, on which I know they wished to know your views. (I have asked Mr Murchison this question so you need not regard it.)

If you will be able to attend to such questions as may arise regarding the propriety of continuing the publication of our 'proceedings in sections' we may perhaps be able to prevail on the [General] Committee to abolish that troublesome and very nearly useless appendage: but having twice tried the force of arguments (backed by Lloyd, Forbes, etc) I despair without a general agreement beforehand. Last year the Committee directed no change to be made in this respect, and I have done my best in consequence to make the account of the proceedings as good as possible. It is probably rather longer than usual.

If the Newcastle meeting, with the discussions which will (I feel sure) there arise, should cause me such intense anxiety as I experienced at Liverpool, it is probable that a regard to my health and powers of usefulness in other ways may compel me to quit my post and take shelter in the ranks. That I should do this in ill-humour you will not believe, but it is very possible that temporary circumstances might have too great weight with me, if there should be no one to advise with that I could *trust*. It is therefore of some consequence to me to know whether you will be at Newcastle, or choose to consult your own quiet by abstaining from its *ball!!* and its 5000 promenaders.

There is no doubt the meeting will be very splendid; as to its scientific value nous verrons. Alas! that we have never yet got our committees into the state of life and reality which was proposed at the York meeting. The Royal Society is now copying our plan of committees of science. Please to present my best compliments to Mrs Harcourt and to receive my best good wishes for yourself and all the young ones.

I have been lecturing to excess this year, very much for the purpose of delivering myself from the pressure of pecuniary wants and shall probably have accomplished my (moderate!) wishes at the end of 1838.

Harcourt MSS

221 *Murchison, 2 Eccleston Street, Belgrave Square, London, to Harcourt, St Clare, Ryde, Isle of Wight, 18 July 1838*

Yesterday we held our last Council previous to the assembly at Newcastle. The chief object I had in calling this meeting was to direct attention to the reply of Herschel to the proposition I was commissioned to make to him, namely 'if he would consent to act as President for the year ensuing, provided he was elected at Newcastle by the General Committee'. His reply was an acquiescence, coupled with the proviso that the wish should be general in his favour and that he should stand in the way of no-one.

I had been in correspondence with Mr Corrie of Birmingham and on communicating to him Herschel's acquiescence, I have received from him and his friends of Birmingham a letter warmly applauding the *initiative* taken by us and saying that such an appointment will be most grateful to the people of Birmingham.

As far as my own feelings are concerned, I should have said that no other scientific man save Herschel would have been adequate to induce *me* to give up the idea of having Sir Robert Peel as Praeses. But if you had been present at the Liverpool meeting you would have witnessed (as I have before explained to you) so strong a demonstration on the part of Lubbock, Robinson, Sedgwick and many others, and if you knew how Babbage, etc, who were not at Liverpool feel in the same cause, you would have perceived that 'coute que coute' it was absolutely essential for the peace of the Association to select on the next occasion, wherever the rendezvous might be, some *cultivator of science*. It struck me that no one except Herschel could obviate all the difficulties, for being a star of the first order, honoured and fêted by princes as well as by the men of science of England, there would be no difficulty in finding 'great guns' to work under him. I also knew, that though no orator (as to physical powers) he would write us an *imperishable address* and thus mark an epoch in our concern. Now the sequitur of this preamble, is, that the Council talked over the probabilities and whom we might perchance induce to take the Vice-chairs at Birmingham; and first it was unanimously opined, that *if Sir Robert Peel* would permit his name to be at the head of the list of Vice-presidents and sit at the right hand of the Astronomer, he would essentially serve us and not as we hope do injustice to himself by taking a post previously occupied by Lord Northampton and the Bishop of Durham and previously *rejected with disdain* by *Lord Durham*!! I was therefore desired to request *you*, who know Sir Robert and have had previous communication with him, to put this matter to him in your best manner.

At first it did appear to me almost hopeless to induce a man of

Peel's station to accept such an office, but the more I reflect on it the more I am disposed to think that he will accept it if judiciously managed and that the case is explained *with tact*. It will, I think, require an abstract of our doings to make him understand our position and why we are debarred from offering him the chair in chief, namely, that the sons of science seeing 3 great lords *in succession* as their rulers, thought they had lost the privilege of having a first Lord of the Treasury chosen from among them. If Peel accepts he will do himself great honour. He knows what it is for a commoner to have been Premier with the Duke of Wellington under him.

If you think I can follow up your application by any *personal* application I am quite ready to do so.

We have prepared our new rules for composition of [the] General Committee which being very liberal will I trust be approved. We have yet to prepare a list of foreign members to fill up vacancies and to extend, and here I confess I do not see my way for there is so much difference of opinion as to whether we should merely elect men of real distinction, or men of work and use, that either we must have two classes or we never shall please the critics.

I have been compelled at the eleventh hour to take a strong measure and in conjunction with my colleague to order Phillips not to print a geological memoir of Mr Heywood at length, which he was going to do, accompanied by a *detailed geological map* and section illustrating the Lancashire coal field!! As we have hitherto specially eschewed all such details, thereby indeed avoiding the reproach of robbing the supplies from other societies and have never published anything more than short abstracts of our morning proceedings, I am wholly at a loss to comprehend the logic of our friend, the more so as he wrote to me (while in some measure apologizing for doing this without *any communication* with Peacock or myself) that he was very anxious to omit on future occasions *all notice whatever* of everything done in the sections, and that he hoped to get your assent to this proposition. Now this [is] a point I never will assent to as long as I hold office. I look upon the morning meetings as the very essence of the Association, for although our reports constitute our real claims in the literature of science, the sections are the chronometers which mark the rate of the current of living enterprise and in short give rise to all our recommendations, reports and so forth.

I hope the health of your daughter will not prevent your attendance at Newcastle. Our kind regards to Mrs Harcourt.

[PS] I have nearly written all my portion of the discussion which we the General Secretaries were ordered to deliver on the first day. NB Write if possible by return of post as Peacock is in town and Peel may bolt.

PS   Being hung up by the last leaves of my book, I shall not leave town till the 6 August.

Harcourt MSS (Harcourt Papers, *xiv. 29–33*)

James Heywood (1810–97), a Manchester banker, was a keen supporter of the Association. This letter is the first of several concerning the Presidency and the Vice-presidencies of the 1839 meeting. In May 1838 Herschel had returned in triumph from the Cape of Good Hope. Murchison's colleague in the General Secretariat was Peacock.

222   *Murchison, 2 Eccleston Street, Belgrave Square, London, to Harcourt, St Clare, Ryde, Isle of Wight, 28 July 1838*

Your announcement of Sir Robert's refusal did not surprise me. I communicated it to Peacock and have since seen Mr Corrie of Birmingham who dined indeed with me yesterday. It was suggested in our last Council that Corrie should be a Vice-president, but he very properly knows his own position too well in Birmingham to wish to take so high an office and begs to be senior Local Secretary, with which opinion I quite coincide, believing that he will better serve the Association in that capacity. With a Mr Barker and an able surgeon of the town, Mr Hodgson, F R S, there will be no difficulty as to [Local] Secretaries. There is however some little difficulty as to Vice-presidents. Herschel being in the chair it would be well to have the V Ps men of influence in the town and neighbourhood. The first names which occur are those of Watt and Boulton but these gentlemen withdraw *from all connection with us*. We are thus left without any great townsmen and, driven to the country, we have only the surrounding nobility. Lord Dartmouth (almost in the suburbs) is an excellent worthy man but without science or literature. He will open his house and I shall have a good quarter there if I am in England, but it would be difficult to manufacture him into a Vice-president. Then we have Lord Ward, the Dudley fossil of high price, young, handsome, generous, of immense local influence and anxious to display; desirous also, I am told, of being connected with science. Mr Corrie seemed very anxious to place this nice young Lord in a high seat but really I think it would be a strong measure. Besides, you have young Lord Lyttleton quite as near at Hagley Park and though he has not the wealth, he is *really* distinguished by having taken the first class honours at Cambridge. But Lord Lyttleton has no love of science.

To get rid of these difficulties it has occurred to me that we might do well to have recourse to our trusty friend, Lord Northampton, and place him as senior V.P. He is a nobleman of *science* and his

oldest property is in Warwickshire. In appointing him we can offend
no other lords, science being the plea. Then, for our second V P,
Babbage as a compliment to the great town of machinery and
manufacture. By adhering to these two we shall avoid dilemmas,
but I do not by any means feel assured of the superiority of the
arrangement and will thank you to think it over and give me your
advice.

Independent of Lord Ward's youth, etc, he is I understand going
abroad. Lord Hatherton has been spoken to concerning Lord Ward.
The former I should conceive to be quite [out] of the question being
too political a character.

I shall be glad to hear better accounts of your sweet little girl and
with Mrs M's kind remembrances to Mrs Harcourt,
PS   We leave town on the 6 August.

Harcourt MSS (Harcourt Papers, *xiv. 34–6*)

George Barker (1776–1845), *DNB*, a Birmingham solicitor; Joseph Hodgson (1788–
1869), *DNB*, a Birmingham surgeon; James Watt (1769–1848), *DNB*, of the engineering firm of Boulton and Watt; William Ward (1817–85), 11th Baron Ward, later
Earl of Dudley; George William Lyttleton, 4th Baron Lyttleton (1817–76), *DNB*;
Edward John Littleton, 1st Baron Hatherton (1791–1863), *DNB*, was Secretary for
Ireland, 1833–4. Babbage's industrial interests were well shown in his *On the economy
of machinery and manufactures* (London, 1832).

223   *Harcourt, St Clare, Ryde, Isle of Wight, to Murchison, 2 August 1838*

I very much approve of your idea of proposing Babbage as a Vice-
president, and I should be inclined to advise in the absence of any
scientific persons of consequence in the neighbourhood of Birmingham, that Baily should be selected for his coadjutor in preference to
either of the young sprigs of nobility you mention. Lord Northampton is as you say a safe card and 'good and [great]' in any post; but
whether he has so much connection and influence in the neighbourhood as to afford a strong reason for calling him a second time to
the same office I do not know. If you take three such distinguished
men of science as Herschel, Baily and Babbage it will extinguish the
cry of too much aristocratic learning which has begun to prevail, as
I guess from the remarks made to me yesterday when I told Dr
Richardson that I thought it likely Herschel might preside at Birmingham. I was glad to find that he, Dr Richardson, is going to
Newcastle, and shall hope to hear from you, by and bye, that the

meeting has been crowned with success. Mrs H sends her kind remembrances to Mrs Murchison.

BL, Add. MSS 37190, f. 505

224 *Murchison, n.p., to Babbage, 3 August 1838*

You will perceive by the enclosed that I have been doing my best
to collect the sense of those who are most qualified to judge of the
future arrangements (in re British Association). It was in this spirit
that I called on you, regretting as I did your absence at the two last
Councils, for I wished you to know what we were talking about at
those meetings.

Herschel's provisional acceptance of the chair removes the great
difficulty. We had next to consider who the men of Birmingham
could suggest as fit and proper persons to fill the Vice chairs and
[Local] Secretariat. In consequence of the favourable impression he
made on the General Committee last year, and in virtue of the very
high opinion entertained of him in his native town, the Council
agreed that it would be very proper to press upon Mr John Corrie
the acceptance of one of these chairs. Mr Corrie having come to
London this step was taken, but he at first begged rather to be
senior Local Secretary, assigning modest reasons for not putting
himself forward. At the same time *he* urged that if *young Lord Ward*!
could be made a Vice-president it would greatly add to the success
of the meeting quoad Birmingham and the expenses etc. On this I
at once remonstrated and convinced him that Lord Ward was too
young and wholly unknown in science. In the same way I said my
particular friend Lord Dartmouth was quite out of the question.
And thus it was that, conceiving it might be desirable to have some
one man of property in the country adjacent, I suggested to Harcourt the possibility of uniting Lord Northampton with you as a
nobleman possessing some science and a thorough devotion to our
cause.

He has however had the honour already and I am quite disposed
to go along with the views of Harcourt, particularly if you will
cordially accept the office of one of the Vice-presidents. The case
would then stand thus: Herschel President; Vice-presidents, Babbage, Baily, Corrie.

No hint has yet been given of it to Baily; for he was at our last
Council and talked of others.

Whatever may be the upshot you of all the men of science are
most appositely called upon to appear in a high station at the great
'atelier' of manufactures. Your appointment will as Mr Corrie as-

sures me be considered a great honour conferred upon the town and I hope you will not refuse what we all so much desire.

If our friend had not returned from the Cape and justly aroused that general enthusiasm among men of science, it was my full intention (indeed if I mistake not I mentioned it to you) to suggest you to occupy the chair on this occasion.

The cause of Herschel's appointment was obvious and I know that no one rejoices in it more than yourself.

Let us all pull together and the British Association will be stronger than ever, and above all let us avoid the semblance of any thing like want of harmony among the rulers of the large camp. Public discussions on points of officers and so forth are dangerous and I sincerely trust that every thing will go on so smoothly that there will be no trace of differences of opinion.

I do not say this with any reference to yourself, for I am unaware of your feeling in any degree opposed to the method and practice proposed.

[PS]   In reference to what you said about Lyell allow me to tell you that from what Horner said to me Lyell will on no account be put into harness [as president of the geological section].

BL, Add. MSS 37190, ff. 507–10

225   *Humphrey Lloyd, Trinity College, Dublin, to Herschel, 4 August 1838*

I rejoice to learn from Major Sabine that you have expressed a strong opinion of the importance of a south polar expedition. May we therefore hope that you will bring the subject forward at the approaching meeting of the British Association?

It is now three years since the Association resolved to recommend to the government to undertake an Antarctic expedition, for the purpose of promoting our knowledge of terrestrial magnetism in a region hitherto little explored, and to establish one or two magnetical observatories in British India. A committee was appointed at the time, to bring the matter under the notice of government; but, though I believe the Lords of the Admiralty were not unfavourable to the former project, nothing was done.

There seems to be every reason to rejoice that this delay has occurred: for the singular discoveries which have resulted from the system of simultaneous observation under the direction of Gauss, and the new and important results obtained by Major Sabine on the distribution of magnetic force over our globe, must give a new direction, as well as a fresh impulse, to investigation. The time however has now arrived; and I cannot but think that by a well directed expedition, on a large and liberal scale, Britain might now redeem, in the course of two or three years, the great distance to which she has suffered herself to fall behind the nations of the Continent in magnetic discovery.

There is every reason to believe that the government will *act*, if the Association should *recommend;* so that the fate of the measure will, in all probability, depend upon the manner in which it is brought forward at Newcastle. If *you* are fully satisfied of its importance, and will undertake to bring it forward, there can be no doubt of the result. In other hands, the measure would probably fall to the ground. I trust, Dear Sir, that this will justify the importunity of the well wishers of this great project.

Herschel Papers, 11.264

Carl Friedrich Gauss (1777-1855), *DSB*, had promoted the Göttingen Magnetische Verein (founded 1834) which soon published important magnetic observations.

226 *Murchison, n.p., to Herschel, 8 August 1838*

Confidential

In the midst of packing and inditing the last corrections of my Siluriana, and with the carriage almost at the door, I write a line or two to say how much I regret not having seen you. I wished to have had five minutes talk with you on British Association affairs, and particularly to request you to *do your best* to keep our friend Babbage in good humour. He has taken umbrage at something in my conduct and although he does not *speak out*, and I cannot ascertain what he is driving at, still I apprehend from *his manner* (which is much altered of *late* to me) that he intends to raise discussions at the Council and even at the General Committee on points of management etc of the Association. I rather presume that he thinks I have been instrumental in 'throwing him overboard', and he never was more mistaken!!

It is quite true that in November last (I think) and when I thought you were going to *Rio* and had not expected to see you for a year, knowing the necessity of having a scientific Praeses at Birmingham I hinted one night to Babbage that he ought to be our man.

Not a step however of any sort was taken, nor am I aware that any other person in the Association ever entertained the same idea as myself.

As soon as you returned, matters were entirely changed. The *subject was discussed in Council* and you were *unanimously* fixed upon.

In giving a little forecast to the probable *Vice-presidents*, I have recommended (which is all I can do) that Lord Northampton and Babbage should fill these offices. But in reply to this application on my part our friend's manner is to say the least of it ungracious, almost unkind, and as I can declare before God that I have had no object but the good of the Association founded on an unceasing connection with it from its establishment, I am of course a good deal mystified at this treatment which I never before experienced from any member of the large body.

It is my intention to resign the office of General Secretary at this meeting.

I always felt the impropriety of a mere geologist holding this onerous and responsible post, but I took it to oblige my friends in *a moment of need*, and without my urgent solicitations we should not have secured Peacock for this year's service.

As it is alas! Peacock is unwell and can do nothing to the address which will either be abandoned or be a failure, for I naturally referred all the physical sciences, chemistry etc to him. I thus have a gloomy prospect and shall consider it an act of real friendship if you can in any way prevent our friend Babbage from overloading the cup of misfortune, for as he is to be your fellow traveller your opinions will have great weight.

Herschel Papers, 12.441

The address was that of the two General Secretaries to be delivered at the 1838 meeting of the Association.

227 *Phillips, Newcastle-upon-Tyne, to Harcourt, St Clare, Ryde, Isle of Wight, 10 August 1838*

Many thanks for your friendly and valued letter. The meeting rapidly approaches and as I am in good health I hope to pass through it without too much mental anxiety; but, frankly, as the numbers and power of the meeting augment, it is difficult not to feel solicitous about the *direction* of its movements, especially as we do not always see at our meetings the same 'familiar faces'. You ask me for news. En! accipe! 1st Dr. Goldfuss of Bonn writes to me as 'The Honourable Professor' etc etc, which very much astonishes my father's son. 2. Newcastle, which was one of the blackest and filthiest old carbonaceous towns in the land, has been utterly transformed so as to rival in many of its parts the best parts of Edinburgh: or rather, to say merely the truth, to *surpass* them. For the style of the buildings is admirable, and their masses really noble. Yet, for me the south has its charms, and if the word *comfort* be unknown over the channel, its meaning is better known in the southern counties than on the border. 3. The meeting now collecting will be enormous. 1246 new members have been elected at Newcastle of whom 1033 live within 15 miles of the town. 214 more than 15 miles off. New applicants (to date) 43. The strangers coming are numerous and among them the best of the English, Irish and Scottish men of science. From Germany we have Ehrenberg, Ertel; from France Gambey and possibly J P *probably* Arago, Gay-Lussac, etc; from America Bache; a small list, but you remember we never had a large one 10 days previous to the meeting. 4. The accommodations here are *not* ample as to lodgings, they are considerable as to private hospitality and ample as to scientific business. The physiciens will meet in a room holding 500. The chemists, naturalists in County Court, 500 each. The geologists and mechanicians, 1000 each. The statisticians and medicals, 300 each. The evening business in a room (quite splendid) built by the man who has transformed Newcastle (Grainger), holding 2700 seats and 300 standings. The promenades, one in Assembly Rooms and one in decorated Green Market which is truly one of the most marvellous rooms ever beheld. It is to be ornamented by *2000* dozen flowers, shrubs and many of them made of paper 'wonderfully well done'.

The dining room holds 800 and I have suggested to ornament its striped calico sides

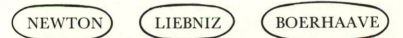

coronals or chaplets of laurel and flowers, along its sides, of foreign and British names *alternately*, as Newton, Leibniz, Davy, Lavoisier, Ray, Linnaeus/Buffon etc. Right or wrong the idea is friendly and is adopted. I had thought of mottos but 'qui vitam excoluere per artes' etc. is too common, and now I rather object to such things at all. The room is dark by day, but will shine in gas light.

Herschel, Babbage, Lyell, Buckland, Sedgwick, Lloyd, Robinson, Robison (Sir J.), Ross, Sabine, Egerton, Cole, Brewster, Forbes, and multitudes of our friends are on the way. Duke Northumberland, Lord Tankerville, Lord Northampton, Howick, Ravensworth and many other nobles and gentles are expected.

Murchison has written to you re Babbage and I hope you have found time to advise him, as the day is at hand.

I have received an important communication from De la Beche which will once again make me plunge into the mystery of organic remains of Devon and Cornwall. If anything extraordinary, and not *too painful*, should arise I will write again, but I rather promise myself to send you newspapers. May I hope Miss Harcourt is better?

And that Mrs H. and all your other valued connections are well (In haste).

[PS]   Many enquiries for you among all ranks of members, who regret your absence and especially the Northumbrians who were at York meeting. Vide Dean's second letter!

Harcourt MSS

Christian Gottfried Ehrenberg (1795–1876), *DSB*, Berlin professor and biologist; Traugott Lebrecht Ertel (1778–1858) German instrument maker; Henri Prudence Gambey (1787–1847), *DSB*, French instrument maker; Alexander Dallas Bache (1806–67), *DSB*, was then President, Girard College, Philadelphia; Joseph Louis Gay-Lussac (1778–1850), *DSB*, the French chemist; Richard Grainger (1798–1861), *DNB*, the architect of classical Newcastle; Gottfried Wilhelm Leibniz (1646–1716), *DSB*, the German philosopher and mathematician; Herman Boerhaave (1668–1738), *DSB*, medical professor at Leyden University; Antoine Laurent Lavoisier (1743–94), *DSB*, the French chemist; Viscount Cole, later 3rd Earl of Enniskillen (1807–86), a keen palaeontologist; Charles Augustus Bennet, 5th Earl Tankerville (1776–1859); Viscount Howick (1802–94), *DNB*, was MP for north Northumberland and Secretary-at-War in the cabinet; Thomas Henry Liddell, Lord Ravensworth (1775–1855). The Dean was William Cockburn (1773–1858), Dean of York Minster, who had attacked the Association in his *A remonstrance, addressed to His Grace the Duke of Northumberland, upon the dangers of peripatetic philosophy* (London, 1838). The Latin phrase, from Virgil's *Aeneid*, refers to those who enobled their life through the arts.

228   *Murchison, Newcastle-upon-Tyne, to Harcourt, St Clare, Ryde, Isle of Wight, 21 August 1838*

Ten thousand thanks for your prompt and effective friendship in producing in so short a time *so brilliant* an oration out of my stony skeleton. It would not however do to take it in all respects as you had written it; for Peacock got rapidly better and is now quite well indeed and for the last 3 days sat with me from morn to night in making the whole [near] well together. He wrote the parts on Russell, etc, etc, and amplified about the don folks. We gave a rex excidica and I added chapters on geology, geography, statistics and zoology. A fine clap-trap was suggested by the new town here, with other local allusions and I finished (as they all tell me) with effect by that sentence about union which I wrote before.

This last sentence was forced on me by the strong desire to preserve unanimity, seeing with pain and vexation the perverse and untoward line which Babbage is taking and *persevering in*.

How, my good friend, did you happen to omit to send me back what I specially called for, the letters and correspondence which I charged you to return? It is now too late to get them and I am unprepared for the furious attack he is going to make on Thursday. He has already roused Dr Robinson of Armagh and the hot-heads upon the point of *interference* of the Council; has already driven Herschel who is [in] utter AWE of him from the chair, for that good, great yet most *weak* (morally) man came to Peacock and self yesterday and declined. Here we are then on the eve of a volcano and all to gratify Babbage's personal vanity and spleen. If he is elected I cannot in decency continue as General Secretary after all the intrigue which he has been carrying on against me, and the probability indeed is that before I can hear from you I shall be compelled as a gentleman to take those steps which will be alone left open to me: forbearance for the Association's sake is one thing, but to support the unforgiving and relentless contumely of Babbage and then serve under him is impossible. Peacock will certainly retire also; Whewell will leave the Association, i.e. I mean not frequent it, and in short Babbage will reign a Mephistopheles over the broken and exploded crucibles of the Association. I write almost in despair.

[PS] Write by return of post. The discourse was admirably received. It will be printed tonight and you will have a copy immediately.

Harcourt MSS (Harcourt Papers, *xiv. 36-8*)

229 *Murchison, n.p. [Newcastle-upon-Tyne], to Harcourt, St Clare, Ryde, Isle of Wight, n.d. [22 August 1838]*

Babbage *refused* the chair distinctly, saying it would compromise him with Herschel, and no *entreaties* could get him to agree to the proposal.

A *few mutual friends, the* most influential in the Association, had however thought of the *only succedaneum* to restore harmony and readjust the elements of an institution about to be scattered, and conceiving the possibility of this refusal had *your* name ready. It acted as a *talisman*!! Babbage came to, and by Lord Northampton's *skill* it was finally brought about that Babbage should propose *W. Vernon Harcourt* as Praeses and that *Herschel* should second it. Carried with rapture and all arranged, and the finale was that after struggle of feeling (both on my part as on that of Babbage) which was very severe, we shook hands as good friends *I hope* as ever.

The Vice-presidents to be Lords Northampton and Dartmouth, Messrs Corrie and Dr Robinson of Armagh; Secretaries 2 or 3 local men.

You, my dear friend, are selected as the peace-maker and as you in your last letter promise attendance there can be no doubt you will heal us. I have pledged myself to it. I shall be [restless] till return of post and your acceptance will rejoice me. Refusal under such circumstances would *paralyse* your own offspring.

[PS] The general affair is progressing *marvellously well*. What I speak of is only an affair of *Council*. Every section is up to *its hilt* in business and Babbage is making an *excellent president* of the mechanical section and last night before 2,000 made us a capital oration on the general subject.

The election takes place *tomorrow*.

Harcourt MSS (Harcourt Papers, *xiv. 41-2*)

This incomplete letter is concerned with discussions in the Council, which preceded the formal meeting of the General Committee.

230 *Babbage, Newcastle-upon-Tyne, to Harcourt, Friday 24 August 1838*

It is necessary that I should make a statement of the facts which led to my proposing your election to the chair of the British Association.

We had a special meeting of the Council on Wednesday last when my co-trustee, Mr Murchison, on communicating Sir J. Herschel's resignation of the Presidency which he had previously accepted, made a statement in which he admitted the following facts.

1st That about Christmas last he (Mr M.) had informed me that he thought it very desirable that I should be the President of the British Association at the meeting at Birmingham, and he strongly pressed me to accept the situation.

2nd That about the middle of June last at a meeting of the Council held on that day he (without the slightest previous communication to me of his altered intentions) HIMSELF proposed that Sir J. Herschel should be invited by the Council to accept the provisional offer of the Presidency. Mr Murchison fully admitted that the Council were totally uninformed by him that he had had any previous communication on the subject with me.

3rdly That some time after, Mr Murchison (meeting me accidentally) informed me that he had at the last meeting of the Council proposed that Sir J.H. should be invited and that the Council had adopted that proposition, that Mr M. did not even at that time make the slightest reference to our previous understanding. That about the 10 August Mr M. called on me when I communicated to him my intention of proposing Sir J.H. at the general meeting at Newcastle. That on the succeeding day Mr M. wrote to me a letter offering me a Vice-presidency and enclosing one from you approving of the proposal and stating that Mr Peacock and Mr Corrie (the representative of Birmingham) wished me to accept it. It was also admitted that neither of these three gentlemen whose opinions had been requested were previously made acquainted with Mr Murchison's first communication to me.

All these facts were either stated by Mr M. or distinctly admitted.

I must now state some other facts which were not within the General Secretary's knowledge. Almost immediately after the first proposal to me of the Presidency I mentioned it to a relative and then foretold that the General Secretary would on the arrival of my friend throw me overboard and adopt him. Soon after Sir J.H.'s arrival he informed me that Mr M. had proposed to him the Presidency of the British Association, that he thought it desirable, and that he proposed conditionally to accept the offer. In these circumstances I considered that the best course I could adopt was MYSELF to propose Sir J.H. as President at the next general meeting at Newcastle. With this determination I arrived at Newcastle.

In the mean time Sir J.H. was on the Monday made acquainted with the fact of Mr Murchison's communication with me but not by me nor with my consent; and at the special Council (where by the way neither President nor any Vice-president appeared and Mr Baily presided) the General Secretary reported that he had received a formal though verbal resignation of Sir J.H.'s acceptance of the Presidency on the ground that the whole affair was larger than he had expected. Sir J. Herschel's letter accepting the office of Presidency was then read and Mr M. then made the statement and admissions I have given in this letter. Upon this statement I remarked that there were two distinct questions.

1st That I had been by the conduct of my co-trustee most unjustifiably brought into a conflicting position with respect to my oldest friend.

2ndly That they the Council had on their former meeting in June been induced to pass a vote proposed by the General Secretary, Mr M., who allowed them all to act in complete ignorance of his previous communication with me. This latter question I left to them to approve or disapprove.

Mr M. then moved that the Council request me to allow myself to be proposed as President. This was seconded by Lord Northampton (who as well as Sir Charles Lemon had been called in to assist). At my request Lord Northampton withdrew his support. The question was however put and carried. To this request I immediately gave a decided and firm refusal. It was impossible that I could ever act in conjunction with my co-trustee, and I was unwilling to allow myself to be placed before the world in a position in which it might be supposed that I had supplanted my friend. I had myself offered to propose Sir J.H. to shield him from the chance of suffering from the same unjust reproach. A second resolution was then carried to recommend you as President and a third was also carried that the Council request Mr Babbage to propose and Sir J.H. to second your nomination. To this request I acceded. It was very unfortunate that the Duke of Northumberland was not in the chair at that meeting of the Council; HE would have seen at once the *impossibility* of my ever acting with Mr M. as my co-trustee and from his position and character would have had great weight in bringing about the only reparation I could receive. If the D of N. had used his influence in prevailing on Mr M. to withdraw from his Trusteeship and on Sir J.H. to make that sacrifice of his time which he disliked, I should then have been most happy to have been one of my friend's Vice-presidents.

Early on the next morning I called on Sir J.H. and having pointed out to him the difficulty in which the British Association was placed and the possibility of some friend of Mr M. suggesting to him to retire, I asked whether he would THEN consent to be President and I offered to be one of his Vice-presidents or to be placed in ANY position that he might think most desirable. This proposition he absolutely declined. I then asked whether if I accepted the offer of being proposed as President he would be a Vice-president. This also he declined. I then said that I wished when he had considered the subject he would send me his decision to the mechanical section of which I was chairman.

On meeting Sir J.H. at the General Committee on that day, he informed me that he would not be a Vice-president, and I then proposed you, and at the same meeting gave notice of my intention to resign the office of Trustee on the grounds which I have already stated.

In this course I intend to persevere in order that at the next general meeting the British Association may have an opportunity of choosing between Mr Murchison and me.

BL, Add. MSS 37190, ff. 522-6

Sir Charles Lemon (1784-1868) led the Cornish mining interest in Parliament.

231   *Murchison, n.p. [Newcastle-upon-Tyne], to Harcourt, n.d. [27 August 1838]*

The newspapers will have communicated to you long ago the result which I prepared you for in my last, *your election as President.*

I wrote a short note to you on Friday and enclosed the discourse of the General Secretaries in a frank but I found them both lying in a corner (unsuspected) this morning. The meeting has gone off *triumphantly* in every sense of the word and if not for the *galling*, *withering*, continued and unrelenting persecution of Babbage I should have enjoyed this meeting more than any one which I ever was at.

His conduct is [so] extravagant and relentless that thank God *every one I know* has rallied round me. He has been I understand showing about the copy of a letter which he wrote to you, and some of my friends who have seen it say that they would require nothing better than [this] to convict him of very bad feeling and egotism out of his own epistle. This grand dispatch was to be decisive of the existence of the British Association.

Sir D. Brewster laughs heartily at this notion and condemns Babbage's conduct in a marked manner (Sir David is *in excellent* humour).

As I told you before every member of Council is with me, and by what Peacock tells me, who has been on an excursion with the Glasgow deputies and others, they all went away impressed with the conviction that his conduct in the General Committee on Thursday (where he made the same declaration against rank and wealth, and a special attack on the government, as he had done *previously* at the Council) was such as to render it very desirable to get rid of all connection with a man of so dangerous a character.

He is resolved I hear to *print*. Let him do so and he shall get such a dressing as he little expects.

In fact the poor man does not or will not know that there are [not] 2 *influential* persons in the Association who are with him.

He told the Duke of Northumberland (who begged him in his excited state to refer the matter to a *friend*) that he had no friend save one here. I think I told you before that he had previously been at Birmingham and Liverpool to pick up stories. The result of enquiry is that no one thought of Babbage but myself; and I really intended to try to carry him, though I never spoke of my intention, until Herschel's unexpected return overthrew like an earthquake all previous thoughts and settled the question of the Birmingham President, supposing he was to be a man of science. But enough of this. Lord Northampton and Peacock, certainly *the* 2 calmest and best judging men in our motley concern, will put you into possession of the case, and I can only say that your ready and cordial acceptance of the chair and your union with all the men who have really supported the Association will entirely remove all difficulty.

I have had much to endure and much to suppress for the sake of harmony and in consequence of my position.

Hoping anxiously to hear from you,

[PS] We are all going to the great Natural History Society dinner today. I shall be at Alnwick Castle from Saturday to Wednesday next.

Harcourt MSS (Harcourt Papers, *xiv. 38-40*)

On 27 Aug 1838 the Natural History Society of Northumberland, Durham, and Newcastle-upon-Tyne held its anniversary meeting and mounted a dinner attended by more than 400 including many leading members of the Association. Alnwick Castle was the home of the Duke of Northumberland.

232   *Peacock, Newcastle-upon-Tyne, to Harcourt, 27 August 1838*

Murchison will have explained to you some of the various and distressing embarrassments in which we have been placed during the last week, and the results to which they have led. The most satisfactory of these is undoubtedly your appointment to the chair of the Association, a position in which it can receive all the benefit of that excellent sense and judgment which has been its principal guide and support from its infancy to its maturity.

Our friend Babbage has been the real cause of all our difficulties and his conduct has been universally condemned. *He* conceived that he was the person tacitly referred to by the speakers in the General Committee at Liverpool who advocated the future appointment of scientific presidents. He conceived likewise that he was the person wished for at Birmingham, and he conceived therefore that Murchison had been the person who had tripped up his heels and compromised his relation with Herschel, who is his most intimate friend. Much of this has been the mere coinage of his own jealous temper and of his extreme and really extravagant vanity. And in the case of any other person, the very handsome and manly apology which was made to him by Murchison, in the presence of the Council, would have been considered more than sufficient to extinguish for ever every vestige of resentment or irritation. As it was, however, his violent resentment was controlled by the unanimous expression of the members of the Council present, and more particularly of Sir Charles Lemon, whom he had selected as his friend to be present at the meeting; but it was by no means eradicated. He agreed, however, very cordially in the propriety of proposing you as possessing the highest claims to preside over the Association, from a consideration of the great services you had rendered the Association.

At the meeting for choosing the officers, the next day, he repeated with great bitterness of language and manner, one of his usual tirades against the government of this country for their neglect of men of science, and ended by proposing you in very handsome terms. This was seconded with great cordiality and warmth by Herschel and you were elected with universal approbation. Whewell in making a motion (for reappointing Murchison and myself) could not conceal his disapproval of Babbage's opinions, and the consequence was that Babbage declared that he would retire from the office of

Trustee, as he found that his opinions found no response in the Association. The friends of peace deprecated (perhaps unwisely) this determination, but on Saturday he repeated his determination, assigning as his ground that he could not act as joint Trustee with Murchison. Murchison referred to his explanation of his conduct before the Council which he hoped was satisfactory to them. And Sir Charles Lemon, who was chairman, very properly and promptly stopped the conversation. Thus has ended this very unhappy affair, but I see no likelihood of any change in Babbage's view of the transaction.

Though one of Babbage's oldest friends, I must consider him totally in the wrong in this affair. I will not attempt to vindicate Murchison from the charge of having been guilty of a great imprudence, but his conduct has been in the highest degree manly and conciliatory and such as has raised him, if possible, in the opinion of all those who have witnessed it. But Babbage is universally condemned and I have heard from every quarter wishes expressed that he would retire altogether from the Association. I have not heard of a single person who approves of what he has done. And I can assure you, that it is with the deepest regret, that I feel compelled to express my concurrence in the general opinion.

I trust indeed that if he again appears in the Association, that it will be with softened feelings and more reasonable views. But if he should hereafter attempt to make the British Association a theatre for the display of his resentments or of his extreme and exaggerated opinions, I believe that the whole body of the Association will oppose him, and come forward cordially and readily in support of the authority of the laws and officers of the Association.

With this single exception, the meeting has been harmonious and successful, beyond all former example. Strangers and natives have been equally charmed with it.

Harcourt MSS (Harcourt Papers, *xiv. 42–5*)

233 *Northampton, Penrith, to Harcourt, St Clare, Ryde, Isle of Wight, 27 August 1838*

You will, of course, have heard from Murchison that you have been elected our President for next year, and I trust that you will not hesitate to accept the office. If you do not, I know not what scrapes we may get into. We have been over a mine of gunpowder and are fortunately not blown up. But a truce to metaphors and I will come to plain facts. We have had very awkward and very delicate discussions, and if there had not been yourself, a person in whom united all suffrages in the Council, we might have had a very fatal dispute as to our next year's President in the general meeting. Babbage, as you probably are well aware, seems to have *no skin at all*. He thinks himself very ill used by Murchison, who, to say the truth, I also think, in one point, did not quite do what was right, and so he himself fairly said at the Council, and in fact made a most handsome and ample apology there for that one fault, but it was with great difficulty that matters could be settled. At last, however, they were arranged *after a fashion*. But Babbage was still so angry that he has declared that he will resign his trusteeship. Dr Robinson of Armagh gave notice last year that he would oppose the nomination of any president not distinguished for science, so there might have been another element of discord had Peel been proposed, as was at one time thought of; but I understand that he had been sounded on the subject of a Vice-presidentship, but stated that he could not as he was generally obliged to rest himself after the parliamentary session, so that was out of the question. Murchison had proposed Herschel, in the first instance, to the Council in London, but he has declined. Babbage himself was afterwards proposed and he also declined. I had the honour of proposing you, and you were elected by accla-mation. The Vice-presidents elect are Mr Corrie of Birmingham, Dr Robinson of Armagh, Lord Dartmouth and myself. I can only say for myself, but I have no doubt that I might also for the others, that they will be diligent ministers as far as they can. Lord Dartmouth indeed is a new recruit and has not yet been with us, but Murchison says that he knows that he is very friendlily disposed to the British Association, and his property comes up to the very confines of Bir-mingham, which was the reason for his being chosen one of the Vice-presidents. As there are four of us we may save you trouble at ordinaries, etc, and at all the evening meetings except the first and last, if you are either fatigued or indisposed; but we shall perhaps have great need of your pilotage through the shoals of the Council and General Committee, in both of which our bark has been in dire peril this meeting. Not only have we had the Babbage Scylla in the Council, but we have had a medical Charybdis in the General Committee where we had a division on Saturday on the question of reversing the decision of the Committee of Recommendations on a *money grant*, which the Committee had rejected. The majority how-ever did support its own Committee, but it was after a long debate; and another attempt was made to increase one of the Committee's grants, but equally defeated. In short, I am sure that when you understand that your election is the highest of all compliments, namely, that the Association asks your assistance because it *needs* it, and because it knows that without the assistance of its original legislator, its constitution may go to wreck and ruin. I am sure you will not refuse your aid. I can only repeat to you what I said in the Council, that I shall be proud to have any share in assisting you, however small. The confidence placed in you has been the means *now* of getting us out of a difficulty which would have been unsurmountable without you, as any other President proposed under existing circumstances would have been sure to have produced discussion and division of a deplorable nature.

Though all the matters, to which I have referred, have in a business point of view been very disagreeable, yet in other respects the meeting at Newcastle has been one of the most brilliant that the Association has yet gone through. Sedgwick exceedingly eloquent. The geological section was particularly strong, with Sedgwick, Lyell, Buckland, Phillips, etc. The foreigners were not very numerous. We had a *ball* which is rather contrary to my ideas of a philosophical meeting. The Duke of Northumberland was unfortunately unwell at the end of the meeting, and could not come the last evening. The Bishop of Durham, as one of the Vice-presidents, occupied the chair instead. I left Newcastle this morning and am now on my way to Ashby but shall pass three days first at the Lakes.

Harcourt MSS (Harcourt Papers, *xiv. 46-9*)

At the 1838 meeting the Committee of Recommendations rejected an application by the medical section for £200 to make experiments on digestion. An unsuccessful attempt was made in the General Committee by the medicals to reverse that decision. Northampton was staying at Halsteads, Penrith, the country home of John Marshall (1765-1845), the Leeds flax-spinner, on his way home to Castle Ashby, Northamptonshire.

234 *Northampton, Halsteads, Penrith, to Harcourt, St Clare, Ryde, Isle of Wight, 28 August 1838*

In writing to you yesterday I think I made one omission. I stated, I think, that I had proposed you in the *Council*, but I doubt whether I mentioned what is important, that you were proposed and seconded at the General Committee by Babbage and Herschel. This was done to show that those who had been thought of themselves for the office were of the same opinion with us all that you ought to be our President. This you ought to know, but probably you may have heard as much already. Pray excuse my boring you with another letter, and show you forgive it by acquiescing in the warm wishes of all that you should preside over us next year.

[PS] I shall be at Castle Ashby (Northampton) the end of this week.

Harcourt MSS (Harcourt Papers, *xiv. 50*)

235   *Harcourt, St Clare, Ryde, Isle of Wight, to Babbage, 2 September 1838*

Whilst I deeply lament that any differences on the subject of the Presidency should have deprived the Association of such services as Sir John Herschel or yourself would have rendered in that office, I certainly cannot but feel gratified by the kind feeling evinced towards me, and return you my sincere thanks for the cordial manner in which I hear you undertook and executed the task of proposing my election, though in other points of view it is not what I should have wished, or could, if I had been present, have consented to.

But now that you have mounted me 'nolens, volens', on this formidable engine, and in such a manner as to make it impossible for me to decline the seat, I entreat and adjure you not to put on the steam and shut down the valve so as to blow me and it into the air. Seriously if any thing could make me repent the ever having had any thing to do with the Association it would be the finding that hostilities arose in it between my friends which no mediation could disarm.

Murchison, I think, was wrong in two respects: in his official capacity he should have refrained from imparting to you his intention of proposing you; and in a private point of view he was bound, after having done so, to come to a full understanding with you before he proposed another. This I learn from Lord Northampton and others he has frankly acknowledged, and made you in open court the 'amende honorable'. 'Habes confitentem reum'. *Public* opinion in such a case requires no more; and though on a point of *private* feeling between you I have no right to interfere, I trust you will forgive me for expressing an earnest hope that, as you have made a sort of peace offering of me in appointing me President, you would allow me to act the part of an effective peace-maker between you. It is not the peace of the Association only which makes me anxious for this 'redintegratio amicitive', but in a much higher degree, I can sincerely assure you, the personal esteem and regard with which I remain

BL, Add. MSS 37190, ff. 547–8

The Latin sentence, from Petronius' *Satyricon*, means: you have a prisoner who admits his crimes.

236   *Babbage, Newcastle-upon-Tyne, to Northumberland, 3 September 1838*

Private

I feel that it is due to my character to state to the members of the

British Association the circumstances which have compelled me to offer my resignation of the office of one of its Trustees.

It is my wish to perform that duty with calmness and to avoid stating anything unnecessary for the vindication of my own conduct.

At a meeting of the Council held at Newcastle on Wednesday the 23rd [22] August my Co-trustee, the General Secretary, stated that Sir J Herschel (who had previously accepted the offer of the Council to be proposed as President of the British Association) had withdrawn his acceptance of the office. The General Secretary then made a statement in which the following facts were either included or were fully admitted by him.

1st. That my Co-trustee the General Secretary had about Christmas last strongly urged me to allow myself to be recommended by the Council as President for the ensuing year at Birmingham.

2nd. That the General Secretary had in the month of June last, without the slightest previous communication with me, HIMSELF proposed to the Council that they should offer the Presidency to Sir J. Herschel. He also fully admitted that he had not mentioned his previous communication with me to any member of that Council which he then induced to recommend Sir J. Herschel.

3rdly. That in the beginning of August the General Secretary wrote to offer me a Vice-presidency and enclosed a letter from Mr William Vernon Harcourt to himself approving of the plan. The General Secretary also informed me that his Co-secretary Mr Peacock, as well as Mr Corrie (the representative of Birmingham) approved of it. But the General Secretary fully admitted that, when he procured these opinions, he had not informed either of those three gentlemen of his previous proposal of the Presidency to myself. The Council then passed a resolution to propose me to the General Committee as President at the ensuing meeting at Birmingham. I immediately declined this offer and the Council then resolved to propose Mr William Vernon Harcourt.

I must now state the line of conduct I adopted. When I was informed by Sir J. Herschel (who was perfectly ignorant of the General Secretary's previous offer to myself) that there were circumstances which made it desirable for him to accept the Presidency, I immediately resolved, not merely on resigning my own pretensions but by appearing at Newcastle in the General Committee as his proposer, to shield him from any unjust imputations, from any appearance of having supplanted his friend.

Early on the morning following the meeting of the Council at which the General Secretary's statement was made, I called on Sir J Herschel and having pointed out what I conceived the only possible method of relieving the British Association from the difficulty in which it was involved, I enquired whether, supposing the General Secretary should be disposed to retire, Sir J.H. would *then* consent to preside: I pressed this point and added that in such a case I would willingly be one of his Vice-presidents or act in *any* other office he might think most desirable.

Finding him absolutely decline this, I then asked whether, in the same contingency, if I were myself to accept the recommendation of the Council to the chair he would be one of the Vice-presidents; this also Sir J.H. declined and at the meeting of the General Committee he having finally declined either plan, I, at the request of the Council, then proposed and Sir J.H. seconded Mr William Vernon Harcourt.

The three Trustees of the British Association are the *only permanent* officers of the institution. As one of those Trustees I am always a member of the Council and must necessarily be in frequent communication with my colleagues the Treasurer and the General Secretary. It is highly important for the interest of the British Association that the most perfect confidence should be maintained between those officers; and it is evident that under the circumstances stated such a feeling is impossible. It is therefore my intention at the meeting at Birmingham formally to execute that resignation of which I have given notice.

BL, Add. MSS 37190, ff. 551–2

237 *Murchison, Alnwick Castle, Northumberland, to Harcourt, St Clare, Ryde, Isle of Wight, 4 September 1838*

Your letter of—received yesterday and I failed not in communicating its contents to the Duke and Duchess and your apologies. Be assured that I am very sensible of your kind feelings towards me as well as of your feelings towards your 'scientific offspring', in wishing to do all that you can to promote peace between Babbage and self. I beg however you will recollect that the overtures conciliatory have all been made by myself, and all rejected with scorn. You know that I commenced these overtures in London and I hope you have not mislaid my letter with enclosures on that occasion. To show you that up to the last moment, and after all the spleen if not vengeance with which I am pursued I have been endeavouring to sooth the angry man, I now enclose you another copy of a letter sent to Woolryche Whitmore, Babbage's brother-in-law, nay your MP for Bridgnorth and a most excellent man. If you attempt reconciliation it is well you should know the status quo and that I *have* done and *am* doing all I can to eradicate this foolish hostility of my quondam friend. At the same time recollect that I can do *no more* and that my measure of concession is full. You are right in your conclusion about the General Secretaries: we should both have retired, had I not been personally attacked. And when at one moment I threatened to go, Peacock immediately said 'then I go likewise', and so we have hung together. I hope with such a premier as we now have our government may be sustained. The point which really offends me most in Babbage is that, *after* the explanation in the Council and after his public declaration in the General Committee on Thursday, he withdrew from the Trusteeship because 'his sentiments met with *no response* among the members of the Association' (that these were the words *every one* can testify though the *Athenaeum* has omitted and perverted them); and that on Saturday he should declare the cause of his retreat to be entirely personal [and then] should name me pointedly after reading the General Committee a lecture on the sort of men which Trustees should be. The real fact is that the more B. is now petted by the press the worse he will become. Lady Tankerville has tried hard to get him to Chillingham, but he has shown no where here. And the last we know of him [is] that he was going to print about these matters or rather about B. and M. I specially request you to take care of my letters, for you have now the only pieces justificatives of which I have copies. Sedgwick and Whewell and your brother Charles are here. We came from Sir Charles' Monday and tomorrow we go to Sir J. Trevelyan's. Thence to Silvertops and my next fixed address is at J. Marshall, Esq., Halsteads, Penrith. After the Lakes we go to Rokeby.

[PS] You never were more mistaken in anything than that Herschel is to be or will be P R S. On this point he has unequivocally declared himself in letter and words to myself. He has better things to do and for want of *nerve*, is as unsuited to it as to lead in the British Association. These things we learn as we move on. Every man of science is *now* aware of the failing of the Astronomer.

Harcourt MSS

William Wolryche Whitmore (1787-1858) had been Whig MP for Bridgnorth, 1826-32; Chillingham Castle, Northumberland, was the seat of the Tankervilles; Charles Harcourt (1798-1870), Anglican minister; Sir Charles was probably Sir Charles Miles Lambert Middleton Monck (1779-1867) of Belsay Castle, Northumberland; Sir John Trevelyan (1761-1846) lived at Wallington Hall, Northumberland; the Silvertop was George Silvertop (1775-1849), High Sheriff of Northumberland, of Minsteracres Hall, Northumberland.

238 *Phillips, York, to Harcourt, St Clare, Ryde, Isle of Wight, 17 September 1838*

Your hypothesis of the cause of my silence was quite correct. I thought it better to let the combatants tell their own story, and not

to weary you with a thrice-told tale of the same disagreeable incidents. May it end well! Sir John Robison is a true knight, but
whether K.H. or St Louis, or the Iron Cross, know I not. He was
in good health and spirits, not a whit changed from the Mr Robison
of 1831. Brewster defended himself on more than one occasion from
some sharp cuts of Whewell; Lardner had to recant (which they say
he did very well) his errors concerning ocean steamers; there were
a few other contentions, besides the great one of which you have
heard enough. Let us view the Association in three lines supposed to
proceed from the Newcastle centre of force. 1. its *vis viva*; 2. the
direction of its movements; 3. the obstacles in its path.

1. As to *number* of men assembled, I think the veriest lover of marvel
will be satisfied with meeting 2400 'men of science!'; he will be glad
that for 7 days, for I can hardly except Sunday (of which anon!)
these men discussed and debated, but could not even by *the greatest
temptation* be led into angry dispute; and if he be like me he will be
a little fearful of a second such experiment.

As to the *quality* of the men, there never was a finer gathering of
all the southern and western intellect, but of the northern we were
a little shortened. The weakened sections were medicine, etc, and
natural history. The strongest was the physical, as for all sound
philosophy I opine that it ought to be, since therein is the largest
field of research, and one that can only be traversed by the aid of
exact science. The geologists did their duty, and the geographers took
quite a considerable share of attention (Greenough wishes this to be
a separate sub- or total section).

The weakest point of the meeting was the evening assembly; yet
it was less weak than at any previous meeting, and if 1/2 the number
of hearers (3000!) had been put in half the space, this would have
been a successful effort, though the parts were not *all* well cast.

The issue of tickets was *easy*: everything as to ordinary, assemblies
for talk, promenades, expeditions to Tynemouth, lists of members,
etc, etc was successful, and even the ball or balls (for I think there
were two) went on without much blame. I think every one was
wonderstruck with the fact that 'canny Newcastle' *could* entertain
such a mighty meeting.

The cost was enormous (£3200 raised), *not lavish* (I assert), but
yet such as to alarm small towns, and make them *measure their rooms*,
before inviting the philosophers. A balance remains, say £500, to
furnish collections etc for the Museum of Natural History.

2. The money received by the Association was not so much as you
might think, yet more than at Liverpool (see *Athenaeum*). Grants
£3600 and more. Reports demanded few, and not particularly good
subjects, I think.

Scientific communications very respectable, but not in general at all remarkable for novelty or unusual depth of view. The best thing was the conviction on every observing mind, that the members generally knew a great deal about the things discussed; knowledge of a high quality is largely dealt out, and largely digested by great bodies of men who are not known as authors, or professors, or doctors. The Association *advances* knowledge *somewhat*, but it *diffuses* new and ameliorates the quality of old knowledge possessed in a tenfold degree. We did not contemplate this as the main *object* at first, but it has been our main *result* for some two or three meetings.

There is a great deal of confidence on the part of the members in the governing body, yet a breath might destroy it, and it has been weakened, I *must say*, by the style in which the appointment of presidents has been managed, since you gave up the reins. Anything not plain and open as the sunlight will not succeed with so free and high-spirited a body as the General Committee, who enter of *right* into the examination of all acts of the officers, though in 99 cases out of a hundred, this right will sleep soundly. Peacock manages well, admirably, because he is perfectly candid and transparent, and if we lose him, it will be hard to find his equal (his health is feeble!).

The new regulations as to the constitution of the General Committee (see *Athenaeum*) appear to me perfect. They were framed by a small committee (I was one) and reconsidered more than once before being hazarded to the meeting. They were all affirmed and in no particular enlarged or contracted, so entire was the feeling of the mass of members that they were right.

3. The obstacles in our way are not slight. The Dean of York has written against us, and his inkhorn has been filled for a second pamphlet: if directed *at me?* it will have a chance of being a Philippic; *The Times* abuses us on account chiefly of the 'Educational Association' which by its assemblying just after us seems a 'consequence' of our proceedings, and we suffer as principals though we are not even accessaries. But we are raising obstacles for ourselves. The indiscriminate admission of all 'respectable' people on paying their sovereign can be shown by rigid deduction to be the fertile source of economic difficulty and perhaps of scientific degradation. It necessitates a great outlay for rooms, produces the *sale* of ladies tickets; fills the sections with idlers (I do not mean the ladies only for they are very attentive) and hangers-on for speeches; and finally lowers our finances; (this paradox I can justify) increases our expenditure in printing, etc; and renders it impossible to deliberate when nothing can prevent confusion but violent and dangerous exertion of the mind on the part of many of the most gifted members of the staff.

If this should go to its full length behold a *vanity fair*! Birmingham is so circumstanced for railways and roads, that upon a week's notice not 2400 but 5000 *members* (as the phrase is) may meet at 11 a.m. on the Monday morning, and I am not sanguine enough to maintain that so great a concourse is needed for the *Advancement of Science*, however useful it may be once in 10 years for the diffusion of the knowledge gathered by a few. Alas for the truth, that knowledge is *gathered* but by few, and our meetings prove that *one year* yields in general but few discoveries of moment.

I was going to add a few more shades to my picture on the subject of our fast growing funds, the possible contest for their appropriation, and the diminishing sale of our books; but all these can be conquered or endured if the great evil of nominal members at £1, which entails in logical order a host of errors, can be managed. Now I have a plan for this which I will explain, if upon reading this essay on the state of our Association, you think my prescription may be trusted, or even worth deciphering.

As to the presidency I leave it to you, but I fear the plan you state will *not be adopted*, whatever benefits it may appear to offer. It might be very inconvenient to subject our free body to the triumvirate you would constitute. If in every case the views of the local authorities were fully ascertained and as much as possible consented to, as was done till you left the car, there would be seldom any great cause of embarrassment. It is generally thought I believe (but am not sure) that by the admixture or alternation of men of rank and men of science as presidents, vice-presidents, etc, the interests of the Association will be consulted. At all events your own chair will be very much respected, as you will sit there of right, and besides have affairs to adjust. If you learn from Mr Babbage and Mr Murchison the truth, and the *whole truth*, of the discussion between them, it seems to me not impossible that you may act as umpire with effect, but I can add nothing to what they ought to tell you, and therefore will not further allude to what is painful. From what I heard at Newcastle, I feared you had no reason to think Miss Harcourt much improved in health, yet I should rejoice to be wrong in this impression. I shall be at home till the 8th October and then lecture at Sheffield, the 40th course I shall have delivered. Forbes passed a few days ago, *well*.

Harcourt MSS (Harcourt Papers *xiv. 51–7*)

At the 1836 meeting of the Association some statisticians formed an Education Committee which in 1837 and 1838 met at the same time and place as the Association. This Committee, closely allied with the Central Society of Education, discussed highly contentious issues. For abuse of the Association, see *The Times*, 24 Aug and 5 Sept 1838.

239 *Murchison, Rokeby Castle, to Harcourt, 9 October 1838.*

I find a packet of the addresses here and, as a Lord of the Treasury is in the house who can frank any sized bundle, I think *you* are well entitled to as many of these as you please.

I have long ago ceased to bother myself about Babbage and the Newcastle schism. I was, I confess, much hurt in discovering the extent of his *rancour*, but I am quite ready to throw it into oblivion. In writing to me on this point, Peacock says that he has heard but one opinion respecting B. and adds, 'If B. informs me that it is his intention to restate his grievances at Birmingham, I will tell him plainly that he will provoke an expression of opinion that will mortify his pride and vanity *most deeply*'.

On my way southwards we go first to Lord Prudhoe's and Lord Tyrconnel's.

We were asked to Bishopthorpe but under existing circumstances I shall not propose it. In our route to Castle Ashby I propose halting a day or two at Sandwell Park, Lord Dartmouth's, specially to see the result of some coal-works through the red sandstone and I will take the same opportunity of replying to some queries propounded to me by the Local Secretary, British Association Birmingham. He asks if I can suggest any improvements on former plans. I have written to ask Phillips for his advice if he has any to offer and shall be delighted if any point strikes you on which I may illuminate the natives.

A letter under cover to the Earl of Dartmouth will reach me towards the end of the month.

Lord Brougham came here for one day by an act of his own volition, and kept us famously alive for a night touching up His Royal Highness, our defunct President, but he disappeared to my sorrow next morning before break of day like an aurora borealis and went to York (65 miles) to breakfast.

H R H is very well and in high spirits, though he is evidently *sorry to abdicate* . . .

Harcourt MSS (Harcourt Papers, *xiv. 57–9*)

The address was that given by Murchison and Peacock to the 1838 meeting. H R H the Duke of Sussex resigned as President of the Royal Society of London, Nov 1838.

240 *Murchison, Sandwell near Birmingham, to Harcourt, Bromley, Kent,*
8 November 1838

I fully intended to have written to you from Bishopthorpe where we passed a few delightful days and where we were not among the least overjoyed to hear that your intense anxiety respecting your dear little girl had been relieved. We trust that the move to Bromley and the skill of Mr Scott may yet prove successful.

I wrote to you some time ago to say that I was coming here to look at the finish of Lord Dartmouth's successful enterprise, and that the Birmingham people wished to take advantage of the circumstance to consult me upon various points connected with the meeting. I have seen Mr Corrie several times, and Lord Dartmouth has asked several of the leading people here to meet me at dinner, so that I pretty well know the temper of men's minds and the materials we have to work upon. In old Corrie we have a kind, benevolent and intelligent man, albeit he was a *dissenting parson*. He is now Esq and a magistrate and co-operates with Lord Dartmouth in the Lepers home and Poor Law Union. Lord D. is willing to do anything which can be useful; and I have therefore suggested that he should take the chair at an early meeting of the Local Council, to give weight and character to the resolutions of that body by which they will invite the nobility, gentry and inhabitants of the surrounding region to flock in at our approaching festival.

Today the *town* meeting was held (the high bailiff in the chair) merely to receive the announcement of the appointment of the meeting at Birmingham and the names of the officers, and two or 3 preliminary resolutions were passed. When a good and influential Local Council is formed sub-committees will be appointed to carry into effect all requisite arrangements.

The [Local] Secretaries may all be made useful in their respective lines. Mr Barker is an eminent solicitor and the most gentlemanlike man in the place, with considerable influence with the high church and Conservative party in the neighbourhood. When I came to Sandwell I found him (by talk after dinner) inclined to retire from the post, alleging his unceasing occupation, but knowing from Lord Dartmouth and Mr Corrie how essential it was to retain him, I persuaded him to adhere to us and he will be invaluable as a local master of the ceremonies. Mr Hodgson is [the] leading surgeon, F R S, and a very pleasing, well-informed, right-minded man, who takes no care of politics. Mr Follett Osler is the clever active youth who invented the anemometer; he is a violent radical in politics. Dr Peyton Blakiston is an incipient physician of the conservative order, not long established in the place, and a bustling person (friend of Peacock's).

Mr Moilliet, the Local Treasurer, is a pleasant old Swiss gentleman who has made a large fortune here; and Mr Russell, the permanent Local Treasurer is a zealous, indefatigable man, ready to slave at anything.

The town bailiff, a chief magistrate's *present* title, a Mr ——— (name forgotten), told the meeting in other places, from what he could learn, politics had not been carefully excluded, but *ere* he was persuaded that *armony* would prevail, and that however much their town was divided they would all unite on this occasion; which sentiment was much cheered. They seem indeed all in good humour and therefore a successful issue is to be looked to. I find that they (as is invariably the case in these democracies) would have preferred an aristocratic leader; and much as I did to point out your value in re 'British Association', I believe that the communication of all your high connections made a much greater impression on them.

Touching places of meeting (or rooms) I think we shall do very well, as the greater number of them are *well together*. Four sections, for example, may sit at the Free Schools, though it will require a good deal of pre-arrangement as the two long halls, though beautiful rooms, are not suited to lecturing and are against *hearing*. The chemicals can be well accommodated in the Theatre of the Philosophical Institution, the medicals in the School of Medicine, the statisticals at the courts. The Town Hall is really a splendid building for the general meetings and I suggested one concert (as more connected with science than balls) to allow the philosophers to hear the fine organ.

There are good halls for exhibition of models and works of art, and a picture gallery will be lighted on one or more evenings. It is proposed to fit up Beardsworth's great Horse Repository as a *refectory*.

As the use of the Schools is essential, the convenience of the Governors must be specially consulted.

August (*alas!*) being fixed upon, all *we* can do is to appoint the precise time, but in doing this the Council must of course account the wishes of the Birminghamers. I had fondly hoped that the last week might be taken but I find that the School holidays range into the 2nd week of August, and therefore the probability is that the first week will be recommended, which will break up the geological summer and hasten me back from my travels.

There is one feature which cannot be brushed out in sketching this picture, or rather there is the want of a feature in Birmingham which was strongly marked at Newcastle. In the latter place we found a sort of aristocratic bourgeoisie of bankers, glass makers etc, who were connected with the best families in the county, rich and influential. Indeed, many of the Northumbrians of the largest landed estates owe their origin to the town. Here there is nothing of the sort, for Boulton and Watt, the Gog and Magog of the new era, have cut all connection with the place and will take no part in the doings; so that the best people in the place are decidedly inferior to the Newcastle auxiliaries. Her Majesty has just granted the town a corporation and before Christmas a *Mayor* and aldermen will be appointed. This will and does occasion a little political feeling and the Conservatives, seeing that they cannot obtain a just balance, intend, as I understand, to take no interest in the election and thus leave it entirely to the other party. Notwithstanding these drawbacks I have no doubt that when the neighbourhood (including the rich and intelligent iron masters and miners of the surrounding towns) is well whipped in, the meeting will be a very good one.

I have now to inform you that the letter to the Duke of Northumberland from Babbage with enclosures from His Grace is in my possession with directions to lay it before the Council.

The Duke explains that he retained this letter and wrote to Mr B., *hoping* that [it] might be intended solely for his private reading, but that he regrets to find it is not so and being directed by Mr B. to forward it he is under the necessity of making this painful communication.

On my arrival in town I shall call a Council and will so time it, by concert with Peacock and Lord Northampton, that they shall both be present, and on that occasion I shall also lay before them a *written* reply to Babbage's assertions and aspersions. In fact my written statement will be the sum of what I said at the Council of the 22nd August at Newcastle, followed by a short comment on what really transpired at that meeting, namely *your* selection and B's cordial acquiescence to be *your proposer*, and then B's letter to the Duke which informs His Grace and the Council that he B, early next morning, endeavoured to reverse all the arrangements and to get either himself or Herschel into the chair, if the General Secretary could only be got rid of. Any observation is unnecessary with such a document before them. It is the Council (to whom he pledged himself), and not *Roderick Impey Murchison* who is now at issue with him for having *done his best* to break his pledge. Of all this we should have known nothing, but for this insane letter.

If you can by possibility attend it is highly desirable you should be present at the Council held on this subject. But if you cannot, still I should hope to be able to consult you on the nature and force of my reply.

We go tomorrow to Castle Ashby where I shall pass 3 or 4 days and be in town on Tuesday next the 13th; a letter to Eccleston Street will be thankfully received.

You would be glad to learn that so good a man as Lord Northampton is selected by the Council as future PRS and that he has accepted the office. As I shall have ample opportunity to consult him on the Babbagian case, I shall abide very much by his recommendations, as he has looked into the subject with the kindest endeavours on his part to prevent B. proceeding to these extremities.

Now it is impossible to allow B's document to be recorded and no reply to come from me. My silence would be an acknowledgment of the accuracy of his version.

Pray offer our kind regards to Mrs Harcourt and in anxious wishes for your dear child

[PS omitted]

Harcourt MSS (Harcourt Papers, *xiv. 59-66*)

Peyton Blakiston (1801-78); James Russell, Birmingham surgeon (1786-1851), *DNB*; John Lewis Moilliet of Geneva settled in Birmingham about 1800 and became a merchant and banker.

241 *Murchison, 2 Eccleston Street, Belgrave Square, London, to Buckland, Christ Church, Oxford, 20 November 1838*

By a note just received from Lady Marian Compton to Mrs Murchison it appears that you have asked Babbage to dine at the Geological Society *Club* tomorrow. If you had known what he has done since the Newcastle meeting, (nay even had you been present at the meetings of Council) you never would I am persuaded have taken such a step. I have not time nor inclination to explain all this affair but I believe in sincerity that there is not a member of the Council of the British Association who does not participate *in my feelings*. They saw and know what efforts (Peacock and Lord Northampton particularly) I made to conciliate Babbage but in vain. His conduct at and before the Newcastle meeting was rancorous and unforgiving in the extreme, but it is as nothing compared with what he has now done *officially*. A full week after the Newcastle meeting he wrote an official letter to the Duke of Northumberland, giving his own version of a part of my statement (to the Council of the Wednesday during the week of our meeting) and then with the utmost *simplicity* he tells His Grace, that he Babbage on the following morning early, waited upon Herschel to induce him to consent to one of two plans: by the first of which Herschel to be President, Babbage Vice-president; by the second Babbage to be President, Herschel Vice-president, but both plans coupled with the condition *that the General Secretary Murchison was to be got rid of as the only means of saving the British Association*!!! Of course Herschel rejected both plans instanter.

Will you believe? can any *gentleman* believe that these propositions were made on Thursday early by the same man, who the day before (*Wednesday*) having rejected the proposal of the Council moved *by myself* that he should be the President (Herschel having retired), had completely and fully agreed to the final arrangement of that meeting, viz that *Vernon Harcourt was to be the President,* which resolution he Babbage *had pledged himself* to the Council to propose on Thursday to the General Committee.

Verbum sat! Every member of the Council who has seen this precious document is astounded!!

On the 1st of December therefore, the day after the Anniversary of the Royal Society, a full meeting of Council will be called and in presenting Mr Babbage's charge I shall of course put in writing the substance of what I formerly stated in words and which has completely satisfied all my friends.

This is no affair of science: it is entirely Babbage's vindictive spirit which has brought up the subject and I am ordered (recollect) by the Duke of Northumberland (most *unwillingly* on His Grace's part for he *remonstrated with B*) to present this document.

One of the objects of the Council will be to accept Babbage's resignation of his Trusteeship *with as much speed as may be.* I had hoped that he who persists in being my inveterate enemy, not being a member of our [Geological] Society nor of the Athenaeum, I might have been spared the being brought into contact with him. I wish however to say nothing myself. Ask any member of the Council (Lord Northampton, J. Taylor, Peacock, Baily, Whewell) who is cognizant of the facts what Babbage's conduct has been and then do not be surprised if I am vexed at being deprived of one of the few though real pleasures I have in attending my first joyous meeting at the Geological. If Babbage's letter had never been written I might have forgotten all, but he pursues me still and I cannot consent to *subscribe my own condemnation.* I shall preside at the Club in Whewell's absence and have a friend coming.

[Written across p. *1*]

N.B. You will at once perceive that under existing circumstances it would be absurd to bring Babbage into the same small party with me, if pleasure to either be the object. Can I *speak* to a person who has expressed the opinion I have alluded to *since* the termination of the Newcastle meeting? At the same time I trust to your discretion not to make me appear averse to meeting him. I have always sought conciliation but his last act compels me to protect my own character.

Indeed I am sure that if he knew I was to be present he would, knowing what he laid to my charge, abstain from coming.
[Written on p. 4]
If your object in asking Babbage was to effect a reconciliation a different method must be taken. He must withdraw his letters to the Duke of Northumberland and Council and believe my statement. If you will consult Peacock and others you will find that our effort to propitiate Babbage has made him worse and that the only step now is to accept his resignation at once.
[Written in in later hand? l.h. margin p. 3]
I do not believe there is even a provincial snob who would have thought of asking Babbage to put his legs under the same mahogany with me.

Murchison Papers

Lady Marian Compton, Northampton's daughter, acted as hostess for her father whose wife had died 1830.

242 *Babbage, n.p., to Harcourt, 28 November 1838*

I have this instant received your letter and hasten to put you in possession of my views.

Having publicly given notice of my intended resignation of the office of Trustee, and having officially written to confirm that intention on grounds which, in my opinion, fully justify it, I cannot withdraw that resignation without admitting it to be wrong, or at least hasty, unless some reasonable ground for the change of intention can be shown.

If, however, the Council, when my letter to the President is read, would request *him* to answer it, and to express the regret of the Council at the occurrence of the circumstances which had induced me to give notice of that resignation, and also to state that they considered my withdrawing from the office of one of the Trustees as injurious to the interests of the British Association, then I think I should have a reasonable ground for remaining, and I think the Council would thereby only express an opinion, not make any apology.

But if this is done I should expect to receive from the Secretary of the *Council* (not from the General Secretary) a copy of the minutes. This is absolutely necessary not for my own use, but for my own defence, as I could better explain when we meet.

I sincerely trust your peaceful efforts may not be impeded by the state of your poor invalid.

Harcourt MSS (Harcourt Papers, *xiv. 66–7*)

243   *Harcourt, Bromley, Kent, to Babbage, 1 Dorset Street, Manchester Square, London, 1 December 1838*

We had a very numerous meeting, all or nearly all the members of the Council (Lord Northampton included) being present. They were apparently unanimous in considering the difference between Murchison and yourself as a personal question not coming within their jurisdiction.

In the conversation, however, which took place on the subject, Lyell, as he has probably informed you, stated the fact which you wished to be known of your having refused M's hand subsequently to Lord N's mediation. The only resolution come to was to the effect of instructing the Treasurer to communicate with you as to the transfer of stock to the remaining Trustees. Nothing passed which could have been in any way offensive to you had you been present; and the relations between M. and yourself remain just where they were except that I have told him I had understood from you that you had no design in what you wrote to the Duke of Northumberland of deviating from the terms on which you parted at Newcastle, on which terms he assures me he is also desirous of remaining, and I conclude therefore that it is so arranged: ill satisfied as I am to be obliged to have matters thus between you, I am glad we are agreed in thinking that wounds which cannot be healed should be kept out of sight.

BL, Add. MSS 37191, ff. 51–2

244   *Northampton, Castle Ashby, to Minto, 6 January 1839*

I have not received any account from the Royal Society as to the result of the interview between a deputation from them and Lord Melbourne. But as after all the question belongs more immediately to your department of the government than to the Treasury, at least that part of the question which concerns the proposed antarctic expedition, I hope you will excuse me for troubling you with a few lines.

I assure you that I have reason to know that the scientific world feels a *very great* anxiety for the dispatch of this expedition, now that the peace is still continuing, and that the services of such an eminent person as Captain James Ross are to be had. I do not say this from any *personal* partiality to him for I hardly know him by sight, or rather I do not, though I have been introduced to him. It would be a great pity indeed if some other nation were to take the start of us, and it seems to me highly probable after the prominent manner in which the British Association and the Royal Society have brought forward the question, that some other nation *will* do so if we allow the present season to pass over. I am sure you must think and know that there are governments who would not grudge the expenditure of a sufficient sum of money for such a purpose, and who would be the more disposed to make such an effort, as it would give them the opportunity of saying that the government of England, the Queen of the Ocean, refused such a boon to the united prayers of her chief men of science, assembled in what may be called their *two parliaments*; a boon, the objects of which are closely connected with those sciences, the interests of which a great naval nation should naturally be most anxious to cultivate. Having given my *general* support to the government, I feel, as it were, a personal interest in its reputation and credit, and it would be to me a source of great gratification that the time when the reins of our navy were held by Lord Minto, was the period during which an expedition most important to science was sent forth to comply with the prayers of the Royal Society and the British Association.

I do not like in a letter on a subject of this nature to refer at all to direct calculations of expense, etc, but if the improvements of our knowledge of magnetism, etc, should at any time save only one ship of the line, the whole expense of an expedition will have been well laid out, without any reference whatsoever to the scientific objects of the expedition.

You have, I have no doubt, seen the report of the joint committee of the Royal Society on the subject, but in case you should not, I enclose one.

Royal Society of London, Miscellaneous Correspondence, 3, no 2

William Lamb, Viscount Melbourne (1779-1848), *DNB*, was Prime Minister, 1835-41. Northampton, as President of the Royal Society of London, enclosed the Dec 1838 report of its joint committee on physics and meteorology. Northampton's intervention was probably decisive in persuading government to pay for an antarctic magnetic expedition and for colonial magnetic observatories.

245 *Murchison, 2 Eccleston Street, Belgrave Square, London, to Harcourt, 23 January 1839 [Murchison wrote 1838]*

I have been a good deal out of town this winter and am going away again for a week on Sunday, which will account for my never having met Babbage since you were so good as to mediate. By accident, however, I learn from Chantrey that I am to meet B at his house at dinner *tomorrow*, and hence I wish to ask you whether it was as distinctly understood by Babbage *as it is by myself* that we are to have social intercourse. I have little doubt from your letter that this is the case, but still I would like to know from you as a friend what we, i.e. wife and self, ought to do? Should we give as courteous a bow or how d ye' do as may he, or ought we to shake hands?

For my own part, believe me, I should be *too happy* if the latter were accomplished and if our intercourse was such that no persons could observe that we had been estranged: but I presume this cannot be *as yet*, and that all *we* can do is to be polite and with as little reserve as possible. In truth, the Chantreys asked us without forecast, but when Sir Francis recollected the feud, he called and asked me if I had any objection to come, to which I said certainly not, and in saying this I trusted to *your* explanation. This season cannot pass without our meeting at other places and the ice must be broken. If, however, you have any reason to think I had better avoid the rencontre, say so. I can only add that I have long ago completely dismissed the subject from my mind and that if the same has been effected in another quarter there can be no objection to our meeting.

Phillips has informed me of his projects of reform and as far as I can judge I like them. They can only apply prospectively, that is they can have no other effect on the Birmingham meeting, except that as we have several untoward subjects to digest there the less these reforms savour of dictation to the mass, the better.

Bozzi Granville and his agriculture must be steadily and decidedly thrown over.

After parliament has met we ought to have at least two meetings of Council to arrange preliminaries and our line of conduct. Again I hope *you* will cast about for a good Glasgow President, and when you have a fitting man let it be broached in the Council and clearly understood. Sir William Hooker is now in London and seems to consider it quite certain that the Association is to go to Glasgow. As the Glasgow people have been especially told not to make any sort of demonstration quoad President without consulting us and have been assured that no one has yet been suggested, the field is quite open. I mentioned the Duke of Hamilton to you but stray doubts as to his fitness may be mentioned. I shall be over the seas and far away, if I live, when that meeting takes place and it is my fixed resolve to resign my post of General Secretary at the close of the Birmingham meeting. Nothing, indeed, but the peculiar circumstances and a feeling connected with my own honour and to support you, would have induced me to remain so long; for I have planned a trip to the Baltic in the spring, not intending to return till August and then to fly again.

Harcourt MSS (Harcourt Papers, *xiv. 26–9*)

Augustus Bozzi Granville (1783–1872), *DNB*, wanted a separate section for agriculture; Alexander Hamilton Douglas, 10th Duke of Hamilton (1767–1852), *DNB*.

246   *Murchison, 2 Eccleston Street, Belgrave Square, London, to Harcourt, Carlton, Pontefract, 21 February 1839*

When I wrote to you last I little thought that I was intruding upon you at a sad moment, and was much vexed with myself for having done so as soon as I heard of the loss you had sustained. I trust that Mrs W. Harcourt and yourself are now recovering from its effects and that you will be able to rouse yourself to attend to a little business, for I am persuaded that on such melancholy occasions exertion is useful.

Phillips went to Birmingham last week and brought back a letter from the Local Secretaries requiring the authority of the London Council to enable them to proceed in forming a Local Council, and I called a meeting yesterday at which we sanctioned the measure they proposed, of starting with a nucleus of names forwarded to us and of adding thereto according to a given plan, the names to be finally approved by us.

A circular signed by Lord Dartmouth will be sent to all the surrounding folks to invite them to join.

We legislated on sundry other points.

1st. We allowed a grant of £500! to the Newcastle folks (in fact John Taylor had left that sum with them) for extra scientific expenditure but not without a great deal of grumbling and remonstrance on my part, that a sum double that which we have paid at former places should be abstracted from our treasury. It is contended that when we go to these commercial towns they have not places to receive us and therefore are put to great expense, but I contend that no town is entitled to *ask us* who cannot *house us* and it is a bad example and precedent to defray any charges of this sort which may be made.

2. We ruled that there shall be only 2 general evening meetings of *science* at Birmingham, viz the opening and the close. On this point we were *unanimous*.

3. That the ladies have access to the galleries only or railed-off spaces in the various halls of the sectional meetings.

4. We talked of having the sectional meeting-rooms open every evening either for the reading of memoirs, or such work as the presidents and committees of the sections might approve of; these evening meetings and the various exhibitions will be the chief attraction for the ladies.

We did not go much into the eating, drinking and festivity department, but in allusion thereto we all agreed that one daily grand ordinary (as at Newcastle) was uncalled for, a bore of the first magnitude to be avoided. These are points for the locals.

I have however written to Mr Corrie (the regular resolutions being forwarded by Yates) to explain our wishes and feelings more fully.

When I was at Birmingham Mr Corrie seemed to dwell much upon *one* great *eating festival* in Beardsworth's Repository or some such place, to which all the surrounding nobility and gentry should be invited; and to this there can be no objection, for if well managed, and that Peel and others will attend, it would impart a good character to the meeting.

Mr Corrie and myself also talked of one general concert in the Town Hall as proceeding entirely from the local authorities and to this I see no objection. Some such thing is required for the neighbourhood, and if we do not attract the great folks around our meeting will have too much of the 'Brummagem'.

Corrie will write to me when the Local Council has schemed a project and I have no doubt that they will attend on every point to our suggestions before such points are decided upon. I have recommended them (being *poor*) to avoid all evening refreshments etc for they are costly and productive of great confusion.

I have suggested that there should be daily ordinaries at each of the great hotels, the officers and presidents of sections to preside, etc.

Johnston has printed or is printing a sort of semi-official portfolio of all the machinery of the Newcastle meeting, the great good of which will be that of a beacon to other towns on the score of expense.

I thought it right to tell you what we are about and, if you can, in the course of the next ten days, give me your opinion on any of these points and before Corrie's reply arrives, we can have another concilium and terminate these preliminaries.

Phillips opened his reform budget, but we did not go into it. T'is a long yarn to spin at the end of a letter and you know his plan of augmenting an entrance fee and of abolishing £1 members. He is to bring it on as a recommendation from the Council to the General Committee at a subsequent meeting. I highly approve his principle but have strong doubts of the feasibility of the measure and dread its unpopularity.

Offer the kindest remembrances of Mrs Murchison and myself to the Archbishop and your family circle.

NB I need scarcely tell you that Babbage and myself met 'comme si de rien n'était' and have since repeatedly met, though we are no longer invited to his Saterd*alia*.

Harcourt MSS (Harcourt Papers, *xiv. 74-8*)

Harcourt's daughter, Louisa, had died in Jan 1839. The Council of the Association gave £500 to the Novocastrians to defray the deficit caused by their lavish hospitality at the 1838 meeting. Johnston's portfolio was *Meeting of the British Association at Newcastle. Report of the Local Secretaries* (Newcastle-upon-Tyne, 1839).

247 *Phillips, 23 Norfolk Street, Strand, London, to Harcourt, Nuneham Courtnay, Oxfordshire, 1 March 1839*

I hope I do not err in supposing it will *now* be useful to try to interest your thoughts in plans for the future good government of the Association, which, in consequence of its very magnitude, and the extreme laxity of the cords which bind together its anomalous parts, needs from time to time the re-examination of the architect. If you remember, I stated to you at York that our condition was *apparently* most prosperous but that the balance of our affairs was delicate. Among the causes of disturbance in our equilibrium the following have appeared to me prominent.

1. The crowd of merely temporary members who pay £1 to 'hear the lectures'.

2. The consequent difficulty of accommodation.

3. The consequent expense of fittings and refreshments.

4. The objectionable mode of raising this money in the towns which receive us.

5. The difficulty of retaining a really scientific character in the midst of such a heterogeneous assembly.

6. The want of sale for our volumes.

7. The general result a *loss of money* to the Association.

For 1. By reason of the great local expenses few persons compound for £5, but most pay £1 and *cease* to pay afterwards.

2. The money raised in the places which entertain us, is never enough and last year we paid £500! for the purpose of covering the deficiency.

3. Our printing and other expenses rise proportionally.

My remedy for all this is

1. To *require* from every new member an admission fee of £5.

2. In consequence to give every such member (paying his annual subscription £1 or a composition of £5) the next and future volumes as a *right*.

3. In case any old member *chooses* to pay £5 admission, he is to have the future volumes supplied gratis.

My plan was mentioned to the Council, and its principle was apparently approved, but the amount of the admission £5 was obviously a source of alarm. If reduced to £2 or £1 even, it would be pro tanto useful and *then we can not give the books* (They do now sell many copies). This will enable you to *consider* the matter, which will be brought forward again in the Council, but I hope not hastily passed, as I think every change of our laws requires great prudence.

Harcourt MSS

248   *Murchison, Reading, to Harcourt, 6 April 1839*

The Ides of March have passed away and we have been propounding various improvements in our Council, of which Phillips will inform you. With another meeting on *the 25 April*, I trust that every point on which the Council can legislate by anticipation will have been attended to and that we shall meet the General Committee with a clear understanding of what we intend to propose and what to *oppose*. These matters, together with notices of members regularly given in at our last meeting, will then be printed in the circular to be sent to every member. I need not say that it is highly desirable you should take cognizance of these subjects and discuss them at length with Phillips before he returns to London, in order that we may be in full possession of your opinion. I had, indeed, hoped that you would have written to me before in answer to my former letters. On the 1st May I leave this country on a summer tour in France and Germany, not intending to return till the eve of the meeting. It is, therefore, desirable that all the little which I can do should be thrown off as soon as may be. It is also essential that you should know that both Peacock and myself have resolved to give up our places as General Secretaries at Birmingham. For my own part my decision has long been made and would have been carried into effect at Newcastle, had not the effort of Babbage to *remove me* compelled me to stand to my guns, for fear that my resignation should have the appearance of being driven out by the Finsbury radical. I have done all that I can to induce Peacock to remain, but he is inexorable and declares that it is solely *with me* that he will act, and that but for the wish to act another year *with me*, he would also have bolted at Newcastle. You have, therefore, to furnish your successor with a brace of ministers and I think you will have no difficulty.

Major Sabine, who is an excellent man of business, will make you one and I have no doubt you can think of several fit men before the time comes.

I have written to the Duke of Hamilton by desire of the last Council to ask His Grace to officiate as President in case the next meeting should be held at Glasgow, and this is done at the suggestion of the most influential persons in and around that city. Should the Duke refuse, are we to apply to the Duke of Montrose?

In reference to the anniversary discourse it is quite clear that you must compose it on this occasion and have all *the honour* which it will bring you. No man can do it better than you and no one is so well qualified to speak out and *to the point*. No one of the Local Secretaries is in the slightest degree entitled or competent to make a general discourse, and neither of the General Secretaries can do it half so well as yourself, so that Peacock says you *must* do it and pronounce it from your own chair. This will give you besides an admirable opportunity of refuting the dull and senseless calumnies which are heaped up upon us by fanatics and fools. As long as such trash was confined to the *British Critic* I despised it, but now that it comes out with all the force of the 'great Thunderer' and that this Jupiter of the daily press foretells that we are to be driven out of Birmingham with infamy, it is high time to buckle on our armour and show the strength of our cause and its goodness. Your discourse and the attendance, even on one day at one of our public dinners, of such a man as Peel will do more to remove these aspersions than all other efforts united (*In limine* I am glad to perceive Sir Robert is a member elect and *has* accepted).

Presuming, however, that we shall overcome all difficulties, it is more than ever essential that when we meet in the great workshop we should give as little rise as possible to subjects which experience has taught us have often been attended with ridicule: I mean general evening lectures and *exhibitions*. The Council has, therefore, I think wisely resolved to recommend that any such concerns must take place in the rooms of the respective sections, subject to the approbation of the president of the section and of the President of the Association.

It is now *utterly impracticable* to have daily general assemblies with all the '*ladies* and *gentlemen*' united, and therefore we suggest that *two* of these only be held at the opening and close of the meeting.

We have been making a little Easter trip and have passed a few days at Christ Church with Buckland, in coming from whom yesterday we saw the Archbishop 'en passant' so I shall send this letter to be franked by His Grace.

We return to town on Wednesday. With Mrs Murchison's kind remembrances to Mrs Harcourt

PS I hoped from what you said and also from what others who were in his confidence have assured me, that Babbage had quite abandoned (and that indeed he never had contemplated), the idea of stirring up a great row at Birmingham. It was, therefore, with sorrow that I heard from Peacock that he B. had been descanting on his grievances to Willis of Cambridge expressing his intention to bring them all out at Birmingham!! On talking to Whewell and others about this I find that any such effort would be met by such a vigorous *settler* at the outset that I have little fear of its producing much effect (particularly as I happen to hear that the Birminghamers are one and all resolved not to allow such personal nonsense to be produced). Still, however, the very mention of this 'decies repetita' and nauseating tale, and the endeavour to create fresh discord is very disgusting. I fear that B. *calculates* upon your indulgence. If you knew the extent to which concession and kindness were carried at Newcastle, you would I believe see the absolute necessity of taking a firm line and of extinguishing at the first any attempt to revive this troubled question. But the thing is too absurd to be thought of and so say all those with whom I am acquainted. For the fulmination of *The Times* see 29th March, 3 columns devoted to our annihilation.

Harcourt MSS (Harcourt Papers, *xiv. 78–83*)

James Graham, 4th Duke of Montrose (1799-1874), *DNB*. At the 1839 meeting of the Association Harcourt gave the key-note address. Babbage stood unsuccessfully as Radical MP for Finsbury, London, in 1832. John William Bowden (1798-1844), *DNB*, 'The British Association for the Advancement of Science', *British Critic*, 1839, xxv. 1-48, provided much ammunition for *The Times*, 29 Mar 1839.

249   *Murchison, n.p., to Harcourt, 12 April 1839*

I have had His Grace of Hamilton's reply and he accepts the conditional offer of the chair, but with conditions of his own. 1st, that he shall be in the country when the meeting takes place. 2ndly, that he be not exposed to a concentration of *light*. I shall bring these points before the Council on the 25th and I presume that they will empower me to ask His Grace to let us know whether or not we may absolutely depend upon him as a leader, provided we assemble at Glasgow of which event I may assure or rather reassure him there is little doubt.

If this be known then we may endeavour not to annoy him too much with gas or tapers by having our general meetings by daylight, to which I see no radical objection. Coupling this with the other data I sent you, I shall be happy to have your opinion before the 24th.

[PS]   To have the President of the British Association extinguished by too great an influx of light!!

Harcourt MSS

250   *Phillips, York, to Harcourt, Bolton Percy near Tadcaster, 20 April 1839*

There has been a double misconception. I thought you were at Stokesley and you did not know that I was in York. I was meditating a visit to you as soon as I found from Miss Cooke my mistake, but I fear that I can not do so until after returning to town to attend a Council of the Association on Thursday next (25th) at 1 p.m. To do this I must leave York on Tuesday afternoon, and unless you find yourself likely to be in York before that I am afraid we shall not meet. There is a Council of Yorkshire Philosophical Society on Monday at 1.

An absurd story has got into the papers in which I have the honour to hold a new appointment etc in a national museum. There is such a museum and such an appointment but it is chiefly of a chemical nature and it is most worthily filled by *Richard* Phillips.

I shall not stay in town more than a few days and propose to return via Birmingham. Possibly you may choose to attend the London Council meeting yourself, as it is the *last* (probably) before we assemble in Birmingham. It is thought by some persons that you might find an occasion of aiding much the cause of the Association in your official address at Birmingham, for it is remarkable how many and persevering though ill-judged and ill-executed attacks, on the score of politics and religion, our gigantic confederation has to endure. I informed you in my last of the *decision* of the Council as to the proposal at Birmingham of an *admission* fee, and they sanctioned my plan regarding the sale of books so far as [to] encourage the receipt of voluntary compositions of £5, which should entitle to future volumes of transactions. To hold the meetings biennially was talked of, but met with no favour. It would now be a dangerous experiment, unless we could command a preponderating majority in favour. I have not been very well and am much in need of repose so that I regret this journey to town extremely. I long to see you and hope you will be able to resume some of your studies in meteorology, now that you are fixed in the county.

Harcourt MSS

In 1839 Richard Phillips was appointed Chemist and Curator at the expanded Museum of Economic Geology (founded 1835). For Harcourt's views on religion and science, see his 1839 Presidential address, *Athenaeum*, 1839, 651–4.

251 *Harcourt, Bolton Percy near Tadcaster, to Murchison, 2 Eccleston Street, Belgrave Square, London, 21 April 1839*

The arrears of business which have accumulated for me here during two or three years of absence from my home and parish have engaged me so much as to make me slow in answering your letters; but having been confined for a day to my bed by indisposition I have run over in my mind the points on which you wish for my opinion.

I agree with Phillips as to the necessity of a change in our pecuniary terms of admission but doubt he goes further than the public will bear. The arrangement that would most simplify our accounts would be to *admit no more annual subscribers*; but to let the payment for all be that which has hitherto been the composition, namely, £5. To remove the objection of *excluding scientific individuals incapable of paying such a sum* the local councils might be empowered to select (subject to the approval of the General Committee) a certain number, say a dozen, honorary members, *pro hoc vice*. With respect to the transactions I see no objection to allowing any one to compound for them for £5, confining the period of application to three or four years.

Of these propositions the last is perfectly innocent; the first would produce *a considerable limitation of numbers*. If the Council shrink from this, the least change that can be made is to raise the first payment of the annual subscriber from £1 to £2.

I think your arrangements for the order of proceeding at Birmingham judicious; but do not feel equally satisfied that you have done well for Glasgow, unless the stiff unpopular Lord Douglas of former years is an altered man. I should have preferred the Rector of the University, who is always some distinguished man, or Brewster, or Brisbane over again. But is it not well worth considering whether the next meeting should not be two years hence, and, for the future, biennial? Faraday suggested to me that our meetings would be improved by being less frequent, and I am inclined to be of this opinion.

As to the address, Peacock ought to write it; if he cannot be persuaded, and *the Council lay it upon me*, I shall do my best. But it is really too much to call upon me to look out for new Secretaries, especially considering that you are living in London and know so much better than myself where to find them. I have not yet got a copy of *The Times* of the 29th. Is South the author of the diatribe or a more formidable adversary?

Murchison Papers (Harcourt Papers, *xiv. 83–5*)

The Duke of Hamilton was previously known as Lord Douglas.

252 *Murchison, London, to Harcourt, 26 April 1839*

Your letters were duly received and the Council was held yesterday.

It had *previously* been decided that it would be impolitic if not impracticable to propose to exclude annual members and the Council had therefore agreed to adopt the succedaneum of £2 for every annual member, such person's name not to be printed in the list as members of the Association except *locally*; and the £5 composition [fee] for the volumes was also adopted.

We yesterday amended and directed to be put into operation certain forms of circular to be sent to each member of the General Committee, with notices of motions to be submitted to them, etc.

You were (by an unanimous expression of the Council) requested to prepare the annual address, to be read from the chair at the first day of meeting. Having heard from Phillips as well as from yourself concerning the suggested propriety of considering whether the meetings should not henceforth be held biennially, I thought it right that the subject should be canvassed fully; and it was the *unanimous* opinion of the Council (a full one, the Marquis Northampton in the chair), that it is *not* desirable to entertain such a project, nor even to speak of it as having ever been before us officially (I beg pardon, little *Yates* was biennially disposed).

Lord Northampton has the strongest possible feeling that such a scheme would operate most disadvantageously in many ways: in rendering the *double* duties to be executed at *one* sitting almost intolerable; in destroying the spirit of the Association by abstracting from it the effect of its *continuous* operations; in preventing the possibility of returning in our orbit to any given place of meeting during the life of man etc; while every one felt that under *existing circumstances* and with the impending prophecy that we are to be extinguished at Birmingham, such a motion on our part would be taken as the first mortal symptom of dissolution.

As far as *I* am concerned I should certainly *like* the meetings to be biennial, and I am also disposed to think (though this is doubtful) that it would have been well to have so regulated them from the beginning. But *now* the project is I think not to be entertained and ought to be postponed until *our cycle is completed*.

Having read His Grace of Hamilton's letter it was resolved that I should write a polite letter to him, stating that after his candid explanation of his inability to sit in a lighted assembly it would to our *deep regret* (not yours) be impossible to avail ourselves of His Grace's invaluable services. This letter is written (recollect His Grace was suggested by the Glasgow folk, not by me).

I then propounded to the Council whether we should take *no* step concerning the chair but leave it to fate and Birmingham; whereon it was unanimously felt that after our experience of the danger of such a proceeding (with the certainty in our minds that we are to visit Glasgow) and after a *well considered* argument of whether it would be possible to offer it to any scientific Scotchman of science

[sic] or the Rector or Principal of the University, we resolved to offer it to the Duke of Montrose whose place is near at hand and who is de facto and for life *Chancellor* of the University of Glasgow.

I happen to know that nothing on earth would induce Brewster to take the chair and also that he has the strongest *objection* to *any man* of science being at our head! In short, this feeling is so strong (in the Association at large) that we never can again venture to propose a mere man of science *except* at the *great* universities. In a mixed great society like that of Glasgow, commercial and agricultural, it is absolutely essential that some public person should be at our head who can influence the masses. The Principal of Glasgow is a worthy good man but of *no power* and only fit to be a Vice-president, in which office he can be placed together with a star of Scotch science like Brewster, while the other Glasgow savans such as Thomson, Hooker, etc, can be placed as presidents of sections, Local Secretaries, etc.

The Rector of the University is generally some *violent party man* of the House of Commons and if we selected him we should be left-handed. But by taking the Chancellor of the University we combine everything which is desired in the Duke of Montrose (who took high honours at Cambridge) and is a steady and sensible man.

If he refuses it is proposed to offer it to Lord Greenock, a good practical geologist and now Commander of the Force in Scotland. You will recollect that this year you appear President as a man of science and ever according to equity we must not have two savans in succession, particularly when the *locals* of Glasgow who came in deputation expressed their horror at such a plan for *their place* frightened as they were by the Babbagean [exhibition]. 'Gude God Sur', said Bailie *Paul*, the Glasgow deputy, to Peacock, 'we trest ye'll no let that Maister Baybidge come amang us'. This shows their feeling about men of science and their liability to squabble.

P S   Do not suppose that the Duke of Hamilton is out and the Duke of Montrose in until I have had an interchange of letters.

Harcourt MSS (Harcourt Papers, *xiv.* 85–9)

The Principal of Glasgow University was Duncan MacFarlan (1771–1857), *DNB.* Henry Paul, manager of the City of Glasgow Bank and a municipal magistrate, had pressed for the 1840 meeting to be held at Glasgow. By cycle Murchison meant the sequence of meetings of the Association until its return to York.

253   *Phillips, n.p.* [*York*], *to Harcourt, Bolton Percy near Tadcaster, 27 April 1839*

After all, when it came within an hour of my starting to London, I found myself so pressed by my own urgent affairs and so involved in the cares of building that I determined to send my package of documents and trust them to Murchison and Yates. The meeting [Council] went off as I learn tonight (Saturday) very well and I am requested by Mr Yates to state to you especially that a proposal which I suggested, viz that you should be requested, as President elect, to deliver an 'address' at Birmingham was adopted, and you are therefore so requested to favour the meeting with an opening discourse for Monday evening the 26th August. Murchison tells me you have already had this mentioned to you and that you were willing to adopt the suggestion. I conceive it may be of great importance.

Mr Murchison will write to you on other points especially the subject of an appointment of two new General Secretaries, for according to his present view, both he and Peacock resign. He has spoken to Sabine who is going to America, and talks of sounding Wheatstone as a successor to Peacock, but says he shall write to you on that matter. I am glad he has so resolved. There is nothing more dangerous than to propose such an office to A or B without a full fore-consideration. A successor to Peacock *should* be eminent as a mathematician, or else as a physicien (as Wheatstone is). Hopkins, Powell, these are the men, as to *species*.

I am detained here till Wednesday at least, but I think I could spend next Thursday and Friday with you at Bolton Percy if you should be at home.

Harcourt MSS

William Hopkins (1793-1866), *DNB*, was a Cambridge private crammer. A physicien was a physicist.

254 *Murchison, n.p., to Harcourt, Bolton Percy near Tadcaster, 4 May 1839*

Your wishes are accomplished inasmuch as after our solicitations to the Duke of Montrose, Chancellor of the University of Glasgow etc, and to Lord Greenock, Commander of the Forces in Scotland, we are again without a 'cheval de bataille' both these personages having declined; the Duke of Montrose in a short note to myself, Lord Greenock in a long and friendly letter pointing out that he is *not* a *competent* President either through his scientific attainments or his influence in society. He, however, is *vastly grateful* for the opinion entertained of him by the Council and expresses his utmost devotedness to the cause of the Association.

Having now the ball at our foot once more, I write to say that I shall call another Council for Thursday of next week (as I leave town for France on the 13th) that we may take some further steps to prevent a dilemma at Birmingham.

We can, it is true, always retire upon old Brisbane, but I should be *sorry* to do so. His astronomical *observations* have been recently corrected to a *great extent*, and if that one merit be taken away from him, I fear we cannot place him in the front rank except as President Royal Society [of] Edinburgh; and really though a good worthy man he is so *thoroughly inefficient* in leading a great body, that I cannot in my conscience approve of him.

The Principal of the University is nil. The *Rector* of next year must be *unknown* until after our Birmingham meeting (and there is always a *political* contest for the post). Lastly I know that Brewster will not hear of it.

So now 'amicus curiae' out with your opinion, these data being offered to you.

Would it be possible to take the Duke of Sutherland? But he has no lands in or near Glasgow and there can be no greater reason for him than the Duke of Buccleuch. Lord Bute has large possessions in the Firth of Clyde. Lord Douglas is a large proprietor and is much liked, but he is old, retired and out of the question. Lord Belhaven is an active country gentleman, a good magistrate in the neighbourhood and popular. If Lord Bute cannot be had or be not approved of, Lord Belhaven (if lords are in the ascendant) is our only resource.

Much however as I prefer the being headed by a personage of local influence to the presidency of any savant I cannot go the length of running out this principle to the extent of taking a small 'milord'.

Hoping that this charming weather agrees with you.

Harcourt MSS (Harcourt Papers, *xiv. 89–91*)

George Granville Leveson-Gower, 2nd Duke of Sutherland (1786-1861), *DNB*, was President of the Highland Society; John Crichton Stuart, 2nd Marquis of Bute (1793-1848); Robert Montgomery Hamilton, 8th Earl Belhaven (1793-1868) of Wishaw House, Lanarkshire. The Lord Douglas was probably Archibald Douglas, Baron Douglas (1773-1844) of Douglas Castle, Lanarkshire.

255 *Murchison, 2 Eccleston Street, Belgrave Square, London, to Harcourt, 6 May 1839*

Thomas Young who forms ministries hath suggested to me that Lord Breadalbane would be a fitting President at Glasgow as he has popular manners and large possessions not very far distant. What say you?

[PS] I have called the Council for Friday at 2. I sail the day after.

Harcourt MSS

Thomas Young (1784-1864) was private secretary to Lord Melbourne; John Campbell, 2nd Marquis of Breadalbane (1796-1862), *D.N.B.*

256 *Murchison, n.p., to Harcourt, 11 May 1839*

I start tomorrow for Paris.

At our Council yesterday (a very full one, Lord Northampton and Sir Charles Lemon both present) it was unanimously resolved to offer the chair at Glasgow to the *Duke of Sutherland*, in virtue of his great possessions and his being President of the Highland Society, and if he refuses (which I have reason to think he will not from what *Loch* says) then to the Breadalbane.

I did not by any means try to lead the Council to this choice.

I know *now* that Lord Breadalbane will take it if offered, but I find by letter from Hooker that he is *not* popular with a certain party in Glasgow.

Dr Thorpe's sermon is unworthy of your notice, it was only a sentence or two of the Dean of York: but the articles in *The Times* and *British Critic* and the *general tendency* of the bigoted party of *clericals* against all science, and geologists in particular, render it imperiously incumbent on you to speak out.

Dean Peacock in his last letter to me (the day before he was promoted to the post of Ely) wrote strongly to me on this head, and now that you have a dignitary of the church as your General Secretary and that you know his sentiments I hope you will not shrink from doing your duty.

The *nursery* at Buckingham Palace is in a strange confusion and what is to become of us with our little 'stamping' Queen is a fearful problem.

If you have anything to write between this and the 15 August when I shall be in town again, write here. My wife will forward on to me.

I shall be at Birmingham some days before the meeting.

[PS] The clergy of Birmingham stand aloof, so says Mr Hodgson who is a capital man.

Harcourt MSS (Harcourt Papers, *xiv. 91-2*)

James Loch (1780-1855), *D.N.B.*, was infamous as the manager of the Sutherland estates; Murchison had been annoyed by a sermon of William Thorpe (1778-1865), minister of Belgrave chapel, Pimlico, London, who supported scriptural geology.

257 *Phillips, York, to Harcourt, Bolton Percy near Tadcaster, 12 June 1839*

I have been continually reproaching myself for what I hope you will not call inattention to your kind note and invitation. The fact is I have been so perplexed with small things that it has been hardly easy to return Mr Taylor's proofs and attend to the troubles of homebuilding. I have been on the point of starting for Bolton [Percy] more than once but among other impediments is the want of the sheets already printed off, which I have instructed Mr Taylor to forward for your use. They must surely come by Monday, and if you are likely to be at home on that day I will be with you early, or on any other day next week that you may appoint. I have found at the Lodge (YPS) a packet some days ago addressed to you, and now enclose it by this parcel to see if you will receive it in due course. It leaves York at 10 a.m. Friday. I also enclose a copy of the Secretaries' address at Newcastle, thinking that you may find somewhat to remark on it; in which case pray write to Peacock (Dr and Dean of Ely!) who is supervising the printing of it, and has looked over much of the other part of the volume.

All the *copy* is now in Taylor's hands, and indeed all but the address is set up.

I think we may breathe before going to Birmingham. The subcommittees of finances, models, etc are described to me by Dr Blakiston, one of the [Local] Secretaries, as working well. £1400 is the sum now raised and if the Chartists will allow us to walk the streets in peace, and the Dean of York does not appear with his thunder against solid rocks and undulating light, we may perhaps far very well. It is however a nervous business to face the General Committee with the questions which you will see in the red circular and others which may arise. I believe we shall have our full strength of conspicuous members, to keep the multitude in awe, and if Peacock and Murchison decline their offices, they will yet help through the meeting.

I have been thinking much upon that part of the request of Mr Murchison to you which invites you to defend geology against theological objections. It is rather too much to ask of you to do this, more particularly as you may not be satisfied with the evidence on which some of the modern antidiluvial views are maintained. What if you take *only two points*, the only ones really of consequence on either side:

1. The pre-Adamitic phases of the earth and organic life;
2. The universality of the diluvial catastrophe.

Of these the former is the very root of all the science of organic remains and will bring consequences of importance down if treated *alone*. It seems *easy*.

P. S.   I find you have carried off the parcel at the Lodge and as I hope you will receive this sooner by post than by train I keep the Secretaries' address till Monday, unless you send for it.

Harcourt MSS

258   *Murchison, Bingen on the Rhine, to Harcourt, Bolton Percy near Tadcaster, 21 July 1839*

When I left London (on the 9th May) I thought that the Council had so prearranged concerning the President elect to succeed you, that no mishap could occur. The post was first to be offered to the Duke of Sutherland and failing of him to the Marquis of Breadalbane. I wrote to the Duke, but happening accidentally to be a day in the same town with him on his way through Germany, I ascertained that in his present state of health and with the load of the Highland Society on his shoulders His Grace could not undertake the office. Thereon I wrote officially to the Marquis of Breadalbane, forwarding my letter through Thomas Young who is well known to his Lordship. Whether the most noble said 'yes' or 'no' is what I know not, for I have been so very migratory that all my letters (even those from Mrs M.) have missed me during the last 3 weeks. I think it is right you should know this state of affairs and perhaps you will communicate with the Dean of Ely thereon . . .

I shall finish my work near Namur, from whence I shall reach London in 2 or 3 days in time to be with you the Friday and Saturday before the meeting at any rate. If you should wish to write to me a letter waiting for me in my home in town may be sufficient, but if any thing should induce you to say a word previously, address me chez M D'Omalius D'Halloy, au Chateau d'Halloy, près de Namur.

Sedgwick will *not* be at Birmingham, having resolved never more to break up a *geological* summer in the middle. The same reason and the 'iam satis' which I am well entitled to say, after never yet missing a meeting, will certainly prevent my being at the next also, if that an autumnal month is fixed upon: at all events I hold steadily to my resolve to retire from the post of General Secretary. I can think of but one to fill the post: Sabine would in my opinion make a very efficient General Secretary as regards the scientific duties and would pull well with Phillips.

Peacock as certainly retires as myself. If you could by any chance succeed in obtaining Whewell you would reanimate the Association, but I fear this is in vain as I did every thing in my power to bring this about at Liverpool, according to your suggestion, and failed.

Peacock is an admirable man and his name and position are at this moment of great use to us.

I only read of the Chartists and Anarchists in the German papers, but I see enough to make me fear that our place of union is not the most secure or agreeable.

I trust that your health is good and that you have found yourself equal to the preparation of such a discourse as will prevent the ship foundering. Forbes told me at Paris that Whewell intended to give us up: but this I cannot believe.

Adieu, my dear friend

[PS] I think I hear your blessing. You see that *M*. has come to the end of his letter without an allusion to *B*. I have I assure you long ago forgotten that affair, but I fear from what I heard before I left town that my former friend is still my bitter foe and is very likely to stir up a new row at Birmingham. If you can, for the love he bears yourself, prevent this you will do great service. If you can make him think of the matter as I do you will do us both a great benefit; for I am persuaded (and so will B. in due time) that the turmoil is vain and injurious only to the good cause in which under different tacks we are both embarked. He who reads the final sentence of my first volume (*Silurian system*) will see where I have placed and how I have estimated Babbage. The quarrel took place long after the sentence was penned and had I been spiteful the cancel of a page would have exonerated me from all *allusion* to him; but having written what I had written, not in flattery but in truth, I of course resolved that the *letter* should remain.

Harcourt MSS (Harcourt Papers, *xiv. 92–6*)

Jean Baptiste Julien D'Omalius D'Halloy (1783–1875), *DSB*, Belgian geologist; Murchison, *Silurian system*, i. 576, referred to Babbage and Herschel as 'two of our first philosophers'.

259   *Phillips, n.p., to Harcourt, 22 July 1839*

By advices from Birmingham I am induced to prefer a few days delay in my journey lest, arriving in the midst of excitement, both the [Local] Committee and myself may have less coolness in our deliberations than the case needs. It appears the *notion* of *postponement* has found entrance in the [Local] Secretary's (Hodgson's) mind: and a cunning gamester might take advantage of this and carry biennial meetings by a ruse of not (very) exceptionable character.

I saw a copy (the original minute of Sabine) of the grants sanctioned by the [General] Committee at Newcastle; in a day or two I fully expect a proof of all this part of the proceedings. In addition to the grants, reports requested: on meteorology of America by Bache; on chemistry as bearing on geology, Johnston; on mollusca, J.E. Gray; on ornithology, Selby; on specific gravity of steam etc, B. Donkin etc; on geographical distribution of mollusca, E. Forbes.

Requests to government: observatory at Cape to be strengthened; to East India Company researches in magnetism for certain geodetical postulates etc; to government for *enlarged* Ordnance maps; to government for mining records establishment.

Committees on meteorology to report, scale of sections for geological purposes to be proposed, fauna of Ireland, certain insects, diseases of lungs in animals.

Committee and section C to be styled henceforth the committee and section of geology and physical geography.

Any section may (if it finds itself too pressed by business) subdivide itself.

These are the principal things: you will see that under many grants many committees are renewed.

I must send the Dean's *pamphlets*, when Mr Sunter has collected them. The only important thing in his *letter to me* was the question 'Tell me the exact state of the globe, 10000 years before the birth of Adam'!

Harcourt MSS

John Edward Gray (1800–75), *DNB*, was assistant keeper of zoology at the British Museum; Bryan Donkin (1768–1855), *DNB*, civil engineer and inventor; Edward Forbes (1815–54), *DNB*, marine biologist. The Dean was William Cockburn, Dean of York. Robert Sunter was a York printer.

260   *Sabine, Woolwich, London, to Harcourt, Bolton Percy near Tadcaster, 7 August 1839*

I hasten to reply to your letter at the first moment of leisure of which I have been able to avail myself since I received it. My time and thoughts are so thoroughly engrossed by the preparation for the departure of the antarctic expedition, and of the officers appointed to conduct the magnetic observatories who are placed under my direction, that I feel very little able to do justice to the subject you propose to me, much as I have it at heart. I am persuaded also that it would be very difficult to rise to the full and fair anticipation of the beneficial consequences, in both a national and a scientific point of view, of the undertakings completed, or in progress, which owe their origin to the meetings of the Association. Beyond all question magnetism has made a most rapid advance, theoretical, practical, and in public interest, in the last 3 or 4 years, during which it has held a prominent place in the attention of the members of the Association; and its prospects, arising from the national undertakings instituted (primarily) at their recommendation, are still more bright. On these perhaps I need not enter, as they are so well described by higher authority in Sir John Herschel's report, which will be presented at Birmingham, and in the two reports made to government by the Royal Society, of which I shall take care that you are immediately furnished with copies. The Royal Society is working zealously, heartily, and most effectively in this cause, but, whilst we delight to recognise and congratulate ourselves on this union of efforts of the two great scientific bodies of the nation, it must not be forgotten that the zeal of the Royal Society, if not awakened by, has at least been greatly *stimulated* by the proceedings of the Association.

We should take an inadequate view of what has really been accomplished were we to limit ourselves to the prospects of the one science alone, or to the incidental gain in other sciences, which cannot fail to result from the magnetic observatories and naval expedition, and is already contemplated in their instructions contained in the second report of the Royal Society. It is from the union so happily established amongst scientific men in this country, in promoting plans of worthy research; from the cordiality and zeal with which they are working together; from the weight which their union, and their disinterested exertions and purposes give them with the government; from the system, so well commenced, of employing officers, of competent intelligence and trained to the exact fulfilment of prescribed instructions, in scientific researches as their public and responsible duty; it is from these admirable consequences, which may be traced legitimately to the Association, that we may anticipate, not merely the advancement of magnetical knowledge which has been now provided for, but the further direction of the same means in promoting researches in every department of science connected with what the French have termed the physique du globe; whereby England will take that lead in all such researches which is her appropriate station, but which she has hitherto cared to take only in the subordinate department of geographical research.

As a direct and immediate *theoretical* consequence of the report on the magnetic intensity published in last year's volume, we may surely instance the very important memoir of M Gauss on the general theory of terrestrial magnetism, the translated sheets of which were sent you last week by Mr Taylor at my request: on page 210 is M Gauss's acknowledgement that the publication of that report stimulated him to undertake and enabled him to complete an investigation, long contemplated but desisted from on account of the deficiency of materials. M Gauss's memoir may assuredly be regarded as the most important contribution yet made to the theory of terrestrial magnetism.

As a *practical* consequence of the report referred to, we may venture to anticipate that more complete knowledge of the phenomena, which Captain Ross's voyage, to which it has given rise, will obtain for us: and to which we may look forward as furnishing the materials and also the test of a yet more perfect theory.

I hope within a week at farthest to send you a copy of the report, designed for the eighth volume of the publications of the Association, on the magnetic survey of the British Islands. The labour which has been bestowed on the observations, and on the calculations, of this report, is very great indeed; and might, when fully apprehended, appear to some disproportionate to the objects. But much more has been accomplished than the mere determination of the phenomena in the British Isles though that in itself might well be deemed a worthy national work, commenced at the instance of the Association and performed by the private exertions of some of its members; and it cannot be doubted that it will become a valuable document to posterity, when the changes which shall have taken place in the phenomena will give a high value to so careful a determination corresponding to the present epoch. The instruments and the modes of observation have received great improvement in the progress of the survey which cannot fail to be of great service in the magnetical researches which are now receiving so wide an extension. The methods of combining such observations to produce general results have also been deeply considered: and as this is the first work of the kind in any country, the endeavour has been made to render it an example worthy of imitation and in some degree a guide to future experimenters.

In this hasty sketch of what has been accomplished for terrestrial magnetism through the instrumentality of the Association, I must not omit to notice the very important service which has been rendered by the £100 granted to Mr Richard Taylor in aid of his *Scientific Memoirs*. The 5th and 6th parts have, in consequence of that grant, contained no less than *nine* distinct papers by Gauss and Weber on magnetical subjects, relating chiefly to those simultaneous affections of the needle which have attracted so much attention of late, and are to form one branch of the investigations undertaken by this country. Besides the general interest and value of these papers, it is obviously of the first importance that those who are to conduct such researches should be in possession of all that has been done and is doing in other countries in regard to them.

I must apologize for having written rather a long letter, being too much pressed by other engagements to write as concisely as I could wish: but I would not venture to make any longer delay in replying to you.

Harcourt MSS

Wilhelm Eduard Weber (1801–91), *DSB*, was professor of physics at Göttingen University 1831–7. In spring 1839 in response to pressure from the Association and the Royal Society of London the government had agreed to establish colonial magnetic observatories and to support an antarctic magnetic expedition. For Herschel's report, see *1839 Report*, 31–42. Sabine's 'Report on the variations of the magnetic intensity observed at different points of the earth's surface', *1837 Report*, 1–85, was used by Gauss in his *Allgemeine theorie des erdmagnetismus* (Göttingen, 1839), translated into English in *Scientific memoirs. Selected from the transactions of foreign academies of science and learned societies, and from foreign journals*, R. Taylor (ed), (London, 1841), ii. 184–251. For Sabine's magnetic survey of Britain, see Sabine et al, 'A memoir on the magnetic isoclinal and isodynamic lines in the British Isles', *1838 Report*, 49–196.

261   *Phillips, Philosophical Institution, Birmingham, to Harcourt, Bolton Percy near Tadcaster, 11 August 1839*

Dear Harcourt,

You must expect very unsatisfactory letters from me, because we are now in the transition state and really impeded in respect of information by the undefined feeling of uneasiness which seems to prevail among the resident and distant members. I can, however, state that in respect of *communications* there appears likely to be a fair supply for the different sections, and some of the offerings appear to me really very good. The number of *local members* enrolled is *very small*, and as our funds are really measured by the addition of new members into each meeting, you must not be overgenerous in grants of money. A curious feature of these *elections* is the fact that not one *life member* (£5) is amongst them. This speaks volumes for the imposition of a small admission fee, and may perhaps prompt other measures tending to render our assemblies rather more exclusive.

As to strangers expected, you know as much or more than we do; Lyell, Lubbock, Horner, Hopkins, are certain to be here and, excepting from Ireland and Scotland, there seems no likelihood of any remarkable deficiency in our ranks except Herschel and Sedgwick (I suppose Whewell will be here). Have you tried Herschel? Can anything be done to stay Babbage in his suicidal course? I hardly know whether, when I see him, I may venture to expostulate or intreat, but he would perhaps attend to you. If not, let the whole affair be discussed and ended, for it is a gangrene we must expel.

As to the state of the town I have only two complaints: twice have I been disturbed from sleep by real or false alarms. Last night

(Saturday 2 a.m.) loud shouts, watchmen's rattles, violent beating of doors, etc awakened me. Then came the tramp and rolling of horse, men, and fire engines, in excessive hurry toward West Bromwich to *put out a fire*. All the house and street, and other houses and streets were alarmed, but I have not yet this morning any further information. If before sending this I can learn whether it was a wilful or accidental fire, you shall know; and I have repeatedly charged the local men to take the first opportunity of acquainting Mr Yates with any event, which in their opinion may augment the embarrassment of the inhabitants and injure the meeting.

I am staying at the hotel you thought of visiting. It is good. Lord Northampton, C.W. Hamilton, and others are coming to it and for anything that yet appears I shall not quit it. The *reason* for my refusing private hospitality (freely offered) is my fear to catch the polemical spirit of the place, and darken my sight with other men's spectacles. Linnaeus describes an unlucky author thus 'Ipse cereus, aliorum occulis videt, si quid videt'.

Harcourt MSS

Charles William Hamilton (d. 1880), Dublin geologist; Linnaeus's tag means that he who is easily moulded sees with the eyes of others if he sees at all.

262 *Phillips, New Royal Hotel, Birmingham, to Ann Phillips, Penley Grove Street, York, 11 August 1839*

As you will be looking with interest on all the smaller events which may influence the success and comfort of our meeting, I will add a few notes to the letter which I suppose you received from me on Thursday. It was written and sent home on Wednesday. Perhaps when I go to the [Birmingham] Institution I may find a return which I greatly desire, a letter from home. As far as yet appears the tranquillity of the town is not likely to be interrupted during our week of wisdom; yet it is but a feverish quiet we can be said to enjoy, amidst men in green and men in red, police staves and cavalry sabres. Two nights ago [there] was a little fire some mile or two off: last night (Saturday) at 2 o clock, a great noise arose: shouts of watchmen, springing of rattles, violent running, alarming knocks at the gates of the Hotel yard. After listening in forced composure some time the uproar became insupportable; windows were flung up, the guests of the Inn tramped along the passages, and even I enquired what was the matter. Sir, it is *a fire* at West Bromwich, and the engine house is near, and they want horses etc. This, after half an hour of wild shouting and galloping, passed away, and I turned to a restless sleep. Mr Russell called this morning, and although he

lives in another street the same alarm of watchmen's rattles woke
him and his vicinity. I have not yet heard what was the cause or
the extent of the fire, but if produced by Chartists, it may deserve
attention.

Among the strangers expected are Agassiz, Schönbein of *Basle;*
among the English, Lubbock, Hopkins, Lyell, Buckland, etc (Herschel does not come) *Babbage!!* (to make a speech) etc. About 300
local members are elected and probably not *one life member among
them all.* About £1700 or more raised, and probably this may be
enough. I am more and more convinced that the most successful
meetings of the Association will be in future held in quieter towns
like our own York, where if prejudices may abound, at least peace,
good order, leisure, favour the expansion of a philosophical spirit. I
am still at the Inn, and it suits the tone of my mind better than to
be at any friend's house, though it is a costly piece of self denial,
and hard to deny one's friends. There is no lack of communications
announced. Unless I hear somewhat more about the fire, you may
conclude it was of no consequence. Tell me somewhat of our own
quiet home; give me a little sunshine amidst the darkness of this
political atmosphere. If you see Mr Taylor, perhaps he may like to
know the state of the place, and if he thinks fit to command me I
will try to get him a lodgment, at about 3 guineas the week. There
is hardly any thing lower that is comfortable.

Phillips Papers, A31

Christian Friedrich Schönbein (1799-1868), *DSB*, professor of chemistry and physics
at Basel university. The Russell was James Russell; the Taylor, William Taylor of
York.

263 *Babbage, 1 Dorset Street, Manchester Square, London, to Harcourt, 26
August 1839*

I have this instant seen by *The Times* that my name appears as one
of the Vice-presidents of the mechanical section of the British
Association. I can only explain this, if it has been recommended by
the Council, by supposing that it is meant as an additional insult,
or else that they wish the public to infer that I do not disapprove of
those principles of intrigue to which they have lent their own support. If my name has been proposed by any individual I have not
authorised him. In either case I request you will withdraw my name
as publicly as it has been proposed and direct the Secretaries to take
care that it may not appear in any of the printed proceedings. I
write this in the confidence that you will not refuse me this justice

and that it would be less disagreeable to you than that I should myself do it in a more formal and public manner.

Harcourt MSS

264 *Harcourt, Revd J.P. Lee's Free School, Birmingham, to Robert Brown, British Museum, London, 8 September 1838*

I sent you a copy of the number of the *Athenaeum* which contains a correct account (with the omission of some dates and references) of my late address to the British Association. If you have taken the trouble of reading it you will perceive that I have taken up in some detail the question between Watt and Cavendish, in my opinion very unfairly as well as incorrectly treated by Arago and Brougham, though of the latter's 'historic notice', appended to the éloge, I have made no direct mention as being less disparaging and somewhat less wide of the truth.

Since I came here I have been told that you have taken some interest in this matter and examined the Mss at the Royal Society. In that case, as my remarks are but too likely to entail some further controversy, I should be obliged by your informing me whether the statements which Brougham has made respecting dates and insertions by Blagden are correct.

We have had a good meeting here notwithstanding the disadvantages under which we met; we created less local expense than at some former meetings and had no disputes.

BL, Add. MSS 33227, ff. 87–8

In his Presidential address at the 1839 meeting of the Association Harcourt had argued that Henry Cavendish (1731-1810), *DNB*, and not James Watt (1736-1819), *DNB*, discovered the composition of water. Sir Charles Blagden (1748-1820), *DNB*, as a Secretary of the Royal Society, was involved in the publication of the papers on this subject by Cavendish and Watt. For Harcourt's speech, see *Athenaeum*, 1839, 651-4; for Arago's defence of Watt, 'Éloge historique de James Watt', published in *Annuaire pour l'an 1839, présenté au Roi, par Le Bureau des Longitudes* (Paris, 1838), 255-410; for Brougham's defence of Watt, his 'Historical note on the discovery of the composition of water' in Arago, *Historical eloge of James Watt translated ... by James Patrick Muirhead* (London, 1839), 157-73.

265 *Murchison, Nursted House, Petersfield, to Harcourt, Bolton Percy near Tadcaster, 24 October 1839*

I arrived 2 days ago from Antwerp (in company with Sedgwick), who has gone to his duties at Cambridge, whilst I have come here to enjoy a little pheasant shooting after my summer toils and before the season of the *fog-baths* of the metropolis. I am anxious to know how you are and whether the good progress you were making when I left you has been followed by a complete restoration of your health?

I found on my table here (among a bundle of letters in my wife's custody) a letter from Peacock of *September 23*, in which 'inter alia' he alludes to some new *dirt* in *The Times* since I started, and after speaking of the productions in question as 'singularly ill written, foolish and gross' adds 'you will of course take no notice of them'.

If these attacks contain nothing personal I shall not be disposed to take up my pen to enter into newspaper strife with so unassailable an antagonist as the leader of *The Times*, but if my character is impeached then for better or worse at him I must. Not having seen the articles in question and not being likely in this district to get a sight of the ponderous file of the mendacious thunderer, I should like to know from you in the mean time what course you would recommend.

Sedgwick is about to write to the editor to correct the lie about himself, and will take that opportunity of reading to that irresponsible *gentleman* a lecture on the real uses and merits of the Association. If he does this advisedly and cautiously, he will do it so much better than myself that I would much prefer to leave the general issue entirely in his hands; reserving to myself simply the privilege of setting the public right on any point on which falsehoods or false insinuations have been propagated concerning *myself*. It is on this point that I crave your advice. The Dean says that he believes the articles are '*South's*' or that the star-light knight furnished the materials for them. If it were possible to bring them home to him, the shortest and I think the best way would be to send a sabreur to him with a laconic message, and if I mistake not we should there after see no more of this bullying blackguardism.

Mrs Murchison unites with me in kind remembrances to Mrs Harcourt and in the hope of hearing good accounts of you.

[PS] The Boulogne meeting was very successful and amiable in its peculiar line. I gave them a grand Silurian lecture in the field, showed that no productive coal works could be made in rocks of that age and stopped speculations which have already ruined many a good citizen.

I induced my agreeable and clever friend D. Verneuil (an admirable naturalist) to accompany me thence to the Rhine where we joined Sedgwick and have been since at work up to the middle of last week.

Harcourt MSS

Philippe Édouard Poulletier de Verneuil (1805-73), *DSB;* an editorial in *The Times*,

29 Aug 1839, claimed that Herschel, Babbage, and Sedgwick had withdrawn from the Association; a further editorial, *Times*, 13 Sept 1839, abused the 'learned gastronomicals' of the Association. In Sept 1839 Murchison had attended the réunion extraordinaire of the Geological Society of France at Boulogne.

266 *Murchison, 16 Belgrave Square, London, to Harcourt, Bolton Percy near Tadcaster, 16 November 1839*

I wrote to you *three weeks* ago from the country and presume that you have never got my letter. Its first object was to enquire after your health, its second to know your opinion on certain thundering peals of *The Times*! I have now no wish to induce you to reply to me on the *latter point*, for I have since been unanimously told by *all my friends* that these low attacks merited no reply particularly after so long an interval. So there I leave them and the *gentlemen* who incited such anonymous slander, while they deal out innuendoes, assist intrigue and so forth which seem to have no existence except in their own dirty machinations.

I have this day directed Yates to call a Council for the 1st December the day following the anniversary of the Royal Society. I should not perhaps have taken this step this early, had I not been urged to do so by sundry councillors. The first point they wish to get settled (and no time can be lost on this) is to curtail the price of the *volume*. This they wish to do by abrogating the printing of the proceedings of the sections and by omitting any document which another journal will print. If this is conceded it will at all events be necessary to *enumerate* simply the memoirs read, with a reference to the periodical each is to be found in. They also talk of omitting any report (such as Mr Russell's say they) which would be better published in the transactions of a philosophical society. Now on this point I see not how we can interfere with the recommendations of the committee thereto appointed, except by occasionally taking exception to some one report which by its method of execution does not come within the scope of our institutions. You know as well as me that these reports are never read and never referred to any one for correction: they come directly to the Secretaries from the author who has been called upon by the Committee of Recommendations to enact such a part. A special case might occur in which the Secretaries might appeal to the Council during the recess, but what other remedy can we have?

The other subjects of reform which are mentioned are mainly those of pre-arrangement of the 'officers of sections' by the Council, i.e. to make enquiries beforehand of individuals as to whether A or B intend to be present. To this there can be no objection though until the last meeting (Chartism having on this occasion thinned our ranks) the want of such a bill of the play was never felt, although I have yet to learn how the *known* absence of some good men who might have been there would have added strength to our lists. The grumbling it appears is from the mechanical section because Mr Carpmael was a secretary.

You have the subject so completely in your head and your judgment is so good in all such matters that I advertise you beforehand of what we are going to do that I may have your rejoinder before the 1st December. I also write to Phillips who will send me the requisite documents and desiderata. Sabine is in town after his return from Berlin where he and Lloyd had a delightful reception from Humboldt: he waits for our meeting on the 1st December, and having talked over the case with him, he is very anxious to know your opinion.

Mrs Murchison begs to offer her kind remembrances to Mrs Harcourt.

In hopes to hear a good account of *yourself*

Harcourt MSS

William Carpmael (1804-67) was a London patent agent. By 1839 it was clear that the voluminous data of John Scott Russell on the shapes of ships would be very expensive if published in full in the *Reports*.

267 *Murchison, 16 Belgrave Square, London, to Harcourt, 6 December 1839*

We held our Council on Monday last (Lord Northampton in the chair) when the requisition of the malcontents being read, Lyell as their organ explained (as well as he could) their views, which are it appears those of *Forbes* who induced the rest of the party to subscribe what to them seemed just and reasonable, namely, reduce the cost of our volumes, seeing that the last had stood us in upwards of £800.

Thereon I read 1st all the prominent part of your letter; 2ndly, a long letter from Phillips; 3rdly, one from the Dean of Ely; and 4thly, gave my own opinion as concurrent with the opinions of the other executive officers and Major Sabine backed it up. By documents obtained from Taylor I showed that the cost of the 'proceedings' in the last part accounted only to £80 and that if one sheet alone were printed enumerating *mere titles* the charge would be £8 to 10, so that in limine I made it appear that all the hubble bubble related to £70. Every one approved of your 2 suggestions of diminishing to *some* extent the number of volumes printed and of not styling the volumes by their respective *numbers*. After a lengthy talk it was agreed that the 'manière de faire' should remain in force as of old, the proceedings intact and the reports also, at the occasional discretion of the General Secretary quoad illustration etc; and further that the number of volumes printed henceforth be 750 and that the volumes be without other number than that of the year.

Sabine introduced after an able preamble an admirable reform, which being approved of *unanimously*, led in fact any dissident to agree to the above as a full measure of practical reform, viz that the volume be in future ready for distribution in *4 months* from the end of the meeting, and that every report not furnished in time to enable the Secretary so to issue the volume, do stand over to the ensuing year. Sabine justly showed that the present system was the great drawback to the *sale* of our volumes, while by their issue at the moment of our meeting no author had justice done to him nor could any one form a just conception of what ought to be proposed in the Committee of Recommendations.

Yates will of course communicate all these important reforms to Phillips. The rule concerning the speedy issue of the volume is of course not to be retrospective, *but* it is *hoped* that the present volume may be out a month or two before we meet at Glasgow, particularly as our next assembly is at so late a period.

The subject of fishing out good sectional officers beforehand was as I supposed little adverted to: a hint on this point is quite enough. In truth people are too apt to judge from a case like Birmingham which thanks to the Chartists was necessarily a thin meeting.

On the whole every thing went off very well and I hope you will approve.

I see the Glasgow folks are already making great efforts to do us honour and I anticipate a capital meeting there. Double letters costing now no more than single I send you this scrawl.

Ready at all times to attend to your suggestions, I shall take good care that no measure of Council is passed without your full concurrence.

We are sitting under the most dense fogs.

Adieu.

[PS] I will write to Phillips soon. I see no occasion for other Councils for a long time.

Harcourt MSS

268 *Murchison, Up Park, Petersfield, to Harcourt, York, 28 December 1839*

On consulting with Sabine as to what ought to be done in reference to the opening speech of our Glasgow parliament, he quite agreed with me that it would be impossible to leave the matter to the Local Secretaries, no one of whom knows anything of us as we know nothing of them. Hereon it was my colleague's opinion that we should apply to *Herschel* and ask his permission to allow us to request the *Council* to beg of him to prepare one of his eloquent effusions. I wrote to H. and have his answer today and stating that he is so shamefully beyond time in his own concerns that, with all his good wishes and doings for us, he feels it to be a moral impossibility to comply with our request. I confess I expected such a reply, but Sabine seemed to think that the sort of composition we were exacting would not cost Herschel a week, or that at all events he could do it more rapidly than any other man alive. As to rapidity and facility I will back Whewell against the baronet. He is the best bottomed hack-hunter that we have ever had in our stable, for all work comes alike to him; no day is too busy and no fence too high. What do you say to my making the same proposition to W. which has been made to H.? I happen to know that his 3rd and *last* volume of the *History of Inductive Philosophy* will be out in March, and from that time till we meet he could prepare half a dozen such fire-works as we require to light up the banks of the Clyde. It does, however, occur to me that if the Council travels out of the record by requesting any one individual (however eminent) to undertake the task, that individual not being pro hoc vice a Secretary or President or Vice-president that some observations might be made thereon as to *inefficiency* of *officers*, etc, etc. For my part I fairly avow that I feel myself incompetent to do justice to the various subjects of the theme. I was in hopes that Sabine would take the oar and do that which I cannot and that out of our duet some tolerably effective harmony might proceed, but he is disposed to think that the General Secretaries should reserve their fire for once in a decade. What think you of proposing the task to Brewster? He is *Vice-president elect* and there would be a peculiar fitness it seems to me in making him our *real* scientific king on this occasion. My voice could give full utterance to Sir David's speech and thus the Scotch would be gratified (Forbes perhaps excepted) and Sir David's 'amour propre' consulted. Forbes had his fling on a former occasion.

What I now write is strictly 'entre nous' and therefore say what you will, for I shall write or speak to no one about it till I hear from you.

And now a word or two about your own 'fair fame' of which I believe you know that I am a good supporter. The bold shot which you fired at Birmingham in re 'Cavendish versus Watt' was, as you might indeed have anticipated, sure to bring down Arago's thunder and lightning on your head. In the meantime Watt himself is much *up*, and with all his friends, or rather they for him, have prepared a refutation of what they consider your misprision of the great steamer. I left town ten days ago, but before I started I happened to hear several little tales. 1st I learnt from Paris that Arago was preparing a smasher, 2nd that Brougham was to be *at work*. From this unpleasant news I was relieved by a long confab with that most excellent and most right-judging man, Robert Brown, who told me that Arago was *quite in the wrong* and that your view was *essentially correct*, only that by one error you had laid yourself open to the French thunderer and he would be *sure* to hit you on it. Moreover I found that Brown was in possession of *many facts* and I was half disposed to think he would print provided the opposite party took a certain course.

Just before I left town new actors appeared on the stage. Watt is you must know a great friend of Chantrey, and I found from the latter that all the Wattites (Babbage included) had taken up your discourse as a downright *attack* upon their hero. Hereon I represented to the sculptor that he and they were all grossly in error; that I was persuaded that such an idea as that of *depreciating* Watt never entered your head, but that you had *chivalrously* started forward to rescue the memory of Cavendish from what you considered to be the unjust fiat of the French philosopher. Chantrey then said he would procure a book out of which he read me a passage or two attempting to refute your position and reflecting on you for having chosen Birmingham for your attack on Watt. Whether this [was] merely the work of one 'Muirhead' which I hear of or not I cannot tell, but Chantrey promised to get me a copy which I hope to find when I return; and if no other friend has put you up to all this *Christmas-boxing*, I will forward it to you if you desire and will also obtain you any information you wish from Brown. Chantrey's house was to be the scene of a Watt conclave on the day of which I speak and Babbage was one of the 'priés'. What transpired at the dinner of course I know not. You are perhaps aware that Babbage and Arago run in the same curricle in science, politics and their views of human nature.

Direct to me 16 Belgrave Square where I shall be on Saturday next. Mrs Murchison unites with me in wishing Mrs Harcourt and yourself many happy new years and prosperity to your family.

Harcourt MSS (Harcourt Papers, *xiv. 100-4*)

James Patrick Muirhead (1813-98), *DNB*, included adverse comments on Harcourt's 1839 address in Arago, *Historical eloge of James Watt*, translated by Muirhead, 114-6. Arago's smasher was delivered on 20 Jan 1840 to the French Academy of Sciences: *Comptes rendus hebdomadaires des séances de l'Académie des Sciences*, 1840, x. 109-11. For Brougham's attack on Harcourt's vindication of Cavendish, see Brougham, *Lives of men of letters and science who flourished in the time of George III* (London, 1845), 400–1. Murchison and Sabine combined to give the key-note address at the 1840 meeting of the Association.

269 *Murchison, 16 Belgrave Square, London, to Harcourt, 22 March 1840*

I see that your last is dated 18 November. Since then we have 'progressed' as the Yankees say in preparing for our next British [Association] meeting.

It was so much the wish of sundry members of the Council and others that as far as possible the sections should be officered, before we went to our rendezvous, that in conjunction with Sabine I bestirred myself in finding out who was likely to be present and also to feel the pulse of the Glasgow Secretaries. Among various good men about whom there could be no doubt, they suggested the name of an eccentric star for whom you have no great devotion, though he calls you his 'excellent friend': I mean *Brougham*. Unknown to us the Glasgow functionaries had elected him by acclamation of all parties as an 'honorary member' of the meeting and as I inferred from their letters had had some communication with him. They further *suggested* that it would add very much to the success of the Glasgow Meeting if *B.* could be prevailed upon to attend by offering him the chair of section *A*. At first I remonstrated with the locals pointing out that there was one thing above all to be avoided and which *we* of the Association would never endure, a display on the part of His Lordship at the expense of the existing President whose opinions and character we deeply respected. The urgent replies of the locals made me fear that we were likely to give umbrage to the place of rendezvous and also to secure a bitter enemy in His Lordship if we did not take the matter into our own hands; and therefore after consulting with Sabine and 3 or 4 in whom I could most confide I opened a correspondence with My Lord, and the first shot *he* fired in reply at once settled the matter and demonstrated the impossibility of having him as one of ourselves. I therefore called a Council and proposed that the 5 following persons should be put in nomination as presidents of the principal sections (to be proposed to the General Committee) and I did this in order to prevent any further doubts and *aspirations*. Forbes mathematics; Thomson, chemistry; Hooker, botany; Lyell, geology; and Robison, mechanical science. These persons have been written to by desire of Council and have accepted, except for Hooker whose family distresses will probably compel him to leave Glasgow. The list so far is Scottish, and this gratifies them, and the Secretaries respond that they are quite gratified with the arrangements and completely understand the propriety of doing without their dear Lord, with whom I have contrived to keep on the best terms while we put Forbes into his intended place.

We shall take 1 local secretary out of 3 for each section. The Vice-presidents [of sections] must as far as possible be English or Irish. Lord Sandon may be president of the statists if he goes, and we may take Abercrombie again if we can get him for the doctors.

I hope you will be able to be present to give up the chair to Lord Breadalbane.

The meeting will, I have no doubt, be very brilliant for the locals have made great exertions and the only difficulty we shall have is to induce them to be quiet enough.

At the next meeting I shall most certainly give up my post and will do my best to find a better man than myself.

Manchester will evidently be the next place of meeting and Lord Northampton ought I think to be the President.

Phillips attended our last meeting when we passed some good rules about our volumes and a better method of distributing them and of relieving our bookshelves.

Lardner's elopement with Mrs Heaviside will abstract (it is probable) a report from our meagre volume of the year, so the General Secretaries will have little enough to say.

I am going to Paris next week but shall be back at or after Easter.

Should you feel disposed to insert anything in the anniversary discourse I should be too happy to avail myself of one or two of your good paragraphs. It is possible that being at Glasgow we may have to say a word of Watt, and if we do so I should like to take that public opportunity of making his admirers feel that in your vindication of the claims of Cavendish to one great discovery, the President of the British Association never thought of disparaging the great mechanist, still less of insulting his memory, *because* the present fat Mr Watt did not open his house or Soho to us at Birmingham!!! This is the *motive* assigned by certain worthy persons for your late discourse in re Watt and Cavendish.

I am going to preside at a dinner today given by the geographers to Guizot and have only time to beg you to offer the kind regards of Mrs Murchison to Mrs Harcourt.

Harcourt MSS (Harcourt Papers, *xiv. 108–11*)

Lord Sandon (1798-1882), MP for Liverpool 1831-47, was a leading member of the Association's statistical section. In March 1840 Lardner eloped with Mary Heaviside, wife of Captain Richard Heaviside of the First Dragoon Guards. Soho, in north Birmingham, was the location of Boulton and Watt's factory.

270   *Harcourt, Scarborough, to Brougham, 13 September 1840*

My dear Lord,

In begging your acceptance of a copy of my address to the British Association and the postscript which I have added to it, I think I ought to tell you of a passage in the address, as delivered at Birmingham, which I have *not printed*, containing an allusion to your 'historical notice' in re Watt versus Cavendish.

The words I believe were these: 'a notice added to it (Arago's attack on Cavendish) by one of his own countrymen, less disparaging indeed to his honesty, but scarcely more just to his fame'.

I considered Arago's attack as a libel on the character of Cavendish addressed to a public body, the national representatives of science in France, and published in their memoirs and under their authority. Such a publication could not in any way have met with so proper and effectual correction as from the chair of the British Association.

Your 'historic doubts' were of a different character, and finding that my allusion to them had not been generally understood I determined on second thoughts to confine my animadversions to my official antagonist. I have touched, however, slightly, you will observe, on one of your remarks in my postscript. If Watt had any merit in this matter it must be found in his *thermal* views of the discovery which Cavendish had made: I prefer Cavendish's reserve respecting matter of heat, and think his notions on this subject more philosophical: but this may possibly admit of dispute which (when you have read my postscript) I conceive you will admit the chemical discovery does not.

In any case nothing can be more unjust than to charge me, as some have foolishly done, with having regard to any other object in dealing with this question than public justice.

I doubt whether Arago has been more just to Watt than to Cavendish: in the matter of steam, he has praised him as an ingenious mechanic rather than as a sagacious philosopher and appears to me to have reserved all the higher praise for his friend Papin, *as before*, scarcely intimating that Watt had any thing to do with the discovery of the laws of heat, or their application.

Brougham Papers, 16002

Denis Papin (1647-1712), *DSB*, worked on steam engines; for Harcourt's address and the long postscript on the Watt-Cavendish controversy, see *1839 Report*, 3-22 and 22-68 respectively.

271   *Whewell, College, Glasgow, to Murchison, 18 September 1840*

The suggestion which you mentioned to me to-day was so utterly different from any thing which had ever entered my mind, that I could not at the moment put my thoughts in order to reply to it with any statement of grounds, and could only express my extreme repugnance to the proposal, my conviction that it would not contribute to the prosperity of the Association, and my general persuasion of its not being advisable. I must try, before I leave Glasgow, to make you perceive that these impressions are very strong in my mind, and I hope that they are well-founded.

My only pretensions to such a position [the Presidency] are what I may have done as a cultivator of science, and my constant attendance upon the business of the Association. With regard to the former point, I venture to say that I can be an impartial and exact judge in my own case, and I know perfectly well that there is nothing of such a stamp, in what I have attempted, as entitles me to be considered an eminent man of science. In the study of the tides, which is my only pretension, I have voluntarily given up all the profounder parts of the subject, and confined myself to collecting laws of phenomena in such a manner as it could be done with little of my own labour. My *History* and *Philosophy* of science are disqualifications, not qualifications, for my being put at the head of the scientific world; for I cannot expect, I know it is impossible, that men of science should assent to my views *at present*: and those who have laboured hard in special fields will naturally feel indignant at having a person put at their head, recommended only by what they think vague and false general views. I believe this would do much to disgust and repel men of science from the meeting.

You spoke of my being a Lancashire man, as a recommendation to my being President, if the [next] meeting were held in that county. It will not so operate. I have lived little in the county, have no connections in it except my own family, and few acquaintances. It could only produce failure and ridicule to have me put in a place which should be occupied by some person of great local position, influence and popularity, and that in a county so populous, rich, and scientific. It would be considered as evidence that you could not find any person coming nearer to the usual conditions, and likely to give the business its usual attractions.

You spoke of my being able to preside over, and, if necessary, to control a large body. Nobody can do that if he be not persuaded that he has the stronger part of the body with him. I should not have that persuasion, for on many points, almost all questionable points, I should be on the losing side (for instance the encroachments of the statistical section, the scenes of display, etc). I should be more likely to irritate than to calm the assemblage, when such points came into controversy.

My own repugnance would not decide me, if I thought I had a

duty to the Association, but the repugnance is very strong. I have in some measure wound up my account with physical science, and turned my thoughts into another field, in which I may, perhaps, do something, but in which, at any rate, I shall probably employ myself seriously for the rest of my life. I have been on this very account gradually unwinding myself from the engagements of the material sciences, and cannot think, without terror and extreme annoyance, of being again plunged in the entanglements I have left. It is not that I do not still love science; but in it I have done all I can; I must go now to 'fresh fields and pastures new'.

But I dare say I am taking more pains than is necessary to convince you that I should never do for your President. I am *not* a man of science, *not* a man of business, *not* a man of popular manners, *not* a man of weight in Lancashire. What other disqualifications can you require?

You will not suspect me of undervaluing your good opinion, and that of the other friends who have overlooked all these disqualifications. I am glad I have friends who can overlook them, for they are obvious enough.

Todhunter, Whewell, *ii. 286–8*

Whewell had recently published his *History of the inductive sciences, from the earliest to the present time* (London, 1837) and *The philosophy of the inductive sciences founded upon their history* (London, 1840).

272 *Sabine, Glasgow, to Murchison, 21 September 1840*

I have read Mr Whewell's letter. I do not think that his reasons could cause a moment's hesitation in any mind but his own, as to the propriety of naming him as our next President. One, and one only, has weight; and if it stood alone, would scarcely I think have been surmountable in his absence. It is where he speaks of [his] own *personal repugnance;* but when he subsequently adds 'that his repugnance would not decide him, if he thought he had a duty to perform to the Association', the objection is neutralised, and falls wholly to the ground.

Mr Whewell says he is not sufficiently eminent as a man of science to be placed '*at the head of the scientific world*'. That is not the position in which he would be placed by being chosen President of the British Association; and there are many qualities required in a suitable president, which are not included in mere scientific eminence. Mr Whewell has decidedly a sufficient scientific eminence to make the propriety of the choice unquestionable on that head.

He says he is not a popular person; popularity has various senses, but he assuredly has that popularity which rests on *universal respect*. He is universally respected, both for the qualities of his character, and for his attainments; and whatever may be the case elsewhere (of which I know nothing for I can boast of no other acquaintance with him than through the Association) I have never heard any one belonging to the Association speak of him in any other terms than those of great respect and *regard*, arising from his sincere attachment and unwearied labours in her cause. I entertain no doubt whatever that his appointment at this time would be the most *popular* one that could be made, and that he would find the conduct of the next meeting an easy task from the strong support that he would receive.

I think therefore that he has not yet 'done all he can' or all that he will hereafter rejoice to have done for science. I think we should elect him, and when he is informed that it is the unanimous wish of the meeting here that 'before he winds up his accounts' he should *preside* over the Association of which he has so long been an unwearied and hard working member, and in which his memory will so long be cherished, I think he *will not refuse us*.

Whewell Papers, a.212[4]

273 *Murchison, Glasgow, to Whewell, 22 September 1840*

In pursuance of my duty I consulted every one of weight and influence connected with the Association respecting our next President and they were *all* of opinion that it was desirable to carry out the idea suggested in the discussion of the General Secretaries *viz.* to place one of ourselves at the head of our band for the next meeting, and they all agreed that this person ought to be yourself. I then proposed the matter in the Council who were unanimous every member thereof adducing some valid reason why you ought to be the man and pointing out how much you could serve us under our existing circumstances.

In the mean time I may tell you that Plymouth was fixed upon to be proposed as the place of meeting on account of our having ascertained from the Manchesterians that 1842 would be more convenient to them than 1841.

We then went before the General Committee with our list and I can assure you that if you had heard the cheer which was given out when your name was proposed you would at once have said, 'I see that however I may estimate myself the feeling is so strong that I can be of service to the British Association that I must accept the office'.

Your refusal under present services would I solemnly assure you place us in *great difficulties*, so that knowing as I do your magnanimity I am confident you will for *one year* hold fast to us and lead us on. Lord Northampton and Sabine read your letter but its perusal only the more convinced them that you must permit *us* to form our estimate of your scientific reputation and of your fitness to be placed in the chair of the Association.

[PS] Write to me by return of post at T Edington's, Phoenix House, Glasgow. The officers of the Plymouth meeting are: President, Revd W Whewell; Vice-presidents, the Earl of Morley, Lord Eliot, Sir C Lemon, Sir Thomas D Acland; [Local] Secretaries, W. Snow Harris, Col. Hamilton Smith, R. Were Fox.

Whewell Papers, a.209[108]

Thomas Edington (d. 1841), a mineralogist and ironfounder who owned the Phoenix Iron Works, Glasgow; Edmund Parker, 2nd Earl Morley (1810–64), *DNB*; Edward Granville Eliot, Lord Eliot (1798–1877), *DNB*; Sir Thomas Dyke Acland (1787–1871) was M P for North Devon; Charles Hamilton Smith (1776–1859), *DNB*, was President of the Natural History Society of Devon and Cornwall.

274 *Lyell, Glasgow, to Whewell, 23 September 1840*

Murchison showed me your letter and we agreed with great regret that it was so strong that it would be impossible to name you next day in spite of it. When we afterward talked it over with Lord Northampton he seemed also to think so, though he declared against *his* being chosen as it is the turn of a scientific man. A few hours after this, early next morning the arrangement as it now stands was proposed to a Council all of whom were with a few exceptions ignorant of what was to be done. Nothing of course was said of your letter by the General Secretary and it was received so completely by all present in a somewhat full Council as the most natural thing imaginable that I said nothing. Its announcement was warmly received by a full General Committee a few hours afterwards and I never knew the meeting more unanimous about anything than all the arrangements both as to officers and the place to go to. If I had ever doubted before, I should have felt satisfied after being present at the election, that every scruple on the ground of your not feeling you should carry with you the general conviction of the Association that *you* were the man for them, their interests, and objects, was unfounded. There has been so much said about our being honoured by so many dukes and marquisses in three speeches by three persons since you left that the naming one Mr Whewell as the next President is the only thing that can redeem our proceedings from the reproach of taking a very low standard in the estimate of the real dignity of scientific men and so may add of the true objects of science, for its defence on the pure utilitarian ground of its application to the arts has been urged in our section till I am weary of hearing such advocacy.

The arrival of Airy, Encke, Agassiz and many others after you were compelled to desert us and the addition of 200 other members put us in such spirits that the bare idea of biennial meetings in future or other treasonable suggestions was never started. My wife desires her kindest regards

Whewell Papers, a. 208[130]

Johann Franz Encke (1791-1865), *DSB*, was Director of the Berlin Observatory.

275 *Murchison, Wishaw House, Glasgow, to Harcourt, 26 September 1840*

Our meeting has been most eminently successful, and by far the most agreeable to me of all the meetings which it has been my lot to attend. I was commander-in-chief at Arran, and we had a glorious field-day, with every part of Goat Fell illuminated, and the day finished by a fête at which old Link of Berlin, Agassiz, Jacobi, and others were placed around the young heir to the house of Douglas. All the surrounding nobility have been heart and hand with us, including our host here (Lord Belhaven, the present Lord High Commissioner); and Hamilton Palace has been the scene of a series of grand feasts, at one of which I assisted, and to three of which I have been invited. We have not had one hitch in our gallop, not one cross word nor one cross shot.

I met all the little objections and reforms with assenting to the propriety of enquiring into this and that, and referred all such to the Council.

In this delirium of our glory we were, however, near shipwreck, for although Manchester had sent us a deputation, I found that the natives really did not wish us to go there till 1842, and that in fact there was a large party against us there.

Sabine gallantly seconding me (and acting throughout with the best possible judgement and the promptest decision) the old soldiers were not long in taking a line, and although we had no formal application from Plymouth, yet, hearing that the inhabitants really wished for us and had passed resolutions to ask us, I announced the fact, stated that some local arrangements wholly unconnected with the British Association prevented the Manchester folks from pressing us to go till a year had elapsed; and, fortified by a letter from Sir C. Lemon, I proposed Devonport and Plymouth as the place, and Whewell as our President. The project was well received. In the meantime I had sounded Whewell, and told him what I was about to do. He (before leaving us, which he did on Sunday last) replied to me in four sides of a sheet to show that he was utterly disqualified for such a post, that he was not a man of science, not an original observer, in short, nothing. Sabine and self resolved that this disclaimer should not put us back, and we found our good account in the great applause which followed the announcement of his name. The [Local] Secretaries, Snow Harris, Hamilton Smith, and R. Fox, will well support him and I have no fears whatever of that meeting; the Vice-presidents being Sir C. Lemon, Sir T. Acland, Lord Morley and Lord Eliot.

We shall place Conybeare in the chair of the geological section, and then all will be in harmony. I found the feeling so strong in favour of my continuing, that, coupling this with your desire, I consented to be re-elected. I now see that even if I should be absent at the next meeting Sabine can do anything, and there will not be the same necessity for a master of the ceremonies as here. I gave your speech to most of the parties you desired; but we had no guns from Ireland, and I have now no doubt that your view of the case *in re* Cavendish will be adopted by every dispassionate man. The foreigners Encke, Link, Agassiz, and Jacobi were good, and we made the most of them; and I particularly put forward my distinguished friend General Tcheffkine, the Russian. Look at the *Athenaeum* of next Saturday for my Russian sketch and section.

This house is full, and we are going on to make a series of pleasant visits, first to Taymouth, whither write to me if you have aught to say.

The kindest regards of wife and self to Mrs Harcourt

PS   I think your reply to Brougham very good. In truth, Mr Muirhead's attack on you in print is quite a justification for any explanation on your own part ...

Harcourt MSS (Harcourt Papers, *xiv. 125-7*)

Heinrich Friedrich Link (1767-1851), *DSB*, German botanist; Moritz Hermann von Jacobi (1801-74), *DSB*, German physicist who worked at the Imperial Academy of Sciences, St Petersburg; the young heir was William Alexander Anthony Archibald Douglas (1811-63), *DNB*, later 11th Duke of Hamilton. Wishaw House was the home of Belhaven, Taymouth that of Breadalbane. At the 1840 meeting a day's geological excursion was made to the Isle of Arran. General Tcheffkine, head of the School of Mines at St Petersburg, gave great help to Murchison's research on the geology of Russia.

276   *Murchison, Hillhead, Glasgow, to Whewell, Trinity College, Cambridge, 29 September 1840*

On my return from Lord Belhaven's yesterday I received your letter of the 25th. The explanation of the circumstances attending the selection of Plymouth and the appointment of the officers which you ask for I willingly offer, and I think you will be perfectly satisfied therewith. After you left Glasgow it was ascertained, that although there was a requisition from Manchester in the town, yet that the said document had been got up with some difficulty and by a *small majority*. The moment I learnt this I saw it would never do for us to go a-begging, and when I further learnt that those who were our friends in the calico metropolis wished us to come in 1842 rather than in the next year (by which time the opposition alluded to would have passed away), it was obvious that Manchester was out of the question. Plymouth stood next on our list of suitors. The application of this year was in the form of an *unanimous expression* of the wishes of the chief officers and inhabitants of the place at a public meeting held this summer in which they state their hope we will take the earliest opportunity convenient with our engagements to visit them. This resolution was communicated in a letter from Snow Harris. We were also given to understand that if the Plymouths had not supposed that we were pledged to Manchester there would have been some stout men here to urge their suit. Backing up this was a letter from Sir Charles Lemon in which he says that 'he trusts we may still decide on coming *next* year to Plymouth'. These circumstances quite decided Sabine and myself: in fact my colleague being in correspondence with Snow Harris and having the highest opinion of his capability and knowing his *anxious desire on this point*, you must allow that being 'rejected of' Manchester (*entre nous soit dit*) we had no other course; Hull—H—and Halifax being places which *I* trust we shall never visit.

Plymouth, Devonport and Stonehouse being the place to be proposed, we debated the subject over in every point of view as to officers. Sir Charles Lemon was talked of but *unanimously* put aside as President, because he neither represented the great men of influence nor [was] the head man of science. All agreed in the propriety of his being a Vice-president and we all know that he would serve in any capacity for which we might [require] him. The same applied but *still more strongly* to Sir T Acland who is less of a man of science than Lemon. Again if both were chosen the two great political parties would be represented and all persons *satisfied*, but the preference of *either* for the Chair would have disgusted one large class. The same principle guided our taking Lord Morley to represent his order in Devonshire (Saltram Park being at the gates of Plymouth), Lord Eliot the lords of Cornwall, while by having the three [Local] Secretaries, Harris, Smith and Fox we balanced the whole concern.

Having been *suddenly* thrown upon Plymouth breakwater, we

the officers had of course no opportunity of consulting the Vice-presidents *previously*, but I have since written to explain to them the circumstances. In doing so, however, I have in no way *let down* Manchester nor permitted to appear *what I unbosom to you*, that we the British Association at the moment of our greatest success (and never was a meeting so *cordial*, more prosperous or *so unanimous*) were on the point of shipwreck, but I simply stated what I commenced with in the General Committee: 'My Lords and gentlemen. Four towns seek the honour of our visit: Manchester, Plymouth, Hull and York. To the first we *ought* to go had it not been communicated to the General Secretaries *unexpectedly*, that 1842 would suit the convenience of that place better than 1841 and knowing that the *second* town on our list *anxiously covets* our attendance we resolved on going thither.' The replies of the Vice-presidents to my letters will be received at Taymouth Castle whither I am going soon but in the mean time I feel quite confident of their all doing their duty cheerfully. They are all personal friends of my own and I am sure not one of them *will jib*. In regard to the Secretaries, it has never been customary to ask them and we know that they will all be too happy to act.

With all that has been now stated I trust, my dear Whewell, to your magnanimity (for it was upon that Sabine and myself relied). We felt sure that when you *knew* that the course on which we were all embarked, *could* only be saved by an energetic devotion of your services and that this was the decided feeling *of those friends of science* whom I know you value, that you would then surrender to us that service which *we* call for. I confess that your letter for a moment shook me and I almost feared to take so bold a step *in face of it*; but when I reflected on the warmth of your feeling for the British Association, I was certain you would eventually see the propriety of allowing on this occasion your friends to judge for you.

Sabine is much to be relied on and his cool judgment was most EARNESTLY put forth to this effect.

In short we had no other course consistent with the dignity and well being of the Association and I am sure that your election will give very general satisfaction. Inter alia I may say that I never saw Sir D. Brewster go away from *any meeting* in such good humour, and he made a speech at our very last dinner the civic fête (upon Rajah of Travancore) which showed that when screwed up he can talk as well as other men. The Devonian region is singularly well fitted for you, backed up by all your Cornish men and supported as you certainly will be by Sedgwick and Conybeare. To the latter I have already written and told him it was my intention to propose to the Council that he be President of section C in his native county. This

I happen to know (from what occurred at Bristol and from *himself*) is the post he covets most; for he disliked particularly being a Vice-president of the whole body which he was at Bristol, and for the chair in chief we all know that he is not suited, from his great peculiarities which can alone pass off in a geological hall.

Verbum sat. I hope that your classical Majesty under whom I glory to serve will now cordially say 'aye' and that we may pull stoutly together is the ardent wish of

[PS] Two points in your letter remain to be adverted to: the statists and the Theatre. On the first, you know as well as myself that the statistical section has always been a difficult card to play. I *fully anticipated* the danger *here*. To endeavour however to *stop* the PUBLIC feeling here was impracticable: our only course was to allow a safety valve and instead of turning Chalmers and Co into our deadly enemies to allow them to pour out the intense feelings which they had been concentrating for many months.

I can assure you that towards the end of the meeting when the people had become slackened in their rage to hear the Doctor, he was *labouring* as zealously with 2 or 3 around him as if he had had a large congregation. Every *local* person agrees in the propriety of having allowed the thing to have a seat, and many persons are pleased with what they call the good of such discussion. At the same time I (and indeed I presume all the Council) agree entirely with you on the principle of keeping the statistical section within the bounds prescribed to it by the *spirit* and *practice* of our body *scientific*. Be therefore assured of two things: first that our next place of meeting differs toto caelo from Glasgow and that you will have no aggravating circumstances, no pressure upon a vast and miserable population which has roused the feelings of a large part of the really good people of this country; and secondly that the Council *will* take preliminary measures so to regulate the march of the section that no such *displays* can be made. The mode I would suggest is to have a firm President who understands our objects and will *not permit* his section to deviate from their straight path of numbers: that man is Sykes. Once installed I know we can trust him.

As to the Theatre it was entirely an accident. The Local Secretaries had but one failing: they were a little too prompt *at the start*, and before they consulted me (knowing there was no hall big enough for us all) they saddled the town with £860!!! for three nights of a theatre!! *I expostulated* but was too late. We have now resolved to draw out a code of instructions for *locals* and for future regulations to be observed at all our meetings by which the British Association shall *insist* on no such expenses and displays: in short to prepare such a scheme that we may be able to go any where without eating up the land. Your aid with Sabine and self will [arrange] this for Council.

We netted £2600 here: (£150 more than at Newcastle) and have employed a very large part of it in grants for scientific researches.

We never had such good work as in our geological section and I am told by Sabine that section A was admirably conducted by Forbes who is I know particularly well pleased with the results. The same may be said of Sir J. Robison, indeed of all. The opportune arrival of Encke, Agassiz and Airy gave a great brilliancy to our last days. The speech of the former at our civic dinner (given after we had closed our scientific accounts) was admirable; indeed Airy and Agassiz both spoke equally well, and from the Duke of Hamilton whose palace has been open daily with dinners of 50 persons down to my hearty friend Thomas Edington there is but one feeling of satisfaction. It is I give you my word the only meeting which I have attended where nothing has been done which I could wish altered save the statistical display: all the rest has been done kindly, cordially and *well*, which I very much attribute to the excellent Lord Provost and the locals who have brought together all classes.

Colquhoun's after dinner speech (at our great feed in the Theatre) was one of the most didactic, elegant and *useful* hits that could have been made *for us*: in short a complete *smasher* for *The Times*. The good, manly and unaffected bearing of our Chief, the very good sense shewn by Lord Greenock in his last opportunity of speaking at the Provost's dinner, the unbounded joy of my Russian friends who kissed me on both cheeks, all these circumstances not omitting the glorious day on Arran when I lectured to a good band of workmen with every peak of Goatfell illumined and marched up at the close of the day to Brodick Castle with the heir of the House of Douglas preceeded by *the piper*; all these things I say have well repaid me for my journey from Nijnii Novgorod and have more than confirmed the anticipations I entertained of the success of the Glasgow meeting.

Airy spoke very well.

[PS   Written crosswise on envelope flap]

I presume the time of meeting next year will be *much earlier*.

Whewell Papers, a. 209[109]

The Lord Provost of Glasgow was Henry Dunlop (1799-1867); John Campbell Colquhoun (1803-70) was MP for Kilmarnock. At the 1840 meeting Chalmers had used the statistical section to oppose Alison's proposal of a compulsory Scottish poor-rate and to have a fling at Popery.

277   *Phillips, n.p., to Harcourt, 29 September 1840*

I send you a few documents from which you may judge of a part of the Glasgovian proceedings. The meeting was a very good substantial assembly of about 1300 persons, yielding £2500; and though a few of the best men were absent as Herschel, Lloyd, Robinson of Armagh, etc yet the staff of every section was really so full and so strong and the method of right proceeding is now so established that the whole of the committee and section work was well done. I feel certain that the business of the sections was on the whole at least as good as at any one of our gatherings. Even the medical men allow this or rather boast of it, and the mechanical section was most successful, as I can testify for sections A and C which I attended. What pleased me most of all was the evident facility with which the audience seized on and entered into such questions as the formation and movement of glaciers, the varying nature of coal, the reason of various quantity of rain, formation of cloud, tornado movement, steam movements, development of ova of fishes, etc etc. This seems to show that our efforts have not been in vain, and that there really is a sort of upwards movement of the standard of mind among the ordinary members of the Association. Grants £2591, 5/-, very fairly proportioned and not one rejected. Our health did not suffer by *feasting*, and what is droll there will be a considerable surplus on the local fund. This is a great nuisance and Sabine and I have been indulging in schemes to utterly extinguish a great part of the injurious mockery of these so-called 'reception funds', which are almost wholly delusive and bring discredit and loss on the meetings. Great part of the money *is never used for our purposes*: witness Birmingham and Glasgow where local benefits result, but we have to deplore a loss both of men and money. Encke, Jacobi, Agassiz, General Tcheffkine, etc and a host of other strangers were at the meeting.

Espy held his own very well in section A under the random shots of Brewster, Stevelly etc.

Agassiz was splendid on glaciers, completely turning Buckland's head. Airy came late but took part in the proceedings.

The invitations from Manchester, Hull, and Plymouth were none of them for 1841 specially, but rather for 1842 or later. We were forced to make an election and as Manchester is politically or municipally divided we preferred Plymouth, Devonport, and Stonehouse.

This was a little beyond our invitation, but we know our men at Plymouth and have had no doubt of the next meeting being a very brilliant and successful one.

Among the sorrows of the meeting I reckon only the hospitality of His Grace of Hamilton who, besides alluring the geologists to a dejeuner at Brodick in Arran, carried out party after party to dine at Hamilton (11 miles from Glasgow). I thought of your own carriage to Drayton and went in what in Glasgow is called a noddy (you can not sleep in it though). We began to eat at 8.30 and rose from table at 11 or 11.30 and reached Glasow at 2 a.m.!, having to rise at 7 to meet a committee! Others who succeeded my coup d'essai at Hamilton on other days went on dining after this absurd fashion of [Chatel-lerault?] till 12 or 1 and reached Glasgow at 3 or later. This was very discreditably stupid.

Lord Breadalbane did very well, Northampton better, His Grace of St Albans made a neat little schoolboy speech, and the Duke of Argyll read a useful memoir.

Harcourt MSS (Harcourt Papers, *xiv. 128–30*)

James Pollard Espy (1785–1860), *DSB*, the American meteorologist, had made the 1840 meeting of the Association the culmination of a tour of Britain; John Stevelly (1794–1868) was professor of natural philosophy at the Royal Belfast Academical Institution; William Aubrey de Vere, 9th Duke of St Albans (1801–49); John Douglas Campbell, 7th Duke of Argyll (1777–1847), read a geological paper and was a Vice-president of the mechanical science section.

278 *Whewell, Trinity College, Cambridge, to Northampton, Castle Ashby, Northampton, 5 October 1840*

I am very much obliged by your letter, and your view of the position of the British Association. I am quite of your opinion that the success of the meeting at Glasgow was such as to promise a highly satisfactory sitting at Plymouth; although I was obliged to leave you before the business had arrived at those occasions which mainly called up the interest and the confidence of those who attended. I certainly could have wished that some other person than myself had been placed at the head of the Association for the ensuing year; and this, not at all from any doubts of the progress of the institution but from my knowledge of my own true position. I cannot conceal from myself that I have no just claim, and cannot be considered by judicious persons as having a just claim, to be placed upon a level with the persons who, as men of eminent science or as patrons of science have hitherto filled the President's chair. Nobody knows better than I do how little I have done in science; and my future exertions will probably be mainly directed to do some little in sciences which do not come within the scope of the Association. Of my *History* of science the principal notice taken by men of science has been of a hostile kind; and I do not think that any practical cultivators of special sciences will feel any deference for a person who has presumed to speculate about them all. But though I would very gladly have avoided this position, I shall not fail to give my best attention and exertion to its duties being now placed in it: and I am very far from insensible to the pleasure of being proposed by you, a person whom I so cordially regard, and whom all the members of the Association have so much reason to look to with gratitude. The expressions of your good opinion and that of other persons whom I esteem, have made my appointment a source of satisfaction to me, as well as of dissatisfaction.

I have no fear that with your assistance and that of the other persons who are associated with me in the direction of the Association, we shall be able to conduct it through the ensuing year in such a way as to make it answer its purposes as well as it has ever done. There is however one point, on which I am far from satisfied; on which I think something should be done, and about which I cannot consult any one so properly as yourself, who have repeatedly presided over the meetings under difficult circumstances, always obtaining my admiration, and I believe that of everybody else, by your temper, fairness, and judgment. It is becoming more evident every meeting that the concourse which the Association produces is used by various persons for purposes which it cannot recognise, and which I doubt whether we ought knowingly and with foresight to further. I have therefore some misgivings when I see a meeting upon the stormy question which now agitates the Church of Scotland to its very foundation combined so closely with our assembly. About this, I say, I have *doubts*. But I have *no doubts* respecting the propriety of having another great question of social economy and legislation, which produces almost as great a storm as the other, agitated within one of our own sections. I cannot doubt that this is an utter violation of all the principles on which we set out, and of all the professions we have made about our objects and maxims. Of course I refer to the question of the Scotch and English Poor Law. If such discussions be allowed, there is nothing in legislation or politics which can be consistently excluded. Dr Chalmers made an attempt to justify or mask this impropriety by saying that it was an example of the value of *numbers*. By the same rule we might have a discussion of schedule A of the Reform Bill; or of the probable majority of ministers in any party question. The absurdity of such a plea is, I think, undeniable; and the inconsistency of such discussions with our fundamental constitution. And this is not a question of form merely. For what kind of an institution do we become, if we allow ourselves to be made an annual ambulatory meeting for agitating in assemblies when both *eminent* and *notorious* men (Dr Chalmers and Robert Owen) address a miscellaneous crowd on the sorest and angriest subjects which occur among the topics of the day? If we cannot get rid of this character, most assuredly I shall be disposed to make my connection with the Association as brief as I can do, without showing myself indifferent to the good opinion of friends like yourself who are good natured enough to think that I can be of service to the genuine interests of the body.

Perhaps you will think then in what I have written, I take the matter more seriously than it is necessary to do. I shall be very glad to have your judgment about this part of the business, when you have leisure to give it me.

I hope by this time you have entirely shaken off your lameness and are able to clamber up the more rugged mass of gothic ruins. You could have found such a mass at Whitby for the tower fell in sometime ago.

I am always truly glad to hear of the welfare of all at Castle Ashby.

Compton Papers, 1150, ff. 202–4

On 23 Sept 1840 Robert Owen (1771–1858), *DNB*, the visionary socialist, had addressed the statistics section of the Association. During the 1840 meeting the supporters of the disestablishment of the Church of Scotland organised a meeting for Breadalbane, then President of the Association, the leading Scottish peer who agreed with disestablishment.

279   *Charles Hamilton Smith, Plymouth, to Phillips, 4 November 1840*

Private

Your letter reached me last night, confirming what I had already seen in the *Athenaeum*, the insertion of my name as one of the Local Secretaries for the next meeting of the British Association to be held in these towns. Not being a member of that learned body, I own that I felt perplexed to account for the honour conferred upon me. Not having been present at any of the meetings of the Association and therefore reduced to the necessity of judging of the proceedings from the published reports, I have always felt apprehensive that this neighbourhood, notwithstanding that it is full of interest to the scientific, nevertheless, from the want of wealth, want of education and political disunion, is not fitted for a satisfactory general meeting of the Association. In general the public here is cant ridden by narrow and scowling sectarians, and the church is not in the least better inclined to the progress of any kind of knowledge. The intelligence, with the exception of Messrs Harris, Prideaux, and Woollcombe is entirely derived from residents who are not natives. The natives are just sufficiently conscious of ignorance to feel their inferiority and therefore averse to appear in the presence of knowledge; especially if it is likely to come upon their pockets. If I were to add my name to the gentlemen just mentioned it will appear that excepting Mr Harris none of us are capable of much exertion. Mr Woollcombe is within a trifle of the same age as myself that is nearly sixty four. Mr Prideaux, a Quaker, is not in health and if he were, is not of a temper to stir in any object that will make an inroad upon his purse or time. From all I hear Mr Woollcombe cannot take upon himself the [Local] Treasurership and as for myself, broken in constitution by age, long services in the field and the tropics, very little exertion overpowers me: I have in consequence already resigned as a member of the [Plymouth] Athenaeum, I look forward with eagerness to the time of being permitted to quit the chair of the town Library committee and I only retain the Presidency of the Natural History Society, because when lately I also sent in my resignation, I was waited upon by the most influential members, with the assurance, that if I withdrew from office the whole Society must break up. Feeling therefore that I could not well cast one hundred and ten members upon so disagreeable a result, I consented to remain; but it is only in my position that the total helplessness of the public is fully perceptible in all questions, in every section, where science is concerned. I find some good-will, I find promise of the future, but there are no heads between the very old and the very young and hence a day seldom passes, that I have not one or more calls to tutor and help the secretaries, while their chairmen are gone fishing, shooting or feeding.

There are some clever men, but their avocations or reserve keeps them in the background. Such is Dr Armstrong of the Naval Hospital and Dr Vaux, who having retired from practice and being of an active disposition, a chemist and experimentalist, might be made a very useful man. Sir David Dixon M.D. is one of your members but I never could perceive much in him beyond an occasional attendance at the Athenaeum where he has never yet spoken. Dr Moore with some love for science has a peculiar obliquity of perception, which makes him mar what he wants to mend. Revd Mr Hore, an ornithologist and active young man, may be made useful.

From all I have said you will see our difficulty as well as my personal inability to attend in London but although I have great doubts of the possibility of our doing anything really satisfactory to the Association, my personal local exertions, as far as my strength can go, will not be wanting in promoting the objects you have in view. We had a private meeting at Mr Harris' on the subject and on Monday next we meet at Mr Woollcombe's to see in what form our project is to be brought forward at a meeting to be held next day in the hall of the Athenaeum; upon the results of which will depend whether we shall or shall not call for a general meeting of the inhabitants, to which the authorities of Plymouth and Devonport will then be specially invited. If this measure be successfully entertained, I would then recommend your Council in London, or wherever it meets, to adopt some suggestions from hence respecting the assistance we require. It may gradually bring on cooperation between the Athenaeum and the Natural History Society; for it is from the last mentioned that the most active and best informed members are mostly to be derived: although among them there are several of the humbler classes, they have unity of purpose, are destitute of the workings of petty jealousies and [have] zeal to carry out their objects. I have practically found the insufficiency of country-town upper classes voting themselves philosophers. I hope in the north that you are better off than we are in this kind of Baeotia. Sir Charles Lemon and Sir Thomas Acland do not comprehend their own county people and I fear that the result of what we are about here will show it. In Cornwall indeed where many of the gentry are enlightened where the Polytechnic Society shows a spirit fostered by the aristocracy, there is life and only a great town is wanting. But here not a single nobleman or gentleman of great fortune or high in station has come forward with any effectual help to science or literature, while in the coteries and at the Athenaeum, tottering as it is, they would not accept such help from some incomprehensible spirit of self admiration.

I make no doubt that Mr Harris will put you au courant of what may be resolved next week; if the issue should be favourable, I would suggest to you in our helpless and penurious state, that you paid us a very early visit to give a true directing impulse to our operations; for excepting Harris and Woollcombe none of us have the least knowledge of the elements of that organisation which will be requisite.

Phillips Papers, 1840/66

John Prideaux (1787-1859), a retired Plymouth chemist and druggist, taught chemistry at the Cornish Mining School 1839-41; Henry Woollcombe (1777-1847), a prominent lawyer, was President of the Plymouth Philosophical Institution 1827-46; Robert Armstrong (d. c. 1860) and Sir David James Hamilton Dixon (1779-1850) were physicians to the Royal Naval Hospital, Plymouth; Edward Moore (d. 1858), a Plymouth surgeon; William Strong Hore (1807-82), Anglican minister, ornithologist, and botanist. The Royal Polytechnic Society of Cornwall was founded in 1833.

280　*Phillips, Plymouth, to Harcourt, 6 July 1841*

As this eleventh meeting of the Association draws near, I have many occasions of reflecting on the style and plan of our earliest sitting at York, and have no doubt that in some respects the experience of so many years is in favour of a recurrence to the simplicity and economy of that meeting. There is reason to think that the attendance here may not be *very large*, and if so we shall undoubtedly find the meeting more manageable, possibly in regard to science more substantial. We shall have little of the noblesse of Devon and Cornwall: ill health carries off Lord Mount Edgecumbe, Parliament Lord Eliot, and it is said the Duke of Somerset is somehow piqued (how, since we never heard of him in these matters before?) The Irish members are *expected* in force, the Scottish men not. As to expenses, there is no need of spending here for the *reception* of the Association above £200–£500, but if they *will* give absurd treats we can not help what we may regret.

Government gives us a launch of the *Hindostan*, and a grand exhibition of naval models, machinery etc. I am hardly aware of the nature or number of papers and reports to be expected, nor do I know who is coming except by mere rumour.

Shall you be willing to recruit yourself (for there will be no hard work for you) here, in this fine season? If so perhaps you will find it a pleasant and useful meeting, and the country is beautiful. Several persons here are anxious to invite you, but I have thought it best to ask whether you will be willing to try an *unexciting* meeting, as I fancy this surely will be. The elections being over, people are getting quiet again.

Harcourt MSS

Ernest Augustus Mount Edgecumbe, 3rd Earl Mount Edgecumbe (1796–1861); Edward Adolphus Seymour, 11th Duke of Somerset (1775–1855), *DNB*, a mathematician and President of the Royal Institution, London, 1827–41. At the meeting the battleship *Hindostan* was launched.

281 *Harcourt, Bishopthorpe near York, to Peel, 6 November 1841*

... I will now venture to take this opportunity of saying a little on the subject of a small item of public expenditure in the department of the Geological Survey going on under the Board of Ordnance.

The general intention of this Survey being to prepare for publication exact delineations of the real areas occupied by rocks of different qualities, and the real directions of mineral veins, beds of coal, limestone etc (a vast work of important bearing on the mining and agricultural interests of the country), the persons employed on the Survey are set to the various tasks of determining every important line of boundary, measuring the thickness of every bed, testing the qualities, and ascertaining the organic remains of each. For the last two years Professor John Phillips has held an *unattached* appointment on the Survey, under which the examination in detail of the real distribution of the remains of plants and animals in the stratified rocks has fallen to his share, an examination so essential to the right understanding of the relations of the mineral masses, that it is not to be considered an ornamental appendage merely to the field-surveyor's work, but a necessary part of the general plan. There is no person so fit as Mr Phillips to execute this task, both on account of his great acquirements, and because as the nephew and pupil of the late W. Smith he has a kindred zeal for these pursuits, like that of Sir J. Herschel for the prosecution of his father's discoveries. Smith, poorly pensioned by the country with £100 a year during the few last years of his life, left no other legacy to his nephew than that of supporting his deranged and destitute widow (for whom no continuance of his pension could be obtained) and working out the problems of which he first began the solution. Should Mr Phillips's present temporary appointment be made *permanent*, as I believe Mr De la Beche has lately suggested to the Board, I am confident that his services will continue to be, as they already have been, of eminent service to the Geological Survey.

BL, Add. MSS 40494, ff. 85–8

In late 1841 Phillips was appointed permanent palaeontologist to the Geological Survey.

282   *Phillips, Llandovery, to Harcourt, 27 December 1841*

Though I think the period of my expatriation for this 'fitto' is nearly ended (for I trust to quit this spot for home in about a week) and therefore I cannot expect any letter from you, it seems quite neces-sary for me to mention for your consideration the state of the ques-tion raised by the Council of the Yorkshire Philosophical Society at the last Association meeting, as to the holding of the meeting in York in 1843. The approaching annual meeting of the Y.P.S. ren-ders it desirable that some understanding should be speedily come to on the part of the early friends of the Society and the Association, and there are two things in particular which it is very material *you* should know. First I believe it is the fact that no *other invitation* will be presented to the Association at Manchester and I know it to be the fact that the cost of a meeting is now very small. Upon these facts the present views of the officers of the British Association, acting on the new arrangement, must be founded. Colonel Sabine and myself have often contemplated such a contingency (only one invi-tation) or rather that a case might arise when *no invitation* should be offered. We formed our plan of reduced expense partly upon that consideration, and concluded from a patient survey of all the data that it would, in such a case, be perfectly competent to the Association to *choose* its own place of meeting wherever rooms and tolerable scientific repute were to be found. From what Lord Northampton, Sabine, and others did say at Plymouth, I think I may say that I know they expect to assemble the Association in York in 1843, not as a pis aller but as the occasion of a very healthy and refreshing meeting. There are only two points for hesitation (as I conceive) among the members of the Council of the Y.P.S.: they may justly regret the paucity of men devoted to science in York; and they may tremble for the pecuniary interests of the Y.P.S., imagining the extra cost of the meeting will, in some way or other, *really* come out of their fair income or *expectancy*. They may think that any £100 raised in subscription for the B.A. might have gone to the pockets of the Treasurer of the Y.P.S. On both these points I have more to say than can be put in a letter. They hang very much together, but in regard to the money question it seems essential that you should know as a fact, that the *necessary expenses* of the meeting are so moderate, that (the greater part being profitably undertaken and paid by the Association) the real sum required to be raised ought not to exceed £250. Of this there is in my mind no doubt. To make this sum suffice nothing is wanted but a strict determination to do nothing for the meeting except what its scientific concerns demand, find sufficiently furnished rooms, attendance, police, etc.

Now really it seems to me this sum will be raised at once, unless by any fatal languor on the part of the Society, the public be led to imagine that the parent is tired of its unruly infant, and willing *anxious* to commit the care and reception of the Association to accident rather than guidance. However, there are other views of this matter which I reserve till I see you, and perhaps on that Sabine will give me a statement of his opinion, which will certainly be important. I have also tried to get Murchison to consider the case.

Harcourt MSS

The 1843 meeting of the Association was not held at York but at Cork.

283 *Phillips, Burford House, Malvern, to Harcourt, 23 May 1842*

I did not reply to your query as to what might be the suitable scale of subscriptions among the members of the Y.P.S. for the purpose of raising £500 to receive the Association. My mind was so undecided and I had so little information that it seemed best to say nothing for fear of saying what was wrong. Perhaps in these cases the best way is to let events have their course. And just now with York Minster,

Hamburg, the income tax and other terrors, it may be best to use only moderate stimuli. I have been so perplexed even in regard to my own subscription that I have requested Meynell to take £10 or £5 according as he may think it most proper and suitable to the scale adopted by others. I have news from Manchester to the effect that they are raising £2500 for us (*it is raised*) and £5627 for Hamburg (*it is raised*).

Murchison and Sabine both count *as a certainty* the visit of the Association to York in 1843. We must therefore be ready. Amongst other things you must appoint at the June Meeting your deputation to Manchester. Kenrick and Creyke I think gave the notice at Plymouth. These would be *very fit* to repeat it at Manchester, where Kenrick is rich in personal friends.

Sabine has asked me if the list of Vice-presidents at York should be Earl Fitzwilliam, Revd W.V. Harcourt, Sir D. Brewster, Revd H. Lloyd (as representing the Provost).

I am afraid you only laughed at my rain gauge plan of putting out fires (may heaven avert them!) in York Minster. If so I shall not be sorry to have caused you even a laugh on a matter which has caused you many a sigh . . .

Harcourt MSS

Thomas Meynell (1805-63) was then a Secretary of the Yorkshire Philosophical Society; John Kenrick (1788-1877), *DNB*, taught at Manchester College which in 1840 had reverted to Manchester from York; Stephen Creyke (1796-1883), prebendary of York Minster. In 1842 Peel introduced income tax. Many towns launched appeals to relieve distress caused by the great fire at Hamburg 5-7 May 1842. York Minster suffered extensive fires in 1829 and 1840; on both occasions appeals were made.

284   *Murchison, 16 Belgrave Square, London, to Harcourt, 3 June 1842*

If you have not heard of it from other quarters, I wish to inform you that your bantling (as Sedgwick would call it) the British Association, has now gained a 'locus a quê' and a tower of strength in the Royal Observatory at Kew which is now in our possession by Her Majesty's command in consequence of an application *we* of the Council made.

The Royal Society rejected the offer of the building, notwithstanding a most beautiful 'rapport raisonné' of Herschel, stressing the great uses in physical science to which it might be applied. The B.A. having voted annual grants for meteorological, acoustical, magnetical and all sorts of physical experiments requiring quiet isolation, it was thought that this building, standing alone in the centre of 450 acres, would be just the place to hoist our flag and be an excellent fortress from whence we could never be expelled so long as physical science flourishes; and in which we could deposit all our gifts, all the instruments used by different experimenters when their duty has been done; also a recipient for a complete set of new and measured instruments to be applied to—etc, etc. We have approved, in short, of a report drawn up by Wheatstone and which Herschel will improve, and which will be our apology to the General Committee for having taken a bold step in which I acknowledge myself a prime conspirator, but which I am sure will be highly approved of by you and by all our real well-wishers. We shall appoint a curator and sub-curator.

The point, however, on which I want to consult you (for the other *is done* for good or for evil) is about our *next* meeting.

Cork! is the only antagonistic place to York and as we can find no one reason for going to the south of Ireland where there is not *one* savant and *no machinery scientific*, it was unanimously resolved at our Council of yesterday that Cork was to be thrown overboard and York approved of. The next step is to organize a staff for the York meeting. I stated to the Council how Lord Fitzwilliam was our first Praeses under your management and left them to judge how far we were compromised to take His Lordship again. He certainly has been our kind good friend and is a very worthy man and of great influence in Yorkshire. On the other hand he has been a hot politician and if we can steer clear of party feud 'tant mieux'.

It is our wish as far as possible to act up to our present system of the alternating presidents representing rank and science. This year we are 'lorded over' and Lord Francis [Egerton] will give us the speech. Next year we thought we might go to one of ourselves, and if so (you having already officiated as Praeses) the Dean of Ely might be the man. Whether we look to Peacock's *very high* station in science, his powers of conducting a great assembly, the urbanity of his manners, his position in the church (*the* scientific Dean) or his facility in writing something worth having, *we* are of opinion that *if* science is to be honoured, there is no man who more deserves the post than the Dean, and we resolved that he should be put into nomination. On speaking to him yesterday, I find that he *shies* the appointment and declares his unfitness. This however could be perhaps got over: but the real thing to know is *what is best to be done to secure a good, strong coalition of all the Yorkshire philosophers, divines and squires. Shall we take a lord or a scientific Dean?* With kind regards to your lady

Harcourt MSS (Harcourt Papers, *xiv. 137-9*)

Lord Francis Egerton (1800–57), *DNB*, presided at the 1842 meeting of the Association. In 1841 government decided to discontinue the Royal Observatory at Kew; next year the Association successfully applied to government for it.

285 *Murchison, 16 Belgrave Square, London, to Harcourt, Bolton Percy near Tadcaster, 7 April 1843*

Putting my great Russian child to sleep for a few months, whilst I voyage to *Warsaw* and elsewhere and launching my long anniversary discourse which you will have very soon, I have not much time left for the British Association. Whether I get back or not for Cork must depend on events and at all events Sabine and Phillips will be there.

We held our *last* Council yesterday, at which, besides settling all the presidents of sections for Cork, we talked over the future of York, and as is customary on such occasions, power was given to me to initiate the appointments of the *grand officers* by asking certain individuals if they would act. We name Peacock as President 'nem con' and Lord Fitzwilliam senior Vice-president if he will act. My first letter is therefore to Lord F.

If he accepts, then a second will be fired at Lord Wharncliffe to ask him if he will make a pendant to Lord F. Lord Northampton suggested Lord Wharncliffe, *but* I was to consult you on this point and as to the other personages.

It was the wish of the Council that Lord Morpeth (and this is particularly my own wish *looking to old times*) should be one of the V.P.s, *yourself another*, Faraday a fifth, and a sixth if you think it desirable may be suggested by you. We think Brewster will be better pleased to be president of section A than to hold a mere honorary office. Faraday 'per contra' owing to his health does not like the drudgery of an office in which there is much to do.

I am off (my wife with me) on Thursday next. Write therefore by return of post.

[PS] Our kindest regards to Mrs Harcourt. If my friends the Tories are *science-haters* why should we bother ourselves about them? Let them learn wisdom at the cat's tail.

Harcourt MSS

James Archibald Stuart Wortley Mackenzie, 1st Baron Wharncliffe (1776–1845), *DNB*. In 1843 Murchison was continuing his work on Russian geology; in early 1843 he had delivered a long presidential address to the Geological Society of London.

286   *Harcourt, Bolton Percy near Tadcaster, to Murchison, Tuesday* [*11 April 1843*]

I think Lord Fitzwilliam would accept the office of Vice-president; I doubt whether Lord Wharncliffe would; and I think we should be better off in all respects with John Wortley and Morpeth, in addition to Lord Fitzwilliam. I hope you will make a point of going to Cork: the Irish will be sore if you do not. It is very seldom that any individual is placed in a position to oblige or disoblige *a nation*; but that is really your position now, as the chief English officer and moving wheel of the Association. I am very serious in the opinion that under all circumstances it is an *important public duty* for you to attend this meeting, and I would venture to predict that the feeling with which you will be received there will repay any sacrifice you may make. I should be very glad to hear of Sedgwick and Buckland going also.

BL, Add. MSS 46126, ff. 379–80

John Stuart Wortley (1801–55), *DNB*, eldest son of Baron Wharncliffe, was MP for the West Riding of Yorkshire 1841–5.

287   *Murchison, n.p., to Harcourt, Bolton Percy near Tadcaster, n.d.* [*12 April 1843*]

Vale. Your powerful support added to my own real wish to do what was right, and the deference of the Corkists to my wishes in deferring the meeting to the 17th August, have quite determined me to be at my post D.V. Nothing in short positive incapacity shall prevent my being there.

In consequence of your note I this day visited a John Wortley and found him a very willing harness horse. I explained to him the full state of the case and he seemed perfectly to agree with you that Lord Wharncliffe would prefer his being in the place.

I told him I should invite Lord Morpeth which he also fully approved.

I asked him if he had any fourth Vice-president to suggest. He replied that as Morpeth might be considered to represent the North Riding [of Yorkshire] and that Lord Fitzwilliam and himself answered for the West, it might be desirable to have one from the *East*. But he laid no stress on this and did not seem to think it essential.

You will therefore concert this point with Phillips and Sabine before another Council at which it will be reported that the Dean assents to the high dignity. V.P.s: Lord Fitzwilliam (whose reply has not yet arrived); Lord Morpeth do do; John Stuart Wortley yes; Faraday ?; W. Vernon Harcourt aye. A sixth therefore may be well added.

We are off tomorrow.

Harcourt MSS

288   *Phillips, Newnham, Worcestershire, to Harcourt, 22 April 1843*

Murchison tells me in his valedictory letter that you have prevailed with him to reinstate J. Wortley instead of Lord Wharncliffe, which is a very good exchange. As he has written to Lord Morpeth, our list will be rich enough in lords, even for Yorkshire, yet he talks of an East Riding representative at Mr Wortley's suggestion. I confess myself very ignorant of what *learned* lords we have in the East Riding, and am rather frightened at such a triplicity of peers. I fear we are forgetting Brewster. Sabine appeared to wish to make him president [of] section A. Thus he has slipped away from his Vice-presidential chair, and another push loses him section A. This would be a great mistake, and a sacrifice of justice which Cambridge has no right to ask.

The Cork people are very active, but I believe are merely working in a circle, the figure usually chosen in preparations for the meetings, till pressure comes on the men as the day draws near and then the figure elongates and ends in a straight line . . .

PS   If an East Riding man is to be chosen, Dr Alderson of Hull might perhaps give good advice. But I suppose you will not think it necessary to be at any trouble about such a fancy.

Harcourt MSS

James Alderson (1794-1882), *DNB*, a physician.

289   *Phillips, Cork, to Harcourt, 23 August 1843*

Everything goes on well here in regard to science, the meeting being very full of papers and animated discussion. The members are fully half English, and the spirit exactly of the old sort. The Dean of Ely is here, and several others not expected have come. Evening lectures have been got up by Owen and E. Forbes, and they have succeeded very well. I speak prophetically of the last, for it is *to be* delivered tonight.

Today we appoint next place of meeting, officers, etc. After much consideration, I have resolved to propose Hatfeild among the [Local] Secretaries, as I am sure of his excellent quality in guiding the preliminary arrangements with a view to the grand principle which I have taken so much pains to teach Meynell and Goldie, viz the principle of so regulating the whole preliminary affairs as to cause a complete renovation of the Yorkshire Museum, fill all its cases with Yorkshire natural history, catalogue all its collections, and make everything near the aspect of a well prepared scientific reception.

The time of the meeting will be proposed, September 19–26 or thereabout.

This will cause an expenditure on the Museum, and on the naming, etc of it of at least £250; well spent it will be I am sure on such an object. If we try to raise £1000 on a distinct plea of this nature, we shall get it, I have no fear. Above all we must have the whole management in the hands of our friends, by a careful selection of a committee based on our Council, but including *county names* from our list of donors to the building, etc. I find the West Riding people will some time or other demand a meeting and look upon this of 1844 as a York Meeting. This being the case we must resolve to make it so.

Harcourt MSS

Richard Owen (1804–92), *DNB*, the anatomist.

290 *Phillips, York, to Harcourt, 8 October 1843*

I apprehend it is true that the expenses, even the necessary expenses, of entertaining the Association in 1844 will be very much greater than those estimated for receiving that body in 1843. The difference of the circumstances in which the meetings of 1843 and 1844 are summoned is the main cause. 1843 is a year of partial success: most of the English and all the Scotch members are absent. All the former are likely and many have already promised to attend in 1844. Many of the Scotch members may be expected, and from all I hear of foreigners they will come in a crowd! This makes it nearly certain that every *large* room in York must be employed and as our own members appear to feel that hospitality must be exercised and a brilliant as well as scientific meeting be aimed at, this demands money. In proportion to the numbers that attend, or rather in a *higher proportion* all the costs rise. If we have 1500 members (and that is below my conjecture) it will cost twice as much as to entertain 1000. I do not find any proposal of mine to restrict the expenditure to plain necessaries at all palatable. Every one seems to think the credit of the city, county and society involved and that there must be some splendour. This being the case I apprehend we must ask larger subscriptions though it is not to be supposed that the mass of our members will be so much interested in the meeting as to augment their 'benevolence' of last year. Hatfeild and Meynell are going to Wentworth next week, and they want to have some information as to what is the Archbishop's thought about the meeting so that they may speak to Earl Fitzwilliam who will probably augment his subscription. As President of Yorkshire Philosophical Society he gave £100. I find in the list of last year, that Meynell prints, above £500 in all. In this list the name of the Archbishop stands for £25 and yours for £10. I should be disposed to advise an increase even at the risk of having a surplus, for the whole management of the subscription is to be in the hands of the Yorkshire Philosophical Society and a committee selected by us, and the Society must spend £300 at least from its own funds independently of the money raised for the Association. This sum it must spend in completing the Museum, on a plan which I have been sketching and beginning, so as to have every thing in a good condition. *We can afford it.* We save £200 this year.

I must not venture to act on your suggestion to announce your subscription, because what is immediately wanted is a point to start from in asking Earl Fitzwilliam, and this can be done only (it appears) by first learning what the Archbishop thinks of it. If you think this is not advisable, Hatfeild will doubtless, at Wentworth, ask the Earl directly, but you must write *him* a note, for I am going to Frome in Somersetshire. I spoke to Earl F. at York the other day but it was on Irish matters, which seemed to me, in an inextricable circle of confusion: a circle having two polarities, laziness in the tenant and ignorance in the landlord; 'each giving each a double charm'.

In Cork and Kerry we passed for twenty miles through districts not naturally rich, where every acre was cultivated and yielding corn (wheat, oats) and potatoes, but not one plough, no farm yard, no team of horses, *no hedge*, hardly a true, decent fence, or good coat except on Sundays. But the roads excellent (and *no turnpikes*, being mended by a county rate). I never saw a country so full of the grossest errors of management on the part of the landlords!

Harcourt MSS

291 *Whewell, Trinity Lodge, Cambridge, to Murchison, 27 February 1844*

I understand that you and the Council of the B.A. are about to discuss the question of the place of meeting for next year. I had, as I stated at Manchester, a very decided opinion that the meeting ought not to be at Cambridge, and ought to be at some new place; and as I retain this opinion very strongly, I should be glad that, if there be occasion, the opinion and my reasons for it should be known to the Council. I conceive the principal utility of the B.A. to consist in the effect it produces upon the places which it visits. It calls out the local men of science and lovers of science, makes them known to the scientific world and acquainted with it, and fixes the attention of such persons upon the proceedings of the B.A. in succeeding years. So long as the B.A. can go on doing this it is a great benefactor to the nation. There remain many places which ought to be visited except it is to renounce this office: for example, Durham (a university town), Leeds, Hull, Lincoln, Norwich, Portsmouth, Exeter. You ought to go to the frontier of Wales, to Swansea or Gloucester, where you are within reach of your own Siluria; to Shrewsbury, where you can see into Cambria. If you cannot go to some of these places the main use of the B.A. is at an end. You wish to meet for the sake of raising money; but I think to meet for that purpose only, without being able to forward the other, would not be right, and I should not wish to share in the plan.

I do not think you ought to go back to the old places, at any rate not till the above and others have been visited. The burthen will be most grievous. The novelty and enthusiasm are past for those places, and you will have a failure. The men of science who have gladly taken a share in your first visit will have a horror of you when they find that they have tied themselves to a wheel which goes round and round catching them every few years whether they will or no, dragging them from their quiet, their plans, their engagements, and making them the instruments of inflicting expense and many annoyances upon their neighbours.

I do not think you will find many Cambridge men who wish you to come here at present. I know of none except Sedgwick and Peacock. All our professors that I have spoken with dislike the thought. I believe that our College, with the exceptions I have mentioned, are unanimous against the plan. I hear that it is not liked in the rest of the University.

I have spoken very candidly as I did at Manchester that you may have the case fully before you. I shall be sorry if we do not ultimately agree; but I am so confident in the strength of my case that I trust we shall. I think I must present my own remembrances to Mrs Murchison. So adieu.

Whewell Papers, O. 15.47[295-6]

At the 1842 meeting in Manchester, Whewell argued that the Association should begin to visit smaller towns and, by implication, not foist itself on Cambridge.

292   *Murchison, 16 Belgrave Square, London, to Whewell, Trinity College, Cambridge, 1 March 1844*

My dear Master,

As you have written to me with perfect candour concerning the future meetings of the British Association, you will I know permit me to reply to you in the same strain. We had a meeting of the Council yesterday and I communicated as you desired your sentiments etc. You must not be surprised when I tell you, that the opinion of all present (and I know it to be the general feeling of the British Association) is opposed to your own, concerning the regulating *principle* of the Association. We repudiate the idea that the chief aim of our existence is to stir up a few embers of latent scientific warmth *in the provinces*. If indeed that were truly our *main* object, I for one would cease to play pantaloon or clown in the strolling company, even if it should have a benefit night, as you suggest, for the followers of Caractacus on the frontiers of Siluria! We think that nearly all the places you enumerate are wholly incapable of receiving the B.A. in its present stature, and if it is to pine away in size (as at Cork) the body can no longer enact the part which entitles it to the nation's confidence.

In such case it could no longer be what *it has been*, a parliament of science which finds the *ways and means* of carrying out researches which without its stimulus would never be undertaken; nor could it with such poor backing as Portsmouth, Shrewsbury, etc., pretend for one moment to act by public opinion upon *the government* of this country. Without we have full meetings our funds fail and we can no longer *institute the first experiments* which, satisfying public men of their usefulness, lead them to adopt our recommendations. This very year the government have taken up works *begun* by us to an extent of £1500!

But how are we to get the guineas, how raise the 'rint' if not supported by the strong voice of the *real science* of England? It is not enough to go about with a begging box *if our O'Connells leave us*. Now admitting with you, that it is by no means necessary or even desirable, that the Association wheel should go the same round, catching up its old friends (none of them we hope *off work*) 'nolentes volentes', still it is essential to our well being, if not to our existence, that we should every now and then secure the embraces of an university; it is I say indispensable to have from time to time a fresh infusion of scientific blood and a rally of our oldest and best friends and if so where (Oxford being lost in her tracts) I say can we obtain such except in your honoured Alma Mater?

But whilst I first argue *my* case 'con amore' I at once admit, that the very *look* of the Master of Trinity when he chides his foster child, is entitled to the greatest respect, and I for one can imagine no good and effective meeting of science *at Cambridge* in which he does not *cooperate*. I know and have known his strong objections to an early meeting there, but I venture to hope that to oblige *all his scientific* friends from whom he differs on *this* point, he will so far relent as to allow us to revisit a place so dear to us, at no very distant day. My proposal therefore is, or rather my urgent request is, that after chastening us and compelling us to break our cabalistic cycle by making us take a new place for our first meeting after York, our good Master will again receive us with open arms and that however repugnant a meeting might be to him in 1845, his opposition having sent us to *fresh pastures* in that year, he will once more put us into *condition* (pardon my old habits) by a Cambridge *training*. Now as clerk of the course which the British Association has to run, I have got the fresh pastures ready for 1845 wherein we may *fatten*. In the name of the Corporation, inhabitants and science (such as it is with Phil Duncan at its head), Bath *has* invited us warmly to visit her in 1845; and with Lord Lansdowne as a President we should there have a good show and collect a good purse, for it is the centre of a network of rail roads, open to Ireland and the south-west, and four hours from London. But good as it may be, the Bath meeting would sound as a great *bath*os in our prospectus, if followed by the poor diets of smaller provincial towns, and then will come the very nick of time when Cambridge can *reinvigorate* us. Pray therefore unite with your scientific friends at Cambridge who are I hear far from being confined to the Dean of Ely and Sedgwick and by allowing us to announce that Cambridge will succeed to Bath, assure the public that we still possess within us *the national scientific strength*.

So much for the public grounds. Excuse me now if whilst writing to you with that openness which I know you like, I speak to you as a friend who respects your character and honours your well earned reputation. I am aware that you are formed of such a mould that once conscious of the propriety and rectitude of your views on any point, you are little likely to be swayed by the opinion of other men; but excuse me when I tell you plainly, that the mass of men of science are perfectly unable to comprehend why you have (as they say) turned your back upon your best friends. That which I grieved to hear at Manchester is now repeated with augmented vexation on account of your continued opposition to what all its supporters (save yourself) consider the first interest of the British Association. The inference among many persons is, that some scholastic or monastic reasons of expediency connected with your new position have led you to cast off your old mantle and with it your best friends. Disbelieving that such motives *can* regulate your conduct, I was delighted to hear from the lips of our valued friend, the Dean, that *you are quite unchanged* and that having honestly adopted the opinions expressed in your letter to me, you adhere to them with your characteristic firmness. But again I say, the world will not believe this without some tangible proof and, having as your friend the strongest desire to eradicate the false impression which has gone abroad, I once more entreat you to reflect upon the power which *you now hold in your own hands* of doing that which will gratify the men of science of England, and bind to you once more those who might become estranged to you. In short my sincere advice is that you 'tak your auld cloak about ye' in the year 1846, and so hug us with your lusty arms as to give us a new spring for the rest of our career.

PS   My wife was delighted with the solution of the riddle. She begs to unite with me in kind remembrances to Mrs Whewell.

My last soirée was very brilliant and the colossal vase from the Emperor 'Geological Russian Exploration' looked well when surrounded by a number of pretty young female specimens.

Whewell Papers, a. 209[118]

Philip Bury Duncan (1772–1863), *DNB*, was Keeper of the Ashmolean Museum, Oxford; Daniel O'Connell (1775–1847), *DNB*, Irish politician. The Association met at Cambridge in 1845.

293   *Harcourt, n.p., to Sabine, n.d.* [*1853*]

I have received from the President of the Philosophical Society of Hull, where, as you know, the British Association is about to meet, a memoir which he has put into public circulation, descriptive of the nature of that body, its early history, and the specific services rendered to it by individuals in its infancy.

The task which Mr Frost has undertaken is one of a difficult and delicate kind; and I was not surprised to find his description of circumstances, with which he had no means of being intimately acquainted, somewhat inaccurate and defective.

Mr Frost informs the public that when in 1831 Sir David, then Dr Brewster, made a proposal that meetings for promoting science by *reunions* of scientific men similar to those which prevailed abroad should be held in England and commenced at York, the country had been duly prepared and predisposed for such cooperation by the severe strictures which he had then recently passed on the actual state of science in this country, and on the conduct and character of its scientific institutions and in particular its universities. It would have been better if these strictures, now forgotten, had not been adverted to, especially with reference to the Association. The truth is, they formed the chief difficulty in the way of carrying such a proposal as had been made into effect. It was clear that any attempt at scientific association not headed or joined by many persons who could not but feel aggrieved by the strictures referred to, and who have been since among the chief lights of the institution, would probably have led to results more mischievous than beneficial to science.

As soon as Dr Brewster's proposal was made, and before it should be acceded to, I thought it needful to enter into correspondence with numerous individuals thus situated, and finding them agreeing for the most part in the opinion that such reunions would operate for the benefit of science, and that, losing sight of all personal feelings they consented to cooperate, I drew up a scheme which was ultimately followed.

It is a mistake to consider this Association as having been formed on any foreign model. My conception of the manner in which a great scientific combination might be effectually worked in England was founded on different principles. No one could be insensible of the advantages to be derived from bringing men of science together to confer and discuss: but even this point I considered it impossible to gain without extending our views considerably further. I did not believe that the great labourers in science would undergo the inconvenience and interruption of travelling to various places to meet one another, as a continuous system, on mere invitation and for the sole purpose of discussion, and I knew that if such men should absent themselves from the meetings they would become no better than *foci* of *sciolism* and vanity.

I therefore proposed to found the Association on the principle of *acquiring funds* to be devoted to the expenses of unremunerative objects of science, of levying such funds from the multitudes of persons who might be expected to feel interest in scientific discussions at populous places, and of its giving the appropriation of them first to the [inspection] of select committee[s] now attached to the various sections of science and secondly to the final determination of the whole body of actual scientific labourers at the meeting assembled in General Committee.

To this principle in the constitution of the British Association its success has been mainly due. To this principle we owed for instance the unintermitting attendance to the time of his lamented decease of one of its ablest members, Mr Baily, under whose direction one of the largest applications of its funds was made to the [sic].

These grants of assistance, conjoined with requests to individuals to execute particular tasks for the interests of science, have given the exertions of the Association as a body a direct utility peculiarly its own, tending far beyond the promiscuous discussions of the sections both to advance material objects and to maintain the attendance at its meetings of persons pursuing such objects.

The wealth, the public spirit, the intelligence, the curiosity, of the great cities of the United Kingdoms offered great encouragement to the financial part of this plan, and by its adoption has enabled the Association to carry out its entire objects, not only in regard to liberal grants for scientific purposes and in defraying all expenses incidental to its operation and essential to its permanence, but even in maintaining an establishment of its own for experimental research. This plan, proposed by me at York, was adopted in all its details, and my acceptance of the office of General Secretary enabled me with able and zealous cooperators to work a machine of great magnitude and complexity with a success surpassing my expectations from 1831 to 1837, during which years I was charged with its chief management and revised all that was printed in its name.

The cordial reception of the first meeting of the B. Association by the city of York, the hospitality of Bishopthorpe, the countenance of the Royal President of the Royal Society, the presence of Lord Fitzwilliam, the aid of Professor Phillips, the attendance of the distinguished philosopher Sir David Brewster with Brisbane, Robison, Forbes, and Johnston, the attendance from London of Murchison, from Dublin of Provost Lloyd, from Oxford of Dr Daubeny, from Manchester of Dalton, the concurrence of Buckland and Whewell and Conybeare and many others of known repute, these incidents helped to launch a/the vessel of the early history of which, if any one would write accurately of that part of its history, he may record with truth that Sir D. Brewster first proposed that a craft should be built which the united crew of British science might sail and manfully embarked in it all his high scientific reputation, but for myself I must be allowed to claim that I manned the ship, that I constructed the charts and piloted the vessel for six years. A labour which I bestowed on this service has since been divided among more capable hands; but none of us could have worked the vessel at all without the constant and invaluable helping hand of the Assistant Secretary, Professor Phillips.

It induces me to put down on paper and transmit to you, as actual President of the Association, a statement of the real facts without the least intention however of involving either you or any one else in controversy on the subject.

Harcourt MSS (Harcourt Papers, *xiii, 228–32*)

Charles Frost (1781–1862), *DNB*, author of *On the prospective advantages of a visit to the town of Hull by the British Association for the Advancement of Science ... read before the Hull Literary and Philosophical Society ... on the 16th of November 1852* (Hull, 1853).

SUBJECT INDEX

NAME AND PLACE INDEX

Dates of birth and death, and brief biographical information, are given on pages indicated by italic entries.